The online curriculum is the most dynamic part of the Cisco Networking Aca [illegible] you begin your study of each chapter with the online material and then move [illegible] this mapping guide to ensure that you get the most from the various components of the program.

CCNA 3 and 4 Companion Guide, Third Edition		CCNA 3 and CCNA 4 Online Curriculum	
Chapter Number	Chapter Title	Mod #	Module Title
Part I	Review		
1	Review: The OSI Reference Model and Routing		
Part II	CCNA 3: Switching Basics and Intermediate Routing		
2	Introduction to Classless Routing	CCNA 3 #1	Introduction to Classless Routing
3	Single-Area OSPF	CCNA 3 #2	Single-Area OSPF
4	Enhanced Interior Gateway Routing Protocol	CCNA 3 #3	EIGRP
5	Switching Concepts and LAN Design	CCNA 3 #4	Switching Concepts
6	Switches	CCNA 3 #5	Switches
7	Switch Configuration	CCNA 3 #6	Switch Configuration
8	Spanning Tree Protocol	CCNA 3 #7	Spanning Tree Protocol
9	Virtual LANs	CCNA 3 #8	Virtual LANs
10	VLAN Trunking Protocol	CCNA 3 #9	Virtual Trunking Protocol
Part III	CCNA 4: WAN Technologies		
11	Scaling IP Addresses	CCNA 4 #1	Scaling IP Address
12	WAN Technologies	CCNA 4 #2	WAN Technologies
13	Point-to-Point Protocol	CCNA 4 #3	PPP
14	ISDN and DDR	CCNA 4 #4	ISDN and DDR
15	Frame Relay	CCNA 4 #5	Frame Relay
16	Introduction to Network Administration	CCNA 4 #6	Introduction to Network Administration
Part IV	CCNA Bonus Material		
17	Optical Networking Fundamentals		
18	Network Management		
19	Network+ Certification Exam Review		
20	CCNA Certification Exam Review		
21	Introduction to Converged Networking		
22	Developing Network Security and Network Management Strategies		
23	Virtual Private Networks		
Part V	Appendixes		
A	Glossary of Key Terms		
B	Check Your Understanding Answer Key		

Cisco Networking Academy Program
CCNA 3 and 4 Companion Guide
Third Edition

Cisco Systems, Inc.

Cisco Networking Academy Program

Cisco Press

201 West 103rd Street

Indianapolis, Indiana 46290 USA

www.ciscopress.com

Cisco Networking Academy Program
CCNA 3 and 4 Companion Guide
Third Edition

Cisco Systems, Inc.

Cisco Networking Academy Program

Copyright © 2003 Cisco Systems, Inc.

Published by:
Cisco Press
201 West 103rd Street
Indianapolis, IN 46290 USA

Printed in the United States of America   2 3 4 5 6 7 8 9 0

Second Printing   August 2003

Library of Congress Cataloging-in-Publication Number: 2003100556

ISBN: 1-58713-113-7

Trademark Acknowledgments

Warning and Disclaimer

Feedback Information

At Cisco Press, our goal is to create in-depth technical books of the highest quality and value. Each book is crafted with care and precision, undergoing rigorous development that involves the unique expertise of members from the professional technical community.

Readers' feedback is a natural continuation of this process. If you have any comments regarding how we could improve the quality of this book, or otherwise alter it to better suit your needs, you can contact us through e-mail at networkingacademy@ ciscopress.com. Please make sure to include the book title and ISBN in your message.

We greatly appreciate your assistance.

Publisher	John Wait
Editor-in-Chief	John Kane
Executive Editor	Carl Lindholm
Cisco Representative	Anthony Wolfenden
Cisco Press Program Manager	Sonia Torres Chavez
Manager, Marketing Communications, Cisco Systems	Scott Miller
Cisco Marketing Program Manager	Edie Quiroz
Production Manager	Patrick Kanouse
Development Editor	Andrew Cupp
Project Editor	San Dee Phillips
Copy Editors	Karen A. Gill, Marcia Ellett, Keith Cline
Technical Editors	Ron Bodtcher, K Kirkendall, Jim Lorenz, Rick McDonald
Assistant Editor	Sarah Kimberly
Cover Designer	Louisa Adair
Compositor	Octal Publishing, Inc.
Indexer	Tim Wright

CISCO SYSTEMS

Corporate Headquarters
Cisco Systems, Inc.
170 West Tasman Drive
San Jose, CA 95134-1706
USA
www.cisco.com
Tel: 408 526-4000
    800 553-NETS (6387)
Fax: 408 526-4100

European Headquarters
Cisco Systems International BV
Haarlerbergpark
Haarlerbergweg 13-19
1101 CH Amsterdam
The Netherlands
www-europe.cisco.com
Tel: 31 0 20 357 1000
Fax: 31 0 20 357 1100

Americas Headquarters
Cisco Systems, Inc.
170 West Tasman Drive
San Jose, CA 95134-1706
USA
www.cisco.com
Tel: 408 526-7660
Fax: 408 527-0883

Asia Pacific Headquarters
Cisco Systems, Inc.
Capital Tower
168 Robinson Road
#22-01 to #29-01
Singapore 068912
www.cisco.com
Tel: +65 6317 7777
Fax: +65 6317 7799

Cisco Systems has more than 200 offices in the following countries and regions. Addresses, phone numbers, and fax numbers are listed on the
Cisco.com Web site at www.cisco.com/go/offices.

Argentina • Australia • Austria • Belgium • Brazil • Bulgaria • Canada • Chile • China PRC • Colombia • Costa Rica • Croatia • Czech Republic
Denmark • Dubai, UAE • Finland • France • Germany • Greece • Hong Kong SAR • Hungary • India • Indonesia • Ireland • Israel • Italy
Japan • Korea • Luxembourg • Malaysia • Mexico • The Netherlands • New Zealand • Norway • Peru • Philippines • Poland • Portugal
Puerto Rico • Romania • Russia • Saudi Arabia • Scotland • Singapore • Slovakia • Slovenia • South Africa • Spain • Sweden
Switzerland • Taiwan • Thailand • Turkey • Ukraine • United Kingdom • United States • Venezuela • Vietnam • Zimbabwe

About the Technical Reviewers

Ronald Bodtcher has been involved with computer networking since college, where he implemented a primitive version of SneakerNet while programming an IBM-360 with punched cards. After graduating from BYU with bachelor's and master's degrees in accounting, Ron actually became a computer and worked as a manager and tax computer specialist for KPMG Peat Marwick. Today, Ron is a consultant for CPAide, a company that provides web services for accounting professionals. Ron is a certified public accountant, and his IT certifications include A+, Network+, and CCNA. He is also a member of the Internet Society, the Association for Computing Machinery, and the IEEE. As a graduate of the Cisco Networking Academy Program at College of the Canyons in Santa Clarita, California, Ron has first-hand experience in mastering basic Cisco Networking and passed the CCNA with flying colors. Ron spends his free time recovering and restoring Ice Age fossils in the paleontology lab at the LaBrea Tar Pits and hiking in Waterton National Park with his wife, Sara, and their three daughters Sara Jr., Alice, and Ronaleah.

K R. Kirkendall is a teacher at Boise State University in Boise, Idaho, has his B.A. degree in business administration from St. Leo College, and is working on his MIS degree at Boise State. At Boise State, K teaches Cisco, Microsoft, and network security courses. He has several industry certifications, including CCNP, CCNA, CCAI, CCDA, MCP, CNA, A+, Network+, and Server+. K and his wife Jeanine have five wonderful children and two super grandsons, Isaiah and Kdren. For the past five years, K has also worked for the Cisco Networking Academy in the assessment division, which writes questions for the Cisco Networking Academy Program and Cisco Certification exams.

Jim Lorenz is a senior technical writer and curriculum developer for the Cisco Networking Academy Program. He has more than 20 years of experience in information systems and has held various IT positions in Fortune 500 companies, including Honeywell and Motorola. Jim has developed and taught computer and networking courses for both public and private institutions for more than 15 years. He is also an editor for the Cisco Networking Academy Program Lab Companion manuals. Jim is a Certified Novell Netware Engineer (CNE), a Microsoft Certified Trainer (MCT), and a Cisco Certified Academy Instructor (CCAI). Jim earned his bachelor's degree in computer information systems from Prescott College.

Rick McDonald earned his CCNP in 2002 and currently teaches CCNP and other computer classes at Central Piedmont Community College in Charlotte, North Carolina. He holds a B.A. degree in English and an M.A. degree in computer education from Gonzaga University in Spokane, Washington. Rick is an avid cyclist who also enjoys reading, but his preferred hobby is travel with his wife, Becky, and his sons, Greg, Paul, and Sam.

Overview

Table of Contents

Cisco Systems Networking Icon Legend

Cisco Systems, Inc. uses a standardized set of icons to represent devices in network topology illustrations. The icon legend that follows shows the most commonly used icons that you might encounter throughout this book.

Router   Bridge   Hub   DSU/CSU

Catalyst Switch   Multilayer Switch   ATM Switch   ISDN/Frame Relay Switch

Communication Server   Gateway   Access Server   Cluster Controller

PC   PC with Software   Sun Workstation   Macintosh   Terminal

File Server   Web Server   Cisco Works Workstation   Modem   Front End Processor

Printer   Laptop   IBM Mainframe

Token Ring   FDDI   Network Cloud

Line: Ethernet   Line: Serial   Line: Switched Serial

Command Syntax Conventions

The conventions used to present command syntax in this book are the same conventions used in the Cisco IOS Software Command Reference. The Command Reference describes these conventions as follows:

- Vertical bars (|) separate alternative, mutually exclusive elements.

- Square brackets ([ ]) indicate optional elements.

- Braces ({ }) indicate a required choice.

- Braces within brackets ([{ }]) indicate a required choice within an optional element.

- **Boldface** indicates commands and keywords that are entered exactly as shown.

- *Italic* indicates arguments for which you supply values.

Foreword

Throughout the world, the Internet has brought tremendous new opportunities for individuals and their employers. Companies and other organizations are seeing dramatic increases in productivity by investing in robust networking capabilities. Some studies have shown measurable productivity improvements in entire economies. The promise of enhanced efficiency, profitability, and standard of living is real and growing.

Such productivity gains aren't achieved by simply purchasing networking equipment. Skilled professionals are needed to plan, design, install, deploy, configure, operate, maintain, and troubleshoot today's networks. Network managers must assure that they have planned for network security and for continued operation. They need to design for the required performance level in their organization. They must implement new capabilities as the demands of their organization, and its reliance on the network, expands.

To meet the many educational needs of the internetworking community, Cisco Systems established the Cisco Networking Academy Program. The Networking Academy is a comprehensive learning program that provides students with the Internet technology skills essential in a global economy. The Networking Academy integrates face-to-face teaching, web-based content, online assessment, student performance tracking, hands-on labs, instructor training and support, and preparation for industry-standard certifications.

The Networking Academy continually raises the bar on blended learning and educational processes. The Internet-based assessment and instructor support systems are some of the most extensive and validated ever developed, including a 24/7 customer service system for Networking Academy instructors. Through community feedback and electronic assessment, the Networking Academy adapts the curriculum to improve outcomes and student achievement. The Cisco Global Learning Network infrastructure designed for the Networking Academy delivers a rich, interactive, and personalized curriculum to students worldwide. The Internet has the power to change the way people work, live, play, and learn, and the Cisco Networking Academy Program is in the forefront of this transformation.

This Cisco Press title is one of a series of best-selling companion titles for the Cisco Networking Academy Program. Designed by Cisco Worldwide Education and Cisco Press, these books provide integrated support for the online learning content that is made available to Academies all over the world. These Cisco Press books are the only authorized books for the Networking Academy by Cisco Systems, and provide print and CD-ROM materials that ensure the greatest possible learning experience for Networking Academy students.

I hope you are successful as you embark on your learning path with Cisco Systems and the Internet. I also hope that you will choose to continue your learning after you complete the Networking Academy curriculum. In addition to its Cisco Networking Academy Program titles, Cisco Press also publishes an extensive list of networking technology and certification publications that provide a wide range of resources. Cisco Systems has also established a network of professional training companies—the Cisco Learning Partners—who provide a full range of Cisco training courses. They offer training in many formats, including e-learning, self-paced, and instructor-led classes. Their instructors are Cisco certified, and Cisco creates their materials. When you are ready, please visit the Learning & Events area on Cisco.com to learn about all the educational support that Cisco and its partners have to offer.

Thank you for choosing this book and the Cisco Networking Academy Program.

Kevin Warner
Senior Director, Marketing
Worldwide Education
Cisco Systems, Inc.

Introduction

Cisco Networking Academy Program CCNA 3 and 4 Companion Guide, Third Edition, supplements your classroom and laboratory experience with the Cisco Networking Academy Program, whose curriculum empowers you to enter employment or further education and training in the computer networking field.

This book is designed to train you beyond the online materials that you have already used in this program. It also covers topics that pertain to the Cisco Certified Network Associate (CCNA) certification exam. This book closely follows the style and format that Cisco has incorporated into the curriculum. Finally, this book is complemented by a CD-ROM, which contains instructional Videos, e-Lab Activities, PhotoZooms, and exam preparation practice questions, all presented in an interactive multimedia format as learning reference materials.

This book introduces and extends your knowledge and practical experience with the design, configuration, and maintenance of switches, local-area networks (LANs), and virtual local-area networks (VLANs). The concepts that are covered in this book enable you to develop practical experience in skills that are related to configuring LANs, wide-area networks (WANs), Interior Gateway Routing Protocol (IGRP), Enhanced Interior Gateway Routing Protocol (EIGRP), and network troubleshooting. In addition, this book extends your knowledge of and practical experience with WANs, Integrated Services Data Network (ISDN), Point-to-Point Protocol (PPP), and Frame Relay design, configuration, and maintenance.

This book not only prepares you for the CCNA certification exam, but it also prepares you for the CompTIA Network+ certification exam.

The Goal of This Book

The goal of this book is to educate you about Cisco-supported networking technologies and to help you understand how to design and build networks and to configure Cisco routers. This book is designed for use in conjunction with the Cisco Networking Academy Program curriculum or as a standalone reference.

The Audience for This Book

This book's main audience is students who are interested in networking technologies. In particular, this book is targeted toward students who are in the Cisco Networking Academy Program. In the classroom, this book can serve as a supplement to the online curriculum.

This book is also appropriate for corporate training faculty and staff members, as well as general users. The book's user-friendly, nontechnical approach is ideal for readers who prefer to stay away from manuals that require a vast amount of technical knowledge.

Book Features

This book contains many helpful features that help facilitate your understanding of computer systems and troubleshooting system problems:

- **Objectives**—Each chapter starts with a list of objectives that should be mastered by the end of the chapter. The objectives provide a reference for the concepts that are covered in the chapter.

- **Figures, Examples, and Tables**—This book contains figures, configuration examples, and tables that help explain theories, concepts, and commands that reinforce concepts and help visualize the content that the chapter covers. In addition, the specific examples provide real-life situations that detail the problem and the solution.

- **Chapter Summaries**—At the end of each chapter is a summary of the concepts that were covered in the chapter. The summary provides a synopsis of the chapter and serves as a study aid. Use it to gauge your mastery of the topics covered in that chapter.

- **Key Terms**—The Key Terms section provides a summary of the most important terms that are covered in the chapter. These terms serve as a study aid. They also reinforce the concepts that were introduced in the chapter. As you read the chapter, any terms that appear in ~~blue~~ are defined in the Key Terms section.

- **Check Your Understanding Questions**—Review questions are presented at the end of Chapters 1–17 to serve as a further assessment. These questions reinforce the concepts introduced in the chapter and help test your understanding before you move on to new chapters.

- **Skill Builders**—Throughout this book are references to worksheet and lab activities that are found in *Cisco Networking Academy Program CCNA 3 and 4 Lab Companion*, Third Edition. These labs allow you to make a connection between theory and practice.

How This Book Is Organized

This book is divided into 23 chapters and two appendixes. Chapter 1 is a review, Chapters 2–10 apply to the CCNA 3 online curriculum, and Chapters 11–16 apply to the CCNA 4 online curriculum. Chapters 17–23 are additional materials that are written to help you prepare for exams, such as the CCNA and CompTIA Network+ exams, and to gain knowledge on emerging technologies. The following provides a summary of each element:

- Chapter 1, "The Review: The OSI Reference Model and Routing"—This chapter presents a review of the Open System Interconnection (OSI) reference model and an overview of network planning and design considerations that are related to routing.

- Chapter 2, "Introduction to Classless Routing"—This chapter presents the fundamentals of variable length subnet mask (VLSM) along with how and why to use it. This chapter describes how to configure VLSM. It also delves into the history of the Routing Information Protocol (RIP) and the basic components of RIPv2. Finally, this chapter covers how to configure, verify, and troubleshoot RIPv2.

- Chapter 3, "Single-Area OSPF"—This chapter discusses the fundamentals of link-state routing protocols, single-area OSPF concepts, and single-area OSPF configuration.

- Chapter 4, "Enhanced Interior Gateway Routing Protocol"—This chapter presents the basic concepts of EIGRP and compares it to IGRP. The steps for configuring, verifying, and troubleshooting are described as well.

- Chapter 5, "Switching Concepts and LAN Design"—This chapter discusses problems in LANs and possible solutions that can improve LAN performance. In addition, this chapter covers the advantages and disadvantages of using bridges, switches, and routers for LAN segmentation and the effects of switching, bridging, and routing on network throughput. Finally, this chapter presents Ethernet, Fast Ethernet, and VLANs and the benefits of these technologies.

- Chapter 6, "Switches"—This chapter presents 802.3 LANs and the pros and cons of LAN segmentation with LAN design. In addition, this chapter describes basic Layer 2 bridging and switching functions.

- Chapter 7, "Switch Configuration"—This chapter describes the processes of LAN switching. It covers the steps for configuring and verifying switch configuration and describes password recovery and firm upgrade procedures.

- Chapter 8, "Spanning Tree Protocol"—This chapter provides an overview of the Spanning Tree Protocol and redundant topologies.

- Chapter 9, "Virtual LANs"—This chapter discusses the basic concepts of VLANs and their benefits. It also describes how to configure, verify, save, delete, and troubleshoot VLANs.

- Chapter 10, "VLAN Trunking Protocol"—This chapter provides an overview of trunking. In addition, it describes the concepts, operation, and configuration of VTP. Finally, it covers the fundamentals of inter-VLAN routing.

- Chapter 11, "Scaling IP Addresses"—This chapter describes the components of scaling networks with NAT and PAT. It also discusses DHCP, its operation, configuration, and steps for troubleshooting.

- Chapter 12, "WAN Technologies"—This chapter presents the various protocols and technologies that are used in WAN environments. It describes the basics of WANs, including common WAN technologies, types of wide-area services, encapsulation formats, and link options. Finally, this chapter discusses point-to-point links, circuit switching, packet switching, virtual circuits, dial-up services, and WAN devices.

- Chapter 13, "Point-to-Point Protocol"—This chapter discusses the basic components, processes, and operations that define PPP communication. In addition, this chapter describes how to configure and verify the configuration of PPP along with PPP authentication.

- Chapter 14, "ISDN and DDR"—This chapter presents the services, standards, components, operation, and configuration of ISDN communication.

- Chapter 15, "Frame Relay"—This chapter discusses Frame Relay services, standards, components, and operation. In addition, this chapter covers the configuration tasks for Frame Relay service, along with the commands for monitoring and maintaining a Frame Relay connection.

- Chapter 16, "Introduction to Network Administration"—This chapter provides an overview of the methodologies that are used to design WANs. It includes a description of WAN communication and the processes and considerations for designing a WAN. It also covers the process for gathering user requirements for WAN design and the benefits of using a hierarchical design model. This chapter discusses basic components of different types of workstations and servers, including Microsoft, UNIX, and Apple systems. In addition, this chapter introduces network management tools, the OSI and network management models, as well as how management software gathers information and records problems.

- Chapter 17, "Optical Networking Fundamentals"—This chapter describes how optical networks provide speed, data transportation, capacity, and scalability. This chapter also discusses the optical network function, the enhanced scalability provided by dense wavelength division multiplexing (DWDM), and the solutions that optical networks provide.

- Chapter 18, "Network Management"—This chapter discusses the basic fundamentals of managing a network. It covers network documentation, network security, network maintenance, data recovery, server administration, server maintenance, and network troubleshooting.

- Chapter 19, "Network Certification Exam Review"—This chapter provides a review of the topics you need to know to successfully pass the Network+ certification exam.

- Chapter 20, "CCNA Certification Exam Review"—This chapter assists in your preparation for the CCNA certification exam by presenting a review of the topics that are covered on the exam.

- Chapter 21, "Introduction to Converged Networking"—This chapter describes how traditional voice, video, and data networks are implemented and explains various types of voice-over-data technologies. This chapter also covers the need for converged voice, video, and data networks. In addition, this chapter introduces Cisco Architecture for Voice, Video and Integrated Data (AVVID) and new applications for converged networks.

- Chapter 22, "Developing Network Security and Network Management Strategies"—This chapter helps you work with your network design customer in the development of effective security strategies. It helps you select the right tools and products to implement the strategies.

- Chapter 23, "Virtual Private Networks"—This chapter establishes virtual private networking as a clear case for security. It covers the basic mechanism for using public networks for private communications.

- Appendix A, "Glossary of Key Terms"—The glossary contains definitions of all the key terms that are used throughout the book.

- Appendix B, "Check Your Understanding Answer Key"—This appendix provides the answers to the "Check Your Understanding" questions that are at the end of each chapter.

About the CD-ROM

A CD-ROM accompanies this book to further enhance your learning experience. The CD-ROM contains a test engine with CCNA practice exam questions, interactive e-Lab Activities, PhotoZooms of networking equipment and hardware, and instructional Videos and animations that highlight potentially difficult concepts. These materials support self-directed study by allowing you to engage in learning and skill-building exercises outside of the classroom. The CD-ROM also provides the following:

- An easy-to-use graphical user interface
- Chapter-by-chapter activities and resources
- Information and activities that are not found online
- Accurate and concise feedback on practice exam questions
- Learner-directed practice and study
- Flexibility for learners of all levels

Finally, these learning tools emphasize not only conceptual material, but also the importance of practicing what you have learned. The CD-ROM helps you understand networking technologies and make the connection between theory and practice.

Part I

Review

Objectives

After reading this chapter, you will be able to

- Describe the OSI reference model's overall function and the problems it solves
- Describe the characteristics of the OSI reference model's physical layer
- Describe the characteristics of the OSI reference model's data link layer
- Describe the characteristics of the OSI reference model's network layer
- Describe the characteristics of the OSI reference model's transport layer
- Describe the function of routing in networks
- Understand the different classes of routing protocols

Chapter 1

Review: The OSI Reference Model and Routing

Networks are complex environments involving multiple media, multiple protocols, and interconnections to networks outside an organization's central office. Well-designed and carefully installed networks can reduce the problems associated with growth as a networking environment evolves.

Designing, building, and maintaining a *network* can be a challenging task, despite improvements in equipment performance and media capabilities. Even a small network that consists of only 50 routing nodes can pose complex problems that lead to unpredictable results. Large networks that feature thousands of nodes can pose even more complex problems.

This chapter provides a review of the Open System Interconnection (OSI) reference model and an overview of network planning and design considerations related to routing. Using the OSI reference model as a guide for network design can facilitate changes. Using the OSI reference model as a hierarchical structure for network design allows you to design networks in layers. The OSI reference model is at the heart of building and designing networks, with every layer performing a specific task to promote data communications. This chapter focuses on Layers 1 through 4. These four layers define the following:

- The type and speed of LAN and WAN media
- How the data is sent across the media
- The type of addressing schemes
- How flow control is accomplished
- The type of routing protocol

Please be sure to look at this chapter's associated e-Lab Activities, Videos, and PhotoZooms that you will find on the CD-ROM accompanying this book. These CD-ROM elements supplement the material and reinforce the concepts introduced in this chapter.

Layered Network Model: OSI Reference Model

Network models use layers to simplify the networking functions. The separation of networking functions is called layering. To understand the importance of *layering*, consider the OSI reference model, a layered model for comprehending and implementing computer communications. By using layers, the OSI reference model simplifies the tasks required for two computers to communicate with each other. Each layer focuses on specific functions, allowing the networking designer to choose the right networking devices and functions for the layer. In the OSI reference model, each of the seven layers represents distinct functions.

Reasons for this division of network functions include the following:

- Layers divide the aspects of network operation into less complex elements.
- Layers define standard interfaces for plug-and-play compatibility.
- Layers enable engineers to concentrate design and development efforts on modular functions.
- Layers promote symmetry in the different network modular functions so they work together.
- Layers prevent changes in one area from affecting other areas, so each area can evolve more quickly.
- Layers divide networking complexities into separate, easy-to-learn operations.

As shown in Figure 1-1, each layer of the OSI reference model serves a specific function:

- *Application layer (Layer 7)*—This layer provides network services to user applications. For example, a word-processing application is serviced by file-transfer services at this layer.
- *Presentation layer (Layer 6)*—This layer provides data representation and code formatting, and negotiates data transfer syntax. It ensures that the application can use the data that arrives from the network, and that information the application sends can be transmitted on the network.
- *Session layer (Layer 5)*—This layer establishes, maintains, and manages sessions between applications.
- *Transport layer (Layer 4)*—This layer provides flow control, windowing, and recovery. It also segments and reassembles data into a data stream. The transport layer has the potential to guarantee a connection and offer reliable transport. The transport layer is also responsible for assigning a port number, which is used to pass information to the higher layers.

- *Network layer (Layer 3)*—This layer determines the best way to move data from one place to another by defining end-to-end delivery of packets using a logical address to identify endpoints. The router operates at this layer. This layer uses logical addressing schemes that can be managed by an administrator. This layer can use the Internet Protocol (IP) addressing scheme or the AppleTalk, DECnet, VINES, and IPX addressing schemes.

- *Data link layer (Layer 2)*—This layer defines physical transmission across the medium. It provides error detection and, in some cases, error recovery, network topology, and flow control. This layer uses *Media Access Control (MAC)* addresses, which are also referred to as physical or hardware addresses.

- *Physical layer (Layer 1)*—This layer provides the electrical, mechanical, procedural, and functional means for activating and maintaining the physical link between systems. This layer uses such physical media as twisted-pair, coaxial, and fiber-optic cable.

Lab Activity   OSI Model and TCP/IP Model

In this exercise, you describe and compare the layers of the OSI and TCP/IP models. You also name the TCP/IP protocols and utilities that operate at each layer.

Lab Activity   OSI Model Encapsulation and Devices

In this exercise, you describe layers and characteristics of the OSI model. You also identify the encapsulation units and devices that operate at each layer.

Figure 1-1 Seven Layer OSI Model

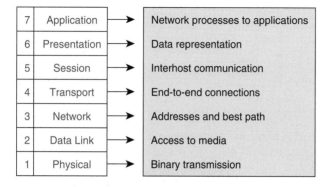

Peer-to-Peer Communication

The OSI reference model defines layer functions that can be used by any network products vendor to help guide the design and development of network products. The OSI reference model describes how information moves from application programs on different computers through a network medium. As the information to be sent descends through the layers of a given system, it looks less and less like a human language, and more and more like the 1s and 0s that a computer understands.

Each layer uses its own protocol to communicate with its peer layer in the other system. Each layer's protocol exchanges information, called *protocol data units (PDUs)*, between peer layers.

Figure 1-2 shows an example of OSI-type communication. In host-to-host, peer-layer protocol communication, the layer below the current layer provides services to the current layer. For example, Host A has information to send to Host B. The application program in Host A communicates with Host A's application layer, which communicates with Host A's presentation layer, which communicates with Host A's session layer, and so on, until Host A's physical layer is reached. The physical layer puts information on (and takes information off) the physical network medium. After the information traverses the physical network medium and is picked up by Host B, it ascends through Host B's layers in reverse order (first the physical layer, then the data link layer, and so on) until it reaches Host B's application layer.

Figure 1-2 OSI Model Communication

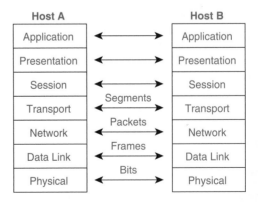

Although each Host A layer communicates with its adjacent layers, each layer in a host has a primary task it must perform. Each layer's primary task is to communicate with its peer layer in Host B. That is, Layer 1's task in Host A is to communicate with Layer 1 in Host B; Layer 2 in Host A communicates with Layer 2 in Host B; and so on.

The OSI reference model's layering prohibits direct communication between peer layers in different hosts. Each layer in Host A must rely on services provided by adjacent Host A layers to help achieve communication with its Host B peer. Assume that Layer 4 in Host A must communicate with Layer 4 in Host B. To do this, Layer 4 in Host A must use the services of Host A's Layer 3. Layer 4 is said to be the service user, and Layer 3 is the service provider. Layer 3 services are provided to Layer 4 at a service access point (SAP), which is a location at which Layer 4 can request Layer 3 services.

As shown in Figure 1-2, the TCP segments become part of the network layer *packets* (also called *datagrams*) exchanged between IP peers. In turn, the IP packets must become part of the data-link frames exchanged between directly connected devices. Ultimately, these frames must become bits as the data is finally transmitted by the physical-layer protocol using hardware.

Data Encapsulation

How does Layer 4 in Host B know what Layer 4 in Host A wants? Layer 4's specific requests are stored as control information, which is passed between peer layers in a *header* block that is attached to the actual application information. Each layer depends on the service function of the OSI reference model layer below it. To provide this service, the lower layer uses encapsulation to put the PDU from the upper layer into its data field; then, it can add whatever headers and trailers the layer will use to perform its function.

The concept of a header and data is relative, depending on the layer currently analyzing the information unit. For example, to Layer 3, an information unit consists of a Layer 3 header and the data that follows. Layer 3's data, however, can potentially contain headers from Layers 4, 5, 6, and 7. Furthermore, Layer 3's header is simply data to Layer 2, as illustrated in Figure 1-3. Finally, not all layers need to append headers. Some layers simply transform the actual data they receive to make the data readable to their adjacent layers.

Figure 1-3 Network Layer

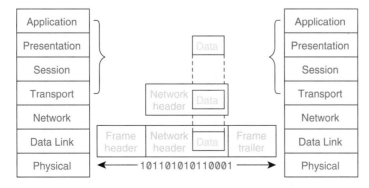

The network layer moves data through the network by encapsulating the data within a header. For example, the network layer provides a service to the transport layer, and the transport layer presents data to the network. The network layer then encapsulates the data within a header. This header contains the information required to complete the transfer, such as the source and destination logical addresses. The data link layer, in turn, provides a service to the network layer, encapsulating the network layer information in a frame. The frame header contains information required to complete the data-link functions. For example, the frame header contains physical addresses. The physical layer also provides a service to the data link layer by encoding the data-link frame into a pattern of 1s and 0s for transmission on the medium (often copper wire or optical fiber).

For example, assume that Host A wants to send the following e-mail to Host B:

The small gray cat ran up the wall to try to catch the red bird.

Five conversion steps occur during data encapsulation, which enables the transmission of the e-mail to the appropriate destination:

Step 1   As a user sends an e-mail message, the message's alphanumeric characters are converted to data, starting at Layer 7 and moving down through Layer 5, and are sent over the network.

Step 2   By using segments at Layer 4, the transport function packages data for the network transport and ensures that the message hosts at both ends of the e-mail system can reliably communicate.

Step 3   The data is placed into a packet (or datagram) at Layer 3 that contains a network header with source and destination logical addresses. Then, the network devices send the packets across the network along a chosen path.

Step 4   Each network device must put the packet into a frame at Layer 2, allowing the connection to the next directly connected network device on the link. Each device in the chosen network path requires framing to connect to the next device. Keep in mind that routers, which are Layer 3 devices, use IP addresses to choose the path a packet must take to reach a destination. After the router chooses a path, it usually sends the packet out one of its Layer 2 interfaces, which has a MAC address, to another router's MAC address.

Step 5   The frame must be converted into a pattern of 1s and 0s for transmission on the medium (often copper wire or optical fiber) at Layer 1. A clocking function enables the devices to distinguish these bits as they traverse the medium. The medium on the physical network can vary along the path used. For example, the e-mail message can originate on a LAN, cross a campus backbone, and go out a WAN link until it reaches its destination on another remote LAN.

Physical Layer

Ethernet and IEEE 802.3 currently maintain the greatest share of any LAN protocol used. Today, the term Ethernet is often used to refer to all carrier sense multiple access collision detect (CSMA/CD) LANs that generally conform to Ethernet specifications, including IEEE 802.3.

Ethernet was designed to fill the middle ground between long-distance, low-speed networks and specialized, computer room networks carrying data at high speeds for very limited distances. Ethernet is good for applications where a local communication medium must carry sporadic, occasionally heavy traffic at high-peak data rates.

Ethernet refers to the family of LAN implementations that includes three principal categories:

- **Ethernet and IEEE 802.3**—LAN specifications that operate at 10 Mbps over coaxial and twisted-pair cable.
- **100-Mbps Ethernet**—Also known as *Fast Ethernet*, it specifies a LAN operating at 100 Mbps over twisted-pair cable.
- **1000-Mbps Ethernet**—Also known as *Gigabit Ethernet*, it specifies a LAN operating at 1000 Mbps (1 Gbps) over fiber-optic and twisted-pair cables.

Ethernet has survived as an essential media technology because of its tremendous flexibility and because it is simple to implement and understand. Although other technologies have been promoted as likely replacements, network managers have turned to Ethernet and its derivatives as effective solutions for a range of campus implementation requirements. To resolve Ethernet's limitations, creative users (and standards organizations) have created bigger and bigger Ethernet pipes. Critics might dismiss Ethernet as a technology that cannot grow, but its underlying transmission scheme continues to be one of the principal means of transporting data for contemporary campus applications.

Ethernet/802.3 Physical Connections

The Ethernet and IEEE 802.3 wiring standards define a bus topology LAN that operates at 10 Mbps.

Figure 1-4 illustrates the three defined wiring standards:

- **10Base2**—Known as *thin Ethernet* or *ThinNet*, 10Base2 allows network segments up to 185 meters on coaxial cable.
- **10Base5**—Known as *thick Ethernet*, 10Base5 allows network segments up to 500 meters on coaxial cable.
- **10BaseT**—10BaseT carries Ethernet frames on inexpensive twisted-pair wiring with individual cable runs of up to 100 meters.

Figure 1-4 10Base2, 10Base5, and 10BaseT Standards

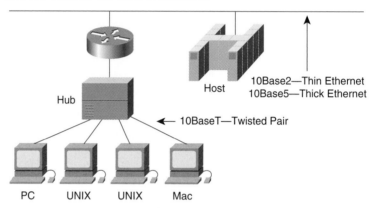

10Base2, 10Base5, and 10BaseT standards provide access for several stations on the same LAN segment. Ethernet and IEEE 802.3 wiring standards specify a bus topology network with a connecting cable between the end stations and the actual network medium. In the case of Ethernet, that cable is called a transceiver cable. The transceiver cable connects to a transceiver device attached to the physical network medium. The IEEE 802.5 configuration is much the same, except that the connecting cable is referred to as an *attachment unit interface (AUI)*, and the transceiver is called a *media attachment unit*. In both cases, the connecting cable attaches to an interface board (or interface circuitry) within the end station.

Stations are attached to the segment by a cable that runs from an AUI in the station to a central concentrating device that is directly attached to the Ethernet coaxial cable. 10BaseT Ethernet also uses a bus topology, but it is a logical bus because it is implemented in the hub or switch's circuitry. Physically, 10BaseT Ethernet uses a star or extended-star topology, with all network nodes connected to the central hub or LAN switch.

Data Link Layer

Access to the networking media occurs at the OSI reference model's data link layer. The data link layer, where the MAC address is located, is adjacent to the physical layer. No two MAC addresses are ever alike. A *Network Interface Card (NIC)* is an expansion board you insert into a computer so that the computer can be connected to a network. Most NICs are designed for a particular type of network, protocol, and media; although, some can serve multiple networks. On a network, the network interface card (NIC) is where a device connects to the medium, and each NIC has a unique MAC address.

Before each NIC leaves the factory, the hardware manufacturer assigns it a MAC address. This address is programmed into a chip on the NIC. Because the MAC address is located on the NIC, if a computer's NIC is replaced, the station's physical address changes to that of the new NIC's MAC address.

MAC addresses are written using a base 16 (hexadecimal) number. MAC addresses have two formats: 0000.0c12.3456 and 00-00-0c-12-34-56.

Imagine that you operate a motel. Room 207 has a lock called Lock A. Key A opens the door to Room 207. Room 410 has a lock called Lock F. Key F opens the door to Room 410.

You decide to swap the locks on Rooms 207 and 410. After you switch the two locks, Key A opens the door to Room 410, and Key F opens the door to Room 207.

In this analogy, the locks are like NICs. When the NICs are swapped, the matching keys must also change. A computer's LAN address is in the NIC card, and if you change the card, the address will also change.

On an Ethernet network, when one device wants to send data to another device, it can open a communication pathway to the other device using its MAC address. When data is sent out on a network by a source, it carries the intended destination's MAC address. As this data travels along the network media, the NIC in each device on the network checks to see if its MAC address matches the physical destination address carried by the frame. If no match is made, the NIC ignores the frame, and the frame continues along the network to the next station.

When a match is made, the NIC makes a copy of the frame, which it places in the computer, where it resides at the data link layer. Even though this copy has been made by the NIC and placed on the computer, the original frame continues along the network where other NICs can determine whether a match can be made.

Ethernet/802.3 Interface

NOTE

Fast Ethernet interfaces on modular routers are designated as Fa0/0 (2600 and others). The abbreviation Fa represents Fast Ethernet and 0/0 represents slot 0 and port or interface 0.

The Ethernet and 802.3 data links provide data transport across the physical link joining two devices. For example, as Figure 1-5 shows, the three devices can be directly attached to each other over the Ethernet LAN. The Apple Macintosh on the left and the Intel-based PC in the middle show MAC addresses used by the data link layer. The router on the right also uses MAC addresses for each of its LAN-side interfaces. To indicate the 802.3 interface on a router, you use the *Cisco Internetwork Operating System (IOS)* interface type abbreviation E, followed by an interface number (for example, FA0).

Figure 1-5 Ethernet/802.3 Interface

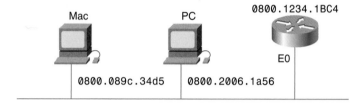

Network Layer

Several protocols operate at the OSI reference model's network layer:

- IP provides connectionless, *best-effort delivery* of routed datagrams (packets). It is not concerned with the datagrams' content; instead, it looks for a way to move the datagrams to their destinations.
- *Internet Control Message Protocol (ICMP)* provides control and messaging capabilities.
- *Address Resolution Protocol (ARP)* determines the data link layer addresses for known IP addresses.
- *Reverse ARP (RARP)* determines network addresses when data link layer addresses are known.

IP Addressing and Subnets

In a TCP/IP environment, end stations communicate with servers, hosts, or other end stations. This occurs because each node using the TCP/IP protocol suite has a unique 32-bit logical address, known as the *IP address*. In addition, within a TCP/IP environment, each network is seen as a single unique address. That address must be reached before an individual host within that network can be contacted.

Networks can be segmented into a series of smaller networks called *subnetworks*, as shown in Figure 1-6. An IP address is broken up into the network number, the subnetwork number, and the host number. Subnets use unique 32-bit subnet addresses that are created by borrowing bits from the host field. Subnet addresses are visible to other devices on the same network, but they are not visible to outside networks because detailed information about subnetting scheme is normally not shared with neighbor routers.

Figure 1-6 Subnetworks

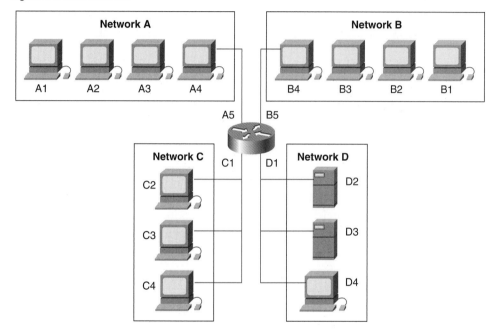

Subnets allow network address space to be used more efficiently. There is no change to how the outside world sees the network, but additional structure exists within the organization. Routers determine the destination network using the subnet address, which limits the amount of traffic on the other network segments. In Figure 1-7, network 172.16.0.0 is subdivided into four subnets: 172.16.1.0, 172.16.2.0, 172.16.3.0, and 172.16.4.0.

Figure 1-7 Subnetting

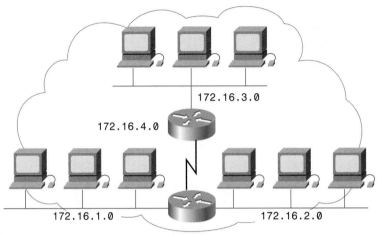

172.16.3.0

172.16.4.0

172.16.1.0

172.16.2.0

Network 172.16.0.0

Path Determination

Path determination is the path traffic should take through the network cloud. The path determination function enables a router to evaluate the available paths to a destination and to establish a packet's preferred handling. As shown in Figure 1-8, routers evaluate the best-known path for traffic. Path determination occurs at Layer 3, the network layer. Routing services use network topology information when evaluating network paths. This information can be configured by the network administrator or collected through dynamic processes running in the network.

The network layer connects to networks and provides best-effort, end-to-end packet delivery services to its user, the transport layer. The network layer sends packets from the source network to the destination network based on the IP routing table. After the router determines which path to use, it can proceed with switching the packet. Switching involves taking the packet the router accepted on one interface and forwarding it to another interface or port that reflects the best path to the packet's destination.

Path Communication

For path communication to be truly practical, a network must consistently represent the paths available between routers. An address must have information about the path of media connections that the routing process uses to pass packets from a source toward a destination. Each line between the routers in Figure 1-9 has a number that represents the subnetwork address that a routing process can use. These addresses must convey information that a routing process can use.

Figure 1-8 Path Determination

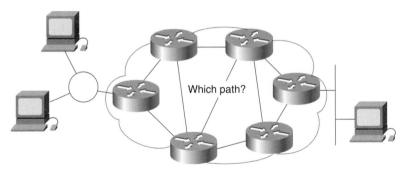

Figure 1-9 Path Communication

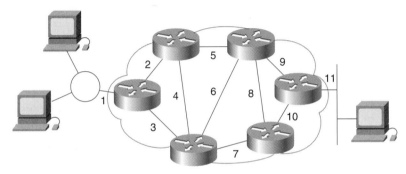

The network address contains both a path and a host part. The path portion identifies a path part used by the router within the network cloud; the host part identifies a specific port or device on the network. The router uses the network address to identify a packet's source or destination address within a network.

Most network-protocol addressing schemes use some form of a host or node address. Figure 1-10 shows three network numbers coming from the router and three hosts sharing the network number 1. For some network layer protocols, a network administrator establishes this relationship by assigning network addresses ahead of time according to a network-addressing plan. For other network layer protocols, assigning addresses is partially or completely dynamic.

The consistency of Layer 3 addresses across the entire network improves bandwidth use by preventing unnecessary broadcasts. Broadcasts cause unnecessary traffic and waste capacity on devices or links that do not need to receive the broadcasts. By using consistent, end-to-end addressing to represent the path of media connections, the network layer can find a path to the destination without unnecessary use of devices or links on the network.

Figure 1-10 Addressing Schemes

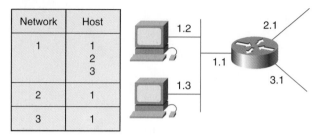

Network	Host
1	1 2 3
2	1
3	1

ICMP

ICMP messages are carried in IP datagrams and are used to send error and control messages. ICMP uses the following types of defined messages; others exist, but are not included in the following list:

- Destination unreachable
- Time exceeded
- Parameter problem
- Source quench
- Redirect
- Echo
- Echo reply
- Timestamp
- Timestamp reply
- Information request
- Information reply
- Address request
- Address reply

The router issues a destination unreachable message indicating that the host, the port, or the network is unreachable. Figure 1-11 shows a router receiving a packet that it is unable to deliver to its ultimate destination; because of this, the router sends the source an ICMP host unreachable message. The message might be undeliverable because no known route exists to the destination. Results of a **ping** command could also include other ICMP messages, such as unreachable and timeout messages.

On the other hand, Figure 1-12 shows an echo reply that is a successful reply to a ping command.

Figure 1-11 Undeliverable Packet

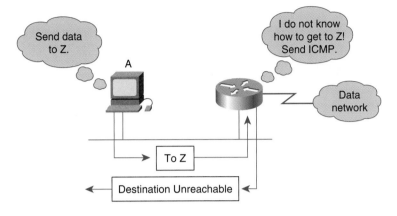

Figure 1-12 Ping Command Results

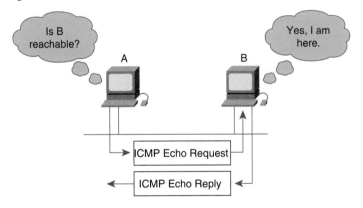

ARP

To communicate on an Ethernet network, the source station must know the destination station's IP and MAC addresses. When the source has determined the IP address for the destination, the source's IP looks into its ARP table to locate the destination's MAC address. If the IP locates a mapping of destination IP address to destination MAC address in its table, it binds the IP address with the MAC address and uses them to encapsulate the data. The data packet is then sent over the networking media to be picked up by the destination.

When a network device wants to send data, it checks its ARP table for the destination address. If the address is not found in the table, the sender broadcasts an ARP request in an attempt to discover the destination's MAC address. Every device on the network receives this broadcast.

Local ARP resolves an address by looking at the subnet mask. The term *local ARP* is used when both the requesting host and the destination host share the same medium, or wire (see Figure 1-13).

Figure 1-13 Local ARP

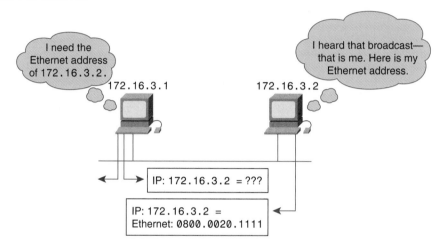

Routing

The network layer must relate to and interface with various lower layers. Routers must be capable of seamlessly handling packets encapsulated into different lower-level frames without changing the packets' Layer 3 addressing. Figure 1-14 shows an example of this with LAN-to-LAN routing. In this example, packet traffic from Host 4 on Ethernet Network 1 needs a path to Host 5 on Network 2.

When the router checks its routing table entries, it discovers that the best path to Network 2 uses outgoing Port To0, the interface to a Token Ring LAN. Although the lower-layer framing must change as the router switches packet traffic from Ethernet on Network 1 to Token Ring on Network 2, the Layer 3 addressing for the source and destination remains the same. The LAN hosts depend on the router and its consistent network addressing to find the best path. In Figure 1-14, the destination address remains Network 2, Host 5, despite the different lower-layer encapsulations.

Figure 1-14 Routing

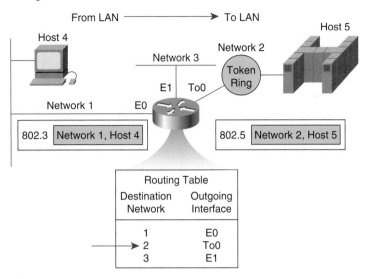

Router Operations

Routers generally relay a packet from one data link to another. To relay a packet, a router uses two basic functions: a path determination function and a switching function. A router passes the packet to the next network along the path and uses the address's network portion to make path selections. Figure 1-15 illustrates how routers use addressing for routing and switching functions.

Figure 1-15 Router Operations

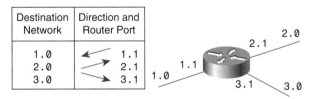

The switching function allows a router to accept a packet on one interface and forward it on a second interface. The path determination function enables the router to select the most appropriate interface for forwarding a packet. The node portion of the address refers to a specific port on the router that leads to an adjacent router in that direction.

When a host application needs to send a packet to a destination on a different network, a data-link frame is received on one of a router's interfaces. The network layer process examines the header to determine the destination network, and then references the routing table that associates networks to outgoing interfaces. The original frame is stripped off and discarded. The packet is again encapsulated in the data-link frame for the selected interface and stored in a *queue* for delivery to the next *hop* in the path.

This process occurs each time the packet switches through another router. At the router connected to the network containing the destination host, the packet is again encapsulated in the destination LAN's data-link frame type and delivered to the destination host.

Static Versus Dynamic Routes

Static routing is administered manually. A network administrator enters the route into the router's configuration. The administrator must manually update this static route entry whenever a network topology change requires an update. Static routing reduces overhead because routing updates are not sent (in the case of RIP, every 30 seconds).

Dynamic routing works differently. After the network administrator enters configuration commands to start dynamic routing, route knowledge is updated automatically at periodic intervals, or whenever new information is received from the network. Changes in dynamic knowledge are exchanged between routers as part of the update process.

Static routing has several useful applications. It allows a network administrator to specify what is advertised about restricted partitions. For security reasons, the administrator can hide parts of a network. Dynamic routing tends to reveal everything known about a network.

Additionally, when a network is accessible by only one path, a static route to the network can be sufficient. This type of partition is called a *stub network*. Configuring static routing to a stub network avoids the overhead of dynamic routing because routing updates are not sent.

Default Route Example

Default routes can be set as the result of the administrator's static configuration. Figure 1-16 shows a use for a *default route*—a routing table entry that is used to direct packets for which the next hop is not explicitly listed in the routing table. In this example, Company X routers possess specific knowledge of Company X's network topology, but not of other networks. Maintaining knowledge of every other network accessible by way of the Internet cloud is unnecessary and unreasonable, if not impossible.

Figure 1-16 Default Route

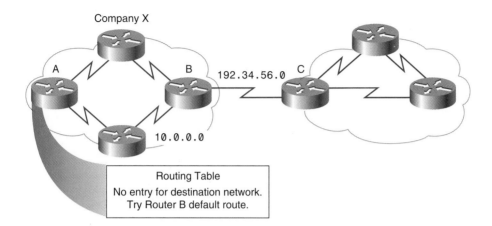

Instead of maintaining specific network knowledge, each router in Company X is informed by the default route that it can reach any unknown destination by directing the packet to the Internet.

Routed Versus Routing Protocols

Confusion often exists between the similar terms *routed protocol* and *routing protocol*. The following definitions differentiate the terms:

- **Routed protocol**—Any network protocol that provides enough information in its network layer address to allow a packet to be forwarded from host to host based on the addressing scheme. Routed protocols define the format and use of the fields within a packet. Packets generally are conveyed from end system to end system. IP is an example of a routed protocol.

- **Routing protocol**—A protocol that supports a routed protocol by providing mechanisms for sharing routing information. Routing protocol messages move between routers. A routing protocol allows the routers to communicate with other routers to update and maintain tables. TCP/IP examples of routing protocols are *Routing Information Protocol (RIP)*, *Interior Gateway Routing Protocol (IGRP)*, *Enhanced Interior Gateway Routing Protocol (EIGRP)*, and *Open Shortest Path First (OSPF)* protocol.

Routing Protocols

The success of dynamic routing depends on two basic router functions:

- Routing table maintenance
- Timely distribution of knowledge in the form of routing updates to other routers

Dynamic routing relies on a routing protocol to share knowledge. A routing protocol defines the set of rules a router uses when it communicates with neighboring routers. For example, a routing protocol describes the following:

- How updates are sent
- What knowledge is contained in these updates
- When to send this knowledge
- How to locate recipients of the updates

Exterior routing protocols communicate between autonomous systems. An autonomous system is a collection of networks under a common administration sharing a common routing strategy. Interior routing protocols are used within a single autonomous system.

IP Routing Protocols

At the network layer (Layer 3) of the OSI reference model, a router can uses IP routing protocols to transmit data to the proper location through the implementation of a specific protocols, which are listed below. Examples of IP routing protocols include the following:

- **RIP**—A distance-vector routing protocol
- **IGRP**—Cisco's distance-vector routing protocol
- **OSPF**—A link-state routing protocol
- **EIGRP**—A balanced-hybrid routing protocol

Routing Protocols

Most interior routing protocols can be classified as one of three basic types: distance vector, link state, or balanced-hybrid routing. The *distance-vector routing protocol* determines the direction (vector) and distance to any link in the network. The *link-state routing protocol* (also called the *shortest path first [SPF] protocol*) approach re-creates the entire network's exact topology (or at least the partition in which the router is situated). The *balanced-hybrid protocol* combines aspects of the link-state and distance-vector protocols.

Convergence

Routing protocols, which are used to determine the best route for traffic from a particular source to a particular destination, are fundamental to dynamic routing. Whenever the network topology changes because of growth, reconfiguration, or failure, the network knowledge base also must change. The knowledge needs to reflect an accurate, consistent view of the new topology. This accurate, consistent view is called *convergence*.

When all routers in a network are operating with the same knowledge, the network is said to have converged. Fast convergence is a desirable network feature because it reduces the period of time that routers have outdated knowledge for making routing decisions that could be incorrect, wasteful, or both.

Distance-Vector Routing

Regular updates between routers communicate topology changes. Distance-vector routing protocols pass periodic copies of a routing table from router to router. For example, in Figure 1-17, each router receives a routing table from its direct neighbor. Router B receives information from Router A. Router B adds a distance-vector number (such as a number of hops), increases the distance vector, and passes the routing table to its other neighbor, Router C. This same step-by-step process occurs in all directions between direct-neighbor routers.

Figure 1-17 Distance-Vector Routing

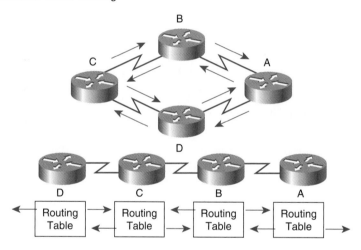

In this way, the protocol accumulates network distances so it can maintain a database of network topology information. Distance-vector protocols do not allow a router to know a network's exact topology.

Link-State Routing

The second basic protocol used for routing is the link-state protocol. Link-state routing protocols maintain a complex database of topology information. Whereas the distance-vector protocol has nonspecific information about distant networks and no knowledge of distant routers, a link-state routing protocol maintains full knowledge of distant routers and how they interconnect.

Link-state routing uses *link-state advertisements (LSAs)*, a topological database, the SPF protocol, the resulting SPF tree, and a routing table of paths and ports to each network. Engineers have implemented this link-state concept in OSPF routing.

Distance-Vector Routing Versus Link-State Routing

You can compare distance-vector routing to link-state routing in several key areas:

- Distance-vector routing gets all topological data from its neighbors' routing table information. Link-state routing obtains a complete view of the network topology by accumulating information from LSAs from both neighboring and distant routers.
- Distance-vector routing determines the best path by adding to the metric value it receives as tables move from router to router. For link-state routing, each router works separately to calculate its own shortest path to destinations.
- With most distance-vector routing protocols, updates for topology changes come in periodic table updates. These tables pass from router to router, often resulting in slower convergence. With link-state routing protocols, updates are usually triggered by topology changes. Relatively small LSAs passed to all other routers usually result in faster convergence on any network topology change.

IP Routing Configuration Tasks

The selection of IP as a routed protocol involves setting global parameters. Global parameters include selecting a routing protocol, such as RIP or IGRP, and assigning IP network numbers without specifying subnet values.

IP Address Configuration

You use the **ip address** command to establish the interface's logical network address. You use the **term ip netmask-format** command to specify the network masks' format for the current session. Format options are bit count, dotted-decimal (the default), and hexadecimal.

Dynamic Routing Configuration

Dynamic routing occurs when routers send periodic routing update messages to each other. Each time such a message is received and it contains new information, the router recalculates the best route and sends update information to other routers.

The commands in Table 1-1 start routing processes.

Table 1-1 Router and Network Commands

Command	Description
router *protocol*	Defines an IP routing protocol, which can be RIP, IGRP, OSPF, or EIGRP.
network	The **network** subcommand is a mandatory configuration command for each routing process.

The **network** command in Table 1-2 is required because it allows the routing process to determine which interfaces will participate in sending and receiving routing updates.

Table 1-2 Network Commands

network Command	Description
network *network-number*	Specifies a directly connected network

RIP

Key characteristics of RIP include the following:

- It is a distance-vector routing protocol.
- Hop count is used as the metric for path selection.
- The maximum allowable hop count is 15.
- Routing updates are broadcast every 30 seconds by default.

Routing updates allow the router to learn the network topology. The **router rip** command selects RIP as the routing protocol. The **network** command assigns an IP-based network address range, which is directly connected to the router. The routing process associates interfaces with the proper addresses and begins packet processing on the specified networks, as shown in Figure 1-18:

- **router rip**—Selects RIP as the routing protocol.
- **network 1.0.0.0**—Specifies a directly connected network.
- **network 2.0.0.0**—Specifies a directly connected network.

The Cisco A router interfaces connected to networks 1.0.0.0 and 2.0.0.0 will send and receive RIP updates.

Figure 1-18 Routing Updates

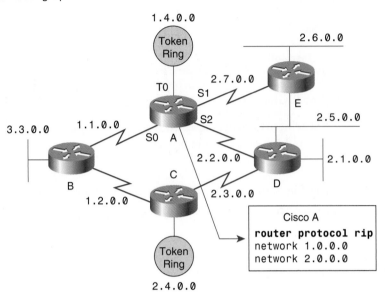

Transport Layer

As the transport layer sends its data segments, it can ensure the data's integrity. One method of doing this is called *flow control*. Flow control avoids the problem of a source host overflowing the buffers in the destination host. Overflows can present serious problems because they can result in the loss of data.

Transport-layer services also allow users to request reliable data transport between hosts and destinations. To obtain such reliable transport of data, a connection-oriented relationship is used between the communicating end systems. Reliable transport can accomplish the following:

- Segment upper-layer applications
- Establish a connection
- Transfer data
- Provide reliability with windowing
- Use acknowledgment techniques

Segmenting Upper-Layer Applications

One reason for using a layered network model is so that several applications can share the same transport connection. Transport functionality is accomplished segment by segment. This means that different applications can send data segments on a first-come, first-served basis. Such segments can be intended for the same destination or for many different destinations.

Establishing a Connection

To establish a connection, one machine places a call that must be accepted by the other. Protocol software modules in the two operating systems communicate by sending messages across the network to verify that the transfer is authorized and that both sides are ready. After all synchronization has occurred, a connection is established, and the transfer of data begins. During transfer, the two machines continue to communicate with their protocol software to verify that data is received correctly.

For data transfer to begin, both the sending and receiving application programs must inform their respective operating systems that a connection will be initiated. Figure 1-19 depicts a typical connection between sending and receiving systems. When you first meet someone, you often greet the person by shaking his or her hand. The act of shaking hands is understood by both parties as a signal for a friendly greeting. We speak of connections on the network in the same way. The first handshake, or greeting, requests synchronization. The second and third handshakes acknowledge the initial synchronization request, as well as synchronize the connection parameters in the opposite direction. The final handshake segment is an acknowledgment used to inform the destination that both sides agree that a connection has been established. After the connection is established, data transfer begins.

Figure 1-19 Network Connection

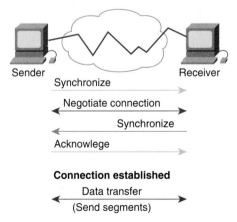

Data Transfer

When data transfer is in progress, congestion can arise for two different reasons. First, a high-speed computer might be able to generate traffic faster than a network can transfer it. Second, if many computers simultaneously need to send datagrams to a single destination, that destination can experience congestion, even though no single source caused the problem.

When datagrams arrive too quickly for a host or gateway to process, they are temporarily stored in memory. Instead of allowing data to be lost, the transport function can issue a "not ready" indicator to the sender. If the traffic continues, the host or gateway eventually exhausts its memory and must discard additional datagrams that arrive. As shown in Figure 1-20, an indicator acts like a stoplight and signals the sender to stop sending data. When the receiver can handle additional data, the receiver sends a "ready" transport indicator, which is like a "go" signal. When the sender receives this indicator, it can resume segment transmission.

Figure 1-20 Data Transfer

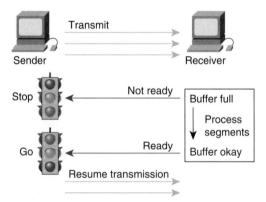

Reliability with Windowing

In the most basic form of reliable connection-oriented data transfer, data packets must be delivered to the recipient in the same order in which they were transmitted. The protocol fails if any data packets are lost, damaged, duplicated, or received in a different order. The basic solution is to have a recipient acknowledge the receipt of every data segment.

If the sender has to wait for an acknowledgment after sending each segment, throughput is low. Because time is available after the sender finishes transmitting the data packet and before the sender finishes processing any received acknowledgment, the interval is used for transmitting more data. The number of data packets the sender is allowed to have outstanding without yet receiving an acknowledgment is known as the *window*.

Windowing is a method to control the amount of information transferred end-to-end. Some protocols measure information in terms of the number of packets; TCP/IP measures information in terms of the number of bytes.

Acknowledgment Techniques

Reliable delivery guarantees that a stream of data sent from one machine will be delivered through a data link to another machine without duplication or data loss. Positive acknowledgment with retransmission is one technique that guarantees reliable delivery of data streams. Positive acknowledgment requires a recipient to communicate with the source, sending back an acknowledgment message when it receives data. The sender keeps a record of each data packet it sends and waits for an acknowledgment before sending the next data packet. The sender also starts a timer when it sends a segment, and it retransmits a segment if the timer expires before an acknowledgment arrives.

Positive acknowledgment requires a recipient to communicate with the source, sending back an acknowledgment message when it receives data.

Figure 1-21 shows the sender transmitting Data Packets 1, 2, and 3. The receiver acknowledges receipt of the packets by requesting Packet 4. Upon receiving the acknowledgment, the sender sends Packets 4, 5, and 6. If Packet 5 does not arrive at the destination, the receiver acknowledges with a request to resend Packet 5. The sender resends Packet 5 and must receive an acknowledgment to continue with the transmission of Packet 7.

Figure 1-21 Acknowledgment Techniques

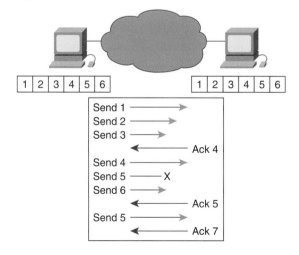

Summary

- By using layers, the OSI reference model simplifies the task required for two computers to communicate.

- Each layer's protocol exchanges information, called PDUs, between peer layers.

- Each layer depends on the service function of the OSI reference model layer below it. The lower layer uses encapsulation to put the PDU from the upper layer into its data field; then, it can add whatever headers and trailers the layer will use to perform its function.

- The term *Ethernet* often refers to all CSMA/CD LANs that generally conform to Ethernet specifications, including IEEE 802.3.

- Ethernet and 802.3 data links provide data transport across the physical link that joins two devices.

- IP provides connectionless, best-effort delivery routing of datagrams. It is not concerned with the datagrams' content, but it looks for a way to move the datagrams to their destination.

- ICMP messages are carried in IP datagrams and are used to send error and control messages.

- ARP maps a known IP address to a MAC sublayer address to allow communication on a multiaccess medium, such as Ethernet.

- The switching function allows a router to accept a packet on one interface and forward it on a second interface.

- Routed protocols are network protocols that provide enough information in the network layer address to allow a packet to be forwarded from host to host based on the addressing scheme.

- Routing protocol supports routed protocols by providing mechanisms for sharing routing information. Routing protocol messages move between the routers.

- Most routing protocols can be classified into one of two basic protocols: distance-vector or link-state.

- Routers must be capable of seamlessly handling packets encapsulated into different lower-level frames without changing the packets' Layer 3 addressing.

- Examples of IP routing protocols include RIP, IGRP, OSPF, and EIGRP.

- Transport-layer services allow users to request reliable data transport between hosts and destinations.

To supplement all that you've learned in this chapter, refer to the chapter-specific Videos, PhotoZooms, and e-Lab Activities on the CD-ROM accompanying this book.

Key Terms

application layer   Layer 7 of the OSI reference model. This layer provides network services to user applications. For example, a word-processing application is serviced by file-transfer services at this layer.

ARP (Address Resolution Protocol)   An Internet protocol used to map an IP address to a MAC address. Defined in RFC 826.

AUI (attachment unit interface)   An IEEE 802.3 interface between a media attachment unit and a network interface card. The term AUI can also refer to the rear panel port to which an AUI cable might attach, such as those found on a Cisco LightStream Ethernet access card. Also called a transceiver cable.

balanced-hybrid protocol   A protocol that combines aspects of the link-state and distance-vector protocols.

best-effort delivery   This delivery occurs when a network system does not use a sophisticated acknowledgment system to guarantee reliable delivery of information.

Cisco IOS (Internetwork Operating System) Software   Cisco system software that provides common functionality, scalability, and security for all products under the CiscoFusion architecture. The Cisco IOS Software allows centralized, integrated, and automated installation and management of internetworks, while ensuring support for a wide variety of protocols, media, services, and platforms.

convergence   The speed and capability of a group of internetworking devices running a specific routing protocol to agree on an internetwork's topology after a change in that topology.

data link layer   Layer 2 of the OSI reference model. This layer provides reliable transit of data across a physical link. The data link layer is concerned with physical addressing, network topology, line discipline, error notification, ordered delivery of frames, and flow control. The IEEE divided this layer into two sublayers: the MAC sublayer and the LLC sublayer. Sometimes, this layer is called simply the link layer. This layer roughly corresponds to the SNA model's data link control layer.

datagram   A logical grouping of information sent as a network layer unit over a transmission medium without prior establishment of a virtual circuit. IP datagrams are the primary information units in the Internet. The terms cell, frame, message, packet, and segment are also used to describe logical information groupings at various layers of the OSI reference model and in various technology circles.

default route   A routing table entry that directs frames for which a next hop is not explicitly listed in the routing table.

distance-vector routing protocol   A routing protocol that iterates on the number of hops in a route to find a shortest-path spanning tree. Distance-vector routing protocols call for each router to send its entire routing table in each update, but only to its neighbors. Distance-vector routing protocols can be prone to routing loops, but are computationally simpler than link-state routing protocols. Also called Bellman-Ford routing algorithm.

dynamic routing   Routing that adjusts automatically to network topology or traffic changes. Also called adaptive routing.

EIGRP (Enhanced Interior Gateway Routing Protocol)   An advanced version of IGRP developed by Cisco. Provides superior convergence properties and operating efficiency, and combines the advantages of link-state protocols with those of distance-vector protocols.

flow control   A technique for ensuring that a transmitting entity does not overwhelm a receiving entity with data. When the buffers on the receiving device are full, a message is sent to the sending device to suspend transmission until the data in the buffers has been processed. In IBM networks, this technique is called pacing.

header   Control information placed before data when encapsulating that data for network transmission.

hop   The passage of a data packet between two network nodes (for example, between two routers).

ICMP (Internet Control Message Protocol)   A network layer Internet protocol that reports errors and provides other information relevant to IP packet processing. Documented in RFC 792.

IGRP (Interior Gateway Routing Protocol   A protocol developed by Cisco to address the problems associated with routing in large, heterogeneous networks.

IP address   A 32-bit address assigned to hosts using TCP/IP. An IP address belongs to one of five classes (A, B, C, D, or E) and is written as four octets separated by periods (that is, dotted-decimal format). Each address consists of a network number, an optional subnetwork number, and a host number. The network and subnetwork numbers together are used for routing, and the host number is used to address an individual host within the network or subnetwork. A subnet mask extracts network and subnetwork information from the IP address. Also called an Internet address.

layering   The separation of networking functions used by the OSI reference model, which simplifies the tasks required for two computers to communicate with each other.

link-state routing protocol   A routing protocol in which each router broadcasts or multicasts information regarding the cost of reaching each of its neighbors to all nodes in the internetwork. Link-state protocols create a consistent view of the network and are not prone to routing loops, but they achieve this at the cost of relatively greater computational difficulty and more widespread traffic (compared with distance-vector routing protocols).

LSA (link-state advertisement)   A broadcast packet used by link-state protocols that contains information about neighbors and path costs. Receiving routers use LSAs to maintain their routing tables. Sometimes called link-state packets (LSPs).

MAC (Media Access Control)   The part of the data link layer that includes the 6-byte (48-bit) address of the source and destination, and the method of getting permission to transmit.

media attachment unit   A device used in Ethernet and IEEE 802.3 networks that provides the interface between a station's AUI port and the Ethernet's common medium. The media attachment unit, which can be built into a station or can be a separate device, performs physical-layer functions, including the conversion of digital data from the Ethernet interface, collision detection, and injection of bits onto the network. Sometimes referred to as a media access unit or a transceiver.

network   A collection of computers, printers, routers, switches, and other devices that are able to communicate with each other over some transmission medium.

network layer   Layer 3 of the OSI reference model. This layer provides connectivity and path selection between two end systems. It's the layer at which routing occurs. Corresponds roughly with the path control layer of the SNA model.

NIC (network interface card)   A board that provides network communication capabilities to and from a computer system. The NIC has a MAC address assigned by the manufacturer that is used as the computer's physical address in a LAN.

OSPF (Open Shortest Path First) protocol   A link-state, hierarchical routing protocol proposed as a successor to RIP in the Internet community. OSPF features include least-cost routing, multipath routing, and load balancing.

packet   A logical grouping of information that includes a header containing control information and (usually) user data. Packets are most often used to refer to network layer units of data. The terms datagram, frame, message, and segment also describe logical information groupings at various layers of the OSI reference model and in various technology circles.

path determination   The decision of which path traffic should take through the network cloud. Path determination occurs at the network layer of the OSI reference model.

PDU (protocol data unit)   The OSI term for a packet.

physical layer   Layer 1 of the OSI reference model. This layer defines the electrical, mechanical, procedural, and functional specifications for activating, maintaining, and deactivating the physical link between end systems. Corresponds with the physical control layer in the SNA model.

presentation layer   Layer 6 of the OSI reference model. This layer provides data representation and code formatting, and negotiates data transfer syntax. It ensures that the application can use the data that arrives from the network, and that the information the application sends can be transmitted on the network.

queue   1. Generally, an ordered list of elements waiting to be processed. 2. In routing, a backlog of packets waiting to be forwarded over a router interface.

RARP (Reverse Address Resolution Protocol)   A protocol in the TCP/IP stack that provides a method for finding IP addresses based on MAC addresses.

RIP (Routing Information Protocol)   A protocol supplied with UNIX BSD systems. The most common Interior Gateway Protocol (IGP) in the Internet. RIP uses hop count as a routing metric.

routed protocol   A protocol that can be routed by a router. A router must be able to interpret the logical internetwork as specified by that routed protocol. Examples of routed protocols include AppleTalk, DECnet, and IP.

routing protocol   A protocol that accomplishes routing through the implementation of a specific routing protocol. Examples of routing protocols include IGRP, OSPF, and RIP.

session layer   Layer 5 of the OSI reference model. This layer establishes, maintains, and manages sessions between applications.

SPF (shortest path first) protocol   A routing protocol that iterates on length of path to determine a shortest-path spanning tree. Commonly used in link-state routing protocols. Sometimes called Dijkstra's algorithm.

static routing   Routing that is explicitly configured and entered into the routing table. Static routes take precedence over routes chosen by dynamic routing protocols.

stub network   A network that has only a single connection to a router.

subnet mask   A mask used to extract network and subnetwork information from the IP address.

subnetwork   A network that is segmented into a series of smaller networks.

transport layer   Layer 4 of the OSI reference model. This layer segments and reassembles data into a data stream. The transport layer has the potential to guarantee a connection and offer reliable transport.

window   The number of bytes a receiver can accept.

Check Your Understanding

1. Which OSI reference model layer best describes 10BaseT standards?

   A. The data link layer

   B. The network layer

   C. The physical layer

   D. The transport layer

2. Which of the following best describes the function of the OSI reference model's transport layer?

   A. It sends data by using flow control.

   B. It provides the best path for delivery.

   C. It determines network addresses.

   D. It allows for network segmentation.

3. Which of the following functions does a router use to relay data packets between networks?

   A. Application and media

   B. Path determination and switching

   C. Broadcast and collision detect

   D. None of the above

4. Which of the following are two basic types of dynamic routing?

    A. Static and default

    B. TCP and UDP exchange

    C. Distance-vector and link-state

    D. None of the above

5. When all the routers in a network are operating with the same knowledge, the network is said to have done which of the following?

    A. Converged

    B. Formalized

    C. Reconfigured

    D. None of the above

6. Describe the purpose of data encapsulation.

7. Describe the main function of the OSI reference model's transport layer.

8. Describe the purpose of ICMP.

9. Describe windowing in a TCP/IP implementation.

10. Describe the main function of the OSI reference model's network layer.

11. What commands are used to associate a network with a RIP routing process?

    A. router rip

    area *area-id*

    B. router rip

    network *network-number*

    C. router rip

    neighbour *ip-address*

    D. router rip

    show ip route *summary*

12. Which of the following best describes the TCP/IP protocol stack?

    A. Maps closely to the OSI reference model in the upper layers

    B. Supports all standard physical standards and data link-protocols

    C. Transfers information in a sequence of datagrams

    D. Reassembles datagrams into complete messages at the receiving location

13. Which best describes the structure of an encapsulated data packet?

   A. Segment header, network header, data, frame trailer

   B. Segment header, network header, data, segment trailer

   C. Frame header, network header, data, frame trailer

   D. Frame header, segment header, data, segment trailer

14. What technique is used with windowing to guarantee that a stream of data sent from one machine will be delivered through a data link to another machine without duplication or data loss?

   A. Acknowledgment and retransmission

   B. Encapsulation and broadcasting

   C. Recovery and flow control

   D. Synchronization and acknowledgment

15. What is one advantage of dynamic routing?

   A. Takes little network overhead and reduces network traffic

   B. Reduces unauthorized break-ins because security is tight

   C. Adjusts automatically to topology or traffic changes

   D. Requires little bandwidth to operate efficiently

16. Which best describes a primary function of the transport layer?

   A. Uses the TCP protocol to segment and reassemble data into a data stream

   B. Establishes, maintains, and manages sessions between applications

   C. Provides network services to user applications

   D. Uses a MAC address to provide physical transmission across media and handles error notification, network topology, and flow control

17. In the IP RIP routing protocol, how often are routing updates sent?

   A. Every 30 seconds

   B. Every 60 seconds

   C. Every 90 seconds

   D. Only when the administrator directs the router to do so

18. Which of the following statements is true?

A. MAC addressing is a hierarchical addressing system, which has unique MAC addresses assigned.

B. IP addresses are used by bridges to enable the traveling of data across the network.

C. The MAC address resides at the data link layer and is hard-coded into the network interface card.

D. If a device is moved from one network to a different network, the device's MAC address changes.

19. What is the advantage of using a layered model of networking?

A. Simplifies the network

B. For the purpose of standardization

C. Divides the complexity of internetworking into discrete, more easily learned operation subsets

D. All of the above

20. A router routing a packet of data performs which of the following functions?

A. Simply adds another header to the packet frame, consisting of the final, resolved destination machine's IP address.

B. Consults its routing tables to determine which of its ports it will need to send the data out on for it to reach its destination network

C. Broadcasts the data frame to all the ports except the port that the data arrived at

D. Performs all the above functions

Part II

CCNA 3: Switching Basics and Intermediate Routing

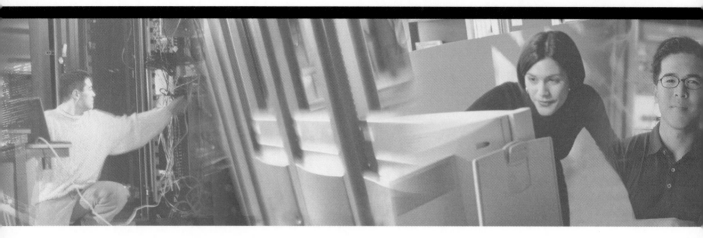

Objectives

After reading this chapter, you will be able to

- Describe classless interdomain routing (CIDR)
- Calculate subnets with variable-length subnet masking (VLSM)
- Describe route aggregation with VLSM
- Describe Routing Information Protocol version 2 (RIPv2)
- Configure RIPv2
- Verify and troubleshoot RIPv2

Chapter 2

Introduction to Classless Routing

This chapter introduces classless routing, classless interdomain routing, variable-length subnet masking, and RIP versions 1 and 2.

Please be sure to look at this chapter's associated e-Lab Activities, Videos, and PhotoZooms that you will find on the CD-ROM accompanying this book. These CD-ROM elements supplement the material and reinforce the concepts introduced in this chapter.

CIDR Overview

With the explosive growth of IP networks, most importantly the Global Internet, the available IP address space was shrinking and the core Internet routers were running out of capacity. CIDR (pronounced "cider") was developed to address these problems.

CIDR replaced the old process of assigning IP addresses based on Class A, B, and C addresses with a generalized network prefix. Instead of being limited to network identifiers (or prefixes) of 8, 16, or 24 bits, CIDR currently uses prefixes from 13 to 27 bits. Blocks of addresses can be assigned to networks as small as 32 hosts, or to those with over 500,000 hosts. This allows for address assignments that more closely fit an organization's specific needs.

With CIDR, IP address notation changed a bit. A CIDR address includes the standard 32-bit IP address and information on how many bits are used for the network prefix. For example, in the CIDR address 206.13.01.48/25, the /25 indicates that the first 25 bits identify the unique network, leaving the remaining bits to identify the specific host. 206.13.01.48/25 can also be written as 206.13.01.48 255.255.255.128.

Why CIDR?

Routers use a form of IPv4 addressing called *classless interdomain routing (CIDR)* that ignores class. In a classful system, a router determines an address's class and then identifies the network and host octets based on that class. With CIDR, a router uses a prefix that describes how many bits are network bits (the bits at the beginning, or prefix, of the address). The remaining bits are host bits. The Prefix number follows a slash (/) at the end of the address; for example, 10.10.10.10/30. The /30 is the prefix. The network and host portions of an address are no longer restricted to using an entire octet.

First introduced in 1993 by RFC 1517, 1518, 1519, and 1520, and later deployed in 1994, CIDR dramatically improves IPv4's scalability and efficiency by providing the following:

- Replacement of classful addressing with a more flexible and less wasteful classless scheme
- Enhanced route aggregation, also known as *supernetting*

The following sections describe route aggregation, supernetting, and address allocation in more detail.

Route Aggregation and Supernetting

By using a bitmask instead of an address class to determine the network portion of an address, CIDR allows routers to aggregate, or summarize, routing information. This shrinks the size of the router's routing tables. In other words, just one address and mask combination can represent the routes to multiple networks.

Without CIDR and route aggregation, a router must maintain individual entries for the Class B networks shown in Table 2-1.

The shaded columns in Table 2-1 identify the 16 bits that, based on class rules, represent the network number. Classful routers are forced to handle Class B networks using these 16 bits. Because the first 16 bits of each of these eight network numbers are unique, a classful router sees eight unique networks and must create a routing table entry for each.

However, these eight networks do have common bits, as shown by the shaded portion of Table 2-2. If the last common bit, which has been bolded in Table 2-1, is defined by the prefix, the router can point to one common number representing many networks. This is known as route summarization and saves space in the routing tables.

Table 2-1 Route Aggregation and Supernetting with 16 Bits

Network Number	First Octet	Second Octet	Third Octet	Fourth Octet
172.24.0.0/16	10101100	00011000	00000000	00000000
172.25.0.0/16	10101100	00011001	00000000	00000000
172.26.0.0/16	10101100	00011010	00000000	00000000
172.27.0.0/16	10101100	00011011	00000000	00000000
172.28.0.0/16	10101100	00011100	00000000	00000000
172.29.0.0/16	10101100	00011101	00000000	00000000
172.30.0.0/16	10101100	00011110	00000000	00000000
172.31.0.0/16	10101100	00011111	00000000	00000000

Table 2-2 shows that the eight example network addresses have the first 13 bits in common.

Table 2-2 Route Aggregation and Supernetting with 13 Bits

Network Number	First Octet	Second Octet	Third Octet	Fourth Octet
172.24.0.0/16	10101100	00011000	00000000	00000000
172.25.0.0/16	10101100	00011001	00000000	00000000
172.26.0.0/16	10101100	00011010	00000000	00000000
172.27.0.0/16	10101100	00011011	00000000	00000000
172.28.0.0/16	10101100	00011100	00000000	00000000
172.29.0.0/16	10101100	00011101	00000000	00000000
172.30.0.0/16	10101100	00011110	00000000	00000000
172.31.0.0/16	10101100	00011111	00000000	00000000

A CIDR-compliant router can summarize routes to these eight networks using a 13-bit prefix, which these eight networks (and only these networks) share:

10101100 00011

To represent this prefix in decimal terms, the rest of the address is padded with 0s and then paired with a 13-bit subnet mask:

10101100 00011000 00000000 00000000 = 172.24.0.0

11111111 11111000 00000000 00000000 = 255.248.0.0

A single address and mask define a classless prefix that summarizes routes to the eight networks: 172.24.0.0/13.

By using a prefix address to summarize routes, you can keep routing table entries manageable, which results in the following:

- More efficient routing
- A reduced number of CPU cycles when recalculating a routing table or when sorting through the routing table entries to find a match
- Reduced router memory requirements

Supernetting is the practice of using a bitmask to group multiple classful networks as a single network address. Supernetting and route aggregation are different names for the same process, although the term supernetting is most often applied when the aggregated networks are under common administrative control.

Recall that the Class A and Class B address space is virtually exhausted, leaving large organizations little choice but to request multiple Class C network addresses from their providers. If a company can acquire a block of contiguous (sequential) Class C network addresses, supernetting can make the addresses appear as a single large network, or supernet.

Supernetting and Address Allocation

Consider Company XYZ, which requires addresses for 400 hosts. Under the classful addressing system, XYZ could apply to a central Internet address authority for a Class B address. If the company got the Class B and then used it to address one logical group of 400 hosts, tens of thousands of addresses would be wasted. A second option for XYZ would be to request two Class C network numbers, yielding 508 (2 * 254) host addresses. The drawback to this approach is that XYZ would have to route between its own logical networks, and default-free Internet routers would need to maintain two routing table entries for XYZ's network, rather than just one.

Under a classless addressing system, supernetting allows Company XYZ to get its required address space without wasting addresses or increasing the routing tables unnecessarily. Using CIDR, XYZ asks for an address block from its Internet service provider, not a central authority such as the InterNIC. The ISP assesses XYZ's needs and allocates address space from its own large CIDR block of addresses. Providers assume the burden of managing address space in a classless system. With this system, Internet routers keep only one summary route, or supernet route, to the provider's network, and the provider keeps routes that are more specific to its customer networks. This method drastically reduces the size of Internet routing tables.

In the following example, XYZ receives two contiguous Class C addresses, 207.21.54.0 and 207.21.55.0. If you examine the shaded portion of Table 2-3, you see that these network addresses have this common 23-bit prefix:

11001111 00010101 0011011

Table 2-3 Supernetting and Address Allocation

Network Number	First Octet	Second Octet	Third Octet	Fourth Octet
207.21.54.0	11001111	00010101	00110110	00000000
207.21.55.0	11001111	00010101	00110111	00000000

When supernetted with a 23-bit mask (207.21.54.0 /23), the address space provides well over 400 host addresses (2^9 or 512 hosts) without the tremendous waste of a Class B address. With the ISP acting as the addressing authority for a CIDR block of addresses, the ISP's customer networks, which include XYZ, can be advertised among Internet routers as a single supernet. In Figure 2-1, the ISP manages a block of 256 Class C addresses and advertises them to the world using the 16-bit prefix 207.21.0.0 /16.

Figure 2-1 Addressing with CIDR

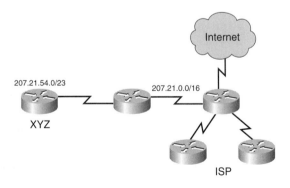

With CIDR enabling ISPs to hierarchically distribute and manage blocks of contiguous addresses, IPv4 address space enjoys the following benefits:

- Efficient address allocation
- Reduced number of routing table entries

Variable-Length Subnet Masking (VLSM)

Variable-length subnet masks (VLSMs) were developed to allow multiple levels of sub-networked IP addresses within a single network. This strategy can be used only when supported by the routing protocol in use, such as Open Shortest Path First (OSPF) and Enhanced Interior Gateway Routing Protocol (EIGRP). RIP version 1 is older than VLSM and cannot support it. RIPv2, however, can support VLSM.

VLSM allows an organization to use more than one subnet mask within the same network address space. Implementing VLSM allows an administrator to "subnet a subnet" and maximize addressing efficiency.

VLSM Features

When an IP network is assigned more than one subnet mask, it is considered a network with variable-length subnet masks, overcoming the limitation of a fixed number of fixed-size subnetworks imposed by a single subnet mask. This section describes the features of variable-length subnet masks.

In Figure 2-2, Network 172.16.14.0/24 is divided into smaller subnets:

- Subnets with one mask—/27.
- One unused /27 is further subdivided into three (3) /30 subnets.

Figure 2-2 VLSM

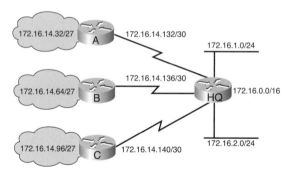

VLSMs provide the ability to include more than one subnet mask within a network and the ability to subnet an already subnetted network address. VLSM offers the following benefits:

- **Even more efficient use of IP addresses**—Without the use of VLSMs, companies must implement a single subnet mask within an entire Class A, B, or C network number.

For example, in Figure 2-2, consider the 172.16.0.0/16 network address divided into subnets using /24 masking, and one of the subnetworks in this range, 172.16.14.0/24, further divided into smaller subnets with the /27 masking. These smaller subnets range from 172.16.14.0/27 to 172.16.14.224/27. In Figure 2-2, one of these smaller subnets, 172.16.14.128/27, is further divided with the /30 prefix, creating subnets with only two hosts to be used on the WAN links. The /30 subnets range from 172.16.14.128/30 to 172.16.14.156/30. In Figure 2-2, the WAN links use the 172.16.14.132/30, 172.16.14.136/30, and 172.16.14.140/30 subnets out of the range.

- **Greater capability to use route summarization**—VLSM allows more hierarchical levels within an addressing plan, allowing more efficient routing using *route summarization* within routing tables. For example, in Figure 2-2, subnet 172.16.14.0/24 summarizes all of the addresses that are further subnets of 172.16.14.0, including those from subnets 172.16.14.0/27 and 172.16.14.128/30.

Consider the subnets created by borrowing 3 bits from the host portion of the Class C address, 207.21.24.0, shown in Table 2-4.

Table 2-4 Table 2-4 Subnetting with One Mask

Subnet Number	Subnet Address
Subnet 0	207.21.24.0/27
Subnet 1	207.21.24.32/27
Subnet 2	207.21.24.64/27
Subnet 3	207.21.24.96/27
Subnet 4	207.21.24.128/27
Subnet 5	207.21.24.160/27
Subnet 6	207.21.24.192/27
Subnet 7	207.21.24.224/27

If you use the **ip subnet-zero** command, this mask creates seven usable subnets of 30 hosts each. You can use four of these subnets to address remote offices in the organization pictured in Figure 2-3, at sites A, B, C, and D.

Figure 2-3 Using Subnets to Address the WAN

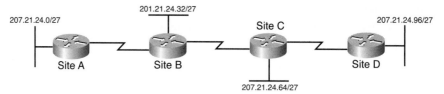

Unfortunately, you have only three subnets left for future growth, and you have yet to address (literally) the three point-to-point WAN links between the four sites. If you assign the three remaining subnets to the WAN links, you completely exhaust your supply of IP addresses. Moreover, squandering the remaining 30-host subnets to address these two-node networks will waste more than a third of your available address space.

As you might have guessed, there are ways to avoid this kind of waste. Over the past 20 years, network engineers have developed three strategies for efficiently addressing point-to-point WAN links:

- Use VLSM
- Use private addressing (RFC 1918)
- Use IP unnumbered

Private addresses and IP unnumbered are discussed further in the "Route Summarization" section of this chapter. This section focuses on VLSM. If VLSM is applied to your addressing problem, your Class C address can be broken into groups (subnets) of various sizes. Large subnets are created for addressing LANs, and very small subnets are created for WAN links and other special cases.

You use a 30-bit mask to create subnets with only two valid host addresses, the exact number needed for a point-to-point connection. Figure 2-4 shows how eight subnets can be made from one subnet by extending the prefix to 30. You can see what happens if you take one of your three remaining subnets (subnet 6, or 207.21.24.192/27) and subnet it again using a 30-bit mask.

Figure 2-4 Subnetting with Variable-Length Masks

Subnet 0	207.21.24.0/27
Subnet 1	207.21.24.32/27
Subnet 2	207.21.24.64/27
Subnet 3	207.21.24.96/27
Subnet 4	207.21.24.128/27
Subnet 5	207.21.24.160/27
Subnet 6	207.21.24.192/27
Subnet 7	207.21.24.224/27

Sub-subnet 0	207.21.24.192/30
Sub-subnet 1	207.21.24.196/30
Sub-subnet 2	207.21.24.200/30
Sub-subnet 3	207.21.24.204/30
Sub-subnet 4	207.21.24.208/30
Sub-subnet 5	207.21.24.212/30
Sub-subnet 6	207.21.24.216/30
Sub-subnet 7	207.21.24.220/30

Subnetting the 207.21.24.192/27 subnet in this way supplies you with eight ranges of addresses to be used for point-to-point networks. For example, the 207.21.24.192/30 network can be used to address the point-to-point serial link between Site A's router and Site B's router, as shown in Figure 2-5. The IP address of 207.21.24.193 could be assigned to Site A's WAN interface, and 207.21.24.194 could be assigned to Site B's WAN interface.

Figure 2-5 Figure 2-5 Using VLSM to Address Point to Point

207.21.24.32/27

207.21.24.192/30

Site A   Site B

Calculating VLSMs

As already discussed, with VLSMs, you can subnet an already subnetted address. Consider, for example, that you have a subnet address 172.16.32.0/20, and you need to assign addresses to a network that has 10 hosts. This allocates 20 bits for the network address and the remaining 12 bits for hosts. With this subnet address, however, you have over 4000 ($2^{12} - 2 = 4094$) host addresses, most of which will be wasted. With VLSMs, you can further subnet the address 172.16.32.0/20 to give you more network addresses and fewer hosts per network. If, for example, you subnet 172.16.32.0/20 to 172.16.32.0/26, you gain 64 (2^6) subnets, each of which could support 62 ($2^6 - 2 = 62$) hosts. Refer to Figure 2-6.

Figure 2-6 Calculating VLSM

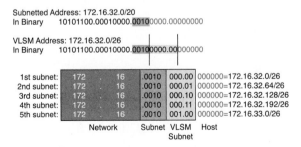

Subnetted Address: 172.16.32.0/20
In Binary   10101100.00010000.00100000.00000000

VLSM Address: 172.16.32.0/26
In Binary   10101100.00010000.00100000.00000000

1st subnet:	172 . 16	.0010	000.00	000000=172.16.32.0/26
2nd subnet:	172 . 16	.0010	000.01	000000=172.16.32.64/26
3rd subnet:	172 . 16	.0010	000.10	000000=172.16.32.128/26
4th subnet:	172 . 16	.0010	000.11	000000=172.16.32.192/26
5th subnet:	172 . 16	.0010	001.00	000000=172.16.33.0/26

Network   Subnet VLSM Host
Subnet

Use this procedure to further subnet 172.16.32.0/20 to 172.16.32.0/26:

Step 1   Write 172.16.32.0 in binary form.

Step 2   Draw a vertical line between the 20th and 21st bits, as shown in Figure 2-6. (/20 was the original subnet boundary.)

Step 3 Draw a vertical line between the 26th and 27th bits, as shown in Figure 2-6. (The original /20 subnet boundary is extended 6 bits to the right, becoming /26.)

Step 4 Calculate the 64 subnet addresses using the bits between the two vertical lines, from lowest to highest in value. Figure 2-6 shows the first five subnets available.

VLSMs are commonly used to maximize the number of possible addresses available for a network. For example, because point-to-point serial lines require only two host addresses, using a /30 subnet will not waste scarce IP addresses.

In Figure 2-7, the subnet addresses used on the Ethernet segments are those generated from subdividing the 172.16.32.0/20 subnet into multiple /26 subnets. Figure 2-7 illustrates where the subnet addresses can be applied, depending on the number of host requirements. For example, the WAN links use subnet addresses with a prefix of /30. This prefix allows only two hosts, just enough hosts for a point-to-point connection between a pair of routers.

Figure 2-7 VLSM Example

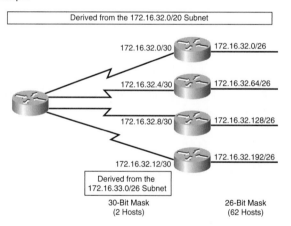

To calculate the subnet addresses used on the WAN links, further subnet one of the unused /26 subnets. In this example, 172.16.32.0/26 is further subnetted with a prefix of /30. This provides four more subnet bits and, therefore, 16 (2^4) subnets for the WANs.

Remember that only unused subnets can be further subnetted. In other words, if you use any addresses from a subnet, that subnet cannot be further subnetted.

Lab Activity   Calculating VLSM Subnets

In this lab, you use VLSM to support more efficient use of the assigned IP address and to reduce the amount of routing information at the top level.

Configuring VLSM

This section shows you how to configure VLSM on a Cisco router. Example 2-1 shows the commands needed to configure Site A's router (RTA) with a 27-bit mask on its Ethernet (e0) port and a 30-bit mask on its serial port (s0).

Example 2-1 *Configure VLSM*

```
RTA(config)#interface e0
RTA(config-if)#ip add 207.21.24.33 255.255.255.224
RTA(config-if)#interface s0
RTA(config-if)#ip add 207.21.24.193 255.255.255.252


RTA#show ip route
Codes:  C-connected, S-static, I-IGRP, R-RIP, M-mobile, B-BGP
        D-EIGRP, EX-EIGRP external, O-OSPF, IA-OSPF inter area
        E1=OSPF external type1, E2=OSPF external type 2, E=EGP
        i-IS-IS, L1-IS-IS level-1, L2-IS-IS level-2,
     *-candidate default


Gateway of last resort is not set
     207.21.24.0 is variably subnetted, 2 subnets, 2 masks
C    207.21.24.32 255.255.255.224 is directly connected, Ethernet0
C    207.21.24.192 255.255.255.252 is directly connected, Serial0
```

For routers in a variably subnetted network to properly update each other, they must send masks in their routing updates. Without subnet information in the routing updates, routers will have nothing but the address class and their own subnet mask to go on. Only routing protocols that ignore address class rules and use classless prefixes will work properly with VLSM. (See Table 2-5.)

Table 2-5 Classful and Classless Routing Protocols

Classful Routing Protocols	Classless Routing Protocols
RIP version 1	Rip version 2
IGRP	EIGRP
EGP	OSPF
BGP 3	IS-IS
	BGP 4

VLSM Using RIP and IGRP

RIP version 1 and IGRP, common interior gateway protocols, cannot support VLSM because they do not send subnet information in their updates. Upon receiving an update packet, these classful routing protocols use one of the following methods to determine an address's network prefix:

- If the router receives information about a network, and if the receiving interface belongs to that same network (but on a different subnet), the router applies the subnet mask that is configured on the receiving interface.
- If the router receives information about a network address that is not the same as the one configured on the receiving interface, it applies the default (by class) subnet mask.

Despite its limitations, RIP is a popular routing protocol supported by virtually all IP routers. RIP's popularity stems from its simplicity and universal compatibility. However, the first version of RIP (RIPv1) suffers from several critical deficiencies:

- RIPv1 does not send subnet mask information in its updates. Without subnet information, VLSM and CIDR cannot be supported.
- Its updates are broadcast, increasing network traffic.
- It does not support authentication.

In 1988, RFC 1058 prescribed the new (and improved) RIP version 2 to address these deficiencies:

- RIPv2 sends subnet information and supports VLSM and CIDR.
- It multicasts routing updates using the Class D address, 224.0.0.9, providing better efficiency.
- It provides for authentication in its updates.

Because of these key features, RIPv2 should always be preferred over RIPv1, unless a legacy device on the network cannot support it.

When RIP is first enabled on a Cisco router, the router listens for version 1 and 2 updates but sends only version 1. To take advantage of version 2 features, you can turn off version 1 support and enable version 2 updates with the command shown in Example 2-2:

Example 2-2 *Configuring RIP Version 2*

```
Router(config)#router rip
Router(router-config)#version 2
```

RIP's straightforward design ensures that it will continue to survive. A new version has already been designed to support future IPv6 networks.

 Lab Activity   Review of Basic Router Configuration with RIP

In this lab, you cable and configure workstations and routers. You set up an IP addressing scheme using the class B networks defined in the table and configure RIP on routers.

Route Summarization

Using CIDR and VLSM not only prevents address waste, but it also promotes route aggregation, or summarization. Without route summarization, Internet backbone routing would likely have collapsed sometime before 1997.

Figure 2-8 illustrates how route summarization reduces the burden on upstream routers. This complex hierarchy of variable-sized networks and subnetworks is summarized at various points using a prefix address until the entire network is advertised as a single aggregate route: 200.199.48.0 /20.

Recall that this kind of route summarization, or supernetting, is possible only if the network's routers run a classless routing protocol, such as OSPF or EIGRP. Classless routing protocols carry the prefix length (subnet mask) with the 32-bit address in routing updates. In Figure 2-8, the summary route that eventually reaches the provider contains a 20-bit prefix common to all of the addresses in the organization: 200.199.48.0 /20 or 11001000 11000111 0001. For summarization to work properly, you must carefully assign addresses in a hierarchical fashion so that summarized addresses share the same higher-order bits.

Figure 2-8 Route Summarization

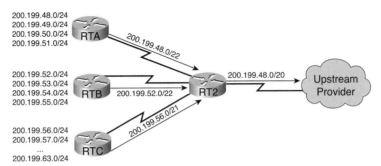

For example, as shown in Figure 2-9, Router A can either send three routing update entries or summarize the addresses into a single network number. Figure 2-9 illustrates how routes 172.16.25.0/24, 172.16.26.0/24, and 172.16.27.0/24 are summarized into 172.16.0.0/16.

Figure 2-9 More Route Summarization

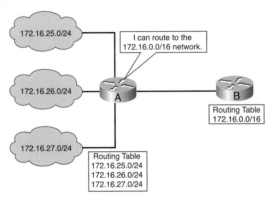

The router in Figure 2-9 can route to network 172.16.0.0/16, including all subnets of that network. However, if other subnets of 172.16.0.0 existed elsewhere in the network (for example, if 172.16.0.0 was discontiguous), summarizing in this way might not be valid. Discontiguous networks and summarization are discussed later in this lesson.

Another advantage to using route summarization in a large, complex network is that it can isolate topology changes from other routers. That is, if a specific link in the 172.16.27.0/24 domain is flapping (going up and down rapidly), the summary route does not change. Therefore, no router external to the domain needs to keep modifying its routing table due to this flapping activity.

Route summarization is most effective within a subnetted environment when the network addresses are in contiguous blocks in powers of two. For example, 4, 16, or 512 addresses can be represented by a single routing entry because summary masks are binary masks—just like subnet masks—so summarization must take place on binary boundaries (powers of two).

Routing protocols summarize or aggregate routes based on shared network numbers within the network. Classless routing protocols, such as RIPv2, OSPF, Intermediate System-to-Intermediate System (IS-IS), and EIGRP, support route summarization based on subnet addresses, including VLSM addressing. Classful routing protocols, such as RIPv1 and IGRP, automatically summarize routes on the classful network boundary, and do not support summarization on any other boundaries.

Summarization is described in RFC 1518, "An Architecture for IP Address Allocation with CIDR."

Summarization Within an Octet

Suppose a router receives updates for the following routes, as shown in Figure 2-10:

> 172.16.168.0/24
>
> 172.16.169.0/24
>
> 172.16.170.0/24
>
> 172.16.171.0/24
>
> 172.16.172.0/24
>
> 172.16.173.0/24
>
> 172.16.174.0/24
>
> 172.16.175.0/24

Figure 2-10 Summarization Within an Octet

172.16.168.0/24 =	10101100	.	00010000	.	10101	000 .	00000000
172.16.169.0/24 =	172	.	16	.	10101	001 .	0
172.16.170.0/24 =	172	.	16	.	10101	010 .	0
172.16.171.0/24 =	172	.	16	.	10101	011 .	0
172.16.172.0/24 =	172	.	16	.	10101	100 .	0
172.16.173.0/24 =	172	.	16	.	10101	101 .	0
172.16.174.0/24 =	172	.	16	.	10101	110 .	0
172.16.175.0/24 =	172	.	16	.	10101	111 .	0

Number of Common Bits = 21
Summary: 172.16.168.0/21

Noncommon
Bits = 11

To determine the summary route, the router determines the number of highest-order bits that match in all the addresses. By converting the IP addresses to binary format, you can determine the number of common bits shared among the IP addresses. In Figure 2-10, the first 21 bits are in common among the IP addresses. Therefore, the best summary route is 172.16.168.0/21. You can summarize addresses when the number of addresses is a power of two. If the number of addresses is not a power of two, divide the addresses into groups and summarize the groups separately.

To allow the router to aggregate the most number of IP addresses into a single route summary, your IP addressing plan should be hierarchical in nature. This approach is particularly important when using VLSMs.

Summarization with a Discontiguous Network

Classful routing protocols summarize automatically at network boundaries. This behavior, which cannot be changed with RIPv1 and IGRP, has important results:

- Subnets are not advertised to a different major network.
- Discontiguous subnets are not visible to each other.

In Figure 2-11, RIPv1 does not advertise the 172.16.5.0 255.255.255.0 and 172.16.6.0 255.255.255.0 subnets because RIPv1 cannot advertise subnets; both Router A and Router B advertise 172.16.0.0. This leads to confusion when routing across network 192.168.14.0. In this example, Router C receives routes about 172.16.0.0 from two different directions, so it cannot make a correct routing decision.

Figure 2-11 Summarization with Discontiguous Subnets

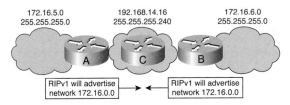

Resolve this situation by using RIPv2, OSPF, IS-IS, or EIGRP, and don't use summarization because the subnet routes would be advertised with their actual subnet masks.

Cisco IOS Software also provides an IP unnumbered feature that permits discontiguous subnets to be separated by an unnumbered link. An unnumbered link is a link that might not yet have an IP address number assigned to it, but can still be visible by other subnets, as to prevent discontiguous links. An unnumbered link without using the IP unnumbered feature could result in discontiguous links.

Route Flapping

Route flapping occurs when a router's interface alternates rapidly between the "up" and "down" states. A number of factors can cause this, including a faulty interface or poorly terminated media.

Summarization effectively insulates upstream routers from route flapping problems. If RTC's interface connected to the 200.199.56.0 network goes down, RTC will remove that route from its table. If the routers were not configured to summarize, RTC would send a triggered update to RTZ about removing network 200.199.56.0. In turn, RTZ would update the next router upstream, and so on. Every time these routers are updated with new information, their processors must go to work. The processors can work hard enough to noticeably impact performance (especially in the case of OSPF routing). Consider the impact on performance if RTC's interface to network 200.199.56.0 comes back up after only a few seconds. The routers update each other and recalculate. In addition, what happens when RTC's link goes back down seconds later? And then back up? This is route flapping, and it can cripple a router with excessive updates and recalculations.

However, the summarization configuration prevents RTC's route flapping from affecting any other routers. RTC updates RTZ about a supernet (200.199.56.0 /21) that includes eight networks (200.199.56.0 through 200.199.63.0). Losing one network does not invalidate the route to the supernet. Although RTC might be kept busy dealing with its own route flap, RTZ (and all upstream routers) do not notice a thing. Summarization effectively insulates the other routers from the route-flapping problem.

RIP Version 2

Networks need to be scalable. In other words, they must be able to grow. The chosen routing protocol can make a vast difference to the network's scalability, so choosing the routing protocol wisely is important. Generally, Routing Internet Protocol (RIP) is considered suitable for small networks but is not scaleable to large networks. RIPv1 is a classful routing protocol, while RIP v2 is a classless routing protocol. A limitation of the classful approach is the need to automatically summarize to the classful network boundary at major network boundaries. This means that RIPv1 does not support VLSM whereas RIPv2 does.

Short History of RIP

In an international network such as the Internet, using a single routing protocol for the entire network is unlikely. Rather, the network will be organized as a collection of autonomous systems (AS). Each of these AS is generally administered by a single entity.

Each AS has its own routing technology, which might differ from other autonomous systems. The routing protocol used within an AS is referred to as an Interior Gateway Protocol (IGP). A separate protocol, called an Exterior Gateway Protocol (EGP), transfers routing information among autonomous systems. RIP was designed to work as an IGP in a moderate-sized AS. It is not intended for use in more complex environments.

RIPv1 is considered a classful IGP. It is a distance-vector protocol that broadcasts its entire routing table to each neighbor router at predetermined intervals (for example, 30 seconds). RIP uses hop count as a metric, with 15 as the maximum number of hops. As previously mentioned, if RIPv1 receives an update packet, it will use one of the following two alternatives to work out an address's network prefix:

- If the router receives information about a network and the receiving interface belongs to the same network but is on a different subnet, the router applies the subnet mask that is configured on the receiving interface.
- If the router receives information about the network address that is NOT the same as the one configured on the receiving interface, it applies the default (by class) interface.

For Class A addresses, the default classful mask is 255.0.0.0.

For Class B addresses, the default classful mask is 255.255.0.0.

For Class C addresses, the default classful mask is 255.255.255.0.

RIPv1 is a common and popular routing protocol because virtually all IP routers support it. Its popularity is based on its simplicity and universal compatibility. RIPv1 is capable of load balancing over as many as six equal-cost paths. (Four paths is the default.)

Recall some of the limitations of RIPv1:

- It does not send subnet masks information in its updates.
- It sends updates as broadcasts on 255.255.255.255.
- It does not support authentication.
- It is not able to support variable-length subnet masking (VLSM) or classless interdomain routing (CIDR).

Example 2-3 shows how to configure RIPv1.

Example 2-3 *Configuring RIP v1*

```
Sydney(config)# router rip
Sydney(config-router)# network 172.16.0.0
Sydney(config-router)# network 192.168.100.0
```

RIP Version 2 Features

RIPv2 is an improved version of RIPv1. It shares the following features with RIPv1:

- Uses hop-count metric—maximum 15 hops
- Is a distance-vector protocol
- Uses hold-down timers to prevent routing loops—default is 180 seconds
- Uses split horizon to prevent routing loops
- Uses 16 hops as a metric for infinite distance
- Transmits subnet mask with route
- Enables VLSM by passing the mask along with each route so that the subnet is exactly defined
- Provides authentication
- Uses both clear text and MD5
- Includes a next-hop router IP address in its routing update
- Uses external route tags
- Provides multicast routing updates

RIPv2 provides prefix routing, which allows it to send out subnet mask information with the route update. RIPv2 supports the use of classless routing in which different subnets within the same network can use different subnet masks (variable-length subnet masking).

RIPv2 provides for authentication in its updates. A set of keys can operate as an authentication check on an interface. RIPv2 allows a choice of the authentication type to be used in RIPv2 packets. The choice can be either clear text or MD5 encryption. Clear text is the default. (MD5 can be used to authenticate a routing update's source.) MD5 is typically used to encrypt and enable secret passwords and it has no known reversal.

RIPv2 multicasts routing updates using the Class D address 224.0.0.9, which provides for better efficiency.

Comparing RIPv1 and RIPv2

RIP uses distance-vector algorithms to determine the direction and distance to any link in the internetwork. If there are multiple paths to a destination, RIP selects the path with the least number of hops. However, because hop count is the only routing metric RIP uses, it does not necessarily select the fastest path to a destination. It counts only the hops.

RIPv1 allows routers to update their routing tables at programmable intervals. The default interval is every 30 seconds. RIPv1's continual sending of routing updates builds network traffic very quickly. To prevent a packet from looping infinitely, RIP has a maximum hop count of 15 hops. If the destination network is more than 15 router hops away, it is considered unreachable and the packet is dropped. This situation creates a scalability issue when routing in large, heterogeneous networks. RIPv1 uses split horizon to prevent loops. This means that RIPv1 advertises routes out an interface only if such routes were not learned from updates entering that interface. It uses hold-down timing to prevent routing loops. Hold-downs ignore any new information about a network for a time equal to the hold-down timer.

The following summarizes the behavior or RIPv1 when used by a router:

- Directly connected subnets are already known to the router, and these routes are advertised to neighboring routers.
- Routing updates are broadcast, and all neighboring routers learn by single broadcast.
- Routers listen for updates to help them learn new routes.
- A metric describes each route in the update, which indicates how "good" the route is.
- If many routes exist, the lowest metric route is used.
- Topology information is in routing updates, which, at a minimum, includes subnet and metric information.
- Periodic updates are expected from neighboring routers.
- Failure to receive updates in a timely manner results in removal of routes previously learned from the neighbor.
- Routes learned from neighboring routers are presumed to be from that neighboring router.

Table 2-6 compares RIPv1 and RIPv2.

Table 2-6 Comparing RIP v2 and RIP v1

RIPv2	RIPv1
Authentication	No authentication
Classless subnet masking, VLSM	Classful masking
Next host	Next gateway
Multicast—224.0.0.9	Broadcast—255.255.255.255
Uses route tags	Does not use route tags
Plus all features of RIPv1	

Configuring RIP Version 2

RIPv2 is a dynamic routing protocol that is configured by naming the routing protocol (RIP version 2) and then assigning IP network numbers without specifying subnet values. This section describes the basic commands used to configure RIPv2 on a Cisco router.

To enable a dynamic routing protocol, you must complete the following tasks:

- Select a routing protocol such as RIPv2.
- Assign IP network numbers without specifying subnet values.
- Assign network or subnet addresses and the appropriate subnet mask to interfaces.

RIPv2 uses multicasts to communicate with other routers. The routing metric helps routers find the best path to each network or subnet.

The **router** command starts a routing process. The **network** command causes the implementation of the following three functions:

- Routing updates are multicast out an interface.
- Routing updates are processed if they enter that same interface.
- The subnet directly connected to that interface is advertised.

The **network** command is required because it allows the routing process to determine which interfaces will participate in sending and receiving routing updates. The **network** command starts the routing protocol on all interfaces that the router has in the specified network. The **network** command also allows the router to advertise that network.

The **router rip** and **version 2** commands combined specify RIPv2 as the routing protocol, while the **network** command identifies a participating attached network.

Referring to Figure 2-12, Router A's configuration includes the following:

- **router rip**—Enables RIP as the routing protocol
- **version 2**—Identifies version 2 as the version of RIP being used
- **network 172.16.0.0**—Specifies a directly connected network
- **network 10.0.0.0**—Specifies a directly connected network

Router A interfaces connected to networks 172.16.0.0 and 10.0.0.0, or their subnets, will send and receive RIPv2 updates. These routing updates allow the router to learn the network topology. Routers B and C have similar RIP configurations but with different network numbers specified.

Figure 2-12 Figure 2-12 RIP Configuration

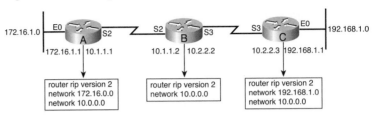

Lab Activity Converting RIP v1 to RIP v2

In this lab, you enable RIP version 1 routing and then convert to RIPv2 routing.

Verifying RIP V2

The **show ip protocols** and **show ip route** commands display information about routing protocols and the routing table. This section describes how to use **show** commands to verify the RIP configuration.

The **show ip protocols** command displays values about routing protocols and routing protocol timer information associated with the router. Example 2-4 displays **show ip protocols** output from Router A in Figure 2-12.

Example 2-4 show ip protocols *Command Output*

```
RouterA#show ip protocols
Routing Protocol is "rip"
Sending updates every 30 seconds, next due in 12 seconds
Invalid after 180 seconds, hold down 180, flushed after 240
Outgoing update filter list for all interfaces is not set
 Incoming update filter list for all interfaces is not set
Redistributing rip
Default Version Control: send version 1 receive any version
    Interface          Send    Receive    Triggard RIP    Key-Chain
    Ethernet0           1       1 2
    Serial2             1       1 2
 EIGRP maximum metric variance 1
Routing for Networks:
    10.0.0.0
    172.16.0.0
 Routing Information Sources:
```

Example 2-4 show ip protocols *Command Output (Continued)*

```
Gateway          Distance     Last Update
(this router)       120       02:12:15
10.1.1.2            120       01:09:01
Distance: (default is 120
```

In Example 2-4, the router is configured with RIP and sends updated routing table information every 30 seconds. (This interval is configurable.) If a router running RIP does not receive an update from another router for 180 seconds or more, it marks the routes served by the nonupdating router as invalid. In Example 2-4, the hold-down timer is set to 180 seconds, so an update to a route that was down and is now up will stay in hold-down "possibly down" state until 180 seconds have passed.

If still no update has occurred after 240 seconds "flush timer setting," the router removes the routing table entries from the router. In Example 2-4, 18 seconds have passed since Router A received an update from Router B.

The router is injecting routes for the networks listed following the "Routing for Networks" line. The router is receiving routes from the neighboring RIP routers listed following the "Routing Information Sources" line.

The distance default of 120 refers to the administrative distance for a RIP route.

You can also use the **show ip interface brief** command to list a summary of an interface's IP information and status.

The **show ip route** command displays the contents of the IP routing table, as shown in Example 2-5.

Example 2-5 show ip route *Command Output*

```
RouterA#show ip route
Codes: C - connected, S - static, I - IGRP, R - RIP, M - mobile, B - BGP
       D - EIGRP, EX - EIGRP external, O - OSPF, IA - OSPF inter area
       N1 - OSPF NSSA external type 1, N2 - OSPF NSSA external type 2
       E1 - OSPF external type 1, E2 - OSPF external type 2, E - EGP
       i - IS-IS, L1 - IS-IS level-1, L2 - IS-IS level-2, ia - IS-IS inter area
       * - candidate default, U - per-user static route, o - ODR
       P - periodic downloaded static route
```

continues

Example 2-5 show ip route *Command Output*

```
Gateway of last resort is not set


    172.16.0.0/16 is subnetted, 1 subnets
C       176.16.1.0/24 is directly connected, Ethernet0
    10.0.0.0/24 is subnetted, 2 subnets
R       10.2.2.0/24 [120/1] via 10.1.1.2, 00:00:07, Serial2
C       10.1.1.0/24 is directly connected, Serial2
R    192.168.1.0/24 [120/1] via 10.1.1.2, 00:00:07, Serial2
```

The routing table contains entries for all known networks and subnetworks, and contains a code that indicates how that information was learned. The output of key fields from this command and their function is explained in Table 2-7.

Table 2-7 Route Table Output Explained

Output	Description
R or C	Identifies the route's source. For example, C indicates the route originated from a directly connected subnet. An R indicates that the route was learned from another RIP-speaking router.
192.168.1.0 10.2.2.0	Indicates the remote networks' address.
120/1	The first number in the brackets is the information source's administrative distance; the second number is the metric for the route (for example, 1 hop).
Via 10.1.1.2	Specifies the next-hop router's address to the remote network.
00:00:07	Specifies the time since the route was updated in hours:minutes:seconds.
Serial 2	Specifies the interface through which the specified network can be reached.

Examine the output to see if the routing table is populated with routing information. If routing information is not being exchanged (that is, if the **show ip route** command's output shows no entries that were learned from a routing protocol), use the **show running-config** or **show ip protocols** privileged EXEC commands on the router to check for a possible misconfigured routing protocol.

Lab Activity   Verifying RIP v2 Configuration

In this lab, you enable RIP Version 1 and 2 routing and verify RIPv2 routing with various **show** commands.

Troubleshooting RIP

This section explains the use of the **debug ip rip** command.

Use the **debug ip rip** command to display RIP routing updates as they are sent and received. The **no debug all** or **undebug all** commands turn off all debugging.

Example 2-6 shows that the router being debugged has received updates from one router at source address 10.1.1.2. That router sent information about two destinations in the routing table update. The router being debugged also sent updates, in both cases to broadcast address 255.255.255.255 as the destination. The number in parentheses is the source address encapsulated in the IP header. Because this is RIPv1, updates are being sent to the broadcast address. RIPv2 would send routing updates to the multi-cast Class D address of 224.0.0.9, which would be more efficient.

Example 2-6 debug ip rip *Command*

```
RouterA#debug ip rip
RIP protocol debugging is on
RouterA#
00:06:24: RIP: received v1 update from 10.1.1.2 on Serial2
00:06:24:      10.2.2.0 in 1 hops
00:06:24:      192.168.1.0 in 2 hops
00:06:33: RIP: sending v1 update to 255.255.255.255 via Ethernet0 (172.16.1.1)
00:06:34:      network 10.0.0.0, metric 1
00:06:34:      network 192.168.1.0, metric 3
00:06:34: RIP: sending v1 update to 255.255.255.255 via Serial2 (10.1.2.1)
00:06:34:      network 176.168.0.0, metric 1
```

Other output sometimes seen from the **debug ip rip** command includes entries such as the following, which appear at startup or when an event occurs, such as an interface transitioning or a user manually clearing the routing table:

```
RIP: broadcasting general request on Ethernet0
RIP: broadcasting general request on Ethernet1
```

An entry such as the following is most likely caused by a malformed packet from the transmitter:

```
RIP: bad version 128 from 160.89.80.43
```

debug ip rip output and meanings are shown in Table 2-8.

Table 2-8 debug ip rip Output Explained

Output	Description
RIP:broadcasting general request on Ethernet0 as startup	Transitioning of interface, or a user manually clearing an interface
RIP:bad version 128 from 160.89.80.43	Malformed packet from 160.89.80.43
RIP:received v2 update from 150.100.2.3 on Serial0	Shows version or RIP that 150.100.2.3 is sending
RIP:sending v1 update to 255.255.255.255 via Serial0 (150.100.2.2)	Shows RIPv1 is configured on Serial0
RIP:ignored v1 packet from 150.100.2.2 (illegal version)	Shows that the router is not configured for RIPv1
RIP:sending v2 update to 224.0.0.9 via FastEthernet0 (150.100.3.1)	Shows RIPv2 configured and sending updates
RIP:build update entries 150.100.2.0/24 via 0.0.0.0, metric 1, tag0	Shows use of default route and tag

Lab Activity   Troubleshooting RIP v2 Using Debug

In this lab, you Configure RIP v2 on both routers. You then use debug commands to verify proper rip operation and analyze data transmitted between routers.

Default Routes

By default, routers learn paths to destinations three different ways:

- *Static routes* are manually defined by the system administrator as the next hop to a destination. These are useful for security and traffic reduction, as no other route is known.

- *Default routes* are also manually defined by the system administrator as the path to take when no known route exists to the destination. Default routes keep routing tables shorter. When an entry for a destination network does not exist in a routing table, the packet is sent to the default network.
- Dynamic routing means that the router learns of paths to destinations by receiving periodic updates from other routers using a routing protocol such as RIP.

A simple, static route can be defined using the command shown in Example 2-7.

Example 2-7 *Static Route*

```
Router(config)# ip route 172.16.1.0  255.255.255.0  172.16.2.1
```

The **ip default-network** command establishes a default route in networks using dynamic routing protocols, as in Example 2-8.

Example 2-8 *Dynamic Default Route*

```
Router(config)#ip default-network 192.168.20.0
```

After the routing table has been set to handle all the networks that must be configured, ensuring that all other packets go to a specific location, such as a router that connects to the Internet, is often useful. This is called the router's default route. All the packets that are not defined in the routing table go to the default router's nominated interface. Figure 2-13 shows the default network where packets would be directed, as defined in Example 2-8.

The **ip-default network** command is usually configured on routers that connect to a router with a static default route.

Figure 2-13 Default Routing w/RIP

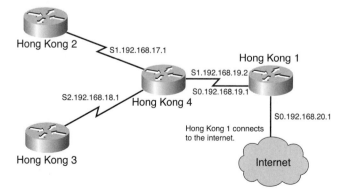

Example 2-9 shows the command to define a static default route that can be used with either static or dynamic routing.

In Figure 2-13, Hong Kong 2 and Hong Kong 3 use Hong Kong 4 as the default gateway. Hong Kong 4 uses interface 192.168.19.2 as its default gateway. Hong Kong 1 routes packets to the Internet for all internal hosts. To allow Hong Kong 1 to route these packets, it is necessary to configure a default route, as shown in Example 2-9.

Example 2-9 *Default Route*

```
HongKong1(config)#ip route 0.0.0.0  0.0.0.0  192.168.20.1
```

The 0s represent any destination network with any mask. Default routes are referred to as quad zero routes. In the diagram, Hong Kong 1 has only one way out to the Internet through the interface 192.168.20.1.

Summary

In this chapter, you learned the following:

- Classless Interdomain Routing (CIDR) replaces the old method of assigning IP addresses based on classful boundaries.
- CIDR was first introduced in 1993 by RFC 1517, 1518, 1519, and 1520, and later deployed in 1994.
- CIDR introduces supernetting and route aggregation.
- VLSM allows network administrators to allocate IP addresses more efficiently. The use of classless routing makes VLSM more efficient because classful network boundaries are no longer necessary.
- Route summarization is most effective in a subnetted network.
- RIPv1 and v2 are distance-vector routing protocols that uses hop count as the metric for route selection and broadcast routing updates every 30 seconds.
- RIPv1 does not send subnet mask information in its updates. Without subnet information, VLSM and CIDR cannot be supported. Its broadcast updates increase network traffic, and it does not support authentication.
- RIPv2 does send subnet information and supports VLSM and CIDR. It multicasts routing updates using the Class D address 224.0.0.9 for better efficiency. It also provides for authentication in its updates.

- The **router RIP** command specifies RIP as the routing protocol.
- The **network** command identifies a participating attached network. RIPv2 supports authentication, subnet masking, next host information, multicasting, and route tagging.

To supplement all that you've learned in this chapter, refer to the chapter-specific Videos, PhotoZooms, and e-Lab Activities on the CD-ROM accompanying this book.

Key Terms

CIDR (classless interdomain routing)   Classless routing protocols based on route aggregation. CIDR allows routers to group routes together to reduce the quantity of routing information the core routers carry. With CIDR, several IP networks appear to networks outside the group as a single, larger entity. With CIDR, IP addresses and their subnet masks are written as four octets separated by periods, followed by a forward slash and a prefix that represents the subnet mask.

default route   A route that a device will automatically select if you do not specify a substitute.

route summarization   Consolidation of advertised addresses in OSPF and IS-IS. In OSPF, this causes a single summary route to be advertised to other areas by an area border router.

static route   A route that is fixed and not capable of action or change.

supernetting   Aggregating IP network addresses advertised as a single classless network address.

VLSM (variable-length subnet mask)   The ability to specify a different subnet mask for the same network number on different subnets. VLSM helps optimize available address space.

Check Your Understanding

1. Which two addresses are valid subnet addresses when 172.17.15.0/24 is subnetted an additional 4 bits? (Choose two.)

    A. 172.17.15.0

    B. 172.17.15.8

    C. 172.17.15.40

    D. 172.17.15.96

    E. 172.17.15.248

2. What is the most efficient subnet mask to use on point-to-point WAN links?

    A. 255.255.255.0

    B. 255.255.255.224

    C. 255.255.255.252

    D. 255.255.255.248

3. Which of the following are features of CIDR? (Choose all that apply.)

   A. Classful addressing

   B. Supernetting

   C. More entries in routing table

   D. Route aggregation

4. What is a summarization address for the networks 172.21.136.0/24 and 172.21.143.0/24?

   A. 172.21.136.0/21

   B. 172.21.136.0/20

   C. 172.21.136.0/22

   D. 172.21.128.0/2

5. Which routing protocol does not contain subnet mask information in its routing updates?

   A. EIGRP

   B. OSPF

   C. RIPv1

   D. RIPv2

6. Which method represents a collection of IP addresses within a single IP address?

   A. Classful routing

   B. Supernetting

   C. Address translation

   D. Route summarization

Objectives

After reading this chapter, you will be able to

- Describe OSPF
- Describe the designated router election process
- List OSPF network types
- Configure OSPF in a single area
- Verify and troubleshoot OSPF

Chapter 3

Single-Area OSPF

Link-state routing protocols are sophisticated and scalable routing protocols. This chapter introduces the industry-standard Open Shortest Path First (OSPF) link-state routing protocol. It describes the OSPF router-election process and how OSPF operates on various networks. Instructions are provided for configuring a basic single-area OSPF network. Procedures for verifying and troubleshooting the OSPF configuration are also covered.

Please be sure to look at this chapter's associated e-Lab Activities, Videos, and PhotoZooms that you will find on the CD-ROM accompanying this book. These CD-ROM elements supplement the material and reinforce the concepts introduced in this chapter.

Single-Area OSPF Concepts

Link-state routing protocols differ from distance vector protocols. Link-state protocols flood link-state information and allow every router to have a complete view of the network topology. With a distance vector protocol, routers do not learn about the complete network topology. OSPF is a link-state protocol.

In OSPF, the shortest path first algorithm (discovered by the computer scientist Dijkstra) determines the best path—the lowest-cost path to a link.

The shortest path first (SPF) algorithm was conceived as an algorithm for point-to-point network connections. To implement OSPF on the variety of today's available networks, OSPF must be aware of the network type in which it operates.

Before link-state information is exchanged, the OSPF protocol establishes a neighbor relationship between routers. The OSPF Hello protocol is used for this purpose.

OSPF is a complex protocol and is described by a set of operational steps.

OSPF Overview

OSPF is a link-state routing protocol based on open standards. Several Internet Engineering Task Force (IETF) standards describe it; the most recent is RFC 2328.

The Open in OSPF means open to the public and non-proprietary. OSPF is becoming the preferred Interior Gateway Protocol (IGP) over Routing Information Protocol (RIP) because it is scalable.

RIP cannot scale beyond 15 hops, it converges slowly, and it can choose slow routes because it ignores critical factors, such as bandwidth, in route determination.

OSPF deals with these limitations and has been proven to be a robust, scalable routing protocol suitable for today's networks. OSPF can be used in a single area for small networks and in multiple areas for large networks.

OSPF can be used for large networks. OSPF routing scales to large networks if hierarchical network design principles are used. Large OSPF networks use hierarchical design principles. Multiple areas connect to a distribution area, Area 0, also called the *backbone*. This design approach allows for extensive control of routing updates. Defining areas reduces routing overhead, speeds up convergence, confines network instability to an area, and improves performance.

OSPF networks are divided into sections, known as *areas*, to efficiently control network operations. The main area is Area 0. All OSPF networks have an Area 0 and use it as the main distribution area.

OSPF Terminology

As a link-state protocol, OSPF operates differently from distance vector routing protocols. Link-state routers identify neighboring routers and communicate with these neighbors. OSPF comes with a new set of terms. These are shown in Figure 3-1.

Figure 3-1 OSPF Terminology

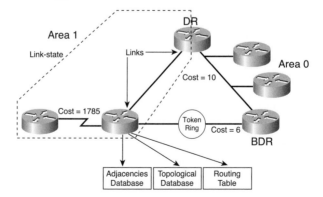

Information gathered from OSPF neighbors is not a complete routing table. Each OSPF router tells about the status of its connections, or links, as shown in Figure 3-2. This information is flooded to all its neighbors. *Flooding* is a process that sends information out all ports, with the exception of the port on which the information was received. An OSPF router advertises its link states and passes on received link states.

Figure 3-2 OSPF Links

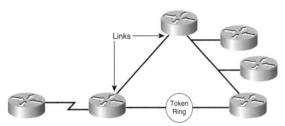

The routers in Area 1 process this information and build a link-state or topological database, as shown in Figure 3-3. Every router in the OSPF area, as in Figure 3-4, has the same link-state database. Every router has the same information about the state of the links and every other router's neighbors. An autonomous system (AS) can be divided into a number of areas, which are groups of contiguous networks and attached hosts. Routers with multiple interfaces can participate in multiple areas. These routers, called Area Border Routers, maintain separate topological databases for each area.

Figure 3-3 OSPF Link-State Topological Database

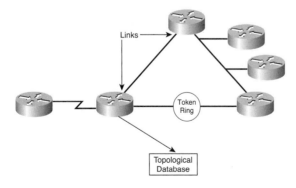

Each router then runs the *shortest path first (SPF) algorithm*, also known as the Dijkstra algorithm, on its copy of the database. This calculation determines the best route to a destination. The SPF algorithm adds up the costs, which is a value usually based on bandwidth, as shown in Figure 3-5. The lowest-path cost is added to the routing table, also known as the forwarding database.

Figure 3-4 OSPF Link-State Area

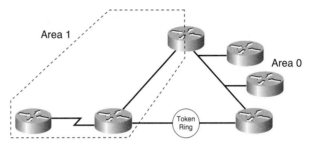

Figure 3-5 OSPF Cost

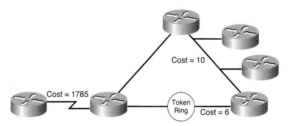

OSPF routers record information about their neighbors in the adjacency database. To reduce the number of routing information exchanges among several neighbors on the same network, OSPF routers elect a *designated router (DR)* and a *backup designated router (BDR)* that serve as focal points for routing information exchange.

OSPF States

OSPF routers establish relationships, or states, with their neighbors for efficiently sharing link-state information. In contrast, distance vector routing protocols, such as RIP, blindly broadcast or multicast their complete routing table out every interface, hoping that a router is out there to receive it. Every 30 seconds, by default, RIP routers send only one kind of message—their complete routing table. OSPF routers, on the other hand, rely on five different kinds of packets to identify their neighbors and to update link-state routing information. Table 3-1 shows the OSPF packet types.

These five packet types make OSPF capable of sophisticated and complex communications. These packet types are discussed in more detail later in the chapter. At this point, you should become familiar with the different relationships that are possible between OSPF routers, the different OSPF network types, and the OSPF Hello protocol.

Table 3-1 OSPF Packet Types

OSPF Packet Type	Description
Type 1—Hello	Establishes and maintains adjacency information with neighbors
Type 2—Database description packet (DBD)	Describes the contents of an OSPF router's link-state database
Type 3—Link State Request	Requests specific pieces of a router's link-state database
Type 4—Link-state update (LSU)	Transports link-state advertisements (LSAs) to neighbor routers
Type 5—Link-state acknowledgement (LSACK)	Acknowledges receipt of a neighbor's LSA

The key to effectively designing and troubleshooting OSPF networks is to understand the relationships, or states, that develop between OSPF routers. OSPF interfaces can be in one of seven states. OSPF neighbor relationships progress through these states, one at a time, from top to bottom in the list presented here:

- Down
- Init
- Two-way
- ExStart
- Exchange
- Loading
- Full adjacency

Down State

In the Down state, the OSPF process has not exchanged information with any neighbor. OSPF is waiting to enter the next state, which is the Init state.

Init State

OSPF routers send Type 1 (Hello) packets at regular intervals (usually 10 seconds) to establish a relationship with neighbor routers. When an interface receives its first Hello packet, the router enters the Init state, which means the router knows a neighbor is out there and is waiting to take the relationship to the next step.

There are two kinds of relationships—Two-way state and adjacency—although many phases occur in between. A router must receive a Hello from a neighbor before it can establish any relationship.

Two-Way State

Using Hello packets, every OSPF router tries to establish a two-way state, or bidirectional communication, with every neighbor router on the same IP network. Among other things, Hello packets include a list of the sender's known OSPF neighbors. A router enters the two-way state when it sees itself in a neighbor's Hello. For example, as shown in Figure 3-6, when RTB learns that RTA knows about RTB, RTB declares that a two-way state exists with RTA.

Figure 3-6 OSPF Two-Way State

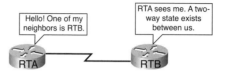

The two-way state is the most basic relationship that OSPF neighbors can have, but routing information is not shared between routers in this relationship. To learn about other routers' link states and eventually build a routing table, every OSPF router must form at least one adjacency. An adjacency is an advanced relationship between OSPF routers that involves a series of progressive states that rely not just on Hellos, but also on the other four types of OSPF packets. Routers that attempt to become adjacent to one another exchange routing information even before the adjacency is fully established. The first step toward full adjacency is the ExStart state.

ExStart State

Technically, when a router and its neighbor enter the ExStart state, their conversation is characterized as an adjacency, but the routers have not become fully adjacent yet. ExStart is established using Type 2 database description (DBD) packets (also known as DDPs). The two neighbor routers use Hello packets to negotiate who is the "master" and who is the "slave" in their relationship, and they use DBD packets to exchange databases, as shown in Figure 3-7.

The router with the highest OSPF router ID becomes the master. (The OSPF router ID is discussed later in this chapter.) When the neighbors establish their roles as master and slave, they enter the Exchange state and begin sending routing information.

Figure 3-7 OSPF Route Discovery

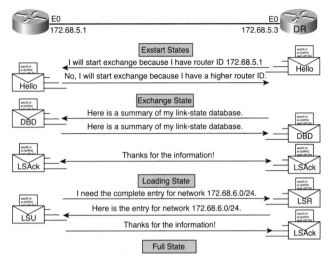

Exchange State

In the Exchange state, neighbor routers use Type 2 DBD packets to send each other their link-state information, as shown in Figure 3-7. In other words, the routers describe their link-state databases to each other. The routers compare what they learn with their existing link-state databases. If either of the routers receives information about a link that is not already in its database, the router requests a complete update from its neighbor. Complete routing information is exchanged in the Loading state.

Loading State

After each router describes its database to the others, , the routers can request information that is more complete by using Type 3 packets, link-state requests (LSRs). When a router receives an LSR, it responds with an update using a Type 4 link-state update (LSU) packet. These Type 4 LSU packets contain the actual link-state advertisements (LSAs), which are the heart of link-state routing protocols. As shown in Figure 3-7, Type 4 LSUs are acknowledged using Type 5 packets, called link-state acknowledgments (LSAcks).

Full Adjacency

With the Loading state complete, the routers are fully adjacent. Each router keeps a list of adjacent neighbors, called the adjacency database. Do not confuse the adjacency database with the link-state database or the forwarding database. Table 3-2 lists the important OSPF databases.

Table 3-2 OSPF Databases

Database	Description
Adjacencies database	List of all the neighbor routers to which a router has established bidirectional communication. This is unique for each router.
Link-state database (topological database)	List of information about all other routers in the network. This database shows the network topology. All routers within an area have identical link-state databases.
Forwarding database (routing table)	List of routes generated when an algorithm is run on the link-state database. Each router's routing table is unique and contains information on how and where to send packets to other routers.

Comparing OSPF with Distance Vector Routing Protocols

OSPF uses link-state technology whereas RIP uses distance vector technology. Link-state routers maintain a common picture of the network and exchange link information upon initial discovery or network changes.

Link-state routers do not broadcast their routing tables periodically as distance vector protocols do, and so use less bandwidth for routing table maintenance.

RIP is appropriate for small networks. OSPF was developed for the needs of large, scalable internetworks. RIP chooses the best path based on hops. This could be the lowest speed path. RIP and other distance vector protocols use simple algorithms to compute best paths. The SPF algorithm is complex. Routers implementing distance vector routing might need less memory and less powerful processors than those running OSPF.

OSPF selects routes based on cost, which is related to bandwidth. The higher the bandwidth, the lower the OSPF cost of the link. OSPF selects the fastest loop free path, the shortest path first tree, as the best path in the network.

OSPF guarantees loop-free routing, whereas distance vector protocols can cause routing loops.

If links are unstable, flooding of link-state information can lead to unsynchronized *link-state advertisements (LSAs)* and inconsistent decisions amongst routers.

OSPF addresses the following issues:

- Speed of convergence
- Support for variable-length subnet masking (VLSM)

- Network size
- Path selection
- Grouping of members

In large networks, RIP convergence can take several minutes because the routing table of each router is copied and shared with directly connected routers. With OSPF, convergence is faster because only changes in the network are flooded to other routers in an area. When only changes in the network are sent, the update is referred to as an *incremental update*.

OSPF is a classless protocol and supports VLSM. RIPv1 does not support VLSM but RIPv2 does. RIP is limited to 15 hops and considers a network that is more than 15 routers away to be unreachable. This limits RIP to small topologies. OSPF has virtually no size limits and is suitable for intermediate to large networks.

RIP selects a path by adding 1 to the hop count to a network that is reported by a neighbor. It compares the hop counts to a destination and selects the path with the smallest distance or hops. This algorithm is simple and does not require a powerful router or much memory. RIP does not take into account the available bandwidth in best path determination.

OSPF selects a path using cost, a metric based on bandwidth. All OSPF routers must obtain complete information about the networks for every router to calculate the shortest path. This is a complex algorithm, and OSPF requires more powerful routers and more memory than RIP.

RIP uses a flat topology, and all routers in a RIP region exchange all information with all routers. OSPF uses areas. A network can be subdivided into clusters of routers. In this way, OSPF limits traffic to these areas, and changes in one area do not affect performance in other areas. This hierarchical approach allows a network to scale efficiently.

Shortest Path First Algorithm

OSPF uses the shortest path first algorithm to determine the best path to a destination. In this algorithm, the best path is the lowest-cost path. The algorithm was created by Dijkstra, a Dutch computer scientist, and was explained in 1959. The algorithm considers a network to be a set of nodes, connected by point-to-point links.

Each link has a cost. Each node has a name. Each node has a complete database of all the links, so complete information about the physical topology is known. The shortest path algorithm then calculates a loop-free topology using the node as the starting point and examining, in turn, the information it has about adjacent nodes.

OSPF Network Types

A neighbor relationship is required for OSPF routers to share routing information; a router will try to become adjacent, or neighbor, to at least one other router on each IP network to which it is connected. Some routers might try to become adjacent to all their neighbor routers, and others might try with only one or two. OSPF routers determine which routers to become adjacent to based on what type of network connects them. After an adjacency is formed between neighbors, link-state information is exchanged. As shown in Figure 3-8 and listed below, OSPF interfaces recognize three types of networks:

- Broadcast multiaccess
- Nonbroadcast multiaccess (NBMA)
- Point-to-point networks

Figure 3-8 OSPF Network Types

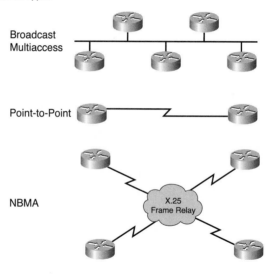

An administrator can configure a fourth type of network, point-to-multipoint, on an interface. Table 3-3 lists the OSPF network types.

In a *multiaccess network*, it cannot be known, in advance, how many routers will be connected. In *point-to-point* networks, only two routers can be connected. If every router had to establish full adjacency with every other router and exchange link-state information with every neighbor, there would be too much overhead. For example, 5 routers would require 10 adjacency relationships and 10 link states to be sent. Ten routers would require 45 adjacencies. In general, for n routers, $(n*n–1)/2$ adjacencies would need to be formed.

Table 3-3 OSPF Network Types

Network Type	Determined Characteristics	DR Election?
Broadcast multiaccess	Ethernet, Token Ring, or FDDI	Yes
Nonbroadcast multiaccess	Frame Relay, X.25, SMDS	Yes
Point-to-point	PPP, HDLC	No
Point-to-multipoint	Configured by an administrator	No

The solution to this overhead is to hold an election for a designated router (DR). This router becomes adjacent to all other routers in the broadcast segment. All other routers on the segment send their link-state information to the DR. The DR acts as the spokesperson for the segment. Using the preceding example numbers, only 5 and 10 sets of link states need be sent, respectively. The DR sends link-state information to all other routers on the segment using the multicast address for all OSPF routers, 224.0.0.5.

Despite the gain in efficiency that electing a DR provides, a weakness still exists. The DR represents a single point of failure. A second router is elected as a backup designated router (BDR) to take over the DR's duties if it fails. Figure 3-9 shows the DR and BDR receiving LSAs. To ensure that both the DR and the BDR see the link states, all routers send on the segment; the multicast address for all designated routers, 224.0.0.6, is used.

Figure 3-9 DR and BDR Receive LSAs

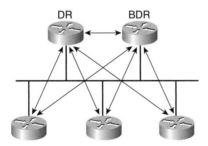

Only two nodes exist On point-to-point networks, and no DR or BDR is elected. Both routers become fully adjacent with each other.

OSPF Hello Protocol

When a router starts an OSPF routing process on an interface, it sends a Hello packet, and continues to send Hellos at regular intervals. The rules that govern the exchange of OSPF Hello packets is called the *Hello protocol*.

At Layer 3 of the OSI model, the Hello packets are addressed to the multicast address 224.0.0.5. This address is "all OSPF routers." OSPF routers use Hello packets to initiate new adjacencies and to ensure that neighbor routers are still functioning. Hellos are sent every 10 seconds, by default, on broadcast multiaccess and point-to-point networks. On interfaces that connect to NBMA networks, such as Frame Relay, Hellos are sent every 30 seconds. On multiaccess networks, the Hello protocol elects a designated router (DR) and a backup designated router (BDR).

Although the Hello packet is small, it contains the OSPF packet header, as shown in Figure 3-10. The Hello packet's type field is set to 1.

Figure 3-10 OSPF Packet Header

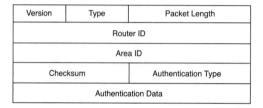

The Hello carries information about which all neighbors must agree to form an adjacency and exchange link-state information, as shown in Figure 3-11.

Figure 3-11 OSPF Hello Header

Network Mask		
Hello Interval	Options	Router Priority
Dead Interval		
Designated Router		
Backup Designated Router		
Neighbor Router ID		
Neighbor Router ID		
(Additional Neighbor Router ID fields can be added to the end of the header, if necessary.)		

Steps in OSPF Operations

OSPF routers progress through five distinct steps of operation:

1. Establish router adjacencies.
2. Elect a DR and BDR (if necessary).
3. Discover routes.
4. Select the appropriate routes to use.
5. Maintain routing information.

The following sections describe each of these steps in detail.

Establishing a Router Adjacency

A router's first step in OSPF operation is to establish router adjacencies. Each of the three routers shown in Figure 3-12 attempts to become adjacent to another router on the same IP network.

Figure 3-12 OSPF Example Topology

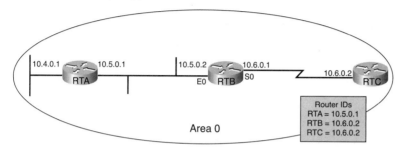

To become adjacent with another router, RTB sends Hello packets, advertising its own router ID.

Assuming that RTB is appropriately configured, RTB multicasts Hello packets out both S0 and E0. RTA and RTC should both receive the Hello packets. These two routers then add RTB to the Neighbor ID field of their respective Hello packets and enter the Init state with RTB.

RTB receives Hello packets from both of its neighbors and sees its own ID number (10.6.0.1) in the Neighbor ID field. RTB declares a Two-Way state between itself and RTA, and a Two-Way state between itself and RTC.

At this point, RTB determines which routers to establish adjacencies with based on the type of network that a particular interface resides on. If the network type is point-to-point, the router becomes adjacent with its sole link partner. If the network type is multiaccess, RTB enters the election process to become a DR or BDR, unless both roles are already established (as advertised in the Hello packet header).

If an election is necessary, OSPF routers proceed as described in the next section. However, if an election is not necessary, the routers enter the ExStart state, as described in the section, "Discovering Routes."

Electing a DR and BDR

Because multiaccess networks can support more than two routers, OSPF elects a DR to be the focal point of all link-state updates and LSAs. The DR's role is critical, therefore a BDR is elected to "shadow" the DR. If the DR fails, the BDR can smoothly take over. Figure 3-13 shows the DR and BDR election process.

Figure 3-13 OSPF DR and BDR Election Process

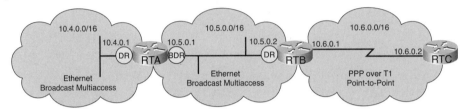

Like any election, the DR/BDR selection process can be rigged. The ballots are Hello packets, which contain a router's ID and priority fields. The router with the highest priority value among adjacent neighbors wins the election and becomes the DR. The router with the second-highest priority is elected the BDR. When the DR and BDR have been elected, they keep their roles until one of them fails, even if additional routers with higher priorities show up on the network. Hello packets inform newcomers of the identity of the existing DR and BDR.

OSPF routers all have the same priority value by default: 1. You can assign a priority from 0 to 255 on any given OSPF interface. A priority of 0 prevents the router from winning any election on that interface. A priority of 255 ensures at least a tie. The Router ID field is used to break ties; if two routers have the same priority, the router with the highest ID is selected. The priority value should be used instead because each interface can have its own unique priority value. You can easily configure a router to win an election on one interface and lose an election on another.

NOTE

DRs and BDRs are elected on a per-network basis. An OSPF area can contain more than one IP network, so each area can (and usually does) have multiple DRs and BDRs.

How does the DR election process affect the example network? As shown in Figure 3-16, RTB and RTC are connected by Point-to-Point Protocol (PPP) on a point-to-point link. A DR isn't necessary on network 10.6.0.0/16 because only two routers can exist on this link.

Because 10.4.0.0/16 and 10.5.0.0/16 networks are multiaccess Ethernet networks, they could potentially connect more than two routers. Even if only one router is connected to a multiaccess segment, a DR is still elected because the potential exists for more routers to be added to the network. A DR must be elected on both 10.4.0.0/16 and 10.5.0.0/16.

In the example topology, RTA serves a dual role as both the DR and the BDR. Because it is the only router on the 10.4.0.0/16 network, RTA elects itself the DR. The 10.4.0.0/16 network is a multiaccess Ethernet network, so a DR is elected because multiple routers could potentially be added to this network. RTA is also the runner-up in the election for 10.5.0.0/16 and, thus, the BDR for that network. Despite claiming equal priority value with RTA, RTB is elected as DR for 10.5.0.0/16 by virtue of the tie-breaker: a higher router ID (10.5.0.2 versus 10.5.0.1).

With elections complete and bidirectional communication established, routers are ready to share routing information with adjacent routers and build their link-state databases. This process is discussed in the next section.

Discovering Routes

On a multiaccess network, the exchange of routing information occurs between the DR or BDR and every other router on the network. As the DR and BDR on the 10.5.0.0 /16 network, RTA and RTB exchange link-state information.

Link partners on a point-to-point or point-to-multipoint network also engage in the exchange process. So, RTB and RTC share link-state data.

However, who goes first? This question is answered in the first stage of the Exchange process. The purpose of ExStart is to establish a master/slave relationship between the two routers.

The router that announces the highest router ID in the Hello packet acts as master, as shown in Figure 3-7. The master router orchestrates the exchange of link-state information, while the slave router responds to prompts from the master. RTB engages in this process with both RTA and RTC.

After the routers define their roles as master and slave, they enter the Exchange state. As shown in Figure 3-7, the master leads the slave through a swap of DBDs that describe each router's link-state database in limited detail.

These descriptions include the link-state type, the advertising router's address, the cost of the link, and a sequence number.

The routers acknowledge the receipt of a DBD by sending an LSAck (Type 5) packet, which echoes back the DBD's sequence number. Each router compares the information that it receives in the DBD with the information it already has. If the DBD advertises a new or more up-to-date link state, the router will enter the Loading state, as in Figure 3-7, by sending an LSR (Type 3) packet about that entry.

In response to the LSR, a router sends the complete link-state information, using an LSU (Type 4) packet. LSUs carry LSAs.

With the Loading state complete, the routers achieve full adjacency (enter into the Full state). As shown in Figure 3-7, RTB is now adjacent to RTA and to RTC.

Adjacent routers must be in the Full state before they can create their routing tables and route traffic. At this point, the neighbor routers should all have identical link-state databases.

Selecting the Best Route

After a router has a complete link-state database, it is ready to create its routing table so that it can forward traffic. As mentioned earlier in the chapter, OSPF uses the metric value cost to determine the best path to a destination (see Figure 3-14). The default cost value is based on media bandwidth. In general, cost decreases as the speed of the link increases. RTB's 10-Mbps Ethernet interface (E0), for example, has a lower cost than its T1 serial line (S0) because 10 Mbps is faster than 1.544 Mbps.

To calculate the lowest cost to a destination, RTB uses the SPF algorithm. In simple terms, the SPF algorithm adds up the total costs between the local router (called the root) and each destination network. If multiple paths exist to a destination, the lowest-cost path is preferred. Figure 3-14 shows this process. By default, OSPF keeps up to four equal-cost route entries in the routing table for load balancing.

Figure 3-14 OSPF Selecting the Best Route

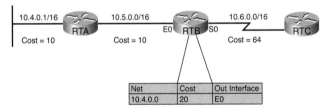

Sometimes a link, such as a serial line, will go up and down rapidly (a condition called flapping). If a flapping link causes LSUs to be generated, routers that receive those updates must rerun the SPF algorithm to recalculate routes. Prolonged flapping can severely affect performance. Repeated SPF calculations can overtax the router's CPU; moreover, the constant updates can prevent link-state databases from converging.

To combat this problem, the Cisco IOS uses an SPF hold timer. After receiving an LSU, the SPF hold timer determines how long a router will wait before running the SPF algorithm. The **timers spf** command enables you to adjust the timer, which defaults to 10 seconds.

After RTB has selected the best routes using the SPF algorithm, it moves into the final phase of OSPF operation.

Maintaining Route Information

When an OSPF router has installed routes in its routing table, it must diligently maintain routing information. When a change occurs in a link state, OSPF routers use a flooding process to notify other routers on the network about the change. The Hello protocol's dead interval provides a simple mechanism for declaring a link partner down. If RTB does not hear from RTA for a time period exceeding the dead interval (usually 40 seconds), RTB declares its link to RTA down.

RTB then sends an LSU packet containing the new link-state information as follows:

- On a point-to-point network, no DR or BDR exists. New link-state information is sent to the 224.0.0.5 multicast address. All OSPF routers listen at this address.

- On a multiaccess network, a DR and BDR exist and maintain adjacencies with all other OSPF routers on the network. If a DR or BDR needs to send a link-state update, it sends the update to all OSPF routers at 224.0.0.5. However, the other routers on a multiaccess network are adjacent only to the DR and the BDR and can send LSUs only to them. For that reason, the DR and BDR have their own multicast address, 224.0.0.6. Non-DR/BDR routers send their LSUs to 224.0.0.6, or all DR/BDR routers.

In Figure 3-15, a router notices a change in a link state and multicasts an LSU packet that includes the updated LSA entry to 224.0.0.6, the all OSPF DRs (and BDR) address.

Figure 3-15 OSPF Link-State Information

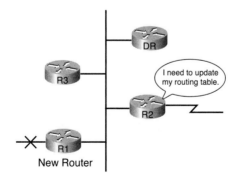

When the DR receives and acknowledges the LSU destined for 224.0.0.6, it floods the LSU to all OSPF routers on the network at 224.0.0.5. Each router acknowledges receipt of the LSU with an LSAck.

If an OSPF router is connected to another network, it floods the LSU to other networks by forwarding the LSU to the multiaccess network's DR, or to an adjacent router if in a point-to-point network. The DR, in turn, multicasts the LSU to the other OSPF routers in that network.

After receiving an LSU that includes new information, an OSPF router updates its link-state database. It then runs the SPF algorithm using the new information to recalculate the routing table. After the SPF hold timer expires, the router switches over to the new routing table.

If a route already exists in a Cisco router, the old route is used while the SPF algorithm is calculating the new information. If the SPF algorithm is calculating a new route, the router will not use that route until after the SPF calculation is complete.

Note that even if a change in link state does not occur, OSPF routing information is periodically refreshed. Each LSA entry has its own age timer. The default timer value is 30 minutes. After an LSA entry ages out, the router that originated the entry sends an LSU to the network to verify that the link is still active.

Single-Area OSPF Configuration

To configure OSPF, you must enable OSPF on the router and configure the router's network addresses and area information, as shown in Figure 3-16, according to the following steps:

Figure 3-16 Basic OSPF Configuration

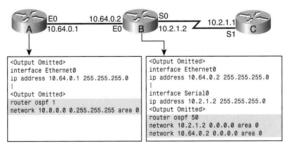

Step 1   Enable OSPF on the router using the following command syntax:

```
router(config)# router ospf process-id
```

The process ID (*process-id* argument) is a process number on the local router. The process ID is used to identify multiple OSPF processes on the same router. The number can be any value between 1 and 65,535. You do not have to start numbering OSPF processes at 1. Most network administrators keep the same process ID throughout the entire AS. You can run multiple OSPF processes on the same router, but doing so is not recommended because it creates multiple database instances that add extra overhead to the router.

Step 2   Identify IP networks on the router using the following command syntax:

```
router(config-router)# network address wildcard-mask area area-id
```

For each network, you must identify the area to which the network belongs. The *address* value can be the network address, subnet, or the interface's address. The router knows how to interpret the address by comparing it to the wildcard mask. A wildcard mask is necessary because OSPF supports CIDR and VLSM, unlike RIPv1 and IGRP. The *area-id* argument is required even when configuring OSPF in a single area. Again, note that more than one IP network can belong to the same area.

Designing and implementing large OSPF networks begins with the ability to configure OSPF routing in a single area. OSPF is configured in a similar way to other routing protocols. Some differences are in the way networks to be advertised are entered in the **network** statement. This is because the protocol is link state.

OSPF requires a *process identifier (process ID)* and a *router identifier (router ID)* for successful operation. The router identifier is taken from an active interface. If that interface fails, the OSPF process cannot continue. To ensure that OSPF is stable, a *loopback* address is configured for use as the router id. Additionally, in broadcast multiaccess networks, a designated router (DR) is elected. This router acts on behalf of other routers in propagating link states to the segment. You might need to ensure that a particular router is elected. Such a router is given a high priority to ensure the election outcome.

Configuring a Loopback Address

When the OSPF process starts, the Cisco IOS uses the highest local IP address as its OSPF router ID. If a loopback interface is configured, that address is used regardless of its value. You can assign an IP to a loopback interface with the following command syntax:

```
router(config)#interface loopback number
router(config-if)#ip address ip-address subnet-mask
```

A loopback-derived router ID ensures stability because that interface is immune to link failure. The loopback interface must be configured before the OSPF process starts to override the highest interface IP address.

Using the loopback address on all key routers in your OSPF-based network is recommended. To avoid routing problems, it is good practice to use a 32-bit subnet mask when configuring a loopback IP address, as shown in Example 3-1.

Example 3-1 *Configuring a Loopback with a Host Mask*

```
router(config)#interface loopback0
router(config-if)#ip address 192.168.1.1 255.255.255.255
```

NOTE

To prevent propagation of bogus routes, OSPF always advertises loopback addresses as host routes, with a 32-bit mask.

A 32-bit mask is sometimes called a host mask, because it specifies a single host and not a network or subnetwork.

Modifying OSPF Router Priority

You can manipulate DR/BDR elections by configuring the priority value to a number other than the default value, which is 1. A value of 0 guarantees that the router will not be elected as a DR or BDR. Each OSPF interface can announce a different priority. You can configure the priority value (a number from 0 to 255) with the **ip ospf priority** command, which has the following syntax:

```
router(config-if)#ip ospf priority number
```

To set a router's E0 with a priority of 0 (so that it can not win DR/BDR elections on that network), use the commands shown in Example 3-2.

Example 3-2 *Setting e0's Priority*

```
RTB(config)#interface e0
RTB(config-if)#ip ospf priority 0
```

For the priority value to figure into the election, it must be set before the election takes place. An interface's priority value and other key information can be displayed with the **show ip ospf** interface command, as shown in Example 3-3. The output in this example tells which routers have been elected the DR and BDR, the network type (in this case, broadcast multiaccess), the cost of the link (10), and the timer intervals specific to this interface. The timer intervals configured are Hello (10), Dead (40), Wait (40), and Retransmit (5). OSPF timers are described in the next section.

The higher the priority, the more likely that router will be elected as the DR. Modify the OSPF priority by entering the **ip ospf priority** command for an interface that is participating in OSPF. For Example 3-3, the command **show ip ospf interface** displays the interface priority value as well as other key information.

Example 3-3 *Using the* show ip ospf interface *Command*

```
Routers#show ip ospf interface e0

Ethernet0 is up, line protocol is up
    Internet Address 10.5.0.2, Area 0
    Process ID 1, Router ID 10.6.0.1, Network Type BROADCAST, Cost:  10
    Transmit Delay is 1 sec, State Dr, Priority 1
    Designated Router (ID) 10.6.0.2, Interface address 10.6.0.1
    Backup Designated router (ID) 10.5.0.1, Interface address 10.5.0.1
    Timer intervals configured, Hello 10, Dead 40, Wait 40, Retransmit 5
        Hello due in 00:00:03
    Index 1/1, flood queue length 0
    Next 0x0(0)/0x0(0)
    Last flood scan length is 1, maximum is 1
    Last flood scan time is 0 msec, maximum is 0 msec
    Neighbor Count is 2, Adjacent neighbor count is 2
        Adjacent with neighbor 10.5.0.1 (Backup Designated Router)
    Suppress hello for 0 neighbor(s)
```

Lab Activity   Configuring the OSPF Routing Process

In this lab, you set up an IP addressing scheme for an OSPF area using two routers. You then configure and verify OSPF routing.

Lab Activity   Configuring OSPF with Loopback Addresses

In this lab, you observe the election process for designated routers, DR and BDR, on a multiaccess network. You configure loopback addresses for OSPF stability and assign each OSPF interface a priority to force the election of a specific router as DR.

Modifying OSPF Cost Metric

OSPF uses cost as the metric for determining the best route. The Cisco IOS automatically determines cost based on the bandwidth of the interface. Cost is calculated using the following formula:

10^8/bandwidth

For OSPF to calculate routes properly, all interfaces connected to the same link must agree on its cost. The cost can be changed to influence the OSPF cost calculation's outcome. The most common situation requiring a cost change occurs in a multivendor routing environment. This is because another vendor's cost value must be matched.

Links have default costs based on the technology implementing the link. An administrator can modify a link's OSPF cost metric. Table 3-4 shows the default link costs.

Table 3-4 OSPF Default Costs

Medium	Cost
56-kbps serial link	1785
T1 (1.544-Mbps serial link)	64
E1 (2.048-Mbps serial link)	48
10 Mbps Ethernet	10
16 Mbps Token Ring	6
100 Mbps Fast Ethernet, FDDI	1

The link cost is set using the following interface configuration command syntax:

```
Router(config-if)#ip ospf cost number
```

The cost *number* can be between 1 and 65,535. An alternative way to influence a link's OSPF cost is to set the bandwidth value on an interface, as in Example 3-4. The lower the number, the better the link.

Example 3-4 *Setting OSPF Bandwidth*

```
Router(config)# interface serial 0/0
Router(config-if)# bandwidth 64
```

The default bandwidth for this serial interface was 1544.

 Lab Activity   Modifying OSPF Cost Metrics

In this lab, you configure and verify OSPF routing. You then modify the OSPF cost metric on the interface.

Configuring OSPF Authentication

Security in networks is enhanced when routing information is guaranteed to be from a particular source. OSPF implementation permits routers to authenticate themselves to each other.

A router, by default, trusts that routing information received has come from a router that should be sending it. A router also trusts that the information has not been tampered with along the way. To guarantee this trust, routers in an area can be configured to authenticate each other.

Authentication is another interface-specific configuration. Each OSPF interface on a router can present a different authentication key, which functions as a password among OSPF routers in the same area. The following command syntax configures OSPF authentication:

```
router(config-if)#ip ospf authentication-key password
```

After a password is configured, you can enable authentication on an area-wide basis with the following syntax, which must be entered on all participating routers:

```
router(config-router)#area number authentication [message-digest]
```

Although the **message-digest** keyword is optional, it is recommended that you always use it with this command. By default, authentication passwords will be sent in clear text over the wire. A packet *sniffer* could easily capture an OSPF packet and decode the unencrypted password. However, if the **message-digest** keyword is used, a message digest, or hash of the password, is sent over the wire in place of the password itself. Unless the recipient is configured with the proper authentication key, that person will not be able to make sense of the message digest.

If you choose to use message-digest authentication, the authentication key is not used. Instead, you must configure a message-digest key on the OSPF router's interface. The syntax for this command is as follows:

```
router(config-if)#ip ospf message-digest-key key-id md5
   [encryption-type] password
```

MD5 authentication creates a message digest. This is scrambled data based on the password and the packet contents. The receiving router uses the shared password and the packet to recalculate the digest. If the digests match, the router believes that the source of the packet and its contents have not been tampered with. The authentication type identifies the authentication, if any, being used. In the case of message-digest authentication, the authentication data field contains the key ID and the length of the message digest that is appended to the packet. The message digest is like a watermark that cannot be faked.

Lab Activity Configuring OSPF Authentication

In this lab, you improve security in an OSPF network by configuring router authentication in the OSPF area.

Configuring OSPF Timers

In some cases, speeding up the reporting of link-state failures might be necessary. In OSPF, this is done by configuring OSPF timers.

For OSPF routers to exchange information, they must have the same Hello intervals and the same dead intervals. By default, the dead interval is four times the value of the Hello interval.

This means that a router has four chances to send a Hello packet before being declared dead.

On broadcast OSPF networks, the default Hello interval is 10 seconds, and the default dead interval is 40 seconds. On nonbroadcast networks, the default Hello interval is 30 seconds, and the default dead interval is 120 seconds. These default values result in efficient OSPF operation, so they need not be modified.

A network administrator does have the freedom to choose these timer values. A justification that OSPF network performance will be improved is needed prior to changing the timers. These timers must be configured to match those of another router.

To configure the Hello and dead intervals on an interface type, use the following command syntax:

```
Router(config-if)# ip ospf hello-interval seconds
Router(config-if)# ip ospf dead-interval seconds
```

 Lab Activity Configuring OSPF Timers

In this lab, you speed up the reporting of link-state failures by configuring OSPF timers.

Configure OSPF over NBMA

Another type of OSPF network, nonbroadcast multiaccess (NBMA), can include more than two nodes and will try to elect a DR and a BDR. Common NBMA implementations include Frame Relay, X.25, and Switched Multimegabit Data Service. (SMDS). NBMA networks follow rules at Layer 2 of the OSI model that prevent the delivery of broadcasts and multicasts. Figure 3-17 summarizes the OSPF network types.

Figure 3-17 OSPF Network Types

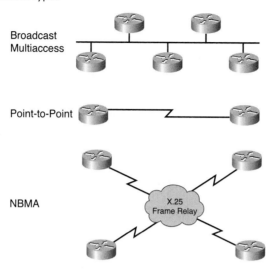

NBMA networks can create problems with OSPF operation, specifically, with the exchange of multicast Hello packets. In the example shown in Figure 3-18, RTA, RTB, and RTC belong to the same IP subnetwork and attempt to elect a DR and a BDR. However, these routers cannot hold a valid election if they cannot receive multicast Hellos from every other router on the network. Without administrative intervention, a strange election takes place. As far as RTA is concerned, RTC is not participating. Likewise, RTC goes through the election process oblivious to RTA. This botched election can lead to problems if the central router, RTB, is not elected the DR.

Figure 3-18 OSPF Neighbor Status in an NBMA Network

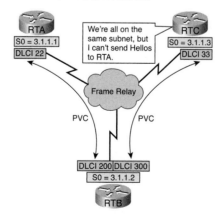

The Cisco IOS offers several options for configuring OSPF to overcome NBMA limitations, including the OSPF **neighbor** command, point-to-point subinterfaces, and point-to-multipoint configuration. The solutions available to you depend on your NBMA network topology.

Before selecting an OSPF configuration strategy for a Frame Relay network (or legacy X.25 network), you must understand the different NBMA topologies. Fundamentally, two possible physical topologies exist for Frame Relay networks:

- Full-mesh topology
- Partial-mesh topology (including the hub-and-spoke topology)

Figure 3-19 shows Frame Relay topologies.

Figure 3-19 OSPF Frame Relay Topologies

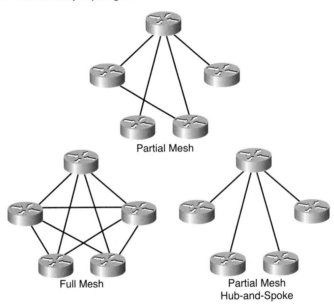

The following sections describe how to configure OSPF in both full-mesh and partial-mesh Frame Relay networks.

Full-Mesh Frame Relay

Organizations deploy Frame Relay primarily because it supports more than one logical connection over a single interface, making it an affordable and flexible choice for WAN links. A full-mesh topology takes advantage of Frame Relay's capability to support multiple permanent virtual circuits (PVCs) on a single serial interface. In a full-mesh topology, every router has a PVC to every other router, as shown in Figure 3-20.

Figure 3-20 OSPF Full Mesh Frame Relay

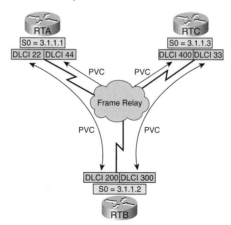

For OSPF to work properly over a multiaccess, full-mesh topology that does not support broadcasts, you must manually enter each OSPF neighbor address on each router, one at a time. The OSPF **neighbor** command tells a router about its neighbors' IP addresses so that it can exchange routing information without multicasts. Example 3-5 illustrates how the **neighbor** command is used:

Example 3-5 *Using the OSPF* neighbor *Command*

```
RTA(config)#router ospf 1
RTA(config-router)#network 3.1.1.0 0.0.0.255 area 0
RTA(config-router)#neighbor 3.1.1.2
RTA(config-router)#neighbor 3.1.1.3
```

Specifying each router's neighbors is not the only option to make OSPF work in this type of environment. The following section explains how configuring subinterfaces can eliminate the need for the **neighbor** command.

Configuring Subinterfaces to Create Point-to-Point Networks

The IOS subinterface feature can be used to break up a multiaccess network into a collection of point-to-point networks.

In Figure 3-21, a different IP subnet is assigned to each PVC.

Figure 3-21 OSPF Full-Mesh Subinterfaces

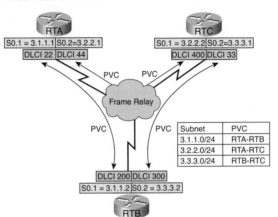

OSPF automatically recognizes this configuration as point-to-point, not NBMA, even with Frame Relay configured on the interfaces. Recall that OSPF point-to-point networks do not elect a DR. Instead, the Frame Relay router uses Reverse Address Resolution Protocol (ARP) or a Frame Relay map to obtain the link partner's address so that routing information can be exchanged.

A full-mesh topology offers numerous advantages, including maximum fault tolerance. Unfortunately, full-mesh topologies can get expensive because each PVC must be leased from a provider. An organization would have to lease 45 PVCs to support just 10 fully meshed routers. If subinterfaces are used to create point-to-point networks, the 45 IP subnets must also be allocated and managed, which is an additional expense.

Partial-Mesh Frame Relay

Because a full-mesh topology is costly, many organizations implement a partial-mesh topology instead. A partial-mesh topology is any configuration in which at least one router maintains multiple connections to other routers, without being fully meshed. The most cost-effective partial-mesh topology is a hub-and-spoke topology, in which a single router (the hub) connects to multiple spoke routers.

The hub-and-spoke topology is a cost-effective WAN solution, however, it introduces a single point of failure (the hub router). Organizations typically deploy Frame Relay because it is inexpensive, not because it is fault-tolerant. Because dedicated leased lines (not Frame Relay links) typically carry mission-critical data, an economical Frame Relay topology, such as hub-and-spoke, makes sense.

Unfortunately, the **neighbor** command that worked with a full-mesh topology does not work as well with the hub-and-spoke topology. The hub router in Figure 3-22 sees all the spoke routers and can send routing information to them using the **neighbor** command, but the spoke routers can send Hellos only to the hub.

Figure 3-22 OSPF Hub-and-Spoke

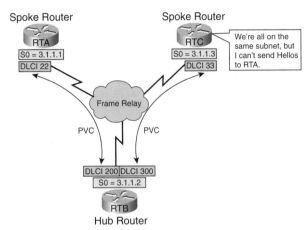

The DR/BDR election will be held, but only the hub router sees all of the candidates. Because the hub router must act as the DR for this OSPF network to function properly, you could configure an OSPF interface priority of 0 on all the spoke routers. Recall that a priority of 0 makes it impossible for a router to be elected as DR or BDR for a network.

A second approach to dealing with this topology is to avoid the DR/BDR issue altogether by breaking the network into point-to-point connections. Point-to-point networks, as in Figure 3-23, do not elect a DR or a BDR.

Although they make OSPF configuration straightforward, point-to-point networks have major drawbacks when used with a hub-and-spoke topology. Subnets must be allocated for each link, which can lead to WAN addressing that is complex and difficult to manage. You can avoid the WAN addressing issue by using IP unnumbered, but many organizations have WAN-management policies that prevent using this feature. Are there any viable alternatives to a point-to-point configuration? Fortunately, the Cisco IOS offers a relatively new alternative. A hub-and-spoke physical topology can be manually configured as a point-to-multipoint network type, as described in the following section.

Figure 3-23 OSPF Hub-and-Spoke Point-to-Point

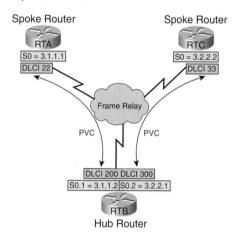

Point-to-Multipoint OSPF

In a point-to-multipoint network, a hub router is directly connected to multiple spoke routers, but all the WAN interfaces are addressed on the same subnet, as shown in Figure 3-24.

Figure 3-24 OSPF Hub-and-Spoke Point-to-Multipoint

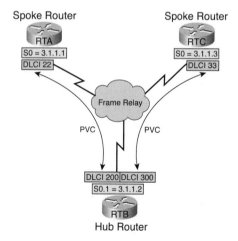

You saw this logical topology earlier in the chapter, but you learned that OSPF does not work properly as an NBMA OSPF network type. By manually changing the OSPF network type to point-to-multipoint, you can make this logical topology work. Routing between RTA and RTC will go through RTB, the router that has virtual circuits to both routers. Note that configuring neighbors when using this feature is unnecessary (Inverse ARP will discover them).

Point-to-multipoint networks have the following properties:

- Adjacencies are established between all neighboring routers. No DR or BDR exists for a point-to-multipoint network. No network LSA is originated for point-to-multipoint networks. Router priority is not configured for point-to-multipoint interfaces or for neighbors on point-to-multipoint networks.

- When originating a router LSA, the point-to-multipoint interface is reported as a collection of point-to-point links to all the interface's adjacent neighbors, together with a single stub link advertising the interface's IP address with a cost of 0.

When flooding out a nonbroadcast interface, the LSU or LSAck packet must be replicated to be sent to each of the interface's neighbors.

To configure point-to-multipoint, you must manually override the detected OSPF network type as follows:

```
router(config-if)#ip ospf network point-to-multipoint
```

You should also configure the interface with a **frame-relay map ip** command, as demonstrated in the following syntax:

```
router(config-if)#frame-relay map ip address dlci broadcast
```

The **broadcast** keyword permits the router to send broadcasts via the specified DLCI to the mapped neighbor or neighbors.

In a point-to-multipoint configuration, OSPF treats all router-to-router connections on the nonbroadcast network as if they were point-to-point links. No DR is elected for the network. You can manually specify neighbors using the **neighbor** command, or they can be dynamically discovered using Inverse ARP.

Ultimately, point-to-multipoint OSPF offers efficient operation without administrative complexity.

Propagating a Default Route

To gain access to networks that are not in the routing table, a default gateway must be set at a border router. This default route information can be propagated to all other routers in the OSPF area.

In OSPF routing, domain routing tables allow all networks in that domain to be reached. Users in an OSPF domain will need to access networks that are not part of the domain (for example the Internet).

A need exists for a default route that will allow routers to send packets of unknown addresses toward a router that might have the packet network address in its routing table.

A configured default route is used by routers to generate a "Gateway of Last Resort." The following static default route configuration syntax uses the network 0.0.0.0 and the subnet mask of 0.0.0.0:

```
Router(config)#ip route 0.0.0.0 0.0.0.0 [interface | next-hop address]
```

This route matches any network address using the rule that the network gateway is determined by ANDing the packet destination with the subnet mask. To propagate this route to all the routers in a normal OSPF area, use the following configuration statement:

```
Router(config-router)# default-information originate
```

All routers in the OSPF area will learn a default route provided that the border router's interface to the default gateway is up.

 Lab Activity   Propagating Default Routes in an OSPF Domain

In this lab, you introduce and propagate default routes in an OSPF network so that all hosts in an OSPF area can connect to outside networks.

Common OSPF Configuration Issues

For effective, rapid, and successful deployment of OSPF, network administrators need to know common configuration problems. OSPF routing for a single area can fail for a number of reasons. An OSPF router must establish a neighbor or adjacency relationship with another OSPF router to exchange routing information. Failure to establish a neighbor relationship can occur for any of the following reasons:

- Hellos are not sent from both neighbors
- Hello and dead interval timers are not the same
- Interfaces are on different network types
- Authentication passwords or keys are different

In OSPF, routing is also important to ensure the following:

- All interfaces have the correct addresses and subnet mask
- **network area** statements have the correct wildcard masks
- **network area** statements put interfaces into the correct area

Verifying the OSPF Configuration

To verify the OSPF configuration, a number of **show** commands are available. Table 3-5 lists these commands.

Table 3-5 OSPF Operation and Statistic Commands

Command	Description
show ip protocol	Displays parameters for timers, filters, metrics, network, and other information for the entire router.
show ip route	Displays the routes known to the router and how they were learned. This is one of the best ways to determine connectivity between the local router and the rest of the internetwork.
show ip ospf interface	Verifies that interfaces have been configured in the intended areas. If no loopback address is specified, the interface address is taken as the router ID. It also gives the timer intervals, including the Hello interval, and shows the neighbor adjacencies.
show ip ospf	Displays the number of times the shortest path first (SPF) algorithm has been executed. It also shows the link-state update interval, assuming no topological changes have occurred.
show ip ospf neighbor detail	Displays detailed lists of neighbors, their priorities, and their state (for example: init, exstart, or full).
show ip ospf database	Displays the contents of the topological database maintained by the router. The command also shows the router ID and the OSPF process ID. A number of database types can be shown with this command using keywords. Refer to www.cisco.com for details about the keywords.
clear ip route*	Clears the entire IP routing table.
clear ip route *a.b.c.d*	Clears only the route specified by *a.b.c.d*.
debug ip ospf	Debugs OSPF operations.

Summary

This chapter discussed the following key points:

- Implementing OSPF routing in a single area is suitable for small networks.

- OSPF is configured in a similar way to other routing protocols. The differences arise because OSPF is a link-state protocol.

- OSPF requires a process identifier and a router identifier.

- OSPF stability is ensured by configuring a loopback address.

- In broadcast multiple access networks, a designated router (DR) is elected. This router acts on behalf of other routers in propagating link states to the segment. OSPF priority is configured on an interface to ensure a preferred router is elected.

- A network administrator can control link cost and timers that affect reporting of link states, and can enhance security by configuring router authentication.

- A common set of OSPF configuration issues and commands verify the OSPF configuration.

- OSPF link-state routing protocol differs from a distance-vector protocol such as RIP. OSPF routers make decisions about best paths based on complete information about the network topology. The metric used by OSPF for best path determination is cost, which is based on link speed. With hierarchical design, OSPF is suitable for large internetworks.

- The shortest path algorithm determines the best loop-free path, the lowest-cost path to a link or network. Because OSPF routers require a complete topology of the network, and the SPF algorithm is complex, more powerful routers with more memory are used.

- The shortest path first (SPF) algorithm was conceived for point-to-point network connections. To implement OSPF on the variety of today's available networks, OSPF must be aware of the network type in which it operates. For efficient multi-access network operations, it is necessary to elect a DR as a focal point for link-state exchanges and a BDR for reliability.

- OSPF makes a neighbor relationship between routers before routing information is exchanged. The OSPF Hello protocol establishes a neighbor relationship between adjacent routers.

To supplement all that you've learned in this chapter, refer to the chapter-specific Videos, PhotoZooms, and e-Lab Activities on the CD-ROM accompanying this book.

Key Terms

backbone   The part of a network that acts as the primary path for traffic that is most often sourced from, and destined for, other networks.

BDR (backup designated router)   Backup to the designated router

DR (designated router)   OSPF router that generates LSAs for a multiaccess network and has other special responsibilities in running OSPF. Each multiaccess OSPF network that has at least two attached routers has a designated router that is elected by the OSPF Hello protocol. The designated router enables a reduction in the number of adjacencies required on a multiaccess network, which reduces the amount of routing protocol traffic and the topological database's size.

flooding   Process that sends information out all ports, with the exception of the port on which the information was received.

Hello protocol   Protocol used by OSPF systems to establish and maintain neighbors.

loopback   A special IP number (127.0.0.1) designated for a machine's software loopback interface. The loopback interface has no hardware associated with it and is not physically connected to a network.

LSA (link-state advertisement)   Broadcast packet used by link-state protocols that contains information about neighbors and path costs. Receiving routers use LSAs to maintain their routing tables. Sometimes called a link-state packet (LSP).

multiaccess network   Network that allows multiple devices to connect and communicate simultaneously.

point-to-point   communication between one receiver and one location.

process ID (process identifier)   A numerical number assigned during the OSPF configuration process that identifies each OSPF process running on a router.

router ID (router identifier)   IP address that identifies a router participating in OSPF. The router ID is taken from the active interface with the highest IP address, or from a configured loopback interface.

sniffer   A program and device that monitors data traveling over a network.

SPF (shortest path first) algorithm   Routing algorithm that iterates on length of path to determine a shortest-path spanning tree. Commonly used in link-state routing algorithms. Sometimes called Dijkstra's algorithm.

Check Your Understanding

1. Which state are OSPF network routers in after the DR and BDR are elected?

   A. ExStart

   B. Full

   C. Loading

   D. Exchange

2. Which OSPF packet type establishes and maintains neighbor adjacencies?

   A. Link-state request

   B. Link-state acknowledgement

   C. Hello

   D. Database description

3. What is the default cost metric for OSPF based on?

   A. Delay

   B. Bandwidth

   C. Efficiency

   D. Network traffic

4. Which multicast address represents all OSPF routers?

   A. 224.0.0.6

   B. 224.0.0.1

   C. 224.0.0.4

   D. 224.0.0.5

5. Which command can change OSPF priority on an interface?

   A. ip priority number ospf

   B. ip ospf priority number

   C. ospf priority number

   D. set priority ospf number

6. Which multicast address is used to send LSUs to all DR/BDR routers?

  A. 224.0.0.6

  B. 224.0.0.1

  C. 224.0.0.4

  D. 224.0.0.5

7. What is a common feature associated with NBMA networks?

  A. Support for only two routers

  B. Support for more than two routers

  C. No election of DRs

  D. Full support for broadcast and multicast packets

8. Which command allows OSPF routers to exchange routing updates without multicasts?

  A. ip ospf neighbor

  B. ospf neighbor

  C. neighbor

  D. ip neighbor

9. Which command displays the routes known to a router and how they were learned?

  A. show ip protocol

  B. show ip route

  C. show ip ospf

  D. show ip ospf neighbor detail

Objectives

After reading this chapter, you will be able to

- Describe EIGRP features and fundamentals
- Describe DUAL
- List EIGRP data structures
- Configure EIGRP
- Verify and troubleshoot EIGRP

Enhanced Interior Gateway Routing Protocol

In this chapter, you learn about Cisco's proprietary implementation of the Enhanced Interior Gateway Routing Protocol (EIGRP). You learn how to configure, verify, and troubleshoot EIGRP. You also compare EIGRP to Interior Gateway Routing Protocol (IGRP). In addition, you survey the key concepts, technologies, and data structures of EIGRP. Following this conceptual overview, you study EIGRP convergence and basic operation using the EIGRP state-of-the-art routing algorithm called Diffusing Update Algorithm (DUAL).

Please be sure to look at this chapter's associated e-Lab Activities, Videos, and PhotoZooms that you will find on the CD-ROM accompanying this book. These CD elements are designed to supplement the material and reinforce the concepts introduced in this chapter.

EIGRP Overview

EIGRP is a Cisco-proprietary routing protocol based on IGRP.

Unlike IGRP, which is a classful routing protocol, EIGRP supports classless interdomain routing (CIDR), which allows network designers to maximize address space by using CIDR and variable-length subnet mask (VLSM). Compared to IGRP, EIGRP boasts faster convergence times, improved scalability, and superior handling of routing loops.

Furthermore, EIGRP can replace Novell Routing Information Protocol (RIP) and AppleTalk Routing Table Maintenance Protocol (RTMP), serving both IPX and AppleTalk networks with powerful efficiency.

EIGRP is often described as a hybrid routing protocol that offers the best of distance-vector and link-state algorithms. EIGRP is an advanced routing protocol that relies on features commonly associated with link-state protocols. Some of the best features of OSPF, such as partial updates and neighbor discovery, are similarly put to use by EIGRP. However, EIGRP is easier to configure than Open Shortest Path First (OSPF).

EIGRP is an ideal choice for large, multiprotocol networks that are built primarily on Cisco routers.

EIGRP Processes and Technology

Cisco released EIGRP in 1994 as a scalable, improved version of its proprietary distance-vector routing protocol, IGRP. The same distance-vector technology found in IGRP is used in EIGRP, and the underlying distance information remains the same.

With EIGRP, convergence properties and operating efficiency have improved significantly. This allows for an improved architecture while retaining the existing investment in IGRP.

Compatibility Mode

IGRP and EIGRP are compatible with each other. This compatibility provides seamless interoperability with IGRP routers. This interoperability is important so that users can take advantage of the benefits of both protocols. EIGRP offers multiprotocol support but IGRP does not.

Metric Calculation

EIGRP and IGRP use different metric calculations. EIGRP scales IGRP's metric by a factor of 256 because EIGRP uses a metric that is 32 bits long, and IGRP uses a 24-bit metric. By multiplying or dividing by 256, EIGRP can easily exchange information with IGRP. Both IGRP and EIGRP use the following metric calculation:

metric = [K1 * bandwidth + (K2 * bandwidth) / (256 − load) + (K3 * delay)] * [K5 / (reliability + K4)]

The following are the default constant values:

K1 = 1

K2 = 0

K3 = 1

K4 = 0

K5 = 0

When K4 and K5 are equal to 0, the [K5 / (reliability + K4)] portion of the equation is not factored in to the metric. Thus, with the default constant values, the metric equation is this:

metric = bandwidth + delay

IGRP and EIGRP use the following equations to determine the values that are used in the metric calculation. (Note that EIGRP scales the value by 256.)

bandwidth for IGRP = (10,000,000 / bandwidth)

bandwidth for EIGRP = (10,000,000 / bandwidth) * 256

delay for IGRP = delay / 10

delay for EIGRP = delay / 10 * 256

Hop Count

EIGRP also imposes a maximum hop limit of 224. This is more than adequate to support today's largest internetworks. IGRP has a maximum hop count of 255, whereas RIP has a maximum of 15.

Automatic Protocol Redistribution

Enabling dissimilar routing protocols, such as OSPF and RIP, to share information requires advanced configuration. However, sharing, or redistribution, is automatic between IGRP and EIGRP as long as both processes use the same autonomous system number.

In Figure 4-1, RTB automatically redistributes EIGRP-learned routes to the IGRP autonomous system, and vice versa.

Figure 4-1 EIGRP and IGRP Share Route Information

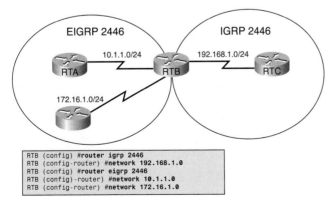

```
RTB (config) #router igrp 2446
RTB (config-router) #network 192.168.1.0
RTB (config) #router eigrp 2446
RTB (config)-router) #network 10.1.1.0
RTB (config-router) #network 172.16.1.0
```

Route Tagging

EIGRP tags routes it learns from IGRP (or any outside source) as external because these routes did not originate from EIGRP routers. IGRP cannot differentiate between internal and external routes.

In the **show ip route** command output for the routers in Example 4-1, EIGRP routes are flagged with 'D', and external routes are denoted by 'EX'. RTA identifies the difference between the network learned via EIGRP (172.16.0.0) and the network that was redistributed from IGRP (192.168.1.0). In RTC's table, the IGRP protocol makes no such distinction.

Example 4-1 show ip route

```
RTA#show ip route
<output omitted>
C       10.1.1.0 is directly connected, Serial0
D       172.16.1.0 [90/2681856] via 10.1.1.1, Serial0
D  EX   192.168.1.1 [170/2681856] via 10.1.1.1, 00:00:04, Serial0


RTC#show ip route
<output omitted>
C       192.168.1.0 is directly connected, Serial0
I       10.0.0.0 [100/10476] via 192.168.1.1, 00:00:04 Serial0
I       172.16.0.0 [100/10476] via 192.168.1.1, 00:00:04, Serial0
```

RTC, which is running IGRP only, just sees IGRP routes (flagged with I), despite the fact that both 10.1.1.0 and 172.16.0.0 were redistributed from EIGRP.

EIGRP Benefits

EIGRP operates quite differently from IGRP. As an advanced distance-vector routing protocol, EIGRP acts like a link-state protocol when updating neighbors and maintaining routing information. The advantages of EIGRP over simple distance-vector protocols include the following:

- **Rapid convergence**—EIGRP routers converge quickly because they rely on a state-of-the-art routing algorithm called *DUAL*. DUAL guarantees loop-free operation at every instant throughout a route computation and allows all routers that are involved in a topology change to synchronize at the same time.

- **Efficient use of bandwidth**—EIGRP makes efficient use of bandwidth by sending partial, bounded updates and through its minimal consumption of bandwidth when the network is stable:
  - **Partial, bounded updates**—EIGRP routers make partial, incremental updates rather than sending their complete tables. This is similar to OSPF operation, but unlike OSPF routers, EIGRP routers send these incremental updates only to the routers that need the information, not to all routers in an area. For this reason, these incremental updates are called bounded updates.
  - **Minimal consumption of bandwidth when the network is stable**—Instead of using timed routing updates, EIGRP routers keep in touch with each other by using small hello packets. Although hello packets are exchanged regularly, they do not consume a significant amount of bandwidth. By contrast, RIP and IGRP send their entire routing tables to neighbors every 30 and 90 seconds respectively.
- **Support for VLSM and CIDR**—Unlike IGRP, EIGRP offers full support for classless IP by exchanging subnet masks in routing updates.
- **Multiple network-layer support**—EIGRP supports IP, IPX, and AppleTalk through protocol-dependent modules (PDMs).

Independence from Routed Protocols

PDMs protect EIGRP from painstaking revision. Evolution of a routed protocol, such as IP, might require a new protocol module, but not necessarily a reworking of EIGRP.

EIGRP Terminology

EIGRP routers keep route and topology information readily available in RAM so that they can react quickly to changes. Like OSPF, EIGRP keeps this information in several tables, or databases.

EIGRP deals with routes in specific ways. Routes are accorded a particular status and can be tagged to provide additional useful information.

Neighbor Table

The *neighbor table* is the most important table in EIGRP. Each EIGRP router maintains a neighbor table that lists adjacent routers. This table is comparable to the adjacency database that OSPF uses. There is a neighbor table for each protocol that EIGRP supports.

When newly discovered neighbors are learned, the address and interface of the neighbor are recorded. This information is stored in the neighbor data structure. When a neighbor sends a hello packet, it advertises a hold time. The hold time is the amount of time that a router treats a neighbor as reachable and operational. In other words, if a hello packet is not heard within the hold time, the hold time expires. When the hold time expires, DUAL, the EIGRP distance-vector algorithm, is informed of the topology change and must recalculate the new topology.

The following fields are found in a neighbor table:

- **Neighbor address (Address)**—The network layer address of the neighbor router.
- **Hold time (Hold Uptime)**—The interval to wait without receiving anything from a neighbor before considering the link unavailable. Originally, the expected packet was a hello packet, but in current Cisco IOS software releases, any EIGRP packets that are received after the first hello reset the timer.
- **Smooth Round-Trip Timer (SRTT)**—The average time that it takes to send and receive packets from a neighbor. This timer determines the retransmit interval (RTI).
- **Queue count (Q Cnt)**—The number of packets that are waiting in queue to be sent. If this value is constantly higher than 0, there might be a congestion problem at the router. A 0 means that there are no EIGRP packets in the queue.
- **Sequence Number (Seq No)**—The number of the last packet that is received from that neighbor. EIGRP uses this field to acknowledge a neighbor's transmission and to identify packets that are out of sequence. The neighbor table supports reliable, sequenced delivery of packets and can be regarded as analogous to the TCP protocol that is used in the reliable delivery of IP packets.

Topology Table

The *topology table* is made up of all the EIGRP routing tables in the autonomous system. The EIGRP distance-vector algorithm, DUAL, takes the information that is supplied in the neighbor and topology tables and calculates the lowest cost routes to each destination. By tracking this information, EIGRP routers can identify, and switch to, alternate routes quickly. This primary route, or successor route, information is placed in the routing table. A copy is also placed in the topology table.

Every EIGRP router maintains a topology table for each configured network protocol. This table includes route entries for all destinations that the router has learned. All learned routes to a destination are maintained in the topology table.

The topology table includes the following fields:

- **Feasible distance (FD is xxxx)**—The *feasible distance (FD)* is the lowest calculated metric to each destination. For example, in Example 4-2, the feasible distance to 32.0.0.0 is 2195456, as indicated by **FD is 2195456**.

Example 4-2 *EIGRP Topology Table*

```
Router#show ip eigrp topology
IP-EIGRP Topology Table for process 100


Codes:    P - Passive, A - Active, U - Update, Q - Query, R - Reply,
    R - Reply Status


P  32.0.0.0/8, 1 successors, FD is 2195456
        via 200.10.10.10 (2195456/281600), Serial1
P  170.32.0.0/16/8, 1 successors, FD is 2195456
        via 199.55.32.10 (2195456/2169856) Ethernet0
        via 200.10.10.5 (2195456/281600), Serial0
P  200.10.10.8/30, 1 successors, FD is 2169856
        via connected, Serial1
P  200.10.10.12/30, 1 successors, FD is 2681856
        via 200.10.10.10 (2681856/2169856), Serial1
P  200.10.10.0/24, 1 successors, FD is 2169856
        via summary (2169856/0), Null0
P  3200.10.10.4/30, 1 successors, FD is 2169856
        via connected, Serial0
P  205.205.205.0/24, 1 successors, FD is 2221056
        via 199.55.32.10 (2221056/2195456), /Ethernet0
        via 200.10.10.5 (2707456/2195456), Serial0
```

- **Route source (via xxx.xxx.xxx.xxx)**—The source of the route is the identification number of the router that originally advertised that route. This field is populated only for routes learned externally from the EIGRP network. Route tagging can be particularly useful with policy-based routing. For example, in Example 4-2, the route source to 32.0.0.0 is 200.10.10.10 via 200.10.10.10.
- **Reported distance**—The *reported distance (RD)* of the path is the distance that an adjacent neighbor reports to a specific destination. As in Example 4-2, the reported distance to 32.0.0.0 is 281600, as indicated by (2195456 / 281600).

- **Interface information**—This is the interface through which the destination is reachable.
- **Route status**—Routes are identified as being either passive (P), which means that the route is stable and ready for use, or active (A), which means that the route is in the process of being recomputed by DUAL, the EIGRP distance-vector algorithm.

EIGRP sorts the topology table so that the successor routes are at the top, followed by feasible successors. At the bottom, EIGRP lists routes that DUAL believes to be loops in the topology table.

Successor

A *successor* is a route that is selected as the primary route to use to reach a destination. DUAL identifies this route from the information contained in the neighbor and topology tables and places it in the routing table. There can be up to four successor routes for any particular route. These can be of equal or unequal cost and are identified as the best loop-free paths to a given destination. A copy of the successor routes is also placed in the topology table.

Feasible Successor

A *feasible successor (FS)* is a backup route. These routes are identified at the same time the successors are identified but are kept in the topology table only. Multiple feasible successors for a destination can be retained in the topology table. It is not mandatory to identify a feasible successor for a destination route.

A router views its feasible successors as neighbors downstream, or closer to the destination than it is. It is the neighbor router's advertised cost to the destination. If a successor route goes down, the router looks for an identified feasible successor. This route is promoted to successor status. A feasible successor must have a lower advertised cost than the existing successor cost to the destination. If a feasible successor is not identified from the existing information, the router places an Active status on a route and sends query packets to all neighbors to recompute the current topology. The router can identify any new successor or feasible successor routes from the new data that is received from the reply packets that answer the query requests. The router then places a Passive status on the route.

Selection of Successors and Feasible Successors

How does an EIGRP router determine which routers are successors and which routers are feasible successors? Assume that RTA's routing table includes a route to Network Z via RTB (see Figure 4-2). From RTA's point of view, RTB is the current successor for

Network Z; RTA forwards packets that are destined for Network Z to RTB. RTA must have at least one successor for Network Z for DUAL to place it in the routing table.

Figure 4-2 EIGRP Successors and Feasible Successors

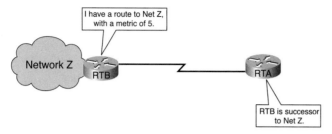

Can RTA have more than one successor for Network Z? If RTC claims to have a route to Network Z with the same metric as RTB, RTA also considers RTC a successor, and DUAL installs a second route to Network Z via RTC (see Figure 4-3).

Figure 4-3 EIGRP Successors and Feasible Successors 2

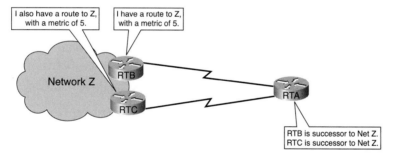

Any of RTA's other neighbors that advertise a loop-free route to Network Z (but with a reported distance higher than the best-route metric and lower than the feasible distance) are identified as feasible successors in the topology table, as shown in Figure 4-4.

Figure 4-4 EIGRP Successors and Feasible Successors 3

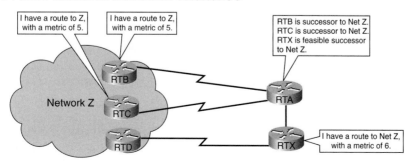

A router views its feasible successors as neighbors that are downstream, or closer, to the destination than it is. If something goes wrong with the successor, DUAL can quickly identify a feasible successor from the topology table and install a new route to the destination. If no feasible successors to the destination exist, DUAL places the route in the Active state. Entries in the topology table can be in one of two states: Active or Passive. These states identify the status of the route indicated by the entry rather than the status of the entry.

A passive route is one that is stable and available for use. An active route is a route that is in the process of being recomputed by DUAL. Recomputation happens if a route becomes unavailable and DUAL cannot find feasible successors. When this occurs, the router must ask neighbors for help in finding a new, loop-free path to the destination. Neighbor routers are compelled to reply to this query. If a neighbor has a route, it replies with information about the successor(s). If not, the neighbor notifies the sender that it does not have a route to the destination either.

Excess recomputation is a symptom of network instability and results in poor performance. To prevent convergence problems, DUAL always tries to find a feasible successor before resorting to a recomputation. If a feasible successor is available, DUAL can quickly install the new route and avoid recomputation.

Stuck in Active Routes

If one or more routers to which a query is sent do not respond with a reply within the active time of 180 seconds (3 minutes), the route, or routes, in question are placed in the *stuck in active* state. When this happens, EIGRP clears the neighbors that did not send a reply and logs a "stuck in active" error message for the route(s) that went active.

Routing Table

EIGRP, through the use of DUAL, chooses the best routes to a destination from the topology table and places these routes in the routing table. Each EIGRP router maintains a routing table for each network protocol.

Route Tagging

The topology table can record additional information about each route. EIGRP classifies routes as either internal or external. EIGRP adds a route tag to each route to identify this classification. Internal routes originate from within the EIGRP autonomous system.

External routes originate outside the EIGRP autonomous system. Routes learned or redistributed from other routing protocols, such as RIP, OSPF, and IGRP, are external.

Static routes that originate outside the EIGRP autonomous system are external. The tag can be configured to a number between 0 and 255 to customize the tag.

All external routes are included in the topology table and are tagged with the following information:

- The identification number (router ID) of the EIGRP router that redistributed the route into the EIGRP network
- The autonomous system number of the destination
- The protocol used in that external network
- The cost or metric received from that external protocol
- The configurable administrator tag

Example 4-3 shows a specific topology table entry for an external route.

Example 4-3 *Viewing Route Tag Information*

```
Router#show ip eigrp topology 204.100.50.0
IP=EIGRP topology entry for 204.100.50.0/24
  State is Passive, Query origin flag is 1, 1 Successor(s), FD is 2297856
  Routing Descriptor Blocks:
  10.1.0.1 {Serial0}, from 10.1.0.1, Send flag is 0x0
    Composite metric is (2297856/128256), Route is External
    Vector metric:
      Minimum bandwidth is 1544 Kbit
      Total delay is 25000 microseconds
      Reliability is 255/255
      Load is 1/255
      Minimum MTU is 1500
      Hop count is 1
    External data:
      Originating router is 192.168.1.1
      AS number of route is 0
      External protocol is Connected, external metric is 0
      Administrator tag is 0 (0x00000000)
```

To develop a precise routing policy, take advantage of the route tagging and, in particular, the administrator tag (shown in the bolded portion of the example). You can configure the administrator tag to be any number between 0 and 255; in effect, this is a custom tag that you can use to implement a special routing policy. External routes can be accepted, rejected, or propagated based on any of the route tags, including the administrator tag. Because you can configure the administrator tag as you see fit, the route-tagging feature affords a high degree of control. This level of precision and flexibility proves especially useful when EIGRP networks interact with Border Gateway Protocol (BGP) networks, which are policy based.

EIGRP Features and Technologies

EIGRP includes many new technologies, each of which represents an improvement in operating efficiency, rapidity of convergence, or functionality relative to IGRP and other routing protocols. These technologies fall into one of the following four categories:

- Neighbor discovery and recovery
- Reliable Transport Protocol
- DUAL finite-state machine algorithm
- Protocol-specific modules

Neighbor Discovery and Recovery

Simple distance-vector routers do not establish a relationship with their neighbors. RIP and IGRP routers merely broadcast or multicast updates on configured interfaces. In contrast, EIGRP routers actively establish relationships with their neighbors, much the same way that OSPF routers do. Figure 4-5 illustrates how EIGRP adjacencies are established. EIGRP routers establish adjacencies with neighbor routers by using small hello packets. Hellos are sent by default every 5 seconds on high-bandwidth links and 60 seconds on low-bandwidth multipoint links. An EIGRP router assumes that, as long as it is receiving hello packets from known neighbors, those neighbors (and their routes) remain viable, or passive.

Figure 4-5 EIGRP Neighbors Exchange Route Information

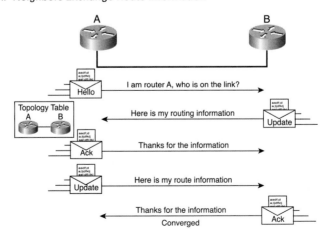

By forming adjacencies, EIGRP routers do the following:

- Dynamically learn of new routes that join their network
- Identify routers that become either unreachable or inoperable
- Rediscover routers that had previously been unreachable

Reliable Transport Protocol

Reliable Transport Protocol is a transport-layer protocol that can guarantee ordered delivery of EIGRP packets to all neighbors. On an IP network, hosts use TCP to sequence packets and ensure their timely delivery. However, EIGRP is protocol independent. (That is, it does not rely on TCP/IP to exchange routing information the way that RIP, IGRP, and OSPF do.) To stay independent of IP, EIGRP uses Reliable Transport Protocol as its proprietary transport-layer protocol to guarantee delivery of routing information.

EIGRP can call on Reliable Transport Protocol to provide reliable or unreliable service as the situation warrants. For example, hello packets do not require the overhead of reliable delivery because they are frequent and should be kept small. Nevertheless, the reliable delivery of other routing information can actually speed convergence because EIGRP routers are not waiting for a timer to expire before they retransmit.

With Reliable Transport Protocol, EIGRP can multicast and unicast to different peers simultaneously, allowing for maximum efficiency.

DUAL Finite-State Machine

The centerpiece of EIGRP is DUAL, EIGRP's route-calculation engine. The full name of this technology is DUAL finite-state machine (FSM). An FSM is an abstract machine, not a mechanical device with moving parts. FSMs define a set of possible states that something can go through, what events cause those states, and what events result from those states. Designers use FSMs to describe how a device, computer program, or routing algorithm reacts to a set of input events. The DUAL FSM contains all the logic used to calculate and compare routes in an EIGRP network.

DUAL tracks all the routes advertised by neighbors and uses the composite metric of each route to compare them. DUAL also guarantees that each path is loop free. The DUAL algorithm then inserts lowest-cost paths into the routing table. These primary routes are known as *successor* routes. A copy of the successor routes is also placed in the topology table.

EIGRP keeps important route and topology information readily available in a neighbor table and a topology table. These tables supply DUAL with comprehensive route information in case of network disruption. DUAL selects alternate routes quickly by using the information in these tables. If a link goes down, DUAL looks for an alternative route path, or *feasible successor,* in the topology table. Packets to the destination network are immediately forwarded to the feasible successor, which, at that point, is promoted to the status of successor, as illustrated in Figure 4-6.

Figure 4-6 EIGRP DUAL Calculation Convergence

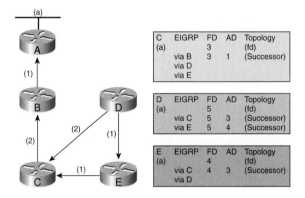

Note in the example in Figure 4-6 that router D does not have a feasible successor identified. The FD (or calculated cost) for router D to router A is 2 and the advertised distance (AD), or reported distance, via router C is 3. Because the AD is smaller than the best-route metric but larger than the FD, no feasible successor is placed in the topology table. Router C has a feasible successor identified as well as router E because the route is loop free and because the AD for the next hop router is less than the FD for the successor.

PDMs

One of the most attractive features of EIGRP is its modular design. Modular, layered designs prove to be the most scalable and adaptable. Support for routed protocols, such as IP, IPX, and AppleTalk, is included in EIGRP through PDMs. In theory, EIGRP can easily adapt to new or revised routed protocols (for example, IPv6) by adding PDMs. Figure 4-7 shows conceptually how PDMs work.

Each PDM is responsible for all functions related to its specific routed protocol. The IP-EIGRP module is responsible for the following:

- Sending and receiving EIGRP packets that bear IP data
- Notifying DUAL of new IP routing information that is received
- Maintaining the results of DUAL's routing decisions in the IP routing table
- Redistributing routing information that was learned by other IP-capable routing protocols

Figure 4-7 EIGRP PDMs

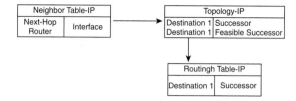

EIGRP Packet Types

Like OSPF, EIGRP relies on several different kinds of packets to maintain its various tables and establish complex relationships with neighbor routers. The five EIGRP packet types are as follows:

- Hello
- Acknowledgment
- Update
- Query
- Reply

Hello Packets

EIGRP relies on hello packets to discover, verify, and rediscover neighbor routers. Rediscovery occurs if EIGRP routers do not receive each other's hellos for a hold time interval but then re-establish communication.

EIGRP routers send hellos at a fixed (and configurable) interval, called the hello interval. The default hello interval depends on the bandwidth of the interface, as shown in Table 4-1.

Table 4-1 Hello Interval

Bandwidth	Example Link	Default Hello Interval	Default Hold Time
1.544 Mbps or less	Multipoint Frame Relay	60 seconds	180 seconds
Greater than 1.544 Mbps	T1, Point-to-Point	5 seconds	15 seconds

EIGRP hello packets are multicast. On IP networks, EIGRP routers send hellos to the multicast IP address 224.0.0.10.

An EIGRP router stores information about neighbors in the neighbor table. The neighbor table includes the Sequence Number (Seq No) field to record the number of the last received EIGRP packet that each neighbor sent. The neighbor table also includes a Hold Time field that records the time of the last received packet. Packets should be received within the Hold Time interval period to maintain a passive—that is, a reachable and operational—status.

If a neighbor is not heard from for the duration of the hold time, EIGRP considers that neighbor down, and DUAL must step in to re-evaluate the routing table. By default, the hold time is three times the hello interval, but an administrator can configure both timers as desired.

OSPF requires neighbor routers to have the same hello and dead intervals to communicate. EIGRP has no such restriction. Neighbor routers learn about each other's respective timers via the exchange of hello packets, and they use that information to forge a stable relationship, despite unlike timers.

Hello packets are always sent unreliably and do not require acknowledgment.

Acknowledgment Packets

An EIGRP router uses acknowledgment packets to indicate receipt of any EIGRP packet during a "reliable" exchange. Reliable Transport Protocol can provide reliable communication between EIGRP hosts. To be reliable, the recipient must acknowledge the sender's message. Acknowledgment packets, which are "dataless" hello packets, are used for this purpose. Unlike multicast hellos, acknowledgment packets are unicast and sent to a specific host. Acknowledgments can be made by piggybacking on other kinds of EIGRP packets, such as reply packets.

Update Packets

Update packets are used when a router discovers a new neighbor. An EIGRP router sends unicast update packets to that new neighbor so that it can add to its topology table. More than one update packet might be needed to convey all the topology information to the newly discovered neighbor.

Update packets are also used when a router detects a topology change. In this case, the EIGRP router sends a multicast update packet to all neighbors, alerting them to the change.

All update packets are sent reliably.

Query and Reply Packets

An EIGRP router uses query packets whenever it needs specific information from one or all of its neighbors. A reply packet is used to respond to a query.

If an EIGRP router loses its successor and cannot find a feasible successor for a route, DUAL places the route in the Active state. Then, the router multicasts a query to all neighbors, searching for a successor to the destination network. Neighbors must send replies that either provide information on successors or indicate that no successor information is available.

Queries can be multicast or unicast, whereas replies are always unicast. Both packet types are sent reliably.

EIGRP Convergence

DUAL's sophisticated algorithm results in EIGRP's exceptionally fast convergence. To better understand convergence by using DUAL, consider the scenario in Figure 4-8. RTA can reach network 24 via three different routers: RTX, RTY, or RTZ.

Figure 4-8 EIGRP Convergence

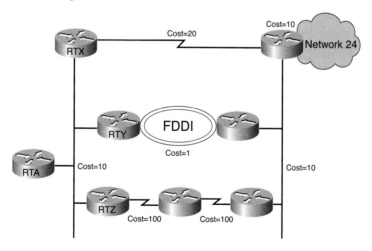

In Figure 4-8, EIGRP's composite metric is replaced by a link cost to simplify calculations. RTA's topology table includes a list of all routes advertised by neighbors. For each network, RTA keeps the real (computed) cost of getting to that network and also keeps the advertised cost (reported distance) from its neighbor, as shown in Table 4-2.

Table 4-2 Composite Metric

Neighbor	Computed Cost to Network 24	Reported Distance to Network 24
RTY	31	21
RTZ	230	220
RTX	40	30

At first, RTY is the successor to network 24 by virtue of its lowest computed cost. RTA's lowest calculated metric to Network 24 is 31; this value is the FD to Network 24.

RTA follows a three-step process to select a feasible successor to become a successor for Network 24:

Step 1 Determine which neighbors have an RD to Network 24 that is less than RTA's FD to network 24. The FD is 31; RTX's RD is 30, and RTZ's RD is 220 (see Table 4-2). Thus, RTX's RD is below the current FD, whereas RTZ's RD is not.

Step 2 Determine the minimum computed cost to Network 24 from among the remaining routes that are available. The computed cost via RTX is 40, whereas the computed cost via RTZ is 230. Thus, RTX provides the lowest computed cost.

Step 3 Determine whether routers that met the criterion in Step 1 also met the criterion in Step 2. RTX has done both, so it is the feasible successor.

With RTY down, RTA immediately uses RTX (the feasible successor) to forward packets to Network 24. The capability to make an immediate switchover to a backup route is the key to EIGRP's exceptionally fast convergence times.

Can RTZ be a feasible successor? Using the same three-step process as before, RTA finds that RTZ is advertising a cost of 220, which is not less than RTA's FD of 31. Therefore, RTZ cannot be a feasible successor (yet). The FD can change only during an active-to-passive transition, and this did not occur, so it remains at 31. At this point, because there has not been a transition to Active state for network 24, DUAL has been performing what is called a *local computation*.

RTA cannot find feasible successors, so it finally transitions from Passive to Active state for Network 24 and queries its neighbors about Network 24. This process is known as a *diffusing computation*. When Network 24 is in Active state, the FD is reset. This allows RTA to at last accept RTZ as the successor to Network 24.

Configuring EIGRP

Common EIGRP configuration procedures are covered in this section. Particular attention is paid to the ways in which EIGRP establishes relationships with adjacent routers, calculates primary and backup routes, and when necessary, responds to failures in known routes to a particular destination.

Configuring EIGRP for IP

Despite the complexity of DUAL, configuring EIGRP can be relatively simple. EIGRP configuration commands vary depending on the protocol that is to be routed. This section covers EIGRP configuration for the IP protocol. Refer to Figure 4-9.

Figure 4-9 Configuring EIGRP for IP

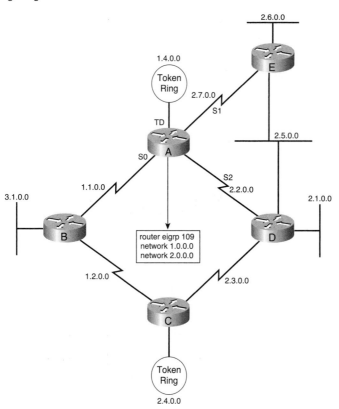

Perform the following steps to configure EIGRP for IP:

Step 1   Use the following command to enable EIGRP and define the autonomous system:

```
router(config)# router eigrp autonomous-system-number
```

The *autonomous-system-number* is the number that identifies the unique autonomous system. It indicates all routers that belong within the internetwork. This value must match all routers within the internetwork.

Step 2   Indicate which networks belong to the EIGRP autonomous system on the local router with the following command:

```
router(config-router)# network network-number
```

The *network-number* is the network number that determines which interfaces of the router are participating in EIGRP and which networks are advertised by the router. The network number is entered by class of IP address. For example, networks 2.2.0.0 and 2.7.0.0 are entered by using the **network** command as follows:

```
Router_A(config-router)#network 2.0.0.0
```

The **network** command configures only connected networks. For example, network 3.1.0.0 (on the far left of Figure 4-9) is not directly connected to Router A. Consequently, that network is not part of Router A's configuration.

Step 3   When configuring serial links using EIGRP, it is important to configure the bandwidth setting on the interface. If the bandwidth for these interfaces is not changed, EIGRP assumes the default bandwidth on the link instead of the true bandwidth. If the link is slower, the router might not be able to converge, routing updates might become lost, or a suboptimal path selection might result. Use the following command to configure the bandwidth setting:

```
router(config-if)# bandwidth kilobits
```

The bandwidth command is ONLY used by the routing process and should be set to match the line speed of the interface.

Step 4   Cisco also recommends adding the following command to all EIGRP configurations:

```
router(config-if)# eigrp log-neighbor-changes
```

This command enables the logging of neighbor adjacency changes to monitor the stability of the routing system and to help detect problems.

Lab Activity   Configuring EIGRP

In this lab, you configure EIGRP on two routers and verify the connection with ping.

Configuring Bandwidth with NBMA

Follow three rules when you configure EIGRP over a nonbroadcast multiaccess (NBMA) cloud such as Frame Relay:

- EIGRP traffic should not exceed the committed information rate (CIR) capacity of the virtual circuit (VC).
- EIGRP's aggregated traffic over all the VCs should not exceed the access line speed of the interface.
- The bandwidth that is allocated to EIGRP on each VC must be the same in both directions.

If these rules are understood and followed, EIGRP works well over the WAN. If care is not taken in the configuration of the WAN, EIGRP can swamp the network.

Configuring Bandwidth over a Multipoint Network

The configuration of the **bandwidth** command in an NBMA cloud depends on the design of the VCs. If the serial line has many VCs in a multipoint configuration, and all of the VCs share bandwidth evenly, set the bandwidth to the sum of all of the CIRs. For example, in Figure 4-10, each VC's CIR is set to 56 Kbps. Because there are 4 VCs, the bandwidth is set to 224 (4×56).

Figure 4-10 EIGRP WAN Configuration Pure Multipoint

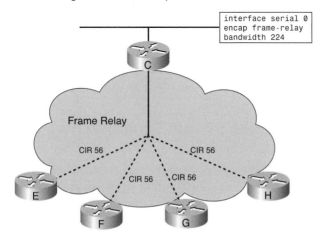

Configuring Bandwidth over a Hybrid Multipoint Network

If the multipoint network has differing speeds allocated to the VCs, a more complex solution is needed. You can take one of two main approaches:

- **Take the lowest CIR and multiply this by the number of VCs**—As shown in Figure 4-11, this is applied to the physical interface. The problem with this configuration is that the higher-bandwidth links might be underutilized.

Figure 4-11 EIGRP WAN Configuration Hybrid Multipoint

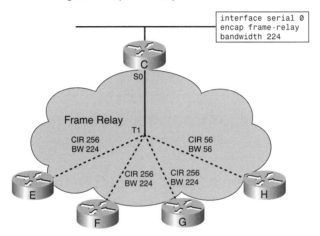

- **Use subinterfaces**—The **bandwidth** command can be configured on each subinterface, which allows different speeds on each VC. In this case, subinterfaces are configured for the links with the differing CIRs. The links that have the same configured CIR are presented as a single subinterface with a bandwidth, which reflects the aggregate CIR of all the circuits. In Figure 4-12, three of the VCs have the same CIR, which is 256 Kbps. All three VCs are grouped together as a multipoint subinterface, serial 0.1. The single remaining VC, which has a lower CIR of 56 Kbps can be assigned a point-to-point subinterface, serial 0.2.

Using the ip bandwidth-percent Command

The **ip bandwidth-percent** command configures the percentage of bandwidth that EIGRP can use on an interface. By default, EIGRP is set to use up to 50 percent of the bandwidth of an interface to exchange routing information. To calculate its percentage, the **ip bandwidth-percent** command relies on the value that the **bandwidth** command sets.

Figure 4-12 EIGRP WAN Configuration Hybrid Multipoint Preferred

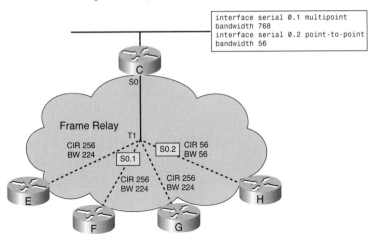

```
interface serial 0.1 multipoint
bandwidth 768
interface serial 0.2 point-to-point
bandwidth 56
```

Use the **ip bandwidth-percent** command when the bandwidth setting of a link does not reflect its true speed. The bandwidth value might be artificially low for a variety of reasons, such as to manipulate the routing metric or to accommodate an oversubscribed multipoint Frame Relay configuration. Regardless of the reasons, configure EIGRP to overcome an artificially low bandwidth setting by setting the **ip bandwidth-percent** to a higher number. In some cases, it might even be set to a number above 100.

For example, assume that the actual bandwidth of a router's serial link is 64 kbps, but the bandwidth value is set artificially low, to 32 kbps. Figure 4-13 shows how to modify EIGRP's behavior so that it limits routing protocol traffic according to the actual bandwidth of the serial interface. The example configuration sets serial 0's bandwidth-percent to 100 percent for the EIGRP process running in autonomous system 24. Because 100 percent of 32 kbps is 32, EIGRP is allowed to use half of the actual bandwidth of 64 Kbps. Figure 4-13 provides details.

Figure 4-13 EIGRP **ip bandwidth-percent** Command

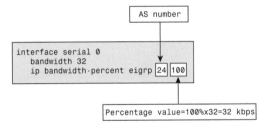

Configuring EIGRP Summarization

EIGRP automatically summarizes routes at the classful boundary (that is, the boundary where the network address ends as defined by class-based addressing). This means that even though RTC is connected only to the subnet 2.1.1.0, it advertises that it is connected to the entire Class A network, 2.0.0.0. In most cases, auto summarization is a good thing; it keeps routing tables as compact as possible (see Figure 4-14).

Figure 4-14 EIGRP Auto Summarization

However, automatic summarization might not be the preferred option in certain instances. If there are discontiguous subnetworks, as shown in Figure 4-15, you must disable auto-summarization for routing to work properly.

To turn off auto-summarization, use the following command:

```
router(config-router)#no auto-summary
```

Figure 4-15 EIGRP Auto Summarization Based on Class

Discontiguous Network with Autosummarization

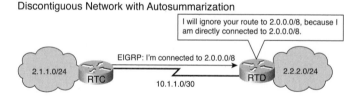

Discontiguous Networks with no Auto-summary

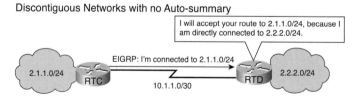

With EIGRP, you can manually configure a prefix to use as a summary address. Manual summary routes are configured on a per-interface basis, so the interface that propagates the route summary must be selected first. Then, the summary address can be defined with the **ip summary-address eigrp** command; the command's syntax follows:

```
router(config-if)#ip summary-address eigrp autonomous-system-number
    ip-address mask administrative-distance
```

EIGRP summary routes have an administrative distance of 5 by default. Optionally, they can be configured for a value between 1 and 255.

RTC can be configured in Figure 4-15 by using the commands shown in Example 4-4.

Example 4-4 *Manual Summarization*

```
RTC(config)#router eigrp 2446
RTC(config-router)#no auto-summary
RTC(config-router)#exit
RTC(config)#interface serial0
RTC(config-if)#ip summary-address eigrp 2446 2.1.0.0 255.255.0.0
Thus, RTC will add a route to its table, as follows:
D   2.1.0.0/16 is a summary, 00:00:22, Null0
```

The summary route is sourced from Null0 and not from an actual interface. This is because this route is used for advertisement purposes and does not represent a path that RTC can take to reach that network. On RTC, this route has an administrative distance of 5.

In the figure, RTD is oblivious to the summarization but accepts the route, and it assigns the route the administrative distance of a "normal" EIGRP route (which is 90, by default). In the configuration for RTC, auto-summarization is turned off with the **no auto-summary** command. If auto-summarization was not turned off, RTD would receive two routes: the manual summary address (2.1.0.0 /16) and the automatic, classful summary address (2.0.0.0 /8).

In most cases, when manually summarizing, the **no auto-summary** command should be issued.

Verifying Basic EIGRP

You can verify EIGRP operation by employing various **show** commands. Table 4-3 lists the key EIGRP **show** commands and briefly discusses their functions.

Table 4-3 Basic EIGRP Show Commands

Command	Description
show ip eigrp neighbors [*type number*] [**details**]	Displays EIGRP neighbor table. Use the type and number options to specify an interface. The **details** keyword expands the output.
show ip eigrp interfaces [*type number*] [*as-number*] [**details**]	Shows EIGRP information for each interface. The optional keywords limit the output to a specific interface or autonomous system. The **details** keyword expands the output.
show ip eigrp topology [*as-number*] | [[*ip-address*] *mask*]	Displays all feasible successors in the EIGRP topology table. Optional keywords can filter output based on an autonomous system number or specific network address.
show ip eigrp topology [**active** | **pending** | **zero-successors**]	Depending on which keyword is used, displays all routes in the topology table that are either active, pending, or without successors.
show ip eigrp topology all-links	Displays all routes, not just feasible successors, in the EIGRP topology.
show ip eigrp traffic [*as-number*]	Displays the number of EIGRP packets that are sent and received. Command output can be filtered by including an optional autonomous system number.

The Cisco IOS **debug** feature also provides useful EIGRP monitoring commands, as listed in Table 4-4.

Table 4-4 Basic EIGRP Debug Commands

Command	Description
debug eigrp fsm	This command helps you observe EIGRP feasible successor activity and determine whether the routing process is installing and deleting route updates.
debug eigrp packet	The output of this command shows transmission and receipt of EIGRP packets. These packet types might be hello, update, request, query, or reply packets. The sequence and acknowledgment numbers that the EIGRP reliable transport algorithm uses are shown in the output.

 Lab Activity   Verifying Basic IGRP Configuration

In this lab, you configure EIGRP on two routers and verify settings using ping and various IGRP commands.

Summary

This chapter discussed the following key points:

- EIGRP is a Cisco-proprietary routing protocol that is based on IGRP.
- EIGRP boasts fast convergence times, improved scalability, and superior handling of routing loops.
- EIGRP can replace Novell RIP and AppleTalk RTMP, serving both IPX and AppleTalk networks with powerful efficiency.
- EIGRP is an advanced distance-vector routing protocol that relies on features that are commonly associated with link-state protocols. Some of the best traits of OSPF, such as partial updates and neighbor discovery, are similarly put to use by EIGRP.
- EIGRP is an ideal choice for large, multiprotocol networks built primarily on Cisco routers.
- This chapter also covered the steps and commands that are used to Configure, verifiy, and troubleshoot EIGRP.

To supplement all that you've learned in this chapter, refer to the chapter-specific Videos, PhotoZooms, and e-Lab Activities on the CD-ROM accompanying this book.

Key Terms

delay   The time between the initiation of a transaction by a sender and the first response that the sender receives. Also, the time required to move a packet from source to destination over a given path.

DUAL (Diffusing Update Algorithm)   Convergence algorithm used in Enhanced IGRP that provides loop-free operation at every instant throughout a route computation. Allows routers involved in a topology change to synchronize at the same time, while not involving routers that are unaffected by the change.

FD (feasible distance)   The lowest calculated metric to each destination.

FS (feasible successor)   A backup route. These routes are identified at the same time that the successors are identified but are kept only in the topology table.

neighbor table   The table that routers running EIGRP use to maintain lists of adjacent routers. There is a neighbor table for each protocol that EIGRP supports.

RD (reported distance)   The distance that an adjacent neighbor reports to a specific destination.

Reliable Transport Protocol   A transport-layer protocol that can guarantee ordered delivery of EIGRP packets to all neighbors.

stuck in active   This refers to the state of a router if one or more routers to which a query is sent do not respond with a reply within the active time of 180 seconds (3 minutes).

successor   A route that is selected as the primary route to use to reach a destination.

topology table   The table that is made up of all the EIGRP routing tables in the autonomous system to provide the router with knowledge of all the destination routes with the autonomous system.

Check Your Understanding

1. How do you configure the automatic redistribution between IGRP and EIGRP?

    A. Configure the two protocols with the different autonomous system numbers.

    B. Configure the two protocols with the different DS numbers.

    C. Configure the two protocols with the same autonomous system numbers.

    D. Configure the two protocols with the same DS numbers.

2. Which protocol combines the advantages of both link-state and distance vector routing protocols?

   A. RIP

   B. OSPF

   C. IGRP

   D. EIGRP

3. Which algorithm is used to achieve rapid convergence?

   A. Dijkstra's algorithm

   B. Diffusing Update algorithm

   C. Convergence algorithm

   D. Dual Convergence algorithm

4. Which protocol does EIGRP support through the use of PDMs?

   A. IS-IS

   B. SNMP

   C. IPX

   D. DHCP

5. Which table includes route entries for all destinations that the router has learned and is maintained for each configured routing protocol?

   A. Topology table

   B. Routing table

   C. Neighbor table

   D. Successor table

6. Which of the following establishes adjacencies in EIGRP?

   A. DUAL finite-state machine

   B. Hello packets

   C. Topology table

   D. Reliable Transport Protocol

7. Which of the following guarantees ordered delivery of EIGRP packets to all neighbors?

   A. DUAL finite-state machine

   B. Hello packets

   C. Topology table

   D. Reliable Transport Protocol

8. What does DUAL do after it tracks all routes, compares them, and guarantees they are loop free?

   A. Inserts up to four lowest-cost paths into the routing table

   B. Determines the optimal path and advertises it to the neighbor routers using hello packets

   C. Supports other routed protocols through PDMs

   D. Sends a unicast query to the neighboring routers

9. How does EIGRP prevent routing loops from occurring with external routes?

   A. By rejecting external routes that are tagged with a router ID identical to their own

   B. By storing the identities of neighbors that are feasible successors

   C. By rejecting all neighboring routers that have an advertised composite metric that is less than a router's best current metric

   D. By storing all neighboring routes that have loops identified in the routing table

10. On higher-bandwidth connections, such as point-to-point serial links and multi-point circuits, how long is the hello interval that EIGRP uses?

    A. 5 seconds

    B. 10 seconds

    C. 60 seconds

    D. 120 seconds

Objectives

After reading this chapter, you will be able to

- Describe Ethernet/802.3 LANs
- Understand LAN switching concepts
- Understand and utilize LAN design concepts
- Describe basic Layer 2 bridging and switching processes

Chapter 5

Switching Concepts and LAN Design

Today, network designers are moving away from using bridges and hubs and are primarily using *switches* and *routers* to build networks.

This chapter discusses problems in a *(LAN)* and possible solutions that can improve LAN performance. You learn about LAN *congestion* and its effect on network performance and the advantages of LAN segmentation in a network. In addition, you learn about the advantages and disadvantages of using bridges, switches, and routers for LAN segmentation and the effects of *switching*, bridging, and routing on network throughput. You learn the basic requirements, goals, and considerations of effective LAN design. Finally, you will learn the benefits of switching technologies such as *Ethernet*, *Fast Ethernet*, *Gigabit Ethernet*, and VLANs and how to apply them to LAN design.

Be sure to look at this chapter's associated e-Lab Activities, Videos, and PhotoZooms that you will find on the CD-ROM that accompanies this book. These CD-ROM elements are designed to supplement the material and reinforce the concepts that are introduced in this chapter.

Ethernet/802.3 LANs

The most common LAN architecture is Ethernet. Ethernet is used to transport data between network devices, such as computers, printers, and file servers.

Ethernet/802.3 LAN Development

The earliest LAN technologies that were installed widely were linear bus-based and used either thick Ethernet or thin Ethernet cabling infrastructures. It is important to understand some of the limitations of these infrastructures so that you can see where LAN switching stands today.

The following is a summarized list of thick Ethernet limitations:

- Limited to 500 meters before signal degradation
- Requires *repeater*s every 500 meters
- Limited number and placement of stations
- Expensive, large, and difficult to pull through buildings
- Relatively simple to add new users
- Provided 10-Mbps shared bandwidth
- Poor connection or break in the linear bus interrupts LAN communications

The following is a summarized list of thin Ethernet limitations:

- Less expensive and requires less space than thick Ethernet
- Still difficult to pull through buildings
- Adding users requires network interruptions
- Provided 10-Mbps shared bandwidth
- Poor connection or break in the linear bus interrupts LAN communications

Adding hubs or concentrators into the network offered an improvement over thick and thin Ethernet technology. A hub is a Layer 1 device and is sometimes referred to as an Ethernet concentrator or a multiport repeater. Introducing hubs into the network allowed greater access to the network for more users. Active hubs, which regenerate the signal, also allowed for the extension of networks to greater distances, as shown in Figure 5-1. A hub does not make decisions when receiving data signals; it simply regenerates and amplifies the data signals that it receives to all connected devices. With linear bus-type networks, a break anywhere in the bus cable or a poor connection to a user workstation could bring down the LAN, making it unavailable. When using newer Ethernet technologies such as hubs or switches, a break in a cable connecting a user does not affect other users on the network. On the other hand, the hub or switch does become a single point of failure.

Ethernet is fundamentally a shared technology with all users on a given LAN segment competing for the same available bandwidth, as shown in Figure 5-2. This situation is analogous to several cars trying to access a one-lane road at the same time. Because the road has only one lane, only one car can access it at a time. The introduction of hubs into a network resulted in more users competing for the same bandwidth.

Figure 5-1 Hubs

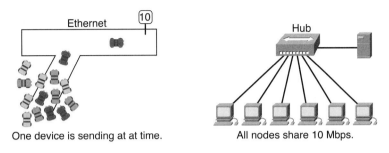

Hub Addressed Many of These Problems

One device is sending at at time.

All nodes share 10 Mbps.

Figure 5-2 Collisions

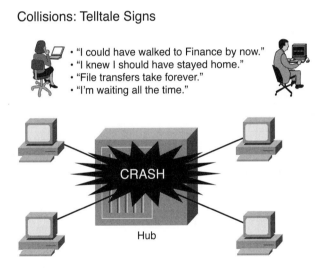

Collisions: Telltale Signs

- "I could have walked to Finance by now."
- "I knew I should have stayed home."
- "File transfers take forever."
- "I'm waiting all the time."

CRASH

Hub

Collisions are a by-product of Ethernet networks. If two or more devices try to transmit at the same time, a collision occurs. This situation is analogous to two cars merging into a single lane and the collision that results. Traffic is backed up until the collision can be cleared. When the number of collisions in a network is excessive, sluggish network response times result, indicating that the network has become too congested or that too many users are trying to access the network at the same time.

Layer 1 devices such as repeaters and hubs simply boost the signal to achieve greater distance. Layer 2 devices are more intelligent than Layer 1 devices. Layer 2 devices make forwarding decisions based on *Media Access Control (MAC) addresses* that are contained within transmitted data frame headers.

A *bridge* is a Layer 2 device that is used to divide (segment) a network and that is capable of collecting and selectively passing data frames between two network segments. Bridges do this by learning the MAC address of all devices on each connected segment. Using this information, the bridge builds a bridging table and forwards or blocks traffic based on that table. This results in smaller *collision domains* and greater network efficiency. Bridges do not restrict broadcast traffic; however, they do provide greater traffic control and a reduction in collisions within a network.

A switch is also a Layer 2 device and can be referred to as a multiport bridge. A switch helps reduce collisions through better traffic control, as shown in Figure 5-3. A switch has the intelligence to make forwarding decisions based on MAC addresses that are contained within transmitted data frames. As do other Layer 2 devices, the switch learns the MAC addresses of devices that are connected to each port; this information is entered into a switching table in content-addressable memory (CAM).

Figure 5-3 Layer 2 Switches

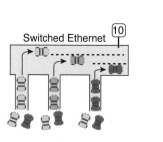
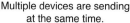
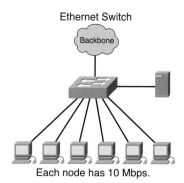

Switches create a virtual circuit between two connected devices that want to communicate. When the virtual circuit is created, a dedicated communication path is established between the two devices. The implementation of a switch on the network provides *microsegmentation*. In theory, this creates a collision-free environment between the source and destination, allowing maximum utilization of the available bandwidth. A switch also can facilitate multiple, simultaneous virtual circuit connections. This is analogous to a highway being divided into multiple lanes, with each car having a dedicated lane. Figure 5-4 illustrates the differences between a Layer 1 hub and a Layer 2 switch.

The disadvantage of Layer 2 devices is that they are compelled to forward frame *broadcasts* to all connected devices on the network. When the number of broadcasts in a network is excessive, sluggish network response times result.

Figure 5-4 Switches and Routers Versus Hubs

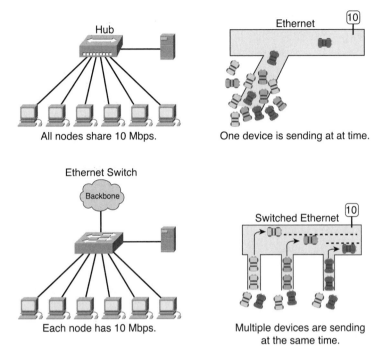

LAN diagrams labeled:
Hub — All nodes share 10 Mbps.
Ethernet (10) — One device is sending at at time.
Ethernet Switch, Backbone — Each node has 10 Mbps.
Switched Ethernet (10) — Multiple devices are sending at the same time.

A router is a Layer 3 device. The router makes decisions based on groups of network addresses as opposed to individual Layer 2 MAC addresses. Routers use *routing tables* to record the Layer 3 addresses of the networks that are accessible. As the network administrator, you can enter these networks manually, or you can learn them via a routing protocol and discovery through neighboring routers.

The purpose of a router is to examine incoming packets (Layer 3 data), choose the best path for them through the network, and then switch them to the proper outgoing port. Routers are not compelled to forward broadcasts. Therefore, routers reduce the size of both the collision domains and the *broadcast domains* in a network. Routers are the most important traffic-regulating devices on large networks. They enable virtually any type of computer to communicate with any other computer anywhere in the world.

LANs typically employ a combination of Layer 1, 2, and 3 devices, as shown in Figure 5-5, which shows a hub (Layer 1), 2 switches (Layer 2), and a router (Layer 3). Implementation of these devices depends on factors that are specific to the particular needs of that organization.

Figure 5-5 Today's LANs

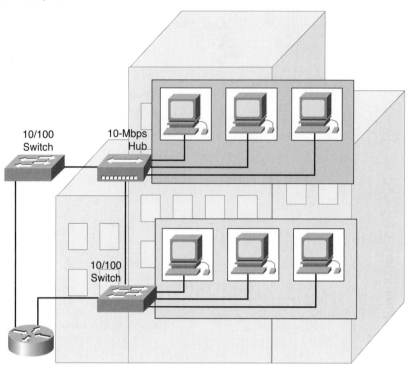

Factors That Impact Network Performance

Today's LANs are becoming increasingly congested and overburdened. In addition to
an ever-growing population of network users, several other factors that are shown in
Figure 5-6 have combined to increase the burden on traditional LANs:

- The multitasking environment that is present in current desktop operating systems (Windows, UNIX, and Mac) allows for simultaneous network transactions.
  This increased capability has lead to an increased demand for network resources.

- With the three most common desktop operating systems (Windows, UNIX, and
  Mac) being able to multitask, users can initiate simultaneous network transactions.
  With the release of Windows 95, which reflected a redesign of DOS/Windows
  that included multitasking, PC users were able to increase their demands for
  network resources.

- Although the use of network-intensive applications such as the World Wide Web
  is increasing, client/server applications allow administrators to centralize information, thus making it easier to maintain and protect. Client/server applications
  free local workstations from the burden of maintaining information and the cost

of providing enough hard disk space to store it. Given the cost benefit of client/ server applications, such applications are likely to become even more widely used in the future.

Figure 5-6 Typical Causes of Network Congestion

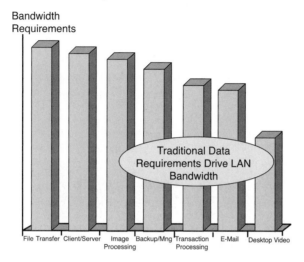

- Too many users on a 10-Mbps segment
- Most users accessing one or two servers
- Network-intensive applications such as color pubishing, CAD/CAM, imaging, and relational databases

Elements of Ethernet/802.3 Networks

The most common LAN architecture is Ethernet. Ethernet is used to transport data between devices on a network, such as computers, printers, and file servers that are connected to the same delivery medium. Ethernet media uses a data frame broadcast method of transmitting and receiving data to all nodes on the shared media, as shown in Figure 5-7.

Figure 5-7 The Ethernet/802.3 Interface

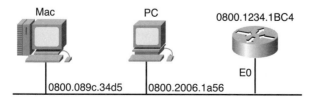

Half-Duplex Ethernet Networks

Basic Ethernet is a half-duplex technology. As shown in Figure 5-8, each Ethernet host checks the network to see whether data is being transmitted before it transmits additional data. If the network is already in use, the transmission is delayed. Despite transmission deferral, two or more Ethernet hosts can transmit at the same time, resulting in a collision. When a collision occurs, the host that first detects the collision sends a jam signal. Upon receiving the jam signal, each host waits a random period of time before attempting to transmit. The network interface card runs a "back-off algorithm" that determines the random amount of time that the host waits before trying to send the message again. As more hosts are added to the network and begin transmitting, collisions are more likely to occur.

Figure 5-8 Half-Duplex Ethernet Design

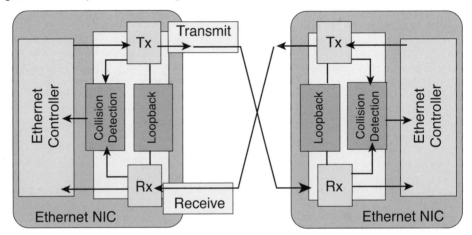

- Most important are receive (Rx), transmit (Tx), and collision detection.
- Ethernet physical connector provides several circuits.

Ethernet LANs become saturated because users run network-intensive software, such as client/server applications, which cause hosts to transmit more often and for longer periods of time. The physical connector (network interface card) that devices use on an Ethernet LAN provides several circuits so that communications between devices can occur.

Full-Duplex Ethernet Networks

Full-duplex Ethernet allows the transmission of a packet and the reception of a different packet at the same time. This simultaneous transmission and reception requires the use of two pairs of wires in the cable and a switched connection between each node. This connection is considered point-to-point and is collision free. Because both nodes can transmit and receive at the same time, there are no negotiations for bandwidth. Full-duplex Ethernet can use an existing shared medium as long as the medium meets the minimum Ethernet standards.

To transmit and receive simultaneously, a dedicated port is required for each node. Full-duplex connections can use 10BASE-T, 100BASE-TX (FastEthernet), or 1000BASE-TX (Gigabit Ethernet) with unshielded twisted-pair (UTP) copper media to create point-to-point connections. Connections can also be made with 100BASE-FX (FastEthernet) or 1000BASE-X (Gigabit Ethernet) using fiber media. The network interfaces (network interface cards, ports, and so on) on all connected devices must have full-duplex capabilities and must be able to support comparable speeds. A 10-Gigabit version of Ethernet has been standardized but only operates over fiber media.

With copper media, the full-duplex Ethernet or Fast Ethernet switch takes advantage of the two pairs of wires in the cable by creating a direct connection between the transmit (TX) at one end of the circuit and the receive (RX) at the other end. With the two stations connected in this manner, a collision-free environment is created as the transmission and receipt of data occurs on separate noncompetitive circuits. Gigabit Ethernet over UTP copper uses all four pairs of wires in the cable to simultaneously transmit in both directions using sophisticated circuitry. All versions of Ethernet that support fiber use two strands: one for TX one for RX.

The use of LAN switching alone reduces collisions because each connection between two ports creates a dedicated virtual circuit. Full-duplex transmission, which effectively doubles the amount of bandwidth between nodes, dramatically improves bandwidth. Full-duplex transmission between stations is achieved by using point-to-point Ethernet connections. This feature can be important, for example, between high-bandwidth consumers, such as a connection between a switch and a server or between two switches. Full-duplex transmission provides a collision-free transmission environment. Because both nodes can transmit and receive at the same time, there are no negotiations for bandwidth.

In 10-Mbps connections, for example, full-duplex transmission provides 10 Mb of transmit capacity and 10 Mb of receive capacity, for effectively 20 Mb of capacity on a single connection. Likewise, a 100-Mbps connection offers effectively 200 Mbps of throughput, as shown in Figure 5-9. Full-duplex communication supports multiple data transmission paths, with speeds up to 2 Gbps.

Figure 5-9 Full-Duplex Technology

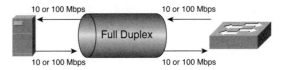

Introduction to LAN Switching

Switching is a technology that decreases congestion in LANs by reducing traffic and increasing bandwidth. *LAN switches* often replace shared hubs and are designed to work with existing cable infrastructures so that they can be installed without disrupting existing network traffic.

LAN switches use microsegmentation to reduce the number of collisions in a LAN and increase the bandwidth. LAN switches also support features such as full-duplex communication and multiple simultaneous conversations. Full-duplex communication enables two devices to communicate with each other simultaneously. Full-duplex communication effectively doubles the throughput that the LAN switch can translate. In a full-duplex switched LAN, no collision occurs.

Three switching modes can be used to forward a frame through a switch: *store-and-forward*, *cut-through*, and fragment-free switching. The *latency* or delay of each switching mode depends on how the switch forwards the frames. The faster the switching mode is, the smaller the latency in the switch.

LAN switches and bridges, operating at Layer 2 of the OSI reference model, forward frames based on the MAC addresses to perform the switching function. If the Layer 2 MAC address is unknown, the device floods the frame in an attempt to reach the desired destination. LAN switches and bridges also forward all broadcast frames. The result could be storms of traffic being looped endlessly through the network. *Spanning Tree Protocol* is a loop-prevention protocol. It is a technology that enables switches to communicate with each other to discover physical loops in the network. Spanning Tree Protocol allows redundant paths to be set up as backups but temporarily disables one of the paths until it is needed.

LAN Segmentation

There are two primary reasons for segmenting a LAN. The first is to isolate traffic between segments, and the second is to achieve more bandwidth per user by creating smaller collision domains.

Without LAN segmentation, LANs that are larger than a small workgroup would quickly become clogged with traffic and collisions and would deliver virtually no bandwidth. LAN segmentation can be implemented through the utilization of bridges, switches, and routers. Each device has particular pros and cons. A network can be divided into smaller units called segments. Each segment uses the *CSMA/CD* access method and maintains traffic between users on the segment.

Figure 5-10 shows an example of a segmented Ethernet network. The entire network has 15 computers (6 file servers and 9 PCs). By using segments in a network, fewer users/devices are sharing the same 10 Mbps when communicating to one another within the segment. Each segment is its own collision domain, as shown in Figure 5-11.

Figure 5-10 Segmented Networks

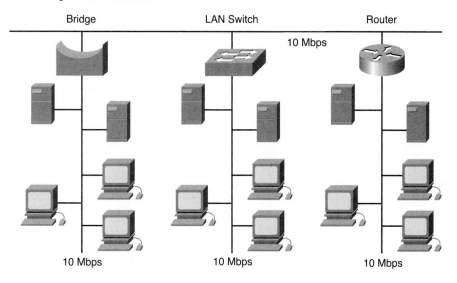

By dividing the network into three segments, a network manager can decrease network congestion within each segment. When transmitting data within a segment, the five devices within each segment are sharing the 10-Mbps bandwidth per segment. In a segmented Ethernet LAN, data that is passed between segments is transmitted on the backbone of the network using a bridge, router, or switch. The backbone (fourth) segment carries frames from all three segments.

Figure 5-11 Collision Domains

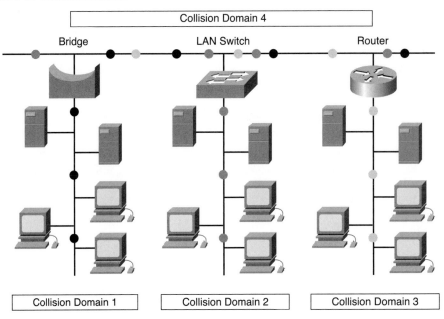

The fundamental concept behind LAN switching is that it provides microsegmentation, which facilitates the creation of a dedicated segment and provides dedicated bandwidth to each user on the network. Each user receives instant access to the full bandwidth; he does not have to contend for available bandwidth with other users. This means that pairs of devices on the same switch can communicate in parallel with a minimum number of collisions. Microsegmentation reduces the number of collisions by reducing the size of collision domains. This increases the capacity for each station that is connected to the network.

LAN Segmentation with Bridges

Ethernet LANs that use a bridge to segment the LAN provide more bandwidth per user because there are fewer users on each segment. In contrast, LANs that do not use bridges for segmentation provide less bandwidth per user because there are more users on a LAN that is not segmented. Figure 5-12 shows an example of a LAN segmented by a bridge.

Figure 5-12 Segmentation with Bridges

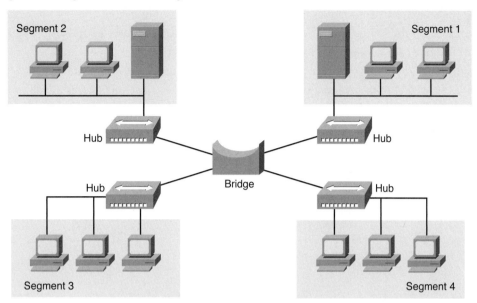

Bridges "learn" a network's segmentation by building address tables that contain the address of each network device and tell which segment to use to reach that device. Figure 5-13 shows an example of how a bridge uses bridging tables to identify the different nodes throughout the network. Bridges are Layer 2 devices that forward data frames according to the frames' MAC addresses. In addition, bridges are transparent to the other devices on the network.

Figure 5-13 Bridging Tables

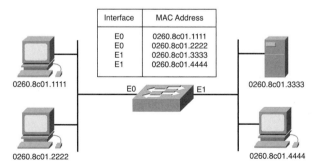

As shown in Figure 5-14, a bridge learns where stations A, B, C, and D are by examining the source MAC addresses. If the bridge sees an incoming frame and does not recognize either the source or the destination address, it adds the source address to its table and forwards the frame to all interfaces except the interface where the bridge received the frame. When the reply comes back, the bridge examines the source address and adds the station to its bridging table. The bridge forwards subsequent communications between devices.

Figure 5-14 Segmentation with Bridges

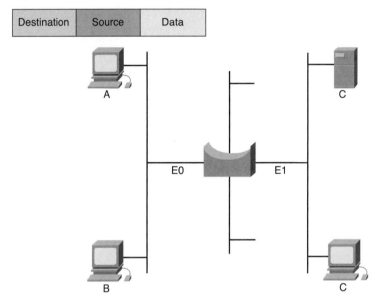

Bridges increase the latency or delay in a network by 10–30 percent. This latency is due to the decision making that is required of the bridge or bridges in transmitting data. A bridge is considered a store-and-forward device because it must examine the destination address field and calculate the cyclic redundancy check (CRC) in the frame check sequence field before forwarding the frame to all ports. If the destination port is busy, the bridge can temporarily store the frame until the port is available.

The time it takes to perform these tasks slows the network transmissions and causes increased latency.

LAN Segmentation with Routers

Routers are more advanced than typical bridges. A bridge is passive on the network and operates at the data link layer. A router operates at the *network layer* and bases all its decisions about forwarding between segments on the network layer protocol address. Routers create the highest level of segmentation by forwarding data to the hub to which workstations are connected. A router makes forwarding decisions to segments by examining the destination address on the data packet and looking in its routing table for forwarding instructions, as shown in Figure 5-15.

Figure 5-15 Segmentation with Routers

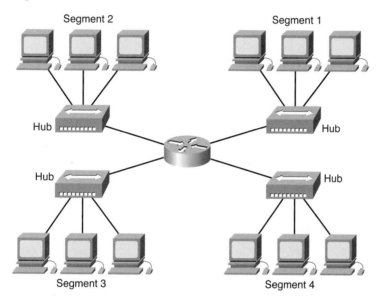

A router must examine a packet to determine the best path for forwarding that packet to its destination. This process takes time. Protocols that require an acknowledgment from the receiver to the sender for every packet as it is delivered (known as acknowledgment-oriented protocols) have a 30–40 percent loss of throughput. Protocols that require minimal acknowledgments (sliding-window protocols) suffer a 20–30 percent loss of throughput. This is because there is less data traffic between the sender and receiver (that is, fewer acknowledgments).

LAN Segmentation with Switches

LAN switching eases bandwidth shortages and network bottlenecks, such as those between several PCs and a remote file server. A switch can segment a LAN into micro-segments, which consist of two hosts, as shown in Figure 5-16. This creates many small collision-free domains from one larger collision domain. Although the LAN switch eliminates collision domains, all hosts that are connected to the switch are still in the same broadcast domain. Therefore, all nodes that are connected through the LAN switch can see a broadcast from just one node. Other advantages include low latency and a high frame-forwarding rate at each interface port, as well as compatibility with existing 802.3 (CSMA/CD) compliant interface cards, hubs, and cabling.

Figure 5-16 Segmentation with Switches

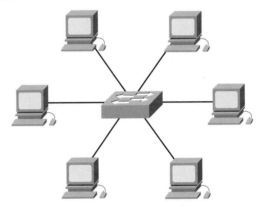

Switched Ethernet is based on Ethernet. Each node is directly connected to one of the switches' ports or a segment that is connected to one of its ports. This creates a 10-Mbps, 100-Mbps, or 1000-Mbps bandwidth connection (depending on which version of Ethernet is being used) between each node and each segment on the switch. A computer that is connected directly to a 10-Mbps Ethernet switch is its own collision domain and accesses the full 10 Mbps. For example, if a 12-port switch has a device connected to each port, 12 collision domains are created.

A LAN that uses a switched Ethernet topology creates a network that behaves as though it has only two nodes: the sending node and the receiving node. These two nodes share the 10-Mbps bandwidth between them, which means that nearly all the bandwidth is available for the transmission of data. Because a switched Ethernet LAN uses bandwidth so efficiently, it can provide more throughput than Ethernet LANs that are connected by bridges or hubs. In a switched Ethernet implementation, the available bandwidth can reach close to 100 percent.

Ethernet switching increases the bandwidth that is available on a network by creating dedicated network segments (that is, point-to-point connections) and connecting those segments in a virtual network within the switch. This virtual network circuit exists only when two nodes need to communicate. This is why it is called a virtual circuit; it exists only when needed and is established within the switch.

One drawback of switches is that they cost more than hubs. However, some businesses might choose to implement switch technology slowly by connecting hubs to switches until such a time that the hubs can be replaced. The speed and capabilities of switches have continued to increase, and the cost has decreased. Nearly all new Ethernet LANs are designed using exclusively switch technology.

The Basic Operations of a Switch

Switching is a technology that decreases congestion in Ethernet, Token Ring, and Fiber Distributed Data Interface (FDDI) LANs by reducing traffic and increasing bandwidth. LAN switches often are used to replace shared hubs. LAN switches are designed to work with cable infrastructures that already exist so that they can be installed without disrupting existing network traffic.

Today in data communications, all switching equipment performs two basic operations:

- **Switching data frames**—This happens when a frame arrives on an input medium and is transmitted to an output medium.
- **Maintaining switching operations**—A switch builds and maintains switching tables.

The term *bridging* refers to a technology in which a device known as a bridge connects two or more LAN segments. Switches were developed using bridging technology and are frequently referred to as multiport bridges. A bridge transmits datagrams from one segment to their destinations on other segments. When a bridge is powered on and begins to operate, it examines the MAC address of the incoming datagrams and builds a table of known destinations. If the bridge knows that the destination of a datagram is on the same segment as the source of the datagram, it drops the datagram because there is no need to transmit it. If the bridge knows that the destination is on another segment, it transmits the datagram on that segment only. If the bridge does not know the destination segment, the bridge transmits the datagram on all segments except the source segment (a technique known as flooding). The primary benefit of bridging is that it limits traffic to certain network segments.

Both bridges and switches connect LAN segments, use a table of MAC addresses to determine the segment on which a datagram needs to be transmitted, and reduce traffic. Switches are more functional in today's networks than bridges because they provide greater connectivity, operate at much higher speeds than bridges, and can support new functionality, such as virtual LANs (VLANs). Bridges typically switch by using software; switches typically switch by using hardware.

This section discusses the fundamental operation of a LAN switch. Figure 5-17 shows a LAN with three workstations, a LAN switch, and the LAN switch's address table. The LAN switch has four interfaces (or network connections). Stations A and C are connected to the switch's Interface 3, and Station B is on Interface 4. Stations A and B would most likely be attached to a hub, which would then be attached to Interface 3. As indicated in Figure 5-17, Station A needs to transmit data to Station B.

Figure 5-17 LAN Switch Operation

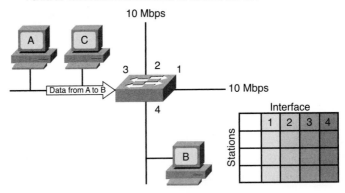

Remember that as this traffic goes through the network, the switch operates at Layer 2, meaning that the switch can look at the MAC layer address. When Station A transmits and the switch receives the frames, the switch looks at the traffic as it goes through to discover the source MAC address and stores it in the address table, as shown in Figure 5-18.

As the traffic goes through the switch, an entry is made in the address table identifying the source station and the interface to which it is connected on the switch. The switch now knows where Station A is connected. When that frame of data is in the switch, it floods to all ports because the destination station is unknown, as shown in Figure 5-19.

Figure 5-18 Building an Address Table

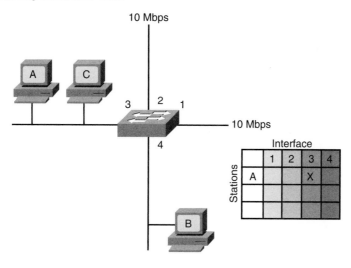

Figure 5-19 Flooding Data to All Switch Ports

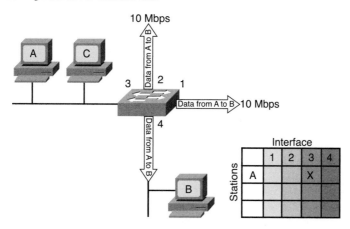

After the address entry is made in the table, however, a response comes back from Station B to Station A. The switch now knows that Station B is connected to Interface 4, as shown in Figure 5-20.

Figure 5-20 Responding to the Flooding Message

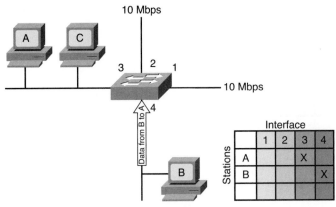

The data is transmitted into the switch, but notice that the switch does not flood the traffic this time. The switch sends the data only out of Interface 3 because it knows where Station A is on the network, as shown in Figure 5-21.

Figure 5-21 Transmitting Data to a Known Station

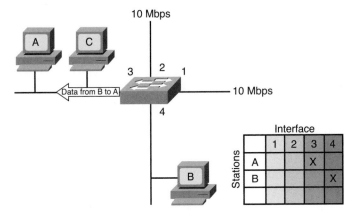

The original transmission indicated where that MAC address came from, enabling the switch to more efficiently deliver traffic in the network.

Ethernet Switch Latency

Each switch that is used on an Ethernet LAN adds latency to the network. However, latency depends on the brand of the switch and on the type of switching used. As explained later, the different switching modes (store-and-forward, fragment free, and *fast forward*) differ on when the decision to switch an incoming frame is made. The latency due to the switch "making its decision" must be added to the time for the frame to enter and exit the switch ports and determines the total latency of the switch.

Note that a hub, which is simply forwarding frames (with no filtering or decision making), has only a port-to-port latency. All these fractions of a second might not seem to matter much, but recall that we are sending data at rates of 10 Mbps (1 bit per 1 ten-millionth of a second), 100 Mbps (1 bit per 1 hundred-millionth of a second), or 1000 Mbps (1 Gbps, 1 bit per 1 billionth of a second). Networking devices are operating at incredibly high speeds, so every nanosecond counts.

Layer 2 and Layer 3 Switching

There are two methods of switching data frames: Layer 2 switching, which is shown in Figure 5-22, and Layer 3 switching, which is shown in Figure 5-23. Switching is the process of taking an incoming frame from one interface and delivering it through another interface. Routers use Layer 3 switching to route a packet; switches (Layer 2 switches) use Layer 2 switching to forward frames.

Figure 5-22 Layer 2 Switching

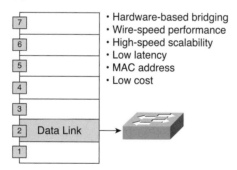

The difference between Layer 2 and Layer 3 switching is the type of information inside the frame that is used to determine the correct output interface. With Layer 2 switching, frames are switched based on MAC address information.

With Layer 3 switching, frames are switched based on network layer information. Layer 2 switching does not look inside a packet for network layer information, as does Layer 3 switching. Layer 2 switching looks at a destination MAC address within a frame. It sends the information to the appropriate interface if it knows the destination address location. Layer 2 switching builds and maintains a switching table that keeps track of which MAC addresses belong to each port or interface.

Figure 5-23 Layer 3 Switching

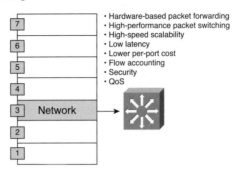

If the Layer 2 switch does not know where to send the frame, it broadcasts the frame out all its ports to the network to learn the correct destination. When the frame's reply is returned, the switch learns the location of the new address and adds the information to the switching table.

The manufacturer of the data communications equipment determines the Layer 2 addresses. They are unique addresses that are derived in two parts: the manufacturing (MFG) code and the unique identifier. The *Institute of Electrical and Electronics Engineers (IEEE)* assigns the MFG code to each vendor. The vendor assigns a unique identifier. Except in Systems Network Architecture (SNA) networks, users have little or no control over Layer 2 addressing because Layer 2 addresses are fixed with a device, whereas Layer 3 addresses can be changed. In addition, Layer 2 addresses assume a flat address space with universally unique addresses.

Layer 3 switching operates at the network layer. It examines packet information and forwards packets based on their network layer destination addresses. Layer 3 switching also supports router functionality.

For the most part, the network administrator determines the Layer 3 addresses. Protocols such as Internet Protocol (IP), Internetwork Packet Exchange (IPX), and AppleTalk use Layer 3 addressing. By creating Layer 3 addresses, you create local areas that act as single addressing units (similar to streets, cities, states, and countries) and assign a number to each local entity. If users move to another building, their end stations obtain new Layer 3 addresses, but their Layer 2 addresses remain the same.

Because routers operate at Layer 3 of the OSI reference model, they can adhere to and create a hierarchical addressing structure. Therefore, a routed network can tie a logical addressing structure to a physical infrastructure, such as through Transmission Control Protocol/Internet Protocol (TCP/IP) subnets or IPX networks for each segment. Traffic flow in a switched (flat) network is inherently different from traffic flow in a routed (hierarchical) network. Hierarchical networks offer more flexible traffic flow than flat networks because they can use the network hierarchy to determine optimal paths and contain broadcast domains.

Implications of Layer 2 and Layer 3 Switching

The increasing power of desktop processors and the requirements of client/server and multimedia applications have created an increased need for greater bandwidth in traditional shared-media environments. These requirements are prompting network designers to replace hubs in wiring closets with switches.

Layer 2 switches use microsegmentation to satisfy the demands for more bandwidth and increased performance, but network designers are now faced with increasing demands for intersubnet communication. For example, every time a user accesses servers and other resources that are located on different subnets, the traffic must go through a Layer 3 device, such as a router. Potentially, there is a tremendous bottleneck, which can threaten network performance. To avoid this bottleneck, network designers can add Layer 3 capabilities throughout the network, which alleviates the burden on centralized routers. Layer 3 switches can be implemented, which include routing technology. A switch improves bandwidth by separating collision domains and selectively forwarding traffic to the appropriate segments of a network.

Symmetric and Asymmetric Switching

Symmetric switching is one way to characterize a LAN switch according to the bandwidth that is allocated to each port on the switch. As shown in Figure 5-24, a symmetric switch provides switched connections between ports with the same bandwidth, such as all 10-Mbps ports or all 100-Mbps ports. As shown in Figure 5-25, an asymmetric LAN switch provides switched connections between ports of unlike bandwidth, such as a combination of 10-Mbps and 100-Mbps or 100-Mbps and 1000-Mbps ports.

Asymmetric switching makes the most of client/server network traffic flows where multiple clients are communicating with a server at the same time, requiring more bandwidth dedicated to the switch port to which the server is connected to prevent a bottleneck at that port. As you will learn in the next section, memory buffering in an asymmetric switch is required to allow traffic from the 100-Mbps port to be sent to a 10-Mbps port without causing too much congestion at the 10-Mbps port. An asymmetric switch also is required to provide high bandwidth links between switches for vertical cabling or backbone segments.

Figure 5-24 Symmetric Switching

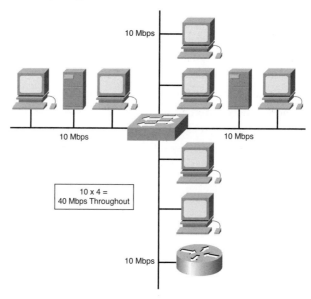

Figure 5-25 Asymmetric Switching

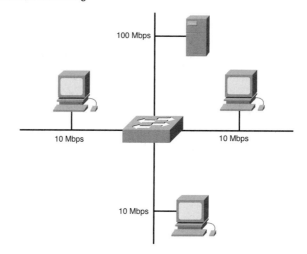

Memory Buffering

An Ethernet switch might use a buffering technique to store and forward packets to the correct port or ports. Buffering might also be used when the destination port is busy. The area of memory where the switch stores the data is called the memory buffer.

This memory buffer can use two methods for forwarding packets: port-based memory buffering and shared memory buffering.

In port-based memory buffering, packets are stored in queues that are linked to specific incoming ports. A frame is transmitted to the outgoing port only when all the frames ahead of it in the queue have been transmitted successfully. A single packet can delay the transmission of all the packets in memory because of a busy destination port. This delay occurs even if the other packets can be transmitted to open destination ports.

Shared memory buffering deposits all packets into a common memory buffer that all the ports on the switch share. The amount of memory that is allocated to a port is determined by how much each port requires. This is called dynamic allocation of buffer memory. The packets in the buffer are then linked dynamically to the transmit port; the packet is linked to the memory allocation of that transmit port. This allows the packet to be received on one port and transmitted on another port, without moving it into a different queue.

The switch maintains a map of the ports to which a packet needs to be transmitted. The switch clears out this map of destination ports only after the packet has been transmitted successfully. Because the memory buffer is shared, the packet is restricted by the size of the entire memory buffer, not just the allocation to one port. This means that larger packets can be transmitted with fewer dropped packets. This is important to asymmetrical switching, where a 100-Mbps port can forward a packet to a 10-Mbps port or a 1000-Mbps port can forward a packet to a 10-Mbps or 100-Mbps port.

LAN Design

Despite improvements in equipment performance and media capabilities, network design is becoming more difficult. The trend is toward increasingly complex environments that involve multiple media types and interconnection to networks outside any single organization's controlled LAN. Keeping these key factors in mind is important. Carefully designing networks can reduce the hardships associated with growth as a networking environment evolves.

One of the most critical steps to ensure a fast and stable network is the design of the network. If a network is not designed properly, many unforeseen problems can arise, and network growth can be jeopardized. This design process is truly an in-depth process. This chapter provides an overview of the LAN design process. It also covers LAN design goals, network design issues, network design methodology, and the development of LAN topologies.

LAN Design Goals

Designing a network can be a challenging task; it involves more than just connecting computers. A network requires many features for it to be reliable, manageable, and scaleable. To design reliable, manageable, and scalable networks, network designers must realize that each of the major components of a network has distinct design requirements.

The first step in designing a LAN is to establish and document the goals of the design. These goals are unique to each organization or situation. The following requirements tend to show up in most network designs:

- **Functionality**—The network must work. The network must allow users to meet their job requirements. The network must provide user-to-user and user-to-application connectivity with reasonable speed and reliability.
- **Scalability**—The network must be able to grow. The initial design should grow without major changes to the overall design.
- **Adaptability**—The network must be designed with an eye toward future technologies, and it should include no element that would limit implementation of new technologies as they become available.
- **Manageability**—The network should be designed to facilitate network monitoring and management to ensure ongoing stability of operation.

These requirements are specific to certain types of networks and more general in other types of networks.

LAN Design Considerations

With the emergence of high-speed technologies such as Gigabit Ethernet and more complex LAN architectures that use LAN switching and VLANs, many organizations have been upgrading existing LANs or planning, designing, and implementing new LANs. Although Asynchronous Transfer Mode (ATM) is a widely used technology in WANs, it is no longer a significant consideration in today's LAN designs.

To maximize available LAN bandwidth and performance, you must address the following LAN design considerations:

- The function and placement of servers
- Segmentation issues
- Broadcast domain issues

Function and Placement of Servers

Servers provide file sharing, printing, communication, and application services. Servers typically do not function as workstations. They run specialized operating systems, such as NetWare, Windows NT/2000/XP, UNIX, and Linux. Each server is usually dedicated to one function, such as e-mail or file sharing.

Servers can be categorized into two distinct classes: *enterprise servers* and workgroup servers. An enterprise server supports all the users on the network by offering services, such as e-mail or Domain Name System (DNS). E-mail or DNS is a service that everyone in an organization would need because it is a centralized function. On the other hand, a workgroup server supports a specific set of users, offering services such as word processing and file sharing, which are services that only a few groups of people would need.

Enterprise servers should be placed in the main distribution facility (MDF). This way, traffic to the enterprise servers has to travel only to the MDF and does not need to be transmitted across other networks. Ideally, workgroup servers should be placed in the intermediate distribution facilities (IDFs) closest to the users who are accessing the applications on these servers. By placing workgroup servers close to the users, traffic has to travel only the network infrastructure to an IDF and does not affect other users on that network segment. Within the MDF and IDFs, the Layer 2 LAN switches should have 100 Mbps or more allocated for these servers.

Segmentation Issues

Segmentation is the process of splitting a single collision domain into two or more collision domains or bandwidth domains, as shown in Figure 5-26. Layer 2 (the data link layer) bridges or switches can be used to segment a logical *bus topology* and create separate collision domains, which results in more bandwidth being available to individual stations. Notice in Figure 5-27 that the entire bus topology still represents a single broadcast domain because, although bridges and switches do not forward collisions, they forward broadcast packets.

All broadcasts from any host in the same Layer 2 broadcast domain are visible to all other hosts in the same broadcast domain. Broadcasts must be visible to all hosts in the broadcast domain to establish connectivity. The scalability of the bandwidth domain depends on the total amount of traffic, and the scalability for a broadcast domain depends on the total broadcast of the traffic. It is important to remember that bridges and switches forward broadcast (FF-FF-FF-FF-FF) traffic, and routers normally do not.

Figure 5-26 Developing a LAN Technology

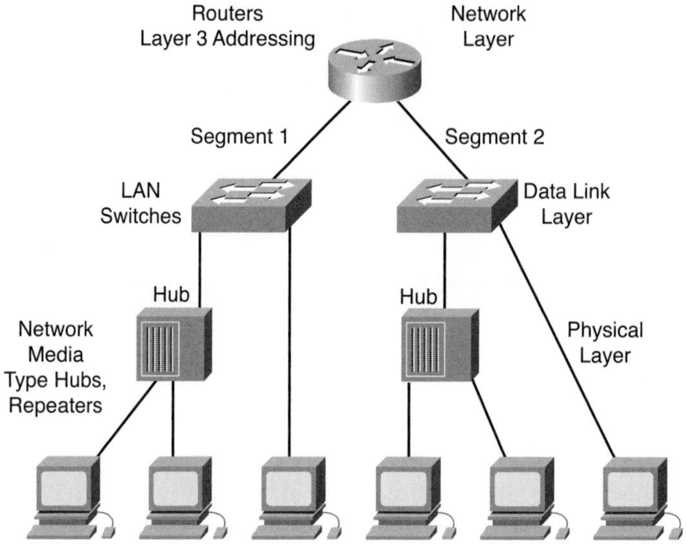

Routers
Layer 3 Addressing

Network
Layer

Segment 1

Segment 2

LAN
Switches

Data Link
Layer

Hub

Hub

Network
Media
Type Hubs,
Repeaters

Physical
Layer

Figure 5-27 Segmentation

Bridging and switching are both used for segmentation.

- Results in multiple collision domains.
- Still a single broadcast domain.
- Stations can get dedicated bandwidth.

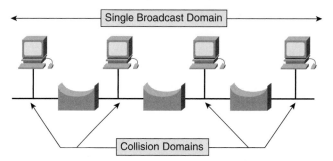

Single Broadcast Domain

Collision Domains

Broadcast Domain Issues

A bandwidth domain is everything that is associated with one port on a bridge or switch. In the case of an Ethernet switch, a bandwidth domain is also known as a collision domain. As shown in Figure 5-28, a switch can create one bandwidth domain per port.

All workstations within one bandwidth domain compete for the same LAN bandwidth resource. All the traffic from any host in the bandwidth domain is visible to all the other hosts. In the case of an Ethernet collision domain, two stations can transmit at the same time, causing a collision.

Figure 5-28 Bandwidth and Broadcast Domains

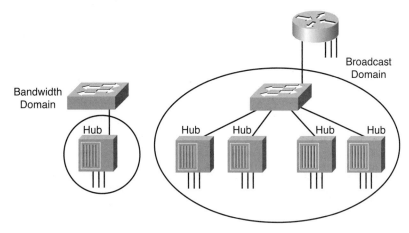

LAN Design Methodology

For a LAN to be effective and serve the needs of its users, it should be designed and implemented according to a planned series of systematic steps, which include the following:

- Gathering the users' requirements and expectations
- Analyzing requirements
- Designing the access layer, distribution layer, and the core layer
- Documenting the logical and physical network implementation

The first step in designing a network should be to gather data about the organizational structure. This information includes the organization's history and current status, projected growth, operating policies and management procedures, office systems and procedures, and the viewpoints of the people who will be using the LAN. You need to answer the following questions: Who are the people who will be using the network? What is their level of skill, and what are their attitudes toward computers and computer applications? Answering these and similar questions will help determine how much training will be required and how many people will be needed to support the LAN.

Ideally, the information gathering process helps clarify and identify the problems. You also need to determine whether documented policies are in place. Has some data been declared mission critical? Have some operations been declared mission critical? (Mission-critical data and operations are those that are considered key to businesses, and access to them is critical to the business running on a daily basis.) What protocols are allowed on the network? Are only certain desktop hosts supported?

Next, you should determine who in the organization has authority over addressing, naming, topology design, and configuration. Some companies have a central Management Information Systems (MIS) department that controls everything. Other companies have small MIS departments and must delegate authority to departments. Focus on identifying the resources and constraints of the organization. Organizational resources that can affect the implementation of a new LAN system fall into two general categories: computer hardware/software and human resources. An organization's existing computer hardware and software must be documented, and projected hardware and software needs must be identified. How are these resources currently linked and shared? What financial resources does the organization have available? Documenting these types of things helps you estimate costs and develop a budget for the LAN. You should make sure you understand performance issues of any existing network.

The next step in designing a network is to analyze the requirements of the network and its users that were gathered in the previous step. Network user needs constantly change. For example, as more voice- and video-based network applications become available, the pressure to increase network bandwidth will become intense.

Another component of the analysis phase is assessing the user requirements. A LAN that is incapable of supplying prompt and accurate information to its users is of little use. Therefore, you must take steps to ensure that the information requirements of the organization and its workers are met.

Factors That Affect Network Availability

Availability measures the usefulness of the network. Many things affect availability, including the following:

- Throughput
- Response time
- Access to resources

Every customer has a different definition of availability. For example, there might be a need to transport voice and video over the network. However, these services require more bandwidth than is available on the network or backbone. You can increase availability by adding more resources, but resources drive up cost. Network design seeks to provide the greatest availability for the least cost.

Designing the Physical Network Topology

After you determine the overall requirements for the network, the next step is to decide on an overall LAN topology that will satisfy the user requirements. In this curriculum, we concentrate on the *star topology* and extended star topology. As you have seen, the star/extended star topology, shown in Figure 5-29, uses Ethernet 802.3 technology. The reason that this curriculum focuses on a CSMA/CD star topology is that it is by far the dominant configuration in the industry.

Figure 5-29 Broadcast Domain

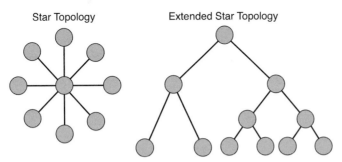

The major pieces of a LAN topology design can be broken into three unique categories of the OSI reference model: the network layer, the data link layer, and the physical layer, shown previously in Figure 5-27. These components are discussed in the following sections.

Layer 1 Design

In this section, you will examine Layer 1 star and extended star topologies, as shown in Figure 5-26.

The physical cabling is one of the most important components to consider when you are designing a network. Design issues include the type of cabling to be used (typically copper or fiber) and the overall structure of the cabling. Layer 1 cabling media include types such as Category 5 UTP and fiber-optic cable, along with the TIA/EIA-568-B standard for layout and connection of wiring schemes, as shown in Figure 5-30.

In addition to distance limitations, you should carefully evaluate various cable types because a network is only as effective as its underlying cable. Layer 1 issues cause most network problems. If you are planning significant changes for a network, you should do a complete cable audit to identify areas that require upgrades and rewiring.

Figure 5-30 Star Topology

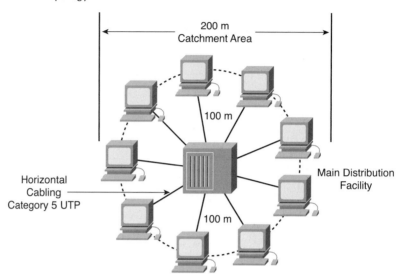

Whether you are designing a new network or recabling an existing one, you should use fiber-optic cable in the backbone and risers, with at least Category 5 UTP cable in the horizontal runs. Also give consideration to the more recent standards of Category 5e and Category 6 UTP. If the network design is to last seven to ten years, the quality of cable should be a priority even if it costs a little more per linear foot. The cable upgrade should take priority over any other needed changes, and enterprises should ensure—without exception—that these systems conform to well-defined industry standards, such as the TIA/EIA-568-b specifications.

The TIA/EIA-568-B standard specifies that every device that is connected to the network should be linked to a central location with horizontal cabling. This is true if all the hosts that need to access the network are within the 100-meter distance limitation for Category 5 UTP Ethernet, as specified by TIA/EIA-568-B standards. Table 5-1 lists cable types and their characteristics.

In a simple star topology with only one wiring closet, the MDF includes one or more horizontal cross connect (HCC) patch panels, as shown in Figure 5-31. HCC patch cables are used to connect the Layer 1 horizontal cabling with the Layer 2 LAN switch ports. The uplink port of the LAN switch, depending on the model, which is unlike other ports because it does not cross over, is connected to the Ethernet port of the Layer 3 router by using patch cable. At this point, the end host has a complete physical connection to the router port.

Table 5-1 *IEEE 802.3* Cable Types and Characteristics

Characteristic	10BASE-T	10BASE-FL	100BASE-TX	100BASE-FX
Data Rate	10 Mbps	10 Mbps	100 Mbps	100 Mbps
Signaling Method	Baseband	Baseband	Baseband	Baseband
Medium Type	Category 5 UTP	Fiber-optic	Category 5 UTP	Multimode fiber (two strands)
Medium Length	100 meters	2000 meters	100 meters	2000 meters

Figure 5-31 Typical MDF in a Star Topology

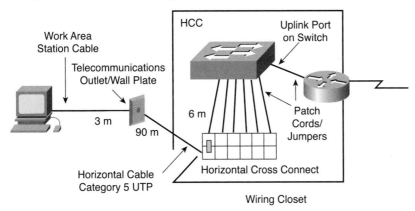

When hosts in larger networks are outside the 100-meter limitation for Category 5 UTP, it is not unusual to have more than one wiring closet. By creating multiple wiring closets, multiple catchment areas are created. The secondary wiring closets are referred to as IDFs. As shown in Figure 5-32, TIA/EIA 568-B standards specify that IDFs should be connected to the MDF by using vertical cabling, also called backbone cabling.

As shown in Figure 5-33, a vertical cross connect (VCC) is used to interconnect the various IDFs to the central MDF. Because the vertical cable lengths typically are longer than the 100-meter limit for Category 5 UTP cable, fiber-optic cabling normally is used, as shown in Figure 5-34.

Figure 5-32 Extended Star Topology in a Multibuilding Campus

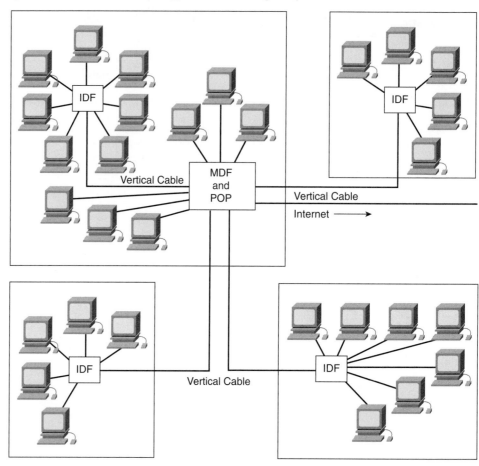

Fast Ethernet is Ethernet that has been upgraded to 100 Mbps. This type uses the standard Ethernet broadcast-oriented logical bus topology of 10BASE-T, along with the familiar CSMA/CD method for MAC. The Fast Ethernet standard is actually several different standards based on copper-pair wire (100BASE-TX) and on fiber-optic cable (100BASE-FX), and it is used to connect the MDF to the IDF, as shown in Figure 5-35. 10BASE-TX switched Ethernet to the desktop and Fast Ethernet backbones are likely to be quite adequate for many network's bandwidth requirements. Newer networks might opt for Gigabit Ethernet using fiber for vertical (backbone) cable runs and Fast Ethernet using CAT 5e horizontal runs to the desktop, depending on budgetary constraints.

Figure 5-33 Extended Star Topology VCC

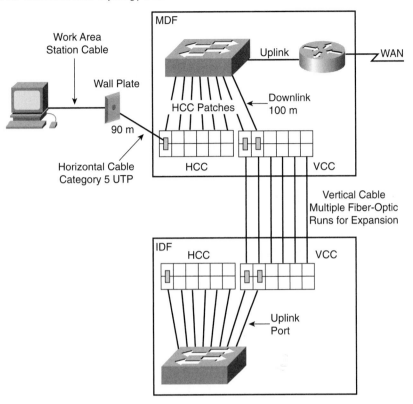

Figure 5-34 Extended Star Topology Vertical Cabling

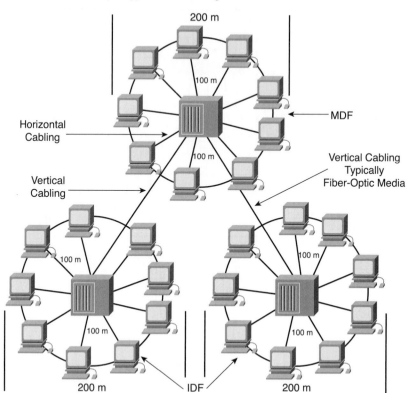

Figure 5-35 MDF to IDF Vertical Cabling

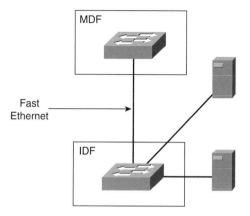

As shown in Figure 5-36, the logical diagram is the network topology model without all the detail of the exact installation path of the cabling. It is the basic roadmap of the LAN. Elements of the logical diagram include the following:

- The exact locations of the MDF and IDF wiring closets.

- The type and quantity of cabling used to interconnect the IDFs with the MDF, along with how many spare cables are available for increasing the bandwidth between the wiring closets. For example, if the vertical cabling between IDF 1 and the MDF is running at 80 percent utilization, you can use two additional pairs to double the capacity.

- Detailed documentation of all cable runs, as shown in Figure 5-37, the identification numbers, and which port on the HCC or VCC that the run is terminated on. For example, say that Room 203 has lost connectivity to the network. By examining the *cut sheet*, you can see that Room 203 is running off cable run 203-1, which is terminated on HCC 1 port 13. You can now test that run by using a cable tester to determine whether the problem is a Layer 1 failure. If it is, you can simply use one of the other two runs to get the connectivity back and then troubleshoot run 203-1.

Figure 5-36 Logical Network Diagram

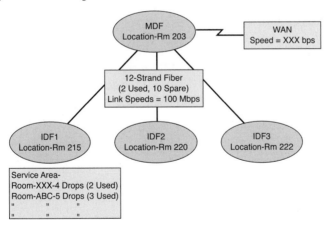

Layer 2 Design

The most common Layer 2 device (other than the network interface card, which every host on the network must have) is the LAN switch. Devices at Layer 2 determine the size of the collision domains and broadcast domains. This section concentrates on the implementation of LAN switching at Layer 2.

Figure 5-37 Cut Sheet

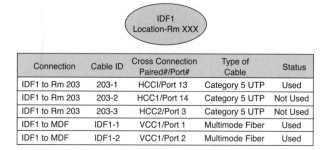

Connection	Cable ID	Cross Connection Paired#/Port#	Type of Cable	Status
IDF1 to Rm 203	203-1	HCCI/Port 13	Category 5 UTP	Used
IDF1 to Rm 203	203-2	HCC1/Port 14	Category 5 UTP	Not Used
IDF1 to Rm 203	203-3	HCC2/Port 3	Category 5 UTP	Not Used
IDF1 to MDF	IDF1-1	VCC1/Port 1	Multimode Fiber	Used
IDF1 to MDF	IDF1-2	VCC1/Port 2	Multimode Fiber	Used

Collisions and collision domain size are two factors that negatively affect the performance of a network. By using LAN switching, you can microsegment the network, thereby eliminating collisions and reducing the size of collision domains. As shown in Figure 5-38, another important characteristic of a LAN switch is how it can allocate bandwidth on a per-port basis, thus allowing more bandwidth to vertical cabling, uplinks, and servers. This type of switching is referred to as asymmetric switching, and it provides switched connections between ports of unlike bandwidth, such as a combination of 10-Mbps and 100-Mbps ports or 100-Mbps and 1000-Mbps ports.

Figure 5-38 Asymmetric Switching

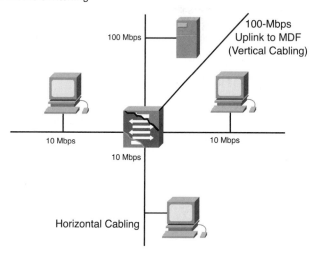

As you have learned, microsegmentation means using switches to boost performance for a workgroup or a backbone. Typically, boosting performance in this manner involves Ethernet switching. Switches can be used with hubs to provide the appropriate level of performance for different users and servers, as shown in Figure 5-39. Due to decreases in cost-per-port pricing, switches are increasingly being used exclusively, especially with new LAN designs.

Figure 5-39 Reducing Network Congestion

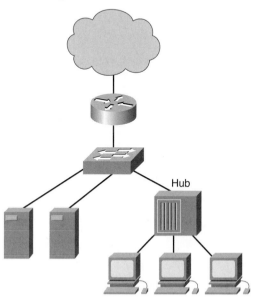

As shown in Figure 5-40, by installing LAN switching at the MDF and IDFs and vertical cable between the MDF and the IDFs, the vertical cable is carrying all the data traffic between the MDF and the IDFs; therefore, the capacity of this run must be larger than that of the runs between the IDFs and workstations. Horizontal cable runs use Category 5 or better UTP, and no cable drop should be longer than 100 meters, which allows links at 10, 100, or 1000 Mbps. In a normal environment, 10 Mbps is usually adequate for the horizontal cable drop, although newer LANs are increasingly standardizing on 10/100-Mbps links to the desktop. Because asymmetric LAN switches allow for mixing 10-Mbps and 100-Mbps or 100-Mbps and 1000-Mbps ports on a single switch, the next task is to determine the number of 10-Mbps, 100-Mbps, and 1000-Mbps ports needed in the MDF and every IDF. You can determine this by going back to the user requirements for the number of horizontal cable drops per room and the number of drops total in any catchment area, along with the number of vertical cable runs. For example, say that user requirements dictate that four horizontal cable runs be installed to each room. The IDF that services a catchment area covers 18 rooms. Therefore, 4 drops × 18 rooms = 72 LAN switch ports.

Figure 5-40 Layer 2 Switching

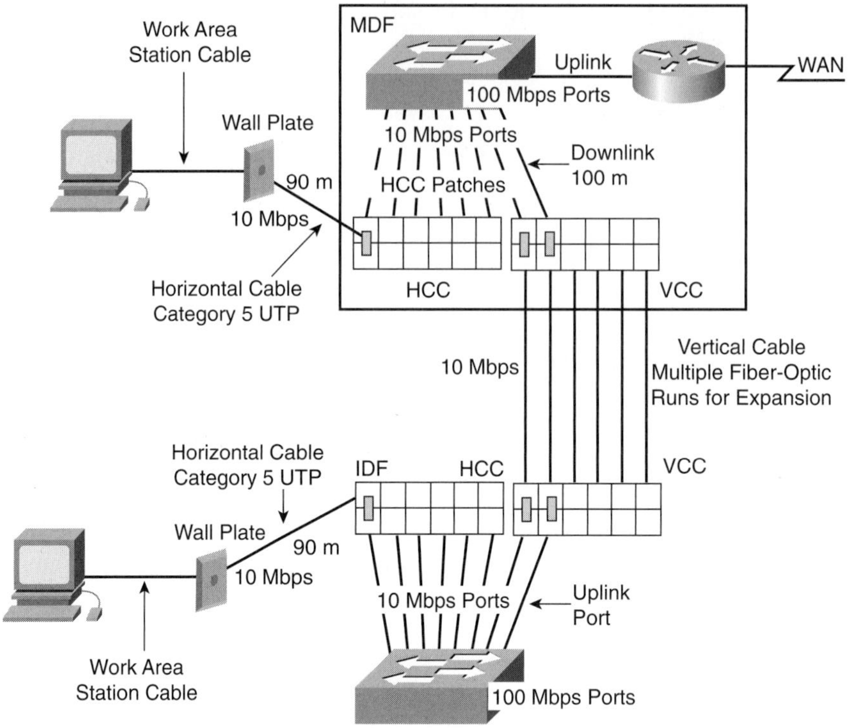

To determine the size of a collision domain, you must determine how many hosts are physically connected to any single port on the switch. This also affects how much network bandwidth is available to any host. In an ideal situation, there is only one host that is connected on a LAN switch port. This would make the size of the collision domain 2 (the source host and destination host). Because of this small collision domain, there should be almost no collisions when any two hosts are communicating with each other. Another way to implement LAN switching is to install shared LAN hubs on the switch ports and connect multiple hosts to a single switch port, as shown in Figure 5-41. As shown in Figure 5-42, all hosts that are connected to the shared LAN hub share the same collision domain and bandwidth. Figure 5-43 is provided as an example to illustrate the calculation of bandwidth to an individual user in a shared Ethernet environment. In newer LAN designs, it would mot be recommended to connect 24 users to a 10-Mbps hub and then connect that hub to a single switch port.

Figure 5-41 Collision Domain Size with Hubs

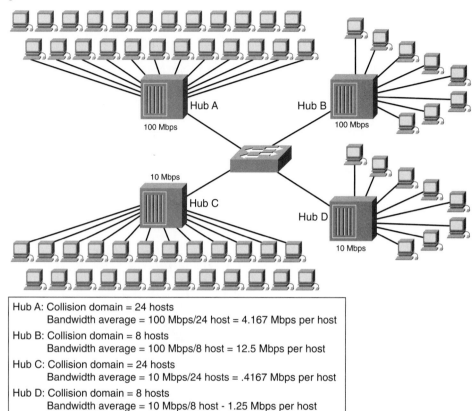

Hub A: Collision domain = 24 hosts
        Bandwidth average = 100 Mbps/24 host = 4.167 Mbps per host
Hub B: Collision domain = 8 hosts
        Bandwidth average = 100 Mbps/8 host = 12.5 Mbps per host
Hub C: Collision domain = 24 hosts
        Bandwidth average = 10 Mbps/24 hosts = .4167 Mbps per host
Hub D: Collision domain = 8 hosts
        Bandwidth average = 10 Mbps/8 host - 1.25 Mbps per host

Figure 5-42 Layer 2 Switch Collision Domains

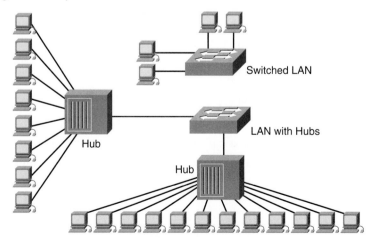

- In a pure switched LAN environment, the size of collision domain is 2 hosts.
- When using hubs, the size of the collision domain increases and bandwidth is shared.

Figure 5-43 Layer 2 Switch with Hubs

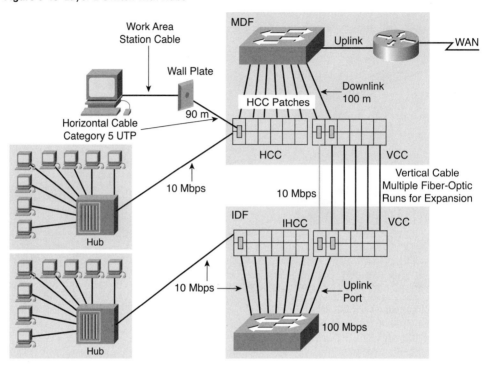

Note that some older switches, such as the Catalyst 1700, do not truly support sharing the same collision domain and bandwidth because they do not maintain multiple MAC addresses mapped to each port. In that case, there are many broadcasts and Address Resolution Protocol (ARP) requests.

Shared-media hubs are generally used in a LAN switch environment to create more connection points at the end of the horizontal cable runs, as shown in Figure 5-43. This is an acceptable solution, but you must ensure that collision domains are kept small and bandwidth requirements to the host are accomplished according to specifications that are gathered in the requirements phase of the network design process.

As the network grows, the need for more bandwidth increases. In the vertical cabling between MDF and IDFs, unused fiber optics can be connected from the VCC to 100-Mbps ports on the switch, as shown in Figure 5-44. The network shown doubles the capacity of the vertical cabling in the network by bringing up another link.

Figure 5-44 Layer 2: Migrate to Higher Bandwidth

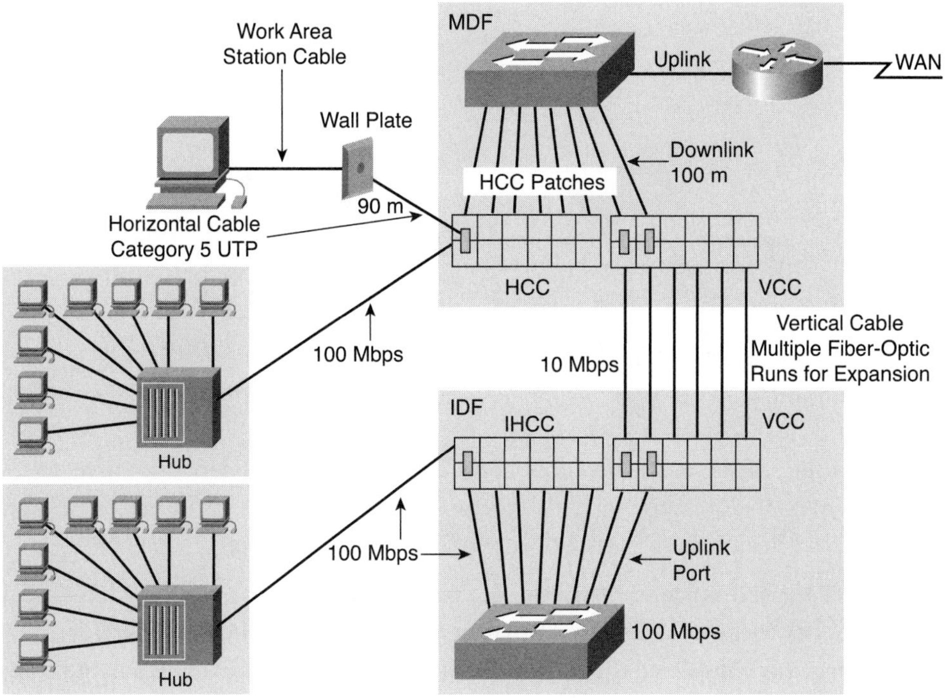

In the horizontal cabling, you can increase the bandwidth by a factor of 10 by repatching from the HCC to a 100-Mbps port on the switch and changing from a 10-Mbps hub to a 100-Mbps hub. When sizing the Layer 2 LAN switch, make sure that there are enough 100-Mbps ports to allow for this migration to higher bandwidth. Document the speed at which each active cable drop is running.

Layer 3 Design

As shown in Figure 5-45, Layer 3 (the network layer) devices, such as routers, can be used to create unique LAN segments and allow communication between segments based on Layer 3 addressing, such as IP addressing. Implementation of Layer 3 devices, such as routers, allows for segmentation of the LAN into unique physical and logical networks. Routers also allow for connectivity to wide-area networks (WANs), such as the Internet.

Figure 5-45 Layer 3 Router Implementation

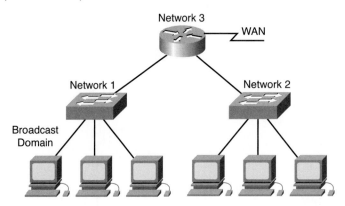

Layer 3 routing determines traffic flow between unique physical network segments based on Layer 3 addressing, such as IP network and subnet. The router is one of the most powerful devices in the network topology.

As you have learned, a router forwards data packets based on destination addresses. A router does not forward LAN-based broadcasts such as ARP requests. Therefore, the router interface is considered the entry and exit point of a broadcast domain and stops broadcasts from reaching other LAN segments.

One important issue in a network is the total number of broadcasts, such as ARP requests. By using VLANs, you can limit broadcast traffic to within a VLAN and create smaller broadcast domains, as shown in Figure 5-46. You also can use VLANs to provide security by creating the VLAN groups according to function, as shown in Figure 5-47.

Figure 5-46 VLAN Communication

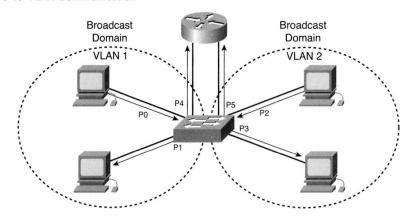

Figure 5-47 VLAN Implementation

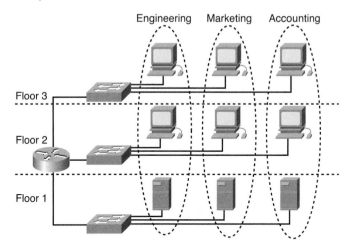

As shown in Figure 5-46, a physical port association is used to implement VLAN assignment. Ports P1, P4, and P6 have been assigned to VLAN 1. VLAN 2 has ports P2, P3, and P5. Communication between VLAN 1 and VLAN 2 can occur only through the router. This limits the size of the broadcast domains and uses the router to determine whether VLAN 1 can talk to VLAN 2. This means that you can create a security scheme based on VLAN assignment.

Routers provide scalability because they can serve as firewalls for broadcasts. In addition, because Layer 3 addresses typically have structure, routers can provide greater scalability by dividing networks and subnets, thereby adding structure to Layer 3 addresses, as shown in Figure 5-48. The ways in which greater structure and scalability in networks can occur are shown in Figure 5-49.

Figure 5-48 Routers Create Logical Structure

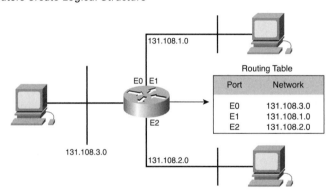

Figure 5-49 Logical Addressing Mapped to a Physical Network

Logical Address	Physical Network Devices
x.x.x.1-x.x.x.10	Router, LAN, and WAN Ports
x.x.x.11-x.x.x.20	LAN Switches
x.x.x.21-x.x.x.30	Enterprise Servers
x.x.x.31-x.x.x.80	Workgroup Servers
x.x.x.81-x.x.x.254	Hosts

When the networks are divided into subnets, the final step is to develop and document the IP addressing scheme to be used in the network. Routing technology filters data-link broadcasts and multicasts. By adding router ports with additional subnet or network addresses, you can segment the internetwork as required. Network protocol addressing and routing provide built-in scaling. When you are deciding whether to use routers or switches, remember to ask the question, "What problem am I trying to solve?" If your problem is protocol related rather than contention oriented, routers are appropriate. Routers solve problems with excessive broadcasts, protocols that do not scale well, security issues, and network-layer addressing. Routers, however, are more expensive and harder to configure than switches.

Routers can be used to create IP subnets to add structure to addresses, as shown in Figure 5-50. With bridges and switches, all unknown addresses must be flooded out of every port. With routers, hosts that are using protocols with network-layer addressing can solve the problem of finding other hosts without flooding. If the destination address is local, the sending host can encapsulate the packet in a data-link header and send a unicast frame directly to the station. The router does not need to see the frame and, of course, does not need to flood the frame. The sending host might have to use ARP. This would cause a broadcast, but the broadcast is only a local broadcast and is not forwarded by the router. If the destination is not local, the sending station transmits the packet to the router (its default gateway). The router sends the frame to the destination or to the next hop, based on its routing table. Given this routing functionality, it is clear that large, scalable LANs need to incorporate some routers.

Figure 5-51 shows an example of an implementation that has multiple physical networks. All data traffic from Network 1 that is destined for Network 2 must go through the router. Network 1 and Network 2 are two separate broadcast domains. The two networks have unique Layer 3 IP addressing network/subnetwork addressing schemes. In a structured Layer 1 wiring scheme, multiple physical networks are easy to create simply by patching the horizontal cabling and vertical cabling into the appropriate Layer 2 switch using patch cables. This implementation provides for robust security. In addition, the router is the central point in the LAN for traffic destination.

Figure 5-50 Using Routers to Impose Logical Structure

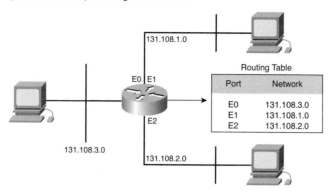

Figure 5-51 Layer 3 Segmentation

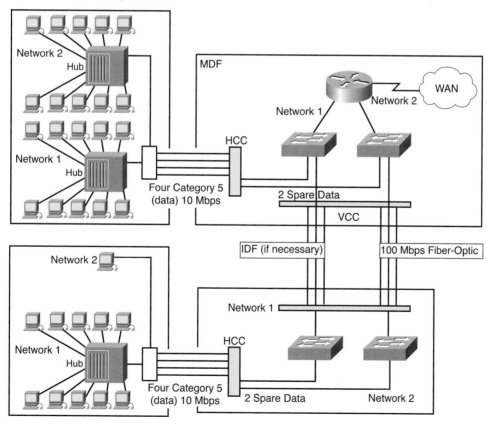

After you have developed the IP addressing scheme for the customer, you should document it by site and by network within the site. Set a standard convention for addressing important hosts on the network, as shown in Figure 5-52. Keep this addressing scheme consistent throughout the entire network. By creating addressing maps, you can get a snapshot of the network, as shown in Figure 5-53. Creating physical maps of the network helps you troubleshoot the network, as shown in Figure 5-54.

Figure 5-52 Addressing Maps

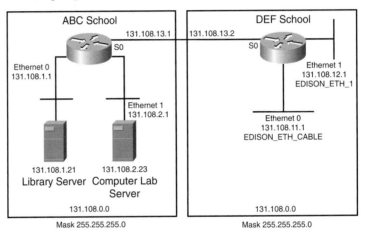

Figure 5-53 Logical Network Maps

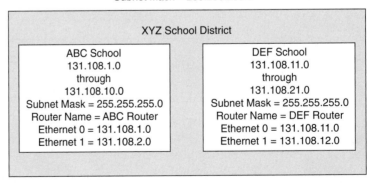

Figure 5-54 Physical Network Maps

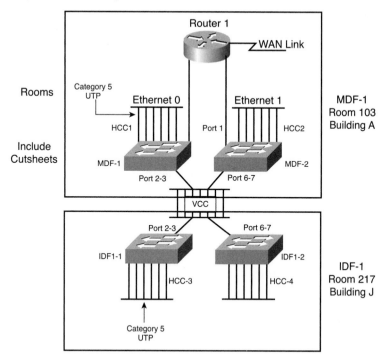

Basic Layer 2 Bridging and Switching

This section covers the functions of switches and bridges, which are classified as Layer 2 devices on the OSI model. It discusses the methods by which switches transmit frames and the way in which frames can be filtered. Interacting with switches and bridges helps users gain an understanding of how these devices learn about addresses. You need to understand the principles of LAN segmentation and collision domains because not every LAN must be segmented. Segmentation is a technique that helps to ensure that a network's performance does not degrade as the size of the LAN grows.

As the network grows in size and the number of users and as users demand more band-width to run their applications, congestion on the network can slow the network to a point at which users no longer have confidence in it. Users are notorious for becoming impatient when an application does not run quickly. One of the most efficient ways to solve the problem of congestion is to break up the network into smaller segments. You can put these segments in place physically by using a bridge or a switch, for example, to limit the number of devices on the network segment.

A switch concentrates connectivity, while making data transmission more efficient. Frames are switched from incoming ports (interfaces) to outgoing ports. Each port can provide the full bandwidth of the connection to the host.

On a typical Ethernet hub, all ports connect to a common backplane or physical connection within the hub, and all devices that are attached to the hub share the bandwidth of the network. If two stations establish a session that uses a significant level of bandwidth, the network performance of all other stations attached to the hub is degraded.

To reduce degradation, the switch treats each interface as an individual segment. When stations on different interfaces need to communicate, the switch forwards frames from one interface to the other at near-wire speed to ensure that each session receives full bandwidth.

To switch frames between interfaces efficiently, the switch maintains an address table. When a frame enters the switch, it associates the MAC address of the sending station (source) with the interface on which it was received.

Following are the main functions of Ethernet switches:

- Isolate traffic among segments
- Achieve greater bandwidth per user by creating smaller collision domains

The first function is to isolate traffic among segments, which is the name given to the smaller units into which the networks are divided by use of such Ethernet switches. Each segment uses the CSMA/CD access method to maintain data traffic flow among the users on that segment. Such segmentation allows multiple users to send information out at the same time on the different segments and not slow down the network.

Ethernet switches filter the traffic by redirecting the datagrams to the right port or ports based on Layer 2 MAC addresses. The second function of an Ethernet switch is to ensure that each user has more bandwidth by creating smaller collision domains.

A Fast Ethernet switch allows for the segmentation of a LAN (break it into smaller collision domains), giving each segment a dedicated network link (like a highway lane) at up to 100 Mbps. High-use servers might have their own 100-Mbps or even 1000-Mbps links. Most often in today's networks, a Fast Ethernet or Gigabit Ethernet switch acts as the "backbone" of the LAN, with 10-Mbps or 100-Mbps Ethernet switches providing the desktop connections in workgroups. As demanding new applications such as desktop multimedia or videoconferencing become more popular, certain individual desktop computers might be given their own dedicated 100-Mbps links to the network. Today's networks are fully switched and use 100 or 1000 backbones and 10/100 megabits to the desktop.

How Switches and Bridges Filter Frames

Bridges are capable of filtering frames based on any Layer 2 fields. For example, a bridge can be programmed to reject (not forward) all frames that are sourced from a particular network. Because link layer information often includes a reference to an upper-layer protocol, bridges usually can filter on this parameter. Furthermore, filters can be helpful in dealing with unnecessary broadcast and multicast packets. Bridging functionality is often built in to a router and might not be provided by the use of a separate device.

After the bridge has built the local address table, it is ready to operate. When the bridge receives a frame, it examines the source address. If the frame's address is local, the bridge ignores it. If the frame is addressed for another LAN, the bridge copies the frame onto the second LAN. Ignoring the frame is called filtering. Copying the frame is called forwarding.

Filtering Types

Basic filtering does the following:

- Keeps local frames local
- Sends remote frames to the other segment

Filtering on specific source and destination addresses does the following:

- Stops one station from sending frames outside of its local LAN
- Stops all "outside" frames that are destined for a particular station, thereby restricting the other stations with which it can communicate

Both types of filtering provide some control over internetwork traffic and can offer improved security.

Most Ethernet bridges can filter broadcast and multicast frames. Occasionally, a device malfunctions and continually sends broadcast frames, which are continuously copied around the network. A *broadcast storm*, as it is called, can bring network performance to zero. If a bridge can filter broadcast frames, a broadcast storm has less opportunity to brew.

Today, bridges are also able to filter according to the Network layer protocol. This blurs the distinction between bridges and routers. A router operates on the Network layer, and it uses a routing protocol to direct traffic around the network. A bridge that implements advanced filtering techniques is usually called a brouter. It filters by looking into the Network layer, but it does not use a routing protocol. Bridging functionality is often built in to a router and might not be provided by the use of a separate device.

Summary

In this chapter, you learned the following:

- The combination of more powerful computers/workstations and network-intensive applications has created a need for bandwidth that is much greater than the 10 Mbps that is available on shared Ethernet/802.3 LANs.

- As more people utilize a network to share large files, access file servers, and connect to the Internet, network congestion occurs.

- In a segmented Ethernet LAN, data that is passed between segments is transmitted across the network by a bridge, switch, or router. A switch segments a LAN into microsegments, creating collision-free domains from one larger collision domain.

- A LAN that uses a switched Ethernet topology creates a network that behaves like it has only two nodes: the sending node and the receiving node.

- Switches achieve high-speed transfer by reading the destination Layer 2 MAC address of the packet, much the way a bridge does.

- Ethernet switching increases the bandwidth that is available on a network by creating dedicated network segments (point-to-point connections) and connecting those segments in a virtual network within the switch.

- Symmetric switching is where all ports have the same bandwidth.

- A VLAN is a grouping of network devices or users that is not restricted to a physical switch segment.

- The main function of the Spanning Tree Protocol is to allow duplicate switched/bridged paths without suffering the latency effects of loops in the network.

- One of the most critical factors in ensuring a fast and stable network is the design of the network. If a network is not designed properly, many unforeseen problems can arise, and network growth can be jeopardized.

- LAN design goals include functionality, scalability, adaptability, and manageability.

The design process includes the following:

- Gathering the users' requirements and expectations
- Determining data traffic patterns now and in the future based on growth and server placements
- Defining all the Layer 1, 2, and 3 devices, along with the LAN and WAN topology
- Documenting the physical and logical network implementation

To supplement all that you have learned in this chapter, refer to the chapter-specific Videos, PhotoZooms, and e-Lab Activities on the CD-ROM that accompanies this book.

Key Terms

bridge   A device that connects and passes packets between two network segments that use the same communications protocol. Bridges operate at the data link layer (Layer 2) of the OSI reference model. In general, a bridge filters, forwards, or floods an incoming frame based on the MAC address of that frame.

bridging   A technology in which a bridge connects two or more LAN segments.

broadcast   A data packet that is sent to all nodes on a network. Broadcasts are identified by a broadcast address. See also broadcast address, broadcast domain, and broadcast storm.

broadcast address   A special address that is reserved for sending a message to all stations. Generally, a broadcast address is a MAC destination address of all 1s. See also broadcast.

broadcast domain   The set of all devices that will receive broadcast frames originating from any device within the set. Routers typically bound broadcast domains because routers do not forward broadcast frames. See also broadcast.

broadcast storm   An undesirable network event in which many broadcasts are sent simultaneously across all network segments. A broadcast storm uses substantial network bandwidth and, typically, causes network time-outs.

bus topology   A linear LAN architecture in which transmissions from network stations propagate the length of the medium and are received by all other stations. Compare with star topology.

collision   In Ethernet, the result of two nodes transmitting simultaneously. The frames from each device collide and are damaged when they meet on the physical medium.

collision domain   In Ethernet, the network area within which frames that have collided are propagated. Repeaters and hubs propagate collisions; LAN switches, bridges, and routers do not. Also called a bandwidth domain.

congestion   Traffic that is in excess of network capacity.

CSMA/CD (carrier sense multiple access collision detect)   A media-access mechanism wherein devices that are ready to transmit data first check the channel for a carrier. If no carrier is sensed for a specific period of time, a device can transmit. If two devices transmit at once, a collision occurs and is detected by all colliding devices. This collision subsequently delays retransmissions from those devices for some random length of time. Ethernet and IEEE 802.3 use CSMA/CD access.

cut sheet   A rough diagram indicating where cable runs are located and the numbers of rooms they lead to.

cut-through   A packet-switching approach that streams data through a switch so that the leading edge of a packet exits the switch at the output port before the packet finishes entering the input port. A device that uses cut-through packet switching reads, processes, and forwards packets as soon as the destination address is looked up and the outgoing port is determined. Also known as on-the-fly packet switching.

enterprise server   A server that supports all the users on a network by offering services such as e-mail or DNS.

Ethernet   A baseband LAN specification that was invented by Xerox Corporation and developed jointly by Xerox, Intel, and Digital Equipment Corporation. Ethernet networks use CSMA/CD and run over a variety of cable types at 10 Mbps. Ethernet is similar to the IEEE 802.3 series of standards.

Fast Ethernet   Any of a number of 100-Mbps Ethernet specifications. Fast Ethernet offers a speed increase 10 times that of the 10BASE-T Ethernet specification, while preserving such qualities as frame format, MAC mechanisms, and maximum transmission unit (MTU). Such similarities allow the use of existing 10BASE-T applications and network management tools on Fast Ethernet networks. Based on an extension to the IEEE 802.3 specification. See also Ethernet.

fast-forward switching   Switching that offers the lowest level of latency by immediately forwarding a packet after receiving the destination address.

Gigabit Ethernet   Any of a number of 1000-Mbps Ethernet specifications. Gigabit Ethernet offers a speed increase 10 times that of the Fast Ethernet specification.

IEEE 802.3   An IEEE LAN protocol that specifies an implementation of the physical layer and the MAC sublayer of the data link layer. IEEE 802.3 uses CSMA/CD access at a variety of speeds over a variety of physical media. Extensions to the IEEE 802.3 standard specify implementations for Fast Ethernet. Physical variations of the original IEEE 802.3 specification include 10BASE-2, 10BASE-5, 10BASE-F, 10BASE-T, and 10BROAD-36. Physical variations for Fast Ethernet include 100BASE-TX and 100BASE-FX. Gigabit Ethernet includes 1000BASE-T, 1000BASE-LX, and 1000BASE-SX.

IEEE (Institute of Electrical and Electronics Engineers)   A professional organization whose activities include the development of communications and network standards. IEEE LAN standards are the predominant LAN standards today.

LAN (local-area network)   A high-speed, low-error data network that covers a relatively small geographic area (up to a few thousand meters). LANs connect workstations, peripherals, terminals, and other devices in a single building or other geographically limited area. LAN standards specify cabling and signaling at the physical and data link layers of the OSI model. Ethernet, FDDI, and Token Ring are widely used LAN technologies.

LAN switch   A high-speed switch that forwards packets between data-link segments. Most LAN switches forward traffic based on MAC addresses. LAN switches are often categorized according to the method they use to forward traffic: cut-through packet switching or store-and-forward packet switching. An example of a LAN switch is the Cisco Catalyst 5000.

latency   The delay between the time that a device requests access to a network and the time that it is granted permission to transmit.

MAC (Media Access Control) address   A standardized data link layer address that is required for every port or device that connects to a LAN. Other devices in the network use these addresses to locate specific ports in the network and to create and update routing tables and data structures. MAC addresses are 6 bytes long, and the IEEE controls them. Also known as a hardware address, a MAC layer address, or a physical address.

microsegmentation   The division of a network into smaller segments, usually with the intention of increasing aggregate bandwidth to network devices.

network layer   Layer 3 of the OSI reference model. This layer provides connectivity and path selection between two end systems. The network layer is the layer at which routing occurs. Corresponds roughly with the path control layer of the SNA model.

repeater   A device that regenerates and propagates electrical signals between two network segments.

router   A network layer device that uses one or more metrics to determine the optimal path along which network traffic should be forwarded. Routers forward packets from one network to another based on network layer information. Occasionally called a gateway (although this definition of gateway is becoming increasingly outdated).

routing table   A table that is stored in a router or some other internetworking device that keeps track of routes to particular network destinations and, in some cases, metrics that are associated with those routes.

Spanning Tree Protocol   Bridge protocol that uses the spanning-tree algorithm, enabling a learning bridge to dynamically work around loops in a network topology by creating a spanning tree. Bridges exchange bridge protocol data unit (BPDU) messages with other bridges to detect loops; then they remove the loops by shutting down selected bridge interfaces. Refers to both the IEEE 802.1 Spanning Tree Protocol standard and the earlier Digital Equipment Corporation Spanning Tree Protocol upon which it is based. The IEEE version supports bridge domains and allows the bridge to construct a loop-free topology across an extended LAN. The IEEE version generally is preferred over the Digital version.

star topology   A LAN topology in which endpoints on a network are connected to a common central switch by point-to-point links. A ring topology that is organized as a star implements a unidirectional closed-loop star instead of point-to-point links. Compare with bus topology.

store-and-forward   A packet-switching technique in which frames are completely processed before being forwarded out the appropriate port. This processing includes calculating the cyclic redundancy check (CRC) and checking the destination address. In addition, frames must be temporarily stored until network resources (such as an unused link) are available to forward the message.

switch   A network device that filters, forwards, and floods frames based on the destination address of each frame. The switch operates at the data link layer of the OSI reference model.

switching   The process of taking an incoming frame from one interface and delivering it out through another interface.

Check Your Understanding

1. Which of the following broadcast methods does an Ethernet medium use to transmit and receive data to all nodes on the network?

   A. A packet

   B. A data frame

   C. A segment

   D. A byte at a time

2. Characteristics of microsegmentation include which of the following?

   A. Virtual paths between sender and receiver hosts

   B. Multiple traffic paths within the switch

   C. All traffic visible on the network segment at once

   D. A and B

3. LAN switches are considered to be which of the following?

   A. Multiport repeaters operating at Layer 1

   B. Multiport hubs operating at Layer 2

   C. Multiport routers operating at Layer 3

   D. Multiport bridges operating at Layer 2

4. Asymmetric switching is optimized for which of the following?

   A. Client/server network traffic, where the "fast" switch port is connected to the server

   B. An even distribution of network traffic

   C. Switches that lack memory buffering

   D. A and B

5. Describe full- and half-duplex Ethernet operation.

6. Describe the main function of the Spanning Tree Protocol.

7. How would each segment be considered in a network that is segmented by switches?

   A. Network

   B. Campus network

   C. Collision domain

   D. WAN

8. In a full duplex Ethernet switch, which of the following is true?

   A. Collisions are virtually eliminated.

   B. Two cable pairs and a switched connection between each node are used.

   C. Connections between nodes are considered point-to-point.

   D. All of the above.

9. Congestion causes which of the following effects?

   A. Lower reliability and low traffic

   B. High rate of collisions

   C. Network unpredictability and high error rates

   D. Lower response times, longer file transfers, and network delays

   E. All of the above

10. Host A transmits to another host, Host B. The communication is such that Host A stops sending information content packets and then Host B begins sending packets. Similarly, Host B stops when Host A starts transmitting again. The transmission type would be classified as which of the following?

    A. Full-duplex

    B. Half-duplex

    C. Simplex

    D. None of the above

11. Which of the following statements concerning packet forwarding in a LAN is not true?

    A. Store-and-forward packet switching is the one in which frames are completely processed before being forwarded to the appropriate port.

    B. Store-and-forward packet switching is slower than cut-through packet switching.

    C. Cut-through packet switching is also known as on-the-fly packet switching.

    D. Buffering is required in cut-through packet switching if the network connection or link is slow.

12. Which of the following is true for a LAN switch?

    A. It repairs network fragments known as microsegments.

    B. It is a high-speed multiport bridge.

    C. Higher latency is made up for by lower bandwidth.

    D. It requires new network interface cards on attached hosts.

13. How many collision domains would a 16-port LAN switch create?

    A. 1

    B. 2

    C. 14

    D. 16

14. By creating a virtual circuit with LAN switching, what will result on that segment?

   A. Increased collisions

   B. Decreased available bandwidth

   C. Increased broadcasts

   D. Increased available bandwidth

15. How do switches learn the addresses of devices that are attached to their ports?

   A. Switches get the tables from a router.

   B. Switches read the source address of a packet that is entering through a port.

   C. Switches exchange address tables with other switches.

   D. Switches are not capable of building address tables.

16. What is the purpose of symmetric switching?

   A. It provides switch connections on ports that have the same bandwidth.

   B. It ensures that the network tables are symmetrical.

   C. It provides switched connections on ports that have different bandwidths.

   D. Switches only provide asymmetrical switching.

17. What device provides logical segmentation of a LAN?

   A. Router

   B. Bridge

   C. Switch

   D. Hub

18. In what ways does a router segment a LAN?

   A. It reduces the broadcast domain.

   B. It creates more logical segments.

   C. It reduces bandwidth.

   D. Both A and B.

19. Which of the following is *not* a benefit of implementing Layer 3 devices in your LAN?

   A. It allows segmentation of the LAN into unique physical and logical networks.

   B. It allows for WAN connectivity.

   C. It provides logical structure to the network.

   D. It increases the size of the LAN.

20. Which of the following is an example of an enterprise server?

A. CAD server at a large company

B. DNS server for a school district

C. Administrative records (grades and transcripts) server at a school

D. Payroll and accounting server

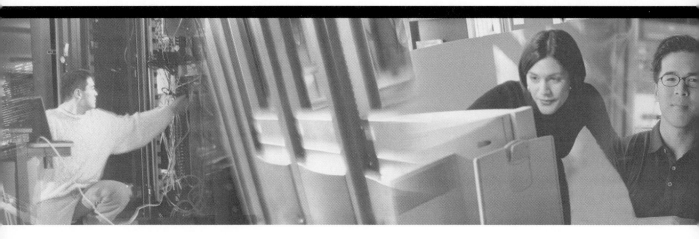

Objectives

After reading this chapter, you will be able to

- Start a switch
- Identify the components of a switch
- Describe and identify where access layer switches are used
- Describe and identify where distribution layer switches are used
- Describe and identify where core layer switches are used

Chapter 6

Switches

This chapter provides a brief comparison between hubs and modern switching technology. It covers physical *switch* characteristics and components, including switch LEDs and their meaning. The switch initialization process, console connection, and command-line help are also discussed. This chapter focuses on the different types and models of switches, hierarchical network design, and the utilization of switches in the access, distribution, and core layers.

Please be sure to look at this chapter's associated e-Lab Activities, Videos, and PhotoZooms that you will find on the CD-ROM accompanying this book. These CD-ROM elements are designed to supplement the material and reinforce the concepts introduced in this chapter.

Overview of Switches

A switch is a Layer 2 network device that acts as the concentration point for the connection of workstations, servers, routers, hubs, and other switches.

A *hub* is an earlier type of concentration device that, like a switch, provides multiple *ports*. Hubs are inferior to switches because all devices that are connected to a hub reside in the same bandwidth domain, and collisions occur. In addition, hubs operate in half duplex mode, which means that they can either send or receive data at any given time.

Switches are multiport bridges that are the standard technology for today's Ethernet local-area networks (LANs), which utilize a star topology. A switch provides a dedicated, point-to-point virtual circuit between two connected networking devices, so collisions do not occur. Switches can operate in full duplex mode, which means that they can send and receive data simultaneously. The ability to understand and configure switches is essential for network support.

LANs span a single room, a building, or a set of buildings that are close together. A set of buildings that are on a site and belong to a single organization are referred to as a campus. The design of larger LANs is assisted by an approach that identifies the following:

- An access layer that connects end users into the LAN
- A distribution layer that provides policy-based connectivity between end user LANs
- A core layer that provides the fastest connection between the distribution points

As the scale of a LAN increases to the size of a campus, there is a need for a variety of LAN switches. Each layer requires switches that are best suited for the tasks of each specific layer. The features, functions, and technical specifications for each switch vary depending on which layer the switch is designed for. Choosing the switches that are best suited for each layer ensures the best network performance for LAN users.

Understanding the role of each layer and the switches used in those layers is important for an effective switched LAN design.

Starting the Switch

Several steps go into transforming a switch from being turned off or brand new out of the box to a fully functioning switch that is managing network traffic around and through the network. This next section outlines what these steps are and how to verify the switch has successfully booted up and performed all the steps required so that it is ready to be configured and placed into production.

Physical Startup of the Catalyst Switch

Switches are dedicated, specialized computers that contain a central processing unit (CPU), random-access memory (RAM), and an operating system. As shown in Figure 6-1, switches usually have several ports for the purpose of connecting hosts, as well as specialized ports for the purpose of management. A switch can be managed by connecting to the console port, shown in Figure 6-2, to view and make changes to the configuration.

Figure 6-1 Cisco Switch Ports

Figure 6-2 Console Connection

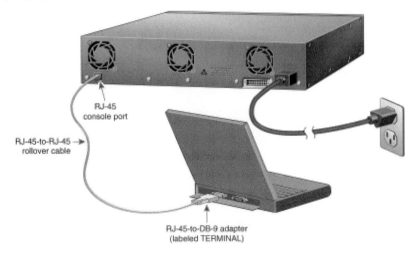

Switches typically have no power switch to turn them on and off, but simply connect or disconnect from a power source. Example 6-1 shows the output of a Cisco switch startup command-line interface (CLI).

Example 6-1 *Cisco Switch Startup Messages*

```
32K bytes of flash-simulated non-volatile configuration memory
Base Ethernet MAC address: 00:04:4D:D2:3D:00
Motherboard assembly number:73-3382-08
Power supply part number:34-0834-01
Motherboard serial number: FAB044685H5
Power supply serial number: DAB04283EPL
Model revision number: A0
Motherboard revision number: C0
Model number: WS-C2924-XL-EN
System serial number: FAB0447S0M2


Press RETURN to get started!


00:00:27: %SYS-5-RESTART: System restarted -
Cisco Internetwork Operating System Software
IOS (tm) C2900XL Software (C2900XL-C3H2S-M), Version 12.0(5.2)XU,
    MAINTENANCE INTERIM SOFTWARE
Copyright (c) 1986-2000 by cisco Systems, Inc.
```

Switch LED Indicators

The front panel of a switch has several lights to help monitor system activity and performance. These lights are called light emitting diodes (LEDs). The front of the switch has the following LEDs:

- System LED
- Remote power supply (RPS) LED
- Port Mode LEDs
- Port Status LEDs

System LED

The System LED, shown previously in Figure 6-1, shows whether the system is receiving power and functioning correctly. Table 6-1 shows the possible states for the system LED.

Table 6-1 System Status LED

Color	System Status
Off	System is not powered on.
Green	System is operating normally.
Amber	System has power but is not functioning properly.

RPS LED

The RPS LED indicates whether the remote power supply is in use. The RPS LED shows the RPS status of the switch. Table 6-2 shows what each of the RPS color modes represent on the switch.

Table 6-2 RPS Status Lights

Color	RPS Status
Off	RPS is off or is not installed.
Solid green	RPS is connected and operational.
Blinking green	RPS is backing up another switch in the stack.
Solid amber	RPS is connected but not functioning correctly.
Blinking amber	Internal power supply in this switch is down. The switch is operating on the RPS.

Port Mode LED

The Mode LEDs indicate the current state of the Mode button. The modes are used to determine how the Port Status LEDs are interpreted. To select or change the port mode, press the Mode button repeatedly until the Mode LEDs indicate the desired mode. The Port Status LEDs have different meanings, depending on the current value of the Mode LED. See Table 6-3.

The Mode button on the front of the switch is used to interpret how the port lights are to be interpreted.

The Mode button has three states:

- STAT (Status)
- UTL (Utilization)
- FDUP (Full Duplex)

If the status light on the switch is flashing orange, it usually means that there is some kind of hardware problem with the port, module, or switch. The same thing is true if the port or module status indicates faulty.

Port Status LEDs

Each port has a Port Status LED or Port LED. These LEDs display information about the switch and the individual ports. Table 6-3 shows what each of the Port modes represents on the switch.

Table 6-3 Port Mode LED Status Lights

Mode LED	Port Mode	Description
STAT	Port status	The port status. This is the default mode.
UTIL	Switch utilization	The current bandwidth in use by the switch.
DUPLX	Port Duplex mode	This can be half duplex or full duplex.
SPEED	Port speed	The port's operating speed (such as 10 or 100 Mbps for 10/100 ports).

To select or change the port mode, you press the Mode button to highlight the mode you want. You release the Mode button to enable the highlighted mode. Table 6-4 shows what each of the Port Mode LED color modes represents in different modes on the switch.

Table 6-4 Port Mode LED Status Lights in Different Modes

Mode LED	Color	Description
STAT Port status	Off	No link.
	Solid green	Link operational.
	Flashing green	Sending or receiving data.
	Alternating green/amber	Link forward.
	Solid amber	The port is not forwarding.

Table 6-4 Port Mode LED Status Lights in Different Modes (Continued)

Mode LED	Color	Description
UTIL Switch utilization	Green	The current backplane utilization.
	Amber	Maximum backplane utilization.
	Green and amber	If all LEDs are green, the switch is using 50% or more of the total bandwidth. It turns amber as utilization is lowered.
DUPLX Port Duplex mode	Off	Half duplex.
	Green	Full duplex.
SPEED Port Speed 10/100 ports	Off	Port is operating at 10 Mbps.
	Green	Port is operating at 100 Mbps.

Verifying Port LEDs During Switch POST

After the power cable is connected, the switch initiates a series of tests called power-on self test (POST) that runs automatically to verify that the switch functions correctly. The System LED indicates the success or failure of POST. If the System LED is off but the switch is plugged in, POST is running. If the System LED is green, POST was successful. If the System LED is amber, POST failed. POST failure is considered to be a fatal error. You should not expect reliable operation of the switch if POST fails.

The Port Status LEDs also change during switch POST. The Port Status LEDs turn amber for approximately 30 seconds as the switch discovers the network topology and searches for loops. If the Port Status LEDs turn green, the switch has established a link between the port and a target, such as a computer. If the Port Status LEDs turn off, the switch has determined that nothing is plugged into the port.

Viewing Initial Bootup Output from the Switch

To configure or check the status of a switch, it is necessary to connect a computer to the switch and establish communication between the switch and the computer. Use a rollover cable to connect the console port on the back of the switch to a COM port on the back of the computer. This is the same cable and process used when connecting to a router console port.

Start HyperTerminal on the computer. A dialog window, shown in Figure 6-3, is displayed. To configure HyperTerminal communication with the switch for the first time, first name the connection. Select the COM port to which the switch is connected using the pull-down menu, and press the OK button, as shown in Figure 6-4. A second dialog window is displayed. Set up the parameters as shown in Figure 6-5, and click the OK button.

Figure 6-3 HyperTerminal

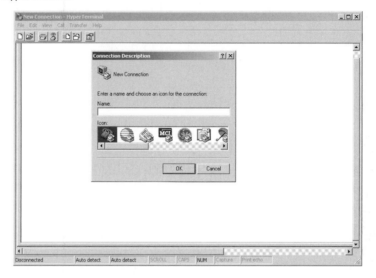

Figure 6-4 Naming the HyperTerminal Session

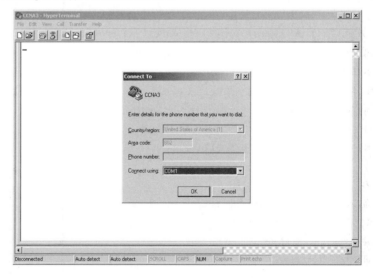

Figure 6-5 HyperTerminal Settings

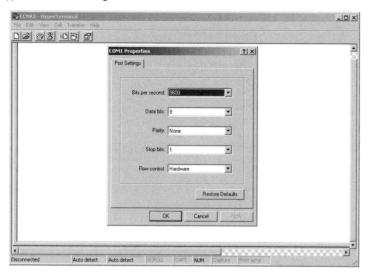

Plug the switch into a surge-protected power supply. The initial bootup output from the switch should be displayed on the HyperTerminal screen. After you have powered on the switch, you should examine the initial bootup output from the switch. This output shows information about the switch, details about POST status, and data about the switch hardware.

Examples 6-2 through 6-4 illustrate the output under the various headings.

Example 6-2 *Loading and Initializing Flash*

```
C2950 Boot Loader (CALHOUN-HBOOT-M) Version 12.0(5.3)WC(1), MAINTENANCE INTERIM
SOFTWARE
Compiled Mon 30-Apr-01 07:56 by devgoyal
WS-C2950-24 starting...
Base ethernet MAC Address: 00:08:e3:2e:e6:00
Xmodem file system is available.
Initializing Flash...
flashfs[0]: 162 files, 3 directories
flashfs[0]: 0 orphaned files, 0 orphaned directories
flashfs[0]: Total bytes: 7741440
flashfs[0]: Bytes used: 2961920
flashfs[0]: Bytes available: 4779520
flashfs[0]: flashfs fsck took 6 seconds.
```

continues

Example 6-2 *Loading and Initializing Flash (Continued)*

```
...done initializing flash.
Boot Sector Filesystem (bs:) installed, fsid: 3
Parameter Block Filesystem (pb:) installed, fsid: 4
Loading "flash:c2950-c3h2s-mz.120-5.3.WC.1.bin"...
################################################################
################################################################

File "flash:c2950-c3h2s-mz.120-5.3.WC.1.bin" uncompressed and installed,
    entry point: 0x80010000
executing...
```

Example 6-3 *POST*

```
Initializing flashfs...
flashfs[1]: 162 files, 3 directories
flashfs[1]: 0 orphaned files, 0 orphaned directories
flashfs[1]: Total bytes: 7741440
flashfs[1]: Bytes used: 2961920
flashfs[1]: Bytes available: 4779520
flashfs[1]: flashfs fsck took 6 seconds.
flashfs[1]: Initialization complete.
Done initializing flashfs.
C2950 POST: System Board Test : Passed
C2950 POST: Ethernet Controller Test : Passed
C2950 POST: MII TEST : Passed

cisco WS-C2950-12 (RC32300) processor (revision B0) with 22260K bytes of memory.
Processor board ID FOC0605W0BH
Last reset from system-reset
```

Example 6-4 *Completion of Initialization*

```
Processor is running Enterprise Edition Software
Cluster command switch capable
Cluster member switch capable
12 FastEthernet/IEEE 802.3 interface(s)


32K bytes of flash-simulated non-volatile configuration memory.
```

Example 6-4 *Completion of Initialization (Continued)*

```
Base ethernet MAC Address: 00:08:E3:2E:E6:00

Motherboard assembly number: 73-5782-08

Power supply part number: 34-0965-01

Motherboard serial number: FOC060502HP

Power supply serial number: PHI05500C5D

Model revision number: B0

Motherboard revision number: B0

Model number: WS-C2950-12

System serial number: FOC0605W0BH



Press RETURN to get started!



C2950 INIT: Complete
```

After the switch has booted and completed POST, prompts for the System Configuration dialog are presented. You can configure the switch manually with or without the assistance of the System Configuration or setup dialog. The System Configuration dialog on the switch is simpler than that on a router. You can access the setup dialog at any time from the privileged command prompt by using the **setup** command.

Examining Help in the Switch Command-Line Interface

The command-line interface for Cisco switches is similar to the command-line interface for Cisco routers.

The help command is issued by entering a question mark. When you enter this command at the system prompt, a list of commands that are available for the current command mode is displayed, as shown in Example 6-5.

Example 6-5 *Output of the ? (Help) Command*

```
Switch>?

access-enable    Create a temporary Access-List entry
 access-profile   Apply user-profile to interface
 clear            Reset functions
```

continues

Example 6-5 *Output of the ? (Help) Command (Continued)*

```
    connect          Open a terminal connection

    disable          Turn off privileged commands

    disconnect       Disconnect an existing network connection

    enable           Turn on privileged commands

    exit             Exit from the EXEC

    help             Description of the interactive help system

    lat              Open a lat connection

    lock             Lock the terminal

    login            Log in as a particular user

    logout           Exit from the EXEC

    mtrace           Trace reverse multicast path from destination to source

    name-connection  Name an existing network connection

    pad              Open a X.29 PAD connection

    ping             Send echo messages

    ppp              Start IETF Point-to-Point Protocol (PPP)

    --more--
```

The help command is flexible. To obtain a list of commands that begin with a particular character sequence, enter those characters followed immediately by the question mark (?). Do not enter a space before the question mark in this case. This form of help is called word help because it completes a word. When using context-sensitive help, the space (or lack of a space) before the question mark is significant. For example, to obtain a list of options for the switch **show** command, enter the command **show** followed by a space and the question mark, as shown in Example 6-6. Example 6-7 shows how to find commands that start with the letter *r* by entering the letter followed immediately by the question mark. (In this case, no space is used.)

Example 6-6 *Output of the* **show** *? Command*

```
Switch>show ?
    class-map        Show QoS Class Map

    clock            Display the system clock

    diags            Show runtime diagnostic info

    exception        exception information

    flash:           display information about flash: file system

    history          Display the session command history
```

Example 6-6 *Output of the* show ? *Command (Continued)*

```
    hosts        IP domain-name, lookup style, nameservers, and host table
    location     Display the system location
    policy-map   Show QoS Policy Map
--more--
Example 6-7Keyword Help Command
Switch>show r?
rmon


Switch>show r_
```

To list keywords or arguments, as shown in Example 6-6, enter a question mark in place of a keyword or argument. Include a space before the question mark. This form of help is called command syntax help because it reminds you which keywords or arguments are applicable based on the command, keywords, and arguments you already have entered.

Like routers, switches have several command modes. The default mode is User EXEC mode, and it is recognized by its prompt, which ends in a greater-than character. The commands that are available in User EXEC mode are limited to those that change terminal settings, perform basic tests, and display system information.

The **enable** command is used to change from User EXEC mode to Privileged EXEC mode. Privileged EXEC mode is also recognized by its prompt, which ends in a pound-sign character, as follows:

```
Switch#
```

The Privileged EXEC mode command set includes those commands that are allowed in User EXEC mode, as well as the **configure terminal, configure memory,** or **configure network** command set through which other command modes are accessed. Because these modes are used to configure the switch, access to Privileged EXEC mode should be password protected to prevent unauthorized use. If the system administrator has set a password, then users are prompted to enter the password before being granted access to Privileged EXEC mode. The password does not appear on the screen, and it is case sensitive. Example 6-7 shows a list of commands that are available in Privileged EXEC mode.

Example 6-7 *Privileged Exec Commands*

```
Switch#?
Exec commands:
access-enable   Create a temporary Access-List entry
access-profile  Apply user-profile to interface
access-template Create a temporary Access-List entry
Archive         manage archive files
clear           Reset functions
clock           Manage the system clock
configure       Enter configuration mode
connect         Open a terminal connection
copy            Copy from one file to another
debug           Debugging functions (see also 'undebug')
delete          Delete a file
dir             List files on a filesystem
disable         Turn off privileged commands
disconnect      Disconnect an existing network connection
enable          Turn on privileged commands
erase           Erase a filesystem
--More--
```

Notice how these commands are different from the ones that are available in User Exec mode.

LAN Switches and Hierarchical Network Design

A hierarchical network design model breaks the complex problem of network design into smaller, more manageable problems. Each level, or tier, in the hierarchy addresses a different set of problems so that network hardware and software can be optimized to perform specific roles. Devices at the lowest tier of the hierarchy are designed to accept traffic into a network and then pass traffic up to the higher layers. Cisco offers a three-tiered hierarchy as the preferred approach to network design.

In the three-layer network design model, network devices and links are grouped according to three layers: core, distribution, and access, as shown in Figure 6-6. Like the Open System Interconnection (OSI) reference model, the three-layer design model is a conceptual framework, an abstract picture of a network.

Figure 6-6 Hierarchical Design Model

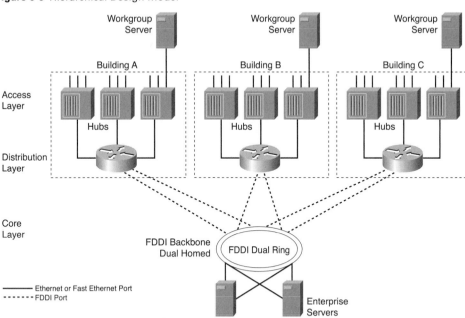

Layered models are useful because they facilitate modularity. Because devices at each layer have similar and well-defined functions, administrators can easily add, replace, and remove individual pieces of the network. This kind of flexibility and adaptability makes a hierarchical network design a scalable network design.

This model applies to any network design. It is important to realize that these three layers might reside in clear and distinct physical entities, but this does not have to be the case. These layers are defined to help create successful network design and represent functionality that must exist in a network.

At the same time, layered models can be difficult to comprehend because the exact composition of each layer varies from network to network. Each layer of the three-tiered design model might include a router, a switch, a link, or some combination of these. In fact, some networks might combine the function of two layers into a single device, or might omit a layer entirely.

The following three sections look at each of the three layers in detail.

The Core Layer

The core of the network has one purpose: to provide an optimized and reliable transport structure by forwarding traffic at high speeds. In other words, the *core layer* should switch packets as quickly as possible. Devices at this layer should not be burdened with access list checking, data encryption, address translation, or any other process that stands in the way of *switching* packets at top speed.

The Distribution Layer

The *distribution layer* sits between the access and core layers and helps differentiate the core from the rest of the network. The purpose of this layer is to provide boundary definition by using access lists and other filters to limit what gets into the core. Therefore, this layer defines policy for the network. A policy is an approach to handling certain kinds of traffic, including routing updates, route summaries, VLAN traffic, and address aggregation. You can use policies to secure networks and to preserve resources by preventing unnecessary traffic.

If a network has two or more routing protocols, such as Routing Information Protocol (RIP) and Interior Gateway Routing Protocol (IGRP), information between the different routing domains is shared, or redistributed, at the distribution layer.

Access Layer

The *access layer* feeds traffic into the network and performs network entry control. End users access the network via the access layer. As a network's "front door," the access layer employs access lists that are designed to prevent unauthorized users from gaining entry. The access layer can also give remote sites access to the network via a wide-area technology, such as Frame Relay, ISDN, or leased lines.

Switched LANs, Access Layer Overview

The construction of a LAN that satisfies the needs of medium- to large-sized organizations is more likely to be successful if a hierarchical design model is used. The use of a hierarchical design model also facilitates easier changes to the network as the organization grows.

The access layer is the entry point for user workstations and servers to the network. In a campus LAN, the device that is used at the access layer can be either a switch or a hub. If a hub is used, bandwidth is shared. If a switch is used, then bandwidth is dedicated. If two or more user workstations or servers are directly connected to switch ports, the full bandwidth of the connection to the switch is available to the connected computers. If two or more computers are connected to a hub, then the available bandwidth to each computer is the total bandwidth divided by the number of computers connected to the hub.

A hub can be connected to a switch port. In such a case, bandwidth is shared between the devices that are connected to the switch port via the hub.

Access layer functions also include the following:

- Shared bandwidth
- Switched bandwidth
- MAC layer filtering
- *Microsegmentation*

MAC layer filtering allows switches to direct frames only to the switch port that is connected to the specified destination device. The switch creates small Layer 2 segments called microsegments. These collision domains can be as small as two devices (that is, a destination device and the connecting switch port). In the access layer, Layer 2 switches are used.

Access Layer Switches

Access layer switches, shown in Figure 6-7, operate at Layer 2 of the OSI model and provide services such as virtual LAN (VLAN) membership. The main purpose of an access layer switch is to allow end users connection to the network. An access layer switch should provide this functionality with low cost and high port density.

Figure 6-7 Access Layer Switches

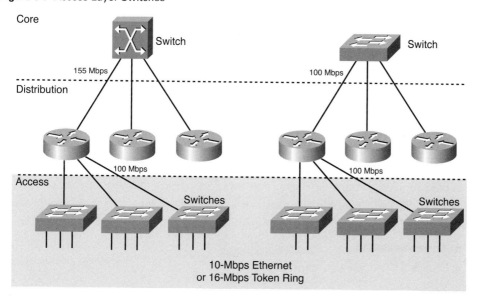

Cisco switches that are commonly used at the access layer include the following:

- Catalyst 1900 series
- Catalyst 2820 series
- Catalyst 2950 series
- Catalyst 4000 series
- Catalyst 5000 series

Features of these access layer switches are outlined in Table 6-5.

The Catalyst 1900 or 2820 series switch is an effective access device in small or medium campus networks. The Catalyst 2950 series switch is effective in providing access for servers and users that require higher bandwidth. This is achieved by providing Fast Ethernet capable switch ports. The Catalyst 4000 and 5000 series switches include Gigabit Ethernet ports and are effective access devices for a larger number of users for large campus networks.

In the noncampus environment, the access layer can give remote sites access to the corporate network via some wide-area technology, such as Frame Relay, ISDN, digital subscriber line (xDSL), or leased lines.

It is often mistakenly thought that the three layers (core, distribution, and access) must exist in clear and distinct physical entities, but this does not have to be the case. The layers are defined to aid successful network design and to represent functionality that must exist in a network. The way the layers are implemented depends on the needs of the network that is being designed. However, it is important to remember that for a network to function optimally and maintain scalability as growth occurs, you must maintain hierarchy.

Distribution Layer Overview

The distribution layer of the network is located between the access and core layers and helps to define and separate the core. The purpose of this layer is to provide a boundary definition in which packet manipulation can take place. This layer segments networks into broadcast domains. Access control lists can apply policy and filter packets. The distribution layer isolates network problems to the workgroups in which they occur and prevents these problems from affecting the core layer. Switches in this layer operate at Layer 2 and Layer 3. It is sufficient at this time to view Layer 3 switching as fast routing. In a switched network, the distribution layer includes several functions, such as the following:

- Aggregation of the wiring closet connections
- Broadcast/multicast domain definition
- VLAN routing
- Any media transitions that need to occur
- Security

Table 6-5 Access Layer Switches

Catalyst	Type	Supported OSI Layers	Ethernet Ports	Fast Ethernet Ports	Gigabit Ethernet	Enterprise Size
1900 series	Fixed configuration	Layer 2	12 or 24	2	0	Small to medium
2820 series	Modular expansion cards	Layer 2	24	2	0	Small to medium
2950 series	Fixed configuration	Layer 2	0	12 or 24 speed configurable	0 or 2	Small to medium
4000 series	Modular multiple slots per chassis	Layer 2 and Layer 3	0	Configurable ports—up to 240	Configurable ports—up to 240	Medium to large
5000 series	Modular multiple slots per chassis	Layer 2 and Layer 3	0	Varies with options chosen	Varies with options chosen	Medium to large

Distribution Layer Switches

Distribution layer switches are the aggregation points for multiple access layer switches. The switch must be able to handle the total amount of traffic from the access layer devices.

The distribution layer switch must have high performance. It is a point at which a broadcast domain is bounded. The distribution layer aggregates VLAN traffic and is a focal point for policy decisions about traffic flow. For these reasons, distribution layer switches operate at both Layer 2 and Layer 3 of the OSI model. Switches in this layer are referred to as multilayer switches. They combine the functions of a router and a switch in one device but are designed to switch traffic to gain higher performance than a standard router does. If these multilayer switches do not have an associated router module, then an external router is used for the Layer 3 functions.

Cisco switches that are suitable for the distribution layer include the following:

- Catalyst 2926G
- Catalyst 5000 family
- Catalyst 6000 family

Distribution-layer devices need fewer *interfaces* and less switching speed than their counterparts in the core because they should handle less traffic. Nevertheless, a lightning-fast core is useless if a bottleneck at the distribution layer prevents user traffic from accessing core links.

The distribution layer of the network divides the access and core layers and helps to define and differentiate the core. (See Figure 6-8.) This layer provides a boundary definition and is the place where packet manipulation takes place. In the campus environment, the distribution layer can include several functions, such as the following:

- Address or area aggregation
- Departmental or workgroup access
- Broadcast/multicast domain definition
- VLAN routing
- Any media transitions that need to occur
- Security

Figure 6-8 Distribution Layer Switch

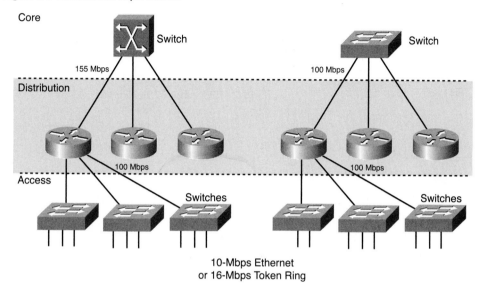

In the noncampus environment, the distribution layer can be a redistribution point between routing domains or the demarcation between static and dynamic routing protocols. It can also be the point at which remote sites access the corporate network. The distribution layer can be summarized as the layer that provides policy-based connectivity.

Core Layer Overview

As the center of the network, the core layer is designed to be fast and reliable. Access lists are avoided in the core because they add latency, or delay. Moreover, end users should not access the core directly. Consider an apple; you cannot get to the seeds in an apple's core without going through the skin first. In a hierarchical network, end users' traffic should reach core routers only after those packets have passed through the distribution and access layers, where access lists can be applied.

Because core routing is done without access lists, address translation, or other packet manipulation, it might seem as though the least powerful routers would work well for so simple a task. However, the opposite is true. The most powerful Cisco routers serve the core because they have the fastest switching technologies and the largest capacity for physical interfaces.

Core Layer Switches

The core layer is the *backbone* of the campus-switched network, as shown in Figure 6-9. The switches in this layer can make use of a number of Layer 2 technologies. Provided that distances between the core layer switches are not too great, the switches can use Ethernet technology. Other Layer 2 technologies, such as Asynchronous Transfer Mode (ATM) cell switching, can be used. In a network design, the core layer can be a routed or Layer 3 core. Core layer switches are designed to provide efficient Layer 3 functionality when needed. Before a core switch choice is made, you should consider factors such as need, cost, and performance.

Figure 6-9 Core Layer Switches

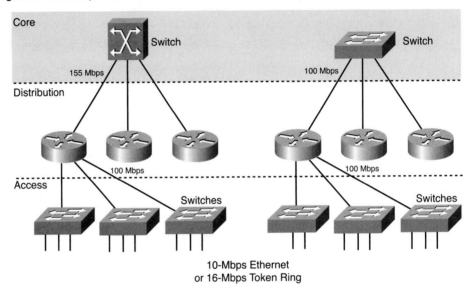

Cisco switches that are suitable for the core layer include these:

- Catalyst 6500 series
- Catalyst 8500 series
- IGX 8400 series
- Lightstream 1010

Marketed by Cisco as enterprise core routers, the 7000, 7200, and 7500 series routers feature the fastest switching modes available. The 12000 series router is also a core router, but it is designed to meet the core routing needs of Internet service providers (ISPs). Unless your company is in the business of providing Internet access to other companies, you are not likely to see a 12000 series router in your telecommunications closet.

Unlike some routers, such as the Cisco 2500 series, the 7000, 7200, and 7500 series routers are modular, so you can add interface modules as needed. The large chassis of this series can accommodate dozens of interfaces on multiple modules for virtually any media type, which makes these routers scalable, reliable core solutions.

One way that core routers achieve reliability is by using redundant links, usually to all other core routers. When possible, these redundant links should be symmetrical (that is, they should have equal throughput) so that equal-cost load balancing can be used. That is why core routers need a relatively large number of interfaces. Another way that core routers achieve reliability is through redundant power supplies. Core routers usually feature two or more "hot-swappable" power supplies, which can be removed and replaced individually without bringing down the router.

Core links should be the fastest, most reliable, and most expensive leased lines in the WAN: T1, T3, OC3, or better. If redundant T1s are used for this WAN core, each router needs four serial interfaces for two point-to-point connections to each site.

With high-end routers and WAN links involved, the core can become a huge expense. Some designers choose not to use symmetrical links in the core to reduce cost. In place of redundant lines, packet-switched and dial-on-demand technologies, such as Frame Relay and ISDN, can be used as backup links. The trade-off for saving money by using such technologies is performance. For instance, if you use ISDN BRIs as backup links, you lose the capability to do equal-cost load balancing.

The core of a network does not have to exist in the WAN. In some cases, a LAN backbone can also be considered to belong to the core layer. Campus networks, or large networks that span an office complex or adjacent buildings, might have a LAN-based core. In this case, switched Fast Ethernet and Gigabit Ethernet are the most common core technologies, and they are usually run over fiber. Enterprise switches, such as the Catalyst 4000, 5000, and 6000 series, shoulder the load in LAN cores because they switch frames at Layer 2 much faster than routers can switch packets at Layer 3. In fact, as modular devices, these switches can be equipped with route switch modules (RSMs), adding Layer 3 routing functionality to the switch chassis.

Summary

In this chapter, you learned a general model that you can use in analyzing and designing networks.

- This model identifies larger networks as being of three layers:
- The access layer

- The distribution layer
- The core layer

You learned that each layer is associated with specialized functions. You also learned that in a switched network design, there are switches that are best suited for each layer. You examined the properties of some switches for each layer. Technology and networking needs for bandwidth and performance change. Devices that seem suitable today might not be suitable for future needs. It is your responsibility as a networking professional to ensure that you can select the most suitable switching devices for your networks.

To supplement all that you have learned in this chapter, refer to the chapter-specific Videos, photozooms, and e-Lab Activities on the CD-ROM that accompanies this book.

Key Terms

access layer   The layer that feeds traffic into the network and performs network entry control. End users access the network via the access layer.

backbone   The structural core of the network, which connects all the components of the network so that communication can occur.

core layer   The backbone of the campus-switched network. The switches in this layer can make use of many Layer 2 technologies.

distribution layer   The layer that provides a boundary definition in which packet manipulation can take place.

hub   Generally, a device that serves as the center of a star-topology network.

interface   1. A connection between two systems or devices. 2. In routing terminology, a network connection.

microsegmentation   The process of splitting a single collision domain into two or more collision domains to reduce collisions and network congestion.

port   An interface on an internetworking device (such as a router). A female plug on a patch panel that accepts the same size plug as an RJ-45 jack. Patch cords are used in these ports to cross-connect computers that are wired to the patch panel. It is this cross-connection that allows the LAN to function.

switch   A network device that filters, forwards, and floods frames based on the destination address of each frame. The switch operates at the data link layer of the OSI reference model.

switching   The process of taking an incoming frame from one interface and delivering it through another interface.

Check Your Understanding

1. What does the access layer provide?

   A. The entry point for users and servers into the network

   B. The point at which all devices connect to the network

   C. All available bandwidth for every user

   D. A connection between the networks high-end routers and switches

2. Which of the following is true of the core layer?

    A. It provides as much packet manipulation as possible to ensure security.

    B. It operates as a high-speed switching backbone to forward traffic from one area to another.

    C. It can only consist of Layer 2 switches.

    D. It provides multiple pathways to slow down the traffic.

3. Which of the following is a benefit of implementing Layer 3 devices in your LAN?

    A. Allows segmentation of the LAN into unique physical and logical networks

    B. Filters data-link broadcasts and multicasts and allows for WAN connectivity

    C. Provides logical structure to the network

    D. All of the above

4. Which of the following devices provides logical segmentation of a LAN?

    A. Router

    B. Bridge

    C. Switch

    D. Hub

5. What does microsegmentation with switches do?

    A. It creates additional broadcast domains.

    B. It decreases network segments.

    C. It creates additional collision domains.

    D. Both A and C.

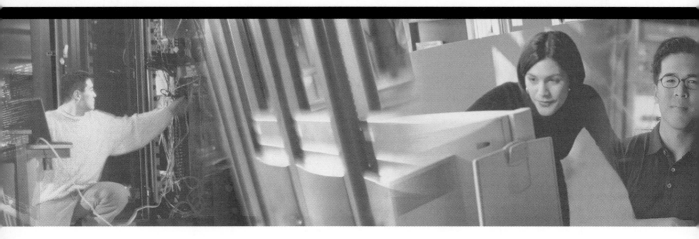

Objectives

After reading this chapter, you will be able to

- Describe microsegmentation
- Describe how a switch learns addresses
- Describe switch forwarding
- Understand switches and collision domains
- Understand switches and broadcast domains
- Configure LAN switches
- Verify LAN switch configuration
- Manage LAN switches

Chapter 7

Switch Configuration

Switches are Layer 2 devices that are used to ease bandwidth shortages and network bottlenecks. A switch can segment a LAN into *microsegments*, which are 2-host segments. This creates collision-free domains out of one larger domain. Although the LAN switch eliminates *collision domains*, all hosts that are connected to the switch are still part of the same *broadcast domain*. Therefore, all nodes that are connected through a LAN switch can see a broadcast from just one node.

This chapter reviews some of the basic attributes of switches as well as operational characteristics. It focuses on basic configuration, verification, and management of an IOS-based switch. Instructions are provided for setting the switch IP address port characteristics and other switch configuration parameters.

Be sure to look at this chapter's associated e-Lab Activities, Videos, and PhotoZooms that you will find on the CD-ROM accompanying this book. These CD-ROM elements are designed to supplement the material and reinforce the concepts introduced in this chapter.

Microsegmentation

There are two primary reasons for segmenting a LAN. The first is to isolate traffic between segments, and the second is to achieve more bandwidth per user by creating smaller collision domains.

There are several reasons and benefits to segmenting a LAN using Layer 2 switches. First, without LAN segmentation, LANs that are larger than a small workgroup would quickly become clogged with traffic and collisions and would deliver virtually no bandwidth.

LAN segmentation can be implemented through the utilization of bridges, switches, and routers. Each device has particular pros and cons.

The addition of such devices segments the LAN into smaller collision domains. In Figure 7-1, four collision domains have been created.

Figure 7-1 Collision Domains

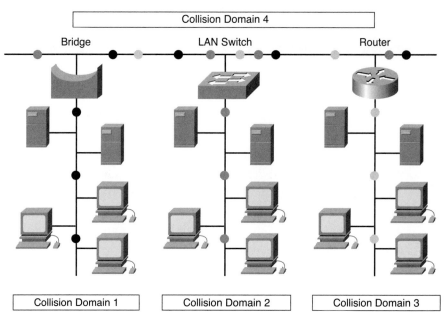

By dividing large networks into self-contained units, bridges and switches provide several advantages. Bridges and switches diminish the traffic that devices experience on all connected segments because only a certain percentage of traffic is forwarded. Bridges and switches increase the number of collision domains while reducing the size of each collision domain. They have no effect on the size of the broadcast domain.

Each interface on the router connects to a separate network, so insertion of the router into a LAN creates smaller collision domains and smaller broadcast domains. This occurs because routers do not forward broadcasts unless they are programmed to do so.

A switch employs microsegmentation to reduce the collision domain on a LAN. It does this by creating dedicated network segments, or point-to-point connections, and connecting these segments in a virtual network within the switch.

This virtual network circuit exists only when two nodes need to communicate. This is called a virtual circuit because it exists only when needed, and it is established within the switch. Figure 7-2 shows a network before and after microsegmentation has been implemented.

Figure 7-2 Microsegmentation of a Network

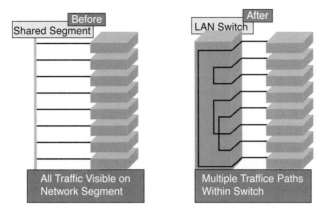

Microsegmentation Implementation

LAN switches are considered multiport bridges with no collision domain because of microsegmentation.

Data is exchanged at high speeds by switching the frame to its destination. By reading the destination MAC address Layer 2 information, switches can achieve high-speed data transfers, much like a bridge does, as shown in Figure 7-3. The frame is sent to the port of the receiving station prior to the entire frame entering the switch. This leads to low latency levels and a high rate of speed for frame forwarding. Figure 7-4 shows a switching table.

Figure 7-3 LAN Switch Operation

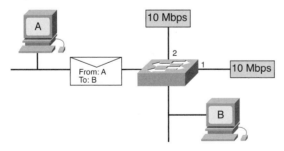

Ethernet switching increases the bandwidth that is available on a network. It does this by creating dedicated network segments, or point-to-point connections, and connecting these segments in a virtual network within the switch. This virtual network circuit exists only when two nodes need to communicate. This is called a virtual circuit because it exists only when needed, and it is established within the switch.

Figure 7-4 Switching Table

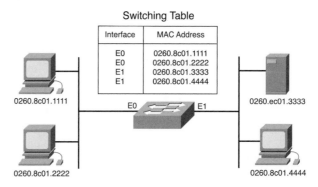

Even though the LAN switch reduces the size of collision domains, all hosts that are connected to the switch are still in the same broadcast domain. Therefore, all other nodes that are connected through the LAN switch see a broadcast from one node.

Switches are data link layer devices that, like bridges, enable multiple physical LAN segments to be interconnected into a single larger network. Similar to bridges, switches forward and flood traffic based on MAC addresses. Because switching is performed in hardware instead of in software, it is significantly faster. Each switch port effectively acts as a microbridge. Each switch port acts as a separate bridge and gives the full bandwidth of the medium to each host. Figure 7-5 shows an example of how a switch can segment a network into a single broadcast domain.

Figure 7-5 LAN Switching Overview

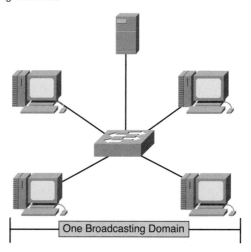

How a Switch Learns Addresses

An Ethernet switch can learn the address of each device on the network by reading the source MAC address of each data frame that is transmitted and noting the port where the frame entered the switch. The switch then adds this information to its forwarding database or switching table. Addresses are learned dynamically. This means that as new addresses are read, they are learned and stored in *content-addressable memory (CAM)*. When a source is read that is not found in the CAM, it is learned and stored for future use.

Each time an address is stored, it is time stamped. This allows for addresses to be stored for a set period of time. Each time an address is referenced or found in the CAM, it receives a new time stamp. Addresses that are not referenced during a set period of time are removed from the list. By removing aged or old addresses, the CAM maintains an accurate and functional forwarding database. This is especially important if the network interface card is replaced in a workstation.

If Station A needs to transmit data to Station B, the frames it sends pass through the switch, as shown in Figure 7-6. Remember that as this traffic goes through the network, the switch operates at Layer 2, meaning that the switch looks at the Media Access Control (MAC) address. The switch looks at the traffic as it goes through to discover the source MAC address and stores it in an address table, as shown in Figure 7-7.

Figure 7-6 LAN Switching Operation Example

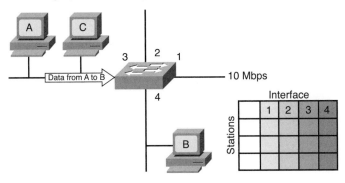

As a packet enters a port, an entry is made in this table indicating the MAC address of the station that sent it and the port on which it resides.

Figure 7-7 Forwarding Table Update

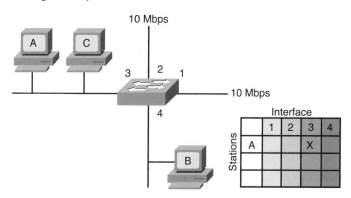

When a switch needs to forward a frame, it examines the destination MAC address of the frame and consults the CAM to see which port is capable of reaching that address. If the switch does not have an entry for that MAC address in its forwarding table, it floods the frame out of all its ports, except the one on which it was received, as shown in Figure 7-8. If Station A sends a frame to Station B, the switch floods that frame out every port because the destination is unknown. When Station B responds to Station A, however, the switch sees Station B's MAC address as the source, and it posts an entry for Station B in the CAM. The switch now knows where Station B is connected to the network.

Figure 7-8 MAC Flooding

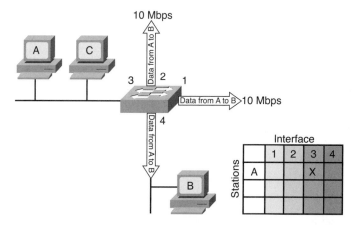

Now data can be sent from Station B to Station A through the switch, but the switch does not flood the traffic this time. The switch only sends the data out of port 3 because it knows where Station A is on the network. As shown in Figure 7-9, B passes data to the switch. In Figure 7-10, the switch passes the data from B to A. The original transmission indicated where that MAC address came from, allowing the switch to deliver traffic more efficiently in the network.

Figure 7-9 Data from B to Switch

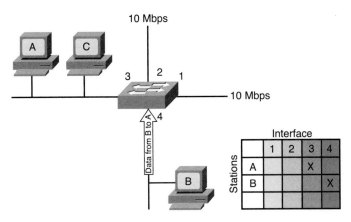

Figure 7-10 Data from B to A

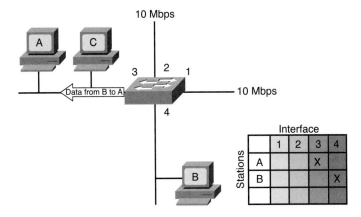

Switch Forwarding

You can use two switching modes to forward a frame through a switch: cut-through and store-and-forward.

Store-and-Forward

When a switch performs *store-and-forward switching*, the entire frame is received before forwarding occurs. The destination or source addresses are read and filters are applied before the frame is forwarded. Latency occurs while the frame is being received. The latency is greater with larger frames because the entire frame takes longer to read. Errors are detected because of the time available for the switch to check for errors while waiting for the entire frame to be received, as shown in Figure 7-11.

Figure 7-11 Frame Header

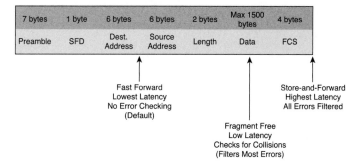

Cut-Through

A switch that performs *cut-through switching* only reads the destination address when receiving the frame. The frame is then forwarded before the entire frame arrives. This mode decreases the latency of the transmission, but has poor error detection, as in Figure 7-12.

Figure 7-12 Store-and-Forward

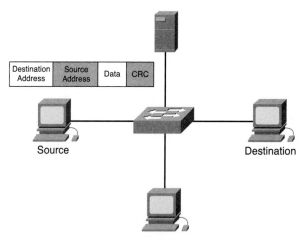

There are two forms of cut-through switching:

- *Fast-forward switching*—This type of switching offers the lowest level of latency by immediately forwarding a packet after receiving the destination address. Because fast-forward switching starts forwarding before the entire packet is received, packets might be relayed with errors. Although this occurs infrequently and the destination network adapter discards the faulty packet upon receipt, the superfluous traffic might be deemed unacceptable in certain environments. Use the fragment-free option to reduce the number of packets forwarded with errors. In fast-forward mode, latency is measured from the first bit received to the first bit transmitted, or first in, first out (FIFO).

- *Fragment-free switching*—This type of switching filters out collision fragments, which are the majority of packet errors, before forwarding begins. In a properly functioning network, collision fragments must be smaller than 64 bytes. Anything greater than 64 bytes is a valid packet and is usually received without error. Fragment-free switching waits until the received packet has been determined not to be a collision fragment before forwarding the packet. In fragment-free mode, latency is measured as FIFO.

The latency of each switching mode depends on how the switch forwards the frames. Faster switching modes result in lower latency for the switch. To accomplish faster frame forwarding, the switch takes less time to check for errors. The trade-off is less error checking, which can lead to a higher number of retransmissions. Store-and-forward switching introduces more latency, but it also ensures data integrity.

Symmetric Switching

Symmetric switching is one way to characterize a LAN switch according to the bandwidth allocated to each port on the switch, as in Figure 7-13. A symmetric switch provides switched connections between ports with the same bandwidth, such as all 10-Mbps ports or all 100-Mbps ports. As shown in Figure 7-14, an asymmetric LAN switch provides switched connections between ports of unlike bandwidth, such as a combination of 10-Mbps and 100-Mbps ports.

Asymmetric Switching

Asymmetric switching makes the most of client/server network traffic flows, where multiple clients are communicating with a server at the same time, requiring more bandwidth dedicated to the switch port to which the server is connected to prevent a bottleneck at that port. As you will learn in the next section, memory buffering in an asymmetric switch is required to allow traffic from the 100-Mbps port to be sent to a 10-Mbps port without causing too much congestion at the 10-Mbps port.

Figure 7-13 Symmetric Switching

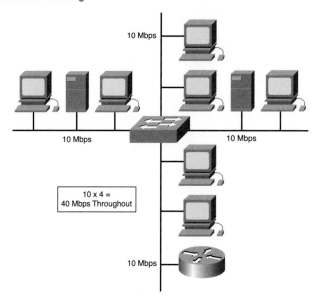

Figure 7-14 Asymmetric Switching

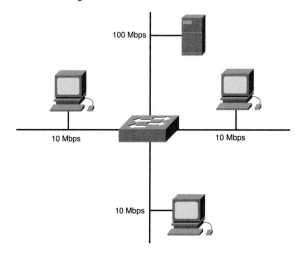

Memory Buffering

An Ethernet switch can use a buffering technique to store and forward packets to the correct port or ports. Buffering can also be used when the destination port is busy. The area of memory where the switch stores the data is called the memory buffer. This memory buffer can use two methods for forwarding packets: port-based *memory buffering* and shared memory buffering

In port-based memory buffering, packets are stored in queues that are linked to specific incoming ports. A packet is transmitted to the outgoing port only when all the packets ahead of it in the queue have been transmitted successfully. A single packet can delay the transmission of all the packets in memory because of a busy destination port. This delay occurs even if the other packets can be transmitted to open destination ports.

Shared memory buffering deposits all packets into a common memory buffer that all the ports on the switch share. The amount of memory that is allocated to a port is determined by how much each port requires. This is called *dynamic allocation of buffer memory.* The packets in the buffer are then linked dynamically to the transmit port; the packet is linked to the memory allocation of that transmit port. This allows the packet to be received on one port and transmitted on another port, without moving it into a different queue.

The switch maintains a map of the ports to which a packet needs to be transmitted. The switch clears out this map of destination ports only after the packet has been successfully transmitted. Because the memory buffer is shared, the packet is restricted by the size of the entire memory buffer, not just the allocation to one port. This means that larger packets can be transmitted with fewer dropped packets. This is important to 10/100 switching, where a 100-Mbps port can forward a packet to a 10-Mbps port.

Switches and Collision Domains

A major disadvantage of Ethernet/802.3 networks is that they are prone to collisions. Collisions occur as a result of two hosts transmitting frames simultaneously. Collisions are especially prevalent with the older bus and hub-based Ethernet implementations. When a collision occurs, the transmitted frames are either corrupted or destroyed. The sending hosts back off from sending further transmissions for a random period of time under the Ethernet/802.3 rules of carrier sense multiple access collision detect (CSMA/CD). Collisions cause network inefficiency, as in Figure 7-15.

A collision domain is the network area within which frames originate and collide. All shared media environments are collision domains, as shown in Figure 7-16.

When a host is connected to a switch port, the switch creates a dedicated connection. This connection is considered an individual collision domain. For example, if a 12-port switch has a device that is connected to each port, 12 collision domains are created.

Figure 7-15 Switches and Collision Domains

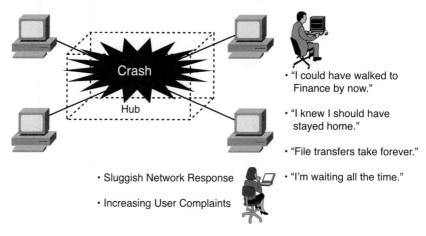

Figure 7-16 Basic Shared Access

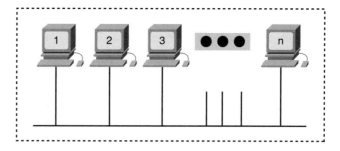

A switch builds a switching table by learning the Layer 2 MAC addresses of the hosts that are connected to each switch port. When two connected hosts want to communicate with each other, the switch looks up the switching table and establishes a virtual connection between the ports. It is called a virtual connection because it exists only when needed. When the virtual circuit is no longer needed, it is disconnected.

This, in turn, creates a microsegment. The microsegment behaves as if the network has only two hosts: one sending and one receiving. This allows for maximum utilization of the available bandwidth.

Thus, switches reduce collisions and increase bandwidth on network segments because they provide dedicated bandwidth to each network segment.

Switches and Broadcast Domains

Communication in a network occurs in three ways. The most common way is by unicast transmissions. In a unicast transmission, one transmitter tries to reach one receiver.

Another way to communicate is multicast transmission. This occurs when one transmitter tries to reach only a subset, or a group, within the entire segment. Only the stations that need to receive multicast traffic participate in the multicast group. Figure 7-17 illustrates switches and various broadcast domains.

Figure 7-17 Switches and Broadcast Domains

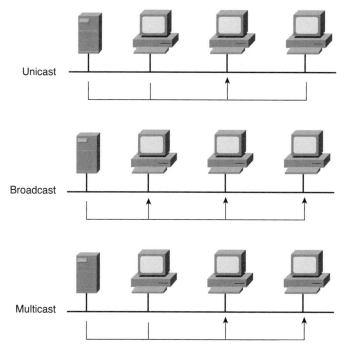

The final way to communicate is by broadcasting. When one transmitter needs to reach all of the receivers in the network, it sends a broadcast. Every host on the segment receives broadcast frames, as in Figure 7-17.

When a device wants to send out a Layer 2 broadcast, the destination MAC address in the frame is set to the highest possible value—that is, to FF:FF:FF:FF:FF:FF. Setting the destination to this value ensures that all devices will accept and process the broadcasted frame.

The broadcast domain at Layer 2 is referred to as the MAC broadcast domain. The MAC broadcast domain consists of all devices on the LAN that receive broadcast frames from a host to all other machines on the LAN.

A switch is a Layer 2 device. When a switch receives a broadcast, it forwards it to each port on the switch except the incoming port. Each attached device must process the broadcast frame. This can lead to reduced network efficiency as available bandwidth is used for broadcasting purposes, as in Figure 7-18.

Figure 7-18 Single Broadcast Domains

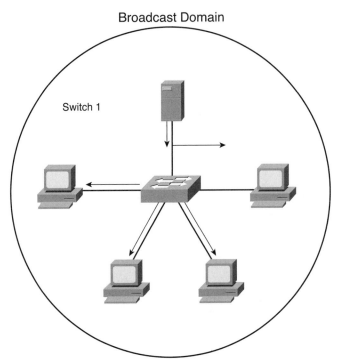

When two switches are connected, the size of the broadcast domain increases. In this example, a broadcast frame is forwarded to all connected ports on Switch 1. If Switch 1 is connected to Switch 2, the frame is propagated to all devices that are connected to Switch 2, as in Figure 7-19.

The overall result is a reduction in available bandwidth because all devices in the broadcast domain must receive and process the broadcast frame.

Routers are Layer 3 devices. Routers do not propagate broadcasts; therefore, they are used to segment both collision and broadcast domains.

Figure 7-19 Multiple Switch Broadcast Domains

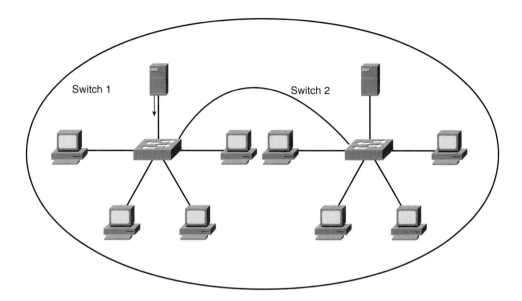

Communication Between Switches and PCs

Switches are Layer 2 devices that use intelligence to learn the MAC addresses of the devices that are attached to the ports of the switch. This data is entered into a switching table. After this table is complete, the switch can read the destination MAC address of an incoming data frame on one port, look up the switching table, and then forward the data frame out of the port that matches the destination MAC address.

> **NOTE**
>
> You must use a straight-through cable when connecting a workstation to a switch.

PC to Switch Transmission

When a PC connects to a LAN, it is unconcerned about the other devices that are connected to the LAN media. The PC simply transmits data frames via a network interface card to the network medium.

The PC could be attached to another PC via a crossover cable or to a network device, such as a hub, switch, or router, via a straight-through cable.

Communication Between Switches

If Host A, with MAC address A, transmits data to Host B, with MAC address B, the transmitted data frame enters Port 1 on Switch A. The switch reads the destination MAC address on the incoming data frame and refers to the switching table. It recognizes that the MAC address of Host B is mapped to Port 2 and switches the frame to this outgoing port.

NOTE

You must use a cross-over cable when you are connecting switches.

Switching tables can have more than one MAC address mapped to a particular port. This is common when a hub that has multiple workstations is attached to a switch port or when switches are interconnected.

A similar process occurs when the transmission needs to pass through two switches. In this case, Host A wants to transmit to Host F, with MAC address F.

Host A transmits the frame to Port A on Switch A. Switch A looks at the switching table and does not recognize the destination MAC address of Host F. The switch then floods all ports with the incoming data frame, except for Port A.

Host B and Host C examine the destination MAC address and ignore the frame because it does not correspond to either of their MAC addresses. The data frame is forwarded to Switch B on Port 2. Switch 2 looks up the switching table and recognizes the destination MAC address. It sends the frame to Host F, with MAC address F, via Port 4.

When Host F replies to Host A, the procedure is reversed. Host A can now update the switching table by mapping Host F to Port 4. Switch 2 can now update the switching table by mapping Host A to Port 2.

Eventually, Switch A will learn that Host D, Host E, and Host F are mapped to Port 4, and Switch B will learn that Host A, Host B, and Host C are mapped to Port 2.

Verifying the Initial Configuration of a Catalyst Switch

A new switch will have a preset configuration with factory defaults. This configuration will rarely be what a network administrator will need. Switches can be configured and managed from a command-line interface. Increasingly, networking devices can also be configured and managed by using a web-based interface and a browser.

A network administrator must be familiar with many tasks to be effective in managing a network with switches. Some tasks are associated with maintaining the switch and its Internetworking Operating System (IOS), whereas tasks are associated with managing its interfaces and tables for optimal, reliable, and secure operation.

Occasionally, a user will forget a password and an administrator must perform password recovery to gain access to the switch. Basic switch configuration, upgrading the IOS, and performing password recovery are essential network administrator skills.

Verifying the Catalyst Switch Default Configuration

When a switch is powered up for the first time, it has default data in the running configuration file. The switch has the default name Switch. No passwords are set on the console or virtual terminal (vty) lines. In Example 7-1, the **show run** command is used to display the default switch configuration for an IOS command-based switch, such as a Cisco 2900 series.

Example 7-1 *Default Switch Configuration*

```
Switch#show run
Building configuration...

Current configuration:
!
version 12.0
no service pad
service timestamps debug uptime
service timestamps log uptime
no service password-encryption
!
hostname Switch
!

!
ip subnet-zero
!

!
interface FastEthernet0/1
!
interface FastEthernet0/2
!
interface FastEthernet0/3
!
interface FastEthernet0/4
```

continues

Example 7-1 *Default Switch Configuration (Continued)*

```
!
interface FastEthernet0/5
!
interface FastEthernet0/6
!
interface FastEthernet0/7
!
<OUTPUT OMITTED>
!
line con 0
 transport input none
 stopbits 1
line vty 5 15
!
end
```

Switch Port Properties

Use the **show interface** command to see the properties for an interface. Remember to specify the slot and port number (such as 0/1). By default, the switch ports (interfaces) are set to auto mode, as shown in Example 7-2. This means that they automatically detect half or full duplex operation and port speed, such as 10 Mbps or 100 Mbps.

Example 7-2 *Interface Default Properties*

```
Switch#show interface FastEthernet0/1
FastEthernet0/1 is down, line protocol is down
  Hardware is Fast Ethernet, address is 0008.e32e.e601 (bia 0008.e32e.e601)
  MTU 1500 bytes, BW 0 Kbit, DLY 100 usec,
     reliability 255/255, txload 1/255, rxload 1/255
  Encapsulation ARPA, loopback not set
  Keepalive not set
  Auto-duplex , Auto Speed , 100BaseTX/FX
  ARP type: ARPA, ARP Timeout 04:00:00
  Last input never, output 00:31:54, output hang never
  Last clearing of "show interface" counters never
  Queueing strategy: fifo
  Output queue 0/40, 0 drops; input queue 0/75, 0 drops
```

Example 7-2 *Interface Default Properties (Continued)*

```
 5 minute input rate 0 bits/sec, 0 packets/sec
 5 minute output rate 0 bits/sec, 0 packets/sec
    1 packets input, 64 bytes
    Received 0 broadcasts, 0 runts, 0 giants, 0 throttles
    0 input errors, 0 CRC, 0 frame, 0 overrun, 0 ignored
    0 watchdog, 0 multicast
    0 input packets with dribble condition detected
    5 packets output, 495 bytes, 0 underruns
    0 output errors, 0 collisions, 1 interface resets
    0 babbles, 0 late collision, 0 deferred
    0 lost carrier, 0 no carrier
```

VLAN Properties

All switch ports are in virtual LAN (VLAN) 1. VLAN 1 is known as the default management VLAN. Use the **show vlan** command to display information about VLANs that are defined in the switch. Example 7-3 shows default properties for VLAN 1. Notice that all 12 ports for this switch are in VLAN 1; by default, all ports belong to VLAN 1 initially.

Example 7-3 *Default Properties for VLAN 1*

```
Switch#show vlan
VLAN Name                             Status    Ports
---- -------------------------------- --------- -------------------------------
1    default                          active    Fa0/1, Fa0/2, Fa0/3, Fa0/4,
                                                Fa0/5, Fa0/6, Fa0/7, Fa0/8,
                                                Fa0/9, Fa0/10, Fa0/11, Fa0/12
1002 fddi-default                     active
1003 token-ring-default               active
1004 fddinet-default                  active
1005 trnet-default                    active


VLAN Type  SAID       MTU   Parent RingNo BridgeNo Stp  BrdgMode Trans1 Trans2
---- ----- ---------- ----- ------ ------ -------- ---- -------- ------ ------
1    enet  100001     1500  -      -      -        -    -        1002   1003
1002 fddi  101002     1500  -      -      -        -    -        1      1003
```

continues

Example 7-3 *Default Properties for VLAN 1 (Continued)*

```
1003 tr    101003  1500 1005  0     -       -     srb  1    1002
1004 fdnet 101004  1500 -     -     1     ibm  -     0    0
1005 trnet 101005  1500 -     -     1     ibm  -     0    0
```

The Flash Directory

Because this is a new switch that has not been configured yet, the flash directory contains no VLAN database file (vlan.dat) and shows no saved configuration file (config.text). The vlan.dat file is used to hold local VLAN information, and the switch uses this file to share VLAN information with other switches. The flash directory, by default, has a file that contains the IOS image (ending in .bin), a file called env_vars, and a subdirectory called html. Use the **dir flash:** command to display the contents of the flash directory, as shown in Example 7-4.

Example 7-4 *Default Flash Directory*

```
Switch#directory flash:

Directory of flash:/

  2  -rwx      1674921   Apr 30 2001 15:09:51  c2950-c3h2s-mz.120-5.3.WC.1.bin
  3  -rwx          269   Jan 01 1970 00:00:57  env_vars
  4  drwx        10240   Apr 30 2001 15:09:52  html
7741440 bytes total (4780544 bytes free)
```

Displaying IOS Version Information

You can verify the IOS version and the configuration register settings with the **show version** command, as in Example 7-5. Other information such as the IOS system image filename, switch model number, serial number, the amount of memory, and the number and type of ports that the switch has is also displayed.

Example 7-5 *Verifying IOS Version and Configuration Register Settings*

```
Switch#show version
Cisco Internetwork Operating System Software
IOS (tm) C2950 Software (C2950-C3H2S-M), Version 12.0(5.3)WC(1),
    MAINTENANCE INTERIM SOFTWARE
Copyright (c) 1986-2001 by cisco Systems, Inc.
Compiled Mon 30-Apr-01 07:56 by devgoyal
```

Example 7-5 *Verifying IOS Version and Configuration Register Settings (Continued)*

```
Image text-base: 0x80010000, data-base: 0x8031A000


ROM: Bootstrap program is CALHOUN boot loader


Switch uptime is 1 hour, 24 minutes
System returned to ROM by power-on
System image file is "flash:c2950-c3h2s-mz.120-5.3.WC.1.bin"
cisco WS-C2950-12 (RC32300) processor (revision B0) with 22260K bytes of memory.
Processor board ID FOC0605W0BH
Last reset from system-reset


Processor is running Enterprise Edition Software
Cluster command switch capable
Cluster member switch capable
12 FastEthernet/IEEE 802.3 interface(s)


32K bytes of flash-simulated non-volatile configuration memory.
Base ethernet MAC Address: 00:08:E3:2E:E6:00
Motherboard assembly number: 73-5782-08
Power supply part number: 34-0965-01
Motherboard serial number: FOC060502HP
Power supply serial number: PHI05500C5D
Model revision number: B0
Motherboard revision number: B0
Model number: WS-C2950-12
System serial number: FOC0605W0BH
Configuration register is 0xF
```

Benefits of Using the Default Configuration

In this default state, the switch has one broadcast domain and can be managed or configured via the console port by using the command-line interface. The spanning tree protocol is also enabled. An additional measure of security exists because the switch has not been assigned an IP address.

For small networks, the default configuration might be sufficient. The benefits of better performance with microsegmentation are obtained immediately.

Lab Activity   Verifying Default Switch Configuration

In this lab, you investigate the settings for a catalyst 29xx switch. You connect as the switch console by using HyperTerminal and use various show commands to gather information about the current switch configuration.

Configuring the Network Settings of the Catalyst Switch

A switch might already be configured and might only require passwords to be entered to access the User EXEC, ENABLE, or PRIVILEGED EXEC modes. Switch configuration mode is entered from PRIVILEDGED EXEC mode. In the command-line interface, the default privileged exec mode is Switch#. In User EXEC mode, the prompt is Switch>.

Resetting the Switch Defaults

You can ensure that a new configuration completely overwrites an existing configuration, as shown in Example 7-6, by doing the following:

- Remove existing VLAN information by deleting the VLAN database file vlan.dat from the flash directory.
- Erase the backup configuration file startup-config. (The example shows how to do this for both the catalyst 2950 and the 1900 switches.)
- Reload the switch.

Example 7-6 *Resetting Switch Defaults in a 2950 and a 1900 Series Switch*

```
Catalyst 2950

Switch#delete flash:vlan.dat

Delete filename [vlan.dat]?

Delete flash:vlan.dat? [confirm]

Switch#erase startup-config


<output omitted>

Switch#reload




Catalyst 1900

Switch#delete nvram
```

Assigning the Switch Host Name and Passwords

Security, documentation, and management are important for every internetworking device.

A switch should be given a host name, and passwords should be set on the console and vty (Telnet) lines, as shown in Example 7-7.

Example 7-7 *Set Switch Host Name and Password-Protect Lines*

```
Switch(config)#hostname ALSwitch
ALSwitch(config)#line configuration 0
ALSwitch(config-line)#password
ALSwitch(config-line)#login
ALSwitch(config-line)#line vty 0 4
ALSwitch(config-line)#password
ALSwitch(config-line)#login
```

Assigning the Switch IP Address and Default Gateway

To allow the switch to be accessible by Telnet and other TCP/IP applications, you need to set IP addresses and a default gateway. Example 7-8 shows how to do this for both Catalyst 2950 and 1900. By default, VLAN 1 is the management VLAN. In a switch-based network, all internetworking devices should be in the management VLAN. This allows a single management workstation to access, configure, and manage all the internetworking devices.

Example 7-8 *Set Switch IP Address and Default Gateway*

```
Catalyst 2950
ALSwitch(config)#interface VLAN1
ALSwitch(config-if)#ip address 192.168.1.2 255.255.255.0



ALSwitch(config)#ip default-gateway 192.168.1.1



Catalyst 1900
ALSwitch(config)#ip address 192.168.1.2 255.255.255.0
ALSwitch(config)#ip default-gateway 192.168.1.1
```

Setting Port Characteristics

The FastEthernet switch ports default to auto-speed and auto-duplex. This allows the interfaces to negotiate these settings. When a network administrator needs to ensure an interface has particular speed (10 or 100) and duplex values (half or full), the values can be set manually, as shown in Example 7-9.

Example 7-9 *Setting Port Speed and Duplex*

```
Switch(config)#interface FastEthernet0/2
Switch(config-if)#duplex full
Switch(config-if)#
00:34:01: %LINK-3-UPDOWN: Interface FastEthernet0/2, changed state to down
00:34:02: %LINEPROTO-5-UPDOWN: Line protocol on Interface FastEthernet0/2,
    changed state to down
00:34:03: %LINK-3-UPDOWN: Interface FastEthernet0/2, changed state to up
00:34:04: %LINEPROTO-5-UPDOWN: Line protocol on Interface FastEthernet0/2,
    changed state to up
Switch(config-if)#speed 100
Switch(config-if)#
00:34:24: %LINK-3-UPDOWN: Interface FastEthernet0/2, changed state to down
00:34:25: %LINEPROTO-5-UPDOWN: Line protocol on Interface FastEthernet0/2,
    changed state to down
00:34:27: %LINK-3-UPDOWN: Interface FastEthernet0/2, changed state to up
00:34:28: %LINEPROTO-5-UPDOWN: Line protocol on Interface FastEthernet0/2,
    changed state to up
```

Another useful option that you can set for a port is **portfast**.

If a switch port is connected only to end user stations (not connected to another switch or bridge), you should enable a Catalyst switch feature called portfast on those end user ports. With portfast, when the port first comes up, it automatically transitions from the blocking state to the forwarding state. Setting portfast can be especially helpful for Novell NetWare clients that need to contact a NetWare server at bootup to log on. Example 7-10 shows how to set portfast. The portfast status is shown in the *Fast-Start* column:

Example 7-10 *How to Enable Portfast on a Port and Verify the Configuration*

```
Switch># set spantree portfast 4/1 enable
Warning: Spantree port fast start should only be enabled on ports connected
to a single host.  Connecting hubs, concentrators, switches, bridges, etc. to
```

Example 7-10 *How to Enable Portfast on a Port and Verify the Configuration (Continued)*

```
a fast start port can cause temporary spanning tree loops.  Use with caution.
Spantree port 4/1 fast start enabled.
Switch>#  show spantree 4/1
Port      Vlan  Port-State       Cost   Priority  Fast-Start  Group-method
--------- ----  --------------   -----  --------  ----------  ------------
 4/1      1     blocking           19        20   enabled
 4/1      100   forwarding         10        20   enabled
 4/1      521   blocking           19        20   enabled
 4/1      522   blocking           19        20   enabled
 4/1      523   blocking           19        20   enabled
 4/1      524   blocking           19        20   enabled
 4/1      1003  not-connected      19        20   enabled
 4/1      1005  not-connected      19         4   enabled
Switch>#
```

Web-Based Interface

Intelligent networking devices can provide a web-based interface for configuration and management purposes. After a switch is configured with an IP address and gateway, you can access it in this way. A browser can be set to point at the IP address and port (default 80) for a web service. You can turn on or off the http service, and you can choose the port address for the service, as in Example 7-11.

Example 7-11 *Enabling HTTP Service and Port*

```
Switch(config)#ip http ?
  access-class     Restrict access by access-class
  authentication   Set http authentication method
  path             Set base path for HTML
  port             HTTP port
  server           Enable HTTP server
Switch(config)#ip http server

Switch(config)#ip http port ?
  <0-65535>  HTTP port

Switch(config)#ip http port 80
Switch(config)#
```

Any additional software (an applet) can be downloaded to the browser from the switch and the network devices managed by a browser-based graphical user interface (GUI).

 Lab Activity   Basic Switch Configuration

In this lab, you configure a switch with an IP address and ensure that access to the command-line interface is secured. You configure switch port speed and duplex properties and then save the active configuration. You also view the switch browser interface.

Managing the MAC Address Table

Switches learn the MAC addresses of PCs or workstations that are connected to their switch ports by examining the source address of frames that are received on that port. These learned MAC addresses are then recorded in a MAC address table. Frames having a destination MAC address that has been recorded in the table can be switched out the correct interface.

To examine the addresses that a switch has learned, enter the privileged exec command in Example 7-12.

Example 7-12 show mac-address-table *Output*

```
Switch#show mac-address-table
Dynamic Address Count:                  2
Secure Address Count:                   0
Static Address (User-defined) Count:    0
System Self Address Count:              13
Total MAC addresses:                    15
Maximum MAC addresses:                  8192
Non-static Address Table:
Destination Address  Address Type  VLAN  Destination Port
------------------   ------------  ----  --------------------
0010.7a60.ad7e       Dynamic          1  FastEthernet0/2
00e0.2917.1884       Dynamic          1  FastEthernet0/5
```

Addresses can be learned dynamically with a switch recording and maintaining thousands of MAC addresses and multiple addresses per port. To preserve memory and optimal operation of the switch, you sometimes need to discard learned entries from the MAC address table. To enable this, all entries in the MAC address table are time-stamped when the packet enters the port. Machines might have been removed from a port, turned off, or moved to another port on the same switch or a different switch. In addition, the network interface card might have been replaced. As a result, there is potential for confusion in frame forwarding. For all these reasons, if no frames are seen with a previously learned address, the MAC address entry is automatically discarded or aged out after 300 seconds.

Rather than wait for a dynamic entry to age out, the administrator has the option of using the privileged exec command **clear mac-address-table.** Example 7-13 shows the output of the **clear mac-address-table** command. MAC address entries that an administrator has configured can also be removed in this way. Clearing the table entries in this way ensures that addresses that are no longer valid are removed immediately.

Example 7-13 clear mac-address-table *Output*

```
Switch#clear mac-address-table
Switch#show mac-address-table
Dynamic Address Count:              0
Secure Address Count:               0
Static Address (User-defined) Count:  0
System Self Address Count:          13
Total MAC addresses:                14
Maximum MAC addresses:              8192
Non-static Address Table:
Destination Address  Address Type  VLAN  Destination Port
-------------------  ------------  ----  -------------------
```

 Lab Activity   Managing the MAC Address Table

In this lab, you create a basic switch configuration and manage switch MAC address tables.

Configuring Static MAC Addresses

It might be decided that a MAC address should be permanently assigned to an interface. The switch will not age out such a MAC address automatically.

A permanent address can be assigned to an interface because a specific server or user workstation must be attached to the port, and the MAC address is known. Security can also be enhanced.

To set a static MAC address entry for a switch interface, use the following command syntax in global configuration mode:

```
Switch(config)#mac-address-table static mac-address-of-host
Switch(config)#interface FastEthernetethernet-number vlan vlan-name
```

To remove this entry, use the **no** form of the command.

Output for the **mac-address-table** command is shown in Example 7-14.

Example 7-14 *Configuring Static MAC Address*

```
Switch(config)#mac-address-table ?
  aging-time  Set MAC address table entry maximum age
  secure      Configure a secure address
  static      Configure a static 802.1d static address
Switch(config)#mac-address-table static 0010.7a60.1884 interface
    FastEthernet0/5 vlan VLAN1


Remove Static MAC Address
Switch(config)#no mac-address-table static 0010.7a60.1884 interface
    FastEthernet0/5 vlan VLAN1
```

 Lab Activity   Configuring Static MAC Addresses

In this lab, you set and clear static MAC addresses on switch ports.

Configuring Port Security

Securing an internetwork is an important responsibility for a network administrator. Access layer switch ports are accessible through the structured cabling at wall outlets in offices and rooms; anyone can plug in a PC or laptop to one of these outlets. This is a potential entry point to the network by unauthorized users. Switches provide a feature called port security. You can limit the number of addresses that can be learned on an interface. You can configure the switch to take an action if this is exceeded, as in Example 7-15. You can set secure MAC addresses statically. However, securing MAC addresses statically can be a complex task that is prone to error.

Example 7-15 *Configuring Port Security*

```
Switch(config)#interface FastEthernet0/2
Switch(config-if)#port security ?
  action         action to take for security violation
```

Example 7-15 *Configuring Port Security (Continued)*

```
    max-mac-count  maximum mac address count
    <cr>


Switch(config-if)#port security action ?
    shutdown  shut down the port from which security violation is detected
    trap      send snmp trap for security violation
```

An alternative approach is to set port security on a switch interface. The first address that the switch learns dynamically becomes the secure address.

To reverse port security on an interface, use the **no** form of the command.

To verify port security status, enter the command **show port security.**

Lab Activity   Configuring Port Security

In this lab, you configure and manage port security for individual Fast Ethernet ports on a Catalyst switch.

Executing Adds, Moves, and Changes

When you add a new switch to a network, configure the switch name, an IP address for the switch in the management VLAN, a default gateway, and line passwords.

When you are adding a new switch, be sure to complete the following tasks:

- Configure the switch name.
- Determine and configure the IP address for management purposes.
- Configure a default gateway.
- Configure administrative access for the console, auxiliary, and virtual terminal (vty) interfaces.
- Configure security for the device.
- Configure the access switch ports as necessary.

When you move a host from one port or switch to another, you should remove configurations that can cause unexpected behavior. Configuration that is required can then be added.

When adding, changing, or moving hosts, be sure to complete the following tasks:

- Adding a MAC address:
  - — Configure port security.
  - — Configure the MAC address.
- Changing a MAC address:
  - — Remove MAC address restrictions.
- Moving a MAC address:
  - — Add the address to a new port.
  - — Configure port security on the new switch.
  - — Configure the MAC address to the port that is allocated for the new user.
  - — Remove the old port configuration.

 Lab Activity Add, Move, and Change MAC Addresses

In this lab, you move a PC from one switch port to another and add a new PC to the switch.

Managing Switch Operating System Images and Device Configuration Files

Document and maintain the operational configuration files for networking devices. Keep backup copies of the most recent **running-configuration** file on a server, or keep a separate copy on a disk. This is essential documentation that is useful if a configuration needs to be rebuilt. You can also use this information as a starting point when you are configuring similar switches.

Back up the IOS to a local server. This allows reloading of the IOS to flash memory if needed.

 Lab Activity Managing Switch Operating System Images

In this lab, you back up the IOS image file to a TFTP server and then restore the IOS to the switch.

 Lab Activity Managing Switch Startup Configuration Files

In this lab, you back up and restore the startup configuration file to a TFTP server and then restore to the switch.

1900/2950 Password Recovery

Any switch-management procedure ensures that passwords are set on the console and vty lines. An enable password and an enable secret password are also set. These practices help ensure that only authorized uses have access to the user exec and privileged exec modes of the switch.

Sometimes, you will achieve physical access to the switch but will be denied access to the user or privileged exec mode because the passwords are not known or have been forgotten.

In these circumstances, you must follow a password recovery procedure.

Lab Activity Password Recovery Procedure for a Catalyst 29XX Switch

In this lab, you regain control of the Catalyst 2900 switch after you have lost your password.

1900/2900 Firmware IOS Upgrade

IOS and firmware images are periodically released with bugs fixed, new features introduced, and performance improved. The network can be made more secure or can operate more efficiently with a new version of the IOS. In these circumstances, you should upgrade the IOS.

To upgrade the IOS, obtain a copy of the new image by downloading it to a local server from the Cisco.com Software Center.

Log in to the site with a customer username and password. After you have downloaded the image, you can install it to the switch.

Lab Activity Firmware Upgrade of a Catalyst 29XX Switch

In this lab, you upgrade the switch IOS and HTML files.

Summary

In this chapter, you learned the following:

- The concept and benefits of using a switch to segment a network
- How a switch learns addresses
- The different methods that a switch uses to forward traffic
- The default settings of a Catalyst switch
- How to set an IP address and default gateway for the switch to allow connection and management over a network
- How to view the switch settings with a web browser
- How to set interfaces for speed and duplex operation
- How to examine and manage the switch MAC address table
- How to configure port security
- How to manage configuration files and IOS images
- How to perform password recovery on a switch
- How to upgrade the IOS of a switch.

To supplement all that you've learned in this chapter, refer to the chapter-specific Videos, PhotoZooms, and e-Lab Activities on the CD-ROM accompanying this book.

Key Terms

asymmetric switching   A switching method that provides switched connections between ports with different bandwidths, such as between 10-Mbps ports and 100-Mbps ports.

broadcast domain   The set of all devices that will receive broadcast frames originating from any device within the set. Broadcast domains are typically bounded by routers because routers do not forward broadcast frames.

CAM (content-addressable memory)   Memory that is accessed based on its contents, not on its memory address.

collision domain   In Ethernet, the network area within which frames that have collided are propagated. Repeaters and hubs propagate collisions; LAN switches, bridges, and routers do not.

cut-through switching   A packet-switching approach that streams data through a switch so that the leading edge of a packet exits the switch at the output port before the packet finishes entering the input port. A device that uses cut-through packet switching reads, processes, and forwards packets as soon as the destination address is looked up and the outgoing port is determined. Cut-through switching is also known as on-the-fly packet switching.

fast-forward switching   A switching method whereby the switching actually starts before the entire packet is received by the switch.

fragment-free switching   A switching method in which the switch filters out the collision fragments, which are the majority of packet errors, before forwarding begins.

memory buffering   A buffering technique whereby packets are stored in memory before forwarding.

microsegment   Division of a network into smaller segments, usually with the intention of increasing aggregate bandwidth to network devices.

store-and-forward switching   A packet-switching technique in which frames are completely processed before being forwarded out the appropriate port. This processing includes calculating the cyclic redundancy check (CRC) and checking the destination address. In addition, frames must be temporarily stored until network resources (such as an unused link) are available to forward the message.

symmetric switching   A switching method that provides switched connections between ports with the same bandwidth, such as all 10-Mbps ports or all 100-Mbps ports.

Check Your Understanding

1. What do characteristics of microsegmentation include? Select all that apply.

   A. Dedicated paths between sender and receiver hosts

   B. Multiple traffic paths within the switch

   C. Increased collisions

   D. Creation of one broadcast domain for LAN

2. How are LAN switches characterized?

   A. Multiport repeaters operating at Layer 1

   B. Multiport hubs operating at Layer 2

   C. Multiport routers operating at Layer 3

   D. Multiport bridges operating at Layer 2

3. For what is symmetric switching optimized?

   A. Client-server network traffic where the "fast" switch port is connected

   B. An even distribution of network traffic

   C. Switches that lack memory buffering

   D. Load balancing between links

4. In _____ switching, the switch checks the destination address and immediately begins forwarding the frame, whereas in _____ switching, the switch receives the complete frame before forwarding it.

   A. Store-and-forward; symmetric

   B. Cut-through; store-and-forward

   C. Store-and-forward; cut-through

   D. Memory buffering; cut-through

5. Fragment-free and fast-forward switching are two forms of _____ switching.

   A. Store-and-forward

   B. Memory-buffering

   C. Cut-through

   D. Symmetric

6. When you connect a workstation to a switch, what is the proper cable?

   A. Straight-through

   B. Cross-over

   C. Null-modem

   D. Standard phone line

7. Which communication method is characterized by one host sending and one host receiving?

   A. Broadcast

   B. Unicast

   C. Multicast

   D. None of the above

Objectives

After reading this chapter, you will be able to

- Describe the goals of redundant topologies
- Define Spanning Tree Protocol (STP)
- Describe the stages of spanning-tree port states and election of designated ports
- Describe the stages of selecting a root bridge
- Describe Path cost
- Set STP timers
- Explain how STP helps convergence
- Describe Rapid Spanning Tree Protocol (RSTP)

Chapter 8

Spanning Tree Protocol

This chapter describes redundant topologies and how important they are for maintaining networks. In addition, this chapter describes the functionality of both Spanning Tree Protocol (STP) and RSTP.

Please be sure to look at this chapter's associated e-Lab Activities, Videos, and PhotoZooms that you will find on the CD-ROM accompanying this book. These CD-ROM elements are designed to supplement the material and reinforce the concepts introduced in this chapter.

Redundant Topology Overview

Having redundancy in a network is important. Redundancy allows for networks to be fault tolerant. Redundant topologies protect against network downtime due to a failure of a single link, port, or networking device. Redundant topologies that are based on switches and bridges are susceptible to broadcast storms, multiple frame transmissions, and *Media Access Control (MAC)* database instability.

What Is Redundancy?

Companies and organizations are relying increasingly on computer networks for their operations. Access to file servers, databases, the Internet, intranets, and extranets is critical for successful businesses. If the network is down, productivity is lost, and customers are dissatisfied.

Companies are looking for 24-hour, 7-day-a-week uptime for their computer networks. Achieving 100 percent uptime is perhaps impossible, but securing a 99.999 percent (or "five nines") uptime is a goal that organizations set. This is interpreted to mean 1 day of downtime, on average, every 30 years, or 1 hour of downtime, on average, every 4000 days, or 5.25 minutes of downtime per year. Also, this applies to many businesses (financial services, hospitals, ISPs, and so on) and comes at a high financial cost. Many others moderate reliability goals to reduce cost.

Achieving a goal of 99.999 percent reliability requires extremely reliable networks. Reliability in networks is achieved by reliable equipment and by designing networks that are tolerant of failures and faults. The network is designed to reconverge rapidly so that the fault is bypassed.

Fault tolerance is achieved by redundancy. Redundancy means being in excess or exceeding what is usual and natural. How does redundancy help achieve reliability? Assume that the only way to get to work is by car. If the car develops a fault that makes it unusable, going to work will be impossible until the car is repaired and returned.

If the car fails and is unavailable on average 1 day in 10, the car has a 90 percent usage rate. Going to work is possible 9 days in every 10. Reliability is 90 percent.

Buying another car will improve matters. There is not a need for two cars just to get to work, however. One of them is in excess of what is needed, but the second is available in case there is a problem with the first car. This insures increased reliability.

Redundant Topologies

The goal of redundant topologies is to eliminate network outages that are caused by a single point of failure. All networks need redundancy for enhanced reliability. The network of roads is a redundant topology. If one road is closed for repair, there is another way to get to the destination.

Consider a small suburb that is separated from the town center by a river. If there is only one bridge across the river, there is only one way into town. The topology has no redundancy.

If the bridge is flooded or damaged by an accident, travel to town across the bridge is impossible. Building a second bridge across the river creates a redundant topology. The town is not cut off from the town center if one bridge is impassable.

Redundant Switched Topologies

Networks that have redundant paths and devices allow for more network uptime. Redundant topologies eliminate single points of failure, as shown in Figure 8-1. If a path or device fails, the redundant path or device can take over the tasks of the failed path or device.

If Switch A fails, traffic can still flow from Segment 2 to Segment 1 and to the router link through Switch B.

If port 1 fails on Switch A, traffic can still flow through port 1 on Switch B.

Figure 8-1 Redundant Switch Topology

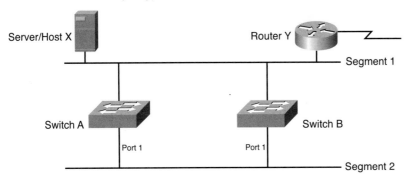

Switches learn the *MAC* addresses of devices on their ports so that data can be properly forwarded to the destination. Until switches learn the MAC addresses of devices, it is good to flood frames for unknown destinations. Broadcasts and multicasts should also be flooded.

A redundant-switched topology causes broadcast storms, multiple frame copies, and MAC address table instability problems.

Broadcast Storms

Broadcasts and multicasts are a potential cause of problems in a switched network. Switches treat multicasts as broadcasts. Broadcast and multicast frames are flooded. The frame is sent out all ports except the one on which the frame was received.

In Figure 8-2, if Host X sends a broadcast, such as an *Address Resolution Protocol (ARP)* request for the Layer 2 address of the router, Switch A forwards the broadcast out all ports. Because Switch B is on the same segment, it also forwards all broadcasts. Switch B sees all the broadcasts that Switch A forwards, and Switch A sees all the broadcasts that Switch B forwards. Switch A sees these new broadcasts and forwards them, as does Switch B. An example is shown in Figure 8-2.

The switches continue to propagate broadcast traffic. This is called a broadcast storm, and it continues until one of the switches is disconnected. The switches and end devices are so busy processing the broadcasts that user traffic is unlikely to flow. The network appears to be down or extremely slow.

Figure 8-2 Broadcast Storm

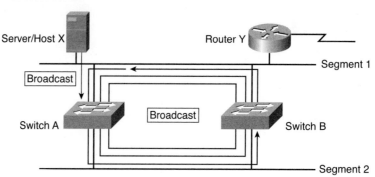

Multiple Frame Transmissions

In a redundant switched network, an end device can receive multiple copies of the same frame (see Figure 8-3).

Figure 8-3 Multiple Frame Transmissions

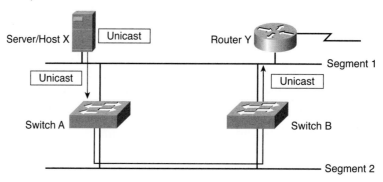

Most protocols are designed to ignore or cope with duplicate transmissions. In general, protocols that make use of a sequence numbering mechanism assume that many transmissions have failed and that the sequence number has recycled. Other protocols attempt to hand the duplicate transmission to the appropriate upper-layer protocol, with unpredictable results. To see how multiple transmissions can occur, refer to Figure 8-3 and consider the following:

- When Host X sends a unicast frame to Router Y, one copy is received over the direct Ethernet connection, segment 1, while Switch A receives a copy and puts it into its buffers.

- If Switch A examines the destination address field in the frame and finds no entry in the MAC address table for Router Y, it floods the frame on all ports except for the originating port.
- When Switch B receives a copy of the frame through Switch A on segment 2, it also forwards a copy of the frame onto segment 1 if there is no entry in the MAC address table for Router Y.
- Router Y receives a copy of the same frame for the second time.

A loop avoidance solution would eliminate the problem of duplicate transmissions by logically breaking the loop and preventing one of the four interfaces from transmitting frames during normal operation.

MAC Database Instability

In a redundant switched network, switches can learn the wrong information. A switch can learn that a MAC address is on a port when it is not. An example of MAC database instability is shown in Figure 8-4.

Figure 8-4 MAC Database Instability

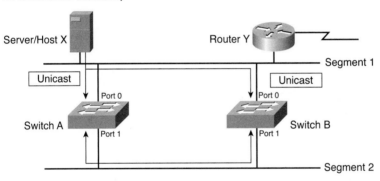

In this example, Switch B installs a mapping between the MAC address of Host X and Port 0, which connects to segment 1 when the first frame arrives. Sometime later, when the copy of the frame that was transmitted through Switch A arrives at port 1 of Switch B, Switch B must remove the first entry and install one that incorrectly maps the MAC address of Station X to the Port 1 that connects to Segment 2.

Depending on the internal architecture of the switch in question, the switch might or might not cope well with rapid changes in its MAC database. In this instance, a loop-avoidance solution would eliminate the problem of the switch not coping well with rapid changes in its MAC database by logically breaking the loop and preventing one of the four interfaces from transmitting frames during normal operation.

Spanning Tree Overview

Spanning Tree Protocol (STP) is a Layer 2 link-management protocol that is used to maintain a loop-free network. The Digital Equipment Corporation (Digital) originally developed STP. The IEEE 802 committee subsequently revised the Digital spanning-tree algorithm and published it in the IEEE 802.1d specification. Digital and the IEEE 802.1d algorithm are not the same and are not compatible. The Cisco switches, such as the Catalyst 1900 and the 2950, use the IEEE 802.1d STP.

The purpose of STP is to maintain a loop-free network topology. A loop-free topology is accomplished when the switch or bridge recognizes a loop in the topology and logically blocks one or more redundant ports automatically.

STP continually probes the network so that a failure or addition of a link, switch, or bridge gets a response. An example is shown in Figure 8-5. When the network topology changes, the switches and bridges that are running STP automatically reconfigure their ports to avoid loss of connectivity or creation of loops.

Figure 8-5 Spanning Tree Protocol

Physical layer loops can cause serious problems in switch-based internetworks. Broadcast storms, multiple frame transmissions, and MAC database instability can make such networks unusable.

Switched networks provide the benefits of smaller collision domains, microsegmentation, and full duplex operation. Put simply, the benefit is performance. STP is used in switched networks to create a loop-free logical topology from a physical topology that has loops. Links, ports, and switches that are not part of the active loop-free topology do not participate in the forwarding of data frames.

When a component of the active topology fails, you must determine a new loop-free topology. You need to recalculate or converge on a new loop-free topology as quickly as possible to reduce the time that end stations lack access to network resources.

STP that is defined in the IEEE 802.1d standard is too slow in converging on a new topology for today's networks. A new standard—IEEE 802.1w, or RSTP—has been defined to overcome known limitations. This chapter discusses both STP and RSTP.

Spanning-Tree Operation

When the network has stabilized, it has converged; each network has one spanning tree.

As a result, the following will be true for every switched network:

- One root bridge exists per network.
- One root port exists per nonroot bridge.
- One designated port exists per segment.
- Undesignated ports are unused.

Root ports and designated ports are used for forwarding (F) data traffic. Undesignated ports discard data traffic. These are called blocking (B) or discarding ports. The root port of a bridge is the port that is closest to the root bridge. Every nonroot bridge must select one root port. Figure 8-6 shows the spanning-tree operation.

Figure 8-6 Spanning-Tree Operation

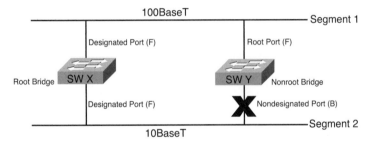

STP initially converges on a logically loop-free network topology by doing the following three steps:

1. **Electing a root bridge.** The protocol has a process to elect a root bridge. Only one bridge can act as the root bridge in a given network. On the root bridge, all ports are designated ports. Designated ports are normally in the forwarding state. When a port is in the forwarding state, it can send and receive traffic. In the example, Switch X is elected as the root bridge.

2. **Selecting the root port on the nonroot bridges.** STP establishes one root port on the nonroot bridge. The root port is the lowest-cost path from the nonroot bridge to the root bridge. Root ports are normally in the forwarding state. Spanning-tree path cost is an accumulated cost that is calculated on the bandwidth. In the example, from switch Y, the lowest-cost path to the root bridge is through the 100BaseT Fast Ethernet.

3. **Selecting the designated port on each segment.** On each segment, STP establishes one designated port. The designated port is selected on the bridge that has the lowest path cost to the root bridge. Designated ports are normally in the forwarding state, forwarding traffic for the segment. In the example, the designated port for both segments is on the root bridge because the root bridge is directly connected to both segments. The 10BASE-T Ethernet port on switch Y is a nondesignated port because there is only one designated port per segment. Nondesignated ports are normally in the blocking state to logically break the loop topology. When a port is in the blocking state, the port is not forwarding traffic, but it can still receive traffic.

Using Spanning Tree to Create a Loop-Free Topology

Redundant networking topologies are designed to ensure that networks continue to function in the presence of single points of failure. Users are less susceptible to interruptions to their work because the network continues to function. Any interruptions that a failure causes should be as short as possible.

Reliability is increased by redundancy. A network that is based on switches or bridges introduces redundant links between the switches or bridges to overcome the failure of a single link. These connections introduce physical loops into the network. An example is shown in Figure 8-7.

Figure 8-7 Bridging Loops

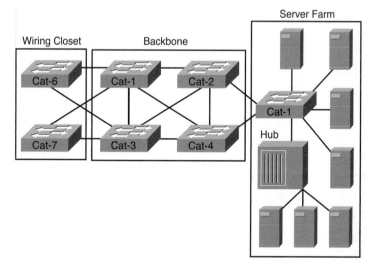

These bridging loops are created so that if one link fails, another can take over the function of forwarding traffic.

Switches operate at Layer 2 of the OSI model, and forwarding decisions are made at this layer. A consequence of this is that switched networks cannot have loops.

Switches flood traffic out all ports when it is for a destination that is not yet known. Broadcast and multicast traffic is forwarded out every port other than the port on which the traffic arrives (floods). This traffic can be caught in a loop. The Layer 2 header has no *time to live (TTL)*. If a frame is sent into a Layer 2 looped topology of switches, it can loop forever, wasting bandwidth and making the network unusable.

At least at Layer 3, the TTL is decremented and the packet is discarded when the TTL becomes 0. There is a dilemma, however. A physical topology that contains switching or bridging loops is necessary for reliability, but a switched network cannot have loops. The solution to this dilemma is to allow physical loops but create a loop-free logical topology.

The loop-free logical topology that is created is called a tree. This topology is a star or extended star logical topology—the spanning tree of the network. The topology is a spanning tree because all devices that are in the network are reachable or spanned. The algorithm that is used to create this loop-free logical topology is the spanning-tree algorithm. This algorithm can take a relatively long time to converge.

Advanced Functions of STP

STP establishes a root node, called the root bridge, and constructs a topology that has one path for reaching every network node. The resulting tree originates from the root bridge. Redundant links that are not part of the shortest path tree are blocked. A loop-free topology is possible because certain paths are blocked. Data frames that are received on blocked links are dropped.

STP requires network devices to exchange messages to detect bridging loops. Links that will cause a loop are put into a blocking state. The messages that switches send that allow the forming of a loop-free logical topology are called *bridge protocol data units (BPDUs)*. BPDUs continue to be received on blocked ports, which ensures that if an active path or device fails, a new spanning tree can be calculated.

The BPDUs contain enough information so that all switches can do the following:

- Select a single switch that will act as the root of the spanning tree.
- Calculate the shortest path from itself to the root switch.

- For each LAN segment, designate one of the switches as the closest one to the root. This bridge is called the designated switch. The designated switch handles all communication from that LAN toward the root bridge.
- Each nonroot switch chooses one of its ports as its root port. This is the interface that gives the best path to the root switch.
- Select ports that are part of the spanning tree, the designated ports. Nondesignated ports are blocked.

When the spanning tree is creating a loop-free logical topology, it always uses the same four-step decision sequence:

1. Lowest root *bridge ID (BID)*
2. Lowest path cost to root bridge
3. Lowest sender bridge ID
4. Lowest port ID

A bridge uses this four-step decision sequence to save a copy of the "best" BPDU that is seen on every port. When a bridge is making this evaluation, it considers all the BPDUs that have been received on the port as well as the BPDU that would be sent on that port. As every BPDU arrives, it is checked against this four-step sequence to see if it is more attractive (that is, lower in value) than the existing BPDU that is saved for that port. If the new BPDU (or the locally generated BPDU) is more attractive, the old value is replaced.

Additionally, this "saving-the-best-BPDU" process controls the sending of BPDUs. When a bridge first becomes active, all of its ports are sending BPDUs every 2 seconds (when using the default timer values). However, if a port hears a BPDU from another bridge that is more attractive than the BPDU it has been sending, the local port stops sending BPDUs. If the more attractive BPDU stops arriving from a neighbor for a period of time (20 seconds by default), the local port can once again resume sending BPDUs.

Selecting the Root Bridge

With STP, the root bridge is the bridge that has the lowest BID. The BID includes the priority and the MAC address of the bridge.

Switches and bridges that are running the spanning-tree algorithm exchange configuration messages with other switches and bridges at regular intervals (every two seconds by default) by using the BPDU. One of the pieces of information that is included in the BPDU is the BID.

STP calls for each bridge to be assigned a unique identifier (BID). Typically, the BID is made up of a priority value (two bytes) and the bridge MAC address (six bytes). The default priority, in accordance with IEEE 802.1d, is 32,768 (1000 0000 0000 0000 in binary, or 0x8000 in hex), which is the midrange value.

In Figure 8-8, both switches use the same default priority; the one that has the lowest MAC address will be the root bridge. In this example, Switch X (SW X) is the root bridge with a bridge ID of 0x8000 (0c00.1111.1111).

NOTE

A Cisco Catalyst switch uses one of its MAC addresses from a pool of MAC addresses that are assigned to either the backplane or to the supervisory module, depending on the switch model.

Figure 8-8 Root Bridge Selection

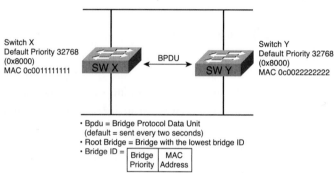

The bridge ID shown in Figure 8-9 consists of a bridge priority that defaults to 32568 and the switch base MAC address.

Figure 8-9 Bridge ID

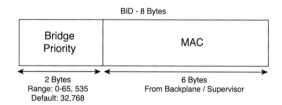

When a switch first starts up, it assumes it is the root switch and sends "inferior" BPDUs. These contain the switch MAC address in both the root and sender BID. All switches see the BIDs sent. As a switch receives a BPDU that has a lower root BID, it replaces that in the BPDUs it sends. All bridges see these and decide that the bridge with the smallest BID value will be the root bridge.

An administrator can influence the decision by setting the switch priority to a smaller value than the default. This makes the bridge ID smaller.

A network administrator might want to influence the outcome of an election for the root bridge. This is often the case when the traffic flow in the network is well understood.

 Lab Activity Selecting the Root Bridge

In this lab, you determine which switch is selected as the root switch with factory default settings. You then force the other switch to be selected as the root switch.

Stages of Spanning-Tree Port States

When STP is enabled, every bridge in the network goes through the blocking and transitory states of listening and learning at powerup. If the ports are properly configured, they then stabilize to the forwarding or blocking state. Forwarding ports provide the lowest-cost path to the root bridge. Two transitional states occur when a bridge recognizes a change in the network topology. During a topology change, a port temporarily implements the listening and learning states. Figure 8-10 shows the spanning-tree port states.

Figure 8-10 Spanning-Tree Port States

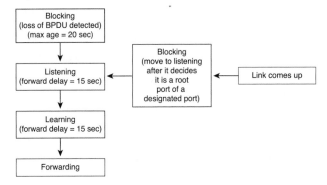

Initially, all bridge ports start in the blocking state where they listen for BPDUs. When the bridge first boots up, it thinks it is the root bridge and transitions to the listening state. An absence of BPDUs for a certain period of time (the max age) can cause a transition from the blocking state to the listening state. When a port is in the transitional listening state, it can send and receive BPDUs to determine the active topology. At this point, no user data is being passed. It is during the listening state that the bridge performs the steps of electing the root bridge, electing the root ports on the nonroot bridges, and electing the designated ports on each segment.

Ports that remain as designated or root ports after 15 seconds (the forward delay) transition to the learning state. Ports that are not the designated or root ports transition back to the blocking state. When a port is in a learning state, it can populate its MAC address table with MAC addresses that are heard on its ports, but it does not forward user frames. The learning state lasts 15 seconds (also the forward delay) by default. At this point, the bridge still does not pass user data.

STP states are as follows:

- **Blocking**—No frames forwarded; BPDUs heard
- **Listening**—No frames forwarded; listening for frames
- **Learning**—No frames forwarded; learning addresses
- **Forwarding**—Frames forwarded; learning addresses
- **Disabled**—No frames forwarded; no BPDUs heard

The learning state reduces the amount of flooding that is required when data forwarding begins. If a port is still a designated or root port at the end of the learning state, the port transitions to the forwarding state. Ports that are not the designated or root ports transition back to the blocking state. In the forwarding state, a port is capable of sending and receiving user data.

The normal time that it takes for a port to transition from the blocking state to the forwarding state is 30 to 50 seconds. You can tune spanning-tree timers to adjust the timing. Normally, you should set these timers to the default value. The default values are put in place to give the network enough time to gather all the correct information about the network topology.

The time that it takes for a port to transition from the listening state to the learning state or from the learning state to the forwarding state is called the forward delay, which has a default value of 15 seconds. The max age, which has a default value of 20 seconds, is the time that a bridge stores a BPDU before discarding it. If a port is in the blocking state and it does not receive a new BPDU within the max age, it transitions from the blocking state to the listening state.

If a switch port is only connected to end user stations (not connected to another switch or bridge), you should enable a Catalyst switch feature called *portfast* on those end user ports. With portfast, when the port first comes up, it automatically transitions from the blocking state to the forwarding state. This is acceptable because no loops can be formed through those ports because there are no other switches or bridges that are connected to it. Figure 8-11 shows a sample network with port states.

Figure 8-11 Sample Network with Port States

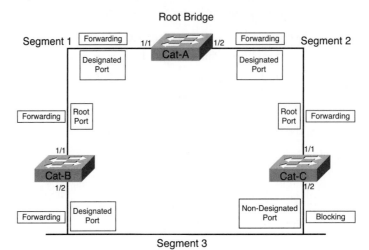

Electing Designated Ports

Each segment in a bridged network has one designated port. This port functions as the single bridge port that both sends and receives traffic to and from that segment and the root bridge. The idea behind this is that if only one port handles traffic for each link, all the loops have been broken. The bridge that contains the designated port for a given segment is referred to as the *designated bridge* for that segment.

At the conclusion of the root war, the switches move on to selecting root ports. The root port of a bridge is the port that is closest to the root bridge. Every nonroot bridge must select one root port.

Again, bridges use the concept of cost to measure closeness. Specifically, bridges track what is referred to as root path cost, which is the cumulative cost of all links to the root bridge. Figure 8-12 shows an example of how root ports are elected and illustrates how this value is calculated across multiple bridges and the resulting root port election process.

When Cat-A (the root bridge) sends BPDUs, the BPDUs will contain a root path cost of 0 (Step 1). When Cat-B receives these BPDUs, it adds the path cost of Port 1/1 to the root path cost that is contained in the received BPDU. Assume that the network is running Fast Ethernet. Cat-B receives a root path cost of 0 and adds in the Port 1/1 cost of 19 (Step 2). Cat-B then uses the value of 19 internally and sends BPDUs with a root path cost of 19 out Port 1/ 2 (Step 3).

Figure 8-12 Electing Root Ports

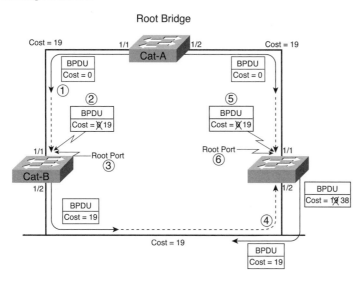

When Cat-C receives these BPDUs from Cat-B (Step 4), it increases the root path cost to 38 (19 + 19). However, Cat-C is also receiving BPDUs from the root bridge on Port 1/1. These BPDUs enter Cat-C Port 1/1 with a cost of 0, and Cat-C increases the cost to 19 internally (Step 5). Cat-C has a decision to make: It must select a single root port—the port that is closest to the root bridge. Cat-C sees a root path cost of 19 on Port 1/1 and 38 on Port 1/2. Therefore, Cat-C Port 1/1 becomes the root port (Step 6). Cat-C then begins advertising this root path cost of 19 to downstream switches (Step 7).

Although Cat-B is not detailed in Figure 8-13, it goes through a similar set of calculations. Cat-B Port 1/1 can reach the root bridge at a cost of 19, whereas Cat-B Port 1/2 calculates a cost of 38. Therefore, Port 1/1 becomes the root port for Cat-B. Notice that costs are incremented as BPDUs are received on a port.

Remember that STP costs are incremented as BPDUs are received on a port, not as they are sent out a port. For example, BPDUs arrive on Cat-B Port 1/1 with a cost of 0 and are increased to 19 "inside" Cat-B.

The loop-prevention part of STP becomes apparent during the third step of initial STP convergence: electing designated ports. Each segment in a bridged network has one designated port. This port functions as the single bridge port that both sends and receives traffic to and from that segment and the root bridge. The idea behind this is that if only one port handles traffic for each link, all the loops have been broken. The bridge that contains the designated port for a given segment is referred to as the *designated bridge* for that segment.

Figure 8-13 Electing Designated Ports

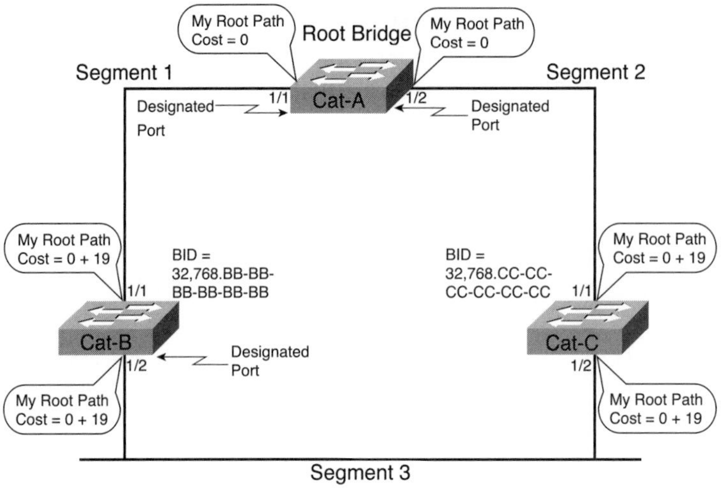

As with the root-port selection, the designated ports are chosen based on cumulative root path cost to the root bridge, as shown in Figure 8-13. In Figure 8-13, locate the designated ports and look at each segment in turn. First look at Segment 1, the link between Cat-A and Cat-B. There are two bridge ports on the segment: Cat-A Port 1/1 and Cat-B Port 1/1. Cat-A Port 1/1 has a root path cost of 0 (after all, it is the root bridge), whereas Cat-B Port 1/1 has a root path cost of 19 (the value 0 received in BPDUs from Cat-A plus the path cost of 19 assigned to Cat-B Port 1/1). Because Cat-A Port 1/1 has the lower root path cost, it becomes the designated port for this link.

For Segment 2 (Cat-A to Cat-C link), a similar election takes place. Cat-A Port 1/2 has a root path cost of 0, whereas Cat-C Port 1/1 has a root path cost of 19. Cat-A Port 1/2 has the lower cost and becomes the designated port. Notice that every active port on the root bridge becomes a designated port. The only exception to this rule is a Layer 1 physical loop to the root bridge. Examples of this occur when two ports on the root bridge are connected to the same hub or two ports are connected via a crossover cable.

Now look at Segment 3 (Cat-B to Cat-C): Both Cat-B Port 1/2 and Cat-C Port 1/2 have a root path cost of 19. There is a tie. When STP is faced with a tie (or any other determination), it always uses the four-step decision sequence that was discussed earlier in the section "Spanning Tree Protocol." Recall that the four steps are as follows:

- Lowest root BID
- Lowest path cost to root bridge
- Lowest sender BID
- Lowest port ID

In the example shown in Figure 8-13, all three bridges agree that Cat-A is the root bridge, causing root path cost to be evaluated next. However, as pointed out in the previous paragraph, both Cat-B and Cat-C have a cost of 19. This causes BID, the third decision criterion, to be the deciding factor. Because the Cat-B BID (32,768.BB-BB-BB-BB-BB-BB) is lower than the Cat-C BID (32,768.CC-CC-CC-CC-CC-CC), Cat-B Port 1/2 becomes the designated port for Segment 3. Cat-C Port 1/2, therefore, becomes a nondesignated port.

Path Cost

Spanning-tree path cost is an accumulated total path cost based on the bandwidth of all the links in the path. Table 8–1 shows some of the path costs that are specified in IEEE 802.1D for various networking technologies such as Token Ring, Ethernet, and SONET. Bridges use the concept of cost to evaluate how close they are to other bridges. The 802.1D standard originally defined cost as 1000 Mbps divided by the bandwidth of the link in Mbps. With the advent of 10 Gigabit Ethernet, this formula is no longer appropriate. Table 8-2 shows previously defined and current link costs for various Ethernet technologies.

Table 8-1 Path Cost for Various Networking Technologies

Bandwidth	STP Cost
4 Mbps	250
10 Mbps	100
16 Mbps	62
45 Mbps	39
100 Mbps	19
155 Mbps	14
622 Mbps	6
1 Gbps	4
10 Gbps	2

Table 8-2 Link Cost Revisions for Ethernet

Link Speed	Cost (Revised IEEE Spec)	Cost (Previous IEEE Spec)
10 Gbps	2	1
1 Gbps	4	1
100 Mbps	19	10
10 Mbps	100	100

You can see from the table how link cost is used by bridges to evaluate how close they are to other bridges. For example, a 10BASE-T link has a cost of 100 (1000/10), and Fast Ethernet and Fiber Distributed Data Interface (FDDI) have a cost of 10 (1000/100). This scheme has served the world well since Radia Perlman first began working on STP in 1983. However, with the implementation of Gigabit Ethernet and OC-48 ATM (2.4 Gbps), a problem has surfaced: The cost is stored as an integer value that does not account for fractional cost values. For example, OC-48 ATM results in 1000 Mbps / 2400 Mbps = 0.41667. 0.41667 is an invalid cost value, which means it would be rounded up to 1, along with every technology that has a bandwidth of 1 Gbps and higher. One option is to use a cost of 1 for all links that are equal to or greater than 1 Gbps. However, this prevents STP from accurately choosing "the best path" in gigabit networks. For a solution, the IEEE decided to modify cost to use a nonlinear scale.

STP Timers

The hello time controls the time interval between the sending of configuration BPDUs. The 802.1D standard specifies a default value of 2 seconds. This value really controls only configuration BPDUs as they are generated at the root bridge. Other bridges propagate BPDUs from the root bridge as they are received. In other words, if BPDUs stop arriving for 2–20 seconds because of a network disturbance, nonroot bridges stop sending periodic BPDUs during this time. If the outage lasts for more than 20 seconds, which is the default max age time, the bridge invalidates the saved BPDUs and begins looking for a new root port. Max age is the time that a bridge stores a BPDU before discarding it.

Forward delay is the time that the bridge spends in the listening and learning states. Forward delay is a single value that controls both states. The default value of 15 seconds was originally derived assuming a maximum network size of seven bridge hops, a maximum of three lost BPDUs, and a hello-time interval of 2 seconds. The forward-delay timer also controls the bridge table age-out period after a change in the active topology.

Recall that each port saves a copy of the best BPDU it has seen. As long as the bridge receives a continuous stream of BPDUs every 2 seconds, the receiving bridge maintains a continuous copy of the BPDU values. However, if the device that is sending this best BPDU fails, a mechanism must exist to allow other bridges to take over. Table 8-3 shows some STP Timers.

Table 8-3 STP Timers

Timer	Purpose	Default
Hello Time	Time between sending of configuration BPDUs by the root bridge	2 seconds
Forward Delay	Duration of listening and learning states	15 seconds
Max Age	Time BPDU stored	20 seconds

In some situations, switches can detect topology changes on directly connected links and immediately transition into the listening state without waiting max age seconds.

For example, assume that the Segment 3 link in Figure 8-14 uses a hub and the Cat-B Port 1/2 transceiver fails. Cat-C has no immediate notification of the failure because it is still receiving an Ethernet "link" from the hub. The only thing Cat-C knows is that BPDUs stop arriving. Twenty seconds (max age) after the failure, Cat-C Port 1/2 ages out the BPDU information that lists Cat-B as having the best designated port for Segment 3. This forces Cat-C Port 1/2 to transition into the listening state in an effort to become the designated port. Because Cat-C Port 1/2 now offers the most attractive access from the root bridge to this link, it eventually transitions all the way into forwarding mode. In practice, it takes approximately 50 seconds (20 max age + 15 listening + 15 learning) for Cat-C to take over after the failure of Port 1/2 on Cat-B.

In some situations, switches can detect topology changes on directly connected links and immediately transition into the listening state without waiting max age seconds. For example, consider Figure 8-15.

In this example, Cat-C Port 1/1 failed. Because the failure results in a loss of link on the root port, it is not necessary to wait 20 seconds for the old information to age out. Instead, Cat-C Port 1/2 immediately goes into learning mode in an attempt to become the new root port. This has the effect of reducing STP convergence time from 50 seconds to 30 seconds (15 listening + 15 learning).

Figure 8-14 Sample Network with Port States Identified

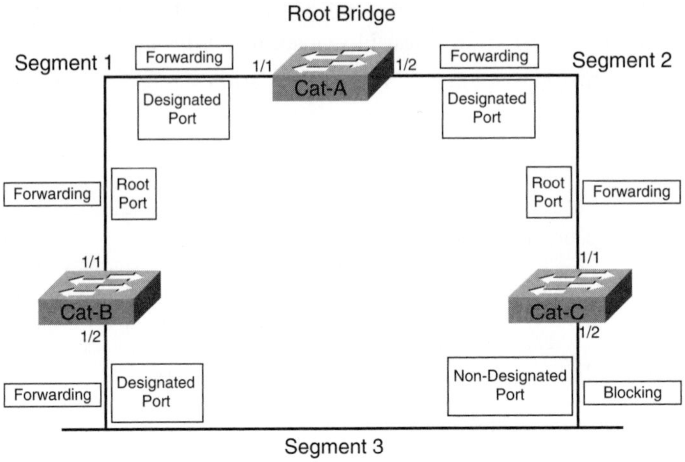

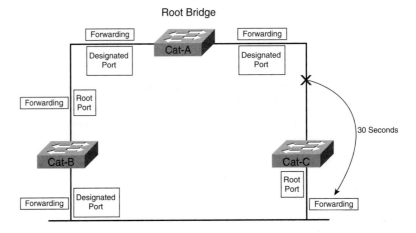

Figure 8-15 Sample Network with Port States Identified

There are two key points to remember about using STP timers. First, do not change the default timer values without careful consideration. When attempting to maximize timer settings, modify only the STP timers on the root bridge because the BPDUs contain three fields where the timer values can be passed from the root bridge to all other bridges in the network. Consider the alternative: If every bridge were locally configured, some bridges could work their way up to the forwarding state before other bridges ever left the listening state. This chaotic approach could quickly lead to an unstable network. By providing timer fields in the BPDUs, the single bridge that is acting as the root bridge can dictate the timing parameters for the entire bridged network.

Spanning-Tree Recalculation

If a change occurs to the network topology, STP maintains connectivity by transitioning some blocked ports to the forwarding state. When there is a topology change due to a bridge or link failure, the spanning tree readjusts the network topology to ensure connectivity by placing blocked ports in the forwarding state.

In Figure 8-16, if Switch X (the root bridge) fails and does not send a BPDU to Switch Y within the max age (default is 20 seconds, which equals 10 missed BPDUs), Switch Y detects the missing BPDU from the root bridge. Then, when the max age timer on Switch Y expires before a new BPDU has been received from Switch X, a new spanning-tree recalculation is initiated. Switch Y transitions its blocking port (port 1) from the blocking state to the listening state to the learning state and then to the forwarding state.

Figure 8-16 Spanning-Tree Recalculation

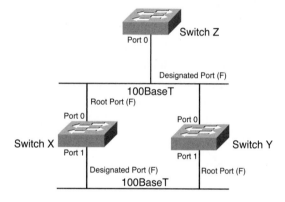

About 50 seconds after the network is converged, Switch Y becomes the root bridge and forwards traffic between the two segments.

Lab Activity   Spanning-Tree Recalculation

In this lab, you observe the behavior of the spanning-tree algorithm in the presence of switched network topology changes.

Convergence

Convergence is a necessity for normal network operations. For a switched or bridged network, a key issue is the amount of time that is required for convergence when network topology changes. Convergence in STP means a state in which all the switch and bridge ports have transitioned to either the forwarding or the blocking state.

Fast convergence is a desirable network feature because it reduces the period of time that bridges and switches have ports in transitional states and are not sending user traffic. The normal convergence time can take from 30 to 50 seconds.

RSTP

(RSTP) is designed to significantly speed the recalculation of the spanning tree when the network topology changes. RSTP defines the additional port roles of alternate and backup and defines port states as discarding, learning, or forwarding.

RSTP (IEEE 802.1w) significantly reduces the time to reconverge the active topology of the network when changes to the physical topology or its configuration parameters occur. RSTP selects one switch as the root of a spanning-tree-connected active topology and assigns port roles to individual ports on the switch, depending on whether the ports are part of the active topology.

RSTP provides rapid connectivity following the failure of a switch, switch port, or a LAN. A new root port and the designated port on the other side of the bridge transition to forwarding through an explicit handshake between them. RSTP allows switch port configuration so that the ports can transition to forwarding directly when the switch reinitializes. RSTP, specified in IEEE 802.1w, supersedes STP specified in 802.1d, while remaining compatible with the STP. To use the RSTP features, you must have the enhanced software image (EI) installed on your switch.

RSTP uses the following definitions for port roles:

- **Root**—A forwarding port that is elected for the spanning-tree topology.
- **Designated**—A forwarding port that is elected for every switched LAN segment.
- **Alternate**—An alternate path to the root bridge to that provided by the current root port.
- **Backup**—A backup for the path that is provided by a designated port toward the leaves of the spanning tree. Backup ports can exist only where two ports are connected together in a loopback by a point-to-point link or bridge with two or more connections to a shared LAN segment.
- **Disabled**—A port that has no role within the operation of the spanning tree.

A root port or designated port role includes the port in the active topology. An alternate port or backup port role excludes the port from the active topology.

RSTP Port States

The port state controls the forwarding and learning processes and provides the values of discarding, learning, and forwarding. Table 8-4 compares STP port states to RSTP port states.

Table 8-4 STP Port States Compared to RSTP Port States

Operational Status	STP Port State	RSTP Port State	Port Included in Active Topology
Enabled	Blocking	Discarding	No
Enabled	Listening	Discarding	No
Enabled	Learning	Learning	Yes
Enabled	Forwarding	Forwarding	Yes
Disabled	Disabled	Discarding	No

In a stable topology, RSTP ensures that every root port and designated port transitions to forwarding, whereas all alternate ports and backup ports are always in the discarding state.

Transition to Forwarding

The rapid transition is the most important feature introduced with IEEE 802.1w. Before the introduction of 802.1w, the spanning-tree algorithm waited passively for the network to converge before transitioning a port to the forwarding state. The new RSTP actively confirms that a port can safely transition to forwarding without relying on a timer configuration. To achieve fast convergence on a port, the protocol relies on two new variables: edge port and link type.

Edge ports are those that are directly connected to end stations. They cannot create bridging loops in the network; therefore, they can go directly to forwarding and skip the listening and learning stages. An edge port does not generate topology changes when its link toggles.

RSTP is only able to achieve rapid transition to forwarding on edge ports and on point-to-point links. On today's switched networks, this is not a big constraint. The link type is automatically derived from the duplex mode of a port. A port that is operating in full-duplex mode is point-to-point, whereas a port that is operating in half-duplex mode is considered shared by default. You can override the automatic link-type setting with an explicit configuration. Figure 8-17 shows an example of rapid transition to forwarding.

Figure 8-17 Rapid Transition to Forwarding

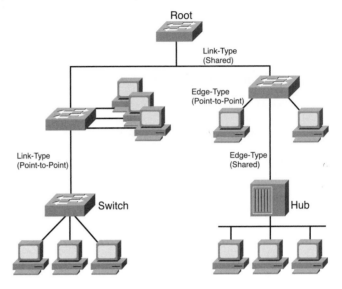

RSTP (IEEE 802.1w) will eventually replace the STP (IEEE 802.1d).

Summary

This chapter covered the following STP topics:

- Discussed issues such as redundant topologies, redundant switched topologies, broadcast storms, multiple frame transmissions, and MAC database instability.
- Redundant topologies provide for more reliable and fault-tolerant networks.
- STP and the spanning-tree algorithm ensure a loop-free logical topology in a physical topology that can have loops.
- Discussed the various concepts that are inportant in how STP works such as, spanning-tree operation, spanning tree, selecting the root bridge, stages of spanning-tree port states, electing designated ports, path cost, STP timers, spanning-tree recalculation, and convergence.
- Discussed issues related to RSTP, RSTP port states, and transition to forwarding.

To supplement all that you've learned in this chapter, refer to the chapter-specific Videos, PhotoZooms, and e-Lab Activities on the CD-ROM accompanying this book.

Key Terms

ARP (Address Resolution Protocol)   Internet protocol used to map an IP address to a MAC address.

BID (bridge ID)   This is the number with which the bridge or switches use to identify priority and root bridge or switch selection. The root bridge is the bridge that has the lowest BID.

BPDU (bridge protocol data unit)   Spanning Tree Protocol hello packet that is sent out at configurable intervals to exchange information among bridges in the network.

designated bridge   The bridge that incurs the lowest path cost when forwarding a frame from a segment to the root bridge.

MAC (Media Access Control)   The lower of the two sublayers of the data link layer that the IEEE defined. The MAC sublayer handles access to shared media, such as whether token passing or contention will be used.

portfast   A command that causes a port to enter the spanning tree forwarding state immediately, bypassing the listening and learning states.

RSTP (Rapid Spanning Tree Protocol)   RSTP defines the additional port roles and defines port states as discarding, learning, or forwarding.

STP (Spanning Tree Protocol)   A Layer 2 link-management protocol that is used to maintain a loop-free network. STP continually probes the network so that a failure or addition of a link, switch, or bridge is responded to.

TTL (time to live)   A field in the IP that specifies how many more hops a packet can travel before being discarded or returned.

Check Your Understanding

1. The goal of redundant topologies is to eliminate network outages that are caused by how many points of failure?

    A. One

    Two

    Three

    Four

2. What is the purpose of Spanning Tree Protocol?

   A. To maintain single loop paths

   B. To maintain a loop-free network

   C. To maintain a multiloop network

   D. To maintain a reduced loop network

3. When the network topology changes, _____.

   A. you must initiate a spanning-tree recalculation

   B. you must reconfigure the top node of the spanning tree

   C. you must reconfigure all devices that are participating in the spanning tree

   D. Spanning Tree Protocol reconfigures switch or bridge ports automatically

4. On the root bridge, all ports are _____.

   A. root ports

   B. blocked ports

   C. designated ports

   D. nondesignated ports

5. How does Spanning Tree Protocol select the root port on a nonroot bridge?

   A. Its root port is the highest-cost path from the nonroot bridge to the root bridge.

   B. The root port is the lowest-cost path from the nonroot bridge to the root bridge.

   C. The root port is the lowest-cost path from the nonroot bridge to the backup root bridge.

   D. The root port is the highest-cost path from the nonroot bridge to the backup root bridge.

6. Which bridge does Spanning Tree Protocol select as the root bridge?

   A. The one that has the lowest priority

   B. The one that has the lowest bridge ID

   C. The one that has the highest bridge ID

   D. The one that has the highest MAC address

7. What composes Spanning Tree Protocol BID?

   A. Bridge priority and bridge IP address

   B. Bridge priority and bridge MAC address

   C. Bridge MAC address and bridge IP address

   D. Bridge MAC address and Ethernet port number

8. In what state can a port populate its MAC address table but not forward user frames?

   A. Learning state

   B. Blocking state

   C. Listening state

   D. Forwarding state

9. In the revised IEEE specification, what is the cost of a 100-Mbps link?

   A. 4

   B. 10

   C. 19

   D. 100

10. What is the definition of convergence for Spanning Tree Protocol?

   A. All the ports have transitioned to the blocking state.

   B. All the ports have transitioned to the forwarding state.

   C. All the ports have transitioned to either the forwarding or the listening state.

   D. All the ports have transitioned to either the forwarding or the blocking state.

11. What is the default max age for Spanning Tree Protocol?

   A. 2 seconds

   B. 15 seconds

   C. 20 seconds

   D. 30 seconds

12. What is Rapid Spanning Tree Protocol equivalent state to the Spanning Tree Protocol blocking state?

   A. Blocking

   B. Dropping

   C. Discarding

   D. Forwarding

13. Which port role specifies a forwarding port that is elected for every switched LAN segment when using Rapid Spanning Tree Protocol?

    A. Root

    B. Backup

    C. Alternate

    D. Designated

14. How does STP provide a loop-free network?

    A. By placing all ports in the blocking state

    B. By placing all bridges in the blocking state

    C. By placing some ports in the blocking state

    D. By placing some bridges in the blocking state

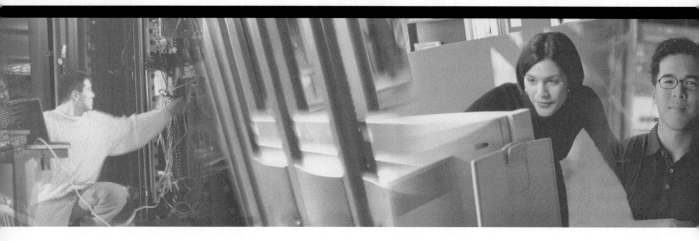

Objectives

After reading this chapter, you will be able to

- Explain what VLANs are
- Cite reasons to create VLANs and describe the benefits of VLANs
- Name and describe the methods of VLAN implementation
- Create, verify, and delete VLAN configurations
- Describe basic VLAN troubleshooting methods

Chapter 9

Virtual LANs

This chapter provides an introduction to virtual local-area networks (VLANs) and discusses the benefits of using a switched VLAN architecture. It also describes the concepts and operations of VLANs. In addition, this chapter provides instructions for the creation, verification, and deletion of VLANs. Finally, this chapter covers troubleshooting steps, which you can use to identify and resolve issues with VLAN implementations.

Be sure to look at this chapter's associated e-Lab Activities, Videos, and PhotoZooms that you will find on the CD-ROM that accompanies this book. These CD-ROM elements are designed to supplement the material and reinforce the concepts that are introduced in this chapter.

VLAN Introduction

A major feature of Ethernet switching technology is called a *VLAN*, where switches are used to cluster workstations and servers into logical groupings. The devices in a VLAN are restricted to communicating with devices on their own VLAN so that the switched network operates like a number of unconnected individual LANs. It is often difficult to get an exact definition for a VLAN because vendors take varied approaches to creating VLANs.

Businesses often use VLANs as a way of ensuring that a particular set of users is logically grouped. Compare this to a traditional workplace where departments were usually grouped in one "local" area; thus, a LAN was a natural development to meet the needs. Now people are not tied to physical spaces, so VLANs have developed "logical" areas. For example, people who work in the Marketing section of the business are placed in the Marketing VLAN, whereas people who work in the Engineering section are placed in the Engineering VLAN.

VLANs address scalability, security, and network management. Routers in VLAN topologies provide broadcast filtering, security, and traffic flow management.

A VLAN is a group of network devices and services that is not restricted to a physical segment or switch. Figure 9-1 shows the logical grouping of workstations in VLANs as compared to the physical grouping of workstations in traditional LANs.

Figure 9-1 VLANs and Physical Boundaries

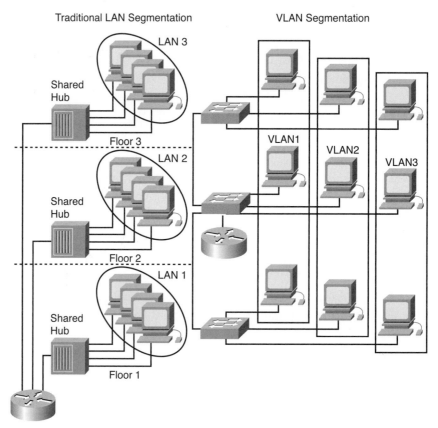

VLANs logically segment switched networks based on an organization's functions, project teams, or applications rather than on a physical or geographical basis. For example, all the workstations and servers that a particular workgroup team uses could be connected to the same VLAN, regardless of their physical connections to the network or location. Figure 9-2 shows a sample physical VLAN design with three VLANs defined across two switches and interconnected by a router. Reconfiguration of the network can be done through software rather than by physically unplugging and moving devices or cables.

Figure 9-2 VLAN Design

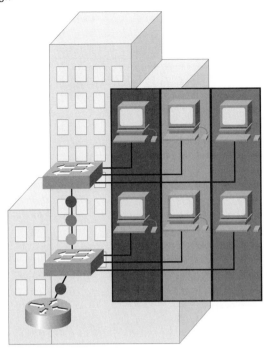

Figure 9-3 shows a physical VLAN design based on different company workgroups and floor locations. In this example, a VLAN is defined for each department (Engineering, Marketing, and Accounting), which spans three switches in three different physical locations.

A client workstation on a VLAN is generally restricted to contacting only file servers that are on the same VLAN. A VLAN can be thought of as a broadcast domain that exists within a defined set of switches. VLANs consist of a number of end systems, either hosts or network equipment (such as bridges and routers), connected by a single bridging domain. The bridging domain is supported on various pieces of network equipment, such as LAN switches that operate bridging protocols, with a separate bridge group for each VLAN.

Figure 9-3 VLANs Span Physical Locations

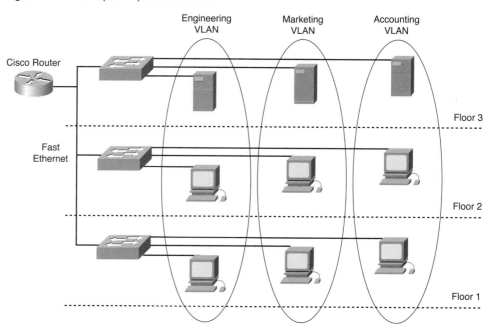

VLANs are created to provide the segmentation services that routers traditionally provide in LAN configurations. Routers in VLAN topologies provide *broadcast* filtering, security, and traffic flow management. Switches might not bridge traffic between VLANs because this would violate the integrity of the VLAN broadcast domain. Traffic should only be routed between VLANs.

Broadcast Domains with VLANs and Routers

A VLAN is a broadcast domain that one or more switches creates.

In the following scenario, the network design requires two separate broadcast domains. In Figure 9-4, two separate broadcast domains are established by using three separate switches—one for each broadcast domain. Note that the router allows the packets to be routed between the broadcast domains, which are like separate Layer 3 groupings. This can be accomplished by using a single or multiple connections to the router.

Figure 9-4 VLAN Broadcast Distribution

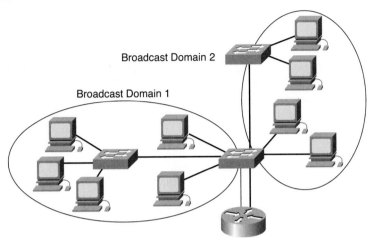

VLAN Operation

A VLAN makes up a switched network that is logically segmented by functions, project teams, or applications, without regard to the physical location of users. Each switch port can be assigned to a VLAN. Ports that are assigned to the same VLAN share broadcasts. Ports that do not belong to that VLAN do not share these broadcasts. This improves the overall performance of the network by reducing unnecessary broadcasts that consume bandwidth after network. There are two methods in which to create VLANs:

- **Static VLANs**—This method is also referred to as port-based membership. Assigning ports to a VLAN creates static VLAN assignments. As a device is connected to the network, it automatically assumes the VLAN of the port. If the user changes ports and needs access to the same VLAN, the network administrator must manually make a port-to-VLAN assignment for the new connection. An example of this is shown in Figure 9-5.

- **Dynamic VLANs**—Dynamic VLANs are created through the use of software packages such as CiscoWorks 2000. With a VLAN Management Policy Server (VMPS), you can assign switch ports to VLANs dynamically based on the source MAC address of the device that is connected to the port. Dynamic VLANs currently allow for membership based on the MAC address of the device. As a device enters the network, it queries a database on the VMPS for VLAN membership. This process is shown in Figure 9-6, with each switch having a unique MAC address.

Figure 9-5 Static VLANs

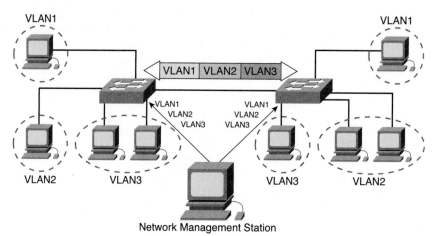

Network Management Station

Static port-based VLAN membership is shown in Figure 9-7. The port is assigned to a specific VLAN that is independent of the user or system that is attached to the port. This means that all users who are attached to the port should be members in the same VLAN. A single user workstation or a hub that has multiple workstations can be connected to a single switch port. The network administrator typically performs the VLAN assignment. The port configuration is static and cannot be automatically changed to another VLAN without manual reconfiguration of the switch. In Figure 9–7, note that each VLAN is on a separate subnet and that the router is used to communicate between them.

When users attach to the same shared segment, as with traditional hub-based Ethernet LANs, all of them share the bandwidth of the segment. For every additional user who is attached to the shared medium, there is less bandwidth available for each user because all users are in the same collision domain. If the sharing becomes too great, excessive collisions can occur and user application performance begins to suffer. Switches reduce collisions by providing dedicated bandwidth between devices using microsegmentation; however, switches still forward broadcasts such as ARP. VLANs offer more bandwidth to users in a shared network by defining separate broadcast domains.

The default VLAN for every port in the switch is VLAN1, or the management VLAN. The management VLAN cannot be deleted; however, additional VLANs can be created and ports can be reassigned to these alternate VLANs.

Figure 9-6 Dynamic VLANs

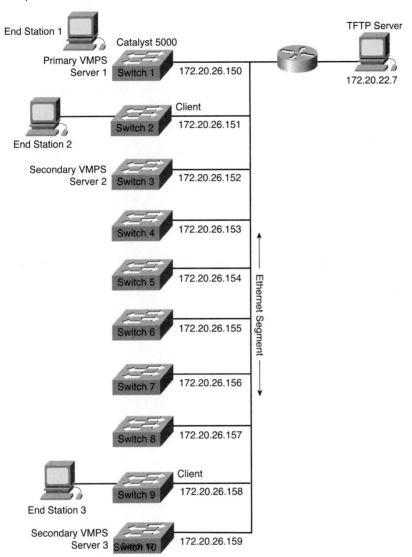

Remember that each interface on a switch behaves like a port on a bridge and that switches are basically considered multiport bridges. Bridges filter traffic that does not need to go to segments other than the source segment. If a frame needs to cross the bridge, and the destination MAC address is known, the bridge forwards the frame to the correct interface and to no others. If the bridge or switch does not know where the destination resides, it floods the frame to all ports in the broadcast domain (VLAN) except the source port.

Figure 9-7 Port-Centric Static VLANs

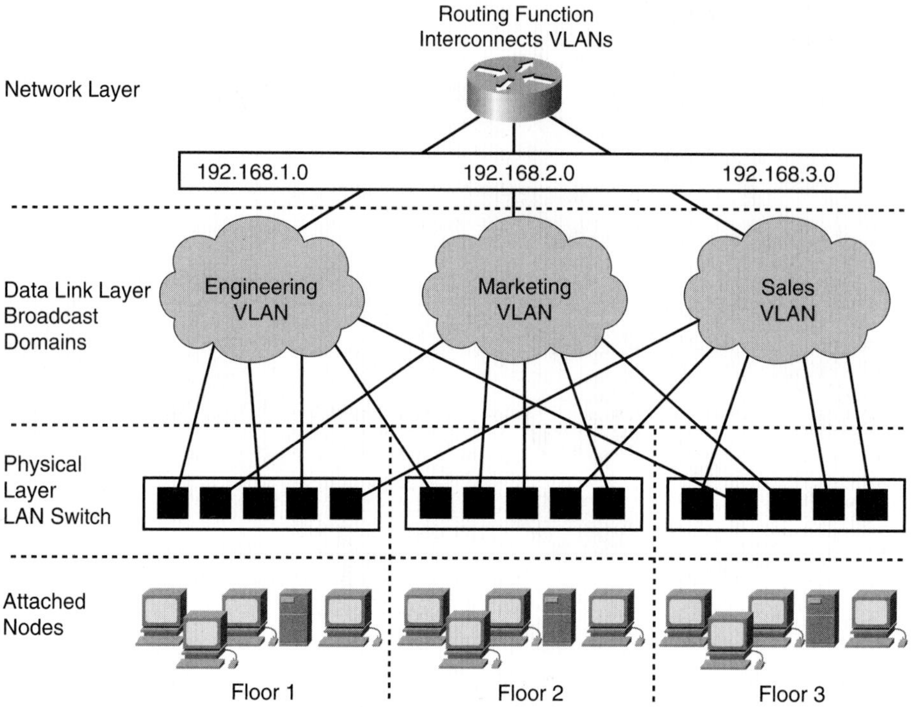

Each VLAN should have a unique Layer 3 network or subnet address assigned. This aids in switching packets between VLANs with routers. VLANs can exist either as end-to-end networks, which span the entire switch fabric, or they can exist inside of geographic boundaries.

End-to-End VLANs

End-to-end VLANs allow devices to be grouped based on resource usage. This includes such parameters as server usage, project teams, and departments. The goal of end-to-end VLANs is to maintain 80 percent of the traffic on the local VLAN. Figure 9-8 shows an example of end-to-end VLANs. An end-to-end VLAN network has the following characteristics:

- Users are grouped into VLANs independent of physical location but dependent on group or job function.
- All users in a VLAN should have the same 80/20 traffic flow patterns.

- As a user moves around the campus, VLAN membership for that user should not change.
- Each VLAN has a common set of security requirements for all members.

Figure 9-8 End-to-End VLANs

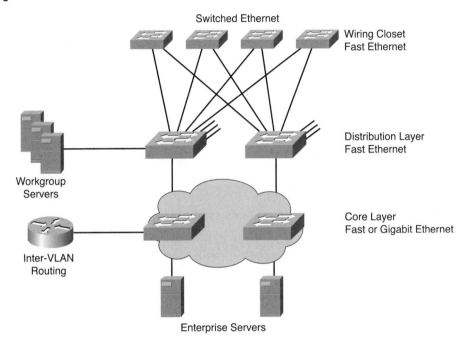

Switched Ethernet

Wiring Closet
Fast Ethernet

Distribution Layer
Fast Ethernet

Workgroup
Servers

Core Layer
Fast or Gigabit Ethernet

Inter-VLAN
Routing

Enterprise Servers

Geographic VLANS

As many corporate networks have moved to centralize their resources, end-to-end VLANs have become more difficult to maintain. Users are required to use many different resources, many of which are no longer in their VLAN. Because of this shift in placement and usage of resources, VLANs are now more frequently being created around geographic boundaries rather than commonality boundaries.

This geographic location can be as large as an entire building or as small as a single switch inside a wiring closet. In a geographic VLAN structure, it is typical to find the new 20/80 rule in effect with 80 percent of the traffic remote to the user and 20 percent of the traffic local to the user. This is the opposite of end-to-end VLAN design. Although this topology means that the user must cross a Layer 3 device (router) to reach 80 percent of the resources, this design allows the network to provide for a deterministic, consistent method of accessing resources.

Geographic VLANs are also considerably easier to manage and conceptualize than VLANs that span different geographic areas.

Benefits of VLANs

Companies are continuously reorganizing. On average, 20–40 percent of the workforce physically moves every year. These moves, additions, and changes are one of a network manager's biggest headaches and one of the largest expenses related to managing the network. Many moves require recabling, and almost all moves require new station addressing and hub and router reconfigurations.

Change Management

VLANs provide an effective mechanism for controlling these changes and reducing much of the cost that is associated with hub and router reconfigurations. Users in a VLAN can share the same network address space (that is, the IP subnet), regardless of their location. When users in a VLAN are moved from one location to another, as long as they remain within the same VLAN and are connected to a switch port, their network addresses do not change. A location change can be as simple as plugging a user into a port on a VLAN-capable switch and configuring the port on the switch to that VLAN. With dynamic VLANs, when the MAC address of the moved workstation's network interface card is looked up on the VMPS, the switch automatically configures the port to be in the correct VLAN.

VLANs and Security

VLANs are an effective mechanism for extending firewalls from the routers to the switch fabric and protecting the network against potentially dangerous broadcast problems. In addition, VLANs maintain all the performance benefits of switching.

You create firewalls by assigning switch ports or users to specific VLAN groups both within single switches and across multiple connected switches. Broadcast traffic within one VLAN is not transmitted outside the VLAN. Figure 9-9 shows an example of broadcast domains. Conversely, adjacent ports do not receive the broadcast traffic that other VLANs generate. This type of configuration substantially reduces the overall broadcast traffic, frees bandwidth for real user traffic, and lowers the overall vulnerability of the network to broadcast storms. Figure 9-10 shows how the router can act as a firewall between VLANs.

Figure 9-9 Broadcast Domains

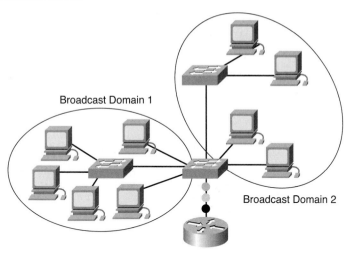

Broadcast Domain 1

Broadcast Domain 2

Figure 9-10 Broadcast Firewall

Broadcast Firewall

One problem of shared LANs is that they are relatively easy to penetrate. By plugging in to a live port, an intrusive user has access to all traffic that is within the segment. The larger the group, the greater the potential access.

One cost-effective and easy administrative technique to increase security is to segment the network into multiple broadcast groups. This allows the network manager to do the following:

- Restrict the number of users in a VLAN group
- Prevent another user from joining without first receiving approval from the VLAN network management application
- Configure all unused ports to a default low-service VLAN

Implementing this type of segmentation is relatively straightforward. Switch ports are grouped together based on the type of applications and access privileges. Restricted applications and resources are commonly placed in a secured VLAN group. On the secured VLAN, the switch restricts access into the group. Restrictions can be placed based on station addresses, application types, or protocol types. An example of VLAN security is shown in Figure 9-11.

Figure 9-11 Secured VLAN

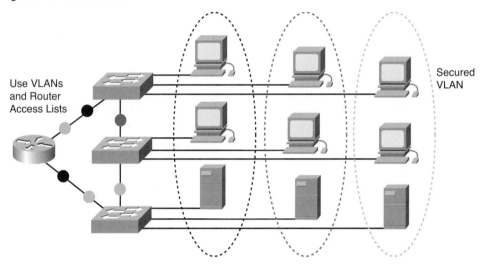

Using Hubs with VLANs

Over the past several years, network administrators have installed a significant number of hubs. Many of these devices are being replaced with newer switching technologies. Because network applications require more dedicated bandwidth and performance directly to the desktop, these hubs still perform useful functions in many existing installations. Network managers can save money by connecting existing hubs to switches. An example is shown in Figure 9-12.

Each hub segment that is connected to a switch port can be assigned to only one VLAN. All stations that share a hub segment become members of the same VLAN group. The switch maintains multiple Media Access Control (MAC) addresses (one for each work-station) that are associated with the port where the hub is attached. If an individual station needs to be reassigned to another VLAN, the station must be relocated to the corresponding hub. The interconnected switch fabric handles the communication between the switching ports and automatically determines the appropriate receiving segments. The more the shared hub can be broken into smaller groups, the greater the microsegmentation and the greater the VLAN flexibility for assigning individual users to VLAN groups. By connecting hubs to switches, you can configure hubs as part of the VLAN architecture. You can also share traffic and network resources that are directly attached to switching ports with VLAN designations.

Figure 9-12 Using Existing Hubs in a Switched VLAN Environment

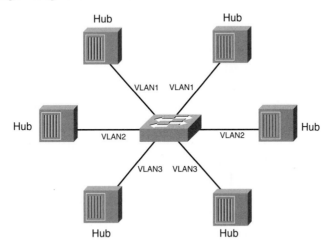

VLAN Types

Three basic models determine and control how a packet is assigned to a VLAN:

- Port-based VLANS (static)
- MAC address-based VLANs (dynamic)
- Protocol-based VLANs (dynamic)

The number of VLANs in the switch might vary greatly, depending on several factors. This includes traffic patterns, types of applications, network management needs, and group commonality. In addition, an important consideration in defining the size of the switch and the number of VLANs is the IP addressing scheme.

For example, suppose that a network uses a 24-bit mask to define a subnet. Given this criterion, a total of 254 host addresses are allowed in one subnet. Because a one-to-one correspondence between VLANs and IP subnets is strongly recommended, there can be no more than 254 devices in any one VLAN.

VLAN Frame Identification

With multiswitch VLANs, the frame headers are encapsulated or modified to reflect a VLAN ID before the frame is sent onto the link between the switches. Before forwarding to the endpoint device, the frame header is changed back to the original format. VLAN identification logically identifies which packets belong to which VLAN group. Multiple trunking methodologies exist, including IEEE 802.1Q, ISL, 802.10, and LANE.

IEEE 802.1Q: Frame Tagging

This protocol is an IEEE standard method for identifying VLANs by inserting a VLAN identifier into the frame header. This process is referred to as frame tagging. Figure 9-13 shows an 802.1Q frame format with the VLAN ID. Every 802.1Q port is assigned to a trunk, and all ports on a trunk are in a native VLAN. Every 802.1Q port is assigned an identifier value that is of its native VLAN ID (default is VLAN 1). All untagged frames are assigned to the LAN that is specified in the ID parameter. An 802.1Q trunk's associated trunk ports have a native VLAN value. 802.1Q does not tag frames for the native VLAN. Therefore, ordinary stations can read the native untagged frames but not other frames because the frames are tagged. IEEE 802.1Q frame tagging is the preferred method for communicating VLAN information between switches.

Figure 9-13 802.1Q Frame Format

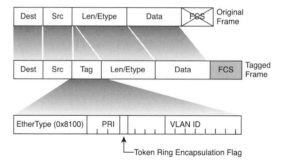

Inter-Switch Link Protocol

Inter-Switch Link (ISL) is a Cisco proprietary encapsulation protocol that interconnects multiple switches; it is supported in switches as well as routers. Figure 9-14 shows an ISL frame format.

The ISL frame tagging that the Catalyst series of switches uses is a low-latency mechanism for multiplexing traffic from multiple VLANs on a single physical path. It has been implemented for connections among switches, routers, and network interface cards used on nodes such as servers. To support the ISL feature, each connecting device must be ISL-configured. A router that is ISL-configured is used to allow inter-VLAN communications. This is discussed in more detail in Chapter 10, "VLAN Trunking Protocol." A non-ISL device that receives ISL-encapsulated Ethernet frames might consider them to be protocol errors if the size of the header plus data frame exceeds the maximum transmission unit (MTU) size. Administrators use ISL to maintain redundant links and load-balance traffic between parallel links using the Spanning Tree Protocol.

Figure 9-14 ISL Frame Format

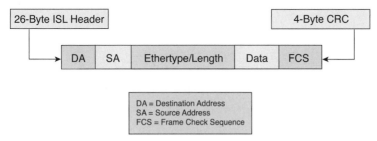

FDDI 802.10

802.10 is a Cisco proprietary method of transporting VLAN information inside the standard IEEE 802.10 frame (FDDI). The VLAN information is written to the security association identifier (SAID) portion of the 802.10 frame. This method is typically used to transport VLANs across Fiber Distributed Data Interface (FDDI) backbones.

LANE

LAN Emulation (LANE) is a standard defined by the ATM Forum that gives two stations attached via ATM the same capabilities they normally have with legacy LANs, such as Ethernet and Token Ring. As the name suggests, the function of the LANE protocol is to emulate a LAN on top of an Asynchronous Transfer Mode (ATM) network. Specifically, the LANE protocol defines mechanisms for emulating either an IEEE 802.3 Ethernet or an 802.5 Token Ring LAN.

The LANE protocol defines a service interface for higher-layer (that is, network layer) protocols that is identical to that of existing LANs. Data that is sent across the ATM network is encapsulated in the appropriate LAN MAC format. In other words, the LANE protocols make an ATM network look and behave like an Ethernet or Token Ring LAN. An example LANE network is shown in Figure 9-15.

Figure 9-15 LANE Network

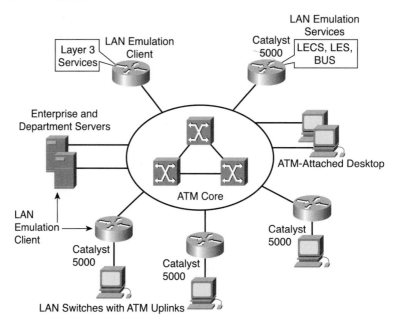

Table 9-1 shows frame tagging and encapsulation methods.

Table 9-1 Frame Tagging and Encapsulation Methods

Identification Method	Encapsulation	Tagging	Media
802.1Q	No	Yes	Ethernet
ISL	Yes	No	Ethernet
802.10	No	No	FDDI
LANE	No	No	ATM

VLAN Configuration

Originally, network administrators thought that VLANs would simplify their work and that VLANs would mean routers would no longer be needed. Unfortunately for network administrators, this was not a correct assumption. VLANs do not eliminate Layer 3 issues. They might allow the administrator to more easily perform some Layer 3 tasks, such as developing simpler access lists, but Layer 3 routing still must exist.

Configuring Static VLANs

Static VLANs are ports on a switch that are manually assigned to a VLAN by using a VLAN management application or by working directly within the switch. These ports maintain their assigned VLAN configuration until you change them. Although static VLANs require manual entry changes, they are secure, easy to configure, and straightforward to monitor. This type of VLAN works well in networks where the following condition occur:

- Moves are controlled and managed.
- There is robust VLAN management software to configure the ports.
- It is not desirable to assume the additional overhead required when maintaining end-station MAC addresses and custom filtering tables.

Dynamic VLANs, conversely, do not rely on ports that are assigned to a specific VLAN. Instead, VLAN assignment is based on MAC addressing, logical addressing, or protocol type.

You must remember the following guidelines when you are configuring static VLANs on Cisco 29xx switches:

- The maximum number of VLANs is switch dependent and is limited by the number of ports on the switch.
- VLAN1 is one of the factory-default VLANs.
- VLAN1 is the default Ethernet VLAN.
- *Cisco Discovery Protocol (CDP)* and *VLAN Trunking Protocol (VTP)* advertisements are sent on VLAN1.
- The same encapsulation protocol, such as 802.1Q or ISL, must be configured on all switch trunks that participate in the VLAN.
- The commands for configuring VLANS vary by model number.
- The Catalyst 29xx IP address is in the VLAN1 broadcast domain.
- The switch must be in VTP server mode to create, add, or delete VLANs.

The creation of a static VLAN on a switch is a straightforward and simple task. If you are using a Cisco IOS command-based switch, enter the VLAN configuration mode with the privileged exec **vlan database** command. The configuration steps that are necessary to create the VLAN are as follows:

```
Switch#vlan database
Switch(vlan)vlan vlan_number [vlan_name]
Switch(vlan)exit
```

A VLAN name can also be configured, if necessary.

Upon exiting, the VLAN is applied to the switch. The next step is to assign the VLAN to one or more interfaces:

```
Switch(config)#interface fastethernet 0/3
```

Catalyst 2900 switch:

```
Switch(config-if)#switchport access vlan 2
```

Catalyst 1900 switch:

```
(config-if)#vlan-membership static 2
```

You can verify the configuration by using the **show running-configuration** command, as shown in Example 9-1.

Example 9-1 show running-configuration *Command*

```
Switch#show running-config

Hostname Switch
!
ip subnet-zero
!
interface FastEthernet0/1
!
interface FastEthernet0/2
!
interface FastEthernet0/3

switchport access vlan 2
--- output omitted ---
```

Lab Activity   Configuring Static VLANs

In this lab, you create a basic switch configuration and verify it. You console into the switch to determine the firmware version, create two VLANs, name them, and assign member ports to them.

Verifying VLAN Configuration

A good practice is to verify VLAN configuration by using the **show vlan** (as in Example 9-2), **show vlan brief,** or **show vlan id** *id_number* commands.

Example 9-2 show vlan *Command*

```
Switch#show vlan
Virtual LAN ID: 300 (IEEE 802.10 Encapsulation)
vLAN Trunk Interface: FDDI 1/1.10
Protocols Configured: Address: Received: Transmitted:
IP 31.108.1.1 642 645
Virtual LAN ID: 400 (ISL Encapsulation)
vLAN Trunk Interface: FastEthernet 2/1.20
Protocols Configured: Address: Received:Transmitted:
IP 171.69.2.2 123456 654321
Bridge Group 50 5190 8234
Virtual LAN ID:500 (ISL Encapsulation)
vLAN Trunk Interface: FastEthernet 2/1.30
Protocols Configured: Address: Received:Transmitted:
IPX 1000 987654 456789
Virtual LAN ID:600 (ISL Encapsulation)
vLAN Trunk Interface: FastEthernet 2/1.30
Protocols Configured: Address: Received:Transmitted:
IP 198.92.3.3 8114 4508
IPX 1001 2 3
Bridge Group 50 8234 5190
```

The following statements apply to VLANs:

- A created VLAN remains unused until it is mapped to switch ports.
- By default, all Ethernet ports are on VLAN 1.
- Do not enter spaces between the port numbers. The switch gives you an error message because a space delimits another argument that is not in the command structure of this command.

Saving a VLAN Configuration

It is useful to keep a copy of the VLAN configuration as a text file for backup or auditing purposes.

You can use a floppy disk to save the VLAN configuration file and then transfer it to different computers. If the VLAN configuration file captures some extraneous characters, delete them before use.

The following steps describe how to copy the VLAN configuration:

Step 1   From the switch console, go to privileged mode on the switch.

Step 2   Go to the Transfer option of the HyperTerminal window.

Step 3   Select Capture Text.

Step 4   Select where the configuration will be saved (such as Desktop).

Step 5   Make the filename VLANconfig.

Step 6   Select Start.

Step 7   On the switch, type **show run**.

Step 8   When the configuration file stops running (press the spacebar a few times to finish it), go back up to the Transfer option in the HyperTerminal window and select Capture Text and Stop to save and close the file.

Step 9   Delete extraneous characters.

 Lab Activity   Verifying VLAN Configurations

In this lab, you create a basic switch configuration and two VLANs. You then name the VLANs and assign multiple member ports to them. You test functionality by moving a workstation from one VLAN to another.

NOTE

When you delete a VLAN, any ports that are assigned to that VLAN become inactive. These ports remain associated with the VLAN (and thus inactive) until you assign them to a new VLAN.

Deleting a VLAN Configuration

To remove a VLAN from a set command-based switch, issue the **clear vlan** *vlan_number* command, as shown in Example 9-3. In this example, VLAN 2 is being removed from the domain by using the command **clear vlan 2**. It is important to note that you must issue this command on a VTP server switch. You cannot delete VLANs from a VTP client switch. If the switch is configured in transparent mode, you can delete the VLAN; however, the VLAN is removed only from the one Catalyst switch and is not deleted throughout the management domain. All VLAN creations and deletions are locally significant only on a transparent switch. VTP domains are covered in Chapter 10.

Example 9-3 *Set Command-Based Switch*

```
Console>(enable) clear vlan 2
This command will deactivate all ports on vlan2
In the entire management domain
Do you want to continue (y/n) [n]?y
Vlan 2 deleted
```

Removing a VLAN from a Cisco IOS command-based switch interface is just like removing a command from a router. In a previous example, you created vlan 2 on FastEthernet 0/3 by using the following command:

```
Switch(config-if)#switchport access vlan 2
```
To remove this VLAN from the interface, use the **no** form of the command, while on interface Fa 0/3:

```
Switch(config-if)#no switchport access vlan 2
```

Lab Activity   Deleting VLAN Configurations

In this lab, you create a basic switch configuration and create two VLANs. You then name them and assign multiple member ports to them. From there, you delete the VLANs and learn why you are not able to delete VLAN 1.

Troubleshooting VLANs

Misconfiguration of a VLAN is one of the most common errors in switched networks. This section describes the most common misconfiguration errors and suggests solutions to help you troubleshoot your switched network.

Table 9-2 shows high-level VLAN problems that can occur with a router or switch. The problem facts or symptoms and the possible problems and action plans might help you identify and solve the problems.

Table 9-2 VLAN Problems

Problem Facts	Possible Problems and Action Plans
Performance on the VLAN is slow or unreliable.	The device has a bad adapter. Check the hardware. *Full-duplex* or *half-duplex* Ethernet settings are incorrect. There is a cabling problem. Check the connected LED. Check whether the correct cable is properly attached and whether the length exceeds the maximum cable distance.
The attached terminal or modem connection cannot communicate with the router or with a switch.	There is a misconfigured terminal and console port. Check that baud rate and character format match. Check whether a default route is needed on the router to reach the switch on a different IP subnet.
Local VLAN devices cannot communicate with remote devices on a VLAN beyond the router.	There is a misconfigured IP addressing or mask. Check with the CDP and **show interface** commands. The default gateway is not specified or is incorrect. Check the router, switch, servers, and clients. VLAN is misconfigured. Check the port assignments. Eliminate unnecessary connections between VLANs if a port belongs to multiple VLANs. There is a VLAN inconsistency problem. Make sure that VLANs match on both sides of a trunk. There is an ISL problem. Make sure that there is proper trunking, use VLAN1, and make sure that no valid VTP server information update has occurred.

When you are faced with poor throughput problems, check to see what type of errors exist. There could be a bad adapter card. Combinations of *frame check sequence (FCS)* and alignment errors and runts generally point to a duplex mismatch; the usual culprit is the autonegotiation between devices or a mismatched setting between the two sides of a link. Consider these questions:

- Is the problem on the local side or the remote side of the link? Remember: A minimum number of switch ports is involved in a link.
- What path is the packet taking? Is it going across trunks or non-trunks to other switches?

If you see that the number of collisions in output from a **show interface** command is increasing rapidly, the problem might just be an overloaded link. There is a myth that switched Ethernet eliminates collisions. The fact is that switches minimize the number of collisions, but if running in half-duplex mode, the collisions still occur because two devices can always attempt to communicate at the same time.

An example is a news server that has many clients attempting to communicate at the same time. The traffic comes through the router and switch to the directly connected server. At the same time, the server is attempting to communicate back to these clients. As the server is answering one client, another client sends a request; as a result, there is the potential for collision. The only cure for collisions on Ethernet is to run in full-duplex mode. Figure 9-16 shows the process for troubleshooting VLANs.

Figure 9-16 Troubleshooting VLANs

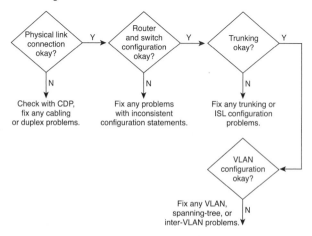

As an example of the troubleshooting process, assume that one device cannot communicate with another device. The following are suggested solutions to the problem:

- Make sure that the IP address, subnet mask, and VLAN membership of the switch interface are correct by using the **show interface** command. To prevent conflicts, make sure that the interfaces are configured with IP addresses and subnet masks in different subnets.
- If the host is in the same subnet as the switch interface, then make sure the switch interface and the switch port to which the host is connected are assigned to the same VLAN. Use the **show interface** and **show port** commands.
- If the host is in a different subnet, then make sure that the default gateway (default route) on the switch is configured with the address of a router in the same subnet as the switch interface. Use the **show ip route** command.

- Check the spanning-tree state on the port by using the **show spantree** (Catalyst 1900) or **show spanning-tree vlan** (Catalyst 2950) command. If the port is in listening or learning mode, wait until the port is in forwarding mode and try to connect to the host again.

- Make sure the speed and duplex settings on the host and the appropriate switch ports are correct. Use the **show port** command.

- If the connected device is an end station:
  - Enable spanning-tree PortFast on the port. Use the **set spantree portfast enable** command. Keep in mind that these commands are not supported on 2900 series switches. PortFast places the port in forwarding mode immediately, bypassing listening and learning modes. (Do not use this feature for connections to non-end station devices.)
  - Disable trunking on the port. Use the **set trunk** command.
  - Disable channeling on the port. Use the **set port channel** command. You must specify a valid port range with this command. You cannot specify a single port.

- Make sure the switch is learning the MAC address of the host. Use the **show cam dynamic** command.

Summary

In this chapter, you learned that VLAN implementation provides the following benefits:

- Easier moves, additions, and changes to device connections
- Greater administrative control by implementing a Layer 3 routing device among the VLANs
- Reduced LAN bandwidth consumption compared to a single broadcast domain
- Reduced unnecessary CPU usage by the reduction in broadcast forwarding

For troubleshooting VLANs, you learned the following:

- A more specific approach in how to troubleshoot VLAN-based networks
- Some of the most common problems when configuring and troubleshooting VLANs
- The prevention of broadcast storms and loops
- The appropriate use of troubleshooting commands

To supplement all that you have learned in this chapter, refer to the chapter-specific Videos, PhotoZooms, and e-Lab Activities on the CD-ROM that accompanies this book.

Key Terms

broadcast   Data packet that is sent to all nodes on a network. Broadcasts are identified by a broadcast address.

CDP (Cisco Discovery Protocol)   Provides a single proprietary command that enables network administrators to access a summary of what the configurations look like on other directly connected routers.

FCS (frame check sequence)   Extra characters that are added to a frame for error control purposes.

full-duplex   Capability for simultaneous data transmission between a sending station and a receiving station.

half-duplex   Capability for data transmission in only one direction at a time between a sending station and a receiving station.

VLAN (virtual local-area network)   Group of devices on one or more LANs that are configured (using management software) so that they can communicate as if they were attached to the same wire, when in fact they are located on several different LAN segments.

VTP (VLAN Trunking Protocol)   VTP reduces administration in a switched network. When you configure a new VLAN on a VTP server, the VLAN is distributed through all switches in the domain. This reduces the need to configure the same VLAN everywhere. VTP is a Cisco-proprietary protocol that is available on most of the Cisco Catalyst Family products.

Check Your Understanding

1. What do VLANs address?

   A. Scalability

   B. Security

   C. Traffic flow management

   D. All of the above

2. Which of the following can a VLAN be considered?

   A. Broadcast domain

   B. Collision domain

   C. Both a broadcast and a collision domain

   D. Domain name

3. What do routers in VLAN topologies provide for?

   A. Broadcast filtering

   B. Security

   C. Traffic flow management

   D. All of the above

4. What does the phrase *microsegmentation with scalability* mean?

   A. The ability to increase network size without creating collisions domains

   B. The ability to put a huge number of hosts on one switch

   C. The ability to broadcast to more nodes at once

   D. All of the above

5. Switches, as the core element of VLANs, provide the intelligence to do which of the following?

   A. They group users, ports, or logical addresses into a VLAN.

   B. They make filtering and forwarding decisions.

   C. They communicate with other switches and routers.

   D. All of the above.

6. Each _____ segment that is connected to a _____ port can be assigned to only one VLAN.

   A. switch; hub

   B. hub; router

   C. hub; switch

   D. LAN; hub

7. Which of the following is *not* an advantage of using static VLANS?

   A. They are secure.

   B. They are easy to configure.

   C. They are easy to monitor.

   D. They automatically configure ports when new stations are added.

8. Which of the following is *not* a criterion on which VLANs can be based?

   A. Port ID.

   B. Protocol.

   C. MAC address.

   D. All of the above are criteria on which VLANs can be based.

9. Which of the following is a beneficial effect of adding a VLAN? Choose all tha apply.

    A. Switches do not need to be configured.

    B. Broadcasts can be controlled.

    C. Confidential data can be protected.

    D. Physical boundaries that prevent user groupings can be removed.

10. Which of the following statements that pertains to virtual LANs is false?

    A. The most common approaches for logically grouping users into distinct VLANs are frame filtering and frame identification.

    B. VLAN benefits include tighter network security with establishment of secure user groups.

    C. Bridges form one of the core components of VLAN communications.

    D. VLANs help in distributing traffic load.

11. Which Layer 3 function on a switch allows you to easily manipulate devices that reside in different IP subnets?

    A. Transparent bridging

    B. Segmentation

    C. Reduction of collision domains

    D. VLANs

12. Which of the following devices is needed for a packet to be passed from one VLAN to another?

    A. Bridge

    B. Router

    C. Switch

    D. Hub

13. In which layer of the OSI model does frame tagging occur?

    A. Layer 1

    B. Layer 2

    C. Layer 3

    D. Layer 4

14. _____ allows switches to share address tables, and _____ assigns a user-defined VLAN ID to each frame.

   A. Frame tagging; frame forwarding

   B. Frame identification; frame removal

   C. Frame filtering; frame tagging

   D. Frame tagging; frame filtering

15. Why is it important to create VLANs?

   A. Moves, adds, and changes are made simpler.

   B. There is less administrative overhead.

   C. The router can switch more quickly.

   D. Both A and B.

Objectives

After reading this chapter, you will be able to

- Understand trunking
- Understand the fundamentals of the VTP and VTP configuration
- Understand inter-VLAN routing
- Configure basic inter-VLAN routing

Chapter 10

VLAN Trunking Protocol

In this chapter, you will learn the origins of trunking and its operation. You will also discover how the VLAN Trunking Protocol (VTP) can solve some of the problems that are related to managing and implementing virtual LANs (VLANs) in a large LAN network environment. Finally, you will be introduced to inter-VLAN routing.

Please be sure to look at this chapter's associated e-Lab Activities, Videos, and PhotoZooms that you will find on the CD-ROM accompanying this book. These CD-ROM elements are designed to supplement the material and reinforce the concepts introduced in this chapter.

Trunking

The history of *trunking* goes back to the origins of radio and telephony technologies. In radio technologies, a trunk is a single communications line that carries multiple channels of radio signals.

In the telephony industry, the trunking concept is associated with the telephone communication path or channel between two points (one usually being a central office). An example is shown in Figure 10-1.

Shared trunks can also be created for redundancy between central offices (COs). (See Figure 10-2.)

The same concept that the telephone and radio industries used was also the first one that the default hardware of telecommunications used. An example on this line is the segment of a communications network in which many lines come together, as shown in Figure 10-3. A backbone is composed of a number of trunks.

Figure 10-1 Trunk Link

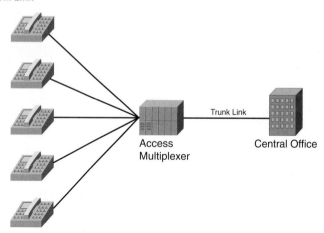

Figure 10-2 Trunk Shared Link

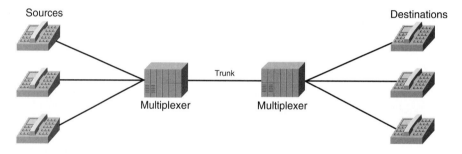

Figure 10-3 Trunks Using Frame Division Multiplexing (FDM)

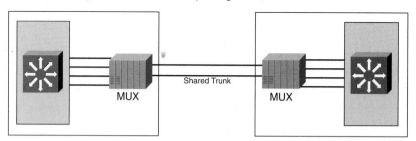

At present, the same principle of trunking has been applied to network switching technologies, whereby a trunk is a physical and logical connection between two switches across which network traffic travels.

Trunking Concepts

A *trunk* is a single transmission channel between two points that are usually switching centers. The trunk is a physical connection that carries (or enables) logical links.

In the context of a VLAN switching environment, a trunk is a point-to-point link that supports several VLANs. The purpose of a trunk is to save ports when creating a link between two devices that are implementing VLANs—typically two switches. Figure 10-4 shows two VLANs that are available on two switches: Sa and Sb.

Figure 10-4 Why Trunking?

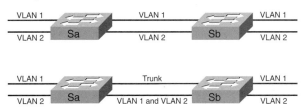

The first method shown in Figure 10-4 creates two physical links between the devices, each one carrying the traffic for a separate VLAN. This first solution does not scale well. If a third VLAN were added, two additional ports would be sacrificed. This design is also inefficient in terms of load sharing; the traffic on some VLANs might not justify a dedicated link. A trunk bundles multiple virtual (logical) links over one physical link.

Trunking Operation

The use of the existing switching tables at both ends of a trunk to make port delivery decisions, based on the destination MAC addresses of the frames, becomes slow and difficult to manage as the number of VLANs traveling across the trunk increases. The larger the tables that a switch has to store, the slower the decision process when switching frames to their respective ports.

To effectively manage the transmission of frames from different VLANs on a single physical line or link between two networking devices, a type of communication/language between these two devices is needed. This communication, or protocol, is used so that the devices can "agree" on the travel and distribution of the frames onto their associated ports at both ends of the trunk. Trunking protocols were created for this purpose.

Trunking protocols allow the traveling of frames from different VLANs through a single physical channel; they manage the distribution of the frames accordingly to their associated VLAN ports. At present, two types of trunking mechanisms exist: frame filtering and frame tagging. This chapter uses frame tagging because this method is the standard trunking mechanism recommended by IEEE. Figure 10-5 shows an example of trunk links.

Figure 10-5 Trunk Links

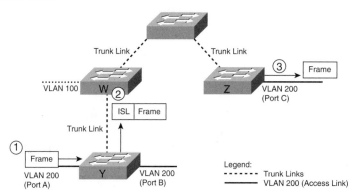

Trunking protocols that use a frame tagging mechanism assign an identifier to the frames to make their management easier, which in turn achieves a faster delivery of the frames. These tags are added on the way out of a trunk link and removed at the other end. They are not broadcast.

The unique physical link between the two switches is able to carry traffic for any VLAN. To achieve this, each frame that is sent on the link is tagged to identify which VLAN it belongs to. Different tagging schemes exist. The most common schemes for Ethernet segments are as follows:

- *Inter-Switch Link (ISL)*—This is the original Cisco proprietary Inter-Switch Link protocol.
- *802.1Q*—This is an IEEE standard method for inserting VLAN membership information into Ethernet frames.

VLANs and Trunking

You need certain rules or protocols to achieve trunking. Trunking mechanisms aid in the expansion of VLAN-switched networks. A *VLAN* is a group of devices on one or more LANs that are configured (using management software) so that they can communicate as if they were attached to the same wire, when, in fact, they are located on a number of different LAN segments. Trunking provides an effective method to distribute VLAN ID information to other switches and for communication between switches in the network, as shown in Figure 10-6.

Figure 10-6 VLANs and Trunking

```
-------  VLAN 1
- - - -  VLAN 2
_____  VLAN 3
```

Frame tagging is the standard trunking mechanism; compared to frame filtering, frame tagging provides a more scalable solution to VLAN deployment that can be implemented campus wide. IEEE 802.1Q states that frame tagging is the way to implement VLANs. An example is shown in Figure 10-7.

Figure 10-7 Frame Tagging

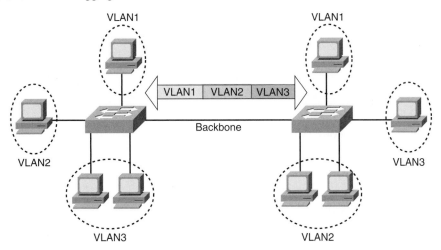

VLAN frame tagging is an approach that has been specifically developed for switched communications. Frame tagging places a unique identifier in the header of each frame as it is forwarded throughout the network backbone. Each switch understands and examines the identifier before any broadcasts or transmissions to other switches, routers, or end-station devices. When the frame exits the network backbone, the switch removes the identifier before the frame is transmitted to the target end station. Frame identification functions at Layer 2 and requires little processing or administrative overhead.

A trunk link does not belong to a specific VLAN. The responsibility of a trunk link is to act as a conduit for VLANs between switches and routers.

The switches in Figure 10-6 communicate with each other using ISL, which is a protocol that maintains VLAN information as traffic flows between the switches. With ISL, an Ethernet frame is encapsulated with a header that contains a VLAN ID.

Switch Command-Line Interfaces

Depending on the switch model you are working with, you can encounter two different types of command entry. The command-line interface (CLI) for Cisco switches is either IOS command-based or set command-based. The first uses IOS commands that are similar to those used with Cisco routers. The second uses set commands to configure the switch. Commands can vary between the two types of CLIs. Both types of commands are provided in the following configuration examples. Switches such as the 2900 Series use IOS-based commands. Switches such as the 4500 and 6500 Series use set-based commands. Older base model switches such as the 1900 Series utilize IOS commands and also have a menu-driven interface. All models of switches provide a graphic web-based management interface that you can access with a browser.

The following is an IOS command-based switch privileged mode prompt and command example:

```
Switch#show trunk
```

The following is a set command-based switch privileged mode prompt and command example:

```
Switch>(enable)set vtp v2 enable
```

Trunking Implementation

To create or configure a VLAN trunk on a Cisco IOS command-based switch, configure the port first as a trunk and then specify the trunk encapsulation. Trunk encapsulation must be the same on both ends. To do this, issue the commands shown in Example 10-1.

Example 10-1 *Configuring VLAN Trunk Commands*

```
Switch(config-if)#switchport mode trunk ?
allowed        Set allowed VLAN characteristics when interface is in trunking
               mode
encapsulation  Set trunking encapsulation when interface is in trunking mode
native         Set trunking native characteristics when interface is in trunking
               mode
pruning        Set pruning VLAN characteristics when interface is in trunking mode
```

Example 10-1 *Configuring VLAN Trunk Commands (Continued)*

```
Switch(config-if)#switchport trunk encapsulation ?
dot1q          Interface uses only 802.1q trunking encapsulation when trunking
isl            Interface uses only ISL trunking encapsulation when trunking

Switch(config-if)#switchport trunk encapsulation isl
```

Lab Activity   Trunking with ISL

In this lab, you create a basic switch configuration and then create multiple VLANs, name them, and assign member ports. You create an ISL trunk line between the two switches and then test the VLANs by moving a workstation from one to the other.

Before you attempt to configure a VLAN trunk on a port, determine what encapsulation the port can support. You can do this by using the **show port capabilities** command on a set command-based switch, as shown in Example 10-2. Notice that Port 2/1 supports only the IEEE 802.1Q encapsulation.

Example 10-2 show port capabilities *Command*

```
Console>(enable) show port capabilities 2/1
Model           WS-X4232-GB-RJ
Port            2/1
Type            No GBIC
Speed           1000
Duplex          full
Trunk encap type    802.1Q
Trunk mode      on,off,desirable,auto,nonegotiate
Channel         2/1-2
Flow control    receive-(off,on,desired),send-(off,on,desired)
Security        yes
Membership      static,dynamic
```

continues

Example 10-2 show port capabilities *Command (Continued)*

```
Fast start          yes

QOS scheduling      rx-(none), tx-(2qlt)

CoS rewrite         no

ToS rewrite         no

Rewrite             no

UDLD                yes

SPAN                source,destination
```

To create or configure a VLAN trunk on a set command-based switch, enter the **set trunk** command to configure the port on each end of the link as a trunk port and to specify the VLANs to be transported on this trunk link:

```
Switch> (enable) set trunk mod_num/port_num [on | off | desirable | auto |
    nonegotiate] vlan_range [isl | dot1q | dot10 | lane | negotiate]
```

You can also use the **set trunk** command to change the mode of a trunk, as shown in Example 10-3.

Example 10-3 set trunk *Command*

```
Console>(enable)

Console>(enable)set trunk 2/1 on dot1q

Port(s) 2/1 trunk mode set to on.

Port(s) 2/1 trunk type set to dot1q
```

Fast Ethernet and Gigabit Ethernet trunking modes by keyword are as follows:

- **on**—This mode puts the port into permanent trunking. The port becomes a trunk port even if the neighboring port does not agree to the change. The on state does not allow for the negotiation of an encapsulation type; therefore, you must specify the encapsulation in the configuration.

- **off**—This mode puts the port into permanent nontrunking mode and negotiates to convert the link into a nontrunk link. The port becomes a nontrunk port even if the neighboring port does not agree to the change.

- **desirable**—This mode makes the port actively attempt to convert the link to a trunk link. The port becomes a trunk port if the neighboring port is set to on, desirable, or auto mode.

- **auto**—This mode makes the port willing to convert the link to a trunk link. The port becomes a trunk port if the neighboring port is set to on or desirable mode. This is the default mode for Fast and Gigabit Ethernet ports. Notice that if the default setting is left on both sides of the trunk link, it will not become a trunk; neither side will be the first to ask to convert to a trunk.

- **nonegotiate**—This mode puts the port into permanent trunking mode but prevents the port from generating Dynamic Trunking Protocol (DTP) frames. You must configure the neighboring port manually as a trunk port to establish a trunk link.

Verify that trunking has been configured and verify the settings by using the **show trunk** [*mod_num/port_num*] command from privileged mode on the switch.

VLAN Trunking Protocol (VTP)

This section explains the concept and operation of the VLAN Trunking Protocol (VTP) as well as its implementation in a VLAN-switched LAN environment.

History of VTP

VTP was created to solve potential operational problems in a VLAN's network-switched environment.

For example, consider a domain that has several interconnected switches that support several VLANs. To create and maintain connectivity within VLANs, each VLAN must be manually configured on each switch. As the organization grows and additional switches are added to the network, each new switch must be manually configured with VLAN information. A single incorrect VLAN assignment could cause two potential problems:

- Cross-connected VLANs due to VLAN configuration inconsistencies
- VLAN configuration conciliations across mixed-media environments such as Ethernet and Fiber Distributed Data Interface (FDDI)

With VTP, VLAN configuration consistency is maintained across a common administration domain. Additionally, VTP reduces the complexity of managing and monitoring VLAN networks.

VTP Concepts

The role of VTP is to maintain VLAN configuration consistency across a common network administration domain. VTP is a messaging protocol that uses Layer 2 trunk frames to manage the addition, deletion, and renaming of VLANs on a single domain.

Further, VTP allows for centralized changes that are communicated to all other switches in the network.

VTP messages are encapsulated in either Cisco proprietary ISL or IEEE 802.1Q protocol frames and then passed across trunk links to other devices. In IEEE 802.1Q frames, a four-byte field is added that tags the frame. Both formats carry the VLAN ID.

Whereas switch ports are normally assigned to only a single VLAN, trunk ports, by default, carry frames from all VLANs.

VTP Benefits

VTP minimizes the possible configuration inconsistencies that arise when changes are made. These inconsistencies can result in security violations because VLANs cross-connect when duplicate names are used; they also can become internally disconnected when they are mapped from one LAN type to another (such as from Ethernet to ATM or FDDI). VTP provides the following benefits:

- VLAN configuration consistency across the network
- Mapping scheme that allows a VLAN to be trunked over mixed media, such as mapping Ethernet VLANs to a high-speed backbone VLAN like ATM LANE or FDDI
- Accurate tracking and monitoring of VLANs
- Dynamic reporting of added VLANs across the network
- Plug-and-play configuration when adding new VLANs

Before creating VLANs on the switch, you must first set up a VTP management domain within which you can verify the current VLANs on the network. All switches in the same management domain share their VLAN information with each other, and a switch can participate in only one VTP management domain. Switches in different domains do not share VTP information.

Using VTP, each Catalyst Family Switch advertises the following on its trunk ports:

- Management domain
- Configuration revision number
- Known VLANs and their specific parameters

VTP Domain

A VTP domain is made up of one or more interconnected devices that share the same VTP domain name. A switch can be in one VTP domain only.

When transmitting VTP messages to other switches in the network, the VTP message is encapsulated in a trunking protocol frame such as ISL or IEEE 802.1Q. Domain names must match (case sensitive) exactly for information to be passed. Figure 10-8 shows the generic encapsulation for VTP within an ISL frame.

Figure 10-8 VTP Encapsulation with ISL Frame

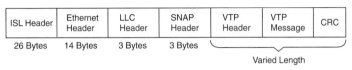

The VTP header varies depending on the type of VTP message, but generally, four items are found in all VTP messages:

- **VTP protocol version**—Will be either Version 1 or 2
- **VTP message type**—Indicates one of four types
- **Management domain name length**—Indicates the size of the name that follows
- **Management domain name**—Indicates the name configured for the management domain

VTP Modes

VTP switches operate in one of three modes:

- Server
- Client
- Transparent

VTP Server (Default Mode)

If a switch is configured for server mode, you can create, modify, and delete VLANs and specify other configuration parameters (such as VTP version and VTP pruning) for the entire VTP domain. VTP servers save VLAN configuration information in Catalyst nonvolatile random-access memory (NVRAM). VTP servers send VTP messages out all trunk ports.

VTP servers advertise their VLAN configuration to other switches in the same VTP domain and synchronize the VLAN configuration with other switches based on advertisements received over trunk links. This is the default mode on the switch.

VTP Client

A switch that is configured as a VTP client cannot create, modify, or delete VLAN information. In addition, clients cannot save VLAN information. This mode is useful for switches that lack sufficient memory to store large tables of VLAN information, as required by VTP servers. VTP clients process VLAN changes as servers do, and they send VTP messages out all trunk ports.

VTP Transparent Mode

Switches configured for transparent mode do not participate in VTP. A VTP transparent switch does not advertise its VLAN configuration and does not synchronize its VLAN configuration based on received advertisements. They forward VTP advertisements (Version 2) received on their trunk ports but ignore information contained in the message. A transparent switch neither modifies its database when updates are received nor sends an update indicating a change in its VLAN status. Except for forwarding VTP advertisements, VTP is disabled on a transparent switch.

VTP Operation

Detecting the addition of VLANs within the advertisements serves as a notification to the switches (servers and clients) that they should be prepared to receive traffic on their trunk ports with the newly defined VLAN IDs, emulated LAN names, or 802.10 security association identifiers (SAIDs).

In Figure 10-9, Switch C transmits a VTP database entry with additions or deletions to Switch A and Switch B. The configuration database has a revision number that is notification +1. A higher configuration revision number indicates that the VLAN information that is being sent is more current than the stored copy. When a switch receives an update that has a higher configuration revision number, the switch overwrites the stored information with the new information being sent in the VTP update. Switch F does not process the update because it is in a different domain.

By default, management domains are set to a nonsecure mode, which means that the switches interact without using a password. Adding a password automatically sets the management domain to secure mode. The same password must be configured on every switch in the management domain to use secure mode.

Figure 10-9 VTP Operation

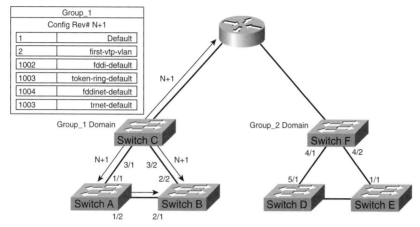

Group_1	
Config Rev# N+1	
1	Default
2	first-vtp-vlan
1002	fddi-default
1003	token-ring-default
1004	fddinet-default
1003	trnet-default

VTP Implementation

With VTP, each switch advertises on its trunk ports its management domain, configuration revision number, the VLANs that it knows about, and certain parameters for each known VLAN. These advertisement frames are sent to a multicast address so that all neighboring devices can receive the frames; however, the frames are not forwarded by normal bridging procedures. All devices in the same management domain learn about any new VLANs that are now configured in the transmitting device. A new VLAN must be created and configured on one device only in the management domain. All the other devices in the same management domain automatically learn this information.

Advertisements on factory-default VLANs are based on media types. User ports should not be configured as VTP trunks. Each advertisement starts as configuration revision number 0. As changes are made, the configuration revision number increments by one (n + 1). The revision number in the management domain continues to increment until it reaches 2,147,483,648, at which point the counter resets back to 0.

Two types of VTP advertisements exist:

- Requests from clients that want information at bootup
- Responses from servers

VTP messages are one of three types:

- **Advertisement request**—Client requests VLAN information
- **Summary advertisement**—Server responds with summary
- **Subset advertisement**—Server responds with subset

These three types of VTP messages are displayed in Figure 10-10.

Figure 10-10 Advertisement Requests

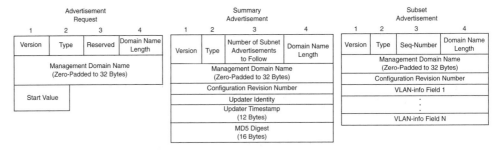

By default, server and client Catalyst switches issue summary advertisements every five minutes. They inform neighbor switches what they believe to be the current VTP revision number. Assuming the domain names match, the receiving server or client compares the configuration revision number. If the revision number in the advertisement is higher than the current revision number in the receiving switch, the receiving switch issues an advertisement request for new VLAN information. See Figure 10-11 for an example of the summary advertisement format.

Figure 10-11 Summary Advertisement Format

Version	Type	Number of Subnet Advertisements to Follow	Domain Name Length
Management Domain Name (Zero-Padded to 32 Bytes)			
Configuration Revision Number			
Updater Identity			
Updater Timestamp (12 Bytes)			
MD5 Digest (16 Bytes)			

Subset advertisements contain detailed information about VLANs, such as VTP version type, domain name and related fields, and configuration revision number. Creating or deleting a VLAN, suspending or activating a VLAN, changing the name of a VLAN, and changing the maximum transmission unit (MTU) of a VLAN can trigger these advertisements. See Figure 10-12 for an example of the subset advertisement format.

Figure 10-12 Subset Advertisement Format

Version	Type	Seq-Number	Domain Name Length
Management Domain Name (Zero-Padded to 32 Bytes)			
Configuration Revision Number			
VLAN-info Field 1			
. . .			
VLAN-info Field N			

The VLAN-info Field contains information for each VLAN
and is formatted as follows:

Info Length	Status	VLAN-Type	VLAN-name Len
ISL VLAN-id		MTU Size	
802.10 Index			
VLAN-name (Padded with 0s to Multiple of 4 Bytes)			

Advertisements might contain some or all of the following information:

- **Management domain name**—Advertisements that have different names are ignored.

- **Configuration revision number**—The higher number indicates a more recent configuration.

- **Message Digest 5 (MD5)**—MD5 is the key that is sent with the VTP when a password has been assigned. If the key does not match, the update is ignored.

- **Updater identity**—The updater identity is the identity of the switch that is sending the VTP summary advertisement.

VTP Configuration

Following are the basic tasks to considered before configuring VTP and VLANs on the network:

Step 1   Determine the version number of VTP that will be utilized.

Step 2   Decide if this switch is to be a member of an existing management domain or if a new domain should be created. If a management domain does exist, determine the name and password of the domain.

Step 3   Choose a VTP mode for the switch.

Configuring the VTP Version

Two different versions of VTP can run in your management domain: VTP Version 1 and VTP Version 2. The two versions are not interoperable. If you choose to configure a switch in a domain for VTP Version 2, you must configure all switches in the management domain to be in VTP Version 2. VTP Version 1 is the default. You might need to implement VTP Version 2 if you require some of the specific features that VTP Version 2 offers that are not offered in VTP Version 1. The most common feature that is needed is Token Ring VLAN support.

To configure the VTP version on a Cisco IOS command-based switch, first enter VLAN database mode. Use the following command to change the VTP version number on a set command-based switch:

```
Switch#vlan database
Switch(vlan)#vtp v2-mode
```

Use the following command to change the VTP version number on a set command-based switch.

```
Switch(enable) set vtp v2 enable
```

VTP Version 2 supports the following features that are unsupported in Version 1:

- **Token Ring support**—VTP Version 2 supports Token Ring LAN switching and VLANs.

- **Unrecognized type/length/value (TLV) support**—A VTP server or client propagates configuration changes to its other trunks—even for TLVs it is not able to parse. The unrecognized TLV is saved in NVRAM.

- **Version-dependent transparent mode**—In VTP Version 1, a VTP transparent switch inspects VTP messages for the domain name and version and forwards a message only if the version and domain name match. Because only one domain is supported in the supervisor engine software, VTP Version 2 forwards VTP messages in transparent mode without checking the version.

- **Consistency checks**—In VTP Version 2, VLAN consistency checks (such as VLAN names and values) are performed only when you enter new information through the CLI or Simple Network Management Protocol (SNMP). Consistency checks are not performed when new information is obtained from a VTP message or when information is read from NVRAM. If the digest on a received VTP message is correct, its information is accepted without consistency checks. A switch that is capable of running VTP Version 2 can operate in the same domain as a switch that is running VTP Version 1 if VTP Version 2 remains disabled on the VTP Version 2-capable switch.

If all switches in a domain are capable of running VTP Version 2, you need to enable VTP Version 2 on only one switch (using the **set vtp v2 enable** command). The version number is propagated to the other VTP Version 2-capable switches in the VTP domain.

Configuring the VTP Domain

If the switch being installed is the first switch in the network, create the management domain. Otherwise, verify the name of the management domain to join. If the management domain has been secured, configure the password for the domain.

To create a management domain, use the following command:

```
Switch(vlan)#vtp domain Cisco
```

The domain name can be between 1 and 32 characters and is case sensitive. The password must be between 8 and 64 characters long.

To add a VTP client to an existing VTP domain, always verify that its VTP configuration revision number is lower than the configuration revision number of the other switches in the VTP domain. Use the **show vtp status** command. Switches in a VTP domain use the VLAN configuration of the switch with the highest VTP configuration revision number. If a switch is added that has a revision number higher than the revision number in the VTP domain, it can erase all VLAN information from the VTP server and VTP domain.

To create a management domain or to add your switch to a management domain on a set command-based switch, use the following command:

```
Switch(enable)set vtp domain domain_name
```

Configuring the VTP Mode

Choose one of the three available VTP modes for the switch. Following are some general guidelines for choosing the switch mode.

If this is the first switch in your management domain and you intend to add additional switches, set the mode to server. The additional switches can learn VLAN information from this switch. You should have at least one server.

If other switches are in the management domain, set your switch mode to client to prevent the new switch from accidentally propagating the incorrect information to your existing network. If you would like this switch to end up as a VTP server, change the mode of the switch to server after it has learned the correct VLAN information from the network.

If the switch is not going to share VLAN information with any other switch on the network, set the switch to transparent mode. In transparent mode, you can create, delete, and rename VLANs at will without the switch propagating changes to other switches. If a large number of people are configuring devices within your network, you run the risk of overlapping VLANs with two different meanings in the network but the same VLAN identification.

To set the correct mode of the Cisco IOS command-based switch, use the following command:

Switch(vlan)#**vtp** {**client** | **server** | **transparent**}

To set the correct mode of your set command-based switch, use this command:

Switch>(enable) **set vtp mode server** | **client** | **transparent**

Verifying VTP Configuration

Example 10-4 shows the output of the **show vtp status** command. This command verifies VTP configuration settings on a Cisco IOS command-based switch.

Example 10-4 show vtp status *Command*

```
Switch#show vtp status
VTP Version                        : 2
Configuration Revision             : 2
Maximum VLANs supported locally    : 68
Number of existing VLANs           : 6
VTP Operating Mode                 : Client
VTP Domain Name                    : Cisco
VTP Pruning Mode                   : Disabled
VTP V2 Mode                        : Enabled
VTP Traps Generation               : Disabled
MD5 Digest                         : 0x35  0x84  0x7B  0x04  0x3D
                                     0x55  0x3B  0xDA
Configuration last modified by 0.0.0.0 at 12-23-02 20:24:33
```

Example 10-5 displays the results of the **show vtp statistics** command on a set command-based switch. This command shows a summary of VTP advertisement messages sent and received, as well as configuration errors detected. Use this command to assist you in troubleshooting VTP.

Example 10-5 show vtp statistics *Command*

```
Switch>(enable) show vtp statistics
VTP statistics:
summary advts received        0
subset advts received         0
request advts received        0
summary advts transmitted     0
subset advts transmitted      0
request advts transmitted     0
No of config revision errors  0
No of config digest errors    0
```

Lab Activity   Trunking with 802.1Q

In this lab, you create a basic switch configuration and then create multiple VLANs, name them, and assign member ports. You create an 802.1Q trunk line between the two switches and then test the VLANs by moving a workstation from one to the other.

Lab Activity   VTP Client and Server Configuration

In this lab you create multiple VLANs, name them, and assign member ports. You create an 802.1Q trunk line between the switches and configure one switch as a VTP server and the other as a client. You then test the VLANs by moving a workstation from one to the other.

VTP Pruning

The default behavior of a switch is to propagate broadcast and unknown packets across the network. This behavior results in unnecessary traffic crossing the network.

VTP pruning enhances network bandwidth use by reducing unnecessary flooding of traffic, such as broadcast, multicast, unknown, and flooded unicast packets. VTP pruning increases available bandwidth by restricting flooded traffic to those trunk links that the traffic must use to access the appropriate network devices. By default, VTP pruning is disabled. If no device from VLAN 3 is available on a remote switch, pruning can keep the switch from sending VLAN 3 traffic out the trunk and wasting bandwidth.

Enabling VTP pruning on a VTP server enables pruning for the entire management domain. VTP pruning takes effect several seconds after you enable it. By default, VLANs 2 through 1000 are pruning eligible. VTP pruning does not prune traffic from VLANs that are pruning ineligible. VLAN 1 is always pruning ineligible; therefore, traffic from VLAN 1 cannot be pruned. You have the option to make specific VLANs pruning eligible or pruning ineligible on the device. To make VLANs pruning eligible on a Cisco IOS command-based switch, enter the following:

```
Switch(vlan)#vtp pruning
```

To make specific VLANs pruning ineligible on a Cisco IOS command-based switch, enter this:

```
Switch(config)#interface fastethernet 0/3
Switch(config-if)#switchport trunk pruning vlan remove vlan-id
```

To make specific VLANs pruning eligible on a set command-based switch, enter the following:

```
Console> (enable) set vtp pruneeligible vlan_range
```

To make specific VLANs pruning ineligible on a set command-based switch, enter the following:

```
Console> (enable) clear vtp pruneeligible vlan_range
```

Inter-VLAN Routing

When a host in one broadcast domain wants to communicate with a host in another broadcast domain, a router must be involved. The same situation exists with VLANS. An example is shown in Figure 10-13.

Port 1 on a switch is part of VLAN 1, and Port 2 is part of VLAN 200. If all of the switch's ports were part of VLAN 1, the hosts that were connected to these ports could communicate. In this case, however, the ports are part of different VLANs: VLAN 1 and VLAN 200. A router must be involved if hosts from the different VLANs need to communicate, as shown in Figure 10-14.

Figure 10-13 Routers and VLANs

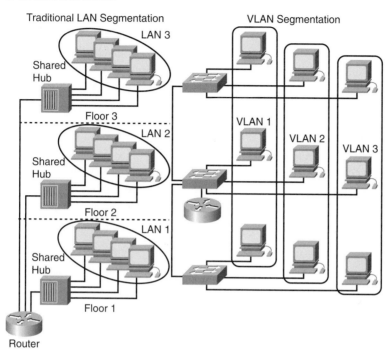

Figure 10-14 Removing Physical Boundaries

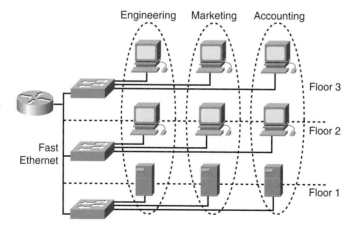

The most important benefit of routing is its proven history of facilitating networks, particularly networks that are large. Although the Internet serves as the obvious example, this point is true for any type of network, such as a large campus backbone. Because routers prevent broadcast propagation and use more intelligent forwarding algorithms than bridges and switches, routers provide much more efficient use of bandwidth. This simultaneously results in flexible and optimal path selection. For example, it is easy to implement load balancing across multiple paths in most networks when you are using routing. On the other hand, Layer 2 load balancing can be difficult to design, implement, and maintain.

If a VLAN spans across multiple devices, a trunk interconnects the devices. A trunk carries traffic for multiple VLANs. For example, a trunk can connect a switch to another switch, a switch to the inter-VLAN router, or a switch to a server that has a special network interface card (NIC) installed that supports trunking.

Remember that when a host on one VLAN wants to communicate with a host on another, a router is necessary.

Inter-VLAN Issues and Solutions

When VLANs are connected, several technical issues arise. Two of the most common in a multiple-VLAN environment are

- The need for end user devices to reach nonlocal hosts
- The need for hosts on different VLANs to communicate

When a device needs to make a connection to a remote host, it checks its routing table to determine if a known path exists. If the remote host falls into a subnet that it knows how to reach, the system checks to see if it can connect along that interface. If all known paths fail, the system has one last option: the default route. This route is a special type of gateway route, and it is usually the only one present in the system. On a router, a default route is indicated by an asterisk (*) in the output of the **show ip route** command. For hosts on a local-area network (LAN), this gateway is set to whatever machine has a direct connection to the outside world, and it is the default gateway listed in the workstation's TCP/IP settings. If the default route is being configured for a router that is functioning as the gateway to the public Internet, the default route points to the gateway machine at an Internet service provider's (ISP) site. Default routes are implemented by using the **ip route** command, as shown in Example 10-6.

Example 10-6 ip route *Command*

```
Router(Config)#ip route 0.0.0.0 0.0.0.0 192.168.1.1
```

In Example 10-6, 192.168.1.1 is the gateway. Inter-VLAN connectivity can be achieved through either logical or physical connectivity. Logical connectivity involves a single connection, or trunk, from the switch to the router. That trunk can support multiple VLANs. This topology is called a "router on a stick" because there is a single connection to the router, but there are multiple logical connections between the router and the switch. An example is shown in Figure 10-15.

Figure 10-15 Router on a Stick

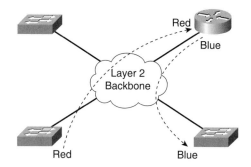

NOTE

In general, the router-on-a-stick approach to inter-VLAN routing is most appropriate when other options are unavailable. This is not to say that the router-on-a-stick design is a poor choice; it is only a reflection that other options tend to provide higher throughput and functionality. Also, because the router-on-a-stick technique functions as if the router were sitting on the edge of the network (at least as far as the Layer 2 network is concerned), it tends to be less tightly integrated with the rest of the campus network.

Isolated Broadcast Domains

In switched networks, Route Processors provide communications between VLANs. These processors provide VLAN access to shared resources and connect to other parts of the network that are either logically segmented with the more traditional subnet approach or require access to remote sites across wide-area links. Route Processors are much like routers, but they can be built into a switch. They might lack physical interfaces, but they are configured with the same IOS commands as regular routers.

Before you can configure routing between VLANs, you must have defined the VLANs on the switches in your network. Issues that are related to network design and VLAN definition should be addressed during your network design phase. The following are issues that you need to consider:

- Sharing resources between VLANs
- Load balancing
- Redundant links
- Logical addressing
- Segmenting the network by using VLANs

Figure 10-16 shows isolated broadcast domains.

Figure 10-16 Isolated Broadcast Domains

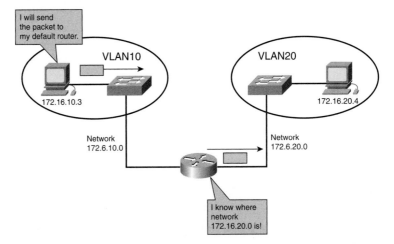

Finding the Route Between VLANs

The *Route Processor* contains most of the system memory components and the main system processor. A *default gateway* is simply a router interface that is normally referenced with an IP address. A *default router* is a router that has at least one interface serving as a default gateway. For DHCP, a default router is a router that provides a pool of IP addresses. A default gateway is shown in Figure 10-17.

Figure 10-17 Default Gateway

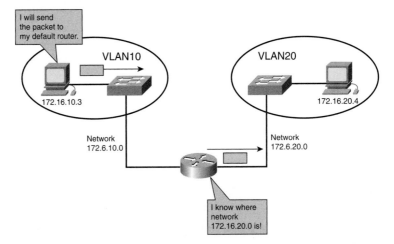

Connecting the separate subnets through a Route Processor introduces the issue of how end user devices can communicate with other devices through multiple LAN segments. Some network devices use routing tables to identify where to deliver packets outside of the local network segment. Even though it is not the responsibility of end user devices to route data, these devices still must be able to send data to addresses on subnets other than their own.

So that each end device does not have to manage its own routing tables, most devices are configured with the IP address of a designated Route Processor. This designated Route Processor is the default router to which all nonlocal network packets are sent. The Route Processor then forwards the packets toward the appropriate destination. A network device's default router IP address depends on which IP subnet contains that network device.

Early VLAN designs relied on external routers connected to VLAN-capable switches. In this approach, traditional routers are connected via one or more links to a switched network. The router-on-a-stick designs employ a single trunk link that connects the router to the rest of the campus network. Inter-VLAN traffic must cross the Layer 2 backbone to reach the router where it can move between VLANs. The traffic then travels back to the desired end station by using normal Layer 2 forwarding. This "out-to-the-router-and-back" flow is characteristic of router-on-a-stick designs.

Physical and Logical Interfaces

In a traditional situation, a network that had four VLANs required four physical connections between the switch and the external router. As technologies such as ISL became more common, network designers began to use trunk links to connect routers to switches. Although any trunking technology such as ISL, 802.1Q, 802.10, or LAN Emulation (LANE) can be used, Ethernet-based approaches are most common (ISL and 802.1Q). On Catalyst 2900 switches, the default is 802.1Q, whereas 29xx switches default to ISL.

The Cisco Proprietary protocol ISL trunks VLANs over Fast Ethernet links.

As the number of VLANs increases on a network, the physical approach of having one router interface per VLAN quickly becomes unscalable. Networks that have many VLANs must use VLAN trunking to assign multiple VLANs to a single router interface.

The primary advantage of using a trunk link is a reduction in router and switch ports. Not only can this save money, but it can also reduce configuration complexity. Consequently, the trunk-connected router approach can scale to a much larger number of VLANs than a one-link-per-VLAN design.

Dividing Physical Interfaces into Subinterfaces

A *subinterface* is a logical interface on a physical interface, such as the Fast Ethernet interface on a router. Multiple subinterfaces can exist on a single physical interface.

Each subinterface supports one VLAN and is assigned one IP address. For multiple devices on the same VLAN to communicate, the IP addresses of all devices must be on the same network or subnetwork. For example, if Subinterface 2 has an IP address of 192.168.1.1, then 192.168.1.2, 192.168.1.3, and 192.1.1.4 are the IP addresses of devices that are attached to Subinterface 2. To route between VLANs with subinterfaces, you must create a subinterface for each VLAN.

Configuring Inter-VLAN Routing

This section demonstrates the commands that are necessary to configure inter-VLAN routing between a router and a switch. Before any of these commands is implemented, check each router and switch to see which VLAN encapsulations they support. For example, Catalyst 2950 switches have supported 802.1Q trunking since the release of Cisco IOS release 12.0(5.2)WC(1), but they do not support ISL trunking. Cisco routers have supported ISL and 802.1Q trunking features since Cisco IOS release 12.0(T). For inter-VLAN routing to work properly, all the routers and switches involved must support the same encapsulation.

On a router, an interface can be logically divided into multiple, virtual subinterfaces. Subinterfaces provide a flexible solution for routing multiple data streams through a single physical interface. To define subinterfaces on a physical interface, perform the following tasks:

1. Identify the interface.

2. Define the VLAN encapsulation.

3. Assign an IP address to the interface.

To identify the interface, use the **interface** command in global configuration mode:

```
Router(config)#interface FastEthernet  port-number subinterface-number
```

The *port-number* identifies the physical interface, and the *subinterface-number* identifies the virtual interface. The router must be able to talk to the switch by using a standardized trunking protocol. This means that both devices that are connected must understand each other. In the example, 802.1Q is used.

To define the VLAN encapsulation, enter the **encapsulation** command in interface configuration mode:

```
Router(config-if)#encapsulation dot1q vlan-number
```

The *vlan-number* identifies the VLAN for which the subinterface carries traffic. A VLAN ID is added to the frame only when the frame is destined for a nonlocal network. Each VLAN packet carries the VLAN ID within the packet header.

To assign the IP address to the interface, enter the following command in interface configuration mode:

```
Router(config-if)#ip address ip-address subnet-mask
```

The *ip-address* and *subnet-mask* are the 32-bit network address and mask of the specific interface.

Lab Activity   Configuring Inter-VLAN Routing

In this lab, you configure an external router to route traffic between multiple VLANs on a switch.

Summary

Trunking is implemented on a VLAN network environment to allow the extension of the VLANs across the network. Trunking is normally implemented among switches by setting at least one of the ports on each of the switches participating on the trunk link to trunking mode.

Two of the most common trunking protocols that allow and manage the flow of different VLANs frames are as follows:

- ISL
- 802.1Q

VLAN Trunking Protocol (VTP) was created to minimize some of the potential problems of a VLAN network environment by maintaining the consistency of the network. VTP provides the following benefits:

- VLAN configuration consistency across the network
- Mapping scheme that allows a VLAN to be trunked over mixed media
- Accurate tracking and monitoring of VLANs
- Dynamic reporting of added VLANs across the network
- Plug-and-play configuration when adding new VLANs

When an end station in one VLAN needs to communicate with an end station in another VLAN, inter-VLAN routing is required.

To supplement all that you've learned in this chapter, refer to the chapter-specific Videos, PhotoZooms, and e-Lab Activities on the CD-ROM accompanying this book."

Key Terms

802.1Q   A trunking protocol that can carry the traffic of more than one subnet down a single cable. The IEEE 802.1Q committee defined this method of multiplexing VLANs in an effort to provide multivendor VLAN support.

default gateway   A router interface that is normally referenced with an IP address.

default router   A router that has at least one interface serving as a default gateway.

ISL (Inter-Switch Link)   A Cisco-specific, proprietary trunking protocol that interconnects multiple switches and maintains VLAN information as traffic travels between switches on trunk links.

Route Processor   Contains most of the system memory components and the main system processor.

subinterface   One of a number of virtual interfaces on a single physical interface.

trunk   A single transmission channel between two points that are usually switching centers.

trunking   A physical and logical connection between two switches across which network traffic travels. A backbone is composed of a number of trunks.

VLAN (virtual LAN)   A group of devices on one or more LANs that are configured (using management software) so that they can communicate as if they were attached to the same wire, when, in fact, they are located on a number of different LAN segments.

VTP (VLAN Trunking Protocol)   VTP is a messaging protocol that uses Layer 2 trunk frames to manage the addition, deletion, and renaming of VLANs on a network-wide basis.

Check Your Understanding

1. What is the primary advantage of using a trunk link?

    A. Provides more bandwidth for each trunk

    B. Efficient use of router and switch ports

    C. c. Allows for a single VLAN on each physical port

    D. d. Creates less overhead on the router

2. Which protocol carries multiple VLANs over a single trunk?

  A. 802.2

  B. 802.3

  C. 802.1Q

  D. 802.11B

3. Which protocol is Cisco proprietary and designed to carry traffic from multiple VLANs?

  A. 802.11A

  B. 802.1Q

  C. VNET

  D. ISL

4. To create or configure a VLAN trunk on a Cisco IOS command-based switch, configure the port first as a trunk and then specify the trunk encapsulation.

  A. True

  B. False

5. VTP messages are encapsulated in either Cisco proprietary Inter-Switch Link (ISL) or what type of frame?

  A. IEEE 802.1Q protocol frames

  B. IEEE 802.1R protocol frames

  C. 802.11D protocol frames

  D. 802.19 protocol frames

6. Using VTP, each Catalyst Family Switch advertises which of the following on its trunk ports?

  A. Management domain

  B. Configuration revision number

  C. Known VLANs and their specific parameters

  D. All of the above

7. VTP switches can operate in which modes?

  A. Server

  B. Client

  C. Transparent

  D. All of the above

8. Two different versions of VTP can run in your management domain: VTP Version 1 and VTP Version 2. The two versions are interoperable.

    A. True

    B. False

9. To create a management domain, use which command?

    A. Switch(vlan)#**domain Cisco**

    B. Switch(vtp)#**domain Cisco**

    C. Switch(vlan)#**vtp domain Cisco**

    D. Switch(vtp)#**vtp domain Cisco**

10. The default behavior of a switch is to propagate broadcasts and unknown _____ across the network.

    A. frames

    B. packets

    C. tags

    D. VLANs

11. Enabling VTP pruning on a VTP server enables pruning for the entire _____ domain.

    A. server

    B. transparent

    C. management

    D. user

12. In switched networks, _____ are used to provide communication between VLANs.

    A. Route Processors

    B. modulators

    C. VTPs

    D. subnets

Part III

CCNA 4: WAN Technologies

Objectives

After reading this chapter, you will be able to

- Explain why scaling IP addresses is necessary
- Describe NAT terminology
- Describe NAT features
- Differentiate between static NAT, dynamic NAT, and PAT
- Configure and verify NAT and PAT
- Troubleshoot NAT and PAT
- Differentiate between BOOTP and DHCP
- Configure and verify DHCP
- Describe DHCP terminology and features
- Troubleshoot DHCP
- Identify and differentiate between public and private IP addresses

Chapter 11

Scaling IP Addresses

An IP address is required for any device that connects to the Internet. The number of devices requiring an IP address is increasing rapidly, yet the number of IP addresses available is limited. This chapter discusses the problem of IP address space depletion and the solutions that have been developed to help alleviate the scaling problems of IP. Solutions presented here include network address translation (NAT), port address translation (PAT), the Dynamic Host Configuration Protocol (DHCP), and the use of private IP addresses. You will learn how to configure, verify, and troubleshoot NAT and DHCP on routers.

Please be sure to look at this chapter's associated e-Lab Activities, Videos, and PhotoZooms that you will find on the CD-ROM accompanying this book. These CD-ROM elements are designed to supplement the material and reinforce the concepts introduced in this chapter.

Internet Protocol Overview

IP is the connectivity protocol of choice. IP applications are being developed at a fast rate, which means that more hosts have the possibility to be connected to the Internet. In the early stages of the Internet, PCs, workstations, servers, and routers were the only devices that were attached to the Internet. An administrator statically assigned IP addresses.

Today, PDAs, laptops, desktops, mainframes, storage devices, routers, switches, video game consoles, and security cameras connect to the Internet. There is even talk of connecting household appliances. It should become clear that without scaling options, the Internet revolution would quickly reach its limits.

Several scaling options have been implemented over the years, including variable-length subnet mask (VLSM), *classless interdomain routing (CIDR)*, and Internet Protocol version 6 (IPv6). In this chapter, three other solutions to the scaling problem of IP are presented: private addressing (RFC 1918), address translation (NAT and PAT), and address pooling (DHCP).

This chapter presents solutions to IP scaling problems.

Two scalability challenges face the Internet today:

- The registered IP address space is being depleted, and size of the Internet continues to increase.
- As the Internet gets bigger, so does the number of IP routes in the backbone Internet routing tables. This poses a scalability problem for routing algorithms.

IP scaling solutions are as follows:

- NAT
- DHCP
- RFC 1918 (private IP addressing)

NAT is a mechanism for conserving registered IP addresses in large networks and simplifying IP addressing management tasks. NAT is standards based and is described in RFC 1631.

As a packet is routed across a Cisco IOS NAT router, the router translates the source IP address on the packet from a private internal network address to a legal IP address so that the packet can be transported over public external networks, such as the Internet. Returning traffic is translated back for delivery within the inside network. NAT is discussed in more detail later in this chapter.

The Internet has grown explosively, and it shows no signs of slowing down. Administrators must assign IP addresses, default gateways, and other necessary information to hosts that connect to the Internet. *DHCP* assists administrators with issuing IP addresses to devices dynamically.

As the global Internet took off, organizations wanted to use IP for connectivity, but they did not want to expose all their hosts to the Internet. RFC 1918 deals with this by defining public and private IP address space.

The Internet Assigned Numbers Authority (IANA) sets aside three blocks of IP addresses, which are shown in Table 11-1. RFC 1918 describes best practices for employing these addresses.

Table 11-1 RFC 1918 Addresses

Class	RFC 1918 Internal Address Range	CIDR Prefix
A	10.0.0.0–10.255.255.255	10.0.0.0/8
B	172.16.0.0–172.31.255.255	172.16.0.0/12
C	192.168.0.0–192.168.255.255	192.168.0.0/16

These three ranges provide more than 17 million private addresses. *Private* means that they are not allowed to be routed through the public Internet, but organizations are free to use them as they want to. Therefore, these addresses are considered on-routable.

Both IPv4 and IPv6 addresses are assigned in a delegated manner. Users are assigned IP addresses by Internet service providers (ISPs). ISPs obtain allocations of IP addresses from a local Internet registry (LIR), national Internet registry (NIR), or from their appropriate regional Internet registry (RIR). These could include Asia Pacific Network Information Centre (APNIC), American Registry for Internet Numbers (ARIN), Latin American and Caribbean IP Address Regional Registry (LACNIC), or Réseaux IP Européens (RIPE NCC).

Anyone can use reserved private IP addresses. That means two networks or two million networks can each use the same private address. RFC 1918 addresses should never be seen on the public Internet; a public Internet router should never route these addresses because ISPs typically configure their routers to prevent privately addressed customer traffic from being forwarded.

If you are addressing a nonpublic intranet, a test lab, or a home network, these private addresses can be used instead of globally unique addresses. Global addresses must be obtained from a provider or a registry at some expense.

RFC 1918 addresses have found a home in production networks as well. With VLSM, you can further subnet one of the subnets left in a Class C network's address space. Although this solution is better than wasting an entire 30-host subnet on each two-host WAN link, it still costs one subnet that could have been used for future growth. A less wasteful solution is to address the WAN links by using private network numbers. In Figure 11-1, the WAN links are addressed by using subnets from the private address space 10.0.0.0 /8.

Figure 11-1 Using Private Addresses in the WAN

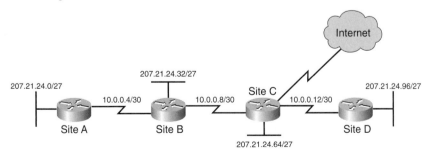

How can these routers use private addresses if LAN users at sites A, B, C, and D expect to access the Internet? End users at these sites should have no problem because they use globally unique addresses from the 207.21.24.0 network. The routers use their serial interfaces with private addresses merely to forward traffic and exchange routing information. Upstream providers and Internet routers see only the source and destination IP addresses in the packet; they do not care if the packet traveled through links with private addresses at some point. In fact, many providers use RFC 1918 network numbers in the core of their network to avoid depleting their supply of globally unique addresses.

One trade-off of using private numbers on WAN links is that these serial interfaces cannot be the original source of traffic bound for the Internet or the final destination of traffic from the Internet. Routers do not normally spend time surfing the web, so this limitation typically becomes an issue only when troubleshooting with ICMP, when using SNMP, or when connecting remotely with Telnet over the Internet. In those cases, the router can be addressed only by its globally unique LAN interfaces.

NAT provides tremendous benefits to individual companies and the Internet. Before NAT, a host with a private address could not access the Internet. With NAT, individual companies can address some or all of their hosts with private addresses and then use NAT to access the public Internet. At the same time, these hosts connect to the Internet without necessarily depleting its address space.

NAT and PAT

NAT is a process of manipulating the addresses in the IP header of a packet so that the destination address, the source address, or both addresses are replaced in the header by different administrator-assigned addresses. A device that is running specialized NAT software or hardware performs this swapping process. Cisco IOS NAT is designed for IP address simplification and conservation because it enables private IP internetworks that use unregistered IP addresses to connect to the Internet by translating those addresses into globally registered IP addresses. Cisco IOS NAT also increases network privacy by hiding internal IP addresses from external networks.

A NAT-enabled device typically operates at the border of a stub network. A stub network is a network that has a single connection to its neighbor network. Figure 11-2 presents a simple example of a stub network. When a host inside the stub network wants to transmit to a host on the outside, it forwards the packet to its border gateway router. In this case, the host's border gateway router is also the NAT box.

Figure 11-2 Stub Network

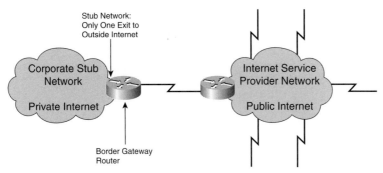

NAT operates on a Cisco router, usually connecting two networks, and it translates the private (inside local) addresses in the internal network to public addresses (inside global) before packets are forwarded to another network, as shown in Figures 11-3 through 11-5.

An internal host (10.0.0.2) wants to communicate with an external host (128.23.2.2). It sends its packet to its gateway RTA, as shown in Figure 11-3.

Figure 11-3 How NAT Works

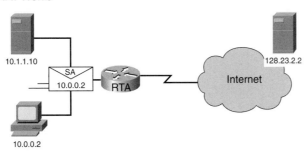

RTA sees the packet is to be routed to the outside Internet. The NAT process chooses a globally unique IP address (179.9.8.80) and replaces the local address in the source field of the pack with the global address. It stores this mapping of local to global address in the NAT table, as shown in Figure 11-4.

The packet is routed to its destination. In this client-server environment, the server might respond with a packet, which will come back to RTA, addressed to the global address 179.9.8.80, as shown in Figure 11-5.

Figure 11-4 How NAT Works: NAT Table

Inside Local IP Address	Inside Global IP Address
10.0.0.2	179.9.8.80
10.0.0.3	179.9.8.81

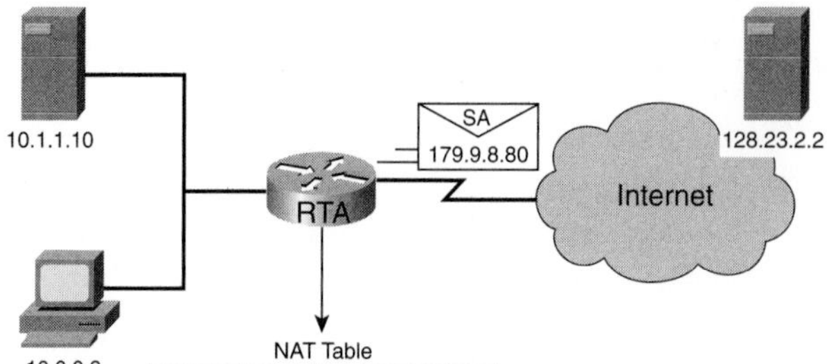

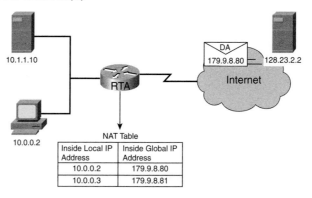

Figure 11-5 How NAT Works: Reply

Inside Local IP Address	Inside Global IP Address
10.0.0.2	179.9.8.80
10.0.0.3	179.9.8.81

In Figure 11-6, the NAT process sees a packet routed from the outside to the inside and consults the NAT table for a mapping of this global address into a local address. The global address in the destination field of the packet is replaced with the local address, and the packet is forwarded internally.

Figure 11-6 How NAT Works: Final

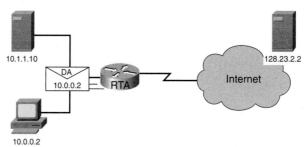

In NAT terminology, the inside network is the set of networks that are subject to translation. The outside network refers to all other addresses. Usually these are valid addresses located on the Internet.

As part of this functionality, NAT can be configured to advertise only one address for the entire network to the outside world. This effectively hides the internal network from the world and provides additional security. This feature of NAT is called static PAT, and it is shown in Figures 11-7 and 11-8. PAT is also referred to as overload in Cisco IOS configuration. Several internal addresses can be translated by using NAT compared to only one or a few external addresses by using PAT. In Figure 11-7, hosts 10.0.0.2 and 10.0.0.3 send packets to the outside world by using the single public IP address of 179.9.8.80. The router keeps track of packets for each host by appending a unique source port number to the outside IP address.

Figure 11-7 How PAT Works

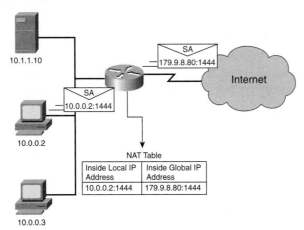

PAT uses unique source port numbers on the inside global IP address to distinguish between translations. Because the port number is encoded in 16 bits, the total number of internal addresses that can be translated into one external address by using PAT could theoretically be as high as 65,536 per IP address. PAT attempts to preserve the original source port. If this source port is already allocated, PAT tries to find the first available port number starting from the beginning of the appropriate port group 0-511, 512-1023, or 1024-65535. If no port is available from the appropriate port group and more than one external IP address is configured, PAT moves to the next IP address and tries to allocate the original source port again. This continues until PAT runs out of available ports and external IP addresses.

Figure 11-8 How PAT Works: Final

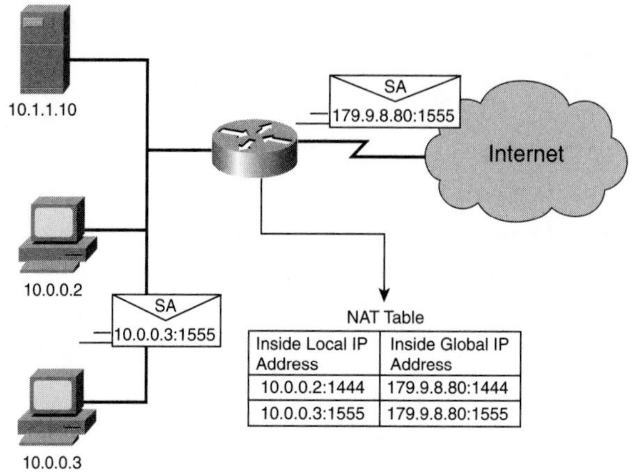

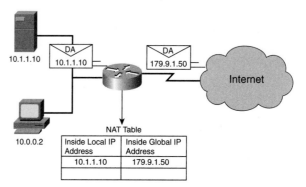

NAT and PAT Features

NAT can occur dynamically or statically, and you can use it for a variety of purposes. Static NAT is designed to allow one-to-one mapping between local and global addresses, as shown in Figure 11-9. This is particularly useful for inside IP hosts that must be accessible from the Internet, such as a DNS server or e-mail server.

Figure 11-9 Static NAT

Dynamic NAT is designed to map an unregistered IP address to a registered IP address from a group of registered IP addresses, as shown in Figure 11-10.

Figure 11-10 Dynamic NAT

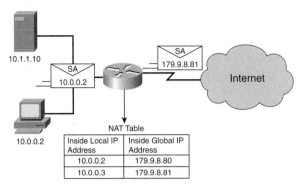

Cisco defines the following NAT terms:

- *Inside local address*—The IP address assigned to a host on the inside network that is likely to be an RFC 1918 private address.

- *Inside global address*—A legitimate IP address that the Regional Internet Registries (RIR) or service provider assigns. It represents one or more inside local IP addresses to the outside world.

- *Outside local address*—The IP address of an outside host as it is known to the hosts in the inside network.

- *Outside global address*—The IP address that the host's owner assigns to a host on the outside network.

NAT offers the following benefits:

- **Eliminates readdressing overhead, such as changing an ISP**—No longer is it necessary to readdress all hosts that require external access, which saves time and money.

- **Conserves addresses through application port-level multiplexing**—With NAT, internal hosts can share a single registered IP address for all external communications. In this type of configuration, relatively few external addresses are required to support many internal hosts, which conserves IP addresses.

- **Protects network security**—Because private networks do not advertise their addresses or internal topology, they remain reasonably secure when they are used in conjunction with NAT to gain controlled external access.

Configuring NAT and PAT

The following configuration topics are covered in this section:

- Static translation
- Dynamic translation
- Overloading NAT (PAT)

Static Translation

Static translation occurs when you specifically configure addresses in a lookup table. A specific inside local address maps to a prespecified inside global address. The inside local and inside global addresses are statically mapped one for one. This means that for every inside local address, static NAT requires an inside global address. To configure static inside source address translation, perform the tasks outlined in Table 11-2.

Table 11-2 Configuring Static NAT

Step	Action	Notes
1.	Establish static translation between an inside local address and an inside global address. Router(config)#**ip nat inside source static** *local-ip global-ip*	Enter the global **no ip nat inside source static** command to remove the static source translation.
2.	Specify the inside interface. Router(config)#**interface** *type number* Mark the interface as connected to the inside. Router(config-if)#**ip nat inside**	When you enter the **interface** command, the CLI prompt changes from (config)# to (config-if)#.
3.	Specify the outside interface. Router(config-if)#**interface** *type number* Mark the interface as connected to the outside. Router(config-if)#**ip nat outside**	

You enter static translations directly into the configuration, and they are shown in the translation table. Example 11-1 gives the command for Cisco IOS routers.

Example 11-1 *Configuring Static NAT*

```
Router(config)#ip nat inside source static 10.1.1.2 192.168.1.2
Router(config)#interface s0
Router(config-if)#ip nat outside
Router(config-if)#interface e0
Router(config-if)#ip nat inside
```

Figure 11-11 shows the use of static NAT. The router translates packets from host 10.1.1.2 to a source address of 192.168.1.2. Example 11-2 provides the gateway configuration.

Figure 11-11 Static NAT Example

Example 11-2 *Gateway Configuration*

```
hostname GW
!
ip nat inside source static 10.1.1. 2 192.168.1.2

!
interface Ethernet0
 ip address 10.1.1.1 255.255.255.0
 ip nat inside
!
interface Serial0
 ip address 192.168.1.1 255.255.255.0
 ip nat outside
!
ip nat inside source static 10.1.1.2 192.168.1.2
```

Dynamic Translation

With Dynamic NAT, translations do not exist in the NAT table until the router receives traffic that requires translation. (An administrator defines such traffic.) Dynamic translations are temporary, and they eventually time out. To configure dynamic inside source address translation, perform the tasks shown in Table 11-3.

Table 11-3 Configuring Dynamic NAT

Step	Action	Notes
1.	Define a pool of global addresses to be allocated as needed. Router(config)#**ip nat pool** *name start-ip end-ip* {**netmask** *netmask* | **prefix-length** *prefix-length*}	Enter the global **no ip nat pool** command to remove the pool of global addresses.
2.	Create an access list to identify hosts for translation. Router(config)#**access-list** *access-list-number* **permit** *source* [*source-wild-card*]	Enter the global **no access-list** *access-list-number* command to remove the access list.
3.	Configure Dynamic NAT based on source address. Router(config)#**ip nat inside source list** *access-list-number* **pool** *name*	Enter the global **no ip nat inside source** command to remove the dynamic source translation.
4.	Specify the inside interface. Router(config-if)#**ip nat inside**	When you enter the **interface** command, the CLI prompt changes from (config)# to (config-if)#.
5.	Specify the outside interface. Router(config-if)#**interface** *type number* Router(config-if)#**ip nat outside**	

Dynamic translation specifies the pool of global addresses that inside addresses can be translated into, as shown in Example 11-3.

Example 11-3 *Configuring Dynamic NAT*

```
Router(config)#ip nat pool nat-pool 179.9.8.80 179.9.8.95
    netmask 255.255.255.0 255.255.255.240
```

The access list must permit only those addresses that are to be translated. Remember that an implicit deny all exists at the end of each access list. An access list that is too permissive can lead to unpredictable results. Cisco highly recommends that you not configure access lists referenced by NAT commands with permit any. Using permit any can result in NAT consuming too many router resources, which can cause network problems.

The following commands configure the appropriate interfaces to take on the role of outside and inside:

```
Router(config)#interface s0
Router(config-if)#ip nat outside
Router(config-if)#interface e0
Router(config-if)#ip nat inside
```

Figure 11-12 translates all source addresses passing access list 1 (having a source address from 10.0.0.0/16) to an address from the pool named nat-pool. The pool contains addresses from 179.9.8.80/28 to 179.9.8.95/28.

Figure 11-12 PAT Example

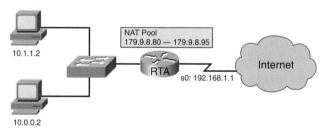

Configuration for GW is shown in Example 11-4.

Example 11-4 *Configuration for GW*

```
<output omitted>
ip nat pool nat-pool1 179.9.8.80 179.9.8.95 netmask 255.255.255.0
ip nat inside source list 1 pool nat-pool1
!
interface fastethernet0/0
 ip address 10.1.1.1 255.255.255.0
 ip nat inside
!
interface Serial0/0
 ip address 192.168.1.1 255.255.255.0
 ip nat outside
 !
```

Overloading NAT

One of the most powerful features of NAT routers is their ability to use PAT. This is sometimes called a "many-to-one" NAT, or address overloading. With address *overloading*, hundreds of privately addressed nodes can access the Internet by using a single global address. The NAT router keeps track of the different conversations by mapping TCP and UDP port numbers in the translation table.

To configure overloading of inside global addresses, perform the tasks shown in Table 11-4.

Table 11-4 Configuring NAT Overload

Step	Action	Notes
1.	Define a standard access list permitting those addresses that are to be translated. Router(config)#**access-list** *access-list-number* **permit** *source* [*source-wildcard*]	Enter the global **no access-list** *access-list-number* command to remove the access list.
2.A	Establish dynamic source translation, specifying the access list that was defined in the prior step. Router(config)#**ip nat inside source list** *access-list-number* **interface** *interface* **overload**	Enter the global **no ip nat inside source** command to remove the dynamic source translation. The **overload** keyword enables PAT.
2.B	Specify the global address (as a pool) to be used for overloading. Router(config)#**ip nat pool** *name* *ip-address* {**netmask** *netmask* | **prefix-length** *prefix-length*} Establish overload translation. Router(config)#**ip nat inside source list** *access-list-number* **pool** *name* **overload**	
3.	Specify the inside interface. Router(config)#**interface** *type number* Router(config-if)#**ip nat inside**	When you enter the **interface** command, the CLI prompt changes from (config)# to (config-if)#.
4.	Specify the outside interface. Router(config-if)#**interface** *type number* Router(config-if)#**ip nat outside**	

Define a standard IP access list permitting those inside local addresses that are to be translated, as shown in Example 11-5.

Example 11-5 *Standard IP Access List*

```
Router(config)#access-list 1 permit 10.0.0.0 0.0.255.255
```

Establish overload translation, specifying the IP address to be overloaded as that assigned to an outside interface, as shown in Example 11-6.

Example 11-6 *Overload with an Interface*

```
Router(config)#ip nat inside source list 1 interface serial0/0 overload
```

Establish overload translation, specifying the IP address to be overloaded as that assigned to a pool name, as shown in Example 11-7.

Example 11-7 *Overload with a Pool*

```
Router(config)#ip nat pool nat-pool2 179.9.8.20 netmask 255.255.255.240
Router(config)#ip nat inside source list 1pool nat-pool2 overload
Router(config)#interface s0
Router(config-if)#ip nat outside
Router(config-if)#interface ethernet 0
Router(config-if)#ip nat inside
```

Lab Activity   Configuring NAT

In this lab, you will configure a router by using NAT to convert internal private IP addresses into outside public addresses.

Lab Activity   Configuring PAT

In this lab, you will configure a router to use PAT to convert internal private IP addresses into outside public addresses.

Lab Activity   Configuring Static NAT Addresses

In this lab, you will configure a router to use PAT to convert internal private IP addresses into outside public addresses. Static IP mapping will also be configured to allow outside access to an internal PC.

Verifying NAT and PAT Configuration

After NAT is configured, verify that it is operating as expected by using the **clear** and **show** commands.

By default, dynamic address translations time out from the NAT table after a period of nonuse. When port translation is not configured, translation entries time out after 24 hours, unless they are reconfigured with the **ip nat translation** command. Clear the entries before the timeout by using one of the commands in Table 11-5.

Table 11-5 Commands for Clearing NAT Table Entries

Command	Description
clear ip nat translation *	Clears all dynamic address translation entries from the NAT translation table
clear ip nat translation inside *global-ip local-ip* [**outside** *local-ip global-ip*]	Clears a simple dynamic translation entry containing an inside translation, or both inside and outside translation
clear ip nat translation protocol inside *global-ip global-port local-ip local-port* [**outside** *local-ip local-port global-ip global-port*]	Clears an extended dynamic translation entry

Translation information can be displayed by performing one of the tasks in EXEC mode, as shown in Table 11-6.

Table 11-6 Commands to Display Translation Information

Command	Description
show ip nat translations	Displays active translations
show ip nat statistics	Displays translation statistics

Alternatively, use the **show run** command and look for NAT, access list, interface, or pool commands with the required values.

Lab Activity   Verifying NAT and PAT configuration

In this lab, you will verify NAT and PAT are functioning correctly using the **clear** and **show** commands.

Troubleshooting NAT and PAT Configuration

When IP connectivity problems exist in a NAT environment, it is often difficult to determine the cause of the problem. Many times, NAT is mistakenly blamed, when in reality, there is an underlying problem.

When you are trying to determine the cause of an IP connectivity problem, it helps to rule out NAT. Follow these steps to verify that NAT is operating as expected:

Step 1 Based on the configuration, clearly define what NAT is supposed to achieve.

Step 2 Verify that correct translations exist in the translation table.

Step 3 Verify that translation is occurring by using **show** and **debug** commands.

Step 4 Review in detail what is happening to the packet and verify that routers have the correct routing information to move the packet along.

Use the **debug ip nat** command to verify the operation of the NAT feature by displaying information about every packet that is translated by the router. The **debug ip nat** *detailed* command generates a description of each packet that is considered for translation. This command also outputs information about certain errors or exception conditions, such as the failure to allocate a global address.

Example 11-8 shows sample **debug ip nat** output for the network in Figure 11-13. In this example, the first two lines show the debugging output that a Domain Name System (DNS) request and reply produced. The remaining lines show the debugging output from a Telnet connection from a host on the inside of the network to a host on the outside of the network.

Figure 11-13 Using NAT Debug Commands

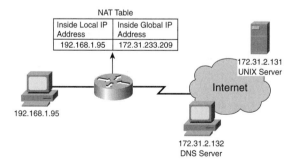

Example 11-8 debug ip nat *Output*

```
Router#debug ip nat

NAT: s=192.168.1.95->172.31.233.209, d=172.31.2.132 [6825]
NAT: s=172.31.2.132, d=172.31.233.209->192.168.1.95 [21852]
NAT: s=192.168.1.95->172.31.233.209, d=172.31.1.161 [6826]
NAT*: s=172.31.1.161, d=172.31.233.209->192.168.1.95 [23311]
NAT*: s=192.168.1.95->172.31.233.209, d=172.31.1.161 [6827]
NAT*: s=192.168.1.95->172.31.233.209, d=172.31.1.161 [6828]
NAT*: s=172.31.1.161, d=172.31.233.209->192.168.1.95 [23313]
NAT*: s=172.31.1.161, d=172.31.233.209->192.168.1.95 [23325]
```

Decode the **debug** output as follows:

- **NAT***—The asterisk (*) next to NAT indicates that the translation is occurring in the fast-switched path. The first packet in a conversation will always go through the slow path (that is, it will be process-switched). The remaining packets will go through the fast-switched path if a cache entry exists.
- **s = *a.b.c.d*—*a.b.c.d* is the source address.
- ***a.b.c.d -> w.x.y.z*—*w.x.y.z* is the address that the source was translated to.
- **d = *a.b.c.d*—*a.b.c.d* is the destination address.
- **[23325]**—The value in brackets is the IP identification number. This information can be useful for debugging because it enables correlation with other packet traces from protocol analyzers, for example.

 Lab Activity Troubleshooting NAT and PAT configuration

In this lab, you will troubleshoot NAT and PAT configurations using the **show** and **debug** commands.

Advantages and Disadvantages of NAT

NAT has several advantages, including the following:

- NAT conserves the legally registered addressing scheme by allowing the privatization of intranets.
- NAT increases the flexibility of connection to the public network. Multiple pools, backup pools, and load sharing/balancing pools can be implemented to help ensure reliable public network connections.

- Deprivatization of a network requires the renumbering of the existing network; the costs can be associated with the number of hosts that require conversion to the new addressing scheme. NAT allows the existing scheme to remain, and it still supports the new assigned addressing scheme outside the private network.

NAT is not without drawbacks. The tradeoff for address translation is a loss of functionality, particularly with any protocol or application that involves sending IP address information inside the IP payload. This requires additional support by the NAT box. NAT disadvantages include the following:

- NAT increases delay. Switching path delays, of course, are introduced because of the translation of each IP address within the packet headers. Performance might be a consideration because NAT is currently accomplished by using process switching. The CPU must look at every packet to decide whether it has to translate it, and then alter the IP header—and possibly the TCP header. It is unlikely that this process will be easily cacheable.

- One significant disadvantage when implementing and using NAT is the loss of end-to-end IP traceability. It becomes much more difficult to trace packets that undergo numerous packet address changes over multiple NAT hops. This scenario does, however, lead to more secure links because hackers who want to determine the source of a packet will find it difficult, if not impossible, to trace or obtain the original source or destination address.

- NAT also forces some applications that use IP addressing to stop functioning because it hides end-to-end IP addresses. Applications that use physical addresses instead of a qualified domain name will not reach destinations that are translated across the NAT router. Sometimes, this problem can be avoided by implementing static NAT mappings.

- NAT supports TCP/UDP traffic that does not carry source or destination IP addresses in the application data stream, such as HTTP, TFTP, and Telnet.

Although the following traffic types carry IP addresses in the application data stream, these are some of the applications that Cisco IOS NAT supports:

- ICMP
- File Transfer Protocol (FTP) (including **PORT** and **PASV** commands)
- NetBIOS over TCP/IP (datagram, name, and session services)
- Progressive Networks' RealAudio
- White Pines' CuSeeMe
- Xing Technologies' Streamworks
- DNS "A" and "PTR" queries

- NetMeeting (2.1, 2.11 & 3.01)
- H.323v2 (H.225/245 message types except RAS - 12.1(5)T)
- VDOLive [11.3(4)/11.3(4)T and later]
- Vxtreme [11.3(4)/11.3(4)T and later]
- IP multicast [12.0(1)T] (source address translation only)

Cisco IOS NAT does *not* support these traffic types:

- Routing table updates
- DNS zone transfers
- BOOTP
- talk, ntalk
- Simple Network Management Protocol (SNMP)
- NetShow

DHCP Overview

Routers, servers, and other key nodes usually require a specific IP configuration. However, desktop clients do not require a specific address, but rather any one in a range of addresses. This range is typically within an IP subnet. A desktop client that is within a specific subnet can have any address within a range, while the other values are defaulted. These default values include the subnet mask, the default gateway, and the DNS server address for the subnet or network.

Configuring a host that is connected to a TCP/IP Internet requires several values:

- An IP address
- A subnet mask
- A default gateway
- A DNS server address

This list is the minimum; there might be other variables depending on the network environment. These variables generally have to be configured manually into every IP host. They are usually stored in a configuration file and accessed by the computer at startup.

In addition, some clients are diskless; the operating system and software are stored on ROM. The manufacturer of the ROM chip is unaware of the IP configuration values at production time; therefore, you cannot configure these values. The configuration must be supplied after booting. In these environments, you can allocate these IP values dynamically when an IP host boots. The DHCP was designed to do this particular task. Because desktop clients typically comprise the bulk of network nodes, DHCP is good news for systems administrators.

Introducing DHCP

DHCP, which works in a client/server mode, enables hosts (DHCP clients) on an IP network to obtain their configurations from a server (DHCP server). This reduces the work necessary to administer an IP network. The most significant configuration option that the client receives from the server is its IP address. The DHCP protocol is described in RFC 2131.

The DHCP client is part of most modern operating systems including Windows 9x/NT/ 2000/XP, Solaris, Linux, and MAC OS. The client part requests the configuration values from the network. The network must have a DHCP server that manages the allocation of the IP configuration values and answers requests from clients. The DHCP server can be responsible for answering requests for many subnets. DHCP is not intended for use in configuring routers, switches, and servers because these hosts need to have static IP addresses.

DHCP works by configuring a server to give out IP information to clients. Clients lease the information from the server for an administratively defined period. When the lease expires, the client must ask for another address, although the client is typically reassigned the same one.

Administrators typically prefer to use a Microsoft NT/2000/XP server or a UNIX computer to offer DHCP services because these solutions are scalable and relatively easy to manage. Even so, a Cisco IOS feature set (Easy IP) offers an optional, fully featured DHCP server that a router can provide. It leases configurations for 24 hours by default. This feature is useful in small offices and home offices where those offices can take advantage of DHCP and NAT without requiring a computer-based server.

Administrators set up DHCP servers to assign addresses from predefined pools. DHCP servers can also offer other information, such as DNS server addresses, WINS server addresses, and domain names. In addition, most DHCP servers allow the administrator to define specifically what client MAC addresses can be serviced and automatically assign them the same IP address each time.

The DHCP client sends a directed IP broadcast, with a DHCP request packet. In the simplest case, a DHCP server is on the same segment, and it will pick up this request. Figures 11-14, 11-15, and 11-16 illustrate the DHCP request/reply process. The server notes that the GIADDR field is blank, so the client is on the same segment. The server notes the client's hardware address in the request packet, as shown in Figure 11-14.

Figure 11-14 DHCP Beginning Process

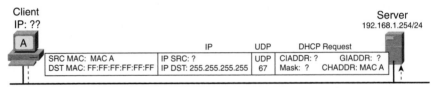

The DHCP server picks an IP address from the available pool for that segment, as well as the other segment and global parameters. The DHCP server then puts them into the appropriate fields of the DHCP packet. The server uses the hardware address of A (in CHADDR) to construct an appropriate frame to send back to the client, as shown in Figure 11-15.

Figure 11-15 DHCP Server Reply

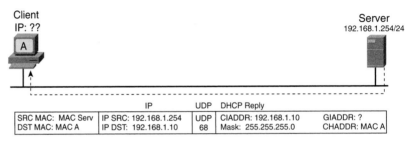

The DHCP client operating system uses the values in the DHCP reply to configure the IP protocol stack of that client, as shown in Figure 11-16.

Figure 11-16 DHCP Completed

DHCP uses UDP as its transport protocol. The client sends messages to the server on port 67, and the server sends messages to the client on port 68.

BOOTP and DHCP Differences

The Internet community first developed the *Bootstrap Protocol (BOOTP)* to configure diskless clients on a network. BOOTP was originally defined in RFC 951 in 1985. The predecessor of DHCP, BOOTP shares some operational characteristics. Both protocols are client-server based, using UDP ports 67 and 68, which are well known as BOOTP ports because BOOTP came before DHCP.

BOOTP provides the basic four IP parameters that have already been mentioned. However, BOOTP is not dynamic. When a client requests an IP address, the BOOTP server searches a predefined table for an entry that matches the client's MAC address. If an entry exists, the corresponding IP address for that entry is returned to the client. This means that the binding between the MAC address and the IP address must have already been configured in the BOOTP server.

DHCP defines mechanisms through which clients can be assigned an IP address for a finite lease period, allowing for reassignment of the IP address to another client later, or for the client to get another assignment if the client moves to another subnet. Clients can renew leases and keep the same IP address.

DHCP provides the mechanism for a client to gather other IP configuration parameters (WINS, domain name) it needs to operate in the TCP/IP network.

Table 11-7 provides a summary of the differences between DHCP and BOOTP.

Table 11-7 DHCP and BOOTP

BOOTP	DHCP
Static mappings	Dynamic mappings
Permanent assignment	Lease assignment
Supports only four configuration parameters	Supports more than 30 configuration parameters
Used to send a bootable operating system to a host	Cannot be used to send a bootable operating system to a host

DHCP Features

Three mechanisms are used to assign an IP address to the client:

- **Automatic allocation**—DHCP assigns a permanent IP address to a client.
- **Manual allocation**—The administrator assigns the client's IP address, and DHCP conveys the address to the client.
- **Dynamic allocation**—DHCP assigns an IP address to the client for a limited period of time (lease).

The focus of this unit is the dynamic allocation mechanism. Some of the configuration parameters available are listed in IETF RFC 1533. A few of these parameters include the following:

- IP address
- Subnet mask
- Router (default gateway)
- Domain name
- Domain name server(s)
- Name server (such as WINS)

Refer to Figure 11-17. The DHCP server creates pools of IP addresses and associated parameters. Pools are dedicated to an individual logical IP subnet, which allows multiple DHCP servers to respond for a subnet; as such, IP clients can be mobile. If multiple servers can respond, a client can get several offers; however, a client can choose only one server. Example 11-9 shows the information the DHCP server sends this DHCP client.

Figure 11-17 DHCP Client and Server

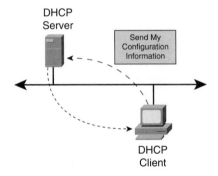

Example 11-9 *DHCP Configuration File*

```
IP Address: 192.204.18.7
Subnet Mask: 255.255.255.0
Default Routers: 192.204.18.1, 192.204.18.3
DNS Servers: 192.204.18.8, 192.204.18.9
Lease Time: 5 days
```

DHCP clients are available for a variety of operating systems and from numerous vendors, including Windows 3.1, Windows 9x, Windows NT, Windows 2000, Windows XP, Solaris, Linux, MAC OS, Novell NetWare, FTP Software, NetManage, and Cisco.

DHCP Operation

The DHCP client configuration process is shown in Figure 11-18.

Figure 11-18 DHCP Discovery Process

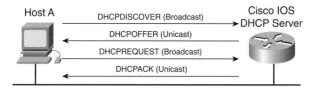

This process follows five steps:

1. **The client sends a DHCPDISCOVER broadcast to all nodes**—A client is preset for DHCP. The client sends a request for a server requesting an IP configuration (typically at boot time). Alternatively, the client can suggest the IP address it wants to use, such as when requesting an extension to a lease. The client tries to locate a DHCP server by sending a broadcast (255.255.255.255) called a DHCPDISCOVER on its local segment.

2. **The server sends a DHCPOFFER unicast to the client**—When the server receives the broadcast, it determines whether it can service the request from its own database. If it cannot service the request, the server might forward the request to another DHCP server(s), depending on its configuration. If it can service the request, the DHCP server offers the client IP configuration information in the form of a unicast DHCPOFFER. The DHCPOFFER is a proposed configuration that might include IP address, DNS server address, and lease time.

3. **The client sends a DHCPREQUEST broadcast to all nodes**—If the client finds the offer agreeable, it will send another broadcast, a DHCPREQUEST, specifically requesting those particular IP parameters. Why does the client broadcast the request instead of unicasting it to the server? A broadcast is used because the first message, the DHCPDISCOVER, might have reached more than one DHCP server. If more than one server makes an offer, the broadcasted DHCPREQUEST lets everyone know which offer was accepted. The accepted offer is usually the first offer received.

4. **The server sends a DHCPACK unicast to the client**—The server that receives the DHCPREQUEST makes the configuration official by sending a unicast acknowledgment, the DHCPACK. Note that it is possible but highly unlikely that the server will not send the DHCPACK because it might have leased that information to another client in the interim. Receipt of the DHCPACK message enables the client to begin using the assigned address immediately.

   If the client detects that the address is already in use on the local segment, it sends a DHCPDECLINE message and the process starts again. If the client receives a DHCPNAK from the server after sending the DHCPREQUEST, it restarts the process.

5. **The client releases the IP address**—If the client no longer needs its IP address, the client sends a DHCPRELEASE message to the server.

Depending on an organization's policies, it might be possible for an end user or an administrator to statically assign a host an IP address that belongs in the DHCP server's address pool. Just in case, the Cisco IOS DHCP server always checks to make sure that an address is not in use before the server offers it to a client. The server issues ICMP echo requests (ping) to a pool address before sending the DHCPOFFER to a client. Although configurable, the default number of pings used to check for potential IP address conflict is two.

If the server is on another segment, you can use a BOOTP relay agent on the router to transport the request to that segment.

Configuring DHCP Operation

Like NAT, DHCP server requires that the administrator define a pool of addresses. The **ip dhcp** pool command defines which addresses are assigned to hosts. The command's syntax is as follows:

```
Router(config)#ip dhcp pool name1
Router(dhcp-config)#network ip-address mask
```

The first command, **ip dhcp pool** *name1*, creates a pool named *name1* and puts the router in a specialized DHCP configuration mode. In this mode, use the network statement to define the range of addresses to be leased. If specific addresses on the network are to be excluded, return to global configuration mode and use the **ip dhcp excluded-address** command. Type **exit** to get out of DHCP configuration mode.

The **ip dhcp excluded-address** command configures the router to exclude an individual address or a range of addresses when assigning addresses to clients. You can use this command to reserve addresses that are statically assigned to key hosts, such as the router's address. The command's syntax is as follows:

```
Router(config)#ip dhcp excluded-address ip-address [end-ip-address]
```

Typically, a DHCP server is configured to assign much more than an IP address. You can set other IP configuration values from the DHCP configuration mode. IP clients will not get far without a default gateway. You can set the gateway by using the **default-router** command. It is possible to configure the address of the DNS server (**dns-server**) and WINS server (**netbios-name-server**) here as well. The IOS DHCP server can configure clients with virtually any TCP/IP information.

A list of the key IOS DHCP server commands, which you enter in DHCP pool configuration mode, is shown in Table 11-8.

Table 11-8 DHCP Pool Commands

Command	Purpose
Router(config)# **ip dhcp pool** *name*	Creates a name for the DHCP server address pool and places you in DHCP pool configuration mode (identified by the config-dhcp# prompt).
Router(config-dhcp)# **network** *network-number* [*mask* | */prefix-length*]	Specifies the subnet network number and mask of the DHCP address pool. The prefix length specifies the number of bits that comprise the address prefix. The prefix is an alternative way of specifying the network mask of the client. The prefix length must be preceded by a forward slash (/).
Router(config-dhcp)# **domain-name** *domain*	Specifies the domain name for the client.
Router(config-dhcp)# **dns-server** *address* [*address2 ... address8*]	Specifies the IP address of a DNS server that is available to a DHCP client. One IP address is required; however, you can specify up to eight IP addresses in one command line.
Router(config-dhcp)# **netbios-name-server** *address* [*address2 ... address8*]	Specifies the NetBIOS WINS server that is available to a Microsoft DHCP client. One address is required; however, you can specify up to eight addresses in one command line.

continues

Table 11-8 DHCP Pool Commands (Continued)

Command	Purpose
Router(config-dhcp)# **default-router** *address* [*address2 ... address8*]	Specifies the IP address of the default router for a DHCP client. One IP address is required, although you can specify up to eight addresses in one command line.
Router(config-dhcp)# **lease** {*days* [*hours*][*minutes*] | **infinite**}	Specifies the duration of the lease. The default is a one-day lease.

Although it is enabled by default on versions of the Cisco IOS that support it, the DHCP server process can be re-enabled by using the **service dhcp** global configuration command. The **no service dhcp** command disables the server.

Verifying DHCP Operation

Table 11-9 lists commands to display DHCP server information, while in EXEC mode, as needed.

Table 11-9 Commands to Display DHCP Server Information

Command	Purpose
Router> **show ip dhcp binding** [*address*]	Displays a list of all bindings created on a specific DHCP server.
Router> **show ip dhcp conflict** [*address*]	Displays a list of all address conflicts recorded by a specific DHCP server.
Router# **show ip dhcp database** [*url*]	Displays recent activity on the DHCP database. Use this command in privileged EXEC mode.
Router> **show ip dhcp server statistics**	Displays count information about server statistics and messages sent and received.

Troubleshooting DHCP Configuration

To enable DHCP server debugging, use the **debug ip dhcp server** privileged EXEC command. Table 11-10 lists commands to debug DHCP server information.

Table 11-10 Commands to Debug a DHCP Server

Command	Purpose
debug ip dhcp server events	Reports server events, such as address assignments and database updates
debug ip dhcp server packets	Decodes DHCP receptions and transmissions
debug ip dhcp server linkage	Displays database linkage information (such as parent-child relationships in a radix tree)

To troubleshoot the operation of the DHCP server, you can use the command **debug ip dhcp server events**, as shown in Example 11-10.

Example 11-10 *DHCP Debug Command*

```
Router#debug ip dhcp server events
Router#
00:22:53: DHCPD: checking for expired leases.
00:23:23: DHCPD: assigned IP address 172.16.13.11 to client 0100.10a4.97f4.6d.
00:27:49: DHCPD: returned 172.16.13.11 to address pool remote.
00:29:59: DHCPD: assigned IP address 172.16.13.11 to client 0100.10a4.97f4.6d.
```

This shows that periodically, the server checks to see if any leases have expired. Also, you can see when addresses are returned and when they are allocated.

DHCP Relay

DHCP clients use IP broadcasts to find the DHCP server on the segment, as seen earlier. What happens when the server and the client are not on the same segment and are separated by a router? Routers do not forward these broadcasts.

DHCP is not the only critical service that uses broadcasts. Cisco routers and other devices can use broadcasts to locate Trivial File Transfer Protocol (TFTP) servers. Some clients might need to broadcast to locate a Terminal Access Controller Access

Control System (TACACS) server. Typically, in a complex hierarchical network, clients reside on the same subnet as key servers. Remote clients broadcast to locate these servers, but routers, by default, do not forward client broadcasts beyond their subnet.

Because some clients are useless without services such as DHCP, one of two choices must be implemented: to place servers on all subnets, or to use the Cisco IOS helper address feature. Running services such as DHCP or DNS on several computers creates overhead and administrative headaches, so the first option is not very appealing. When possible, administrators use the **ip helper-address** command to relay broadcast requests for these key UDP services.

By using the helper address feature, a router can be configured to accept a broadcast request for a UDP service and then forward it as a unicast to a specific IP address. By default, the **ip helper-address** command forwards the eight UDP services:

- Time
- TACACS
- DNS
- BOOTP/DHCP Server
- BOOTP/DHCP Client
- TFTP
- NetBIOS Name Service
- NetBIOS Datagram Service

In the particular case of DHCP, a client broadcasts a DHCP discover packet on its local segment. Figure 11-19 shows what the DHCP message format looks like. The gateway picks up this packet, and if a helper address is configured, the DHCP packet is forwarded to the specified address.

Figure 11-19 DHCP Message Format

OP Code	Hardware Type	Hardware Length	HOPS
Transaction ID (XID)			
Seconds		Flags	
Client IP Address (CIADDR)			
Your IP Address (YIADDR)			
Server IP (SIADDR)			
Gateway IP (GIADDR)			
Client Hardware Address (CHADDR)—16 Bytes			
Server Name (SNAME)—64 Bytes			
Filename—128 Bytes			
DHCP Options			

Before forwarding the packet, the router fills in the GIADDR field of the packet with the router's IP address for the segment. This address will be the gateway address for the DHCP client when it gets the IP address, as shown in Figure 11-20.

Figure 11-20 DHCP Client Gets an IP Address

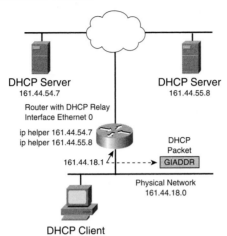

The DHCP server receives the discover packet and uses the GIADDR field to index in to the list of address pools; it is looking for a pool that has the gateway address set to the value in GIADDR. This pool is then used to supply the client with its IP address. Figure 11-21 shows a DHCP client broadcast, and Figure 11-22 shows a DHCP server unicast.

Figure 11-21 DHCP Client Broadcast

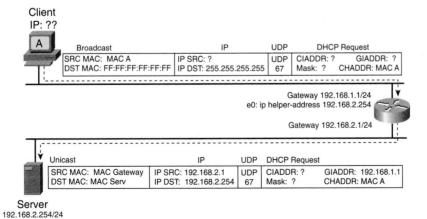

Figure 11-22 DHCP Server Unicast

Client
IP: ??

Broadcast	IP	UDP	DHCP Reply	
SRC MAC: MAC Gateway	IP SRC: 192.168.2.254	UDP	CIADDR: 19.168.1.10	CHADDR: MAC A
DST MAC: MAC A	IP DST: 192.158.1.10	68	Mask: 255.255.255.0	GIADDR: 192.168.1.1

Gateway 192.168.1.1/24
e0: ip helper-address 192.168.2.254

Gateway 192.168.2.1/24

Unicast	IP	UDP	DHCP Reply	
SRC MAC: MAC Serv	IP SRC: 192.168.2.254	UDP	CIADDR: 192.168.1.10	CHADDR: MAC A
DST MAC: MAC Gateway	IP DST: 192.168.1.10	68	Mask: 255.255.255.0	GIADDR: 192.168.1.1

Server
192.168.2.254/24

Lab Activity Configuring DHCP

In this lab, you configure a router for DHCP, which then dynamically assigns addresses to attached hosts.

Lab Activity Configuring DHCP Relay

In this lab, you configure a router for DHCP and then add the ability for workstations to remotely obtain DHCP addresses and dynamically assign addresses to the attached hosts.

Summary

This chapter covered the following:

- As the Internet becomes larger, so does the number of IP routes in the backbone Internet routing tables. This poses a scalability problem for routing algorithms. Three solutions to the scaling problem of IP were presented.

- RFC 1918 provides background on the allocation of IP addresses for private Internets. It also provides implementation guidelines for companies that want to implement IP but do not want full connectivity to the Internet.

- NAT allows for translating private addresses into publicly usable addresses to be used within the Internet. Examples of NAT configuration and verification were shown.

- PAT allows a group of inside hosts to communicate to outside hosts and share the overloaded address in a NAT configuration. Examples of PAT configuration and verification were shown.

- DHCP provides a mechanism for allocating IP addresses dynamically so that addresses can automatically be reused when hosts no longer need them. Examples of configuration and troubleshooting were shown.

To supplement all that you've learned in this chapter, refer to the chapter-specific Videos, PhotoZooms, and e-Lab Activities on the CD-ROM accompanying this book.

Key Terms

BOOTP (Bootstrap Protocol) Originally defined in RFC 951 in 1985. BOOTP is the predecessor of DHCP, and it shares some operational characteristics. Both protocols use UDP ports 67 and 68, which are well known as "BOOTP ports" because BOOTP came before DHCP.

CIDR (classless interdomain routing) Allows routers to group routes together to reduce the quantity of routing information carried by the core routers. With CIDR, several IP networks appear to networks outside the group as a single, larger entity.

DHCP (Dynamic Host Configuration Protocol) Provides a mechanism for allocating IP addresses dynamically so that addresses can be reused automatically when hosts no longer need them.

inside global address In a NAT configuration, the IP address that the inside local address gets translated to.

inside local address In a NAT configuration, the IP address that is translated.

NAT (network address translation) Only globally unique in terms of the public internet. A mechanism for translating private addresses into publicly usable addresses to be used within the public Internet. An effective means for hiding actual device addressing within a private network.

outside global address The IP address of an outside host as it is known to the hosts in the inside network.

outside local address The IP address that the host's owner assigns to a host on the outside network.

overloading (also known as PAT) Uses TCP port numbers to allow a group of inside hosts to communicate to outside hosts and "share" the overloaded address in a NAT configuration.

Check Your Understanding

1. Private addresses are assigned by what?

   A. The network administrator from RFC 1918.

   B. ARIN.

   C. RIPE.

   D. Any address can be a private address.

2. Which of the following are valid RFC 1918 private addresses?

   A. 10.0.0.0/7

   B. 10.0.0.0/8

   C. 192.168.0.0/16

   D. 172.16.0.0/12

3. The BOX Company maintains its own public web server, and it is about to implement NAT. Which type of NAT should be used for the web server?

   A. Dynamic

   B. Static

   C. PAT

   D. No NAT at all

4. Which of the following applications does Cisco IOS NAT support?

   A. ICMP

   B. DNS zone transfers

   C. BOOTP

   D. FTP (including **PORT** and **PASV** commands

5. Which of the following traffic types does Cisco IOS NAT *not* support?

   A. ICMP

   B. DNS zone transfers

   C. BOOTP

   D. FTP (including PORT and PASV

6. BOOTP supports _____ whereas DHCP supports
   _____.

   A. Static mappings

   B. Dynamic mappings

   C. PAT

   D. NAT

7. Place the following DHCP messages in the correct order as they appear in the process.

    A. DHCPACK

    B. DHCPREQUEST

    C. DHCPOFFER

    D. DHCPDISCOVER

8. What does DHCP stand for?

    A. Dynamic Host Configuration Protocol

    B. Dynamic Hosting Configuration Protocol

    C. Dynamic Host Computer Protocol

    D. Dynamic Host Computer Port

9. NAT conserves the legally registered addressing scheme by allowing the privatization of intranets.

    A. True

    B. False

10. DHCP is not intended for use in configuring routers, switches, and servers because these hosts need to have static IP addresses.

    A. True

    B. False

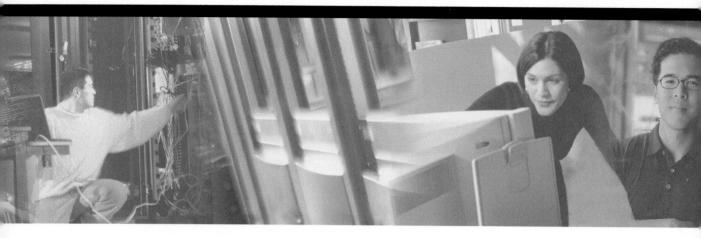

Objectives

After reading this chapter, you will be able to

- Understand the differences between a LAN and WAN
- Identify the devices used in a WAN
- List WAN standards
- Describe WAN encapsulation
- Classify the various WAN link options
- Differentiate between packet-switched and circuit-switched WAN technologies
- Describe the steps in WAN design

Chapter 12

WAN Technologies

As the enterprise grows beyond a single location, it becomes necessary to interconnect the LANs in the various branches to form an enterprise wide-area network (WAN). This chapter examines some of the available options for these interconnections, the hardware needed to make them, and the terminology used in discussing them.

Be sure to look at this chapter's associated e-Lab Activities, Videos, and PhotoZooms that you will find on the CD-ROM accompanying this book. These CD-ROM elements are designed to supplement the material and reinforce the concepts introduced in this chapter.

WAN Technologies Overview

A WAN is a data communications network that operates beyond the geographic scope of a local-area network (LAN). One primary difference between a WAN and a LAN is that a company or organization must subscribe to an outside WAN service provider to use WAN carrier network services. A WAN typically uses data links that are provided by carrier services to access bandwidth over wide-area geographies. A WAN connects the locations of an organization to each other, to locations of other organizations, to external services (such as databases), and to remote users. WANs generally carry a variety of traffic types, such as voice, data, and video. Telephone and data services are the most commonly used WAN services.

Devices on a subscriber's premises, as shown in Figure 12-1, are called *customer premises equipment (CPE)*, which can be owned by the subscriber or leased to the subscriber by the service provider. Copper or fiber cabling connects the CPE to the service provider's nearest exchange or *central office (CO)*. This cabling is often called the local loop or "last-mile." A dialed call is connected locally to other local loops, or nonlocally through a trunk to a primary center, then to a sectional center, and then to a regional- or international-carrier center as the call travels the long distance to its destination. Figure 12-2 illustrates the WAN service provider.

Figure 12-1 CPE

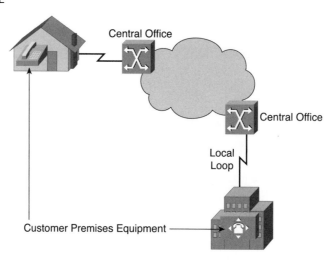

Figure 12-2 WAN Service Provider

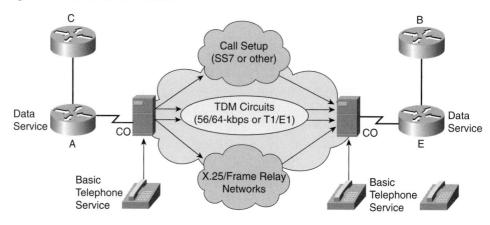

If the local loop is to carry data, it needs a device such as a modem to prepare the data for transmission. Devices that put data on the local loop are called *data circuit-terminating equipment* or *data communications equipment (DCE)*. The customer devices that pass the data to the DCE are called *data terminal equipment (DTE)*. Figure 12-3 shows examples of DCE and DTE devices. The DCE primarily provides an interface for the DTE into the communication link in the WAN cloud. The DTE/DCE interface uses various physical layer protocols (such as High-Speed Serial Interface [HSSI] and V.35) that establish the codes that the devices use to communicate with each other, as shown in Figure 12-4.

Figure 12-3 DTE/DCE

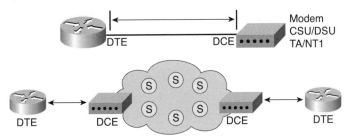

Figure 12-4 Physical Layer WANs

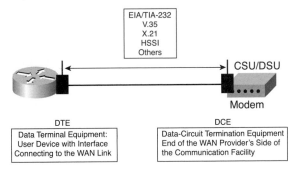

WAN links can be ordered from the WAN provider at various speeds that are stated in bits per second (bps), kilobits per second (kbps, 1000 bps), megabits per second (Mbps, 1000 kbps) or gigabits per second (Gbps, 1000 Mbps). The bps figures are generally full duplex, so an E1 line can carry 2 Mbps, or a T1 can carry 1.5 Mbps, in each direction simultaneously. Note that 1 kbps is 1000 bits per second, whereas a kB (kilobyte) is 1024 bytes. Data transfer rates are measured using the decimal meaning of K, whereas data storage is measured using the binary (powers-of-2) meaning of K. Technically, kbps should be spelled with a lowercase k to indicate that it is decimal, but almost everyone spells it with a capital K. Table 12-1 shows common WAN circuit types and bandwidths.

Table 12-1 WAN Circuit Types and Bandwidths

Line Type	Signal Standard	Bit Rate Capacity
56	DS0	56 kbps
64	DS0	64 kbps
T1	DS1	1.544 Mbps
E1	ZM	2.048 Mbps
J1	Y1	2.048 Mbps
E3	M3	34.064 Mbps
T3	DS3	44.736 Mbps
OC-1	SONET	51.840 Mbps
OC-3	SONET	155.520 Mbps
OC-9	SONET	466.560 Mbps
OC-12	SONET	622.08 Mbps
OC-18	SONET	933.12 Mbps
OC-24	SONET	1244.16 Mbps
OC-36	SONET	1866.24 Mbps
OC-48	SONET	2488.32 Mbps
OC-96	SONET	4976.640 Mbps
OC-192	SONET	9953.280 Mbps

WAN Devices

WANs are, essentially, groups of LANs connected together with communications links from a service provider. Because the communications links cannot plug directly into the LAN, it is necessary to identify the various pieces of interfacing equipment.

LAN-based computers with data to transmit send it to a router with both LAN and WAN interfaces, as shown in Figure 12-5. The router uses the address information to deliver the data on the appropriate WAN interface. Routers are active and intelligent network devices and therefore can participate in managing the network. Routers manage networks by providing dynamic control over resources and supporting the tasks and goals for networks. These goals are connectivity, reliable performance, management control, and flexibility.

Figure 12-5 WANs and LANs Connected Through Routers

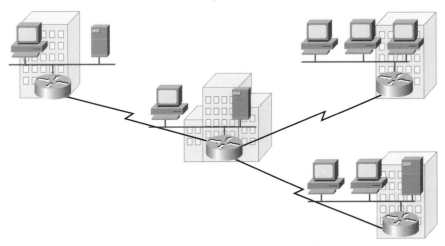

The communications link needs signals that are appropriately formatted. For digital lines, a *channel service unit (CSU)* and a *data (or digital) service unit (DSU)* are required. In practice the two are often combined into a single piece of equipment, the CSU/DSU, as Figure 12-6 illustrates. Sometimes the CSU/DSU is built in to the interface card in the router.

Figure 12-6 WAN CSU/DSU

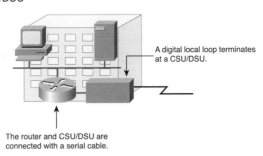

A digital local loop terminates at a CSU/DSU.

The router and CSU/DSU are connected with a serial cable.

If the local loop is analog rather than digital, a modem is needed, as Figure 12-7 shows. A modem transmits data over voice-grade telephone lines by modulating and demodulating the signal. The digital signals are superimposed on an analog voice signal (modulated) for transmission. The modulated signal can be heard by turning on the internal speaker in the modem. It is heard as a series of whistles and hissing sounds. At the receiving end, the analog signals are returned to their digital form, a process called demodulation.

Figure 12-7 WANs and Modems

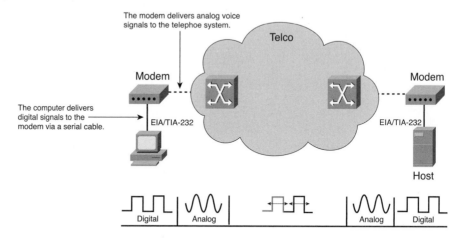

When Integrated Services Digital Network (ISDN) is used as the communications link, all equipment attached to the ISDN bus must be ISDN compatible. Generally, this compatibility is built in to the interface, either in the computer for direct-dial connections or the router for LAN-to-WAN connections. Older equipment may not have an ISDN interface, in which case an ISDN terminal adapter (TA) can be used.

Communication servers, which concentrate dial-in user communication, are used for remote access to a LAN. They may have a mixture of analog and digital (ISDN) interfaces, and support dozens or hundreds of simultaneous users.

WAN Standards

WANs use the OSI layered reference model, just as LANs do, but they are mainly focused on the lower two layers. WAN standards typically describe both physical layer delivery methods and data link layer requirements, including addressing, flow control, and encapsulation. WAN standards are defined and managed by a number of recognized authorities.

The physical layer protocols describe how to provide electrical, mechanical, operational, and functional connections to the services provided by a communications service provider. The device to be connected to the WAN, typically a router, is referred to as DTE, and the device at the other end of the connection, which provides the interface to the service provider, is referred to as DCE. Table 12-2 lists some of the common physical layer standards and their connectors illustrated in Figure 12-8.

Table 12-2 WAN Physical Layer Standards

Standard	Description
EIA*/TIA* 232	Allows signal speeds of up to 64 kbps on a 25-pin D connector over short distances. It was formerly known as RS-232. The ITU-T v.24 specification is effectively the same.
EIA/TIA 449 EIA-530	A faster (up to 2 Mbps) version of EIA/TIA 232, it uses a 36-pin D connector and is capable of longer cable runs. There are several versions. Also known as RS-422 and RS-423.
EIA/TIA 612/613	The High Speed Serial Interface (HSSI), which provides access to services at up to 52 Mbps on a 50-pin D connector.
V.35	An ITU* standard for high-speed synchronous data exchange. In the United States, V.35 is the interface standard used by most routers and DSUs that connect to T1 carriers.
X.21	An ITU-T* standard for synchronous digital communications. It uses a 15-pin D connector. This type of connector is mostly used in Europe and Japan.

*EIA = Electronic Industries Association
*TIA = Telecommunications Industry Association
*ITU = International Telecommunication Union
*ITU-T = International Telecommunication Union Telecommunication Standardization Sector

The data link layer protocols define how data is encapsulated for transmission to remote sites, and the mechanisms for transferring the resulting frames. A variety of different technologies are used, such as ISDN, Frame Relay, and Asynchronous Transfer Mode (ATM), but they nearly all use the same basic framing mechanism, High-Level Data Link Control (HDLC), an ISO standard, or one of its subsets or variants, as shown in Figure 12-9.

Figure 12-8 WAN Connectors

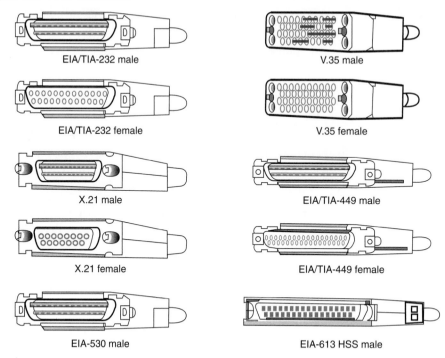

EIA/TIA-232 male

V.35 male

EIA/TIA-232 female

V.35 female

X.21 male

EIA/TIA-449 male

X.21 female

EIA/TIA-449 female

EIA-530 male

EIA-613 HSS male

Figure 12-9 WAN Data Link Layer Protocols

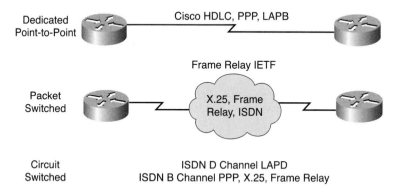

Dedicated Point-to-Point

Cisco HDLC, PPP, LAPB

Frame Relay IETF

Packet Switched

X.25, Frame Relay, ISDN

Circuit Switched

ISDN D Channel LAPD
ISDN B Channel PPP, X.25, Frame Relay

WAN Encapsulation

Data from the network layer is passed to the data link layer for delivery on a physical link, normally point to point. The data link layer builds a frame around the network layer data so that it can apply the necessary checks and controls. Each WAN connection type uses a Layer 2 protocol to encapsulate traffic while it is crossing the WAN link. To ensure that the correct encapsulation protocol is used, the Layer 2 encapsulation type to use for each serial interface on a router must be configured. The choice of encapsulation protocol depends on the WAN technology and the communicating equipment. Most framing is based on the HDLC standard.

HDLC framing is designed to give reliable delivery of data over unreliable lines, and so includes signaling mechanisms for flow and error control. The frame always starts and ends with an 8-bit flag field: the bit pattern 01111110, or $7E_{16}$ (7E in base 16, hexadecimal). Because the likelihood exists that this pattern occurs in the actual data, the sending HDLC system always inserts a 0 bit after every five 1s in the data field, so in practice the flag sequence can only occur at the frame ends. The receiving system strips out the inserted bits. Where one frame is transmitted immediately after another, the end flag of the first frame is used as the start flag of the next.

The address field is not needed for WAN links, which are almost always point-to-point, but is still present. It may be 1 or 2 bytes long. The control field indicates the frame type, which may be information, supervisory, or unnumbered. Unnumbered frames carry line setup messages, information frames carry network layer data, and supervisory frames control the flow of information frames, and if necessary request data retransmission in the event of an error. The control field is normally 1 byte, but for extended sliding windows systems will be 2 bytes. Together the address and control fields are called the frame header.

Following the control field is the encapsulated data, and then a frame check sequence (FCS) using the cyclic redundancy check mechanism to give a 2- or 4-byte field. Several data-link protocols including subsets and proprietary versions of HDLC are in use, and shown in Figure 12-10. Both PPP and the Cisco version of HDLC have an extra field in the header, used to identify the network layer protocol of the encapsulated data.

Figure 12-10 WAN Frame Encapsulation Formats

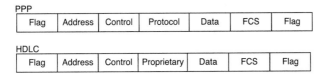

WAN Link Options

The following sections discuss various technologies most used for WAN connections. It is helpful to have an overview or classification of these options.

Circuit-Switched Connections

Circuit switching can be used to establish a connection for voice or data between two geographically separate points. Before useful communication can start, it is necessary to establish the connection by setting switches. This is done by the telephone system, using the dialed number with ordinary voice-grade lines and ISDN digital lines.

To avoid the delays associated with setting up a connection, telephone service providers also offer permanent circuits through their systems. These dedicated or leased lines offer higher bandwidth than is available with a switched circuit. Examples of circuit-switched connections include the following:

- Public Switched Telephone Network (PSTN)
- ISDN Basic Rate Interface (BRI)
- ISDN Primary Rate Interface (PRI)

Packet-Switched Connections

Many WAN users do not make efficient use of the fixed bandwidth that is available with dedicated circuits, whether switched or permanent, as their data flows are in bursts. To more appropriately service these users, communications providers make available data networks, where the data is moved in labeled cells, frames, or packets through a packet-switched network. Because the internal links between the switches are shared among many users, the costs of *packet switching* are lower than those of circuit switching. Because the links are shared, and packets must be entirely received at one switch before they can start moving to the next, delays (latency) and variability of delay (jitter) are greater in packet-switched than in circuit-switched networks. Despite the latency and jitter inherent in shared networks, modern technology allows satisfactory transport of voice and even video communications on such networks.

Packet-switched networks might establish routes through the switches for particular end-to-end connections. If the routes are established when the switches are started, these routes are called *permanent virtual circuits (PVCs)*; if they are established on demand, they are called *switched virtual circuits (SVCs)*. If the routing is not pre-established but worked out by each switch for each packet, the network is called connectionless.

To connect to a packet-switched network, a subscriber needs a local loop to the nearest location where the provider makes the service available, the point of presence (POP) of the service. Normally, this is a dedicated leased line. It is much shorter than the leased line that would be needed to directly connect the subscriber's locations, and often several virtual circuits (VCs) are carried on it. Because it is likely that not all the VCs will have their maximum demand simultaneously, the capacity of the leased line can be smaller than the sum of the individual VCs. Examples of packet- or cell-switched connections include the following:

- Frame Relay
- X.25
- ATM

Packet and Circuit Switching

Packet-switched networks were developed to overcome the expense of public circuit-switched networks and to provide a more cost-effective WAN technology.

When a subscriber makes a telephone call, the number dialed is used to set switches in the exchanges along the route of the call so that there is a continuous circuit from the caller's handset to that of the called party. Because of the switching operation used to establish the circuit, the telephone system is called a circuit-switched network. If the handsets are replaced with modems connected to computers, the switched circuit can carry computer data. Figure 12-11 shows an example of circuit switching.

Figure 12-11 Circuit Switching

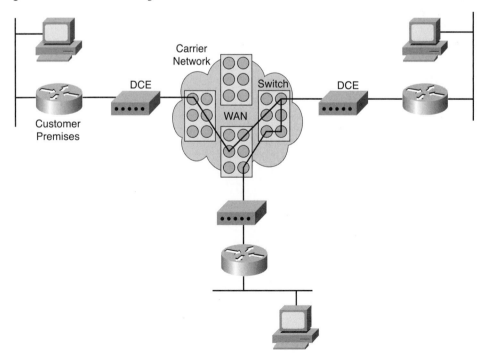

In practice the circuit may be partially media other than copper, such as optical fiber or microwave. Internally, the path taken by the circuit between exchanges will be shared by a number of conversations, so *time-division multiplexing (TDM)* is used to give each conversation a share of the connection in turn. TDM ensures that a fixed-capacity connection is made available to the subscriber.

If the circuit is used to carry computer data, the usage of this fixed capacity may not be efficient. If the circuit is used to access the Internet, for example, a burst of activity occurs on the circuit while a web page is transferred, then no activity occurs while the user reads the page, and then another burst of activity occurs while the next page is transferred. This variation in usage between none and maximum is typical of computer network traffic. Because the subscriber has sole use of the fixed-capacity allocation, switched circuits are generally an expensive way to move data.

An alternative is to allocate the capacity to the traffic only when it is needed, and share the available capacity among many users. With a circuit-switched connection, the data bits put on the circuit are automatically delivered to the far end, because the circuit is already established. If the circuit is to be shared, there must be some mechanism to label the bits, so that the system knows where to deliver them. Because it is difficult to label individual bits, they are gathered into groups variously called cells, frames, or packets, and the resulting labeled parcel or packet can be passed from exchange to exchange through the provider's network for delivery. Networks implementing this system are called packet-switched networks. Figure 12-12 shows an example of packet switching.

Figure 12-12 Packet Switching

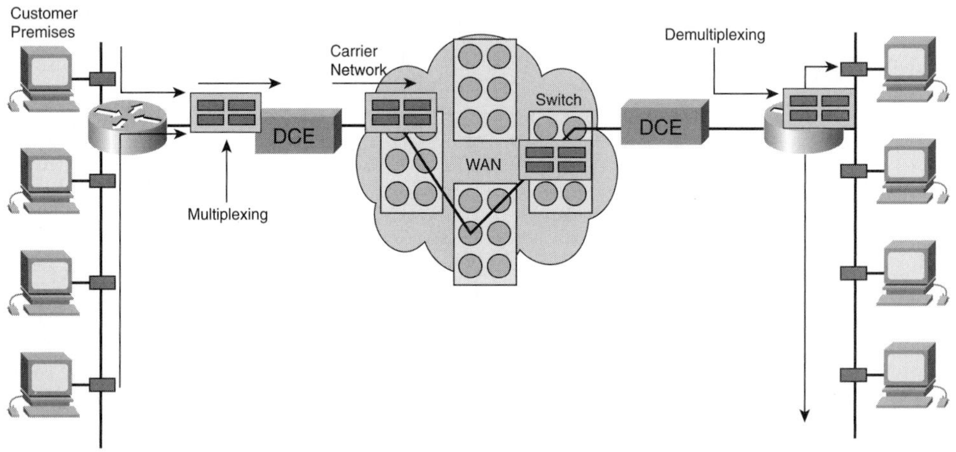

Because the links connecting the exchanges or switches in the provider's network are only allocated to an individual subscriber when there is data from that subscriber, many subscribers can share the links, and the cost to each subscriber can be significantly lower than for a dedicated circuit-switched connection. On the other hand, because an individual packet may have to wait at a switch until some other subscriber's packet is off the link, data on packet-switched networks is subject to unpredictable delays.

The switches in a packet-switched network must be able to determine, from addressing information in each packet, which link the packet must be sent on next. There are two approaches to this link determination, connectionless or connection-oriented. Connectionless systems, such as the Internet, carry full addressing information in each packet. Connection-oriented systems predetermine the route for a packet, and each packet need only carry an identifier. In the case of Frame Relay, these are called data-link connection identifiers (DLCIs). The switch determines the onward route by looking up the identifier in tables held in memory. The set of entries in all the tables identify a particular route or circuit through the system; if this "circuit" is only physically in existence while a packet is traveling it, however, it is called a virtual circuit (VC).

The table entries that constitute a VC can be established by sending a connection request through the network, in which case the resulting circuit is called a switched virtual circuit (SVC). Data that is to travel on SVCs must wait until the table entries have been set up, although once established an SVC may be in operation for hours, days, or weeks. Where a circuit is required to be always available a permanent virtual circuit (PVC) is established. The switches load the table entries at boot time, and so the PVC is always available.

WAN Technologies

The following sections discuss some of the various WAN technologies that are used to set up WAN connections such as analog dialup, ISDN, leased line, X.25, Frame Relay, ATM, DSL, and cable. Also included in these sections are the advantages, disadvantages, and certain scenarios in which these WAN technologies should be used.

Analog Dialup

When intermittent, low-volume data transfers are needed, modems and analog dialed telephone lines provide low-capacity, switched, dedicated connections. (See Figure 12-13.)

Figure 12-13 WANs with Modems

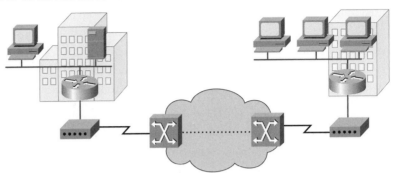

Traditional telephony connects the telephone handset in the subscriber's premises to the PSTN with a copper cable called the local loop. The signal on the local loop during a call is an electrical copy of the subscriber's voice and is a continuously varying signal.

The local loop is not suitable for direct transport of binary computer data, but a modem can send computer data through the voice telephone network. A modem modulates the binary data onto the analog signals and demodulates the analog signals to binary data.

The rate of this signaling is limited by physical characteristics of the local loop and its connection to the PSTN with an upper limit of around 33 kbps. The rate can be increased to around 56 kbps provided that the signal is coming from a digital connection.

For small businesses, this can be adequate for such activities as exchange of sales figures, prices, routine reports, and e-mail. Users can take advantage of low off-peak tariffs by using automatic dialup at night or on weekends for large file transfers and data backup. Tariffs are based on the distance between the endpoints, time of day, and the duration of the call.

The advantages of a modem and analog lines are simplicity and low implementation cost. The disadvantage is the low data rate and a relatively long connection time. Often in the situations in which a modem is used, the long connection setup time is not a problem. The continuous dedicated circuit will show no delay or jitter for point-to-point traffic, but voice or video traffic will not operate adequately at the low bit rates.

ISDN

The internal connections or trunks of the PSTN have changed from carrying analog frequency-division multiplexed signals, and now carry time-division multiplexed

(TDM) digital signals. An obvious next step is to make the local loop carry digital signals resulting in higher-capacity, switched connections.

Integrated Services Digital Network (ISDN) turns the local loop into a TDM digital connection. The connection has 64-kbps bearer channels (B) for carrying voice or data and a signaling (delta or D) channel for call setup and other purposes.

Basic Rate Interface (BRI) ISDN is intended for the home and small enterprise, provides 2 B channels with a 16-kbps D channel. For larger installations, Primary Rate Interface (PRI) ISDN is available. PRI delivers 23 B channels and 1 D channel in North America for a total bit rate of up to 1.544 Mbps. (This includes some additional overhead for synchronization.) In Europe, Australia, and other parts of the world, ISDN PRI provides 30 B channels and 1 D channel for a total bit rate of up to 2.048 Mbps (including synchronization overhead). The PRI D channel is 64 kbps, shown in Figure 12-14. Note that the rate of a North American PRI corresponds to a T1 connection. The rate of the international PRI corresponds to an E1 connection.

Figure 12-14 ISDN Channels

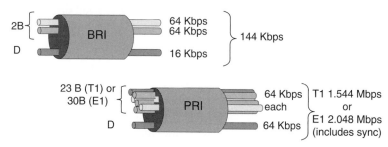

The BRI D channel is very underutilized, with only two B channels to control. Some providers allow it to be used to carry data at low bit rates, such as X.25 connections at 9.6 kbps.

For small WANs, the BRI ISDN can provide an ideal connection mechanism. BRI has a short call setup time (typically subsecond) and its 64-kbps B channel provides greater capacity than that of an analog modem link. Figure 12-15 shows WANs using ISDN. If greater capacity is required, a second B channel can be activated, giving 128 kbps. Although inadequate for video, this increase permits several simultaneous voice conversations in addition to data traffic.

Another common application of ISDN is to provide additional capacity as needed to an existing leased-line connection. The leased line is sized to carry average traffic loads, and ISDN is added during the peaks. ISDN can also be used as a backup when occasional leased-line failures occur.

Figure 12-15 WANs with ISDN

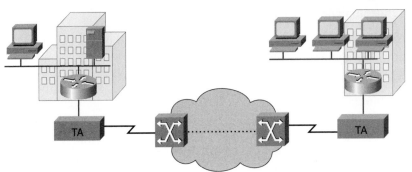

ISDN tariffs are similar to those of analog voice connections on a per-B channel basis. That is, two simultaneous 64-kbps connections cost twice as much as one.

With PRI ISDN, multiple B channels can be connected between two endpoints allowing for videoconferencing and high-bandwidth data connections with no latency or jitter. Multiple connections can become very expensive over long distances.

Leased Line

When permanent dedicated connections are required, leased lines are used with capacities ranging up to 2.5 Gbps.

A point-to-point link provides a pre-established WAN communications path from the customer premises through a carrier network, such as a telephone company, to a remote network. Point-to-point lines are usually leased from a carrier and therefore are often called leased lines. Leased lines are available at many different capacities. These dedicated circuits are generally priced based on bandwidth required and distance between the two connected points. Point-to-point links are generally more expensive than shared services such as Frame Relay. The cost of leased-line solutions can become significant when they are used to connect many sites. The dedicated capacity gives no latency or jitter between the endpoints. Constant availability is essential for some applications such as electronic commerce.

A router serial port is required for each leased-line connection. A CSU/DSU and the actual circuit from the service provider are also required. Leased lines are extensively used for building WANs, as in Figure 12-16, and give permanent dedicated capacity. Traditionally they have been the connection of choice, but they do have a number of disadvantages. WAN traffic is often variable and leased lines have a fixed capacity, which results in the bandwidth of the line seldom being exactly what is needed. In addition, each endpoint needs an interface in the router, so the router at the hub of a multipoint star will be expensive. Any changes to the leased line generally require a site visit by the carrier to change capacity.

Figure 12-16 WANs with Leased Lines

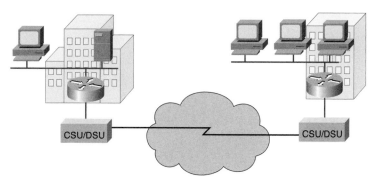

Leased lines can be used to provide direct point-to-point connections between enterprise LANs. Leased lines are also used to connect individual branches to a packet-switched network. Several connections can be multiplexed over such a link resulting in shorter links and the hub routers requiring fewer interfaces.

X.25

In response to the expense of leased lines, telecommunications providers introduced packet-switched networks where shared lines reduce the cost. The first of these packet-switched networks was standardized as the X.25 group of protocols. X.25 provides a low bit rate, shared, variable capacity that may be either switched or permanent. Figure 12-17 shows an X.25 WAN.

Subscribers are provided with a network address. VCs can be established through the network with call request packets to the target address. The resulting SVC is identified by its channel number. Data packets labeled with the channel number are delivered to the corresponding address. Multiple channels can be active on a single connection.

Subscribers connect to the X.25 network with either leased lines or dialup connections. X.25 networks can also have pre-established channels between subscribers, providing a PVC.

Figure 12-17 WANs with X.25

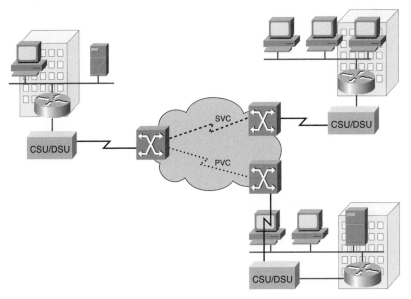

X.25 can prove very cost effective because tariffs are based on the amount of data delivered rather than connection time or distance. Data can be delivered at any rate up to the connection capacity. This provides some flexibility. X.25 networks are usually low capacity with a maximum of 48 kbps. In addition, the data packets are subject to the delays typical of shared networks.

Frame Relay

With increasing demand for higher-bandwidth and lower-latency packet switching, communications providers introduced Frame Relay (FR). Although the network layout appears similar to that for X.25, available data rates are commonly up to 4 Mbps, with some providers offering higher rates. (See Figure 12-18.)

Frame Relay differs from X.25 in several respects. Most importantly, it operates a much simpler protocol at the data link. The term *frame* is used for units at the data link layer.

Figure 12-18 WANs with Frame Relay

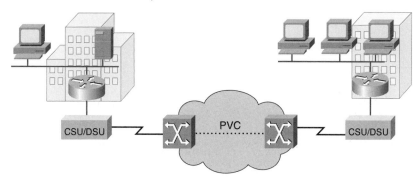

Frame Relay implements no error or flow control. The simplified handling of frames leads to reduced latency. Measures taken to avoid frame buildup at intermediate switches help reduce jitter.

Most FR connections are based on PVCs rather than SVCs. The connection to the network edge is often a leased line. The ISDN D channel is used to set up an SVC on one or more B channels. Frame Relay tariffs are based on the capacity of the connecting port at the network edge and the agreed capacity or committed information rate (CIR) of the various PVCs through the port.

Frame Relay provides permanent, shared, medium-bandwidth connectivity carrying both voice and data traffic. Frame Relay is ideal for connecting enterprise LANs together. The router on the LAN needs only a single interface, even when multiple VCs are used, and the short access line, or local loop, to the FR network edge allows cost-effective connections between widely scattered LANs.

ATM

In parallel with the development of FR, communications providers saw a need for a permanent shared networking technology that offers very low latency and jitter at much higher bandwidths than had previously been available. Their solution was Asynchronous Transfer Mode (ATM). ATM has data rates up to 155 Mbps. As with the other shared technologies, X.25 and FR, diagrams for WANs look the same, as in Figure 12-19, but the technology provides connectivity solutions at very high traffic levels. ATM is particularly useful when the nature of the traffic is intolerant of delay, such as video.

Figure 12-19 WANs with ATM

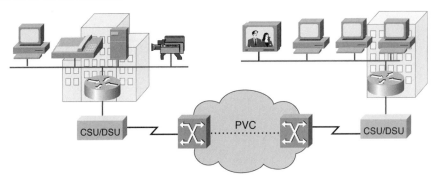

Asynchronous Transfer Mode (ATM) is a technology that is capable of transferring voice, video, and data through private and public networks. It is built on a cell-based architecture rather than on a frame-based architecture. ATM cells are always a fixed length of 53 bytes. The 53-byte ATM cell contains a 5-byte ATM header followed by 48 bytes of ATM payload. Small, fixed-length, 53-byte cells are well suited for carrying voice and video traffic because voice and video traffic are intolerant of delay. Video and voice traffic do not have to wait for a larger data packet to be transmitted.

The 53-byte ATM cell is less efficient than the bigger frames and packets of FR and X.25, with at least 5 bytes overhead for a 48-byte payload. When the cell is carrying broken-up network layer packets, the overhead is higher because the ATM switch must be able to reassemble the packets at the destination. A typical ATM line needs almost 20-percent greater bandwidth than FR to carry the same volume of network layer data.

ATM offers both PVCs and SVCs, although WANs more commonly use PVCs. As with the other shared technologies, ATM allows multiple virtual circuits on a single leased-line connection to the network edge.

DSL

The telephone system places a bandwidth limit on the local loop. Decoupling the local loop from the system can allow much greater bandwidth without having to install new cable. Figure 12-20 illustrates a DSL connection.

Figure 12-20 DSL

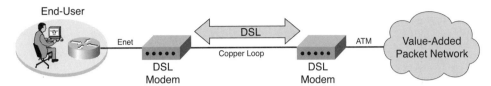

Digital subscriber line (DSL) technology disconnects the local loop from the switch in the CO or local exchange. Instead DSL connects it, along with the local loops of other DSL subscribers in the area, to a digital subscriber line access multiplexor (DSLAM), also in the CO. To maintain ordinary phone service, the DSLAM is connected back to the telephone switch. It is also connected, generally by ATM, back to the DSL provider's Internet service.

DSL provides a full-time connection. As soon as users turn on their computers that are connected to the DSL modem, they are connected. This setup removes the time and effort of dialing in to establish a connection.

The two basic types of DSL technologies are asymmetric (ADSL) and symmetric (SDSL). All forms of DSL service are categorized as one or the other, and there are several varieties of each type. The term xDSL is sometimes used to refer generically to any of the various forms of DSL that exist. Asymmetric service provides a higher download or downstream speed (toward the user) than upstream speed (toward the provider). Symmetric service provides the same speed in both directions.

The different varieties of DSL give different bandwidths, with most exceeding those of a T1 or E1 leased line. The rates achievable in practice depend significantly on the actual length of the local loop and the type and condition of its cabling. For satisfactory service, the loop must be less than about 5.5 kilometers (3.5 miles). DSL availability is far from universal, and with the wide variety of types, standards, and emerging standards, it is not at present a popular choice for enterprise computer departments for supporting home workers. Further, the subscriber cannot choose to connect to the enterprise network directly, but must first connect to an ISP and then make an IP connection through the Internet to the enterprise. This limitation presents security risks.

Cable Modem

In urban areas, coaxial cable is extensively used to distribute television signals. The cable television network can also be used for network access, allowing much greater bandwidth than the conventional telephone local loop. Figure 12-21 shows cable modem connections.

Figure 12-21 Cable Modem

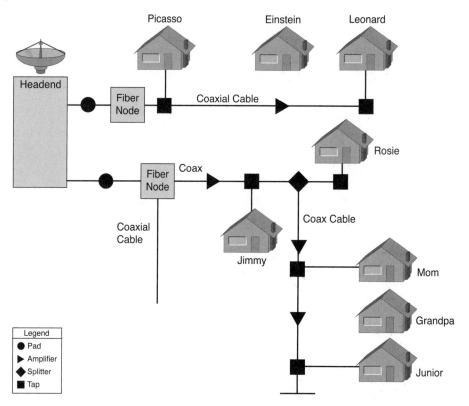

Cable modems enable two-way, high-speed data transmissions using the same coaxial lines that transmit cable television. Some cable service providers are promising data speeds up to 6.5 times that of T1 leased lines. This speed makes cable an attractive medium for transferring large amounts of digital information quickly, including video clips, audio files, and large amounts of data. Information that would take 2 minutes to download using ISDN BRI can be downloaded in 2 seconds through a cable-modem connection.

Cable modem access provides speeds superior to leased lines, with lower costs and simpler installation. Cable modems provide a full-time connection. As soon as users turn on their computers, they are connected to the Internet. This setup removes the time and effort of dialing in to establish a connection. However, the "always-on" cable connection means that connected computers are vulnerable to hackers at all times and need to be suitably secured with firewalls.

A cable modem is capable of delivering up to 30 to 40 Mbps of data in one 6-MHz cable channel. This is almost 500 times faster than a 56-kbps modem.

With a cable modem, a subscriber can continue to receive cable television service while simultaneously receiving data to be delivered to a personal computer. This is accomplished with the help of a simple one-to-two splitter, as shown in Figure 12-22.

Figure 12-22 Cable Modem Two-Way Splitter

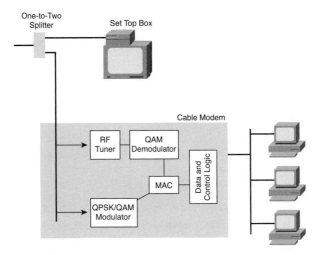

As with DSL, the subscriber has no choice but to use the Internet service provider (ISP) associated with the cable modem connection, and connection to the enterprise network will be by a TCP/IP application such as Telnet. A further disadvantage is that all the local subscribers are sharing the cable bandwidth, as is the case with coaxial Ethernet connections. As more users take up the service, actual bandwidths may be considerably below the expected cable rate. An even more severe problem with security exists: The home computer is vulnerable not just to the rest of the Internet, but also to the users on its own cable. Therefore, some form of local firewall protection is essential.

To address security concerns, cable modem services provide capabilities for using virtual private network (VPN) connections to a VPN server, which is typically located at the corporate site.

WAN Communication

Today's network administrators must manage complex WANs to support the growing number of software applications that are built around the Internet Protocol (IP) and the web. These WANs place a great demand on network resources and require high-performance networking technologies. WANs are environments that incorporate multiple media, multiple protocols, and interconnection to other networks such as the

Internet. Growth and manageability of these network environments are achieved by the often complex interaction of protocols and features.

Despite improvements in equipment performance and media capabilities, WAN design is becoming more difficult. Carefully designed WANs can reduce problems associated with a growing networking environment. To design reliable, scalable WANs, network designers must keep in mind that each WAN has specific design requirements. This following section provides an overview of the methodologies utilized for WAN communication and design.

WANS are considered as a set of data links connecting routers on LANs. User end stations and server machines on LANs exchange data. The routers, as necessary, pass data between the LANs across the data links.

WAN communication occurs between geographically separated areas. When a local end station wants to communicate with a remote end station (that is, an end station located at a different site), information must be sent over one or more WAN links. Routers within WANs are connection points of a network. These routers determine the most appropriate path through the network for the required data streams.

It is generally the case that for both cost and legal reasons the data links that constitute a WAN will be owned by a communications provider or common carrier and made available to the enterprise for a fee.

Circuit-switching and packet-switching technologies are two types of WAN services, each of which has advantages and disadvantages. For example, circuit-switched networks offer users dedicated bandwidth that cannot be infringed upon by other users. In contrast, packet switching is a method in which network devices share a single point-to-point link to transport packets from a source to a destination across a carrier network. Packet-switched networks have traditionally offered more flexibility and used network bandwidth more efficiently than circuit-switched networks. These links, interconnecting LANs or connecting them to other networks, will normally provide data transfer speeds (bandwidth) considerably slower than the 100 Mbps that is common on a LAN. The charges for link provision are the major cost element of a WAN, and the design must aim to provide acceptable bandwidth at acceptable cost. With user pressure to provide more service access at higher speeds and management pressure to contain cost, determining the optimal WAN configuration is not an easy task.

WANs can carry a variety of traffic types, such as voice, data, and video, and the design selected must provide adequate capacity and transit times to meet the requirements of the enterprise. This will involve specifying, among other things, the topology of the connections between the various sites, the nature of those connections, and their capacity.

Where older WANs often consisted of data links directly connecting geographically separated mainframe computers, today's WANs connect geographically separated LANs. End-user stations, servers, and routers are on LANs with the WAN data links terminating at the routers. By exchanging information about their connected LANs, routers determine the most appropriate path through the network for the required data streams. Routers can also provide quality of service (QoS) management, giving differing priorities to the different traffic streams.

Compared to current WANs, the new WAN infrastructures must be more complex, based on new technologies, and able to handle an ever-increasing (and rapidly changing) application mix with required and guaranteed service levels. In addition, with a 300-percent traffic increase expected in the next five years, enterprises will feel even greater pressure to contain WAN costs.

Network designers are using WAN technologies to support these new requirements. WAN connections generally handle important information and are optimized for price and performance bandwidth. The routers connecting the campuses, for example, generally apply traffic optimization, multiple paths for redundancy, dial backup for disaster recovery, and QoS for critical applications. Table 12-3 summarizes the various WAN technologies that support such WAN requirements.

Table 12-3 Summary of WAN Technologies

WAN Technology	Typical Uses
Leased line	Leased lines can be used for Point-to-Point Protocol (PPP) networks and hub-and-spokes topologies, or for backup for another type of link.
Integrated Services Digital Network (ISDN)	ISDN can be used for cost-effective remote access to corporate networks. It provides support for voice and video as well as a backup for another type of link.
Frame Relay	Frame Relay provides a cost-effective, high-speed, low-latency mesh topology between remote sites. It can be used in both private and carrier-provided networks.

Because the WAN is merely a set of interconnections between LAN-based routers, there are no services on the WAN, so WAN technologies function at the three lowest layers of the OSI reference model: the physical layer, the data link layer, and the network layer, as shown in Figure 12-23. Routers determine the destination of the data from the network layer headers and pass the packets down to the appropriate data-link connection for delivery on the physical connection.

Figure 12-23 WANs Operate at Layers 1, 2, and 3

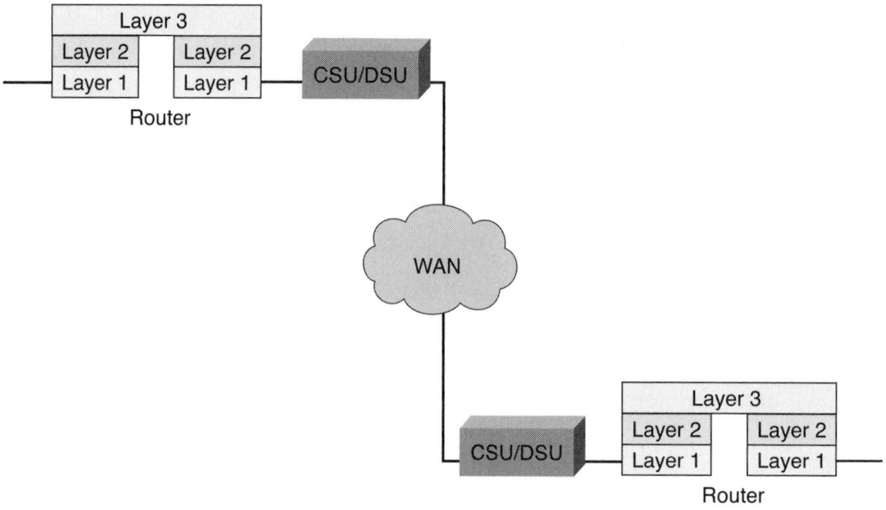

Traditionally, relatively low throughput, high delay, and high error rates have characterized WAN communication. WAN connections are also characterized by the cost of renting media (that is, wire) from a service provider to connect two or more campuses together. Because the WAN infrastructure is often rented from a service provider, WAN network designs must optimize the cost of bandwidth and bandwidth efficiency. For example, all technologies and features used in WANs are developed to meet the following design requirements:

- Optimize WAN bandwidth
- Minimize cost
- Maximize the effective service to the end users

Recently, traditional shared-media networks are being overtaxed because of the following new network requirements:

- Network usage has increased as enterprises utilize client/server, multimedia, and other applications to enhance productivity.
- The rate of change in application requirements has accelerated and will continue to do so (for example, Internet "push" technologies).
- Applications increasingly require distinct network qualities of service due to services they provide end users.
- An unprecedented number of connections are being established among offices of all sizes, remote users, mobile users, international sites, customers/suppliers, and the Internet.

- The explosive growth of corporate intranets and extranets has created a greater demand for bandwidth.
- The increased use of enterprise servers continues to grow to serve the business needs of organizations.

LAN/WAN Integration

Distributed applications need increasingly more bandwidth, and the explosion of Internet use is driving many LAN architectures to the limit. Voice communications have increased significantly, with more reliance being placed on centralized voice-mail systems for verbal communications. The network is the critical tool for information flow. Networks are being required to cost less, yet support the emerging applications and larger number of users with increased performance.

Until now, local and wide-area communications have remained logically separate. In the LAN, bandwidth is free and connectivity is limited only by hardware and implementation costs. In the WAN, bandwidth is the overriding cost, and delay-sensitive traffic such as voice has remained separate from data.

Internet applications such as voice and real-time video require better, more predictable LAN and WAN performance. These multimedia applications are fast becoming an essential part of the business productivity toolkit. As companies begin to consider implementing new intranet-based, bandwidth-intensive multimedia applications, such as video training, videoconferencing, and voice over IP, the impact of these applications on the existing networking infrastructure will become a serious concern.

If a company has relied on its corporate network for business-critical IP traffic and wants to integrate an online video-training application, for example, the network must be able to provide guaranteed QoS. This QoS must deliver the multimedia traffic, but not allow it to interfere with the business-critical traffic. Consequently, network designers need greater flexibility in solving multiple internetworking problems without creating multiple networks or writing off existing data communication investments.

Identifying and Selecting Network Capabilities

After you understand your networking requirements, you must identify and then select the specific capabilities that fit your computing environment. The following sections will help you with these tasks: essentially selecting an interconnection pattern or layout for the links between the various locations and selecting the technologies for those links to meet the enterprise requirements at an acceptable cost.

Many WANs use a star topology, often for historical reasons. As the enterprise has grown, and new branches have been added, the branches have been connected back to the head office, giving the traditional star layout. Sometimes, for reliability or latency or other reasons, some of the star endpoints will have been cross-connected, leading to a mesh or partial mesh topology. Between a star and a full mesh, there are many possible layouts for the interconnections. When designing a new WAN, or, more commonly, re-evaluating or modifying an existing WAN, a topology must be selected that meets the design requirements.

In selecting a layout, there are several factors to consider. More links generally cost more. Having multiple paths between destinations gives increased reliability. The more nodes or routers that data must pass through between destinations, the longer it takes, as it is generally the case that each chunk or packet of data must be completely received at one network device before it can start being delivered to the next.

A range of different technologies with different features is available for the data links, as shown in Table 12-4.

Table 12-4 WAN Technologies

Data Link Type	Provider Charge	Bandwidth	Type of Connection
Dedicated private line	Distance, capacity	Unlimited	Permanent/Fixed capacity
Telephone line	Distance, time	33–56 kbps	Dialed, slow connection
ISDN	Distance, capacity	64–128 kbps	Dialed, medium-speed connection
X.25	Volume	Less than 48 kbps	Switched/Fixed capacity
Frame Relay	Capacity	Less than 4 Mbps	Permanent/Fixed capacity
ATM	Capacity	Less than 155 Mbps	Permanent/Fixed capacity

Technologies that require the establishment of a connection before data can be transmitted, such as basic telephone, ISDN, or X.25, are not suitable for WANs that require low response time or latency (although once established ISDN and telephone are low-latency, low-jitter circuits). ISDN, in particular, often finds application for connecting small or home offices (SOHO) back to the enterprise network, giving fast connections and adaptable bandwidth. ISDN is also useful as a backup link for primary connections and for providing bandwidth-on-demand connections in parallel with a primary connection. A feature of these technologies is that they only cost when they are being used.

The different parts of the enterprise might be directly connected with leased lines, or they might be connected with an access link to the nearest point-of-presence (POP) of a shared network. X.25, Frame Relay, and ATM are examples of shared networks. Leased lines will generally be much longer and, therefore, more expensive than access links but are available at virtually any bandwidth. They provide very low latency and jitter.

ATM, Frame Relay, and X.25 networks carry traffic from several customers over the same internal links. The enterprise has no control over the number of links or hops that its data must traverse in the shared network or the time its data must wait at each network device before it can move on the next link. This uncertainty in latency and jitter makes these technologies unsuitable for some types of network traffic. However, the disadvantages of a shared network may often be outweighed by the shared cost. Because several customers are sharing the link, the cost to each is generally substantially less than the cost of a direct link of the same capacity.

Although ATM is a shared network, it has been designed to give a minimal latency and jitter, through the use of high-speed internal links sending easily manageable units of data, called cells. ATM cells have a fixed length of 53 bytes, 48 for data and 5 for the header. It is widely used for carrying delay-sensitive traffic. Frame Relay may also be used for delay-sensitive traffic, often using QoS mechanisms to give priority to the more sensitive data.

A typical WAN uses a combination of technologies that are usually chosen based on traffic type and volume. ISDN, Frame Relay, or leased lines are used to connect individual branches into an area. Frame Relay, ATM, or leased lines are used to connect areas back to the backbone; ATM or leased lines form the WAN backbone.

Identifying and Selecting a Networking Model

Hierarchical models for network design enable you to design networks in layers. To understand the importance of layering, consider the OSI reference model, a layered model for understanding computer communications. By using layers, the OSI reference model simplifies the tasks required for two computers to communicate. Hierarchical models for network design also use layers to simplify the tasks required for internetworking. Each layer can be focused on specific functions, thereby enabling the networking designer to choose the right systems and features for the layer.

Using a hierarchical design can facilitate changes. Modularity in network design enables you to create design elements that can be replicated as the network grows. Also because networks will require upgrades, the cost and complexity of making the upgrade are constrained to a small subset of the overall network. In large, flat or meshed network architectures, changes tend to affect a large number of systems. You can also facilitate the identification of failure points in a network by structuring the network into small, easy-to-understand elements. Network managers can easily understand the transition points in the network, and that understanding helps them identify failure points.

The Hierarchical Network Design Model

Network designs tend to follow one of two general design strategies: mesh or hierarchical. In a mesh structure, the network topology is flat; all routers perform essentially the same functions, and there is usually no clear definition of where specific functions are performed. Expansion of the network tends to proceed in a haphazard, arbitrary manner. In a hierarchical structure, the network is organized in layers, each of which has one or more specific functions. Benefits to using a hierarchical model include the following:

- **Scalability**—Networks that follow the hierarchical model can grow much larger without sacrificing control or manageability because functionality is localized and potential problems can be recognized more easily. An example of a very large-scale hierarchical network design is the Public Switched Telephone Network.

- **Ease of implementation**—A hierarchical design assigns clear functionality to each layer, thereby making network implementation easier.

- **Ease of troubleshooting**—Because the functions of the individual layers are well defined, the isolation of problems in the network is less complicated. Temporarily segmenting the network to reduce the scope of a problem also is easier.

- **Predictability**—The behavior of a network using functional layers is fairly predictable, which makes capacity planning for growth considerably easier; this design approach also facilitates modeling of network performance for analytical purposes.

- **Protocol support**—The mixing of current and future applications and protocols is much easier on networks that follow the principles of hierarchical design because the underlying infrastructure is already logically organized.

- **Manageability**—All the benefits listed here contribute to greater manageability of the network.

The Three-Layer Design Models

A hierarchical network design includes the following three layers:

- The core layer, which provides optimal transport between sites
- The distribution layer, which provides policy-based connectivity
- The access layer, which provides workgroup and user access to the network

Figure 12-24 shows a high-level view of the various aspects of a hierarchical network design.

Figure 12-24 A Hierarchical Network Design

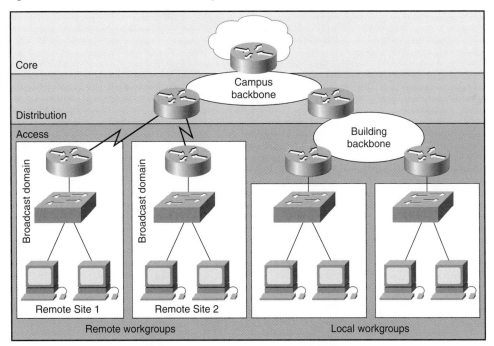

Imagine an enterprise, a financial institution perhaps, which is operational in every country of the European Union, with a branch in every town with a population of more than 10,000. Each branch has a LAN, and it has been decided to interconnect the branches into a WAN. A mesh network is clearly not feasible, because nearly half a million links would be needed for the 900 centers. A simple star will be very difficult to implement, needing a router with 900 interfaces at the hub or a single interface carrying 900 virtual circuits to a packet-switched network.

Consider instead a hierarchical design model, where a group of LANs in an area are interconnected, several areas are interconnected to form a region, and the various regions are interconnected to form the core of the WAN.

The area could be based on the number of locations to be connected, with an upper limit of approximately 30 to 50, or it could follow traditional geographic boundaries. The area would have a star topology, as shown in Figure 12-25, with the hubs of the stars linked to form the region, possibly again in a star. Regions would be geographic, connecting between 3 and 10 areas, and the hub of each region could be linked point to point, as shown in Figures 12-26 and 12-27.

Figure 12-25 Hierarchical Network

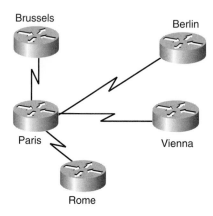

Figure 12-26 Network Connecting Several Areas 1

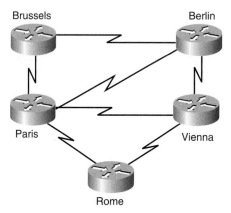

This three-layer model follows the sort of hierarchy used in telephone systems. The links connecting the various sites in an area, giving the sites access to the enterprise network, are called the access links or access layer of the WAN. Traffic between areas is distributed by the distribution links, and where necessary is moved onto the core links to travel to other regions.

Figure 12-27 Network Connecting Several Areas 2

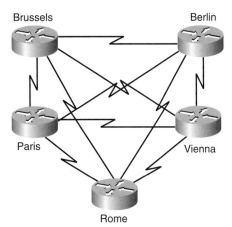

This hierarchy often proves useful where the network traffic mirrors an enterprise's branch structure, with the enterprise divided into regions, areas, and branches. It also proves useful where there is some central service to which all branches must have access, but traffic levels are insufficient to justify direct connection of a branch to the service.

The LAN at the hub of the area may have servers providing area-based, as well as local, service. Depending on the traffic volumes and types, the access connections may be dialup (for example, ISDN), leased, or Frame Relay. Frame Relay facilitates some meshing for redundancy without requiring additional physical connections. Distribution links would be Frame Relay or ATM, and the network core ATM or leased line.

Three-Layer Model Components

A layer is identified as a point in the network where an OSI reference model Layer 3 (network layer) boundary occurs: The three layers are bound by Layer 3 devices or other devices that separate the network into broadcast domains. The three-layer model consists of core, distribution, and access layers, each of which has specific functions:

- **Core layer**—The core layer provides fast wide-area connections between geographically remote sites, tying a number of campus networks together in a corporate or enterprise WAN. Core links are usually point to point, and there are rarely any hosts in the core layer. Core services (for example, T1/T3, Frame Relay, SMDS) typically are leased from a telecom service provider.

- **Distribution layer**—The distribution layer gives network services to multiple LANs within a WAN environment. This layer is where the campus backbone network is found, and it is typically based on Fast Ethernet. This layer is implemented on large sites and is used to interconnect buildings.

- **Access layer**—The access layer is usually a LAN or a group of LANs, typically Ethernet or Token Ring, that provide users with frontline access to network services. The access layer is where almost all hosts are attached to the network, including servers of all kinds and user workstations. Chapter 5, "Switching Concepts and LAN Design," focuses on the design of the access layer.

A three-layer model can meet the needs of most enterprise networks. However, not all environments require a full three-layer hierarchy. In some cases, a two-layer design may be adequate, or even a single-layer flat network. In these cases, however, a hierarchical structure should be planned to allow these network designs to expand to three layers as the need arises. The following sections discuss in more detail the functions of the three layers. Then the discussion moves on to one- and two-layer hierarchies.

Core Layer Functions

The core layer's function is to provide a fast path between remote sites, as shown in Figure 12-28. This layer of the network should not perform any packet manipulation, such as using access control lists and performing filtering, which would slow down the switching of packets. The core layer is usually implemented as a WAN. The WAN needs redundant paths so that the network can withstand individual circuit outages and continue to function. Load sharing and rapid convergence of routing protocols are also important design features. Efficient use of bandwidth in the core is always a concern.

Figure 12-28 The Core Layer

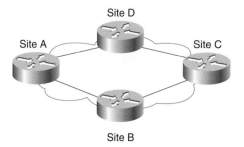

Distribution Layer Functions

The distribution layer of the network is the demarcation point between the access and core layers and helps to define and differentiate the core. The purpose of this layer is to provide boundary definition, and it is the layer at which packet manipulation occurs. In the WAN environment, the distribution layer can include several functions, such as the following:

- Address or area aggregation
- Departmental or workgroup access to the core layer

- Broadcast/multicast domain definition
- Virtual LAN (VLAN) routing
- Any media transitions that need to occur
- Security

The distribution layer would include the campus backbone with all its connecting routers, as shown in Figure 12-29. Because policy is typically implemented at this level, we can say that the distribution layer provides policy-based connectivity. Policy-based connectivity means that the routers are programmed to allow only acceptable traffic on the campus backbone. Note that good network design practice would not put end stations (such as servers) on the backbone. Not putting end stations on the backbone frees up the backbone to act strictly as a transit path for traffic between workgroups or campus-wide servers.

Figure 12-29 The Distribution Layer

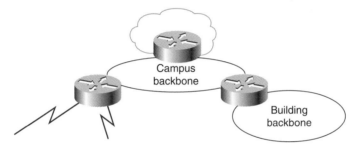

In noncampus environments, the distribution layer can be a point at which remote sites access the corporate network. The distribution layer can be summarized as the layer that provides policy-based connectivity.

Access Layer Functions

The access layer is the point at which local end users are allowed into the network, as shown in Figure 12-30. This layer can also use access control lists or filters to further optimize the needs of a particular set of users. In the campus environment, access layer functions can include the following:

- Shared bandwidth
- Switched bandwidth
- MAC layer filtering
- Microsegmentation

Figure 12-30 The Access Layer

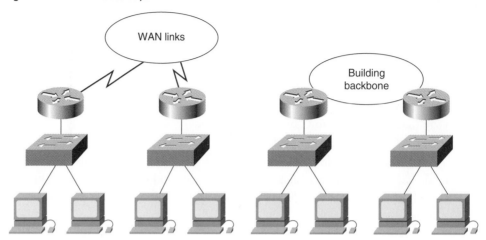

The access layer connects users into LANs, and LANs into WAN backbones or WAN links. This approach enables designers to distribute services of devices operating at this layer. The access layer allows logical segmentation of the network and grouping of users based on their function. Traditionally, this segmentation is based on organizational boundaries (such as Marketing, Administration, or Engineering). However, from a network management and control perspective, the main function of the access layer is to isolate broadcast traffic to the individual workgroup or LAN. In noncampus environments, the access layer can give remote sites access to the corporate network via some wide-area technology, such as Frame Relay, ISDN, or leased lines.

Hierarchical WAN Design Advantages

One of the advantages of a hierarchical WAN design is that it provides a method for controlling data traffic patterns by putting Layer 3 routing points throughout the network. Because routers have the capability to determine paths from the source host to destination hosts based on Layer 3 addressing, data traffic flows up the hierarchy only as far as it needs to find the destination host, as shown in Figure 12-31.

If Host A were to establish a connection to Host B, the traffic from this connection would travel to Router 1 and be forwarded back down to Host B. Notice in Figure 12-32 that this connection does not require that any traffic be placed on the link between Router 1 and Router 2, thus conserving the bandwidth on that link.

In a two-layer WAN hierarchy, which is shown in Figure 12-33, the traffic only travels up the hierarchy as far as needed to get to the destination, thus conserving bandwidth on other WAN links.

Figure 12-31 Routers Are Data Path Decision Points

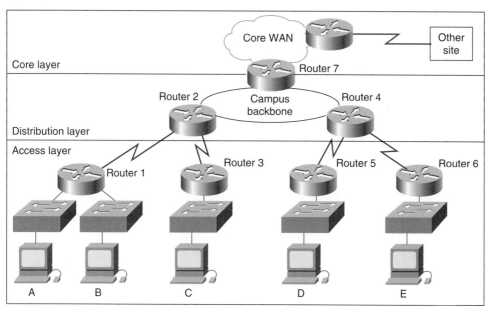

Figure 12-32 Data Flow Based on Source/Destination Addressing

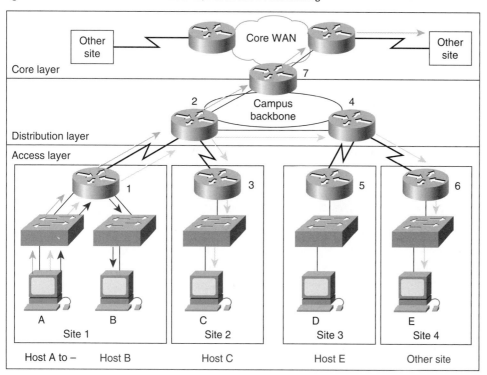

Figure 12-33 Two-Layer WAN Hierarchy

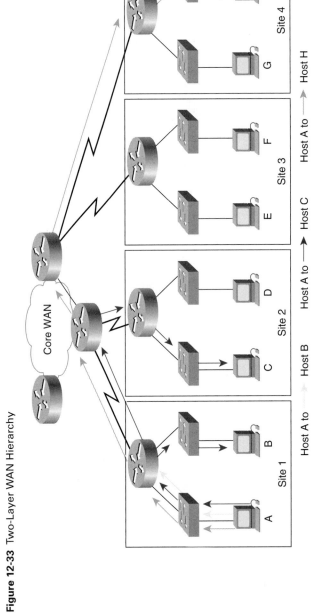

Server Placement

The placement of servers as it relates to who will be accessing them affects traffic patterns in the WAN. If you place an enterprise server in the access layer of Site 1, as shown in Figure 12-34, all traffic destined for that server is forced to go across links between Routers 1 and 2. This consumes major quantities of bandwidth from Site 1.

Figure 12-34 Placement of an Enterprise Server in the Access Layer

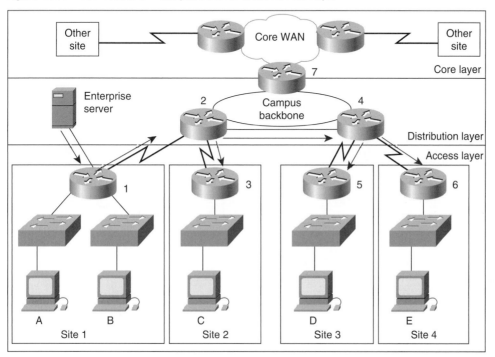

If you place the enterprise server at a higher layer in the hierarchy, as shown in Figure 12-35, the traffic on the link between Routers 1 and 2 is reduced and is available for users at Site 1 to access other services. In Figure 12-36, a workgroup server is placed at the access layer of the site where the largest concentration of users is located, and traffic crossing the WAN link to access this server is limited. Thus, more bandwidth is available to access resources outside the site.

Figure 12-35 Placement of an Enterprise Server at a Higher Layer

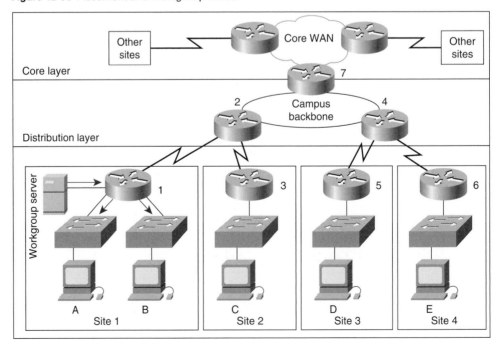

Figure 12-36 Placement of a Workgroup Server

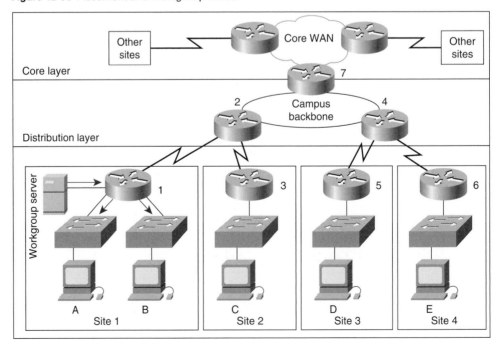

WAN Design

If all the data flows in the enterprise are within a single building, a LAN can be used to carry them. If some data must flow between buildings on a single campus, the buildings can be interconnected with high-speed data links to form a campus LAN. Individual remote access to the LAN and connection of the LAN to the Internet are separate study topics, not considered here. If data must be transferred between geographically separate locations, however, a WAN is needed to carry the data.

Most students will not have the opportunity to design a new WAN, but many will be involved in designing extensions or upgrades to existing WANs and will be able to apply the techniques learned here.

Steps in Designing a WAN

Designing a WAN can be a challenging task. Approaching it in a systematic manner can lead to superior performance at a reduced cost. Many WANs have evolved over time rather than being initially designed following the guidelines discussed here. However, every time a modification to an existing WAN is considered, the steps outlined here should be taken. WAN modifications may arise from change, such as expansion in the enterprise the WAN serves or accommodation of changed work practices or business methods.

Businesses and corporations install WANs because they need to move data in a timely manner between the various branches of the enterprise. Meeting this business need incurs costs, principally provision and management of data links.

To design the WAN, you must know what data traffic must be carried, from where, and to where. WANs carry a variety of traffic types with varying requirements for bandwidth, latency, and jitter. For each pair of endpoints and for each traffic type, information is needed on various traffic characteristics. Determining this may involve extensive studies of, and consultation with, the various network users. The design often involves upgrading, extending, or modifying an existing WAN. Much of the data needed can come from existing network management statistics.

Knowing the various endpoints allows the selection of a topology or layout for the WAN. The topology will be influenced by geographic considerations but also by requirements, such as availability. For instance, high requirement for availability requires extra links to provide alternative data paths.

With the endpoints and their links chosen, the necessary bandwidth for the links can be estimated with some carrying only their own traffic and others carrying aggregated traffic from several sources.

The traffic on the links will have varying requirements for latency and jitter, and these, with the bandwidths already determined, allow the selection of suitable technologies for the links. Installation and operational costs for the WAN can be determined and compared with the business need driving the WAN provision.

The discussions that follow outline several areas that you should carefully consider when planning a WAN implementation. The steps described here can lead to improved WAN cost and performance. Businesses can continually improve their WANs by incorporating these steps into the planning process.

Two primary goals drive WAN design and implementation:

- **Application availability**—Networks carry application information between computers. If the applications are not available to network users, the network is not doing its job.

- **Total cost of ownership**—Information Systems (IS) department budgets often run in the millions of dollars. As large businesses increasingly rely on electronic data for managing business activities, the associated costs of computing resources will continue to rise. A well-designed WAN can help to balance these objectives. When properly implemented, the WAN infrastructure can optimize application availability and allow the cost-effective use of existing network resources.

In general, WAN design needs to take into account three general factors:

- **Environmental variables**—Environmental variables include the location of hosts, servers, terminals, and other end nodes; the projected traffic for the environment; and the projected costs for delivering different service levels.

- **Performance constraints**—Performance constraints consist of network reliability, traffic throughput, and host/client computer speeds (for example, network interface cards and hard drive access speeds).

- **Networking variables**—Networking variables include the network topology, line capacities, and packet traffic. Characterizing network traffic is critical to successful WAN planning, but few planners perform this key step well, if at all.

In WAN design, nothing is more critical than characterizing the types of traffic that will be carried by the WAN.

Types of traffic include the following:

- Voice/fax
- Transaction data (for example, SNA)
- Client/server data
- Messaging (for example, e-mail)

- File transfers
- Batch data
- Network management
- Videoconferencing

Analyzing and categorizing traffic is the basis for key design decisions. Traffic drives capacity, and capacity drives cost. Time-proven processes for measuring and estimating traffic exist for traditional networks, but not for WANs.

Traffic characteristics include the following:

- Peak and average volume
- Connectivity and volume flows
- Connection orientation
- Latency tolerance, including length and variability
- Network availability tolerance
- Error-rate tolerance
- Priority
- Protocol type
- Average packet length

Because many network planners do not have the planning and design techniques needed to deal with WAN traffic complexities and uncertainties, they typically guess the bandwidth capacity, which results in costly, overengineered networks or poorly performing, underengineered ones.

The overall goal of WAN design is to minimize cost based on these elements while delivering service that does not compromise established availability requirements. You face two primary concerns: availability and cost. These issues are essentially at odds. Any increase in availability must generally be reflected as an increase in cost. Therefore, you must carefully weigh the relative importance of resource availability and overall cost.

The first step in the design process is to understand the business requirements, which are covered in the following sections. WAN requirements must reflect the goals, characteristics, business processes, and policies of the business in which they operate.

Gathering Requirements

When designing a WAN, you need to start by gathering data about the business structure and processes. Then, you need to determine who the most important people are to help you design the network. You need to speak to major users and find out their geographic location, their current applications, and their projected needs. The final network design should reflect the user requirements.

In general, users primarily want application availability in their networks. The chief components of application availability are response time, throughput, and reliability:

- Response time is the time between entry of a command or keystroke and the host system's execution of the command or delivery of a response. Applications in which fast response time is considered critical include interactive online services, such as automated tellers and point-of-sale machines.

- Throughput-intensive applications generally involve file-transfer activities. However, throughput-intensive applications also usually have low response-time requirements. Indeed, they can often be scheduled at times when response-time-sensitive traffic is low (for example, after normal work hours).

- Although reliability is always important, some applications have genuine requirements that exceed typical needs. Organizations that conduct all business activities online or over the telephone require nearly 100-percent uptime. Financial services, securities exchanges, and emergency, police, and military operations are a few examples. These situations require a high level of hardware and redundancy. Determining the cost of downtime is essential in determining the importance of reliability to your network.

You can assess user requirements in a number of ways. The more involved your users are in the process, the more likely your evaluation will be accurate. In general, you can use the following methods to obtain this information:

- **User community profiles**—Outline what different user groups require. This is the first step in determining network requirements. Although many general users have the same requirements of e-mail, they may also have different needs, such as sharing local print servers in their area.

  Interviews, focus groups, and surveys build a baseline for implementing a network. Understand that some groups might require access to common servers. Others might want to allow external access to specific internal computing resources. Certain organizations might require IS support systems to be managed in a particular way, according to some external standard.

  The least formal way to obtain information is to conduct interviews with key user groups. You can also use focus groups to gather information and generate discussion among different organizations with similar (or dissimilar) interests. Finally, formal surveys can be used to get a statistically valid reading of user sentiment regarding a particular service level.

- **Human factors tests**—The most expensive, time-consuming, and possibly revealing way to assess user requirements is to conduct a test involving representative users in a lab environment. This is most applicable when you're evaluating response-time requirements. For example, you might set up working systems and have users perform normal remote host activities from the lab network. By evaluating user reactions to variations in host responsiveness, you can create benchmark thresholds for acceptable performance.

After gathering data about the corporate structure, you need to determine where information flows in the company. Find out where shared data resides and who uses it. Determine whether data outside the company is accessed.

Make sure you understand the performance issues of any existing network. If time permits, analyze the performance of the existing network.

Analyzing Requirements

You need to analyze network requirements, including the customer's business and technical goals. What new applications will be implemented? Are any applications Internet based? What new networks will be accessed? What are the success criteria? (How will you know whether the new design is successful?)

Availability measures the usefulness of the network. Many things affect availability, including throughput, response time, and access to resources. Every customer has a different definition of availability. You can increase availability by adding more resources, but resources drive up cost. Network design seeks to provide the greatest availability for the least cost.

The objective of analyzing requirements is to determine the average and peak data rates for each source over time. Try to characterize activity throughout a normal workday in terms of the type of traffic passed, level of traffic, response time of hosts, and the time to execute file transfers. You can also observe utilization on existing network equipment over the test period.

Depending on the traffic type, use one of the following four techniques to analyze and measure traffic:

- **Network management software**—For some types of traffic, you can use network management software to analyze traffic statistics.

- **Existing measurements**—You can place network analysis equipment on servers and analyze packet flows from router statistics for existing network segments.

- **The estimation process**—Where existing measurements cannot be attained (for example, the application does not yet exist), you can use an estimation process.

Work with the application developers and the network administrator to estimate transaction rates, lengths, and flows to derive traffic statistics.

■ **Comparative sources**—You can find a known source that is likely to have similar characteristics and adjust the traffic statistics accordingly.

If the tested network's characteristics are close to those of the new network, you can estimate the new network's requirements based on the projected number of users, applications, and topology. This is a best-guess approach to traffic estimation given the lack of tools to measure detailed traffic behavior.

In addition to monitoring an existing network, you can measure activity and traffic generated by a known number of users attached to a representative test network and then use your results to predict activity and traffic for your anticipated population.

One problem with defining workloads on networks is that it is difficult to accurately pinpoint traffic load and network device performance as functions of the number of users, type of application, and geographic location. This is especially true without a real network in place.

Consider the following factors that influence the dynamics of the network:

■ **The time-dependent nature of network access**—Peak periods can vary; measurements must reflect a range of observations that includes peak demand.

■ **Differences associated with the type of traffic**—Routed and bridged traffic place different demands on network devices and protocols; some protocols are sensitive to dropped packets; some application types require more bandwidth.

■ **The random nature of network traffic**—Exact arrival time and specific effects of traffic are unpredictable.

Each traffic source has its own metric, and each must be converted to bits per second. You should standardize traffic volumes to obtain per-user volumes. Finally, you should apply a factor to account for protocol overhead, packet fragmentation, traffic growth, and safety margin. By varying this factor, you can conduct what-if analyses. For example, you could run Microsoft Office from a server and then analyze the traffic volume generated from users sharing the application on the network. This volume will help you determine the bandwidth and server requirements to install Microsoft Office on the network.

Sensitivity Testing

From a practical point of view, sensitivity testing involves breaking stable links and observing what happens. When working with a test network, this is relatively easy. You can disturb the network by removing an active interface, and monitor how the change is handled by the network: how traffic is rerouted, the speed of convergence, whether any connectivity is lost, and whether problems arise in handling specific types of traffic. You can also change the level of traffic on a network to determine the effects on the network when traffic levels approach media saturation.

WAN Topology

The topology of a network is the layout of the interconnections. Although many different topologies are possible, they are based on a few simple layouts.

Where two LANs are connected by a single link, the topology is called point to point, and is shown in Figure 12-37. Additional LANs can be connected while maintaining a point-to-point topology. It is simple to implement but has the disadvantage that traffic from one end to the other must pass through all the intervening nodes. As an advantage, it will probably have the shortest total distance of interconnections, an important factor if the lines are to be leased.

Figure 12-37 WAN Point-to-Point Topology

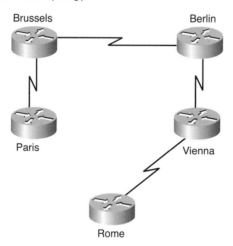

To minimize the delays in getting from any LAN to any other, the interconnections can be rearranged to form a star. The number of links is the same, but each leaf point of the star is now only two hops from each other leaf point. The length of the links will probably be greater and so will cost more. The router at the center of the star will need an interface for each leaf point, but the leaf-point routers will each need only a single WAN interface.

If redundancy or minimal delay is required, you can add more links to give a mesh topology, as in Figure 12-38. Now each LAN is only one hop from each other LAN, and the network is also more robust, because no single node failure can prevent other nodes from communicating. The low latency and robustness come at a price, because many more interfaces and links are required.

Figure 12-38 WAN Full Mesh

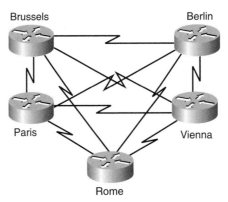

The number of links for a point-to-point or a star WAN is one less than the number of nodes, so N nodes requires (N – 1) links. For a mesh the formula is $N \times (N – 1)/2$. A WAN with 50 nodes requires 49 links for a star, but it requires 1225 links for a mesh. Mesh topologies are unlikely to be economic for more than the smallest WANs.

Various combinations of these topologies are possible. Often the basic configuration will be a star, but some of the leaf nodes will be cross-connected to form a partial mesh, as in Figure 12-39, providing redundancy in the event of failure. As networks grow, these basic topologies are not very scalable, and for larger networks a more structured approach is required. A hierarchical topology is considered in a later section.

Figure 12-39 WAN Partial Mesh

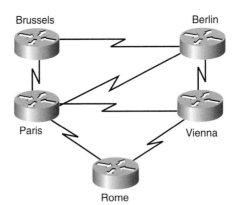

How to Identify and Select Networking Capabilities

Designing a WAN essentially consists of selecting an interconnection pattern or layout for the links between the various locations and selecting the technologies for those links to meet the enterprise requirements at an acceptable cost.

All the technologies, except telephone, ISDN, DSL, and cable, require a dedicated leased line. The leased lines may connect different parts of the enterprise directly together, or they may connect them to their nearest point of presence (POP) on a shared network, such as X.25, Frame Relay, or ATM. Direct connections are generally much longer, and therefore, more expensive, but they are available at virtually any bandwidth. Direct dedicated connections give very low latency and jitter.

ATM, Frame Relay, and X.25 networks carry traffic from several customers over the same internal links. The enterprise has no control over the number of links or hops that its data must traverse in the shared network or the time its data must wait at each network device before it can move on the next link. This uncertainty in latency and jitter makes these technologies unsuitable for some types of network traffic. However, the disadvantages of a shared network may often be outweighed by the shared cost. Because several customers are sharing the link, the cost to each is generally substantially less that the cost of a direct link of the same capacity.

Although ATM is a shared network, it has been designed to give a minimal latency and jitter, particularly through its use of very small data frames (cells) and high-speed internal links. It is widely used for carrying delay-sensitive traffic. Frame Relay may also be used for delay-sensitive traffic, often using QoS mechanisms to give priority to the more sensitive data.

A typical WAN uses a combination of technologies that are usually chosen based on traffic type and volume. ISDN, Frame Relay, or leased lines are used to connect individual branches into an area. Frame Relay, ATM, or leased lines are used to connect areas back to the backbone; ATM or leased lines form the WAN backbone.

Other WAN Design Considerations

Many enterprise WANs will have connections to the Internet. This poses security problems but also provides an alternative for interbranch traffic.

Part of the traffic that must be designed for is going to or coming from the Internet. Because access to the Internet probably exists everywhere that the enterprise has LANs, this traffic can be carried in two principal ways. Each LAN can have a connection to its local ISP, or there can be a single connection from one of the core routers to an ISP. The advantage of the first method is that Internet traffic is carried on the Internet rather than on the enterprise network, possibly requiring lower bandwidth WAN links. The disadvantage of permitting multiple links, however, is that the whole enterprise WAN is open to Internet-based attacks, and it is difficult to monitor and secure the many connection points. The single connection point is more easily policed and secured, even though the enterprise WAN will be carrying some traffic that would otherwise have been carried on the Internet.

If each LAN in the enterprise has a separate Internet connection, another possibility is opened for the enterprise WAN. Where traffic volumes are relatively small, the Internet itself can be used as the enterprise WAN, with all interbranch traffic going via the Internet. Securing the various LANs will be an issue, but the savings in WAN connections may compensate for the additional security.

As far as possible, servers should be placed in the location that most uses them. Frequent replication of servers, with arrangement for off-peak interserver updates, reduces the required link capacity. Location of Internet-accessible services will depend on the nature of the service, anticipated traffic, security issues, and so on. It is a specialized design topic that need not be considered here.

Summary

In this chapter, the following key points were discussed:

- There are many options for connecting WANs.
- WANs carry data between geographically separated LANs.
- Generally, the data links used by WANs are owned by communications providers or common carriers and made available to an enterprise for a fee.
- WANs carry a variety of traffic types, such as voice, data, and video; therefore, the WAN design must provide adequate capacity and transit times to meet the requirements of the enterprise.
- Because the WAN is merely a set of interconnections between LAN-based routers, there are no services on the WAN; therefore, WAN technologies function at the three lowest layers of the OSI reference model.
- WAN design often involves upgrading, extending, or modifying an existing WAN.
- Many different WAN topologies are possible, such as point-to-point, star, and meshed topologies.
- A typical WAN uses a combination of technologies, such as ISDN, Frame Relay, ATM, and leased lines.
- For large WANS, a hierarchical solution with three layers offers many advantages.
- Connecting WANs to the Internet provides an alternative for interbranch traffic.

- Remote individual access from the home office to an enterprise network is available through an analog modem, ISDN, DSL, or cable modem.

- An analog, ISDN, or DSL connection utilizes existing telephone lines, whereas cable modem uses a coaxial cable network.

- Analog and ISDN are dialup and provide connectivity only as required. DSL and cable modem are connected full time as long as the computer is turned on.

- Bandwidth varies among the technologies, with DSL and cable modem transfer rates far exceeding those of analog and ISDN.

To supplement all that you've learned in this chapter, refer to the chapter-specific Videos, PhotoZooms, and e-Lab Activities on the CD-ROM accompanying this book.

Key Terms

ATM (Asynchronous Transfer Mode)   International standard for cell relay in which multiple service types (such as voice, video, or data) are conveyed in fixed-length (53-byte) cells. Fixed-length cells allow cell processing to occur in hardware, thereby reducing transit delays. ATM is designed to take advantage of high-speed transmission media such as E3, SONET, and T3.

circuit switching   Switching system in which a dedicated physical circuit path must exist between sender and receiver for the duration of the "call." Used heavily in the telephone company network.

(CO) central office   Local telephone company office to which all local loops in a given area connect and in which circuit switching of subscriber lines occurs.

(CPE) customer premises equipment   Terminating equipment, such as terminals, telephones, and modems, supplied by the telephone company, installed at customer sites, and connected to the telephone company network.

(CSU) channel service unit   Digital interface device that connects end-user equipment to the local digital telephone loop. Often referred to together with DSU, as CSU/DSU.

(DCE) data circuit-terminating equipment (EIA expansion) or *data circuit-terminating equipment* (ITU-T expansion)   The devices and connections of a communications network that comprise the network end of the user-to-network interface. The DCE provides a physical connection to the network, forwards traffic, and provides a clocking signal used to synchronize data transmission between DCE and DTE devices. Modems and interface cards are examples of DCE.

(DSU) digital service unit   Device used in digital transmission that adapts the physical interface on a DTE device to a transmission facility such as T1 or E1. The DSU is also responsible for such functions as signal timing. Often referred to together with CSU, as CSU/DSU.

(DTE) data terminal equipment   Device at the user end of a user-network interface that serves as a data source, destination, or both. DTE connects to a data network through a DCE device (for example, a modem) and typically uses clocking signals generated by the DCE. DTE includes such devices as computers, protocol translators, and multiplexers.

packet switching   Networking method in which nodes share bandwidth with each other by sending packets.

(PVCs) permanent virtual circuits   Virtual circuit that is permanently established. PVCs save bandwidth associated with circuit establishment and tear

down in situations where certain virtual circuits must exist all the time. Called a permanent virtual connection in ATM terminology.

(SVCs) switched virtual circuits   Virtual circuit that is dynamically established on demand and is torn down when transmission is complete. SVCs are used in situations where data transmission is sporadic. Called a switched virtual connection in ATM terminology.

(TDM) Time-Division Multiplexing   Technique in which information from multiple channels can be allocated bandwidth on a single wire based on preassigned time slots. Bandwidth is allocated to each channel regardless of whether the station has data to transmit.

Check Your Understanding

1. Analog dialed connections are not suitable for which of the following traffic types?

   A. E-mail

   B. Low-volume file transfers

   C. Reports

   D. Video

2. Which of the following statements pertaining to ISDN is true?

   A. The ISDN BRI offers two B channels and one D channel.

   B. The D channel, operating at 16 kbps, is meant to carry user data.

   C. The ISDN BRI offers 23 B channels and 1 D channel in North America.

   D. The total bit rate of the ISDN BRI is 2.533 Mbps.

3. A leased line is a _____ link that provides a single previously established WAN communication path from the customer to a remote network.

   A. Point-to-point

   B. Point-to-multipoint

   C. Analog

   D. Digital

4. Which of these statements about X.25 networks is not true?

   A. Bit rates are low.

   B. Data packets are not subject to delay.

   C. Widely used in EDI applications.

   D. Charges relate to quantity of data.

5. How does Frame Relay handle multiple conversations on the same physical connection?

   A. Frame Relay multiplexes the circuits.

   B. Multiple conversations are not allowed.

   C. Frame Relay duplexes the conversation.

   D. Frame Relay converts it to an ATM cell.

6. Which of the following is *not* true about ATM technology?

   A. It is capable of transferring voice, video, and data.

   B. ATM offers higher bandwidth than Frame Relay.

   C. It is based on a cell-based architecture rather than on a frame-based architecture.

   D. ATM cells are always a fixed length of 35 bytes.

7. Equipment on a subscriber's premises that connects to a service provider's central office is called:

   A. DTE

   B. DCE

   C. CPE

   D. None of the above

8. Devices that put data on the local loop are called:

   A. DTE

   B. DCE

   C. CPE

   D. None of the above

9. The customer devices that pass the data to the DCE are called:

   A. DTE

   B. DCE

   C. C. CPE

   D. D. None of the above

10. For digital lines a _____ and a _____ are required.

   A. CSU and DSU

   B. DTE and DCE

   C. T1 and E1

   D. None of the above

11. For analog WAN services a _____ is required?

   A. DCE

   B. DTE

   C. Modem

   D. NIC

12. Circuit-switched connections include the following except _____?

   A. Public Switched Telephone Network (PSTN)

   B. ISDN Basic Rate Interface (BRI)

   C. ISDN Primary Rate Interface (PRI)

   D. SONET

13. In a packet-switched network, routes established when the switches are started are called:

   A. Permanent virtual circuits (PVCs)

   B. Switched virtual circuits (SVC)

   C. Permanent virtual service (PVS)

   D. Switched virtual service (SVS)

14. In a packet-switched network, routes that are established on demand are called:

   A. Permanent virtual circuits (PVCs)

   B. Switched virtual circuits (SVC)

   C. Permanent virtual service (PVS)

   D. Switched virtual service (SVS)

15. Which type of service characterizes an ISDN connection?

   A. Asynchronous dialup

   B. Asynchronous leased line

   C. Synchronous dialup

   D. Synchronous leased line

16. Which of the following is a DCE device?

   A. Router

   B. Modem

   C. Switch

   D. Hub

17. At which OSI layer does PPP operate?

   A. Network

   B. Data link

   C. Application

   D. Transport

18. Frame Relay operates at which layer of the OSI model?

   A. Layer 1

   B. Layer 2

   C. Layer 4

   D. Layer 3

19. ISDN BRI is composed of which of the following?

   A. 2 B channels and 2 D channels

   B. 2 B channels and 1 D channel

   C. 23 B channels and 1 D channel

   D. 30 B channels and 1 D channel

Objectives

After reading this chapter, you will be able to

- Identify and describe the basic components that define Point-to-Point Protocol (PPP) communication
- Define and describe the use of link control protocol (LCP) and Network Control Protocol (NCP) frames in PPP
- Understand the process for configuring and verifying PPP
- Describe and explain PPP authentication
- Define and describe the use of password authentication
- Define and describe the use of Challenge Handshake Authentication Protocol (CHAP)

Chapter 13

Point-to-Point Protocol

In this chapter, you will learn about the basic components, processes, and operations that define *(PPP)* communication. In addition, you will learn about the use of *LCP* and *Network Control Protocol* frames in PPP. Finally, you will learn how to configure and verify the configuration of PPP. Along with PPP authentication, you will learn to use Password Authentication Protocol (PAP) and CHAP.

PPP, which is documented in RFC 1661, is a good solution for dial-up Internet connections, including Integrated Services Digital Network (ISDN). PPP is a layered protocol, starting with an LCP for link establishment, configuration, and testing. After the LCP is initialized, one or many of several Network Control Protocols can be used to transport traffic for a particular protocol suite. The IP Control Protocol (IPCP), which is documented in RFC 1332, permits the transport of IP packets over a PPP link. Other NCPs exist for AppleTalk (RFC 1378), OSI (RFC 1377), DECnet Phase IV (RFC 1762), Vines (RFC 1763), XNS (RFC 1764), and transparent Ethernet bridging (RFC 1638).

Following are some of the key PPP features that will be discussed in this chapter:

- **Address notification**—This allows a server to inform a dial-up client of its IP address for that link, but the mechanism is powerful enough for clients to request IP addresses and support fallback configurations. SLIP required the user to configure this information manually. PPP options also have been specified (RFC 1877) for notification of name server addresses—both Internet and NetBIOS.

- **Authentication**—This is available as an option with PAP or CHAP. Both are documented in RFC 1334.

- **Multiple protocols**—Multiple protocols can interoperate on the same link simply by running additional NCPs. For example, both IP and IPX traffic can share a PPP link.

- **Link monitoring**—These facilities include a link-level echo facility that can periodically check link operation.

Be sure to look at this chapter's associated e-Lab Activities, Videos, and PhotoZooms that you will find on the CD-ROM that accompanies this book. These CD-ROM elements are designed to supplement the material and reinforce the concepts that are introduced in this chapter.

PPP Layered Architecture

PPP provides router-to-router and host-to-network connections over both synchronous and asynchronous circuits. Figure 13-1 shows PPP encapsulation being used in the WAN. PPP is one of the most widely used and most popular WAN protocols because it offers all the following features:

- Control of data link setup
- Assignment and management of IP addresses
- Network protocol multiplexing
- Link configuration and link quality testing
- Error detection

Figure 13-1 Point-to-Point Protocol in the WAN

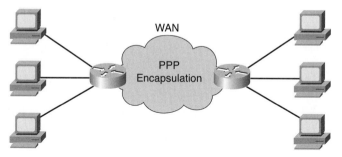

PPP uses a layered architecture. An architecture is simply a logical model, design, or blueprint. A layered architecture aids in communication between interconnecting layers. The OSI model is the layered architecture that is used in networking. PPP provides a method for encapsulating multiprotocol datagrams over a point-to-point link and uses the data link layer for testing the connection. Therefore, PPP uses three of the OSI layers in its architecture. Figure 13-2 shows how PPP fits within the OSI model. Figure 13-3 shows PPP layer functions.

- The physical layer is used for the actual point-to-point connection.
- The data link layer is used to establish and configure the connection.
- The network layer is used to configure different network layer protocols.

Figure 13-2 PPP and the OSI Model

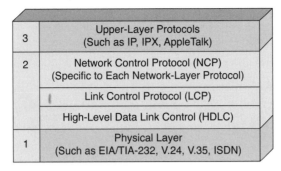

Figure 13-3 PPP Layer Functions

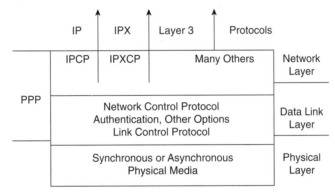

You can configure PPP on the following types of physical interfaces:

- Asynchronous serial
- Synchronous serial
- High-Speed Serial Interface (HSSI)
- ISDN

PPP uses its LCP to negotiate and set up control options on the wide-area network (WAN) data link. PPP uses the Network Control Program component to encapsulate and negotiate options for multiple network layer protocols.

LCP sits on top of the physical layer and is used to establish, configure, and test the data link connection. PPP also uses LCP to automatically agree upon encapsulation format options such as the the following:

- **Authentication**—Authentication options require that the calling side of the link enter information to help ensure the caller has the network administrator's permission to make the call. (See Figure 13-4.) Peer routers exchange authentication messages. Following are two alternatives:

— PAP

— CHAP

Figure 13-4 Authentication

- **Compression**—Compression options increase the effective throughput on PPP connections by reducing the amount of data in the frame that must travel across the link. The protocol decompresses the frame at its destination. (See Figure 13-5.) Two compression algorithms that are available in Cisco routers are Stacker and Predictor.

Figure 13-5 Compression

- **Error-detection**—Error-detection mechanisms with PPP enable a process to identify fault conditions. The Quality and Magic Number options help ensure a reliable, loop-free data link.

- **Multilink**—Cisco IOS Release 11.1 and later supports multilink PPP. This alternative provides load balancing over the router interfaces that PPP uses. (See Figure 13-6.)

Figure 13-6 Multilink

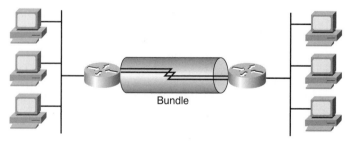

- **PPP callback**—To further enhance security, Cisco IOS Release 11.1 offers callback over PPP. With this LCP option, a Cisco router can act as a callback client or as a callback server. The client makes the initial call, requests that it be called back, and terminates its initial call. The callback router answers the initial call and makes the return call to the client based on its configuration statements.

LCP also handles varying limits on packet size, detects common misconfiguration errors, terminates the link, and determines when a link is functioning properly and when it is failing.

PPP permits multiple network layer protocols to operate on the same communications link. For every network layer protocol that is used, a separate Network Control Protocol is provided. For example, Internet Protocol (IP) uses IPCP, and Internetwork Packet Exchange (IPX) uses the IPCP. NCPs include functional fields that contain standardized codes to indicate the network layer protocol type that PPP encapsulates.

The fields of a PPP frame are shown in Figure 13-7 and are described as follows:

- **Flag**—Indicates the beginning or end of a frame and consists of the binary sequence 01111110.
- **Address**—Consists of the standard broadcast address, which is the binary sequence 11111111. PPP does not assign individual station addresses.
- **Control**—1 byte that consists of the binary sequence 00000011, which calls for transmission of user data in an unsequenced frame. A connectionless link service that is similar to that of *Logical Link Control (LLC)* Type 1 is provided.
- **Protocol**—2 bytes that identify the protocol that is encapsulated in the data field of the frame. Table 13-1 lists some of the PPP Field protocol numbers.

Table 13-1 PPP Field Numbers

Value (in Hex)	Protocol Name
8021	IPCP
8023	OSI Network Layer Control Protocol
8029	AppleTalk Control Protocol
802b	Novell IPX Control Protocol
c021	LCP
c023	PAP
c223	CHAP

More Information
You can find additional PPP field assignments that are not included in the preceeding table at http://www.iana.org/assignments/ppp-numbers.

- **Data**—0 or more bytes that contain the datagram for the protocol that is specified in the protocol field. You can find the end of the data field by locating the closing flag sequence and allowing 2 bytes for the frame check sequence (FCS) field. The default maximum length of the data field is 1500 bytes.

- **FCS**—Normally 16 bits (2 bytes). Refers to the extra characters that are added to a frame for error-control purposes.

Figure 13-7 PPP Frame Format

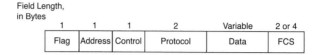

Establishing a PPP Session

PPP provides a method of establishing, configuring, maintaining, and terminating a point-to-point connection. To establish communications over a point-to-point link, PPP goes through four distinct phases:

1. **Link establishment and configuration negotiation**—An originating PPP node sends LCP frames to configure and establish the data link.

2. **Link-quality determination**—The link is tested to determine whether the link quality is sufficient to bring up network layer protocols. Note that this is an optional phase.

3. **Network layer protocol configuration negotiation**—The originating PPP node sends NCP frames to choose and configure network-layer protocols. The chosen network-layer protocols—such as IP, Novell IPX, and AppleTalk—are configured, and packets from each network layer protocol can be sent.

4. **Link termination**—The link remains configured for communications until LCP or NCP frames close the link or until some external event occurs (for example, an inactivity timer expires or a user intervenes).

There are three classes of LCP frames:

- Link-establishment frames are used to establish and configure a link.
- Link-termination frames are used to terminate a link.
- Link-maintenance frames are used to manage and debug a link.

An example of PPP link negotiation is shown in Figure 13-8.

Figure 13-8 PPP Link Negotiation

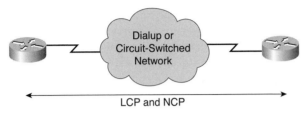

Table 13-2 describes the four PPP session establishment phases.

Table 13-2 PPP Session Establishment Phases

Phase	Description
1. Link establishment	In this phase, each PPP device sends LCP frames to configure and test the data link. LCP frames contain a Configuration Option field that allows devices to negotiate the use of options such as the maximum transmit unit (MTU), compression of certain PPP fields, and the link authentication protocol. If a configuration option is not included in an LCP packet, the default value for that configuration option is assumed.
	Before network layer packets can be exchanged, LCP must first open the connection and negotiate the configuration parameters. This phase is complete when a configuration acknowledgment frame has been sent and received.
2. Link quality determination	After the link has been established and the authentication protocol has been decided on, the peer can be authenticated. Authentication, if used, takes place before the network layer protocol phase is entered.
	As part of this phase, LCP also allows for an optional link-quality determination test. The link is tested to determine whether the link quality is good enough to bring up network layer protocols.

continues

Table 13-2 PPP Session Establishment Phases (Continued)

Phase	Description
3. Network layer protocol	In this phase, the PPP devices send NCP packets to choose and configure one or more network layer protocols, such as IP. After each of the chosen network layer protocols has been configured, packets from each network layer protocol can be sent over the link.
	If LCP closes the link, it informs the network layer protocols so that they can take appropriate action. When PPP is configured, using the **show interfaces** command can check its LCP and NCP states.
4. Link termination	LCP can terminate the link at any time. This is usually done at the request of a user but can happen because of a physical event, such as the loss of a carrier or a timeout.

PPP Authentication Protocols

The authentication phase of a PPP session is optional. After the link has been established and the authentication protocol has been chosen, the peer can be authenticated. If it is used, authentication takes place before the network layer protocol configuration phase begins.

The authentication options require that the calling side of the link enter authentication information to help ensure that the user has the network administrator's permission to make the call. Peer routers exchange authentication messages.

When you are configuring PPP authentication, you can select *PAP* or *CHAP*. In general, CHAP is the preferred protocol.

Password Authentication Protocol

PAP provides a simple method for a remote node to establish its identity by using a two-way handshake. After the PPP link establishment phase is complete, a username/password pair is repeatedly sent by the remote node across the link until authentication is acknowledged or the connection is terminated. An example is shown in Figure 13-9.

PAP is not a strong authentication protocol. Passwords are sent across the link in clear text, and there is no protection from playback or repeated trial-and-error attacks. The remote node is in control of the frequency and timing of the login attempts.

Figure 13-9 PAP Authentication

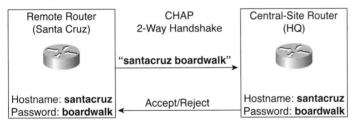

CHAP

CHAP is used at the startup of a link and periodically to verify the identity of the remote node using a three-way handshake. CHAP is done upon initial link establishment and can be repeated any time after the link has been established.

After the PPP link establishment phase is complete, the local router sends a "challenge" message to the remote node. The remote node responds with a value that is calculated by using a one-way hash function (typically the MD5 Message-Digest algorithm) based on the password and challenge message. The local router checks the response against its calculation of the expected hash value. If the values match, the authentication is acknowledged. Otherwise, the connection is terminated immediately. An example is shown in Figure 13-10.

Figure 13-10 CHAP Authentication

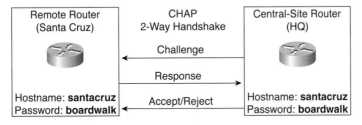

CHAP provides protection against playback attack through the use of a variable challenge value that is unique and unpredictable. Because the challenge is unique and random, the resulting hash value is also unique and random. The use of repeated challenges is intended to limit the time of exposure to any single attack. The local router or a third-party authentication server is in control of the frequency and timing of the challenges.

PPP Encapsulation and Authentication Process

When you are configuring PPP authentication, you can select either PAP or CHAP. When a user enters the **encapsulation ppp** command, the system determines the type of authentication that is configured. If no authentication is required, the PPP session starts immediately. Otherwise, the process proceeds to the next step. The authentication process is shown in Figure 13-11.

Figure 13-11 Authentication Process

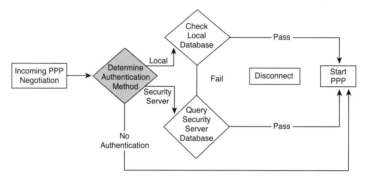

The process then determines the authentication method to be used.

The local database or security server (established with the username password commands) is checked to see if the given username and password pair matches (CHAP or PAP).

The process checks the authentication response sent back from the local database. If it is a positive response, the PPP session is started. If it is a negative response, the user is rejected immediately.

After the PPP link establishment phase is complete in PAP, the remote node repeatedly sends a username and password pair to the router until authentication is acknowledged or the connection is terminated.

After the PPP link establishment phase is complete in CHAP, the local router sends a challenge message to the remote node. The remote node responds with a value that is calculated by using a one-way hash function (typically MD5). The local router checks the response against its own calculation of the expected hash value. If the values match, the authentication is acknowledged. Otherwise, the connection is terminated immediately.

The following steps and figures show the series of events that occur during a CHAP authentication between two routers. These do not represent the actual messages seen in the **debug ppp negotiation** output. For more information, refer to the document "Understanding debug ppp negotiation Output" at www.cisco.com/warp/public/471/debug_ppp_negotiation.html.

The following steps are shown in Figure 13-12:

Step 1   The call comes in to 3640-1. The incoming interface is configured with the **ppp authentication chap** command.

Step 2   LCP negotiates CHAP and MD5.

Step 3   A CHAP challenge from 3640-1 to the calling router is required on this call.

Figure 13-12 First Step of CHAP Authentication Process

Figure 13-13 illustrates the following steps in the CHAP authentication between the two routers:

Step 1   A CHAP challenge packet is built with the following characteristics:

- 01 = Challenge packet type identifier
- id = Sequential number that identifies the challenge
- random = A reasonably random number that the router generates
- 3640-1 = The authentication name of the challenger

Step 2   The id and random values are kept on the called router.

Step 3   The challenge packet is sent to the calling router. A list of outstanding challenges is maintained.

Figure 13-13 Second Step of CHAP Authentication Process

Challenge

766-1   User Dials In   3640-1

| 01 | id | random | 3640-1 |

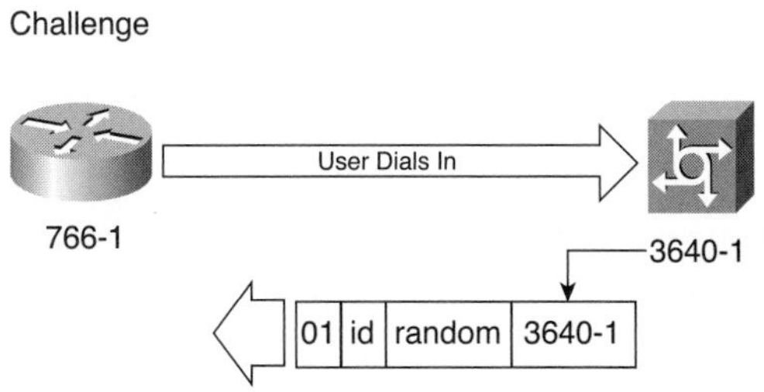

Figure 13-14 illustrates the receipt and MD5 processing of the challenge packet from the peer.

Figure 13-14 Third Step of CHAP Authentication Process

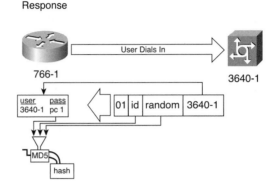

The router processes the incoming CHAP challenge packet in the following manner:

Step 1 The id value is fed into the MD5 hash generator.

Step 2 The random value is fed into the MD5 hash generator.

Step 3 The name 3640-1 is used to look up the password. The router looks for an entry that matches the username in the challenge. In this example, it looks for the following:

username 3640-1 password pc1

Step 4 The password is fed into the MD5 hash generator.

The result is the one-way MD5-hashed CHAP challenge that will be sent back in the CHAP response.

Figure 13-15 illustrates how the CHAP response packet sent to the authenticator is built. The following steps are shown in this figure:

Step 1 The response packet is assembled from the following components:

- 02 = CHAP response packet type identifier.
- id = Copied from the challenge packet.
- hash = The output from the MD5 hash generator (the hashed information from the challenge packet).
- 766-1 = The authentication name of this device. This is needed for the peer to look up the username and password entry that are needed to verify identity. (We will look at this in more detail later.)

Step 2   The response packet is then sent to the challenger.

Figure 13-15 Fourth Step of CHAP Authentication Process

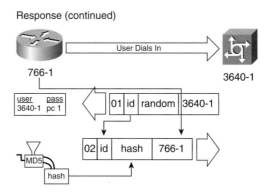

Figure 13-16 shows how the challenger processes the response packet.

Figure 13-16 Fifth Step of CHAP Authentication Process

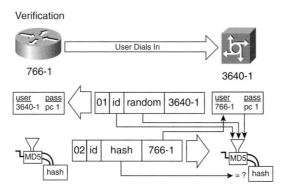

The CHAP response packet is processed (on the authenticator) in the following manner:

Step 1   The id is used to find the original challenge packet.

Step 2   The id is fed into the MD5 hash generator.

Step 3   The original challenge random value is fed into the MD5 hash generator.

Step 4   The name 766-1 is used to look up the password from one of the following sources:

- Local username and password database
- Remote Authentication Dial-In User Service (RADIUS) or Terminal Access Controller Access Control System (TACACS+) server

Step 5   The password is fed into the MD5 hash generator.

Step 6   The hash value that is received in the response packet is then compared to the calculated MD5 hash value. CHAP authentication succeeds if the calculated and received hash values are equal.

Figure 13-17 illustrates the success message being sent to the calling router.

Figure 13-17 Sixth Step of CHAP Authentication Process

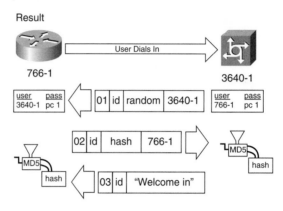

If authentication is successful, a CHAP success packet is built from the following components:

- 03 = CHAP success message type.
- id = Copied from the response packet.
- "Welcome in" is simply a text message that provides a user-readable explanation.

If authentication fails, a CHAP failure packet is built from the following components:

- 04 = CHAP failure message type
- id = Copied from the response packet
- "Authentication failure" or other text message, providing a user-readable explanation

The success or failure packet is then sent to the calling router.

NOTE

This example depicts a one-way authentication. In a two-way authentication, this entire process is repeated, but the calling router initiates the initial challenge.

Serial Point-to-Point Links

Almost all WAN technologies are based on serial transmission at the physical layer. This means that the bits of a frame are transmitted one at a time over the physical medium.

The bits that make up the Layer 2 frame are signaled one at a time by physical layer processes onto the physical medium. The signaling method (NRZ-L, HDB3, AMI), among other things, differentiates between one serial communication method and another. Some of the many different serial communications standards are the following:

- RS-232-E
- V.35
- HSSI

Time-Division Multiplexing

Time-division multiplexing (TDM) is the transmission of several sources of information by using one common channel, or signal, and then the reconstruction of the original streams at the remote end.

Figure 13-18 shows that there are three sources of information, and that these are carried in turn down the output channel. First, a chunk of information is taken from each input channel. The size of this chunk might vary; but typically it is either a bit or a byte at a time. Depending on whether bits or bytes are used, this type of TDM is called bit-interleaving or byte-interleaving.

Figure 13-18 TDM Source Information

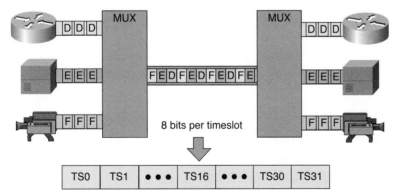

Each of the three input channels has its own capacity. For the output channel to be able to accommodate all the information from the three inputs, the output channel's capacity must be no less than the sum of the inputs.

In TDM, the output timeslot is always there whether or not the TDM input has information to transmit. TDM output can be compared to a train with, for example, 32 cargo trailers. A different shipping company owns each trailer. Every day, the train leaves with its 32 trailers attached. If the shipping company has product to ship, it puts it in a cargo container, puts the container on its trailer, and the train moves the trailer. If a shipping company has nothing to ship, its trailer remains empty, but it is still part of the convoy.

Finally, TDM is a physical layer concept. It has no regard for the nature of the information that is being multiplexed onto the output channel. As such, it is independent of the Layer 2 protocol that the input channels are using.

A good TDM example is ISDN. ISDN Basic Rate Interface (BRI), for example, has three channels, consisting of two 64-kbps B-channels (B1 and B2) and a 16-kbps D-channel. In Figure 13-19, the TDM has nine timeslots, repeated. This allows the telco to actively manage and troubleshoot the local loop as the demarcation point occurs after the NTU.

Figure 13-19 TDM

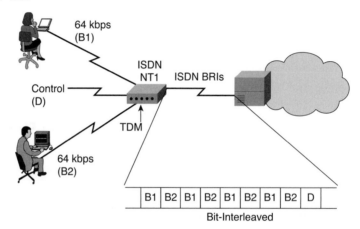

Demarcation Point

The demarcation point, or demarc as it is commonly known, is the point in the network where the responsibility of the service provider, or telco, ends. This differs between the U.S. and non-U.S. telco providers. In the U.S., a telco provides the local loop into the customer's premises, but the customer provides the active equipment (CSU/DSU) on which the local loop is terminated. This termination often occurs in a telecommunications closet. In this case, the customer is responsible for maintaining the hardware and replacing it if it fails.

In North America, the network termination type 1 (NT1) device is a customer premises equipment (CPE) device. In most other parts of the world, the NT1 is part of the network that the carrier provides and manages. This allows the telco to actively manage and troubleshoot the local loop. The demarcation point occurs after the NT1. The customer connects a CPE device—such as a router or frame relay access device—into the NT1, typically by using a serial interface such as V.35 or RS-232. An example of demarc is shown in Figure 13-20.

Figure 13-20 Demarc

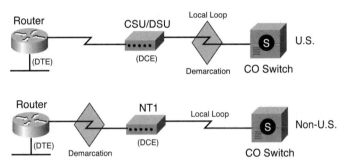

DTE and Data Communications Equipment Devices

In any WAN connection, devices are usually found at each end of the connection. A DTE device and data communications equipment device are at one end of the connection, and a corresponding DTE and data communications equipment are at the other end, as shown in Figure 13-21. Connecting the two data communications equipment is the WAN service provider's transmission network. The CPE, which is often a router, is the DTE. Other examples could be a terminal, computer, printer, or fax machine.

Figure 13-21 Data Communications Equipment

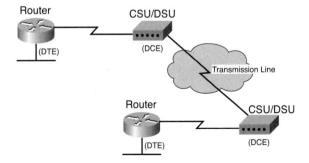

The DCE, commonly a modem or channel service unit/data service unit (CSU/DSU) is the device that is used to convert the user data from the DTE into a form that is acceptable to the WAN service provider's transmission link. This signal is received at the remote DCE, which decodes the signal back into a sequence of bits, which are in turn signaled to the remote DTE. The two DCEs must be configured to understand each other. In other words, they must use the same encoding scheme and data transfer rate.

Many standards have been developed to allow DTEs to communicate with DCEs. Bodies such as the Electronic Industries Association (EIA) and the International Telecommunication Union Telecommunication Standardization Sector (ITU-T) have been most active in the development of these standards. An example of network connections at the CSU/DSU is shown in Figure 13-22.

Figure 13-22 Network Connections at the CSU/DSU

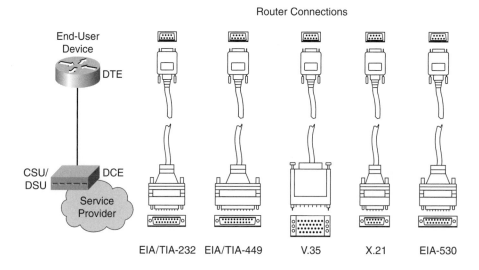

The DTE-DCE interface for a particular standard defines the following specifications:

- **Mechanical**—Physical—number of pins, connector type, and so on.
- **Electrical**—Defines voltage levels for 0/1.
- **Functional**—Specifies the functions that are performed by assigning meanings to each of the signaling lines in the interface. For example, in EIA/TIA-232, DB-25, line 2—transmit DTE to DCE; line 3—receive at DTE from DCE; line 15—transmitter clocking.
- **Procedural**—Specifies the sequence of events for transmitting data.

Suppose that two DTEs must be connected, like two computers or two routers in the lab. A special cable called a null-modem (which is actually two cables rolled together into a single cable) is necessary to eliminate the need for DCE. For synchronous connections, where a clock signal is needed, either an external device or one of the DTEs must generate the clock signal. A DCE normally performs this function.

The synchronous serial port on the router is configured as DTE or DCE depending on the attached cable, which is ordered as either DTE or DCE to match the router configuration. If the port is configured as DTE, which is the default setting, external clocking is required from the CSU/DSU or other DCE device.

The cable for the DTE to DCE connection is a shielded serial transition cable. The router end of the shielded serial transition cable might be a DB-60 connector, which connects to the DB-60 port on a serial WAN interface card. The other end of the serial transition cable is available with the connector that is appropriate for the standard that is used. The WAN provider or the CSU/DSU usually dictates this cable type. Cisco devices support the EIA/TIA-232, EIA/TIA-449, V.35, X.21, and EIA/TIA-530 serial standards.

To support higher densities in a smaller form factor, Cisco has introduced a smart serial cable. The serial end of the smart serial cable is a 26-pin connector that is much smaller than the DB-60 connector.

HDLC Encapsulation

The initial serial communications were based on character-oriented communications. Bit-oriented communications are more efficient, but the initial bit-oriented protocols were proprietary. In 1979, International Organization for Standardization (ISO) standardized on High-Level Data Link Control (HDLC) as a standard bit-oriented data link layer protocol that encapsulates data on synchronous serial data links. This standardization led to other committees adopting it and extending the protocol. Since 1981, ITU-T has developed a series of HDLC derivative protocols, called link access protocols. Link Access Procedure, Balanced (LAPB) for X.25, Link Access Procedure on the D channel (LAPD) for ISDN, Link Access Procedure for Modems (LAPM), PPP for modems, and Link Access Procedure for Frame Relay (LAPF) are examples of these derivative protocols.

HDLC uses synchronous serial transmission. It provides error-free communications between two points over an unreliable physical layer. HDLC defines a Layer 2 framing structure that allows for flow control and error control by using acknowledgements and a windowing scheme. Each frame has the same format, whether it is a data frame or a control frame.

Standard HDLC does not inherently support multiple protocols on a single link because it does not have a way to indicate which protocol it is carrying. Cisco offers a proprietary version of HDLC. The Cisco HDLC frame uses a proprietary type field that acts as a protocol field, which makes it possible for multiple network layer protocols to share the same serial link. HDLC is the default Layer 2 protocol for Cisco router serial interfaces.

HDLC defines three types of frames, as shown in Figure 13-23, each with a different control field format:

- **Information frames (I-frames)**—Carry the data to be transmitted for the station. Additional flow and error control data can be piggybacked on an information frame.

- **Supervisory frames (S-frames)**—Provide request/response mechanisms when piggybacking is not used.

- **Unnumbered frames (U-frames)**—Provide supplemental link control functions, such as connection setup. The code field identifies the U-frame type.

Figure 13-23 HDLC Frames

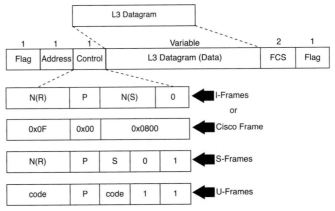

The first one or two bits of the control field serve to identify the frame type. In the control field of an Information (I) frame, the send-sequence number refers to the number of the frame to be sent next. The receive-sequence number provides the number of the frame to be received next. Both sender and receiver maintain send- and receive-sequence numbers.

Configuring HDLC Encapsulation

By default, Cisco devices use the Cisco HDLC serial encapsulation method on synchronous serial lines. However, if the serial interface is configured with another encapsulation protocol, and the encapsulation must be changed back to HDLC, enter the interface configuration mode of the serial interface. Then enter the **encapsulation hdlc** interface configuration command to specify HDLC encapsulation on the interface:

```
Router(config-if)#encapsulation hdlc
```

Cisco's HDLC is a point-to-point protocol that you can use on leased lines between two Cisco devices. When you are communicating with a non-Cisco device, synchronous PPP is a more viable option.

Troubleshooting a Serial Interface

The output of the **show interfaces serial** command displays information that is specific to serial interfaces. Use the **show interface serial** command to verify proper configuration of HDLC or PPP encapsulation. When HDLC is configured, "Encapsulation HDLC" should be reflected in the output of the show interface serial command.

When PPP is configured, you can check its LCP and NCP states by using the **show interface serial** command, as shown in Example 13-1.

The first example shows HDLC encapsulation and the second shows PPP encapsulation.

Example 13-1 show interface s0/0 *Command*

```
Router#show interface s0/0
Serial 0 is up, line protocol is up
  Hardware is MCI Serial
  Internet address is 131.108.156.98, subnet mask is 255.255.255.240
  MTU 1500 bytes, BW 1544 Kbit, DLY 20000 usec, rely 255/255, load 1/255
  Encapsulation HDLC, loopback not set, keepalive set (10 sec)
  Last input 0:00:00, output 0:00:00, output hang never
  Last clearing of "show interface" counters never
--- output omitted ---


Router#show interface s0/0
Serial0 is up, line protocol is up
  Hardware is HD64570
```

continues

Example 13-1 show interface s0/0 *Command*

```
Internet address is 10.140.1.2/24
MTU 1500 bytes, BW 1544 Kbit, DLY 20000 usec, rely 255/255, load 1/255
Encapsulation PPP, loopback not set, keepalive set (10 sec)
LCP Open
Open: IPCP, CDPCP
Last input 00:00:05, output 00:00:05, output hang never
Last clearing of "show interface" counters never
--- output omitted ---
```

Table 13-3 identifies possible problem states that you can identify in the interface status line of the **show interfaces serial** display:

```
Serial x is down, line protocol is down
Serial x is up, line protocol is down
Serial x is up, line protocol is up (looped)
Serial x is up, line protocol is down (disabled)
Serial x is administratively down, line protocol is down
```

Table 13-3 Possible Problem States

Status Line	Condition Possible	Problem Solution
Serial x is up, line protocol is up	This is the proper status line condition.	No action is required.
Serial x is down, line protocol is down (DTE mode)	The router is not sensing a CD signal. (That is, the CD is inactive.) A telephone company problem has occurred; the line is down or is not connected to the CSU/DSU. The cabling is faulty or incorrect. Hardware failure has occurred (CSU/DSU).	1. Check the LEDs on the CSU/DSU to see whether the CD is active, or insert a breakout box on the line to check for the CD signal. 2. Verify that you are using the proper cable and interface. (See your hardware installation documentation.) 3. Insert a breakout box and check all control leads. 4. Contact your leased-line or other carrier service to see whether there is a problem. 5. Swap faulty parts. 6. If you suspect faulty router hardware, change the serial line to another port. If the connection comes up, the previously connected interface has a problem.

Table 13-3 Possible Problem States (Continued)

Status Line	Condition Possible	Problem Solution
Serial *x* is up, line protocol is down (DTE mode)	A local or remote router is misconfigured. The remote router is not sending keepalives. A leased-line or other carrier service problem has occurred (noisy line, misconfigured, or failed switch). A timing problem has occurred on the cable. (SCTE is not set on CSU/DSU.) A local or remote CSU/DSU has failed. Router hardware (local or remote) has failed.	1. Put the modem, CSU, or DSU in local loopback mode and use the **show interfaces serial** command to determine whether the line protocol comes up. If the line protocol comes up, the telephone company or a failed remote router is the likely problem. 2. If the problem appears to be on the remote end, repeat Step 1 on the remote modem, CSU, or DSU. 3. Verify all cabling. Make certain that the cable is attached to the correct interface, the correct CSU/DSU, and the correct telephone company network termination point. Use the **show controllers** exec command to determine which cable is attached to which interface. 4. Enable the **debug serial interface** exec command. 5. If the line protocol does not come up in local loopback mode, and the output of the **debug serial interface** exec command shows that the keepalive counter is not incrementing, a router hardware problem is likely. Swap router interface hardware. 6. If the line protocol comes up and the keepalive counter increments, the problem is *not* in the local router. 7. If you suspect faulty router hardware, change the serial line to an unused port. If the connection comes up, the previously connected interface has a problem.

continues

Table 13-3 Possible Problem States (Continued)

Status Line	Condition Possible	Problem Solution
Serial *x* is up, line protocol is down (DCE mode)	The **clockrate** interface configuration command is missing. The DTE device does not support or is not set up for SCTE mode (terminal timing). The remote CSU or DSU has failed. The **clockrate** interface configuration command is missing. The DTE device does not support or is not set up for SCTE mode (terminal timing). The remote CSU or DSU has failed.	1. Add the **clockrate** interface configuration command on the serial interface: **clock rate** *bps* *bps* is the desired clock rate in bits per second: 1200, 2400, 4800, 9600, 19200, 38400, 56000, 64000, 72000, 125000, 148000, 250000, 500000, 800000, 1000000, 1300000, 2000000, 4000000, or 8000000 2. Set the DTE device to a serial clock transmit external (SCTE) modem if possible. If your CSU/DSU does not support SCTE, you might have to disable SCTE on the Cisco router interface. 3. Verify that the correct cable is being used. 4. If the line protocol is still down, there is a possible hardware failure or cabling problem. Insert a breakout box and observe leads. 5. Replace faulty parts, as necessary.

Table 13-3 Possible Problem States (Continued)

Status Line	Condition Possible	Problem Solution
Serial *x* is up, line protocol is up (looped)	A loop exists in the circuit. The sequence number in the keepalive packet changes to a random number when a loop is initially detected. If the same random number is returned over the link, a loop exists.	1. Use the **show running-config** privileged exec command to look for any **loopback** interface configuration command entries. 2. If you find a **loopback** interface configuration command entry, use the **no loopback** interface configuration command to remove the loop. 3. If you do not find the **loopback** interface configuration command, examine the CSU/DSU to determine whether they are configured in manual loopback mode. If they are, disable manual loopback. 4. Reset the CSU or DSU, and inspect the line status. If the line protocol comes up, no other action is needed. 5. If the CSU or DSU is not configured in manual loopback mode, contact the leased-line or other carrier service for line troubleshooting assistance.
Serial *x* is up, line protocol is down (disabled)	A high error rate has occurred due to a telephone company service problem. A CSU or DSU hardware problem has occurred. Router hardware (interface) is bad.	1. Troubleshoot the line with a serial analyzer and breakout box. Look for toggling Clear to Send and data set ready (DSR) signals. 2. Loop CSU/DSU (DTE loop). If the problem continues, it is likely that there is a hardware problem. If the problem does not continue, it is likely that there is a telephone company problem. 3. Swap out bad hardware, as required (CSU, DSU, switch, local, or remote router).

continues

Table 13-3 Possible Problem States (Continued)

Status Line	Condition Possible	Problem Solution
Serial *x* is administratively down, line protocol is down	The router configuration includes the **shutdown** interface configuration command. A duplicate IP address exists.	1. Check the router configuration for the **shutdown** command. 2. Use the **no shutdown** interface configuration command to remove the **shutdown** command. 3. Verify that there are no identical IP addresses that use the **show running-config** privileged exec command or the **show interfaces** exec command. 4. If there are duplicate addresses, resolve the conflict by changing one of the IP addresses.

The **show controllers** exec command is another important diagnostic tool when you are troubleshooting serial lines. The command syntax, depending on platform, is as follows:

- For serial interfaces on Cisco 7000 series routers, use the **show controllers cbus** exec command.
- For Cisco access products, use the **show controllers** exec command.

On access products such as the Cisco 1700, 2000, 2500, 2600, 3000, and Cisco 4000 series access servers and routers, use the **show controllers** exec command. Example 13-2 shows the **show controllers** command output from the serial interface on a Cisco 2621 access server.

Example 13-2 show controllers *Command*

```
Router#show controllers serial 0/0
Interface Serial0/0
Hardware is PowerQUICC MPC860
DTE V.35 TX and RX clocks detected.
idb at 0x81414E2C, driver data structure at 0x8141753C
SCC Registers:
General [GSMR]=0x2:0x00000030, Protocol-specific [PSMR]=0x8
Events [SCCE]=0x0000, Mask [SCCM]=0x001F, Status [SCCS]=0x06
Transmit on Demand [TODR]=0x0, Data Sync [DSR]=0x7E7E
```

The **show controllers** output indicates the state of the interface channels and whether a cable is attached to the interface. Note that serial interface 0/0 has a V.35 DTE cable attached.

If the electrical interface is displayed as UNKNOWN (instead of V.35, EIA/TIA-449, or some other electrical interface type), an improperly connected cable is the likely problem. A problem with the internal wiring of the card is also possible. If the electrical interface is unknown, the corresponding display for the **show interfaces** serial exec command shows that the interface and line protocol are down.

Following are some **debug commands** that are useful when troubleshooting serial and WAN problems:

- **debug serial interface**—Verifies whether HDLC keepalive packets are incrementing. If they are not, a possible timing problem exists on the interface card or in the network. Example 13-3 shows network debugging output.

- **debug arp**—Indicates whether the router is sending information about or learning about routers (with ARP packets) on the other side of the WAN cloud. Use this command when some nodes on a TCP/IP network are responding, but others are not.

- **debug frame-relay lmi**—Obtains Local Management Interface (LMI) information that is useful for determining whether a Frame Relay switch and a router are sending and receiving LMI packets.

- **debug frame-relay events**—Determines whether exchanges are occurring between a router and a Frame Relay switch.

- **debug ppp negotiation**—Shows PPP packets that are transmitted during PPP startup, where PPP options are negotiated.

- **debug ppp packet**—Shows PPP packets that are being sent and received. This command displays low-level packet dumps.

- **debug ppp errors**—Shows PPP errors (such as illegal or malformed frames) that are associated with PPP connection negotiation and operation.

- **debug ppp chap**—Shows PPP CHAP and PAP packet exchanges.

> **CAUTION**
>
> Because debugging output is assigned high priority in the CPU process, it can render the system unusable. For this reason, debug commands should be used only to troubleshoot specific problems or during troubleshooting sessions with Cisco technical support staff. Moreover, it is best to use debug commands during periods of lower network traffic and fewer users. Debugging during these periods decreases the likelihood that increased debug command processing overhead will affect system use.

Example 13-3 debug serial interface *Command*

```
Router#debug serial interface
Serial network interface debugging is on
Router#
00:06:47: Serial0/0: HDLC myseq 29, mineseen 29*, yourseen 29, line up
```

continues

Example 13-3 debug serial interface *Command*

```
00:06:57: Serial0/0: HDLC myseq 30, mineseen 30*, yourseen 30, line up
00:07:07: Serial0/0: HDLC myseq 31, mineseen 31*, yourseen 31, line up
00:07:17: Serial0/0: HDLC myseq 32, mineseen 32*, yourseen 32, line up


Router#undebug all
All possible debugging has been turned off
Router#
```

 Lab Activity   Troubleshooting a Serial Interface

In this activity, you configure the serial interfaces on two routers. You then use show commands to troubleshoot connectivity issues.

Configuring PPP

Configurable aspects of PPP include methods of authentication, compression, and error detection, as well as whether or not multilink is supported. This chapter describes the different configuration options for PPP.

Cisco routers that use PPP encapsulation might include the LCP configuration options shown in Table 13-4.

Table 13-4 LCP Configuration Options

Option	Function	Protocol	Command
Authentication	Authentication options require that the calling side of the link enter information to help ensure that the caller has the network administrator's permission to make the call. Peer routers exchange authentication messages. Two alternatives are as follows: PAP and CHAP	PAP CHAP	ppp authentication pap ppp authentication chap

Table 13-4 LCP Configuration Options (Continued)

Option	Function	Protocol	Command
Compression	Compression options increase the effective throughput on PPP connections by reducing the amount of data in the original frame that must travel across the link. The protocol decompresses the frame at its destination. Two compression protocols available in Cisco routers are Stacker and Predictor.	Stacker or Predictor	ppp compress stacker ppp compress predictor
Error Detection	Error-detection mechanisms with PPP enable a process to identify fault conditions. The Quality and Magic Number options help ensure a reliable, loop-free data link.	Quality, Magic Number	**ppp quality** *number_1-100*
Multilink	Cisco IOS Release 11.1 and later support PPP Multilink Protocol (MP). This feature is sometimes referred to as Multilink PPP. This alternative provides load balancing over the router interfaces that PPP uses. MP provides packet fragmentation and sequencing that splits the load for PPP and sends fragments over parallel circuits. In some cases, this "bundle" of multilink PPP pipes functions as a single logical link, improving throughput and reducing latency between peer routers.	MP	ppp multilink

Configuring PPP Encapsulation

The following enables PPP encapsulation on serial interface 0:

```
Router# config terminal
Router(config)# interface serial 0
Router(config-if)# encapsulation ppp
```

Point-to-point software compression can be configured on serial interfaces that use PPP encapsulation. Compression is performed in software and might significantly affect system performance. If the majority of the traffic is already compressed files, it is recommended that compression not be used.

To configure compression over PPP, perform the following tasks in interface configuration mode:

```
Router(config)# interface serial 0
Router(config-if)# encapsulation ppp
Router(config-if)# compress [predictor | stac]
```

Enter the following to monitor the data that is dropped on the link, which avoids frame looping:

```
Router(config)# interface serial 0
Router(config-if)# encapsulation ppp
Router(config-if)# ppp quality number_1-100
```

The following commands perform load balancing across multiple links:

```
Router(config)# interface serial 0
Router(config-if)# encapsulation ppp
Router(config-if)# ppp multilink
```

 Lab Activity   Configuring PPP Encapsulation

In this lab, you configure a serial interface on two routers with the PPP encapsulation and then test the link.

Configuring PPP Authentication

The procedure outlined in Table 13-5 describes how to configure PPP encapsulation and PAP/CHAP Authentication protocols.

Table 13-5 Configuring PAP/CHAP

Step	Action	Results and Notes
1.	Assign a host name by using the **hostname** *name* command in global configuration mode: Router(config)#**hostname SantaCruz**	This name must match the user name that the router at the other end of the link expects. Note - The hostname command is case sensitive.
2.	Define the username and password to expect from the remote router using the **username** *name* **password** *password* global configuration command: Router(config)#**username HQ password cisco**	On Cisco routers, the password must be the same for both routers. In pre-11.2 IOS software, this password was an encrypted, secret password. To encrypt passwords on your IOS router, enter the **service password-encryption** command while in global configuration mode.
3.	Enable PPP encapsulation on an interface by using the **encapsulation ppp** interface configuration command: Router(config-if)#**encapsulation ppp**	Additional configuration steps are required to enable PPP on an asynchronous serial interface.
4.	Configure PPP authentication by using the **ppp authentication {chap | chap pap | pap chap | pap}** interface configuration command: Router(config-if)#**ppp authentication chap**	If both methods are enabled, the first method specified will be requested during link negotiation. If the peer suggests using the second method or simply refuses the first method, the second method will be tried.
5.	Verify proper configuration using the show interface command: Router#**show interface s0**	When PPP is configured, LCP and NCP states can be checked using this command.

Correct configuration is essential because PAP and CHAP use these parameters to authenticate.

Figure 13-24 is an example of a two-way PAP authentication configuration. Both routers authenticate and are authenticated, so the PAP authentication commands mirror each other. The PAP username and password that each router sends must match those specified with the **username** *name* **password** *password* command of the other router.

Figure 13-24 PAP Configuration

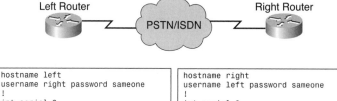

```
hostname left
username right password sameone
!
int serial 0
  ip address 10.0.1.1 255.255.255.0
  encapsulation ppp
  ppp authentication PAP
  ppp pap sent-username username
    password password
```

```
hostname right
username left password sameone
!
int serial 0
  ip address 10.0.1.2 255.255.255.0
  encapsulation ppp
  ppp authentication PAP
  ppp pap sent-username username
    password password
```

In Figure 13-25, with CHAP, a two-way authentication occurs. The host name on one router must match the username that the other router has configured. The passwords must match as well.

Figure 13-25 CHAP Configuration

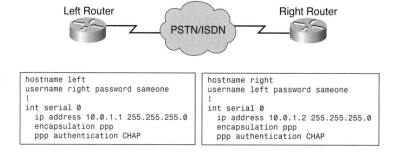

```
hostname left
username right password sameone
!
int serial 0
  ip address 10.0.1.1 255.255.255.0
  encapsulation ppp
  ppp authentication CHAP
```

```
hostname right
username left password sameone
!
int serial 0
  ip address 10.0.1.2 255.255.255.0
  encapsulation ppp
  ppp authentication CHAP
```

The following methods can be used to simplify CHAP configuration tasks on the router:

- **You can use the same host name on multiple routers**—When you want remote users to think they are connecting to the same router when authenticating, configure the same host name on each router:

  `Router(config-if)# ` **`ppp chap hostname`** `hostname`

- **You can use a password to authenticate to an unknown host**—This is to limit the number of username/password entries in the router. To use this, configure a password that will be sent to hosts that want to authenticate the router:

  `Router(config-if)# ` **`ppp chap password secret`**

Lab Activity   Configuring PPP Authentication

In this lab, you configure a PPP authentication by using CHAP on two routers.

Verifying the Serial PPP Encapsulation Configuration

Use the **show interface** command to verify proper configuration of HDLC or PPP encapsulation, as shown in Example 13-4. When HDLC is configured, "Encapsulation HDLC" should be reflected in the output of the **show interface** command. When PPP is configured, you can use this command to check its LCP and NCP states.

Example 13-4 *Verifying Serial PPP Encapsulation Configuration*

```
Router#show interface s0
Serial0 is up, line protocol is up
  Hardware is HD64570
  Internet address is 10.140.1.2/24
  MTU 1500 bytes, BW 1544 Kbit, DLY 20000 usec, rely 255/255, load 1/255
  Encapsulation PPP, loopback not set, keepalive set (10 sec)
  LCP Open
  Open: IPCP, CDPCP
  Last input 00:00:05, output 00:00:05, output hang never
  Last clearing of "show interface" counters never
--- output omitted ---
```

Table 13-6 lists commands that are used when enabling, configuring, and verifying PPP.

Table 13-6 PPP Commands

Command	Description
encapsulation ppp	Enables PPP on an interface
ppp authentication pap	Enables PAP authentication on an interface
ppp authentication chap	Enables CHAP authentication on an interface
username *username* **password** *password*	Establishes a username-based authentication system

continues

Table 13-6 PPP Commands (Continued)

Command	Description
show interfaces	Displays statistics for all interfaces that are configured on the router or access server
debug ppp authentication	Debugs the PAP or CHAP authentication process
undebug all	Turns off all debugging displays

Lab Activity   Verifying PPP Configuration

In this lab, you configure serial interfaces on two routers with the PPP protocol and then verify the link.

Troubleshooting the Serial PPP Encapsulation Configuration

The **debug ppp authentication** command displays the authentication exchange sequence. Example 13-5 illustrates the left router output during CHAP authentication with the router on the right when **debug ppp authentication** is enabled. With two-way authentication configured, each router authenticates the other, and messages appear for both the authenticating process and the process of being authenticated. CHAP is defined as a one-way authentication method. However, using CHAP in both directions creates a two-way authentication. Therefore, with two-way CHAP, each side initiates a separate three-way handshake. This command can be used to display the exchange sequence as it occurs.

Example 13-5 *Troubleshooting Serial PPP*

```
·4d20h: %LINK-3-UPDOWN: Interface Serial0, changed state to up
·4d20h: Se0 PPP: Treating connection as a dedicated line
·4d20h: Se0 PPP: Phase is AUTHENTICATING, by both
·4d20h: Se0 CHAP: O CHALLENGE id 2 len 28 from "left"
·4d20h: Se0 CHAP: I CHALLENGE id 3 len 28 from "right"
·4d20h: Se0 CHAP: O RESPONSE id 3 len 28 from "left"
·4d20h: Se0 CHAP: I RESPONSE id 2 len 28 from "right"
·4d20h: Se0 CHAP: O SUCCESS id 2 len 4
·4d20h: Se0 CHAP: I SUCCESS id 3 len 4
·4d20h: %LINEPROTO-5-UPDOWN: Line protocol on Interface Serial0, changed state
to up
```

Table 13-7 highlights the left router output for a two-way PAP authentication.

Table 13-7 PAP Authentication

Output	Description
Se0 PPP: Phase is AUTHENTICATING, by both	Two way authentication
Se0 PAP: O AUTH-REQ id 4 len 18 from "left"	Outgoing authentication request
Se0 PAP: I AUTH-REQ id 1 len 18 from "right"	Incoming authentication request
Se0 PAP: Authenticating peer right	Authenticating incoming
Se0 PAP: O AUTH-ACK id 1 len 5	Outgoing acknowledgement
Se0 PAP: I AUTH-ACK id 4 len 5	Incoming acknowledgement

The **debug ppp** command is used to display information about the operation of PPP. The **no** form of this command disables debugging output. Table 13-8 shows various options that can be used to extend the use of the **debug ppp** command.

```
debug ppp {packet | negotiation | error | chap}
no debug ppp {packet | negotiation | error | chap}
```

Table 13-8 debug ppp Command Options

Command Option	Definition
packet	Used with the **debug ppp** command to display PPP packets being sent and received
negotiation	Used with the **debug ppp** command to display PPP packets transmitted during PPP startup, where PPP options are negotiated
error	Used with the **debug ppp** command to display protocol errors and error statistics that are associated with PPP connection negotiation and operation
chap	Used with the **debug ppp** command to display CHAP and PAP packet exchanges

Lab Activity   Troubleshooting PPP Configuration

In this lab, you configure PPP on two routers and then use show and debug commands to troubleshoot connectivity issues.

Summary

In this chapter, you learned the following:

- PPP is the most widely used WAN protocol.
- PPP addresses the problems of Internet connectivity by providing an LCP and a family of NCPs to negotiate optional configuration parameters and facilities.
- A PPP session has four phases:
  - Link establishment
  - Link-quality determination
  - Network layer protocol configuration negotiation
  - Link termination
- You can select PAP or CHAP when you are configuring PPP authentication.
- PAP is not a strong authentication protocol.
- CHAP provides protection against playback attacks through the use of a variable challenge value that is unique and unpredictable.
- You configure the interface for PPP encapsulation by using the **encapsulation ppp** command.
- When PPP is configured, you can check its LCP and NCP states by using the **show interfaces** command.

To supplement all that you have learned in this chapter, refer to the chapter-specific Videos, PhotoZooms, and e-Lab Activities on the CD-ROM that accompanies this book.

Key Terms

CHAP (Challenge Handshake Authentication Protocol)   A security feature that is supported on lines using PPP encapsulation that prevents unauthorized access. CHAP does not prevent unauthorized access, but it identifies the remote end; the router or access server then determines whether that user is allowed access.

LCP (Link Control Protocol)   A protocol that provides a method of establishing, configuring, maintaining, and terminating the point-to-point connection.

LLC (Logical Link Control)   The higher of the two data link layer sublayers that the IEEE defines. The LLC sublayer handles error control, flow control, framing, and MAC-sublayer addressing. The most prevalent LLC protocol is IEEE 802.2, which includes both connectionless and connection-oriented variants.

Network Control Program   A program that routes and controls the flow of data between a communications controller and other network resources.

PAP (Password Authentication Protocol)   An authentication protocol that allows PPP peers to authenticate one another. The remote router that attempts to connect to the local router is required to send an authentication request. Unlike CHAP, PAP passes the password and host name or username in cleartext (that is, unencrypted). PAP does not prevent unauthorized access, but it identifies the remote end; the router or access server then determines whether that user is allowed access. PAP is supported only on PPP lines.

PPP (Point-to-Point Protocol)   A successor to SLIP, a protocol that provides router-to-router and host-to-network connections over synchronous and asynchronous circuits.

Check Your Understanding

1. What does the first step in establishing connections over PPP links involve?

   A. The originating PPP node sending a session startup message to the nearest PPP neighbor

   B. Routers along the path negotiating authentication facilities prior to PPP link activation

   C. PPP nodes advertising for dynamic address allocation or querying servers for address assignment

   D. The originating node sending LCP frames to configure the data link

2. In PPP, what happens if LCP terminates a link?

   A. The destination node attempts to establish a new link.

   B. NCP sends a link maintenance frame.

   C. The originating node re-establishes connection sessions.

   D. LCP informs the network layer protocols.

3. Which of the following is the network layer protocol that PPP supports?

   A. Novell IPX

   B. IP

   C. AppleTalk

   D. All of the above

4. PPP uses NCPs to do which of the following?

   A. Establish links

   B. Encapsulate multiple protocols

   C. Convert packets into cells

   D. Establish connections

5. In a PPP frame, what field identifies whether you have encapsulated IPX or IP?

   A. Flag

   B. Control

   C. Protocol

   D. FCS

6. When would PPP most likely be used at a local workstation for Internet connectivity?

   A. When the workstation is directly connected to a LAN.

   B. When the workstation is directly connected to a router.

   C. When the workstation needs dial-up access to the Internet.

   D. PPP would never be used on a workstation.

7. When you are running PPP, LCP is responsible for which of the following?

   A. Establishment, maintenance, and termination of the point-to-point connection

   B. Maintenance of several links

   C. Router updates

   D. Compression

8. How many phases are involved in PPP session establishment?

   A. Two

   B. Three

   C. Four

   D. One

9. What type of handshaking occurs when PAP is the selected PPP authentication protocol?

   A. One-way

   B. Two-way

   C. Three-way

   D. Four-way

10. What command on the router can you use to check the LCP and NCP states for PPP?

    A. router> **show interfaces**

    B. router(config)# **show interfaces**

    C. router# **show interfaces**

    D. router(config-if)# **show interfaces**

11. What protocol would you use to establish a remote connection over ISDN?

    A. PPP

    B. SLIP

    C. PAP

    D. CHAP

12. When PPP is load balancing across several links, what feature is being taken advantage of?

    A. PAP

    B. Stacker

    C. Compression

    D. Multilink

13. What does the PPP link establishment require the LCP to do after opening a connection?

   A. Negotiate configuration parameters and send and receive a configuration acknowledgment frame.

   B. Test the link and determine whether the link quality is sufficient to bring up network protocols.

   C. Poll PPP nodes and determine whether a path to a Network Control Protocol server exists.

   D. Query the nearest adjacent upstream PPP neighbor to obtain routing metrics (such as hop count).

Objectives

After reading this chapter, you will be able to

- Describe Integrated Services Digital Network (ISDN) architecture
- Describe ISDN protocol layers
- Configure ISDN
- Configure dial-on-demand routing (DDR)
- Verify and troubleshoot ISDN
- Verify and troubleshoot DDR

Chapter 14

ISDN and DDR

This chapter introduces and describes a group of technologies called *ISDN*, which were first proposed more than 30 years ago. Recognizing the inherent limitations of Public Switched Telephone Network (PSTN), developers envisioned that ISDN would provide a digital pipeline offering integrated access to the broadest range of services. These services were to include voice, packet switching, and even video.

Be sure to look at this chapter's associated e-Lab Activities, Videos, and PhotoZooms that you will find on the CD-ROM that accompanies this book. These CD-ROM elements are designed to supplement the material and reinforce the concepts that are introduced in this chapter.

ISDN Standards

Many ISDN standards have been agreed to over the years. These standards have promised to bring high-speed digital service to homes and businesses. Despite ISDN's extensive array of standards, carriers have not uniformly implemented the technology. Consequently, ISDN configurations and pricing might vary in significant ways from region to region.

Today, customers deploy ISDN primarily as a wide-area network (WAN) backup technology and to provide remote access to telecommuters and small offices, as Figure 14-1 shows. Service providers and large companies use ISDN *Primary Rate Interface (PRI)* to support several POTS (analog modem) or ISDN *Basic Rate Interface (BRI)* calls. Although ISDN boasts a much faster call setup and higher throughput than POTS, many potential BRI customers are turning to digital subscriber line (DSL) and cable technologies. These typically offer much higher throughput at a lower cost.

Figure 14-1 Integrated Services

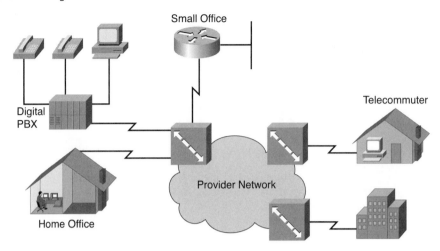

Despite these emerging technologies, ISDN remains a viable remote access solution for several reasons:

- ISDN is more widely available than DSL or cable.
- Many companies and service providers have made a significant investment in ISDN equipment and training and plan to continue leveraging that investment.
- Remote offices that are using ISDN can connect to central offices (COs) directly, without traversing the public Internet. Most DSL and cable implementations require the remote host communicate with the central site using a Virtual Private Network (VPN) over the Internet.

ISDN Overview

Several WAN technologies are used to provide network access from remote locations. This chapter deals with the services, standards, components, operation, and configuration of ISDN communication. ISDN is specifically designed to solve the low bandwidth problems that small offices or dial-in users have with traditional telephone dial-in services.

The traditional PSTN was based on an analog connection between the customer's premises and the local exchange, also called the local loop, as shown in Figure 14-2. This analog signaling introduces limitations on the bandwidth that can be obtained on the local loop. Bandwidth restrictions do not permit analog data to travel faster than 3000 Hz. Removal of the bandwidth restriction has permitted the use of digital signaling on the local loop and has resulted in better access speeds for the remote users, as shown in Figure 14-3. However, users who have analog dial-up modems still utilize the 3 kHz bandwidth of the analog voice local loop system, which limits them to about 56 kbps download and 33 kbps upload speeds.

Figure 14-2 Local Loop

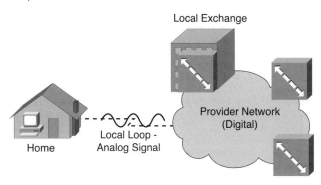

Figure 14-3 Digital Communications with ISDN

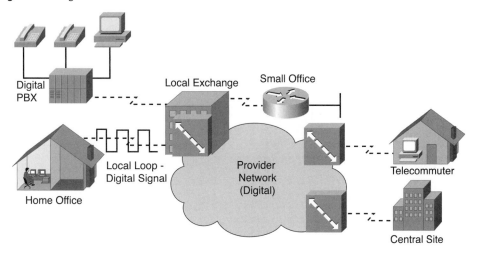

Telephone companies developed ISDN with the intention of creating a totally digital network. ISDN allows digital signals to be transmitted over existing telephone wiring. This became possible when the telephone company switches were upgraded to handle digital signals. ISDN is generally used for telecommuting and networking small and remote offices into the corporate LAN.

Telephone companies developed ISDN as part of an effort to standardize subscriber services. This included the User-Network Interface (UNI), better known as the local loop. The ISDN standards define the hardware and call setup schemes for end-to-end digital connectivity, which help achieve the goal of worldwide connectivity by ensuring that ISDN networks easily communicate with one another. In an ISDN network, the digitizing function is done at the user site rather than at the telephone company.

As its name implies, ISDN uses digital technology. ISDN replaces traditional analog telephone equipment with high-speed digital equipment that provides the customer with a digital local loop. Figure 14-4 shows analog versus digital communications. Therefore, ISDN transmissions are digital from end to end. Because POTS uses an analog local loop, the carrier must use pulse code modulation (PCM) to encode the analog signals for digital transmission. This type of analog-to-digital conversion introduces undesired latency and, potentially, noise.

Figure 14-4 Analog Versus Digital

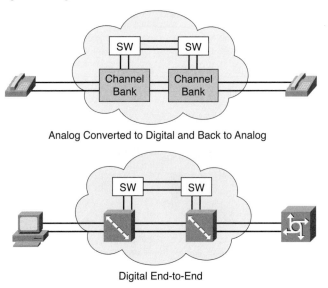

ISDN brings digital connectivity to local sites, which has many benefits, including the following:

- It carries many types of network traffic (such as data, voice, and video).
- It sets up calls faster than basic telephone service.
- It has faster data rates than traditional modems.

Customers can connect to the ISDN carrier via two different physical interfaces: BRI and PRI. A single BRI or PRI interface provides a multiplexed bundle of B and D channels, as shown in Figure 14-5.

Figure 14-5 ISDN Services

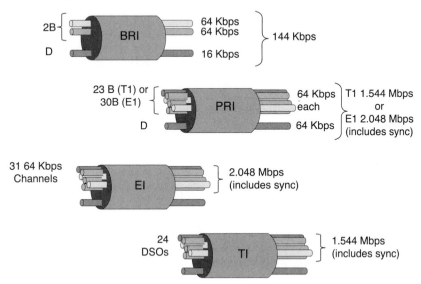

ISDN B channels are called bearer channels because they carry voice, data, and fax transmissions. B channels carry information in frame format, using either High-Level Data Link Control (HDLC) or Point-to-Point Protocol (PPP) as the Layer 2 protocol.

The D channel, or delta channel, is used for out-of-band signaling. The D channel carries control messages, such as call setup and teardown. Typically, the D channel employs *Link Access Procedure on the D channel (LAPD)* at Layer 2.

BRI service is provided over a local copper loop that traditionally carries analog phone service. The maximum length of most ISDN local loops in North America is about 18,000 feet (or 5.5 kilometers).

BRI has the following characteristics:

- Two 64-kbps bearer channels
- One 16-kbps delta channel
- 48 kbps of framing and synchronization information
- Total speed of 192 kbps

When discussing ISDN BRI bandwidth, it is important to know which of the BRI characteristics is being referenced. If you are discussing the bandwidth that is available for user data, ISDN BRI provides 128 kbps (two 64-kbps B channels). If you are discussing the bandwidth of both B channels and the D channel, ISDN BRI provides 144 kbps. Although it is not commonly done, you can reference the total bandwidth of an ISDN BRI, including framing and synchronization, which is 192 kbps.

ISDN PRI service is provided over T1 and E1 leased lines between the *customer premises equipment (CPE)* and the ISDN switch. The ISDN switch is typically a Class 5 Telco switch in a CO, which also handles voice calls.

A T1 is referenced as a DS1, which is made up of 24 DS0 channels of 64 kbps each, as shown in Table 14-1. A single BRI B channel is one DS0. PRI over T1 specifies the following:

- 23 64-kbps bearer channels
- One 64-kbps D channel, carried in timeslot 24
- 8 kbps of framing and synchronization information
- Total speed of 1.544 Mbps

PRI over E1 provides the following:

- 30 64-kbps bearer channels
- One 64-kbps D channel, carried in timeslot 16
- 64 kbps of framing and synchronization information
- Total speed of 2.048 Mbps

Table 14-1 Digital Signal Levels

Digital Signal Level	Speed	T Designation	Channels or DS0s*
DS0	64 Kbps	—	1
DS1	1.544 Mbps	T1	24
DS2	6.312 Mbps	T2	96
DS3	44.736 Mbps	T3	672
DS4	274.176 Mbps	T4	4032

DS0 = digital service zero (0)

ISDN Standards and Access Methods

Work on standards for ISDN began in the late 1960s. A comprehensive set of ISDN recommendations was published in 1984 and is continuously updated by the International Telecommunication Union Telecommunication Standardization Sector (ITU-T), formerly known as the Consultative Committee for International Telegraph and Telephone (CCITT). The ISDN standards are a set of protocols that encompass digital telephony and data communications. The ITU-T groups and organizes the ISDN protocols according to the following general topic areas:

- **E Protocols**—Recommend telephone network standards for ISDN. For example, the E.164 protocol describes international addressing for ISDN.
- **I Protocols**—Deal with concepts, terminology, and general methods. The I.100 series includes general ISDN concepts and the structure of other I-series recommendations. I.200 deals with service aspects of ISDN. I.300 describes network aspects. I.400 describes how the UNI is provided.
- **Q Protocols**—Cover how switching and signalling should operate. The term signalling in this context means the process of establishing an ISDN call.

ISDN standards define two main channel types, each with a different transmission rate. The bearer channel (B channel) is defined to be a clear digital path of 64 kbps. It is said to be "clear" because it can be used to transmit any type of digitized data, such as a digitized voice call, in full-duplex mode. The second channel is called a delta channel (D channel) and can be either 16 or 64 kbps. The D channel is 16 kbps for BRI and 64 kbps for PRI. ISDN access options are shown in Figure 14-6. The D channel is used to carry control information for the B channel. Remember: When a TCP connection is established, there is an exchange of information, called the connection setup. This information was exchanged over the same path as the eventual data would be transmitted. Both the control information and the data share the same pathway. This is called in-band signaling. ISDN uses a separate channel for control information: the D channel. This is called out-of-band signaling.

ISDN specifies two standard access methods: BRI and PRI. A single BRI or PRI interface provides a multiplexed bundle of B and D channels.

BRI uses two 64-kbps bearer (B) channels plus one 16-kbps delta (D) channel. The B channels carry user data, and the D channel is used for signaling and control information. BRI operates with many Cisco routers. Because it uses two B channels and one D channel, BRI is sometimes written as *2B+D*.

Figure 14-6 ISDN Access Options

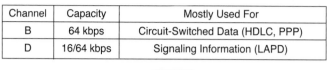

Channel	Capacity	Mostly Used For
B	64 kbps	Circuit-Switched Data (HDLC, PPP)
D	16/64 kbps	Signaling Information (LAPD)

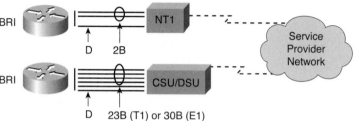

The B channels can be used for digitized speech transmission. In this case, specialized methods are used for the voice encoding. Also, the B channels can be used for relatively high-speed data transport. In this mode, the information is carried in frame format by using either HDLC or PPP as the Layer 2 protocol. PPP is much more robust than HDLC because it provides an excellent mechanism for authentication and negotiation of compatible link and protocol configuration.

Narrowband ISDN is considered a circuit-switched connection. The B channel is the elemental circuit-switching unit.

The D channel carries signaling messages, such as call setup and teardown, to control calls on B channels. Traffic over the D channel employs the LAPD protocol. LAPD is a data link protocol that is based on HDLC. In North America and Japan, PRI offers 23 64-kbps B channels and 1 64-kbps D channel.

In Europe and much of the rest of the world, PRI offers 30 B channels and a D channel so that it can offer the same level of service as an E1 circuit. PRI uses a DSU/CSU for T1/E1 connections.

ISDN 3-Layer Model and Protocols

ISDN utilizes a suite of ITU-T standards spanning the physical, data link, and network layers of the OSI reference model, as shown in Table 14-2:

- The ISDN BRI and PRI physical layer specifications are defined in ITU-T I.430 and I.431, respectively.
- The ISDN data link specification is based on LAPD and is formally specified in ITU-T Q.920, ITU-T Q.921, ITU-T Q.922, and ITU-T Q.923.

- The ISDN network layer is defined in ITU-T Q.930 (also known as I.450) and ITU-T Q.931 (also known as I.451) to specify user-to-user, circuit-switched, and packet-switched connections.

Table 14-2 ISDN Protocols

OSI Layer	D-Channel	B Channel
3	Q.931-ISDN network layer between terminal and switch	IP
2	Q.921-LAPD Link Access Procedure on the D channel	PPP HDLC
1	I.430/I.431—ISDN physical layer interfaces: I.430 for the basic interface; I.431 for the primary interface	

BRI service is provided over a local copper loop that traditionally carries analog phone service. There is only one physical path, yet for BRI, there are three separate information paths (2B+D). Information from the three channels is multiplexed into the one physical path.

ISDN physical layer (Layer 1) frame formats differ depending on whether the frame is outbound (from terminal to network—the TE frame format) or inbound (from network to terminal—the NT frame format), as shown in Figure 14-7. Each frame contains 16 bits from the B1 channel, 16 bits from the B2 channel, 4 bits from the D channel, and 12 bits of overhead, giving a frame size of 48 bits. Four thousand of these frames are transmitted every second, so channels B1 and B2 have a capacity of $16 \times 4000 = 64$ kbps, and channel D has a capacity of $4 \times 4000 = 16$ kbps.

The overhead bits of an ISDN physical layer frame are used as follows:

- Framing bit—Provides synchronization
- Load balancing bit—Adjusts the average bit value
- Echo of previous D channel bits—Used for contention resolution when several terminals on a passive bus contend for a channel
- Activation bit—Activates devices
- Spare bit—Unassigned
- 8 added channel bit counts bits

Figure 14-7 ISDN Physical Layer Frame Formats

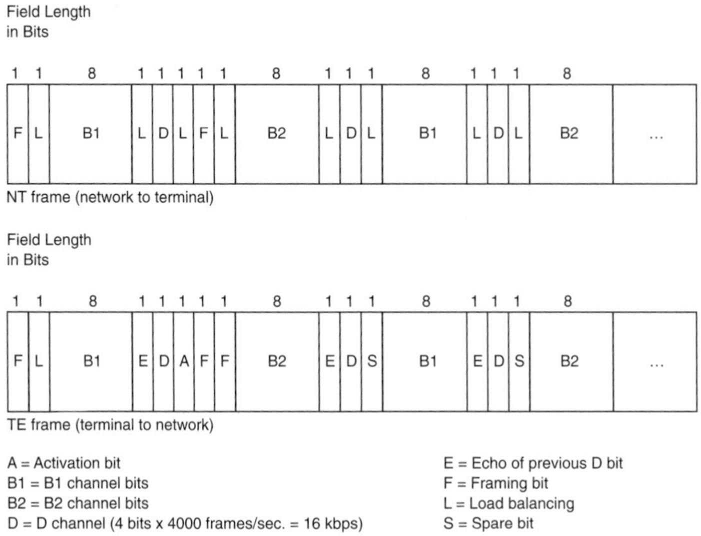
Field Length
in Bits
1 1 8 1 1 1 1 1 8 1 1 1 8 1 1 1 8
F L B1 L D L F L B2 L D L B1 L D L B2 ...
NT frame (network to terminal)
Field Length
in Bits
1 1 8 1 1 1 1 1 8 1 1 1 8 1 1 1 8
F L B1 E D A F F B2 E D S B1 E D S B2 ...
TE frame (terminal to network)
A = Activation bit
B1 = B1 channel bits
B2 = B2 channel bits
D = D channel (4 bits x 4000 frames/sec. = 16 kbps)
E = Echo of previous D bit
F = Framing bit
L = Load balancing
S = Spare bit

Note that the physical bit rate for the BRI interface is $4000 \times 48 = 192$ kbps. The effective rate is $4000 \times 36 = 144$ kbps = 64 kbps + 64 kbps + 16 kbps (2B+D).

Layer 2 of the ISDN signaling protocol is LAPD. LAPD is similar to HDLC. LAPD is used across the D channel to ensure that control and signaling information flows and is received properly.

The LAPD flag and control fields are identical to those of HDLC, as shown in Figure 14-8. The LAPD address field is 2 bytes long. The first address field byte contains the service access point identifier (SAPI), which identifies the portal at which LAPD services are provided to Layer 3. The command/response (C/R) bit indicates whether the frame contains a command or a response. The second byte contains the ***terminal endpoint identifier (TEI)***. Each piece of terminal equipment in the customer's premises needs a unique identifier. You can assign the TEI statically at installation (0-63), or the switch can dynamically assign it when the equipment is involved in a call (64-126). All 1s (127) in the TEI field indicate a broadcast.

The TEI works together with the SAPI to complete the Layer 2 address. The SAPI is a 6-bit number that is used to identify and manage different data types for the same individual device connecting to the ISDN network. Remember: Some ISDN messages are for call setup or teardown, whereas others are actual data. Thus, the TEI represents the specific ISDN device, and the SAPI represents the specific process that is running on that device. For example, the SAPI value 0 is used to identify call-control procedures, whereas the SAPI value 63 identifies a Layer 2 management function.

Figure 14-8 ISDN Data Link Layer

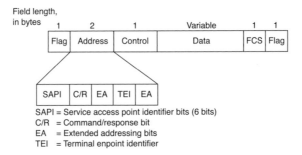

Just as an Ethernet II frame contains the destination Media Access Control (MAC) address and the protocol type information, the LAPD frame contains a TEI and a SAPI value.

ISDN Call Setup

For one router to connect to another via ISDN, several exchanges must occur. To establish an ISDN call, the D channel is used between the router and the ISDN switch, and Signaling System 7 (SS7) signaling is used between the switches within the service provider's network.

The D channel between the router and the ISDN switch is always up. Q.921 describes the ISDN data-link processes of the LAPD, which functions like Layer 2 processes in the Open System Interconnection (OSI) reference model. The D channel is used for call control functions such as call setup, signaling, and termination. These functions are implemented in the *Q.931* protocol. Q.931 specifies OSI reference model Layer 3 functions. The Q.931 standard recommends a network layer connection between the terminal endpoint and the local ISDN switch, but it does not impose an end-to-end recommendation. Because some ISDN switches were developed before Q.931 was standardized, the various ISDN providers and switch types can and do use various implementations of Q.931. Because switch types are not standard, routers must have commands in their configurations specifying the ISDN switch to which they are connecting.

An ISDN call can be placed in numerous ways. In an ISDN call, the calling party requests a call setup, as shown in Figure 14-9. Before the actual connect and call proceeding, you might see several different messages, such as a progress message. This optional message indicates how your call is proceeding.

Figure 14-9 ISDN Q.931 Call Setup

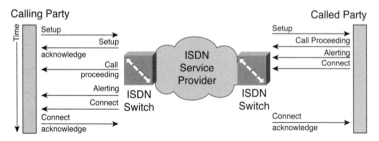

The same is true for the alerting message, which is typical of telephone messages but is not required. Alerting messages are not typical with data transmissions. Most of the time, you see connection messages with data calls.

Different ISDN switches use different call setup and teardown procedures. Depending on the switch type, you might or might not get all the steps shown in Figure 14-9. At a minimum, setup, call proceeding, connect, and connect acknowledge messages should be exchanged.

The following sequence of events occurs during the establishment of a BRI or PRI call:

- The D channel is used to send the called number to the local ISDN switch.
- The local switch uses the SS7 signaling protocol to set up a path and pass the called number to the remote ISDN switch.
- The remote ISDN switch signals the destination over the D channel.
- After the remote router indicates that it will receive the call, the remote ISDN switch uses SS7 to send a call-connect message to the local switch.
- One B channel is connected end-to-end, leaving the other B channel available for a new conversation or data transfer. You can use both B channels simultaneously.

Similar to call setup, the call teardown request is not an end-to-end function, but instead is processed by the ISDN switch. The release procedures are based on a three-message approach:

- Disconnect
- Release
- Release complete

The release message is transmitted through the network as quickly as possible. Figure 14-10 assumes that the called party is generating the release. The process is triggered by a disconnect message on the D channel, between the calling and called parties. After receipt of this message, the exchange immediately starts the release of the switch path that supports the B-channel circuit. A release message is also sent to the succeeding exchange at the same time. The message is passed through the network from all intermediate exchanges to the terminating exchange.

Figure 14-10 ISDN Q.931 Call Teardown

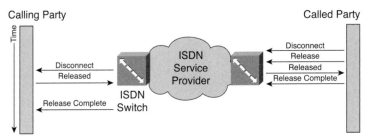

As the involved exchanges release the call, a released message is eventually transmitted to the terminating exchange. This transmission causes the following actions:

- It issues a disconnect message to the calling party.
- It starts a timer to ensure receipt of a released message.
- It disconnects the switched path.
- When a released message is received from the preceding exchange, it returns a release complete message to the preceding exchange.

ISDN Functions and Reference Points

ISDN standards define functions as a device or piece of hardware that enables the user to access the services of the BRI or PRI. Vendors can create hardware that supports one or more functions. ISDN specifications define four *reference points* that connect one ISDN device to another. Each device in an ISDN network performs a specific task to facilitate end-to-end connectivity.

To connect devices that perform specific functions, the interface between the two devices needs to be well defined. These interfaces are called reference points, and they are shown in Figure 14-11. A reference point defines a connection type between two functions. The reference points that affect the customer side of the ISDN connection are as follows:

- R—References the connection between a non-ISDN–compatible device (*TE2*) and a terminal adapter, such as an RS-232 serial interface.
- S—References the points that connect into the customer switching device (*NT2*) and enable calls between the various types of CPEs.

- **T**—Electrically identical to the S interface, it references the outbound connection from the NT2 to the ISDN network or *NT1*.

- **U**—References the connection between the NT1 and the ISDN network that the telephone company owns.

Figure 14-11 ISDN Reference Points

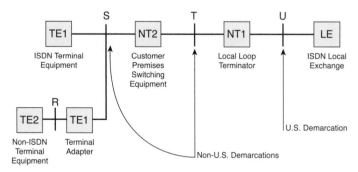

Because the S and T references are electrically similar, some interfaces are labeled S/T interfaces. Although the references perform different functions, the port is electrically the same and can be used for either function.

With all the ISDN abbreviations and acronyms, you might be thoroughly confused. To set up and troubleshoot ISDN, you need to know what all of these components and reference points look like in the real world.

As shown in Figure 14-12, a connection is made from the wall jack with a standard two-wire cable to the NT1 and then out of the NT1 with a four-wire connection to your ISDN phone, terminal adapter, Cisco ISDN router, or ISDN fax. The S/T interface is implemented by using an eight-wire connector to allow for powering the NT and TE.

Because all these connectors look similar (such as RJ-11, RJ-45s, and so on), you must be careful about what you plug in and where. The S/T reference point is a four-wire interface (TX and RX). It is point-to-point and multipoint (passive bus). It uses the ITU I.430 specification. The S/T interface defines the interface between a TE1 or *terminal adapter (TA)* and an NT.

The U interface defines the two-wire interface between the NT and the ISDN cloud. The R interface defines the interface between the TA and an attached non-ISDN device (TE2).

An NT1 and NT2 combination device is sometimes referred to as an NTU.

Figure 14-12 ISDN BRI Physical Reference Points

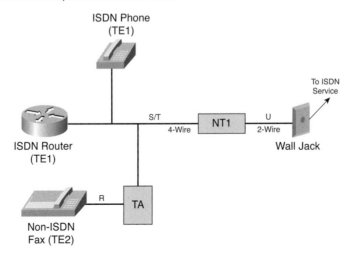

A regular ISDN S interface can have several endpoint devices with different capabilities occupying the same bus (the "S" bus). When the switch can communicate with multiple devices, it is typically referred to as "multipoint." Unfortunately, this creates complexity in both ISDN device setup and call processing. This complexity requires the use of service profile identifiers (SPIDs) and endpoint identifiers (EIDs).

When you are selecting ISDN equipment, it is important that you know the reference point that defines the type of ISDN interface that you need. In the United States, you will typically need a U interface to connect to your provider. That means if you purchase an ISDN router with an S/T interface, you will have to buy additional equipment (an NT1) to connect to your provider's network. Also, if you mistakenly connect a router with a U interface to an NT1, you can cause permanent damage to devices. Thus, knowing the ISDN reference points is key to properly selecting and installing ISDN devices.

Determining the Router ISDN Interface

In the United States, the customer is required to provide the NT1. In Europe and various other countries, the telephone company provides the NT1 function and presents an S/T interface to the customer. In these configurations, the customer is not required to supply a separate NT1 device or integrated NT1 function in the terminal device. Equipment such as router ISDN modules and interfaces must be ordered accordingly.

To select a Cisco router with the appropriate ISDN interface, do the following:

Step 1 Determine whether the router supports ISDN BRI.

Step 2 Determine the provider of the NT1. An NT1 terminates the local loop to the CO of the ISDN service provider. In the United States, the NT1 is CPE, meaning that it is the responsibility of the customer. In Europe, the service provider typically supplies the NT1.

Step 3 If the NT1 is CPE, make sure that the router has a U interface. If the router has an S/T interface, it will need an external NT1 to connect to the ISDN provider.

If the router has a connector labeled "BRI," it is already ISDN-enabled. With a native ISDN interface already built in, the router is a TE1. If the router has a U interface, it also has a built-in NT1.

If the router does not have a connector labeled "BRI" and it is a fixed-configuration (nonmodular) router, it must use an existing serial interface. With nonnative ISDN interfaces such as serial interfaces, an external TA device must be attached to the serial interface to provide BRI connectivity.

If the router is modular, it might be possible to upgrade to a native ISDN interface, providing it has an available slot. Note that a router that has a U interface should never be connected to an NT1. It will most likely damage the interface.

ISDN Switch Types

Routers must be configured to identify the type of switch with which they will communicate. Available ISDN switch types vary, depending in part on the country in which the switch is being used. This a consequence of various implementations of Q.931, the D channel signaling protocol in use in switches that are manufactured by different vendors.

Services offered by ISDN carriers vary considerably from country to country or from region to region. Just like modems, each switch type operates slightly differently and has a specific set of call setup requirements. As a result, before the router can be connected to an ISDN service, it must be configured for the switch type that is used at the CO. This information must be specified during router configuration so that the router can communicate properly with the switch and place ISDN network-level calls and send data. Table 14-3 lists countries and the ISDN switch types in use in those countries.

Table 14-3 ISDN Switch Types Around the World

Country	Switch Type
United States and Canada	AT&T 5ESS and 4ESS; Northern Telecom DMS-100
France	VN2, VN3
Japan	NTT
United Kingdom	Net3 and Net5
Europe	Net3

In addition to learning about the switch type that the service provider is using, it might also be necessary to know what *SPIDs* the Telco has assigned. A SPID is a number that the ISDN carrier provides to identify the line configuration of the BRI service. SPIDs allow multiple ISDN devices, such as voice and data equipment, to share the local loop. National ISDN-1 switches and SMS-100 require SPIDs.

SPIDs are used only in North America and Japan. The ISDN carrier provides a SPID to identify the line configuration of the ISDN service. In many cases when you are configuring a router, you must enter the SPIDs.

Each SPID points to line setup and configuration information. SPIDs are a series of characters that usually resemble telephone numbers. SPIDS identify each B channel to the switch at the CO. After they are identified, the switch links the available services to the connection. Remember: ISDN is typically used for dial-up connectivity. The SPIDs are processed when the router initially connects to the ISDN switch. If SPIDs are necessary, but they are not configured correctly, the initialization fails, and the ISDN services cannot be used.

ISDN Configuration

ISDN defines the data and control information that is passed between the ISDN CPE and the carrier's switch. ISDN service providers use a variety of switch types for their ISDN services. Each switch type operates slightly differently and has a specific set of call setup requirements. The ISDN CPE must be configured with knowledge of the switch type with which it is to communicate at the CO. This information must be configured on the router so that ISDN calls can be placed and data can be transmitted and received. ISDN configuration is the focus of this section.

There are two types of ISDN access: BRI and PRI. BRI and PRI will be covered separately for the purposes of configuration. This section will examine the commands used to verify that the configuration is correct. This section covers the following topics:

- Configuring ISDN BRI
- Configuring ISDN PRI
- Verifying the ISDN configuration
- Troubleshooting the ISDN configuration

You must specify global and interface parameters to prepare the router for operation in an ISDN environment. This section focuses on configuring BRI for access routers.

In global configuration mode, you must specify the ISDN service provider's switch type. There are approximately 10 different switches to choose from, depending on the country where the connection is established.

The interface ISDN addressing tasks include assigning the IP address, dialer group (for DDR), and ISDN service profile statements (SPID numbers). You also must include a **dialer map** command that associates a statically mapped destination to a destination IP address, host name, and ISDN dial number.

Configuring ISDN BRI

You can configure the command **isdn switch-type** *switch-type* at the global or interface command mode to specify the provider ISDN switch.

Configuring the **isdn switch-type** command in the global configuration mode sets the ISDN switch type identically for all ISDN interfaces. Individual interfaces can be configured after the global configuration command to reflect an alternate switch type. Table 14-4 lists ISDN BRI switch types.

Table 14-4 ISDN BRI Switch Types

Switch Type	Description
basic-5ess	AT&T basic rate switches (U.S.)
basic-dms 100	NT DMS-100 (North America)
basic-ni	National ISDN (North America)
basic-1tr6	German 1TR6 ISDN switches
basic-nwnet3	Norwegian Net3 switches
basic nznet3	New Zealand Net3 switches

Table 14-4 ISDN BRI Switch Types (Continued)

Switch Type	Description
basic-ts013	Australian TS013 and TS014 switches
basic-net3	Switch type for NET3 in United Kingdom and Europe
ntt	NTT ISDN switch (Japan)

Different ISDN providers use different switch types. In fact, some providers use one type of switch hardware to emulate another type of switch in software. Your ISDN provider will provide you the appropriate switch type information. If your router is not configured with the correct switch type information, it will not be able to communicate with the ISDN switch by using Q.931 at Layer 3. In other words, no ISDN call can be dialed or received.

You set the switch type by entering the **isdn switch-type** command. However, you must decide whether to enter this command in global or interface configuration mode.

The global **isdn switch-type** command sets all ISDN interfaces on the router to be configured for the same switch type:

```
Router(config)#isdn switch-type type
```

When you issue the **isdn switch-type** command in interface configuration mode, only the interface that you are configuring assumes the switch type:

```
Router(config-if)#isdn switch-type type
```

Note that the interface configuration command overrides the global-level command.

Typically, you specify the switch type in global configuration mode by using the **isdn switch-type** command. However, in some cases, you might need to specify two different ISDN switch types. This is necessary when the same router connects to both BRI and PRI. For this reason, Cisco extended the use of the command to the interface configuration mode, beginning with IOS release 11.3(T).

The **interface bri** *interface-number* command designates an ISDN interface on a router that natively supports ISDN (TE1). Therefore, to configure the first ISDN interface with the AT&T basic rate switch type, you would enter the commands shown in Example 14-1.

Example 14-1 *ISDN Interface BRI Command*

```
RTA(config)#interface bri 0
RTA(config-if)#isdn switch-type basic-5ess
```

If the router does not have a native BRI (if it is a TE2 device), it must use an external ISDN terminal adapter. On a TE2 router, use the **interface serial** *interface-number* command.

When the ISDN service is installed, the service provider issues information about the switch type and SPIDs. SPIDs are used to define the services that are available to individual ISDN subscribers. Depending on the switch type, these SPIDs might have to be added to the configuration. National ISDN-1 and DMS-100 ISDN switches require SPIDs to be configured, but the AT&T 5ESS switch does not. SPIDs must be specified when using the Adtran ISDN simulator. An Adtran ISDN simulator is a device that can be used in labs and testing environments to simulate an ISDN connection without having to actually set up an account with an access provider.

The format of the SPIDs can vary depending on the ISDN switch type and specific provider requirements. Use the **isdn spid1** and **isdn spid2** interface configuration mode commands to specify the SPID that the ISDN network requires when the router initiates a call to the local ISDN exchange. Table 14-5 describes the two commands.

Table 14-5 **isdn spid1** and **isdn spid2** Command Parameters

Command Parameter	Description
spid-number	Number identifying the service subscribed to. The ISDN service provider assigns this value.
ldn	(Optional.) Local dial number. This number must match the called-party information coming in from the ISDN switch to use both B channels on most switches.

The argument *switch-type* indicates the service provider switch type. To disable the switch on the ISDN interface, specify **isdn switch-type none**. Example 14-2 illustrates configuration of National ISDN BRI switches in the global configuration mode.

Example 14-2 *National ISDN BRI Configuration*

```
Router(config)#isdn switch-type basic-ni
```

To define SPIDs, use the **isdn spid#** command in the interface configuration mode to define the SPID numbers that have been assigned for the B channels:

```
Router(config-if)#isdn spid1 spid-number [ldn]
Router(config-if)#isdn spid2 spid-number [ldn]
```

The optional *ldn* argument defines a local dial directory number. On most switches, the number must match the called party information coming in from the ISDN switch. SPIDs are specified in interface configuration mode.

To enter interface configuration mode, use the **interface bri** command in the global configuration mode:

```
Router(config)#interface bri slot/port
```

The *slot/port* argument describes the port-adapter-slot-number/interface-port-number. The numbers are assigned at the factory at the time of installation or when they are added to a system. The numbers can be displayed by using the **show interfaces** command.

To configure SPIDs for both B channels on BRI 0/0, use the syntax shown in Example 14-3.

Example 14-3 *Configuring SPIDS on a BRI Interface*

```
Router(config)#interface bri0/0
Router(config-if)#isdn spid1 51055540000001 5554000
Router(config-if)#isdn spid2 51055540010001 5554001
```

Lab Activity   Configuring ISDN BRI

In this lab, an ISDN router is configured to make a successful connection to a local ISDN switch. An Adtran Atlas550 ISDN emulator is used to simulate the switch/ISDN cloud.

Configuring ISDN PRI

ISDN PRI is delivered via a leased T1 or E1 line. The main PRI configuration tasks are as follows:

Step 1   Set the ISDN switch type. Specify the correct PRI switch type that the router interfaces with at the provider's CO.

Step 2   Select the controller. Specify the T1/E1 controller, framing type, and line coding for the provider's facility.

Step 3   Establish the interface port to function as PRI. Set a PRI group timeslot for the T1/E1 facility and indicate the speed used.

Because routers connect to PRI by using T1/E1, there is no "interface pri." Instead, the physical interface on the router that connects to the leased line is called a T1 controller (or E1 controller, if an E1 line is being used). This controller must be configured properly to interface with the carrier network. The ISDN PRI D and PRI B channels are configured separately from the controller by using the **interface serial** command.

Use the **isdn switch-type** command to specify the provider's ISDN switch to which the PRI connects. As with BRI, this command can be issued globally or in interface configuration mode. Table 14-6 shows the switch types that are available for ISDN PRI configuration.

Table 14-6 ISDN PRI Switch Types

Switch Type	Description
primary-5ess	AT&T basic rate switches (USA)
primary-dms100	Northern Telecom DMS-100 (North America)
primary-ni	National ISDN (North America)
primary-net5	Switch type for Net5 in United Kingdom, Europe, and Australia
primary-ntt	NTT ISDN switch (Japan)

Configuring a T1 or E1 controller is done in four parts:

Step 1   Specify the controller and the slot/port in the router where the PRI card is located, in global configuration mode:

```
Router(config)#controller {t1 | e1} {slot/port}
```

Step 2   Configure the framing, line coding, and clocking, as dictated by the service provider. The **framing** command is used to select the frame type that the PRI service provider uses. For T1, use the following command syntax:

```
Router(config-controller)#framing {sf | esf}
```

For E1 lines, use the **framing** command with the following options:

```
Router(config-controller)#framing {crc4 | no-crc4} [australia]
```

Use the **linecode** command to identify the physical-layer signaling method on the provider's digital facility:

```
Router(config-controller)#linecode {ami | b8zs| hdb3}
```

North America uses the B8ZS signaling method for T1 carrier facilities. It allows a full 64 kbps for each ISDN channel. Europe typically uses **hdb3** encoding.

Step 3   Configure the specified interface for PRI operation and the number of fixed timeslots that are allocated on the provider's digital facility:

```
Router(config-controller)#pri-group [timeslots range]
```

For T1, the range of timeslots used is 1–24; for E1, the range is 1–31.

Step 4   Specify an interface for PRI D-channel operation. The interface is a serial interface to a T1/E1 on the router:

```
Router(config)#interface serial {slot/port: | unit:} {23 | 15}
```

Within an E1 or T1 facility, the channels start numbering at 1 (1–31 for E1 and 1–24 for T1). Serial interfaces in the Cisco router start numbering at 0. Therefore, channel 16, the E1 signaling channel, is serial port subinterface 15. Channel 24, the T1 signaling channel, becomes serial subinterface 23. Therefore, **interface serial 0/0:23** refers to the D channel of a T1 PRI.

Subinterfaces, which are commonly used with Frame Relay, are designated with a dot (period). For example, S0/0.16 is a subinterface. Do not confuse the channels of a T1 or E1 with subinterfaces. Channels use a colon instead of a dot to indicate the channel number, such as the following:

- S0/0.23 refers to a subinterface.
- S0/0:23 refers to a channel.

After DDR (or a user) creates an end-to-end path over the ISDN, some method of datagram encapsulation is needed for data to be transported. Available encapsulations for ISDN include the following:

- PPP
- HDLC
- Frame Relay
- *Link Access Protocol, Balanced (LAPB)*
- Combinet Proprietary Protocol (CPP)

LAPB can also be used for datagram delivery over the D channel.

As noted earlier in this chapter, you will most likely use PPP as the Layer 2 encapsulation protocol.

The **encapsulation** command is used to configure encapsulation for your ISDN interface:

```
Router(config-if)#encapsulation [ppp | labp | hdlc | x25 | cpp]
```

If you configure PPP encapsulation, you must use Password Authentication Protocol (PAP) or Challenge Handshake Authentication Protocol (CHAP) if you receive calls from more than one dial-up source. Example 14-4 represents a typical BRI encapsulation configuration that PPP with CHAP.

Example 14-4 *Sample BRI Encapsulation*

```
Router(config)#interface bri 0
Router(config-if)#encapsulation ppp
Router(config-if)#ppp authentication chap
```

Verifying the ISDN Configuration

The **show** commands are used to verify that the ISDN configuration is functioning correctly:

```
Router#show isdn status
Router#show interfaces bri0/0
Router#show isdn active
```

To confirm BRI operations, use the **show isdn status** command to inspect the status of the BRI interfaces. You can use this command after configuring the ISDN BRI to verify that the TE1 (router) is communicating correctly with the ISDN switch. The sample output in Example 14-5 shows that the TEIs have been negotiated successfully and that ISDN Layer 3 (end-to-end) is ready to make or receive calls.

Example 14-5 show isdn status *Command*

```
Cork#show isdn status

Global ISDN Switchtype = basic-ni
ISDN BRI0/0 interface

    dsl 0, interface ISDN Switchtype = basic-ni

    Layer 1 Status:
    ACTIVE

    Layer 2 Status:
    TEI = 64, Ces = 1, SAPI = 0, State = MULTIPLE_FRAME_ESTABLISHED

    TEI = 65, Ces = 2, SAPI = 0, State = MULTIPLE_FRAME_ESTABLISHED

    Spid Status:
    TEI 64, ces = 1, state = 5(init)

        spid1 configured, no LDN, spid1 sent, spid1 valid
```

Example 14-5 show isdn status *Command (Continued)*

```
        Endpoint ID Info: epsf = 0, usid = 70, tid = 1

   TEI 65, ces = 2, state = 5(init)

      spid2 configured, no LDN, spid2 sent, spid2 valid

      Endpoint ID Info: epsf = 0, usid = 70, tid = 2

   Layer 3 Status:
   0 Active Layer 3 Call(s)

   Activated dsl 0 CCBs = 0

   The Free Channel Mask:  0x80000003
   Total Allocated ISDN CCBs = 0
```

Configuration of ISDN BRI is a mix of global and interface commands. To configure the ISDN switch type, enter global configuration mode and use the **isdn switch-type** *switch-type* command, as Example 14-6 shows.

Example 14-6 *ISDN Partial Configuration*

```
Router(config)# isdn switch-type basic-ni
!
<Output Omitted>
!
interface BRI0/0
   isdn switch-type basic-ni
   isdn spid1 51055540000001 5554000
   isdn spid2 51055540010001 5554001
```

Verify that Layer 1 status is ACTIVE and that the Layer 2 status state MULTIPLE_FRAME_ESTABLISHED appears. This command also displays the number of active calls.

The **show isdn active** command displays current call information, including the called number, the time until the call is disconnected, advice of charge (AOC), charging units used during the call, and whether the AOC information is provided during calls or at end of calls.

The **show dialer** command displays information about the dialer interface. This includes information such as current call status, dial-up timer values, dial reason, and the remote device that is connected.

The **show interfaces bri0/0** command displays statistics for the BRI interface that is configured on the router. Channel-specific information is displayed by putting the channel number at the end of the command. The **show interfaces bri0/0:1** command shows that the B channel is using PPP encapsulation, LCP has negotiated and is open, and two Network Control Protocols are running: IP Control Protocol (IPCP) and CDP Control Protocol (CDPCP). Example 14-7 shows a sample output of the BRI interface.

Example 14-7 *show interfaces bri0/0 Command*

```
BranchF#show interface bri0/0: 1 2
BRI0:1 is up, line protocol is up
  Hardware is BRI
  MTU 1500 bytes, BW 64 Kbit, DLY 20000 usec, rely 255/255, load 1/255
  Encapsulation PPP, loopback not set, keepalive set (10 sec)
  LCP Open
  Open: IPCP, CDPCP
  Last input 00:00:01, output 00:00:01, output hang never
  Last clearing of "show interface" counters never
  Input queue: 0/75/0 (size/max/drops); Total output drops: 0
  Queueing strategy: weighted fair
  Output queue: 0/1000/64/0 (size/max total/threshold/drops)
     Conversations  0/1/256 (active/max active/max total)
     Reserved Conversations 0/0 (allocated/max allocated)
  5 minute input rate 0 bits/sec, 0 packets/sec
  5 minute output rate 0 bits/sec, 0 packets/sec
     82 packets input, 2844 bytes, 0 no buffer
     Received 82 broadcasts, 0 runts, 0 giants, 0 throttles
     0 input errors, 0 CRC, 0 frame, 0 overrun, 0 ignored, 0 abort
     82 packets output, 2838 bytes, 0 underruns
     0 output errors, 0 collisions, 0 interface resets
     0 output buffer failures, 0 output buffers swapped out
     5 carrier transitions
(output omitted)
```

Troubleshooting the ISDN Configuration

The following commands are used to debug and troubleshoot the ISDN configuration:

- **debug isdn q921**—Shows data link layer messages (Layer 2) on the D channel between the router and the ISDN switch. Use this debug if the **show isdn status** command does not display Layer 1 and Layer 2 up.

- **debug isdn q931**—Shows the exchange of call setup and teardown messages of the ISDN network connection (Layer 3).

- **debug ppp authentication**—Displays the PPP authentication protocol messages, including CHAP packet exchanges and PAP exchanges.

- **debug ppp negotiation**—Displays information on PPP traffic and exchanges while negotiating the PPP components, including link control protocol (LCP), authentication, and Network Control Protocol. A successful PPP negotiation opens the LCP state, authenticates, and then negotiates Network Control Protocol.

- **debug ppp error**—Displays protocol errors and error statistics that are associated with PPP connection negotiation and operation.

DDR Routing

DDR refers to a collection of Cisco features that allows two or more routers to establish a dynamic connection over a simple dial-up network. DDR is used for low-volume, periodic network connections over an ISDN network or the PSTN. DDR also allows the exchange of routing updates on an as-needed basis, although static routing is used most often.

Traditionally, dedicated WAN lines are dedicated connections between two sites used for a considerable amount of time per day to be cost effective. DDR addresses the need for periodic network connections over a circuit-switched WAN service. DDR is flexible in that it can connect to several endpoints and it uses WAN connections only as needed, reducing WAN costs.

DDR is the process of a router connecting via a dial-up network when there is traffic to send and then disconnecting when the data transfer is complete (see Figure 14-13). DDR is typically used for the following situations:

- Telecommuters needing to connect to the company network periodically during the day

- Remote offices needing to send small amounts of data—such as sales transactions or inventory status requests—periodically to a main computer at the CO

- Customers using an automated order system

- Periodic retrieval of e-mail from the ISP on a scheduled basis

Figure 14-13 DDR

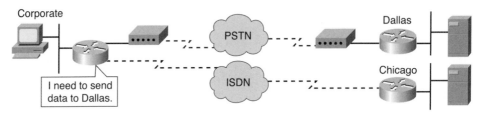

DDR Operation

The receipt of traffic on a DDR-configured interface triggers DDR. If the traffic is "interesting," a call is initiated. This traffic can be defined as IP traffic of a particular protocol type, packets from a particular source address or destination, or other criteria. The network administrator defines interesting traffic. The call is terminated after the interesting traffic has been transmitted and the applicable idle timeout period has elapsed.

The key to efficient DDR operation is in the definition of interesting traffic. There are several mechanisms to define interesting traffic by including dialer and access lists. Even traffic that is not "interesting" can be forwarded if the connection to the destination is active.

DDR is implemented in Cisco routers in the following steps:

Step 1   The router receives traffic, performs a route table lookup to determine if there is a route to the destination, and identifies the outbound interface.

Step 2   If the outbound interface is configured for DDR, the router does a lookup to determine if the traffic is "interesting." The network administrator must predefine interesting traffic.

Step 3   The router identifies the dialing information that is necessary to make the call by using a dialer map to access the next-hop router.

Step 4   The router then checks to see if the dialer map is in use. If the interface is currently connected to the desired remote destination, the traffic is permitted. After a connection is established, any traffic to that destination is permitted; however, only interesting traffic resets the idle timer. If the interface is not currently connected to the remote destination, the router sends call-setup information via the BRI by using the D channel. After the link is enabled, the router transmits both interesting and uninteresting traffic. Uninteresting traffic can include data and routing updates.

Step 5   The idle timer starts when no interesting traffic is seen during the idle timeout period and disconnects the call based on the idler timer configuration.

This process is shown in Figure 14-14.

Figure 14-14 Generic DDR Operation

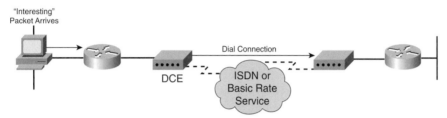

Legacy DDR

Legacy DDR is a term that is used to define basic DDR configurations in which a single set of dialer parameters is applied to an interface. If multiple unique dialer configurations are needed on one interface, you should use dialer profiles.

To configure legacy DDR, perform the following steps:

Step 1   Define static routes.

Step 2   Specify interesting traffic.

Step 3   Configure the dialer information.

Defining Static Routes for DDR

To forward traffic, routers need to know what route to use for a given destination. When a dynamic routing protocol is used, the DDR interface dials the remote site for every routing update or "hello" message if these packets are defined as interesting traffic. To prevent the frequent or constant activation of the DDR link that is necessary to support dynamic routing protocols, the necessary routes should be configured statically.

To configure a static route for IP, use the following command:

```
Router(config)#ip route net-prefix mask {address | interface}
    [distance] [permanent]
```

Figure 14-15 shows the Central router defining a static route to the LAN (10.40.0.0) of the Home router. The Home router has two static routes defined for the two subnets on the Central LAN. If the Home router is responsible for a "stub" network (the route is not local), all traffic should be sent to Central and a default route would be a better choice for the Home router:

```
Home(config)#ip route 0.0.0.0 0.0.0.0 10.1.0.2
```

Figure 14-15 Defining Static Routes

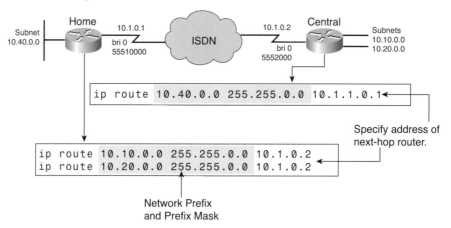

When you are configuring static routes, consider the following:

- A defined static route always takes precedence over a dynamic route. All dynamic routes are ignored if a static route is present in a routing table for the same network.
- To reduce the number of static route entries, define a summarized or default static route.

Specifying Interesting Traffic for DDR

DDR calls are triggered by "interesting" traffic. This traffic can be defined as IP traffic of a particular protocol type, packets with a particular source address or destination, or other criteria. The network administrator defines interesting traffic.

Use the **dialer-list** global command to identify interesting traffic:

```
Router(config)#dialer-list dialer-group-num protocol protocol-name
    {permit | deny | list access-list-number}
```

In Example 14-8, **dialer-list 1 protocol ip permit** allows all IP traffic to trigger a call. In Example 14-8, there are two examples of specifying interesting traffic: one without access lists and the other with them. In the first example (without access lists), the **dialer-list** command allows all IP traffic to trigger a call. In the second example (with access lists), FTP and Telnet traffic are not considered "interesting" and do not activate the DDR link. Any other IP packet does initiate the DDR link.

Example 14-8 dialer-list 1 protocol ip permit *Command*

```
dialer-list 1 protocol ip permit


dialer-list 1 protocol ip list 101


access-list 101 deny tcp any any eq ftp
access-list 101 deny tcp any any eq telnet
access-list 101 permit ip any any
```

Configuring DDR Dialer Information

Several steps are involved in configuring the DDR interface. PPP is configured on the dialer interface in a similar way to the PPP configuration on a serial interface. PPP is the data link protocol that is operating on the B channels. Example 14-9 shows how to configure PPP on the DDR interface.

Example 14-9 *Configuring PPP on a DDR Interface*

```
Home(config)#username Central password cisco
Home(config)#interface bri0/0
Home(config-if)#encapsulation ppp
Home(config-if)#ppp authentication chap
Home(config-if)#ip address 10.1.0.1 255.255.255.0



Home#show running-config
hostname Home
!
isdn switch-type basic-5ess
!
!
username Central password cisco
interface BRI0
  ip address 10.1.0.1 255.255.255.0
```

continues

Example 14-9 *Configuring PPP on a DDR Interface (Continued)*

```
 encapsulation ppp
 dialer idle-timeout 180
 dialer map ip 10.1.0.2 name Central 5552000
 dialer-group 1
 no fair-queue
 ppp authentication chap
!
router rip
network 10.0.0.0
!
no ip classless
ip route 10.10.0.0 255.255.0.0 10.1.0.2
ip route 10.20.0.0 255.255.0.0 10.1.0.2
!
dialer-list 1 protocol ip permit
```

You need to associate a dialer-list specifying the interesting traffic for this DDR interface with the DDR interface. You can do this by using the **dialer-group** *group-number* command, as shown in Example 14-10.

Example 14-10 dialer-group *group-number Command*

```
Home(config-if)#dialer-group 1

Home#show running-config
hostname Home
!
isdn switch-type basic-5ess
!
username central password cisco
interface BRI0
 ip address 10.1.0.1 255.255.255.0
 encapsulation ppp
 dialer idle-timeout 180
 dialer map ip 10.1.0.2 name Central 5552000
 dialer-group 1
 no fair-queue
```

Example 14-10 dialer-group *group-number Command*

```
 ppp authentication chap
!
router rip
network 10.0.0.0
!
no ip classless
ip route 10.10.0.0 255.255.0.0 10.1.0.2
ip route 10.20.0.0 255.255.0.0 10.1.0.2
!
!
dialer-list 1 protocol ip permit
```

In the command, *group-number* specifies the number of the dialer group to which the interface belongs. The group number can be an integer from 1 to 10. This number must match the dialer-list *group-number*. Each interface can have only one dialer group, but the same dialer list can be assigned to multiple interfaces (by using the **dialer-group** command).

You must specify the correct dialing information for the remote DDR interface. You can do this by using the **dialer map** command, as shown in Figure 14-16.

Figure 14-16 Dialer Map

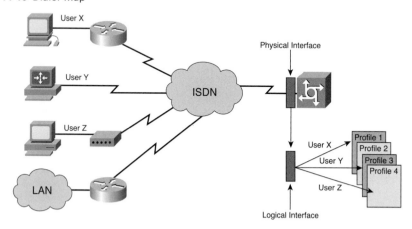

The **dialer map** command maps the remote protocol address to a telephone number. This command is necessary to dial multiple sites:

```
Router(config-if)#dialer map protocol next-hop-address
    [name hostname] [speed 56 | 64] [broadcast] dial-string
```

If you are dialing only one site, use an unconditional dialer string command that always dials the one phone number regardless of the traffic destination; this step is unique to Legacy DDR. Although the information is always required, the steps to configure destination information are different when you are using dialer profiles instead of Legacy DDR.

You can use the **dialer idle-timeout** *seconds* command to specify the number of idle seconds before a call is disconnected. The *seconds* represent the number of seconds until a call is disconnected after the last interesting packet is sent. The default is 120.

 Lab Activity   Configuring Legacy DDR

In this lab, an ISDN router is configured to make a Legacy DDR call to another ISDN-capable router. An Adtran Atlas550 ISDN emulator is used to simulate the switch/ISDN cloud. Only HTTP traffic brings up the link.

Dialer Profiles

There are a number of limitations to Legacy DDR because the configuration is applied directly to an interface. This means that there is a one-to-one correspondence between the two DDR interfaces at each end of the link. If the IP address is applied directly to the interface, only DDR interfaces that are configured in that specific subnet can establish a DDR connection with that interface.

Dialer profiles remove the configuration from the interface that is receiving or making calls and bind the configuration to the interface on a per-call basis. This allows physical interfaces to dynamically take on different characteristics based on incoming or outgoing call requirements. Dialer profiles can define encapsulation and access control lists, determine minimum or maximum calls, and turn features on or off.

Dialer profiles aid in the design and deployment of more complex and scalable circuit-switched internetworks by implementing a new DDR model in Cisco routers and access servers. Dialer profiles separate the logical portions of DDR, the network layer, encapsulation, and dialer parameters from the physical interface that places or receives calls.

Using dialer profiles, you can perform the following tasks:

- Configure B channels of an ISDN interface with different IP subnets.
- Use different encapsulations on the B channels of an ISDN interface.
- Set different DDR parameters for the B channels of an ISDN interface.
- Eliminate the waste of ISDN B channels by letting ISDN BRI interfaces belong to multiple dialer pools.

A dialer profile consists of the following elements:

- **Dialer interface**—A logical entity that uses a per-destination dialer profile.
- **Dialer pool**—Each dialer interface references a dialer pool, which is a group of one or more physical interfaces associated with a dialer profile.
- **Physical interfaces**—Interfaces in a dialer pool are configured for encapsulation parameters and to identify the dialer pools to which the interface belongs. Encapsulation type, PPP authentication, and multilink PPP are configured on the physical interface.

An "interesting packet" is routed to a remote DDR IP address. The router checks the configured dialer interfaces for one that shares the same subnet as the remote DDR IP address. If one exists, the router looks for an unused physical DDR interface in the dialer pool. The configuration from the dialer profile is then applied to the interface, and the router attempts to create the DDR connection. When the connection is terminated, the interface is returned to the dialer pool for the next call.

Configuring Dialer Profiles

Multiple dialer interfaces can be configured on a router. Each dialer interface is the complete configuration for a destination. The **interface dialer** global command creates a dialer interface and enters interface configuration mode.

To configure the dialer interface, perform the following tasks:

Step 1 Configure one or more dialer interfaces with all the basic DDR commands, such as IP address, encapsulation type and authentication, idle-timer, and dialer-group for "interesting traffic."

Step 2 Configure a dialer string and dialer remote-name to specify the remote router name and phone number to dial it. The dialer pool associates this logical interface with a pool of physical interfaces.

Step 3   Configure the physical interfaces and assign them to a dialer pool by using the dialer pool-member command. You can assign an interface to multiple dialer pools by using this command to specify several dialer pool numbers. If more than one physical interface exists in the pool, use the priority option of the dialer pool-member command to set the interface's priority within a dialer pool, which is only used when dialing out.

You can use a combination of synchronous, serial, BRI, or PRI interfaces with dialer pools.

Verifying the DDR Configuration

The **show dialer interface** command displays information in the same format as the legacy DDR statistics on incoming and outgoing calls.

The message "Dialer state is data link layer up" suggests that the dialer came up properly, and the interface bound to profile Dialer1 indicates that interface bri0 is bound to the dialer profile Dialer1, as in the sample output shown in Example 14-11.

Example 14-11 show dialer interface *Command*

```
Router# show dialer interface bri 0
BRI0 - dialer type = ISDN
Dial String Successes Failures Last called Last status
0 incoming call(s) have been screened.
BRI0: B-Channel 1
Idle timer (120 secs), Fast idle timer (20 secs)
Wait for carrier (30 secs), Re-enable (15 secs)
Dialer state is data link layer up
Dial reason: ip (s=10.1.1.8, d=10.1.1.1)
Interface bound to profile Dialer0
Time until disconnect 102 secs
Current call connected 00:00:19
Connected to 5773872 (wolfman)
BRI0: B-Channel 2
Idle timer (120 secs), Fast idle timer (20 secs)
Wait for carrier (30 secs), Re-enable (15 secs)
Dialer state is idle
```

The **show isdn active** command displays information about the current active ISDN calls. (Sample output is shown in Example 14-12.) In this output, the ISDN call is outgoing to a remote router named Seattle.

Example 14-12 show isdn active *Command*

```
Phoenix#show isdn active
- - - - - - - - - - - - - - - - - - - - - - - - - - - - - - - - - - - - - - - - - - -
                            ISDN ACTIVE CALLS
- - - - - - - - - - - - - - - - - - - - - - - - - - - - - - - - - - - - - - - - - - -
History table has a maximum of 100 entries.
History table data is retained for a maximum of 15 Minutes.
- - - - - - - - - - - - - - - - - - - - - - - - - - - - - - - - - - - - - - - - - - -
- -
Call    Calling     Called      Remote  Seconds Seconds Seconds Charges
Type    Number      Number      Name    Used    Left    Idle    Units/Currency
- - - - - - - - - - - - - - - - - - - - - - - - - - - - - - - - - - - - - - - - - - -
Out                 5551000     Seattle   87      41      78      0
- - - - - - - - - - - - - - - - - - - - - - - - - - - - - - - - - - - - - - - - - - -
```

The **show isdn status** command displays information about the three layers of the BRI interface. In this output, ISDN Layer 1 is active, ISDN Layer 2 is established with SPID1 and SPID2 validated, and there is one active connection on Layer 3.

Use **debug** commands to help troubleshoot problems with a DDR configuration.

 Lab Activity Configuring Dialer Profiles

In this lab, ISDN dialer profiles are configured on the routers. This enables you to make a DDR call from two remote routers simultaneously into a central ISDN BRI router. An Adtran Atlas550 ISDN emulator is used to simulate the switch/ISDN cloud.

Summary

In this chapter, you learned the following:

- ISDN provides an integrated voice/data capability that uses the public switched network.
- ISDN components include terminals, TAs, NT devices, and ISDN switches.

- ISDN reference points (R, S, T, and U) define logical interfaces between functional groupings, such as TAs and NT1s.
- A suite of ITU-T standards addresses ISDN, spanning the physical, data link, and network layers of the OSI reference model.
- The two most common encapsulation choices for ISDN are PPP and HDLC.
- ISDN has many uses, including remote access, remote nodes, and SOHO connectivity.
- There are two ISDN services: BRI and PRI.
- ISDN BRI delivers a total bandwidth of a 144-kbps line into three separate channels and a usable bandwidth of 128 kbps.
- BRI configuration involves the configuration of a BRI interface, an ISDN switch type, and ISDN SPIDs.
- DDR establishes and releases circuit-switched connections as needed.

To supplement all that you have learned in this chapter, refer to the chapter-specific Videos, PhotoZooms, and e-Lab Activities on the CD-ROM that accompanies this book.

Key Terms

2B+D   In reference to the ISDN BRI service, two B channels and one D channel.

BRI (Basic Rate Interface)   An ISDN interface that is composed of two B channels and one D channel for circuit-switched communication of voice, video, and data.

CPE (customer premises equipment)   Terminating equipment, such as terminals, telephones, and modems, that is supplied by the telephone company, installed at customer sites, and connected to the telephone company network.

ISDN (Integrated Services Digital Network)   A communication protocol offered by telephone companies that permits telephone networks to carry data, voice, and other source traffic.

LAPB (Link Access Procedure, Balanced)   A data link layer protocol in the X.25 protocol stack. LAPB is a bit-oriented protocol that is derived from HDLC.

LAPD (Link Access Procedure on the D channel)   An ISDN data link layer protocol for the D channel. LAPD was derived from LAPB and is designed primarily to satisfy the signaling requirements of ISDN basic access. Defined by ITU-T Recommendations Q.920 and Q.921.

NT1 (Network Termination type 1)   A device that connects four-wire ISDN subscriber wiring to the conventional two-wire local loop facility.

NT2 (Network Termination type 2)   A device that directs traffic to and from different subscriber devices and the NT1. The NT2 is an intelligent device that performs switching and concentrating.

PRI (Primary Rate Interface)   An ISDN interface to primary rate access. Primary rate access consists of a single 64-kbps D channel plus 23 (T1) or 30 (E1) B channels for voice or data.

Q.931   A protocol that recommends a network layer between the terminal endpoint and the local ISDN switch. Q.931 does not impose an end-to-end recommendation. The various ISDN providers and switch types can and do use various implementations of Q.931.

reference point   Several reference points that are defined to characterize the different interfaces for ISDN that are defined in ITU recommendation I.411 (V, U, T, S, and R reference points) will be defined (physical and electrical characteristics).

SPID (service profile identifier)   A number that some service providers use to define the services to which an ISDN device subscribes. The ISDN device uses the SPID when accessing the switch that initializes the connection to a service provider.

TA (terminal adapter)   A device that is used to connect ISDN BRI connections to existing interfaces, such as EIA/TIA-232. Essentially, a TA is an ISDN modem.

TE1 (Terminal Equipment type 1)   A device that is compatible with the ISDN network. A TE1 connects to a network termination of type 1 or type 2.

TE2 (Terminal Equipment type 2)   A device that is not compatible with ISDN and that requires a terminal adapter.

Check Your Understanding

1. In ISDN, what is the channel over which data is transferred?

    A. The bearer channel with 16 kbps capacity

    B. The delta channel with 16 kbps capacity

    C. The bearer channel with 64 kbps capacity

    D. The delta channel with 64 kbps capacity

2. Which channel is used for ISDN out-of-band signaling?

    A. Data

    B. Bearer

    C. Local loop

    D. Delta

3. What is the first dynamically assigned TEI value?

    A. 64

    B. 127

    C. 0

    D. 1

4. What mechanism is used to pass call control information between two ISDN switches?

    A. D channel

    B. SS7

    C. B channel

    D. Q.921

5. What is the primary purpose of the D channel in processing an ISDN call?

   A. To carry data traffic

   B. To carry voice traffic

   C. To carry video traffic

   D. To carry call signaling

6. To use a router in North America as a dial-in server using ISDN BRI, which ISDN interface is needed?

   A. ISDN PRI E1

   B. ISDN BRI U

   C. ISDN PRI T1

   D. ISDN BRI S/T

7. If a router has a U interface, what does that indicate?

   A. It has a built-in TA.

   B. It has a built-in TE1.

   C. It has a built-in NT1.

   D. It has a built-in BRI.

8. Which of the following switch types is used in European BRI connections?

   A. Net3

   B. Net5

   C. Northern Telecom DMS-100

   D. VN3

9. Which of the following provides SPIDs?

   A. The router manufacturer

   B. The ISDN switch

   C. The ISDN carrier

   D. The network administrator

10. What is DDR used for?

   A. Low-volume, periodic network connections over Frame Relay

   B. Low-volume, periodic network connections over ISDN

   C. Low-volume, permanent network connections over ISDN

   D. High-volume connections over ISDN

11. Which of the following statements about DDR is false? (Choose four.)

   A. DDR is connecting a router to a dial-up network.

   B. DDR creates permanent connections between two sites.

   C. DDR allows a router to connect to only one endpoint.

   D. DDR reduces WAN costs if usage is low.

   E. DDR is the correct technology to deploy if you have a permanent WWW server.

   F. DDR applies only to ISDN.

12. What is the main limitation with Legacy DDR?

   A. There is no support for PPP authentication.

   B. Dialer maps must be used.

   C. Configuration is applied directly to the physical interface.

   D. Legacy DDR is limited to IP applications.

Objectives

After reading this chapter, you will be able to

- Describe Frame Relay services, standards, and components
- Understand Local Management Interface (LMI) features
- Describe the use of Frame Relay subinterfaces
- Configure basic Frame Relay

Chapter 15

Frame Relay

You have learned that Point-to-Point Protocol (PPP) and Integrated Services Digital Network (ISDN) are two types of wide-area network (WAN) technologies that can be implemented to solve connectivity issues between geographically distant locations. In this chapter, you will learn about another type of WAN technology, *Frame Relay*, which can also be implemented to solve connectivity issues for users who need access to geographically distant locations.

In this chapter, you learn about Frame Relay services, standards, components, and operation. In addition, you explore the configuration tasks for Frame Relay service, along with the commands for monitoring and maintaining a Frame Relay connection.

Be sure to look at this chapter's associated e-Lab Activities, Videos, and PhotoZooms that you will find on the CD-ROM that accompanies this book. These CD-ROM elements are designed to supplement the material and reinforce the concepts that are introduced in this chapter.

Frame Relay Overview

Frame Relay is an International Telecommunication Union Telecommunication Standardization Sector (ITU-T) (formerly the Consultative Committee for International Telegraph and Telephone (CCITT) and American National Standards Institute (ANSI) standard that defines the process for sending data over a *public data network*. It is a high-performance, efficient data-link technology that is used in networks throughout the world. Frame Relay is a way of sending information over a WAN by dividing data into packets. Each packet travels through a series of switches in a Frame Relay network to reach its destination. It operates at the physical and data link layers of the Open System Interconnection (OSI) reference model, but it relies on upper-layer protocols such as TCP for error correction.

Frame Relay was originally conceived as a protocol for use over ISDN interfaces. Today, Frame Relay is an industry-standard, switched data link layer protocol that handles multiple virtual circuits (VCs) using High-Level Data Link Control (HDLC) encapsulation between connected devices. Frame Relay uses VCs to make connections through a connection-oriented service.

The network that is providing the Frame Relay interface can be either a carrier-provided public network or a network of privately owned equipment, serving a single enterprise. Frame Relay provides a packet-switching data communication capability that is used between user devices (such as routers, bridges, and host machines) and carrier network equipment (such as Frame Relay switching nodes). As you have learned, user devices are often referred to as data terminal equipment (DTE), whereas network equipment that interfaces to DTE is often referred to as data circuit-terminating equipment, as shown in Figure 15-1.

Figure 15-1 User Devices

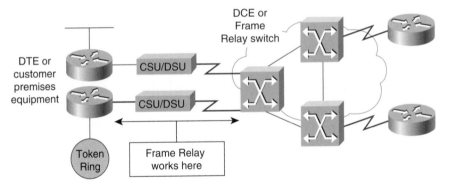

Frame Relay Terminology

The connection through the Frame Relay network between two DTEs is called a logical connection, or VC. VCs can be established dynamically by sending signaling messages to the network. In this case, they are called switched virtual circuits (SVCs), but this is uncommon. Generally, *permanent virtual circuits (PVCs)* that are preconfigured by the carrier are used. The switching information for a VC is stored in the memory of the switch.

Because it was designed to operate on high-quality digital lines, Frame Relay provides no error-recovery mechanism. As in Ethernet local-area network (LAN) technology, if there is an error in a frame, it is discarded without notification.

A Frame-Relay-capable interface device, also called a Frame Relay assembler/disassembler, or a router that is connected to the Frame Relay network can have multiple VCs connecting it to various endpoints. This makes it a cost-effective replacement for a mesh of leased lines because each endpoint needs only a single shorter leased line and interface. Further savings arise because the capacity of the leased line is based on the average bandwidth requirement of the VCs, rather than on the maximum bandwidth.

The various VCs on a single physical access line can be distinguished because each has a data-link connection identifier (DLCI). The DLCI is stored in the address field of every frame that is transmitted. The DLCI has local significance only, and it might be different at each end of a VC.

Following are some terms that are used in this chapter to discuss Frame Relay (refer to Figure 15-2):

- *Local access rate*—This is the clock speed (port speed) of the connection (local loop) to the Frame Relay cloud. It is the rate at which data travels into or out of the network.
- *DLCI*—This is a number that identifies the logical circuit between the source and the destination device. The Frame Relay switch maps the DLCIs between each pair of routers to create a PVC.

Figure 15-2 DLCI Value

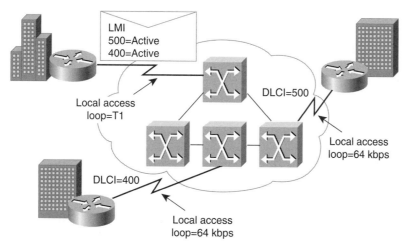

- *LMI*—This is a signaling standard between the customer premises equipment (CPE) device and the Frame Relay switch that is responsible for managing the connection and maintaining status between the devices. LMIs can include support for a keepalive mechanism, which verifies that data is flowing. Also includes support for a multicast mechanism, which can provide the network server with its local DLCI. Multicast addressing, which provides a few DLCIs to be used as multicast (multiple destination) addresses and the ability to give DLCIs global (whole Frame Relay network) significance, rather than just local significance (DLCIs used only on the local switch). A status mechanism is included which provides an ongoing status for the DLCIs that are known to the switch. There are several LMI types, and routers need to be told which LMI type is being used. Three types of LMIs are supported: cisco, ansi, and q933a.

- *Committed information rate (CIR)*—The CIR is the guaranteed rate, in bits per second, that the service provider commits to providing.

- *Committed burst (Bc)*—This is the maximum number of bits that the switch agrees to transfer during any committed rate measurement interval.

- *Excess burst (Be)*—This is the maximum number of uncommitted bits that the Frame Relay switch attempts to transfer beyond the CIR. Excess burst depends on the service offerings that the vendor has available, but it is typically limited to the port speed of the local access loop. This data (Be) generally is delivered with a lower probability than Bc. The network treats Be data as discard eligible.

- *Forward explicit congestion notification (FECN)*—When a Frame Relay switch recognizes congestion in the network, it sends an FECN packet to the destination device, indicating that congestion has occurred.

- *Backward explicit congestion notification (BECN)*—As shown in Figure 15-3, when a Frame Relay switch recognizes congestion in the network, it sends a BECN packet to the source router, instructing the router to reduce the rate at which it is sending packets. If the router receives BECNs during the current time interval, it decreases the transmit rate by 25%.

Figure 15-3 Frame Relay Switch Sending BECNs

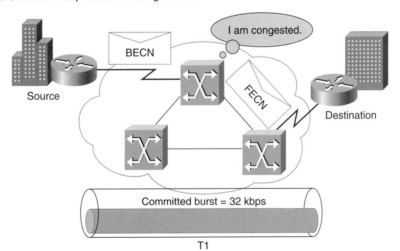

- Discard eligibility (DE) indicator—When the router detects network congestion, the Frame Relay switch drops packets with the DE bit set first. The DE bit is set on the oversubscribed traffic (that is, the traffic that was received after the CIR was met).

Frame Relay Operation

Frame Relay can be used as an interface to either a publicly available carrier-provided service or to a network of privately owned equipment. You deploy a public Frame Relay service by putting Frame Relay switching equipment in the central office (CO) of a telecommunications carrier. In this case, users get economic benefits from traffic-sensitive charging rates, and they do not have to spend the time and effort to administer and maintain the network equipment and service.

No standards for interconnecting equipment inside a Frame Relay network currently exist. Therefore, the support of Frame Relay interfaces does not necessarily dictate that the Frame Relay protocol is used between the network devices in the cloud. Thus, traditional circuit switching, packet switching, or a hybrid approach combining these technologies can be used, as shown in Figure 15-4.

Figure 15-4 Interconnecting Equipment

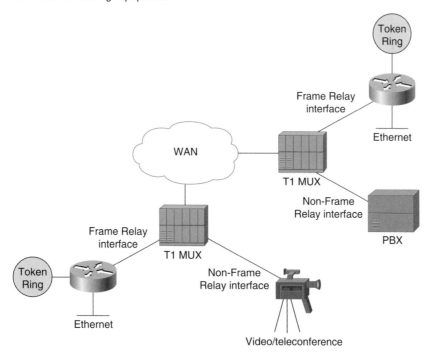

The lines that connect user devices to the network equipment can operate at a speed that is selected from a broad range of data rates. Speeds between 56 kbps and 2 Mbps are typical, although Frame Relay can support lower and higher speeds.

As an interface between user and network equipment, as shown in Figure 15-5, Frame Relay provides a means for multiplexing many logical data conversations (referred to as VCs) through a shared physical medium by assigning DLCIs to each pair of DTE devices.

Figure 15-5 Single Physical Connection

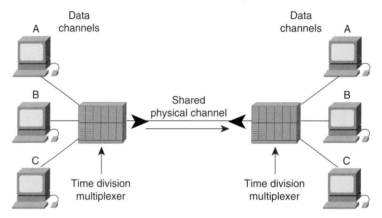

Frame Relay's multiplexing provides more flexible and efficient use of available bandwidth. Therefore, Frame Relay allows users to share bandwidth at a reduced cost. For example, say that you have a WAN using Frame Relay, and the Frame Relay is equivalent to a group of roads. The phone company usually owns and maintains the roads. You can choose to rent a road (or path) exclusively for your company (dedicated), or you can pay less to rent a path on shared roads. Of course, Frame Relay could also be run entirely over private networks; however, it is rarely used in this manner.

Frame Relay standards address PVCs that are administratively configured and managed in a Frame Relay network. Frame Relay PVCs are identified by DLCIs, as shown in Figure 15-6. They have local significance; that is, the values are not unique in the Frame Relay WAN. Two DTE devices that are connected by a VC might use a different DLCI value to refer to the same connection.

Figure 15-6 End Devices

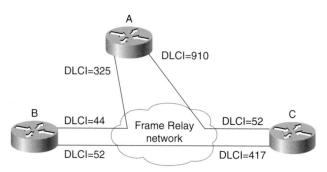

When Frame Relay provides a means for multiplexing many logical data conversations, the service provider's switching equipment first constructs a table mapping a DLCI value to outbound ports. When a frame is received, the switching device analyzes the connection identifier and delivers the frame to the associated outbound port. Finally, the complete path to the destination is established before the first frame is sent.

The Frame Relay frame format is shown in Figure 15-7. The flag fields indicate the beginning and end of the frame. Following the leading flag field are 2 bytes of address information. 10 bits of these 2 bytes make up the actual circuit ID (that is, the DLCI).

Figure 15-7 Flag Fields

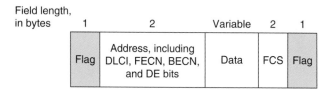

The following are the Frame Relay frame fields:

- **Flag**—Indicates the beginning and the end of the Frame Relay frame.
- **Address**—Indicates the length of the Address field. Although Frame Relay addresses are currently 2 bytes long, the address bits allow for the possible extension of address lengths in the future. The eighth bit of each byte of the address field is used to indicate the address. The address contains the following information:
  - **DLCI value**—Indicates the DLCI value. Consists of the first 10 bits of the Address field.

— **Congestion control**—The last 3 bits in the address field, which control the Frame Relay congestion notification mechanisms. These are the FECN, BECN, and DE bits.

- **Data**—Variable-length field that contains encapsulated upper-layer data.

- **FCS**—*Frame check sequence*, which is used to ensure the integrity of transmitted data.

For example, in Figure 15-8, assume two PVCs, one between Atlanta and Los Angeles, and one between San Jose and Pittsburgh. Los Angeles uses DLCI 22 to refer to its PVC with Atlanta, whereas Atlanta refers to the same PVC as DLCI 82. Similarly, San Jose uses DLCI 12 to refer to its PVC with Pittsburgh, and Pittsburgh uses DLCI 62. The network uses internal mechanisms to keep the two locally significant PVC identifiers distinct. Los Angeles and San Jose use different DLCIs, so the two identifiers are distinct without the actions of internal mechanisms.

Figure 15-8 Using DLCIs

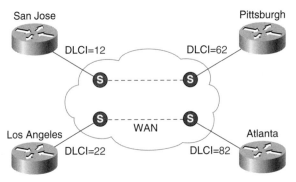

DLCI address space is limited to 10 bits. This creates a possibility of 1024 DLCI addresses. The LMI type that is used determines the usable portions of these addresses. The Cisco LMI type supports a range of DLCI addresses from DLCI 16-1007 for carrying user data. The remaining DLCI addresses are reserved for vendor implementation. This includes LMI messages and multicast addresses.

The number of interface descriptor blocks (IDBs) that your version of Cisco IOS supports limits the total number of interfaces and subinterfaces per system. An IDB is a portion of memory that holds information about the interface, such as counters, status of the interface, and so on. IOS maintains an IDB for each interface that is present on a platform and maintains an IDB for each subinterface. Higher-speed interfaces require more memory than lower-speed interfaces. Each platform contains different amounts of maximum IDBs, and these limits can change with each Cisco IOS release.

Frame Relay LMI

There was a major development in Frame Relay's history in 1990 when Cisco Systems, StrataCom, Northern Telecom, and Digital Equipment Corporation formed a group to focus on Frame Relay technology development and accelerate the introduction of interoperable Frame Relay products. This group developed a specification that conformed to the basic Frame Relay protocol, but it extended the specification with features that provided additional capabilities for complex internetworking environments. These Frame Relay extensions are referred to as LMI.

LMI Operations

The primary purposes of the LMI process are as follows:

- To determine the operational status of the various PVCs that the router knows about.
- To transmit keepalive packets to ensure that the PVC stays up and does not shut down due to inactivity, as shown in Figure 15-9.

Figure 15-9 LMI

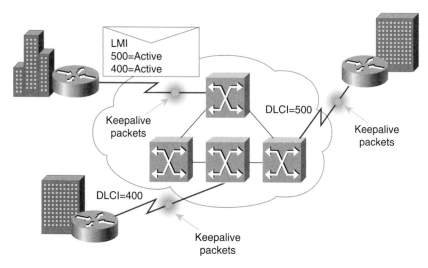

- To tell the router what PVCs are available.
- Three LMI types can be invoked by the router commands: **ansi, cisco,** and **q933a.**

The Frame Relay specification also includes the LMI procedures. LMI messages are sent in frames that are distinguished by LMI-specific DLCIs (defined in the consortium specification as DLCI = 1023). The LMI frame format is shown in Figure 15-10.

Figure 15-10 LMI Frames

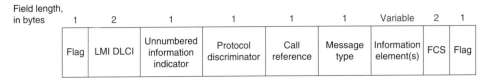

After the flag and LMI DLCI fields, the LMI frame contains 4 mandatory bytes. The first of the mandatory bytes (unnumbered information indicator) has the same format as the Link Access Procedure, Balanced (LAPB) unnumbered information (UI) frame indicator, with the poll/final bit set to zero. The next byte is referred to as the protocol discriminator, which is set to a value that indicates LMI. The third mandatory byte (call reference) is always filled with 0s.

The final mandatory byte is the message type field. Two message types have been defined: status-enquiry messages and status messages. Status messages respond to status-enquiry messages. Keepalives (messages that are sent through a connection to ensure that both sides will continue to regard the connection as active) and PVC status messages are examples of these messages and are the common LMI features that are expected to be a part of every implementation that conforms to the Frame Relay specification.

Together, status and status-enquiry messages help verify the integrity of logical and physical links. This information is critical in a routing environment because routing protocols make decisions based on link integrity.

Next is an information element (IE) field of a variable number of bytes. Following the message type field is some number of IEs. Each IE consists of a 1-byte IE identifier, an IE length field, and 1 or more bytes that contain actual data.

LMI Extensions

In addition to the basic Frame Relay protocol functions for transferring data, the Frame Relay specification includes LMI extensions that make supporting large, complex internetworks easier. Some LMI extensions are referred to as common and are expected to be implemented by everyone who adopts the specification. Other LMI functions are referred to as optional. A summary of the LMI extensions follows:

- **Virtual circuit status messages (common)**—Provide communication and synchronization between the network and the user device, periodically reporting the existence of new PVCs and the deletion of already existing PVCs, and generally providing information about PVC integrity. Virtual circuit status messages prevent the sending of data over PVCs that no longer exist.

- **Multicasting (optional)**—Allows a sender to transmit a single frame but have the network deliver it to multiple recipients. Thus, multicasting supports the efficient conveyance of routing protocol messages and Address Resolution Protocols (ARPs) that typically must be sent to many destinations simultaneously.

- **Global addressing (optional)**—Gives connection identifiers global rather than local significance, allowing them to be used to identify a specific interface to the Frame Relay network. Global addressing makes the Frame Relay network resemble a LAN in terms of addressing; therefore, ARPs perform over Frame Relay exactly as they do over a LAN.

- **Simple flow control (optional)**—Provides for an XON/XOFF flow control mechanism that applies to the entire Frame Relay interface. It is intended for devices whose higher layers cannot use the congestion notification bits and that need some level of flow control.

Global Addressing

In addition to the common LMI features, several optional LMI extensions are extremely useful in an internetworking environment. The first important optional LMI extension is global addressing. With this extension, the values that are inserted into the DLCI field of a frame are globally significant addresses of individual end user devices (such as routers). This is implemented as shown previously in Figure 15-8.

As noted earlier, the basic (nonextended) Frame Relay specification supports only values of the DLCI field that identify PVCs with local significance. In this case, there are no addresses that identify network interfaces, or nodes attached to these interfaces. Because these addresses do not exist, traditional address resolution and discovery techniques cannot discover them. This means that with normal Frame Relay addressing, static maps must be created to tell routers which DLCIs to use to find a remote device and its associated internetwork address.

In Figure 15-8, each interface has its own identifier. Suppose that Pittsburgh must send a frame to San Jose. The identifier for San Jose is 12, so Pittsburgh places the value 22 in the DLCI field and sends the frame into the Frame Relay network. At the exit point, the network changes the DLCI field contents to 62 to reflect the source node of the frame. Each router interface has a distinct value as its node identifier so that individual devices can be distinguished. This permits routing in complex environments. Global addressing provides significant benefits in a large, complex network. The Frame Relay network now appears to the routers on its periphery like any LAN.

Multicasting

Multicasting is another valuable optional LMI feature. Multicast groups are designated by a series of four reserved DLCI values (1019 to 1022). Frames that a device sends by using one of these reserved DLCIs are replicated by the network and sent to all exit points in the designated set. The multicasting extension also defines LMI messages that notify user devices of the addition, deletion, and presence of multicast groups. In networks that take advantage of dynamic routing, routing information must be exchanged among many routers. Routing messages can be sent efficiently by using frames with a multicast DLCI. This allows messages to be sent to specific groups of routers.

Inverse ARP

The Inverse ARP mechanism allows the router to automatically build the Frame Relay map that associates DLCIs and router network addresses, as shown in Figure 15-11. The router learns the DLCIs that are in use from the switch during the initial LMI exchange. The router then sends an Inverse ARP request to each DLCI for each protocol that is configured on the interface if the protocol is supported. The return information from the Inverse ARP is then used to build the Frame Relay map.

Figure 15-11 Inverse ARP

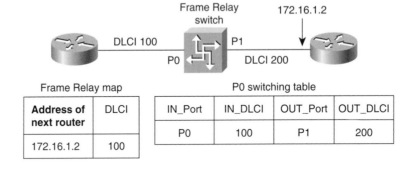

Stages of Inverse ARP and LMI Operation

LMI status messages combined with Inverse ARP messages allow a router to associate network layer and data link layer addresses.

When a router that is connected to a Frame Relay network is started, it sends an LMI status inquiry message to the network. The network replies with an LMI status message containing details of every VC that is configured on the access link.

Periodically, the router repeats the status inquiry, but subsequent responses include only status changes. After a set number of these abbreviated responses, the network sends a full status message.

If the router needs to map the VCs to network-level addresses (IP in most cases), it sends an Inverse ARP message on each VC. The Inverse ARP message includes the router's own network-level address so that the remote DTE (router) can also perform the mapping. The Inverse ARP reply allows the router to make the necessary mapping entries in its Address to DLCI map table. If several network layer protocols (such as IP and IPX) are supported on the link, Inverse ARP messages are sent for each.

Frame Relay Mapping

The router next-hop address that is determined from the routing table must be resolved to a Frame Relay DLCI, as shown in Figure 15-12. The resolution is done through a data structure called a Frame Relay map. The routing table is then used to supply the next-hop protocol address or the DLCI for outgoing traffic. This data structure can be statically configured in the router, or the Inverse ARP feature can be used for automatic setup of the map.

Figure 15-12 Responses to Inverse ARP Requests

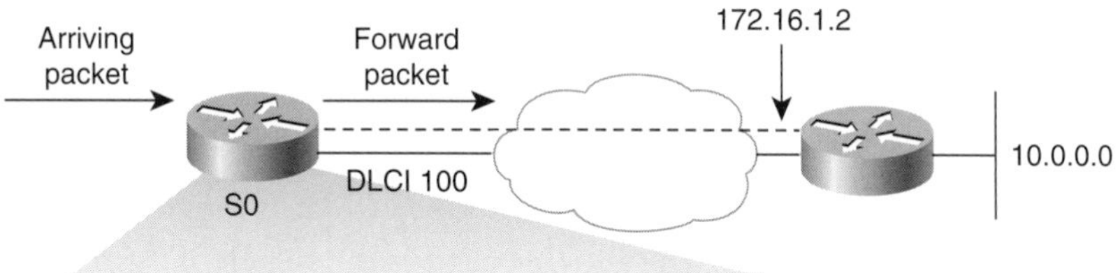

Routing table

Network	Address of next router	Interface
10.0.0.0	172.16.1.2	S0

Main memory

Frame Relay map

Address of next router	DLCI
172.16.1.2	100

Physical interface

Frame Relay Switching Tables

The Frame Relay switching table consists of four entries: two for incoming port and DLCI, and two for outgoing port and DLCI, as shown in Figure 15-13. The DLCI could, therefore, be remapped as it passes through each switch; the fact that the port reference can be changed is why the DLCI does not change even though the port reference might.

Figure 15-13 Frame Relay Switching Table

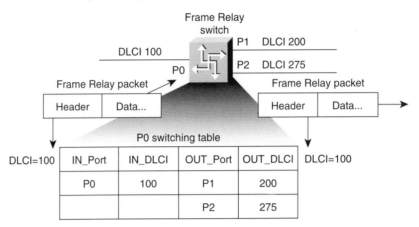

Frame Relay Operation Summary

Now that you have learned the basic Frame Relay operations, you can use the following steps, which are illustrated in Figures 13-14 and 13-15 to implement Frame Relay:

Step 1   Order Frame Relay service from a service provider or create a private Frame Relay cloud.

Step 2   Connect each router, either directly or through a channel service unit/digital service unit (CSU/DSU), to the Frame Relay switch.

Step 3   When the CPE router is enabled, it sends a Status Inquiry message to the Frame Relay switch. The message notifies the switch of the router's status and asks the switch for the connection status of the other remote routers.

Step 4   When the Frame Relay switch receives the request, it responds with a status message that includes the DLCIs of the remote routers to which the local router can send data.

Step 5   For each active DLCI, each router sends an Inverse ARP request packet, introducing itself and asking for each remote router to identify itself by replying with its network layer address.

Step 6   For every DLCI that the router learns about through an Inverse ARP message, a map entry is created in the router's Frame Relay map table. This includes the local DLCI, the remote router's network layer address, and the state of the connection. Note that the DLCI is the router's locally configured DLCI, not the DLCI that the remote router is using. Three possible connection states appear in the Frame Relay map table:

- **Active state**—Indicates that the connection is active and that routers can exchange data.

- **Inactive state**—Indicates that the local connection to Frame Relay switch is working, but the remote router's connection to Frame Relay switch is not working.

- **Deleted state**—Indicates that no LMI is being received from the Frame Relay switch or that no service between the CPE router and Frame Relay switch is occurring.

Step 7   Every 60 seconds, the routers exchange Inverse ARP messages.

Step 8   By default, every 10 seconds or so (this is configurable), the CPE router sends a keepalive message to the Frame Relay switch. The purpose of the keepalive message is to verify that the Frame Relay switch is still active.

Figure 15-14 Configuring the Routes of Remote Routers

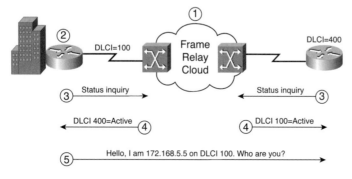

Figure 15-15 Changing the Status of Each DLCI

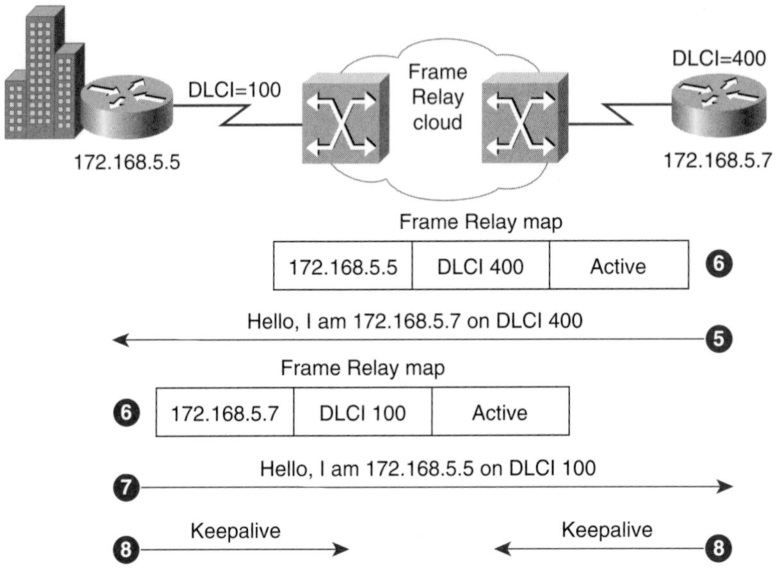

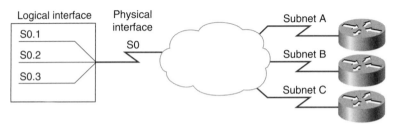

Frame Relay Subinterfaces

To enable the sending of complete routing updates in a Frame Relay network, you can configure the router with logically assigned interfaces called subinterfaces. Subinterfaces are logical subdivisions of a physical interface. In a subinterface configuration, each PVC can be configured as a point-to-point connection, which allows the subinterface to act as a dedicated line, as shown in Figure 15-16.

Figure 15-16 Routing Updates

Early implementation of Frame Relay required that a router (that is, a DTE device) have a WAN serial interface for every PVC, as shown in Figure 15-17. By logically dividing a single physical WAN serial interface into multiple virtual subinterfaces, the overall cost of implementing a Frame Relay network can be reduced. As shown in Figure 15-18, a single router interface can service many remote locations through individual unique subinterfaces.

Figure 15-17 Unique DLCI Numbers

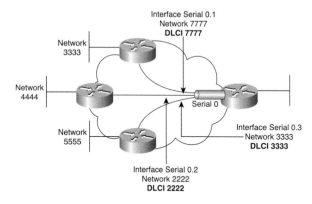

Figure 15-18 Split Horizon

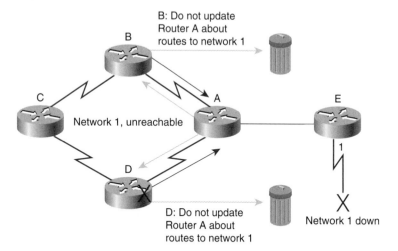

Split Horizon Routing Environments

In split horizon routing environments, routes that are learned on one subinterface can be advertised on another subinterface. Therefore, split horizon reduces routing loops by not allowing a routing update that is received on one physical interface to be advertised through the same physical interface, as shown in Figure 15-19. As a result, if a remote router sends an update to the headquarters router that is connecting multiple PVCs over a single physical interface, the headquarters router cannot advertise that route through the same physical interface to other remote routers, as shown in Figure 15-20.

Figure 15-19 Split Horizon Routers Updates

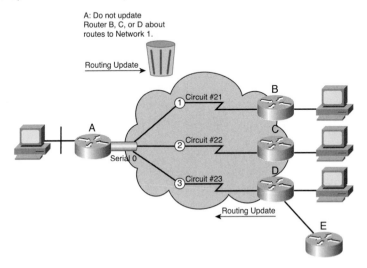

Figure 15-20 Reliable Connections

Point-to-Point Subinterface

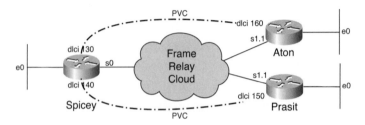

Multipoint Subinterfaces

Resolving Reachabilty Issues with Subinterfaces

You can configure subinterfaces to support the following connection types:

Point-to-point—A single subinterface is used to establish one PVC connection to another physical interface or subinterface on a remote router. In this case, the interfaces would be in the same subnet, and each interface would have a single DLCI. Each point-to-point connection is its own subnet. In this environment, broadcasts are not a problem because the routers are point-to-point and act like a leased line.

Multipoint—A single subinterface is used to establish multiple PVC connections to multiple physical interfaces or subinterfaces on remote routers. In this case, all the participating interfaces would be in the same subnet, and each interface would have its own local DLCI. In this environment, because the subinterface is acting like a regular Frame Relay network, routing updates are subject to split horizon.

Basic Frame Relay Configuration

A basic Frame Relay configuration assumes that you want to configure Frame Relay on one or more physical interfaces and that LMI and Inverse ARP are supported by the remote router(s). In this type of environment, the LMI notifies the router about the available DLCIs. Inverse ARP is enabled by default, so it does not appear in configuration output. Use the following steps to configure basic Frame Relay:

Step 1   Select the interface and go into interface configuration mode:

```
router(config)# interface serial 0
```

Step 2   Configure a network layer address, such as an IP address:

```
router(config-if)# ip address 192.168.38.40 255.255.255.0
```

Step 3   Select the encapsulation type used to encapsulate data traffic end-to-end:

```
router(config-if)# encapsulation frame-relay [cisco | ietf]
```

where **cisco** is the default, which you use if you are connecting to another Cisco router. If you are connecting to a non-Cisco router, you use **ietf**.

Step 4   If you are using Cisco IOS Release 11.1 or earlier, specify the LMI type that the Frame Relay switch uses:

```
router(config-if)# frame-relay lmi-type {ansi | cisco | q933i}
```

where **cisco** is the default. With IOS Release 11.2 or later, the LMI type is autosensed, so no configuration is needed.

Step 5   Configure the bandwidth for the link:

```
router(config-if)# bandwidth kilobits
```

This command affects routing operation by protocols such as IGRP because it is used to define the metric of the link.

Step 6   If Inverse ARP was disabled on the router, re-enable it. (Inverse ARP is on by default.)

```
router(config-if)# frame-relay inverse-arp [protocol] [dlci]
```

protocol is the supported protocols, including IP, IPX, AppleTalk, DECnet, VINES, and XNS. *dlci* is the DLCI on the local interface that you want to exchange Inverse ARP messages.

Now that the basic Frame Relay configuration steps have been outlined, use them to configure Frame Relay on the serial interface of a Cisco 1600 router.

Configuring the Serial Interface

Use the following steps shown to configure the serial interface for Frame Relay packet encapsulation:

Step 1   Enter configuration mode for the serial interface:

```
1600(config)# interface serial 0
```

Step 2   Set the encapsulation method on this interface to Frame Relay:

```
1600(config-if)# encapsulation frame-relay
```

Step 3   Enable the configuration changes on this interface:

```
1600(config-if)# no shutdown
```

Verifying the Serial Interface Configuration

You can verify your configuration to this point by confirming that a PVC is active on the Frame Relay line, as follows:

Step 1   Wait 60 seconds after entering the **encapsulation frame-relay** command.

Step 2   From privileged EXEC mode, enter the **show frame-relay pvc** command.

Step 3   Confirm that the PVC STATUS=ACTIVE message (shaded in the following example) appears in the command output:

```
1600# show frame-relay pvc
PVC Statistics for interface Serial0 (Frame Relay DTE)
DLCI = 17, DLCI USAGE = LOCAL, PVC STATUS = ACTIVE, INTERFACE =
  Serial0.1
input pkts 45 output pkts 52 in bytes 7764
```

```
out bytes 9958 dropped pkts 0 in FECN pkts 0
in BECN pkts 0 out FECN pkts 0 out BECN pkts 0
in DE pkts 0 out DE pkts 0
pvc create time 00:30:59, last time pvc status changed 00:19:21
```

Step 4   Record the number shown in the DLCI = message. (In this example, the number is 17.) You use this number to finish configuring the Frame Relay interface.

Step 5   If there is no output after you enter the command, use the **show interfaces serial** 0 command to determine whether the serial interface is active. The first line of the command output should be this:

```
Serial0 is up, line protocol is up
```

If the first line of the command output is Serial0 is up, line protocol is down, then you should confirm that the LMI type for the Frame Relay switch is correct by checking for the LMI type is CISCO message in the same command output.

Step 6   To continue configuration, re-enter global configuration mode.

Verifying Operation and Confirming Connectivity

After you configure Frame Relay, you can verify that the connections are active by using the **show** commands in Table 15-1.

Table 15-1 show Commands

Command	Description
show interfaces serial	Displays information about the multicast DLCI, the DLCIs used on the Frame Relay–configured serial interface, and the LMI DLCI used for the LMI.
show frame-relay pvc	Displays the status of each configured connection as well as traffic statistics. This command is also useful for viewing the number of BECN and FECN packets that the router receives.
show frame-relay map	Displays the network layer address and associated DLCI for each remote destination to which the local router is connected. This command is not enabled for point-to-point subinterfaces. It is useful for multipoint interfaces and subinterfaces only.
show frame-relay lmi	Displays LMI traffic statistics. For example, it shows the number of status messages exchanged between the local router and the Frame Relay switch.

Confirming That the Line Is Up

Complete the following steps to confirm that the line is up:

Step 1   From the privileged EXEC command mode, enter the **show interfaces serial 0** command, as follows:

```
1600# show interfaces serial 0
Serial0 is up, line protocol is up
Hardware is QUICC Serial
MTU 1500 bytes, BW 1544 Kbit,
    DLY 20000 usec, rely 255/255, load 1/255
Encapsulation FRAME-RELAY,
    loopback not set, keepalive set (10 sec)
LMI enq sent 163, LMI stat recvd 136,
    LMI upd recvd 0, DTE LMI up
LMI enq recvd 39, LMI stat sent 0, LMI upd sent 0
LMI DLCI 1023 LMI type is CISCO frame relay DTE
Broadcast queue 0/64, broadcasts sent/dropped 27/0,
    interface broadcasts 28
Last input 00:00:01, output 00:00:05, output hang never
Last clearing of "show interface" counters never
Input queue: 0/75/0 (size/max/drops);
    Total output drops: 0
Queuing strategy: weighted fair
Output queue: 0/64/0 (size/threshold/drops)
Conversations 0/1 (active/max active)
Reserved Conversations 0/0 (allocated/max allocated)
5 minute input rate 0 bits/sec, 0 packets/sec
5 minute output rate 0 bits/sec, 0 packets/sec
1813 packets input, 109641 bytes, 0 no buffer
Received 1576 broadcasts, 0 runts, 0 giants
13 input errors, 0 CRC, 13 frame, 0 overrun,
    0 ignored, 0 abort
1848 packets output, 117260 bytes, 0 underruns
0 output errors, 0 collisions, 32 interface resets
0 output buffer failures, 0 output buffers swapped out
29 carrier transitions
DCD=up DSR=up DTR=up RTS=up CTS=up
```

Step 2   Confirm that the following messages (shaded) appear in the command output:

- **Serial0 is up, line protocol is up**—The Frame Relay connection is active.

- **LMI enq sent 163, LMI stat recvd 136**—The connection is sending and receiving data. The number shown in your output will probably be different.

- **LMI type is CISCO**—The LMI type is configured correctly for the router.

Step 3   If the message does not appear in the command output, take the following steps:

- Confirm with the Frame Relay service provider that the LMI setting is correct for your line.
- Confirm that keepalives are set and that the router is receiving LMI updates.

Step 4   To continue configuration, re-enter global configuration mode.

Confirming the Frame Relay Maps

Complete the following steps to confirm the Frame Relay maps:

Step 1   From privileged EXEC mode, enter the **show frame-relay map** command. Confirm that the status defined, active message (shaded) appears for each serial subinterface:

```
1600# show frame-relay map
Serial0.1 (up): point-to-point dlci, dlci 17(0x11,0x410),
    broadcast,
status defined, active
```

Step 2   If the message does not appear, follow these steps:

- Confirm that the central-site router is connected and configured.
- Check with the Frame Relay carrier to verify that the line is operating correctly.

Step 3   To continue configuration, re-enter global configuration mode.

Confirming Connectivity to the Central Site Router

Complete the following steps to confirm connectivity to the central site (HQ) router:

Step 1   From privileged EXEC mode, enter the **ping** command, followed by the IP address of the central site router.

Step 2   Note the percentage in the Success rate... line (shaded):

```
1600# ping 192.168.38.40
Type escape sequence to abort.
Sending 5, 100-byte ICMP Echos to 192.168.38.40,
    timeout is 2 seconds:
!!!!!
Success rate is 100 percent (5/5),
    round-trip min/avg/max = 32/32/32 ms
1600#
```

If the success rate is 20% or greater, this verification step is successful.

Step 3   To continue configuration, re-enter global configuration mode.

Lab Activity Configuring Frame Relay

In this lab, a router is configured to make a successful connection to a local Frame Relay switch. An Adtran Atlas550 Frame Relay emulator is used to simulate the switch/Frame Relay cloud.

Lab Activity Configuring Frame Relay PVC

In this lab, two routers are configured back-to-back as a Frame Relay PVC. This is done manually, in the absence of a frame relay switch and LMI.

Configuring Subinterfaces

To configure subinterfaces on a physical interface, as shown in Figure 15-21, complete the following steps:

Step 1 Select the interface on which you want to create subinterfaces and get into interface configuration mode.

Step 2 Remove any network layer address that is assigned to the physical interface. If the physical interface has an address, the local subinterfaces will not receive frames.

Step 3 Configure Frame Relay encapsulation, as discussed in the section "Basic Frame Relay Configuration."

Step 4 Select the subinterface that you want to configure:

```
router(config-if)# interface serial number.subinterface-number
    {multipoint | point-to-point}
```

where *number.subinterface-number* is the subinterface number in the range 1 to 4,294,967,293. The interface number that precedes the period must match the interface number to which this subinterface belongs.

multipoint is used if you want the router to forward broadcasts and routing updates that it receives. Select this if you are routing IP and you want all routers in the same subnet, as shown in Figure 15-22.

point-to-point is used if you do not want the router to forward broadcasts or routing updates and if you want each pair of point-to-point routers to have its own subnet, as shown in Figure 15-23.

Figure 15-21 Point-to-Point Subinterfaces

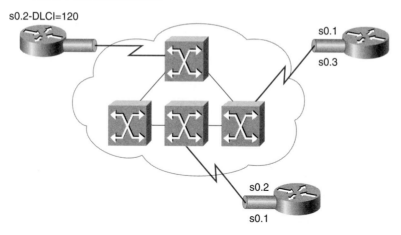

Figure 15-22 Multipoint Configuration

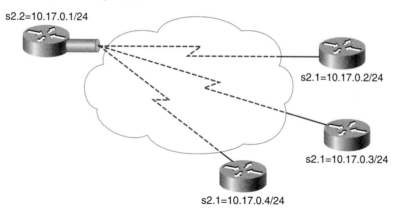

Figure 15-23 Subinterface Configuration

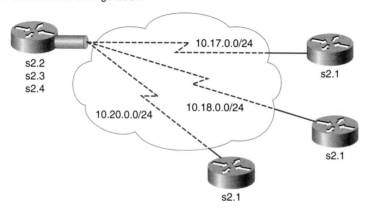

You are required to select either **multipoint** or **point-to-point**; there is no default.

Step 5   Configure a network layer address on the subinterface. If the subinterface is point-to-point and you are using IP, you can use the **ip unnumbered** command:

```
router(config-if)# ip unnumbered interface
```

If you use this command, it is recommended that the interface be the loopback interface. This is because the Frame Relay link does not work if this command is pointing to an interface that is not fully operational, and a loopback interface is not likely to fail.

NOTE

If you defined a sub-interface for point-to-point communication, you cannot reassign the same sub-interface number to be used for multipoint communication without first rebooting the router. Instead, you can avoid using that subinterface number and use a different subinterface number.

Step 6   If you configured the subinterface as multipoint or point-to-point, you must configure the local DLCI for the subinterface to distinguish it from the physical interface:

```
router(config-if)# frame-relay interface-dlci dlci-number
```

where *dlci-number* defines the local DLCI number that is being linked to the subinterface. This is the only way to link an LMI-derived PVC to a subinterface because LMI does not know about subinterfaces.

This command is required for all point-to-point subinterfaces. It is also required for multipoint subinterfaces for which Inverse ARP is enabled. This command is not required for multipoint subinterfaces that are configured with static route maps.

Do not use this command on physical interfaces.

Lab Activity   Configuring Frame Relay Subinterfaces

In this lab, you configure three routers in a full-mesh Frame Relay network by using an Adtran Atlas 550 Frame Relay emulator to simulate the switch/Frame Relay cloud.

Configuring Optional Commands

You can use the following commands when necessary for enhanced router operation:

```
router(config-if)#frame-relay map protocol protocol-address dlci
    [broadcast ][ietf | cisco | payload-compress packet-by-packet]
```

Table 15-2 describes the syntax of **frame-relay map**.

Table 15-2 frame-relay map Command Syntax

Parameter	Description
protocol	Defines the supported protocol, bridging, or logical link control.
protocol-address	Defines the network-layer address of the destination router interface.
dlci	Defines the local DLCI that is used to connect to the remote protocol address.
broadcast	(Optional) Forwards broadcasts to this address when multicast is not enabled. Use this if you want the router to forward routing updates.
ietf	**cisco**	(Optional) Select the Frame Relay encapsulation type for use. Use **ietf** only if the remote router is a non-Cisco router. Otherwise, use **cisco**.
payload-compress packet-by-packet	(Optional) Compresses Packet-by-packet payload using the Stacker method.

Normally, Inverse ARP is used to request the next-hop protocol address for a specific connection. Responses to Inverse ARP are entered in an address-to-DLCI map (that is, Frame Relay map) table, as shown in Figure 15-24. The table is then used to route outgoing traffic. When the remote router does not support Inverse ARP, when you are configuring OSPF over Frame Relay, or when you want to control broadcast traffic while using routing, you must define the address-to-DLCI table statically. The static entries are referred to as static maps.

With Frame Relay, you can increase or decrease the keepalive interval. You can extend or reduce the interval at which the router interface sends keepalive messages to the Frame Relay switch. The default is 10 seconds, and the following is the syntax:

```
router(config-if)# keepalive number
```

where *number* is the value, in seconds, that is usually 2 to 3 seconds faster (a shorter interval) than the setting of the Frame Relay switch to ensure proper synchronization.

Figure 15-24 Responses to Inverse ARP

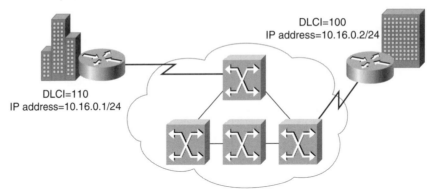

If an LMI type is not used in the network or when you are doing back-to-back testing between routers, you need to specify the DLCI for each local interface by using the following command:

```
router(config-if)# frame-relay local-dlci number
```

where *number* is the DLCI on the local interface to be used.

Summary

In this chapter, you learned the following:

- Frame Relay WAN technology provides a flexible method of connecting LANs over Frame Relay WAN links.
- Frame Relay provides a packet-switching data communication capability that is used across the interface between user devices (such as routers, bridges, and host machines) and network equipment (such as switching nodes).
- Frame Relay uses VCs to establish connections across the WAN.
- The main purposes of the LMI process are as follows:
  - Determine the operational status of the various PVCs that the router knows about
  - Transmit keepalive packets to ensure that the PVC stays up and does not shut down due to inactivity
  - Tell the router what PVCs are available
- The Inverse ARP mechanism allows the router to automatically build the Frame Relay map.

- The router next-hop address that is determined from the routing table must be resolved to a Frame Relay DLCI.

- Frame Relay can divide a single physical WAN interface into multiple subinterfaces.

- Split horizon reduces routing loops by not allowing a routing update that is received on one physical interface to be advertised through the same physical interface.

To supplement all that you have learned in this chapter, refer to the chapter-specific Videos, PhotoZooms, and e-Lab Activities on the CD-ROM that accompanies this book.

Key Terms

Bc (committed burst)   Negotiated tariff metric in Frame Relay internetworks. The maximum amount of data (in bits) that a Frame Relay internetwork is committed to accept and transmit at the CIR.

Be (excess burst)   Negotiated tariff metric in Frame Relay internetworks. The number of bits that a Frame Relay internetwork attempts to transmit after Bc is accommodated. Be data, in general, is delivered with a lower probability than Bc data because the network can mark Be data as DE.

BECN (backward explicit congestion notification)   A bit set by a Frame Relay network in frames traveling in the opposite direction of frames encountering a congested path. DTE devices that receive frames with the BECN bit set can request that higher-level protocols take flow control action as appropriate.

CIR (committed information rate)   The rate (in bits per second) at which the ingress access interface trunk interfaces, and egress access interface of a Frame Relay network transfer information to the destination Frame Relay end system under normal conditions. The rate is averaged over a minimum time interval Tc.

DLCI (data-link connection identifier)   A value that specifies a PVC or an SVC in a Frame Relay network. In the basic Frame Relay specification, DLCIs are locally significant. (That is, connected devices can use different values to specify the same connection.) In the LMI extended specification, DLCIs are globally significant. (That is, DLCIs specify individual end devices.)

FCS (Frame Check Sequence)   The standard 16-bit cyclic redundancy check (CRC) that is used for HDLC and Frame Relay frames. The FCS detects bit errors that occur in the bits of the frame between the opening flag and the FCS and is only effective in detecting errors in frames that are no larger than 4096 octets.

FECN (forward explicit congestion notification)   A bit set by a Frame Relay network to inform DTE devices that are receiving the frame that congestion was experienced in the path from source to destination. DTE devices that receive frames with the FECN bit set can request that higher-level protocols take flow-control action as appropriate.

Frame Relay   An industry-standard, switched data link layer protocol that handles multiple VCs using HDLC encapsulation between connected devices. Frame Relay is more efficient than X.25, the protocol for which it is generally considered a replacement.

local access rate   The clock speed (port speed) of the connection (local loop) to the Frame Relay cloud. It is the rate at which data travels into or out of the network.

LMI (Local Management Interface)   A set of enhancements to the basic Frame Relay specification. LMI includes support for a keepalive mechanism, which verifies that data is flowing; a multicast mechanism, which provides the network server with its local DLCI and the multicast DLCI; global addressing, which gives DLCIs global rather than local significance in Frame Relay networks; and a status mechanism, which provides an ongoing status report on the DLCIs known to the switch.

PVC (permanent virtual circuit)   A VC that is permanently established. PVCs save bandwidth associated with circuit establishment and teardown in situations where certain VCs must exist all the time.

public data network   A network that is operated either by a government (as in Europe) or by a private concern to provide computer communications to the public, usually for a fee. Public data networks enable small organizations to create a WAN without all the equipment costs of long-distance circuits.

Check Your Understanding

1. How does Frame Relay handle multiple conversations on the same physical connection?

    A. It duplexes the conversations.

    B. It multiplexes the circuits.

    C. It converts data to an ATM cell.

    D. Multiple conversations are not allowed.

2. Which of the following protocols does Frame Relay use for error correction?

    A. Physical and data link protocols.

    B. Upper-layer protocols.

    C. Lower-layer protocols.

    D. Frame Relay does not do error correction.

3. Which of the following does Frame Relay do to make its DLCIs global?

    A. It broadcasts them.

    B. It sends out unicasts.

    C. It sends out multicasts.

    D. DLCIs cannot become global.

4. Which of the following is the data rate at which the Frame Relay switch agrees to transfer data?

   A. Committed information rate

   B. Data transfer rate

   C. Timing rate

   D. Baud rate

5. Which of the following assigns DLCI numbers?

   A. The end user

   B. The network root

   C. A DLCI server

   D. The service provider

6. DLCI information is included in which of the following fields of the Frame Relay header?

   A. The Flag field

   B. The Address field

   C. The Data field

   D. The Checksum field

7. Which of the following does Frame Relay use to keep PVCs active?

   A. Point-to-point connections.

   B. Windows sockets.

   C. Keepalives.

   D. They become inactive.

8. How does Frame Relay use Inverse ARP requests?

   A. It maps IP addresses to MAC addresses.

   B. It maps MAC addresses to IP addresses.

   C. It maps MAC addresses to network addresses.

   D. It uses the IP address-to-DLCI mapping table.

9. Which of the following does Frame Relay use to determine the next hop?

   A. An ARP table

   B. A RIP routing table

   C. A Frame Relay map

   D. An IGRP routing table

10. For which of the following does Frame Relay use split horizon?

   A. To increase router updates.

   B. To prevent routing loops.

   C. To raise convergence times.

   D. Frame Relay does not use split horizon.

11. Frame Relay operates at which of the following layers?

   A. Layer 2

   B. Layer 3

   C. Layer 4

   D. Layer 1

12. Which of the following statements is correct?

   A. The purpose of DTE equipment is to provide clocking and switching services in a network.

   B. Proposals for the standardization of Frame Relay were initially presented to the Consultative Committee for International Telegraph and Telephone (CCITT).

   C. The older versions of Frame Relay are referred to collectively as the LMI.

   D. Switched VCs are permanent connections that are used in situations requiring only sporadic data transfer between DTE devices across Frame Relay.

13. Which command is used (at the config mode prompt) to enter the configuration mode for the serial interface for Frame Relay packet encapsulation?

   A. # configure terminal

   B. # encapsulation frame-relay

   C. # frame-relay interface dlci *number*

   D. # interface serial0

14. If a **show interface serial 0** command is executed and the message that appears is "Serial line is up, line protocol is up," what is the correct interpretation of the message?

   A. The connection is sending and receiving data.

   B. The LMI is configured correctly for the router.

   C. The Frame Relay connection is active.

   D. The central-site router is up and connected.

15. What does show interfaces serial do?

A. It displays information about the multicast DLCI, the DLCIs that are used on the Frame Relay-configured serial interface, and the LMI DLCI that is used for the LMI.

B. It displays the status of each configured connection and traffic statistics. This command is also useful for viewing the number of DECN and FECN packets that the router receives.

C. It displays the network layer address and associated DLCI for each remote destination to which the local router is connected.

D. It displays LMI traffic statistics. For example, it shows the number of status messages exchanged between the local router and the Frame Relay switch.

16. What are FECN and BECN?

A. Error-checking mechanisms

B. Congestion-notification mechanisms

C. Flow-control mechanisms

D. Keepalive mechanisms

17. Which of the following is true of Frame Relay VCs?

A. They require session establishment and teardown.

B. They are used only when data transfer is sporadic.

C. They provide permanent communication paths across Frame Relay networks.

D. They provide a logical, bidirectional communication path between network devices.

18. Why does Frame Relay implement a CRC?

A. To perform flow control across VCs

B. To perform error-checking functions

C. To manage address resolution functions

D. To manage BECN and FECN operation

19. Which of the following is *not* one of the Frame Relay LMI extensions?

A. Algorithmically generated MAC addresses

B. Multicast groups

C. Global addressing

D. Virtual circuit status messages

Objectives

After reading this chapter, you will be able to

- Explain important aspects of Windows, UNIX, and Linux workstations
- Explain the functions of network servers
- Understand network operating systems (NOSs)

Chapter 16

Introduction to Network Administration

The term "network administration" covers many aspects and details of the many jobs and responsibilities that are involved when managing a computer network. This chapter focuses on some of the tasks that are involved in managing the desktop/NOSs and provides an overview of some of the popular server options to deploy to manage the enterprise's network resources. This chapter covers the advantages and disadvantages of the available hardware and software options as well as recommendations for which environments these different options work best in. This chapter also provides information on how you can use the Open System Interconnection (OSI) model and Simple Network Management Protocol (SNMP) to help manage the network.

Be sure to look at this chapter's associated e-Lab Activities, Videos, and PhotoZooms that you will find on the CD-ROM that accompanies this book. These CD-ROM elements are designed to supplement the material and reinforce the concepts that are introduced in this chapter.

Overview of Desktop and Server Operating Systems

The first personal computers (PCs) were designed as standalone desktop systems. The operating system software allowed one user at a time to access files and system resources. The user had physical access to the PC. As PC-based computer networks gained popularity in the workplace, software companies developed specialized NOSs. Developers designed NOSs to provide file security, user privileges, and resource sharing among multiple users. The explosive growth of the Internet compelled developers to build the NOSs of today around Internet-related technologies and services, such as the World Wide Web.

Within a decade, networking has become of central importance to desktop computing. The distinction between modern desktop operating systems, now loaded with networking features and services, and their NOS counterparts has blurred. Now, most popular operating systems, such as Microsoft Windows 2000 and Linux, are found on high-powered network servers and on the desktops of end users.

Workstations

A workstation is a client computer that is used to run applications and is connected to a server from which it obtains data shared with other computers. A server is a computer that runs an NOS. A workstation uses special software such as a network shell program to do the following:

- Intercept user data and application commands.
- Decide if the command is for the local operating system or for the NOS.
- Direct the command to the local operating system or to the network interface card for processing and transmission onto the network.
- Deliver transmissions from the network to the application that is running on the workstation.

Windows NT, Windows 2000, and Windows XP Professional operating systems can run on a personal computer. Any system that is running one of these is referred to as either a workstation, shown in Figure 16-1, or a server, shown in Figure 16-2. A PC is a system that is running any of the other popular operating systems that are designed for the PC, such as DOS, Windows 95, Windows 98, Windows ME, or Windows XP Home.

Figure 16-1 Typical Workstation

Figure 16-2 Typical Server

UNIX or Linux can serve as a desktop operating system, but they are most commonly found on high-end computers. These workstations are employed in engineering and scientific applications, which require dedicated high-performance computers. Some of the specific applications that are frequently run on UNIX workstations are included in the following list:

- Computer-aided design (CAD)
- Electronic circuit design
- Weather data analysis
- Computer graphics animation
- Telecommunications equipment management

Most current desktop operating systems include networking capabilities and support multiuser access. For this reason, it is becoming more common to classify computers and operating systems based on the types of applications they run. This classification is based on the role or function that the computer plays, such as workstation or server. Typical desktop or low-end workstation applications might include word processing, spreadsheets, and financial management. On high-end workstations, the applications might include graphical design or equipment management and others, as listed previously.

A diskless workstation is a special class of computer that is designed to run on a network. As the name implies, a diskless workstation has no disk drives but does have a monitor, keyboard, memory, booting instructions in ROM, and a network interface card. The software that is used to establish a network connection is loaded from the bootable ROM chip that is located on the network interface card.

Because a diskless workstation does not have disk drives, you cannot upload data from the workstation or download anything to it. A diskless workstation cannot pass a virus onto the network, nor can it be used to take data from the network by copying this information to a disk drive. As a result, diskless workstations offer greater security than ordinary workstations. For this reason, such workstations are used in networks where security is paramount.

Laptops can also serve as workstations on a LAN and can be connected through a docking station, external LAN adapter, or a PCMCIA card. A docking station, shown in Figure 16-3, is an add-on device that turns a laptop into a desktop.

Figure 16-3 Docking Station

Servers

In an NOS environment, many client systems access and share the resources of one or more servers. Desktop client systems are equipped with their own memory and peripheral devices, such as a keyboard, monitor, and disk drive. The server systems must be equipped to support multiple concurrent users and multiple tasks as clients make demands on the server for remote resources.

NOSs have additional network management tools and features that are designed to support access by several simultaneous users. On all but the smallest networks, NOSs are installed on powerful servers. Many users, known as clients, share these servers. Servers usually have high-capacity/high-speed disk drives, large amounts of RAM, high-speed network interface cards, and in some cases, multiple central processing units (CPUs). These servers are typically configured to use the Internet family of protocols, Transmission Control Protocol/Internet Protocol (TCP/IP), and offer one or more TCP/IP services.

Servers that run NOSs are also used to authenticate users and provide access to shared resources, as shown in Figure 16-4. These servers are designed to handle requests from many clients simultaneously. Before a client can access the server resources, the client must be identified and be authorized to use the resource. You do this by assigning each client an account name and password. The account name and password are then verified by an authentication service acting as a sentry to guard access to the network. By centralizing user accounts, security, and access control, server-based networks simplify the work of network administration.

Figure 16-4 Sharing Resources

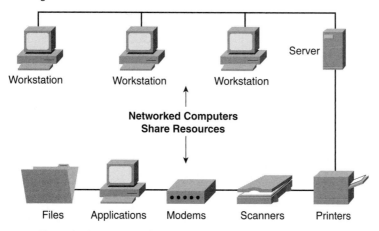

Networked computers share data, software and hardware resources.

Servers are typically larger systems with additional memory to support multiple tasks that are all active, or resident, in memory at the same time. Additional disk space is required on servers to hold shared files and to function as an extension to the internal memory on the system. Also, servers typically require extra expansion slots on their system boards to connect shared devices, such as printers and multiple network interfaces.

Another feature of systems that are capable of acting as servers is the processing power. Ordinarily, computers have a single CPU, which executes the instructions that make up a given task or process. To work efficiently and deliver fast responses to client requests, an NOS server requires a powerful CPU to execute its tasks or programs. Single-processor systems that have one CPU can meet the needs of most servers if they have the necessary speed. To achieve higher execution speeds, some systems are equipped with more than one processor. Such systems are called multiprocessor systems. They are capable of executing multiple tasks in parallel by assigning each task to a different processor. The aggregate amount of work that the server can perform in a given time is greatly enhanced in multiprocessor systems.

Because servers function as central repositories of resources that are vital to the operation of client systems, as shown in Figure 16-5, the servers must not only be efficient but also be robust. The term "robust" indicates that the server systems are able to function effectively under heavy loads. It also means that the systems are able to survive the failure of one or more processes or components without experiencing a general system failure. This objective is met by building redundancy into server systems. Redundancy is the inclusion of additional hardware components that can take over if other components fail. Redundancy is a feature of fault-tolerant systems that are designed to survive failures and even be repaired without interruption while they are up and running. Because an NOS depends on the continuous operation of its server, the extra hardware components justify the additional expense.

Server applications and functions include web services using Hypertext Transfer Protocol (HTTP), file transfer services using File Transfer Protocol (FTP), and host identification services using Domain Name System (DNS). Standard e-mail protocols that network servers support include Simple Mail Transfer Protocol (SMTP), Post Office Protocol (POP), and Internet Message Access Protocol (IMAP). File-sharing protocols include Sun Network File System (NFS) and Microsoft Server Message Block (SMB).

Network servers also frequently provide print services. A server can also provide Dynamic Host Configuration Protocol (DHCP), which automatically allocates Internet Protocol (IP) addresses to client computers. In addition to running services for the clients on the network, servers can be set to act as a basic firewall for the network. This is accomplished by using proxy or network address translation (NAT), both of which hide internal private network addresses from the Internet. Server applications such as these are not normally implemented on a LAN workstation.

Figure 16-5 Servers Support Several Client Systems

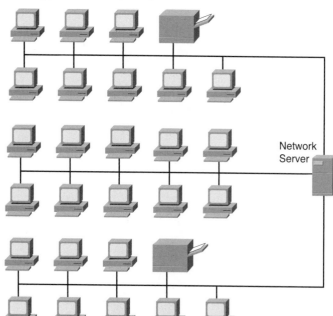

Network
Server

Multiple users and devices can be managed by a network server.

One server that is running an NOS might work well when serving only a handful of clients. However, most organizations find that they must deploy several servers to achieve acceptable performance, as shown in Figure 16-6. A typical design separates services so that multiple servers are responsible for e-mail, another server is responsible for file sharing, and a third server is responsible for FTP.

The concentration of network resources such as files, printers, and applications on servers, shown in Figure 16-7, also makes the data they generate easier to back up and maintain. Rather than having these resources spread around on individual machines, they can be located on specialized, dedicated servers for easier access and backup.

Figure 16-6 Client-Server Environment

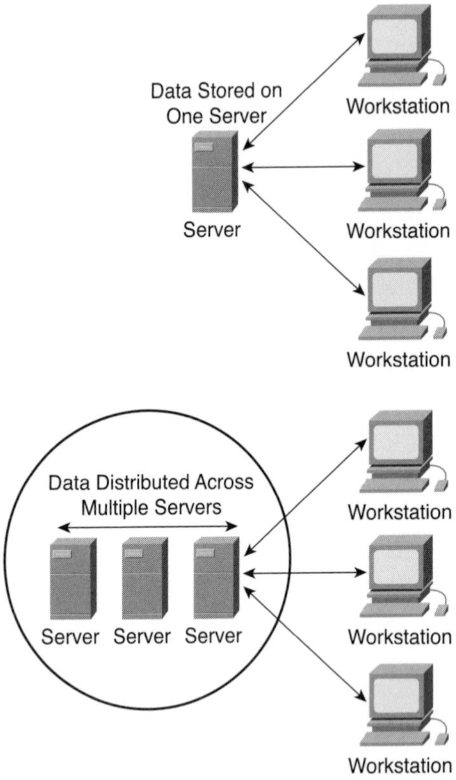

Data can be located on one server or located across a number of servers.

Client/Server Relationship

The client/server computing model distributes processing over multiple computers. Distributed processing enables access to remote systems for the purpose of sharing information and network resources. In a client/server environment, the client and server share or distribute processing responsibilities. Most NOSs are designed around the client/server model to provide network services to users. A computer on a network can be referred to as a host, a workstation, a client, or a server. A computer that is running TCP/IP, whether it is a workstation or a server, is considered a host computer. The following list describes some of the main points that are involved in a client-server relationship:

- The local host is the machine on which the user currently is working.
- A remote host is a system that a user is accessing from another system.
- A server provides resources to one or more clients by means of a network.
- A client is a machine that uses the services from one or more servers on a network.

Figure 16-7 Server Farm

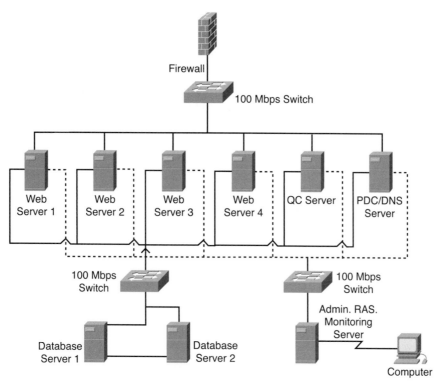

A simple example of a client/server relationship is an FTP session. FTP is a basic industry standard method of transferring a file from one computer to another. For the client to transfer a file to or from the server, the server must be running the FTP daemon or service. In this case, the client requests the file to be transferred. The server provides the services that are necessary to receive or send the file, as shown in Figure 16-8.

Figure 16-8 Client-Server Interaction

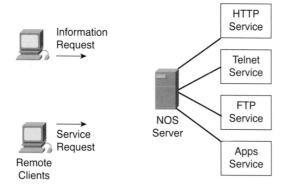

The Internet is also a good example of a distributed processing client/server computing relationship. The client or front end typically handles user presentation functions such as screen formatting, input forms, and data editing. This is done with a browser such as Netscape or Internet Explorer. Web browsers send requests to web servers. When the browser requests data from the server, the server responds, and the browser program receives a reply from the web server. The browser then displays the HTTP data it received in its window. The server or back end handles the client's requests for web pages and provides HTTP or World Wide Web services.

Another example of a client/server relationship is a database server and a data entry or query client in a local-area network (LAN). The client or front end might be running an application that is written in the C or Java language, and the server or back end could be running Oracle or other database management software. In this case, the client also would handle formatting and presentation tasks for the user. The server would provide database storage and data retrieval services for the user.

In a typical file server environment, the client might have to retrieve large portions of the database files to process the files locally. This retrieval of the database files can cause excess network traffic. With the client/server model, the client presents a request to the server, and the server database engine might process 100,000 records and pass only a few back to the client to satisfy the request. Servers are typically much more powerful than client computers and are better suited to processing large amounts of data. With client/server computing, the large database is stored and the processing takes place on the server. The client must deal only with creating the query. A relatively small amount of data or results might be passed across the network. This satisfies the client's query and results in less usage of network bandwidth.

The distribution of functions in client/server networks brings substantial advantages but also incurs some costs. Although the aggregation of resources on server systems brings greater security, simpler access, and coordinated control, the server introduces a single point of failure into the network. Without an operational server, the network cannot function. In addition, servers require trained expert staff to administer and maintain them, which increases the expense of running the network. Server systems require additional hardware and specialized software that adds substantially to the cost.

NOSs

A computer operating system is the software foundation on which computer applications and services run on a workstation. Similarly, an NOS enables communication between multiple devices and the sharing of resources across a network. An NOS is, generally, an operating system that runs on a network server, such as a UNIX server, Microsoft Windows NT server, or Windows 2000 server. Table 16-1 shows some of the different operating systems that these various companies offer.

Table 16-1 Available Network Operating Systems

Novell	UNIX	Windows	Linux
NetWare	HP-UX	NT	Red Hat
IntraNetWare	Sun Solaris	2000 Server	SCO
GroupWise	BSD	.NET Server	SuSE
	SCO		Debian
	AIX		Mandrake
			Xandros

The function of an operating system on a workstation is to control the computer hardware, program execution environment, and user interface. The operating system performs these functions for a single user or a number of users who share the machine serially rather than concurrently. An administrator can set up accounts for more than one user, but multiple users cannot log on to the system at the same time.

In contrast, NOSs distribute their functions over several networked computers. An NOS depends on the native operating system in each computer. The NOS then adds functions that allow access to shared resources by multiple users concurrently.

Workstations function as clients in an NOS environment. By using the functions of the workstations' native operating system, the user can access resources that are local to the workstation. These include applications, files, and devices that are directly attached, such as printers. When a workstation becomes a client in an NOS environment, additional specialized software enables the local user to access nonlocal or remote resources as if these resources were a part of the local system. The NOS enhances the reach of the client workstation by making remote services available as extensions of the local native operating system.

Although several users can have accounts on a workstation, only a single account is active on the system at any given time. In contrast, an NOS supports multiple user accounts at the same time and enables concurrent access to shared resources by multiple clients. Servers must support multiple users and act as repositories of resources that many clients share. Servers require specialized software and additional hardware.

NOS computers take on specialized roles to accomplish concurrent access to shared resources. Client systems contain specialized software that allows them to request shared resources that are controlled by server systems responding to a client request.

A system that is capable of operating as an NOS server must be able to support multiple users concurrently. The network administrator creates an account for each user, allowing the user to connect to and log into the server system. The user account on the server enables the server to authenticate that user and to allocate the resources that the user is allowed to access. Systems that provide this capability are called multiuser systems. UNIX, Linux, and Windows NT/Windows 2000/Windows XP support this multiuser capability.

An NOS server is a multitasking system. Internally, the operating system must be capable of executing multiple tasks or processes at the same time. Server operating systems accomplish this with scheduling software that is built into the execution environment. The scheduling software allocates internal processor time, memory, and other elements of the system to different tasks in a way that allows them to share the system's resources. Each user on the multiuser system is supported by a separate task or process internally on the server. These internal tasks are created dynamically as users connect to the system and are deleted when users disconnect.

The main features to consider when selecting an NOS include performance, management and monitoring tools, security, scalability, and robustness/fault tolerance. The following section briefly defines each of these features.

Performance

An NOS must perform well at reading/writing files across the network between clients and servers. It must be able to sustain fast performance under heavy loads when many, perhaps hundreds, of clients are making requests. An NOS must respond to client requests for access to server databases, such as a transaction request to extract records from a database that is housed in the NOS server system. Consistent performance under heavy demand is an important benchmark for an NOS.

Management and Monitoring Tools

The management interface on the NOS server provides the tools for server monitoring, client administration, file and print management, and disk storage management. The management interface provides tools for the installation of new services and the configuration of those services. In addition, servers require regular monitoring and adjustment.

Security

An NOS must protect the shared resources that are under its control. Security includes authenticating user access to services to prevent unauthorized access to the network resources. Security also performs encryption for the protection of information as it travels between clients and servers.

Scalability

Scalability is the ability of the NOS to grow without degradation in performance. The NOS must be capable of sustaining its performance as new users join the network and new servers are added to support them.

Robustness/Fault Tolerance

A measure of robustness is the ability to deliver NOS services consistently under heavy load and to sustain its services if components or processes fail. Using redundant disk devices and balancing the workload across multiple servers can improve NOS robustness.

Windows NT, Windows 2000, and Windows .NET

The following section discusses the various NOSs that Microsoft offers. Windows NT Workstation was the first Microsoft desktop operating system that was aimed at the corporate market. Windows NT 4 has a user interface that is similar to the one in Windows 95 and was designed to provide an environment for mission-critical business that would be more stable than the Microsoft consumer operating systems.

Windows 2000 Operating Systems

Windows 2000 Professional is a more recent Microsoft operating system for the corporate desktop. Like the Windows 2000 Server products, Windows 2000 is based on the NT kernel and includes many enhanced features. For example, Windows 2000 Professional provides a high level of security and stability for mission-critical tasks.

Windows 2000 supports plug-and-play technology. It can be installed on hard disks that use FAT32, and it includes file encryption for securing data on the hard disk. Plug-and-play technology is a useful tool that allows an administrator to quickly and easily add components to the system. The operating system automatically recognizes and installs the drivers for the device. Essentially, after the component is "plugged" into the system, it "plays" automatically without additional configuration from the administrator. Previously, when you added a new component, you had to install drivers and configure the device manually. Windows 2000 comes with a huge database of drivers for common plug-and-play devices.

Other advantages of Windows 2000 Professional as a desktop operating system and network client include the following:

- It offers better support for mobile users through advanced power management (APM) and Advanced Configuration and Power Interface (ACPI). Windows NT does not support ACPI.

- It provides for more secure Virtual Private Networking (VPN) with the Layer 2 Tunneling Protocol (L2TP) and IP Security (IPSec). Earlier versions of Windows supported only the Point-to-Point Tunneling Protocol (PPTP) for VPNs.

- The offline folders feature enables users to copy and synchronize documents from the network to the local system so that they can be accessed when the computer is not connected to the network.

- The Internet Printing Protocol (IPP) enables users to print to a uniform resource locator (URL) and manage printers through a web browser interface.

- Built-in disk defragmenters and other tools and utilities help users maintain and manage the operating system. Users have to purchase these separately from third parties for Windows NT.

- It supports Kerberos security (developing standard for authenticating network users) and the features of a Windows 2000 domain as an Active Directory client.

- It offers easier and more effective Account administration in Windows 2000.

Administrative tasks in Windows 2000 use a common framework: the Microsoft Management Console (MMC). This tool uses snap-ins, which are modules that contain the tools for specific administrative functions. Users and groups are created and managed with the Active Directory Users (ADUs) and Computers MMC snap-in. You can access the MMC by choosing **Start > Programs > Administrative Tools > Active Directory Users and Computers**. Windows 2000, unlike Windows NT 4.0, enables objects such as users and resources to be placed into container objects called organizational units (OUs). Administrative authority over each OU can be delegated to a user or group. This feature allows more specific control than was possible with Windows NT 4.0.

Windows 2000 and .NET Server Operating Systems

The Windows 2000 and .NET operating systems include Windows 2000 Server, Windows 2000 Advanced Server, and most recently Windows .NET Server. The specific needs of the network determine the best version of Windows 2000 for the installation.

Windows 2000 Server

Windows 2000 Server is an ideal option for small- to medium-sized networks and includes many new server-specific functions. Windows 2000 Server has a multitude of server functions including file, print, and web server services, as well as application server services. What separates Windows 2000 Server from previous releases of Microsoft's Server operating systems is a complete set of infrastructure services based on Active Directory services. Active Directory is fully integrated with Windows 2000 Server and serves as a centralized point of management of users, groups, security services, and network resources. Many network administrators who are familiar with Novell might recognize the similarity of Active Directory to Novell Directory Services. Windows 2000 Server has the capability to support four-way Symmetric Multiprocessing (SMP) systems and allows up to 4 gigabytes of physical memory. For this reason, Windows 2000 Server is intended for use in small- to medium-sized environments. Other enhancements that come with Windows 2000 Server are built-in support for the major network protocols that are in use throughout networks today, such as TCP/IP and Internetwork Packet Exchange (IPX)/Sequenced Packet Exchange (SPX).

Windows 2000 Advanced Server

Windows 2000 Server and Windows 2000 Advanced Server are the same except that Advanced Server provides hardware and software support that a system administrator needs in an enterprise-sized network. Advanced Server is a more powerful, departmental, and application server operating system that includes all the functions of Windows 2000 Server and adds the advanced high availability and improved scalability that are required for larger networks. Windows 2000 Advanced Server supports eight-way SMP, which would be ideal for database-intensive work. Advanced Server also provides support for higher-end hardware supporting an *enterprise network*. For example, Advanced Server provides support for more than 4 GB of physical memory.

Windows .NET Server

Microsoft has developed Windows .NET Server with the ability to provide a secure and reliable system to run enterprise-level web and FTP sites to compete with the Linux and UNIX Server operating systems. However, Windows .NET Server does provide unique features. For example, with the growing emergence of e-commerce, web-based companies and companies that are expanding their services to the Internet, there is a need for a server operating system that is capable of providing secure and reliable web and FTP services. Windows .NET Server, which is built on the Windows 2000 Server kernel, is specifically tailored to provide these types of services. Windows .NET Server provides XML Web Services to companies that run medium- to high-volume web traffic. This feature is designed to allow companies to run all their software and services straight through their servers while the end user desktop systems act as nothing more than a "dumb-terminal" which uses all the software and services straight from the server via an Internet connection and integration with the companies intranet or Internet. This feature is supposed to enhance security and reliability. The .NET Server provides support for companies that are just getting started in this new generation of business as well as businesses that have been providing Internet-based business solutions for some time.

UNIX and Linux

UNIX and Linux server operating systems, although similar, have some distinct differences. The following section outlines some of the different versions of both UNIX and Linux and provides examples of which environments each one might be better suited for. The specific needs of the network determine the best version of UNIX or Linux for the installation.

Origins of UNIX

UNIX is the name of a group of operating systems that trace their origins back to 1969 at Bell Labs. Since its inception, UNIX was designed to support multiple users and multitasking. UNIX was also one of the first operating systems to include support for Internet networking protocols. The history of UNIX, which now spans more than 30 years, is complicated because many companies and organizations have contributed to its development.

UNIX was first written in assembly language, a primitive set of instructions that control the internal instructions of the computer. However, UNIX could only run on a specific computer. In 1971, Dennis Ritchie created the C language. In 1973, Ritchie and fellow Bell Labs programmer Ken Thompson rewrote the UNIX system programs in C language. Because C is a higher-level language, UNIX could be moved (or ported) to another computer with far less programming effort. The decision to develop this portable operating system proved to be the key to the success of UNIX. During the 1970s, UNIX evolved through the development work of programmers at Bell Labs and several universities, notably the University of California, at Berkeley.

When UNIX first started to be marketed commercially in the 1980s, it was used to run powerful network servers, not desktop computers. Today, there are dozens of different versions of UNIX, including the following:

- HP-UX (Hewlett Packard's UNIX)
- Berkeley Software Design, Inc., (BSD UNIX, which has spawned derivatives such as FreeBSD)
- Santa Cruz Operation (SCO) UNIX
- Sun Solaris
- AIX (IBM's UNIX)

In general, UNIX in its various forms continues to advance its position as the reliable, secure operating system of choice for mission-critical applications that are crucial to the operation of a business or other organization. UNIX is also tightly integrated with TCP/IP. TCP/IP basically grew out of UNIX because of the need for LAN and wide-area network (WAN) communications.

The Sun Microsystems Solaris Operating Environment and its core operating system, SunOS, is a high-performance, versatile, 64-bit implementation of UNIX. Solaris runs on a wide variety of computers, from Intel-based personal computers to powerful mainframes and supercomputers. Solaris is currently the most widely used version of UNIX in the world for large networks and Internet websites. Sun is also the developer of the "Write Once, Run Anywhere" Java technology.

Despite the popularity of Microsoft Windows on corporate LANs, much of the Internet runs on powerful UNIX systems. Although UNIX is usually associated with expensive hardware and is considered "user unfriendly," recent developments, including the creation of Linux, have changed that image.

Origins of Linux

In 1991, a Finnish student named Linus Torvalds began work on an operating system for an Intel 80386-based computer. Frustrated with the state of desktop operating systems such as DOS and the expense and licensing issues associated with commercial UNIX, Torvalds set out to develop an operating system that was "UNIX-like" in its operation but used software code that was open and completely free.

Although it was not his original intention, Torvalds' work led to a worldwide collaborative effort to develop Linux, an open-source operating system that looks and feels like UNIX. By the late 1990s, Linux had become a viable alternative to UNIX on servers and Windows on the desktop. The popularity of Linux on desktop PCs has also contributed to interest in using UNIX distributions, such as FreeBSD and Sun Solaris, on the desktop. Versions of Linux can now run on almost any 32-bit processor, including the Intel 80x86, Motorola 68000, Alpha, and PowerPC chips.

As with UNIX, Linux has numerous versions. Some are free downloads from the web, and others are commercially distributed. The following are a few of the most popular Linux versions:

- RedHat Linux, distributed by RedHat Software
- SCOLinux, distributed by SCO
- Xandros Linux
- Slackware

- Debian GNU/Linux
- SuSE Linux

Linux is one of the most powerful and reliable operating systems in the world. Because of this, Linux has already made inroads as a platform for power users and in the enterprise server arena. Linux is less often deployed as a corporate desktop operating system. Although graphical user interfaces (GUIs) are available to make Linux user friendly, most beginning users find Linux more difficult to use than MacOS or Windows. Currently, many companies (such as RedHat, SuSE, SCO, and Xandros) are striving to make Linux a viable operating system for the desktop.

Application support must be considered when Linux is implemented on a desktop system. The number of business productivity applications is limited as compared to Windows. However, some vendors provide Windows emulation software (such as WABI and WINE) that enables many Windows applications to run on Linux. Additionally, companies such as Corel are making Linux versions of their office suites and other popular software packages.

Networking with Linux

Recent distributions of Linux have networking components built in for connecting to a LAN, establishing a dial-up connection to the Internet or other remote network. In fact, TCP/IP is integrated into the Linux kernel instead of being implemented as a separate subsystem.

Some advantages of Linux as a desktop operating system and network client include the following:

- It is a true 32-bit operating system.
- It supports preemptive multitasking and virtual memory.
- The code is open source and available for anyone to enhance and improve.
- Linux is available at no expense under the GNU General Public License (GPL), as are other versions of UNIX such as FreeBSD and NetBSD. Linux is open source software, which means that the source code is publicly available and can be modified to suit specific needs. Linux also can be distributed freely among users. This concept is the opposite of commercial software, where the source code is not publicly available and each user must pay a license fee. Commercial software is based on copyright laws, which seek to limit what the user can do with respect to source code and distribution. Linux can be downloaded at no cost from various websites.

Linux Distributions

Many for-profit companies and non-profit organizations make Linux available along with various combinations of applications, utilities, and other software. These combinations of the operating system and software are called distributions. As an example, Red Hat, Inc. bundles the Linux CDs, source code, and manuals along with a collection of applications and other products for a modest fee. These additional products include an office suite, a choice of graphical desktops, web server software, and so on. A level of customer support also is provided. Red Hat includes the Sun StarOffice suite of productivity software.

The primary component of any distribution is the Linux kernel. In addition to the kernel and applications, other components in a distribution include installation tools, the boot loader, and utility programs. Some distributions are more graphical and oriented toward the new user. Others are more basic and focus on developers and people who are already familiar with UNIX. Here is an alphabetical list of some of the more common Linux distributions and their websites:

- **SCO OpenLinux**—www.sco.com
- **Xandros Desktop Linux**—www.xandros.com
- **Debian GNU/Linux**—www.debian.org
- **Mandrake Linux**—www.mandrakelinux.com
- **Red Hat Linux**—www.redhat.com
- **Slackware Linux**—www.slackware.com
- **SuSE Linux**—www.suse.com
- **Turbo Linux**—www.turbolinux.com
- **United Linux**—www.unitedlinux.com

Linux/UNIX GUI

Both UNIX and Linux are capable of running GUIs. Because there are so many different versions of both UNIX and Linux, there are literally dozens of popular graphical interfaces from which to choose. For example, the default installation of Red Hat 8.x installs the GNOME Desktop Environment, shown in Figure 16-9, and uses GNOME as the default GUI for all users.

Figure 16-9 Gnome Desktop Enviroment

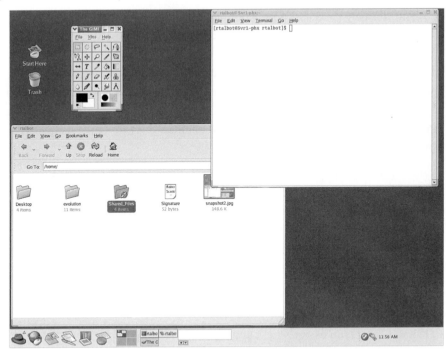

Although other desktop environments, such as K Desktop Environment (KDE), shown in Figure 16-10, can be configured and used with Linux, GNOME rapidly is gaining industry acceptance as a "standard" UNIX and Linux GUI.

Both UNIX and Linux rely on the X Window System to display the GUI. The X Window System is software that works with the system hardware and graphical applications, including the window manager. The window manager is the software that is responsible for sizing, positioning, and rendering the graphical windows in which programs run.

Macintosh OS X

Apple Macintosh computers were designed for easy networking in a peer-to-peer (workgroup) situation. In fact, network interfaces are included as part of the hardware and networking components that are built into the Macintosh operating system. Ethernet and Token Ring network adapters also are available for the Macintosh.

Figure 16-10 KDE Desktop

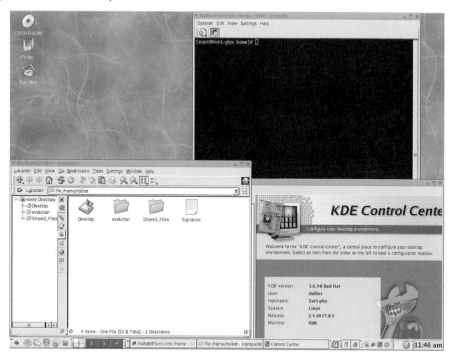

The Macintosh, or Mac, is popular in many educational institutions and corporate graphics departments. Macs can be connected to one another in workgroups and can access AppleShare file servers. Macs also can be connected to PC LANs that include Microsoft, NetWare, or UNIX servers. The Macintosh operating system, Mac OS X, is sometimes referred to as Apple system 10.

Some of the features of MAC OS X are in the GUI called Aqua. The Aqua GUI resembles a cross between the Microsoft Windows XP and Linux X Window System GUI. The MAC OS X is designed to provide features such as Internet browsing, video and photo editing, and games for the home computer, while still providing features that provide powerful and customizable tools that IT professionals need in an operating system.

MAC OS X is fully compatible with older versions of the MAC operating systems. MAC OS X provides a new feature that allows for AppleTalk and Windows connectivity. The MAC OS X core operating system called Darwin is a UNIX-based, powerful system that provides stability and performance. These enhancements provide MAC OS X with support for protected memory, preemptive multitasking, advanced memory management, and symmetric multiprocessing. This makes Mac OS X a formidable competitor among operating systems.

Concept of Service on Servers

NOSs are designed to provide network processes to clients and peers. Network services include the World Wide Web, file sharing, mail exchange, directory services, remote management, and print services. Remote management is a powerful service that allows administrators to configure networked systems that are miles apart. It is important to understand that these network processes are referred to as "services" in Windows 2000 and "daemons" in UNIX and Linux. Essentially, they all provide the same functions, but the way that they are loaded and interact with the NOS is different in each operating system.

Depending on the NOS, some of these key network processes might be enabled during a default installation. Most popular network processes rely on the TCP/IP suite of protocols. Because TCP/IP is an open, well-known set of protocols, TCP/IP-based services are especially vulnerable to unauthorized scans and malicious attacks. Denial-of-service (DoS) attacks, computer viruses, and fast-spreading Internet worms have forced NOS designers to reconsider which network services are started automatically.

Recent versions of popular NOSs, such as Windows 2000 and Red Hat Linux 8.X, restrict the number of network services that are "on" by default. When deploying an NOS, key network services must be enabled manually.

When a user decides to print in a networked printing environment, the job is sent to the appropriate queue for the selected printer. Print queues stack the incoming print jobs and service them using a first-in, first-out (FIFO) order. That is, when a job is added to the queue, it is placed at the end of the list of waiting jobs and is printed after all other previous jobs before it. The wait for a print job can sometimes be long, depending on the size of the print jobs entered into the queue before it. A network print service provides system administrators with the necessary tools to manage the large number of print jobs being routed throughout the network. This includes the ability to prioritize, pause, and even delete print jobs that are waiting to be printed.

File Sharing

The ability to share files over a network is an important network service. Many file-sharing protocols and applications are in use today. Within a corporate or home network, files are typically shared by using Windows File Sharing or the Network File Sharing protocol. In such environments, an end user might not even know if a given file is on a local hard disk or on a remote server. Windows File Sharing and Network File Sharing allow users to easily move, create, and delete files in remote directories.

FTP and File Transfer

Many organizations make files available to remote employees, customers, and to the general public via FTP. FTP services are made available to the public in conjunction with web services. For example, a user can browse a website, read about a software update on a web page, and then download the update using FTP. Smaller companies might use a single server to provide FTP and HTTP services, whereas larger companies might choose to use dedicated FTP servers.

Although FTP clients must log in, many FTP servers are configured to allow anonymous access. When users access a server anonymously, they do not need to have a user account on the system. The FTP protocol allows users to upload, rename, and delete files, so administrators must be careful to configure an FTP server to control levels of access.

FTP is a session-oriented protocol. Clients must open an application layer session with the server, authenticate, and then perform an action such as download or upload. If the client's session is inactive for a certain length of time, the server disconnects the client. This inactive length of time is called an idle timeout. The length of an FTP idle timeout varies depending on the software.

Web Services

The World Wide Web is now the most visible network service. In less than a decade, the World Wide Web has become a global network of information, commerce, education, and entertainment. Millions of companies, organizations, and individuals maintain websites on the Internet. Websites are collections of web pages that are stored on a server or a group of servers.

The World Wide Web is based on a client-server model. Clients attempt to establish TCP sessions with web servers. After a session is established, a client can request data from the server. HTTP typically governs client requests and server transfers. Web services and grown to include, not just HTML that is translated by the web browser and read by humans, but generates XML scripts that computer programs use. Recall from the previous discussion on Microsoft's .NET server how servers are using XML with web services. Web client software includes GUI web browsers, such as Netscape Navigator and Internet Explorer.

Web pages are hosted on computers that are running web services software. The two most common web server software packages are Microsoft Internet Information Services (IIS) and Apache Web Server. Microsoft IIS can only be run on a Windows platform, whereas Apache Web Server is typically used on UNIX and Linux platforms.

Dozens of other web server programs are available. Some kind of web service is available for virtually all operating systems that are currently in production.

DNS

DNS translates an Internet name (such as www.cisco.com) into an IP address. Many applications rely on the directory services that DNS provides to do this work. Web browsers, e-mail programs, and file transfer programs use the names of remote systems. The DNS protocol allows these clients to make requests to DNS servers in the network for the translation of names to IP addresses. Applications can then use the addresses to send their messages. Without this directory lookup service, the Internet would be almost impossible to use.

DHCP

The purpose of DHCP is to enable individual computers on an IP network to learn their TCP/IP configurations from the DHCP server or servers. These DHCP servers have no exact information about the individual computers until information is requested. The overall purpose of this is to reduce the work that is necessary to administer a large IP network. The most significant piece of information that is distributed in this manner is the IP address that identifies the host on the network. DHCP also allows for recovery and the ability to automatically renew network IP addresses through a leasing mechanism. This mechanism allocates an IP address for a specific time period, releases it, and then assigns a new IP address. DHCP allows a DHCP server to do all this, which saves the system administrator considerable amounts of time.

Network Management

As a network evolves and grows, it becomes a more critical and indispensable resource to the organization, as shown in Figure 16-11. However, the more resources that the network offers its users and the more complex the network gets, the more things that can go wrong. However, loss of network resources, or even to have the network perform poorly, is not acceptable to the users. The network administrator, must actively manage the network, diagnose problems, prevent situations from occurring, and provide the best performance of the network for the users. At some point, networks become too large to manage without automated network management tools.

Figure 16-11 Network Evolution

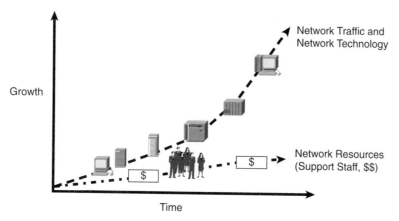

Network management includes the following:

- Network availability monitoring
- Improved automation
- Response time monitoring
- Security features
- Traffic rerouting
- Restoration capability
- User registration

The driving forces behind network management are explained next:

- **Controlling corporate assets**—Without effective control of network resources, these network resources will not provide the payback that the management requires.

- **Controlling complexity**—With massive growth in the number of network components, users, interfaces, protocols, and vendors, loss of control of the network and its resources threatens management.

- **Improving service**—Users expect the same or improved service as the network grows and the resources become more distributed.

- **Balancing various needs**—Users must be provided with various applications at a given level of support, with specific requirements in the areas of performance, availability, and security.

- **Reducing downtime**—Ensure high availability of resources by proper redundant design.

- **Controlling costs**—Monitor and control resource utilization so that user needs can be satisfied at a reasonable cost.

OSI and Network Management Model

A more in-depth analysis of these requirements was needed. The International Organization for Standardization (ISO) created a committee to produce a model for network management, under the direction of the OSI group.

This model has four parts:

- Organization
- Information
- Communication
- Functional

This is a view of network management from the top down, divided into four submodels and recognized by the OSI standard, as shown in Figure 16-12.

Figure 16-12 Network Evolution

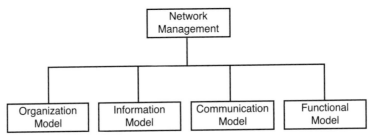

The Organization model describes the components of network management (manager, agent, and so on) and their relationships. The arrangement of these components leads to different types of architecture, which will be discussed later.

The Information model is concerned with structure and storage of management information of network objects. This information is stored in a database, called a Management Information Base (MIB). The industry standard focuses on the Structure of Management Information (SMI) to define the syntax and semantics of management information that are stored in the MIB. MIBs and SMI will be covered in more depth later.

The Communication model deals with how the management data is communicated between the agent and manager process. It considers the transport protocol, the application protocol, and commands and responses between peers.

The Functional model addresses the network management applications that reside upon the network management system (NMS). The OSI network management model categorizes five areas of function (sometimes referred to as the FCAPS model):

- Fault
- Configuration
- Accounting
- Performance
- Security

This network management model has gained broad acceptance by vendors as a useful way of describing the requirements for any network management system.

Standards: SNMP and CMIP

To allow for interoperability of management across many different network platforms, network management standards are required so that vendors can implement and adhere to these standards. Two main standards have emerged:

- **SNMP**—IETF community
- **Common Management Information Protocol (CMIP)**—Telecommunications community

SNMP actually refers to a set of standards for network management, including a protocol, a database structure specification, and a set of data objects. SNMP was adopted as the standard for TCP/IP Internets in 1989 and became very popular. An upgrade, known as SNMP version 2c (SNMPv2c) was adopted in 1993. SNMPv2c could provide support for centralized and distributed network management strategies, and it included improvements in SMI, protocol operations, management architecture, and security. This was designed to run on OSI-based networks as well as TCP/IP-based networks. Since then, SNMPv3 has been released. To solve the security shortcomings of SNMPv1 and SNMPv2c, SNMPv3 provides secure access to MIBs by authenticating and encrypting packets over the network. CMIP is an OSI network management protocol that was created and standardized by the ISO for the monitoring and control of heterogeneous networks.

SNMP Operation

SNMP is an application layer protocol that was designed to facilitate the exchange of management information between network devices. By using SNMP to access management information data packets per second sent on an interface or number of open TCP connections, network administrators can more easily manage network performance and find and solve network problems.

Today, SNMP is the most popular protocol for managing diverse commercial, university, and research internetworks. Standardization activity continues even as vendors develop and release state-of-the-art SNMP-based management applications. SNMP is a relatively simple protocol, yet its feature set is sufficiently powerful to handle the difficult problems that management of heterogeneous networks presents.

The organizational model for SNMP-based network management includes four elements:

- Management station
- Management agent
- MIB
- Network management protocol

The NMS is usually a standalone workstation, but it can be implemented over several systems. NMS includes a collection of software called the network management application. The network management application includes a GUI interface to allow authorized network managers to manage the network. It responds to user commands and issued commands to management agents throughout the network. The management agents are key network platforms and devices, other hosts, routers, bridges, and hubs that are equipped with SNMP so that they can be managed. They respond to requests for information and requests for actions from the NMS (polling) and can provide the NMS with important but unsolicited information (traps). All the management information of a particular agent is stored in the MIB on that agent. An agent might keep track of the following:

- Number and state of its virtual *circuits*
- Number of certain kinds of error messages received
- Number of bytes and packets in and out of the device
- Maximum output queue length (for routers and other internetworking devices)
- Broadcast messages sent and received
- Network interfaces going down and coming up

The NMS performs a monitoring function by retrieving the values from the MIB. The NMS can cause an action to take place at an agent or can change an agent's configuration. The communication between the manager and the agent is carried out by an application layer network management protocol. The SNMP protocol operates over UDP by using port 151/152. It is based on an exchange of messages. Three message types are common:

- **Get**—Enables the management station to retrieve the value of MIB objects from the agent

- **Set**—Enables the management station to set the value of MIB objects at the agent
- **Trap**—Enables the agent to notify the management station of significant events

This model is referred to as a two-tier model, as shown in Figure 16-13. However, it assumes that all network elements are manageable by SNMP. This is not always the case because some devices have a proprietary management interface. In these cases, a three-tiered model is required, as shown in Figure 16-14. A network manager who wants to obtain information or control this proprietary node communicates with a proxy agent. The proxy agent then translates the manager's request into a form that is appropriate to the target system and uses whatever proprietary management protocol is appropriate to communicate with the target system. Responses from the target back to the proxy are similarly translated back into SNMP messages and communicated back to the manager.

Figure 16-13 Components of the Organization Model

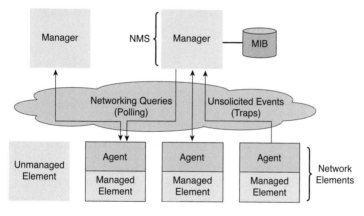

Figure 16-14 Components of the Organization Model

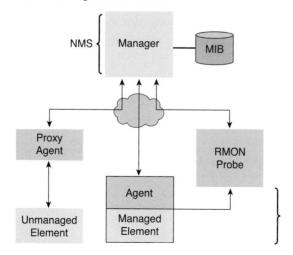

Another common network management application is to offload some network management functionality to a Remote Monitoring (RMON) probe, let it gather management information locally, and then for the manager to periodically retrieve summary information of the data gathered.

The NMS is an ordinary workstation that runs a typical operating system, as shown in Figure 16-15. It usually has a large amount of RAM to hold all the management applications that are running at one time. The manager runs a typical network protocol stack, such as TCP/IP. The network management applications rely on the host operating system and on the communication architecture. Examples of network management applications are CiscoWorks2000, HP OpenView, and SNMPc.

Figure 16-15 Organization Model

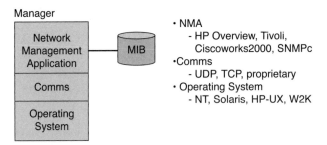

As discussed before, the manager might be a standalone, centralized workstation sending out queries to all agents, no matter where they are located, as shown in Figure 16-16. In a distributed network, a decentralized architecture is more appropriate, with local NMS at each site. These distributed NMSs can act in a client-server architecture, where one NMS acts as a master server, the others are clients, and the clients pass their data back to the master server for centralized storage, as shown in Figure 16-17. An alternative is that all distributed NMSs have equal responsibility, each with its own manager databases, so that the management information is distributed over the peer NMSs, as shown in Figure 16-18.

Structure of Management Information and MIBs

An MIB is used to store the structured information that represents network elements and their attributes. The structure is defined in the SMI, which defines the data types that can be used to store an object, how those objects are named, and how they are encoded for transmission over a network.

Figure 16-16 Centralized Network Management Architecture

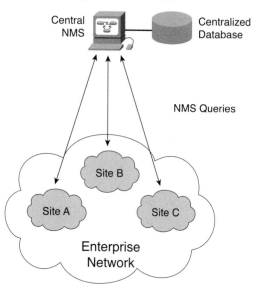

Figure 16-17 Hierarchical Network Management Architecture

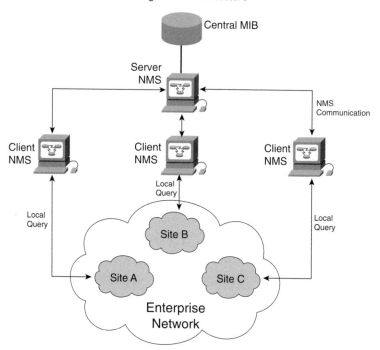

Figure 16-18 Distributed Network Management Architecture

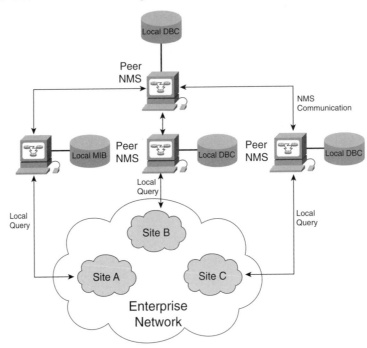

MIBs are highly structured depositories for information about a device. Many standard MIBs exist, but more MIBs that are proprietary exist to uniquely manage different vendors' devices. The original SMI MIB was categorized into eight different groups, totaling 114 managed objects. More groups were added to define MIB-II, which now replaces MIB-I.

All managed objects in the SNMP environment are arranged in a hierarchical or tree structure, as shown in Figure 16-19. The leaf objects of the tree are the actual managed objects, each of which represents some resource, activity or related information that is to be managed. A unique object identifier identifies each managed object, which is a number in dot notation, that traverses the SMI tree. Each object identifier is described by using ASN.1 (abstract syntax notation).

SNMP uses these object identifiers to identify the MIB variables to retrieve or modify. Objects that are in the public domain are described in MIBs introduced in Request For Comments (RFCs).

Vendors are encouraged to make their MIB definitions known. After an assigned enterprise value has been given, the vendor is responsible for creating and maintaining subtrees.

Figure 16-19 Object Identifiers

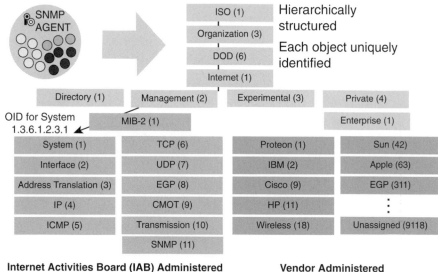

OID for System 1.3.6.1.2.3.1

Internet Activities Board (IAB) Administered   **Vendor Administered**

SNMP Protocol

The agent is a software function that is embedded in most networked devices, such as routers, switches, hubs, printers, and servers, as shown in Figure 16-20. The agent is responsible for processing SNMP requests from the manager. It is also responsible for the execution of routines that maintain variables as defined in the various supported MIBs.

Figure 16-20 Object Identifiers

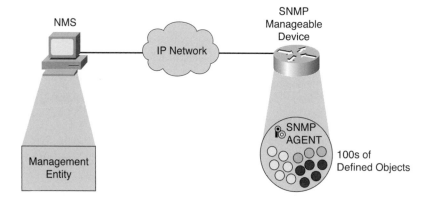

Interaction between the manager and the agent is facilitated by the "question and answer protocol," or SNMP. The term "simple" comes from the restricted number of message types that are part of the initial protocol specification. The strategy was designed to make it easier for developers to build management capabilities into network devices. The initial protocol specification is referred to as SNMPv1 (version 1).

Three types of SNMP messages are issued on behalf of an NMS: GetRequest, GetNextRequest, and SetRequest, as shown in Figure 16-21. The agent acknowledges all three messages in the form of a GetResponse message. In addition, an agent might issue a Trap message in response to an event that affects the MIB and the underlying resources.

Figure 16-21 Object Identifiers

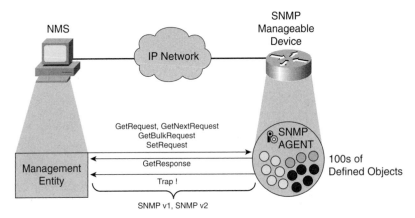

The development of SNMPv2c (version 2c) was quick to address observed limitations in SNMPv1. The most noticeable enhancements were the introduction of the GetBulk Request message type and the addition of 64-bit counters. Retrieving information with GetRequest and GetNextRequest was an inefficient method of collecting information from device tabular data structures. Only one variable at a time could be solicited with SNMPv1. The GetBulk Request addresses this weakness by receiving a "bulk" of information using a single request. The 64-bit counters to the MIB addressed the issue of counters rolling over too quickly, especially with higher speed links such as Gigabit Ethernet.

The management entity is also referred to as the manager or NMS, as shown in Figure 16-22. It is responsible for soliciting information from the agent. The solicitations are based on specific requests. The manager processes the retrieved information in several generic ways. You can log the retrieved information for later analysis, display it via a graphing utility, or compare it with preconfigured values to test whether a threshold condition has been met.

Figure 16-22 Object Identifiers

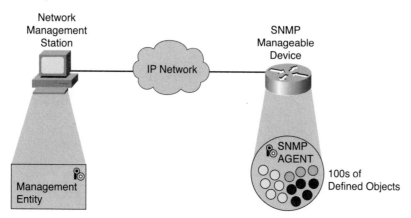

Not all manager functions are based on data retrieval. There is also the ability to issue changes of a value in the managed device. This enables configuration control over the managed device.

The interaction between the manager and the managed device introduces traffic to the network. You should take a cautious approach when introducing managers onto the network. Aggressive monitoring strategies can affect network performance. Bandwidth utilizations will increase and might be an issue for WAN environments. Another impact is associated with the devices that are being monitored. The devices need to process manager requests; this activity should not take precedence over production services.

The rule of thumb is that a minimum amount of information should be polled as infrequently as possible. Therefore, determine which devices and *links* are most critical and what type of granularity of data is required.

SNMP uses User Datagram Protocol (UDP) as a transport protocol. Therefore, it is possible for SNMP to lose messages. SNMP has no provision for guarantee of delivery, so it is up to the application that is using SNMP to cope with a lost protocol data unit (PDU).

Each SNMP message contains a cleartext string (community string), such as a password, to restrict access to managed devices, as shown in Figure 16-23. Although the concept was nice, because the community strings were cleartext, security became an issue. Currently, SNMPv3 (version 3) has been more successful in addressing security concerns.

Figure 16-23 Object Identifiers

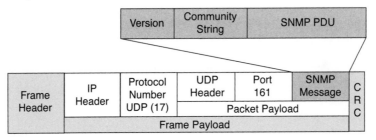

An example of what the SNMPv2c message looks like is illustrated in Figure 16-24. You can find a detailed presentation of the protocol in the Internet standard RFC 1157.

Figure 16-24 Object Identifiers

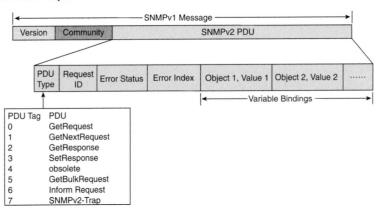

The fact that the community string is cleartext is no surprise to anyone who has studied the IP protocol suite. All fields that are specified in the protocol suite are cleartext except for security authentication and encryption specifications.

The community string was essentially a security placeholder until the SNMPv2 working group could ratify security mechanisms. The efforts were soon put off to the SNMPv3 working group. Consequently, all SNMP-based management applications need to be configured to use the appropriate community strings. In addition, several organizations frequently change the community string values to reduce the risk of malicious activity from the unauthorized use of the SNMP service.

In spite of the weakness associated with community-based authentication, management strategies are still based on SNMPv1. Cisco devices support SNMPv3 message types and consequently the increased security capabilities, but most management software applications do not support SNMPv3, as shown in Figure 16-25.

Figure 16-25 Configuring SNMP

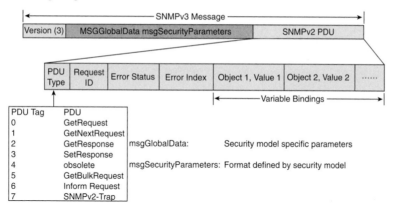

Configuring SNMP

To have the NMS communicate with networked devices, the devices must have SNMP enabled and the SNMP community strings configured. Following is a review of the command line syntax on how to configure these devices.

More than one read-only string is supported. The default on most systems for this community string is public. It is not advisable to use the default value in an enterprise network. To set the read-only community string that the agent uses, use the following command:

```
Router(config)#snmp-server community string ro
```

string is the community string that acts like a password and permits access to the SNMP protocol.

ro (optional) specifies read-only access. Authorized management stations are only able to retrieve MIB objects.

More than one read-write string is supported. All SNMP objects are available for write access. The default on most systems for this community string is private. You should not use this value in an enterprise network. To set the read-write community string that the agent uses, employ the following command:

```
Router(config)#snmp-server community string rw
```

rw (optional) specifies read-write access. Authorized management stations can retrieve and modify MIB objects.

Several strings can be used to specify location of the managed device and the main system contact for the device:

```
Router(config)#snmp-server location text
Router(config)#snmp-server contact text
```

text is the string that describes the system location information. These values are stored in the MIB objects sysLocation and sysContact.

RMON

RMON is a major step forward in internetwork management. It defines an RMON MIB that supplements MIB-II and provides the network manager with vital information about the network. The remarkable feature of RMON is that although it is simply a specification of a MIB, with no changes in the underlying SNMP protocol, it provides a significant expansion in SNMP functionality.

With MIB-II, the network manager can obtain information that is purely local to individual devices. Consider a LAN that has several devices on it, each with an SNMP agent. An SNMP manager can learn of the amount of traffic into and out of each device, but with MIB-II, it cannot easily learn about the traffic on the LAN as a whole. For the purposes of network management in an internetworked environment, there would typically need to be one monitor per subnetwork.

The RMON standard that was originally designated as IETF RFC 1271 (now RFC 1757) was designed to provide proactive monitoring and diagnostics for distributed LAN-based networks. Monitoring devices, called agents or probes, on critical network segments allow for user-defined alarms to be created and a wealth of vital statistics to be gathered by analyzing every frame on a segment.

The RMON standard divides monitoring functions into nine groups to support Ethernet topologies and adds a tenth group in RFC 1513 for Token Ring-unique parameters. The RMON standard was crafted to be deployed as a distributed computing architecture, where the agents and probes communicate with a central management station (a client) via SNMP. These agents have defined SNMP MIB structures for all 9 or 10 (Ethernet or Token Ring) RMON groups, allowing interoperability between vendors of RMON-based diagnostic tools. RMON Groups include the following:

- **Statistics group**—Maintains utilization and error statistics for the subnetwork/ segment that is being monitored. (Examples include bandwidth utilization, broadcast, multicast, CRC/alignment, fragments, and so on.)

- **History group**—Holds periodic statistical samples from the statistics group and stores them for later retrieval. (Examples include utilization, error count, and packet count.)

- **Alarm group**—Allows the administrator to set a sampling interval and threshold for any item that the agent records. (Examples include absolute or relative values and rising or falling thresholds.)

- **Host group**—Defines the measurement of various types of traffic to and from hosts that are attached to the network. (Examples include packets sent/received, bytes sent/received, errors, and broadcast and multicast packets.)

- **Host TopN group**—Provides a report of TopN hosts based on host group statistics.

- **Traffic matrix group**—Stores errors and utilization statistics for pairs of communicating nodes of the network. (Examples include errors, bytes, and packets.)

- **Filter group**—Generates a packet stream from frames that match the pattern the user specifies.

- **Packet capture group**—Defines how packets that match filter criteria are buffered internally.

- **Event group**—Allows the logging of events (generated traps) to the manager, together with time and date. (An example is generating customized reports based on the type of alarm.)

Syslog

The Cisco syslog logging utility is based on the UNIX syslog utility. System events are usually logged to the system console unless it is disabled. The syslog utility is a mechanism for applications, processes, and the operating system of Cisco devices to report activity and error conditions. The syslog protocol is used to allow Cisco devices to issue these unsolicited messages to a network management station.

Every syslog message is associated, at the time of logging, with a timestamp, a facility, a severity, and a textual log message. These messages are sometimes the only means of gaining insight into device misbehaviors.

The severity level indicates the critical nature of the error message, as shown in Figure 16-26. There are eight levels of severity (0–7), with level 0 being the most critical and level 7 being the least critical. The levels are as follows:

- 0—Emergencies
- 1—Alerts
- 2—Critical

- 3—Errors
- 4—Warnings
- 5—Notifications
- 6—Informational
- 7—Debugging

Figure 16-26 Syslog Facility

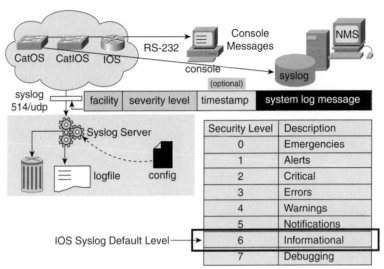

The facility and severity level fields are used for processing the messages. Local 0 to local 7 are facility types provided for custom log message processing. Cisco IOS defaults to severity level 6. This setting is configurable.

To have the NMS receive and record a device's system messages, the devices must have Syslog configured. Following is a review of the command-line syntax on how to configure these devices.

To enable logging to all supported destinations, use the following command:

```
Router(config)#logging on
```

To send log messages to a syslog server host, such as CiscoWorks2000 use the following command:

```
Router(config)#logging hostname | ip address
```

To set logging severity level to level 6 (informational) use the following command:

```
Router(config)#logging trap informational
```

To include a timestamp with a syslog message use the following command:

```
Router(config)#service timestamps log datetime
```

Summary

This chapter covered the following key points and topics:

- The functions of a workstation and a server
- The roles of various equipment in a client/server environment
- The development of NOS
- An overview of the various Windows platforms
- An overview of some of the alternatives to Windows operating systems
- Identify the reasons for network management
- The layers of OSI and the network management model
- The type and application of network management tools
- The role that SNMP and CMIP play in network monitoring
- How management software gathers information and records problems
- How to gather reports on network performance

To supplement all that you have learned in this chapter, refer to the chapter-specific Videos, PhotoZooms, and e-Lab Activities on the CD-ROM that accompanies this book.

Key Terms

circuit   A communications path between two or more points.

enterprise network   A corporation, agency, school, or other organization's network that ties together its data, communication, computing, and file servers.

Frame Relay   An industry-standard, switched data link layer protocol that handles multiple virtual circuits by using HDLC encapsulation between connected devices. Frame Relay is more efficient than X.25, the protocol for which it is generally considered a replacement.

link   A network communications channel that consists of a circuit or transmission path and all related equipment between a sender and a receiver. Link is most often used to refer to a WAN connection. It is sometimes referred to as a line or a transmission link.

Check Your Understanding

1. A network baseline is the comparison value to measure a network's what?

   A. Security

   B. Design

   C. Structure

   D. Performance

2. A peer-to-peer network establishes what type of relationship between end stations?

   A. Client-to-client

   B. Client-to-server

   C. Server-to-server

   D. Server-to-Internet

3. Which type of file system does Windows NT use for security purposes?

   A. FAT 16

   B. FAT 32

   C. NTFS

   D. NFS

4. In a client server network, a user's ability to access certain files while not being able to access other files is the user what?

   A. Accesses

   B. Rights

   C. Abilities

   D. Securities

5. What is the IP address of the internal loopback?

   A. 10.10.10.1

   B. 255.255.255.0

   C. 127.0.0.1

   D. 192.0.0.1

6. What is one way to prevent static electricity damage?

   A. Turn off the electricity when you are working on the computer.

   B. Wear rubber gloves to insulate the equipment

   C. Use only plastic tools

   D. Use a grounding strap

7. Which protocol supports network management?

   A. SMTP

   B. NFS

   C. SNMP

   D. FTP

   E. IPX

8. To list your IP setting on a Windows NT computer, you would run the _____ command.

   A. ip

   B. ipconfig

   C. winipcfg

   D. show ip

   E. config

9. What is one troubleshooting method used in network troubleshooting?

    A. Loopback readout

    B. Divide and conquer

    C. Ping of death test

    D. Trace the fault

    E. Reset the server

10. If the server is set up by using IP, the clients must use which protocol to communicate with it?

    A. IPX

    B. UDP

    C. IP

    D. Telnet

    E. HTTP

11. RMON is an extension of what protocol?

    A. SNMP

    B. UDP

    C. IPX

    D. PING

    E. SMTP

12. What does the *-n* protocol option stand for in the **ping** command?

    A. The network number of the ping area

    B. The no repeat option

    C. Count *x* number of pings

    D. Never stop until interrupted

    E. Nothing

13. How is the remote data gathered with RMON?

    A. Commands

    B. Tables

    C. Lists

    D. Probes

    E. User interaction

14. The cost of _____ equipment for mission-critical operations needs to be added to the cost of maintaining the network.

  A. Redundant

  B. Expensive

  C. Mechanical

  D. Security

  E. Welding

Part IV

CCNA Bonus Material

Objectives

After reading this chapter, you will be able to

- Identify the key business drivers of optical networks
- Describe the features of fiber-optic systems
- Describe the communication components in an optical communication system
- Identify the features of the light-emitting devices used in optical transmission
- Describe important design characteristics of fiber and the index of refraction
- Identify the main components of a fiber-optic cable
- Describe the features of multimode fiber and single-mode fiber
- Explain the possible fiber geometry problems
- Describe loss factors in fiber
- Identify the effects of different types of dispersion
- Describe the optical filter technology and functions of the optical amplifier
- Describe how erbium-doped fiber amplifiers (EDFAs) work
- Describe Synchronous Optical Network (SONET) technology
- Describe SONET/Synchronous Digital Hierarchy (SDH)
- Describe dense wavelength division multiplexing (DWDM) systems
- Explain how electrical/optical/electrical (E/O/E) conversion (transponder) works
- Describe fiber-optic data transmission
- Describe the advantages of DWDM and the features of metropolitan DWDM

Chapter 17

Optical Networking Fundamentals

This chapter provides in-depth coverage of the fundamentals of optical networks. Optical networks are far superior to other more traditional networks in many ways, such as reliability and security. Reliability and security features are two of the most important aspects that government agencies and businesses look for, and they are the main reason why optical technology is becoming a leader and the standard in the computer networking industry.

Basics of Optical Networks

Traffic on the Internet alone is exploding at a rate that far outpaces the growth of traditional voice traffic. The IP bandwidth demands on a network backbone are pushing a service provider's network architecture to its limits and sometimes even beyond its capacity.

Service providers need the capability to provision new services quickly, deliver high-value applications at a fraction of the time and cost, and build scalable, fail-safe infrastructures at reduced operating costs. The answer lies in fiber-optic technology. Optical networks are an extremely efficient means of conveying data such as text, video, and voice.

This chapter describes the key business drivers of the optical networks and the features of fiber-optic systems. This chapter also discusses the components and features of optical transmission.

Optical Business Drivers

Networks must be capable of transmitting data and video quickly, efficiently, and cost effectively. In comparison to any other resource, fiber optics is the most efficient medium for transmitting information. Fiber optics offers the highest bandwidth capacity for network traffic. As demand increases for high-bandwidth capacity and high transmission speeds, it is expected that the usage of fiber optics will grow quickly.

The burgeoning Internet economy and surging amounts of data traffic call for scalable, multiservice platforms with the capability to support next-generation, IP-based services and security. Today, service providers demand certain characteristics from their networks, as described in Table 17-1.

Table 17-1 Optical Business Drivers

Key Driver	Description
Capacity/scalability	Efficiently meet capacity and scalability requirements in both metropolitan and long-haul network infrastructures
Reliability	Scale with the rapid growth of the Internet while providing unrivaled reliability
Accelerated profits	Reduce costs and accelerate profitable new service revenue simultaneously
Broad coverage	Reach long distances
End-to-end flexibility	Provide the capability to build a flexible, end-to-end optical solution that meets the requirements of carrier-class reliability
Adaptability	Be adaptable through an open system architecture
Space efficiency	Reduce point-of-presence (POP) physical space requirements
Security	Support IP-based security

Fiber-Optic Systems

Fiber-optic technology is the core of today's high-speed networks. Connecting both distant cities and many points within a metropolitan area, optical-fiber networks are made of thin glass strands that carry rapid light pulses faster and more reliably than copper wires at speeds of up to 10 gigabits per second (Gbps). Work is under way to increase speeds to 40 Gbps.

Information is transmitted at the speed of light in optical fiber. The time units that are used in measuring light are extremely small. Although optical fibers are small, they can also be long. At approximately the diameter of a human hair, optical fiber can carry a tremendous amount of information.

Fiber-Optic Transmission System

All communication systems have three things in common: a signal source, a medium for the signal to travel through, and a receiver. This system can be as simple as using a pair of tin cans that are connected by a string to talk with a friend. In fiber optics, the transmitter is a light source, the medium is a light guide (optical fiber), and the receiver is an optical sensor (see Figure 17-1).

Figure 17-1 Fiber-Optic Communication Systems

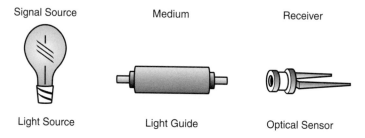

Signal Source	Medium	Receiver
Light Source	Light Guide	Optical Sensor

Optical Transmitter

An optical *transmitter* is simply a source of light, like a light bulb (see Figure 17-2). Lasers and light emitting diodes (LEDs) are used for optical transmitters. An electrical signal such as a voice, data, or video transmission is converted to light by using the electrical signal to turn the light on and off for a digital signal, or to vary the intensity of the light for an analog signal. In a digital signal, the presence of light is a 1, and the absence of light is a 0. In an analog signal, the intensity of the light matches the strength of the electrical signal level.

Figure 17-2 Optical Transmitter

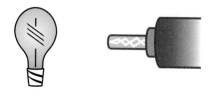

Light On and Off = Digital
Variable Intensity = Analog

Optical Receiver

The receiver is a semiconductor that changes light into a corresponding electrical signal. It is generically called an *optical-to-electrical converter*, or O-E converter. In a digital signal, the presence of light produces an electrical signal of a certain high level. The absence of light produces a lower electrical signal level (see Figure 17-3). In an analog system, the electrical level corresponds to the level (power) of the light hitting the O-E converter.

Figure 17-3 High-Level and Low-Level Signals

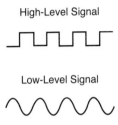

Even with no light hitting an O-E converter, an electrical signal will still be present. The dark current that exists in all detector circuits causes this signal. The dark current is the electrical noise that naturally occurs in the circuit.

Some receiver circuits have lower noise levels than others. The noise level of the receiver depends on its design. Lower noise levels are a result of better designs. (See Figure 17-4.)

Figure 17-4 Dark Current

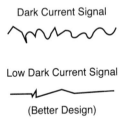

Light

Light can be described in several ways. Consider the way light bulbs are rated at 60 or 100 watts. In fiber optics, the wattage is in the thousandths, millionths, or billionths of a watt: milliwatt (mW), microwatt (µW), or nanowatt (nW). It is usually more convenient to work with decibels (dB), which is a set of units related to watts. The expression "decibels relative to 1 milliwatt" (dBm) defines signal strength in wires and cables at radio frequency and audio frequency.

Light can be described by its color, which is determined by the wavelength of the electromagnetic signal. For example, blue is about 300 nanometers (nm), and red is at 700 nm wavelength. Fiber optics has three wavelength values: 850, 1300, and 1550 nm. Multimode systems use only 850 and 1300 nm, whereas single-mode systems use only 1300 and 1550 nm. (See Figure 17-5.)

Figure 17-5 Fiber-Optic Wavelength

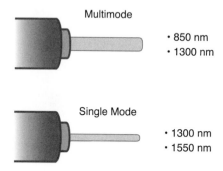

The power in a light determines its brightness. The higher the wattage is, the brighter the light will be. In fiber-optic systems, the benchmark power is 1 milliwatt (mW), which is 0 dBm. Higher values, such as 4 mW, would be +6 dBm. A change of 3 dB means a doubling of the wattage. A change of negative 3 dB (–3 dB) means cutting the wattage in half. For example, 0.250 mW would be –6 dBm. (See Figure 17-6.)

Figure 17-6 Fiber-Optics Power

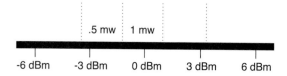

The power levels found in fiber systems range from about +20 dBm, which is the output of hot lasers, to approximately –70 dBm, which is the amount of power returning after making a round trip down a 100-mile-long fiber.

Optical Transmission

In fiber optics, information is carried by modulating the light power, not the wavelength or frequency of the light. As a result, the wavelength remains constant. It is possible to mix two wavelengths of light on the same fiber without interference between them. This is called *wavelength division multiplexing (WDM)*, which allows more than one wavelength to be sent over a single fiber, thereby increasing the capacity of the fiber (see Figure 17-7). WDM is discussed in more detail later in this chapter.

Figure 17-7 WDM

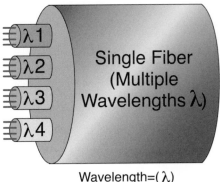

Wavelength=(λ)

The light source that is used in the design of a system is an important consideration because it can be one of the most costly elements. The characteristics of the light source often constitute a strong limiting factor in the final performance of the optical link. Light-emitting devices that are used in optical transmission must be compact, monochromatic, stable, and long lasting.

Three general types of light-emitting devices are used in optical transmission: LEDs, laser diodes, and semiconductor lasers. (See Figure 17-8.) LEDs are relatively slow devices that are suitable for use at speeds of less than 1 Gbps. LEDs exhibit a relatively wide spectrum width and transmit light in a relatively wide cone.

Figure 17-8 Light-Emitting Devices

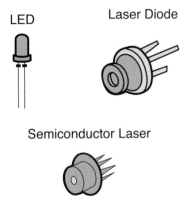

LEDs and laser diodes are inexpensive devices that are often used in multimode fiber communications. Semiconductor lasers, on the other hand, have performance characteristics that are better suited to single-mode fiber applications.

Reflection and Refraction

Light is described sometimes as traveling as a ray. *Reflection* is a light ray that bounces off the interface of two materials at the same angle it hits. Reflection occurs when a flashlight beam bounces off a window or mirror. (See Figure 17-9.) The beam of light comes off at the same angle it hits.

Refraction is the bending of the light ray as it changes speed going from one material to another. When a light ray hits another material at a steep enough angle, most of the light goes through the interface into the other material. (See Figure 17-10.) If the materials have a different density, then the light bends, or refracts, at a fixed angle. This angle of refraction depends on the difference in density of the two materials. For example, when light comes out of water into the air, it bends. When you stick a fishing pole into the water, the pole looks like it bends. However, the pole is not bending; the light hitting the pole is bending.

Figure 17-9 Reflection

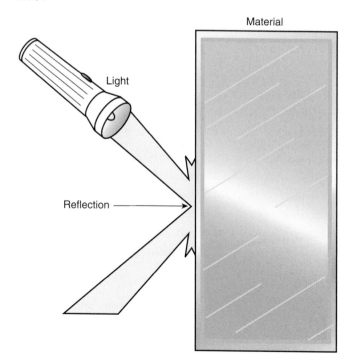

Figure 17-10 Refraction

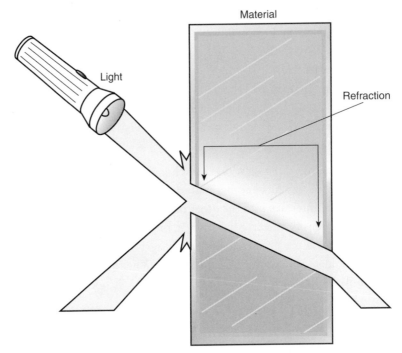

IOR

One of the most important design characteristics of fiber is its *IOR,* which is the ratio of the speed of light in a vacuum to the speed of light in a fiber. IOR is a measure of the density of a fiber because denser materials (higher IOR) cause light to travel more slowly. For optical fiber, the typical IOR values are between 1.4 and 1.5.

Each fiber manufacturer has a slightly different IOR because each makes its fibers using a different process. Even within a single fiber, the IOR might vary. The IOR value reported by manufacturers is the average IOR. Two fibers with different IOR values might work together. Remember, however, that different IORs have different effects on distance measurements. Denser materials cause light to travel more slowly.

Optical Fibers

Fiber-optic cable is a networking medium that uses modulated light for data transmissions through thin strands of glass. Signals that represent data bits are converted into beams of light. Many characteristics of fiber optics make this media superior to copper.

Fiber is not susceptible to EMI or RFI. Fiber has higher data transmission rates, significantly greater transmission distances, no grounding concerns, and better resistance to environmental factors. Those characteristics make fiber a more attractive choice over copper in some implementations.

To understand how fiber-optic media works, you must have a basic knowledge of some important characteristics of light as it relates to the way it is transmitted (propagated) through materials such as glass. This section describes two main types of fiber: single mode and multimode. This section also discusses possible fiber geometry problems, loss factors in fiber optics, and causes of attenuation. In addition, this section introduces two fiber filter technologies: fiber bragg grating and dielectric filter.

Fiber Types

A fiber-optic cable has three components, as shown in Figure 17-11:

- **Protective outer coating**—This is also known as buffer coating.
- **Inner cladding**—The cladding is of a different density than the core, so the light bounces against it.
- **Fiber core**—The core is doped with chemicals that enhance its transmission properties.

Figure 17-11 Components of Fiber-Optic Cable

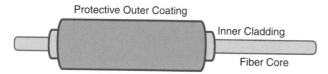

Telecom fiber is classified into multimode or single mode. The only physical difference between the two is the size of the core (see Figure 17-12). Because of the core size, the performance characteristics are different. With its smaller core, single-mode fiber can carry information over long distances and can handle substantially more information than multimode. Also, single-mode fiber exhibits less loss than multimode fiber.

Figure 17-12 Fiber Types

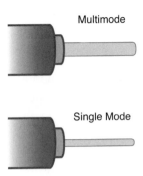

Multimode

Multimode fiber is used to transmit many signals per fiber. Multimode allows many paths or modes for the light. The larger core of multimode fiber allows light to break up into many different modes. Some modes will make it to the far end faster than others, causing the original signal to be broadened out in time. In a time-division multiplexing (TDM) digital signal, the variance of light speed limits the spacing between bits of information and the rate at which bits can be sent. This is known as *dispersion*. Typical multimode rates are in the hundreds of megabits per second (Mbps).

Single Mode

Single-mode fiber is used to transmit one signal per fiber. Single-mode fiber allows only one path for the signal to travel down the middle of the fiber. The entire signal travels the length of the fiber at the same rate, allowing for much higher data rates. Typical single-mode rates are in the millions and billions of bits per second (bps).

Fiber Geometry

Fiber manufacturing continues to improve, making fiber less expensive and of better quality. However, there are some allowable variations in the physical structure of fiber. One of the most important characteristics related to splicing (and testing) is the shape and location of the core within the cladding.

Because light travels only in the core of the fiber, it is necessary for fiber cores to link up when splicing them. In some cases, the fiber cores might not match up well. They might be slightly off center from the cladding center, they might be of different sizes, or they might not be round. (See Figure 17-13.) In some cases, it might not be possible to make a splice better than 0.20 dB loss because of the mismatch in fiber characteristics.

Figure 17-13 Fiber Geometry Problems

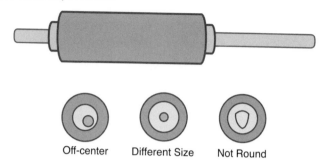

Off-center   Different Size   Not Round

Loss Factors

When light is injected into a fiber, you need to be concerned about how well it will be transmitted and whether it will be lost before it gets to the other end. The amount of signal loss in a fiber is its most critical performance characteristic. If light is too weak coming out of the receiver end of fiber, the entire system might not work properly. The following sections describe major loss factors in fibers, including the following:

- Connector loss
- Macrobending
- Microbending
- Absorption

Connector Loss

Connector loss depends on passing light from one core to another. Because a connector relies on the capability of the bulkhead to line up the two fiber ends, it allows for some different loss factors than with field splices. If two fiber ends are separated, loss occurs because of the spreading of light as it comes out of the first core. This is called *end-face separation*.

Even when the gap is small, some light might be lost. The wider the gap is, the more loss there will be. If the bulkhead is worn and allows some play in the alignment of two fibers, then some light might be lost because the cores are not lined up completely. This is called *angular separation*. Core misalignment is the same for splices.

Figure 17-14 illustrates the three causes of connector loss described in this section.

Figure 17-14 Connector Losses

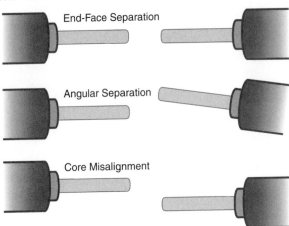

Macrobending

A macrobend is a bend that you can see. When you bend fiber, you can cause some of the light rays to exceed the critical angle, allowing light to leak out of the core and into the cladding. When light is in the cladding, it cannot easily get back into the core; it then leaks out through the buffer. (See Figure 17-15.)

Figure 17-15 Macrobending

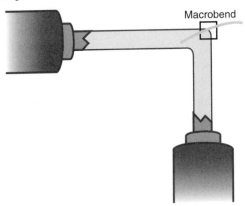

Macrobending loss is more severe at longer wavelengths. (For example, a nickel-size bend might leak out 0.5 dB of light at 1310 nm but might cause a loss of 2.0 dB at 1550 nm.) You can reduce macrobending by eliminating tight bends in the fiber and cable.

Microbending

Microbending produces the same effect as macrobending; it causes the light to exceed the critical angle and leak out of the core. (See Figure 17-16.) Microbending occurs on a microscopic scale and is invisible to the eye.

Figure 17-16 Microbending

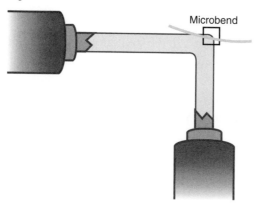

Microbending appears as a wrinkle in the fiber caused by temperature variations during manufacturing. It can also be caused by extreme temperature swings in installed cable when the different materials in the cable structure expand and contract at different rates. This causes the fiber to be squeezed or stretched, in turn causing microbending.

Absorption

Some light is always absorbed into the glass structure. Certain wavelengths exhibit higher absorption rates than others. The user can neither change nor control absorption. Absorption is an intrinsic loss characteristic of fiber. (See Figure 17-17.)

Figure 17-17 Absorption

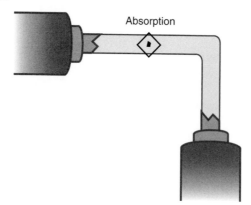

The most serious absorption in glass occurs close to the operating wavelength windows of 1310 and 1550 nm. These areas often show high levels of absorption because of the hydroxyl (OH−) ion, which is produced as a result of the manufacturing process. The absorption peaks can grow in certain conditions and can cause increased attenuation in the operating wavelength windows.

Attenuation

Attenuation refers to the decrease in the strength of a signal during transmission. Attenuation is a natural consequence of signal transmission over long distance. Attenuation in optical fiber is caused by extrinsic factors, including stress from the manufacturing process, the environment, and physical bending. Attenuation in optical fiber is also caused by intrinsic factors, primarily scattering and absorption.

The most common form of scattering, Rayleigh scattering, is caused by small variations in the density of glass as it cools. Scattering affects short wavelengths more than long wavelengths and limits the use of wavelengths below 800 nm.

Attenuation as the result of absorption is caused by the intrinsic properties of the material. Impurities in the glass or atomic defects in the glass can cause absorption. These impurities absorb the optical energy, causing the light to become dimmer. Whereas Rayleigh scattering is an important factor at shorter wavelengths, intrinsic absorption is an issue at longer wavelengths.

Following are the two primary factors that affect attenuation in optical fibers:

- Length of the fiber
- Wavelength of the light

Figure 17-18 shows the loss in decibels per kilometer (dB/km) by wavelength from Rayleigh scattering, intrinsic absorption, and total attenuation from all causes. Based on the attenuations response, the two choices of operation are 1310 or 1550 nm. The 1550-nm window is preferred for long-haul applications because it has less attenuation.

Figure 17-18 Attenuation

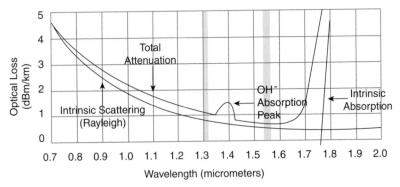

Optical Filters

Optical filters are used to identify different wavelengths or lambdas. Fiber bragg grating and the dielectric filter are examples of optical filters (see Figure 17-19).

Figure 17-19 Optical Filter Technology

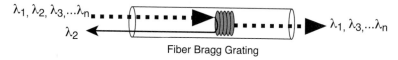

Fiber Bragg Grating

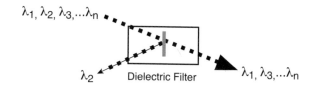

Dielectric Filter

Fiber bragg gratings are spectral filters that reflect light over a narrow wavelength range and transmit all other wavelengths. Fiber bragg gratings are a low-cost approach in which gratings are written directly into standard single-mode fiber. These gratings have the advantage of being ultra narrow. However, it is hard to control the filter shape by using fiber bragg gratings.

Dielectric filter is based on semiconductor processing, in which alternating layers of quarter-wavelength thick dielectric stacks are laid down. Dielectric filters reflect one or more lights and transmit others. Unlike fiber bragg gratings, the filter shape is easily controlled with dielectric filters.

Optical filters are used in optical add drop multiplexers (OADMs) to drop the appropriate channel by essentially reflecting it out. (See Figure 17-20.)

Figure 17-20 Optical Add Drop Multiplexers

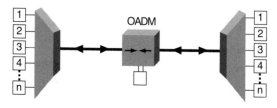

Optical Amplifiers

The *optical amplifier (OA)* is a device that amplifies an input optical signal terahertz (THz) of optical bandwidth near 1550 nm, which is nearly ideal noise performance, low signal distortion and crosstalk, and high-output saturation power. OA is also simple and efficient. (See Figure 17-21.)

Figure 17-21 Optical Amplifier

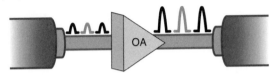

The optical pulse begins to deteriorate as it travels farther. To prevent this deterioration, an electrical regenerator is used to perform the three Rs: restore the signal level, reshape the pulse, and retime the pulse. Electrical regenerators are expensive, introduce latency, and are channel specific.

EDFAs, unlike electrical regenerators, do not convert the signal back to electric before boosting it. EDFA is a device that consists of the following four parts:

- Erbium-doped fiber
- Optical pump
- Coupler
- Isolator

The signal path in an EDFA is entirely passive. The pump laser is the only active part.

In an EDFA, optical fibers are doped with erbium, which is a rare element that can amplify light in the 1550-nm region when pumped by an external laser. (See Figure 17-22.)

Figure 17-22 EDFAs

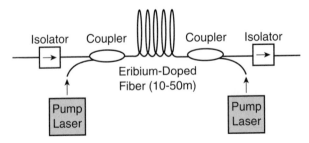

Optical Transmission and Multiplexing

SONET is the standard for synchronous data transmission on optical media used in North America. SDH is the international equivalent of SONET. Service providers who are using a ring topology primarily deploy SONET. The two prevalent types of rings in networks today are unidirectional path switched rings (UPSRs) and bidirectional line switch rings (BLSRs).

DWDM is a technology that transmits multiple signals simultaneously at different wavelengths, allowing a single fiber to operate as if it were multiple fibers. DWDM works in conjunction with optical networks to make data transmission fast and cost effective. DWDM is a scalable solution that increases the information-carrying capacity of existing fiber.

This section introduces the SONET/SDH technology, SONET overhead hierarchy, and SONET/SDH multiplexing hierarchy. In addition, this section describes how DWDM systems work and discusses the benefits of DWDM systems.

SONET Technology

SONET is a standard for optical transport formulated by the Exchange Carriers Standards Association (ECSA) for the American National Standards Institute (ANSI), which sets industry standards in the United States for telecommunications and other industries. Bellcore initiated the SONET standard on behalf of the regional Bell operating companies (RBOCs) and others to ensure compatibility of equipment by all vendors that manufacture to the *midspan meet* standard. Midspan meet refers to the capability to connect different vendors' equipment on a communication network and have them function properly with each other.

SONET was also designed to standardize synchronous networking-enhanced operations, administration, management, and provisioning (OAM&P), and standards-based survivable rings. SONET defines optical carrier (OC) levels and electrically equivalent Synchronous Transport Signals (STSs) for the fiber optic–based transmission hierarchy.

SDH is the international equivalent of SONET. Together, SONET and SDH are a set of global standards that interface equipment from different vendors. SONET uses substantial overhead information, which allows simpler multiplexing and greatly expanded OAM&P capabilities. The following section introduces the SONET overhead hierarchy.

SONET Overhead Hierarchy

The SONET overhead information has several layers, which are shown in Figure 17-23. Enough information is contained in the overhead to allow the network to operate and allow OAM&P communications between the network controller and the nodes. The following describes the three levels of SONET overhead hierarchy:

- **Section overhead (SOH)**—A section is a link between two network elements. Section overhead is used for communications between adjacent network elements, such as regenerators.

- **Line overhead (LOH)**—A line is one or more sections connecting two network elements that multiplex and demultiplex SONET STS signals. Line overhead is for the STS-N signal between STS-N multiplexers.

- **Path overhead (POH)**—A path is one or more lines connecting two network elements that assemble and disassemble traffic. Path overhead, which includes information such as path status, is carried from end to end.

Figure 17-23 SONET Overhead Hierarchy

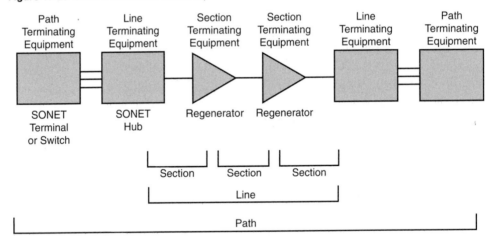

The section-terminating equipment (STE) is usually a regenerator. An STE is capable of originating, accessing, modifying, or terminating the section overhead. The line-terminating equipment (LTE) is a network element that can originate, access, modify, or terminate the line overhead. The path-terminating equipment (PTE) originates accesses, modifies, or terminates the path overhead.

SONET Rings

Most carriers provide two types of SONET services: point-to-point dedicated SONET lines and SONET rings. Both deliver high-speed data transfer, but only dual fiber rings guarantee automatic rerouting around outages. Many types of rings are possible. The two prevalent types in networks today are UPSR and BLSR. (See Figure 17-24.)

Figure 17-24 UPSR and BLSR Configurations

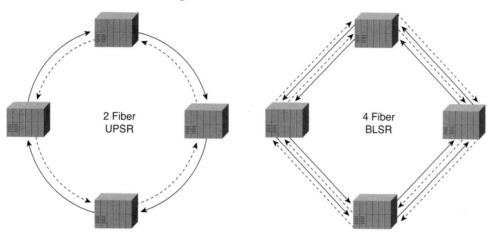

In a unidirectional ring, all working traffic travels around the ring in the same direction. In a bidirectional ring, all working traffic between two nodes travels in both directions (clockwise and counterclockwise).

UPSRs, deployed in metropolitan-area networks (MANs), have two fibers (two counter-rotating rings). One ring is reserved for automatic protection of the working traffic. BLSRs, which are deployed in WANs or backbones, use two pairs of fiber, with one pair designated for working traffic and one pair designated for protection. In BLSR, half the bandwidth in each direction in a ring is reserved for the shared protection of all traffic in the reverse direction of the ring.

SONET Automatic Protection Switching

SONET line automatic protection switching (APS) protects the entire facility at the line layer. A network element can monitor a working line and switch to a spare (protection) line in the event of failure. An APS of 1:1 provides one protection line for each working line. An APS of 1:N provides one protection line for every N working lines.

SONET/SDH–Based TDM Transport

SONET/SDH–based TDM offers an accepted transport architecture that provides performance monitoring and logical point-to-point over the physical ring. (See Figure 17-25.) Multiservice is via TDM, which is not an optimal use of bandwidth for data transmission. However, TDM offers good protection.

Figure 17-25 SONET/SDH–Based TDM Transport

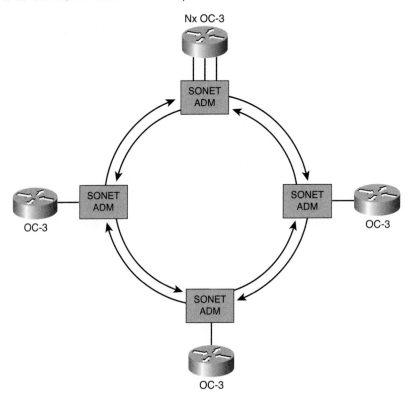

SONET Multiplexing Hierarchy

SONET has a hierarchical multiplexing structure. SONET defines a technology for carrying many signals of different capacities through a synchronous, flexible, optical hierarchy. This is accomplished by means of a byte-interleaved multiplexing scheme.

The first step in the SONET multiplexing process involves the generation of the lowest level or base signal. In SONET, this base signal is referred to as Synchronous Transport Signal level 1, or simply STS-1, which operates at 51.84 Mbps. Higher-level signals are integer multiples of STS-1, creating the family of STS-N and Synchronous Transport Module (STM)-N signals. (STS-N is the SONET hierarchy, and STM-N is the SDH hierarchy.) The optical counterpart for each STS-N signal is the designated optical carrier level N, or OC-N. (See Table 17-2.)

Table 17-2 SONET/SDH Multiplexing Hierarchy

SONET/SDH Multiplexing Hierarchy Optical Carrier	SONET/SDH Signal	Bit Rate	Capacity
OC-1	STS-1	51.84 Mbps	28 DS1s or 1 DS3
OC-3	STS-3/STM-1	155.52 Mbps	84 DS1s or 3 DS3s
OC-12	STS-12/STM-4	622.08 Mbps	336 DS1s or 12 DS3s
OC-48	STS-48/STM-16	2488.32 Mbps	1344 DS1s or 48 DS3s
OC-192	STS-192/STM-64	9953.28 Mbps	5379 DS1s or 192 DS3s

DWDM Systems

The origin of optical networks is linked to WDM, which arose to provide additional capacity on existing fibers. With WDM, several optical transmission signals that operate at different wavelengths, or "colors," are combined onto a single fiber. The difference between WDM and DWDM is fundamentally one of only degree. DWDM spaces the wavelengths more closely than does WDM; therefore, DWDM has a greater overall capacity.

DWDM puts data from many different sources together on an optical fiber, with each signal carried on its own separate wavelength. Using DWDM, more than 200 separate wavelengths or channels of data can be multiplexed into a light stream that is transmitted on a single optical fiber. (See Figure 17-26.)

Most DWDM systems support standard SONET/SDH short-reach optical interfaces to which compliant client devices can attach. In today's long-haul WDM systems, this is most often an OC-48c/STM-16c interface operating at 1300 nm wavelength. The clients can be SONET/SDH terminals or add/drop multiplexers (ADMs), ATM switches, or routers.

Figure 17-26 DWDM Systems

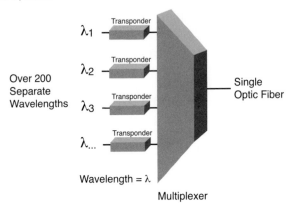

E/O/E Conversion

A light beam can travel through a network that is not 100 percent optical fiber. The E/O/E conversion begins when data traffic from the edge of the optical network enters the core of the network as an electrical signal and is converted into an optical signal for transmission across the optical network. The optical signal travels across the network and is converted back into an electrical signal at a transit point.

Within the DWDM system, a device called a transponder converts the SONET/SDH–compliant optical signal from the client back to an electrical signal. The electrical signal then is used to drive a WDM laser. The WDM laser is a precise laser that operates within the 1500 nm wavelength range. Each transponder within the system converts its client's signal to a slightly different wavelength. The wavelengths from all the transponders in the system are then optically multiplexed onto a single fiber. In the receive direction of the DWDM system, the reverse process occurs. Individual wavelengths are filtered from the multiplexed fiber and are fed to individual transponders, which convert the signal to electrical and drive a standard SONET/SDH interface to the client. (See Figure 17-27.)

Data Transmission

In a DWDM system, with each channel carrying 10 Gbps (10 billion bits per second), the optical fiber can deliver up to 2 trillion bps. (See Figure 17-28.) Because each channel is demultiplexed at the end of the transmission back into the original source, different data formats can be transmitted together at different data rates.

Figure 17-27 E/O/E Conversion

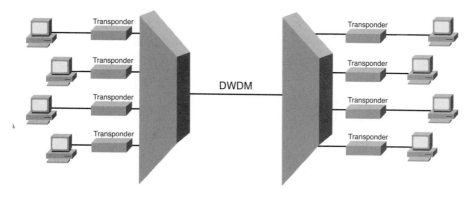

Figure 17-28 Data Transmission

DWDM

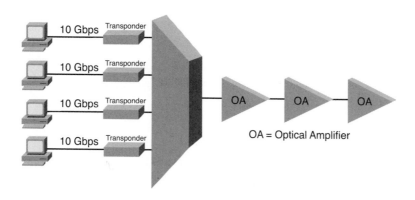

DWDM Advantages

From both technical and economic perspectives, the capability to provide potentially unlimited transmission capacity is the most obvious advantage of DWDM technology. The current investment in fiber plant can be preserved and optimized. As demands change, more capacity can be added without expensive upgrades, either by performing simple equipment upgrades or by increasing the number of lambdas on the fiber.

Bandwidth aside, the following list describes the most compelling technical advantages of DWDM:

- **Flexibility**—DWDM is extremely flexible. Specifically, Internet Protocol (IP), SONET, and Asynchronous Transfer Mode (ATM) data can be traveling at the same time within the optical fiber.

- **Transparency**—Because DWDM is a physical layer architecture, it can transparently support both TDM and data formats such as ATM, Gigabit Ethernet, Enterprise System Connection (ESCON), and Fibre Channel with open interfaces over a common physical layer.

- **Scalability**—DWDM provides economical, scalable bandwidth growth. DWDM can take advantage of the abundance of dark fiber in many metropolitan-area and enterprise networks. DWDM can meet demand for capacity quickly on point-to-point links and on spans of existing SONET/SDH rings.

- **Dynamic provisioning**—Fast and simple dynamic provisioning of network connections gives providers the capability to provide high-bandwidth services in days rather than months.

Traditional ways of increasing bandwidth include using faster electronics, which are expensive, or using more fiber. The problems with the latter include a slower time to market, expensive engineering, limited right of way, and duct exhaust. WDM increases bandwidth without these issues while maintaining fiber compatibility. DWDM provides fiber capacity release, a fast time to market, a lower cost of ownership, and the utilization of existing TDM equipment.

Metro DWDM

Metropolitan (metro) DWDM maximizes the service density, or revenue potential per wavelength, by supporting both subwavelength TDM services and wavelength services, such as Gigabit Ethernet, fiber connectivity (FICON), ESCON, and more on a single DWDM backbone. Metro DWDM is fundamentally different from long-haul DWDM; metro DWDM is driven by demand for fast service provisioning, not fiber exhaust. (See Figure 17-29.) Table 17-3 shows a comparison of metro DWDM and long-haul DWDM.

Figure 17-29 Metro Versus Long-Haul DWDM

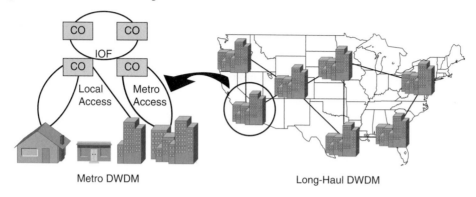

Metro DWDM   Long-Haul DWDM

Table 17-3 Metro DWDM Versus Long-Haul DWDM

	Metro DWDM	**Long-Haul DWDM**
Connectivity	Local-area access, mesh, and centrally homed configuration	Intercity connectivity
Distance	Less than 50 km between central offices (COs)	Greater than 50 km between COs
Design	Cost-driven; low-cost SONET/DWDM equipment	Capacity-driven; employs expensive DWDM technology
Fiber Usage	Fiber typically leased and readily available	Severely fiber constrained; not easy to install additional fiber

Summary

In this chapter, you learned the following key points:

- Information is transmitted at the speed of light in optical fiber.
- The O-E converter converts light into a corresponding electrical signal.
- Multimode optical fiber systems use wavelengths at 850 and 1300 nanometers (nm). Single-mode systems use only 1300 and 1550 nm.
- In fiber optics, information is carried by modulating the light power. The wavelength remains constant.
- IOR is one of the most important design characteristics of fiber.

- A fiber-optic cable has three components: a protective outer coating, an inner cladding, and a fiber core.

- Telecom fiber is classified into two modes: multimode and single mode.

- Typical multimode transmission rates are in the hundreds of megabits per second; typical single-mode transmission rates are in the millions and billions of bits per second.

- The loss factors in fiber include connector losses, macrobending, microbending, and absorption.

- Attenuation in optical fiber can be caused by scattering, absorption, stress from the manufacturing process, the environment, and physical bending.

- Dispersion causes the light pulse to spread as it travels along the fiber.

- The OA is a device that amplifies an input optical signal without converting it to electrical form.

- EDFAs do not convert the signal back to electric before boosting it.

- SONET/SDH are standards for optical transport. The SONET standard is used in North America, whereas the SDH standard is the international equivalent of SONET.

- DWDM puts data from different sources together on an optical fiber.

- A transponder is a device that converts the SONET/SDH–compliant optical signal to electrical signal, and vice versa.

- DWDM can transmit different data formats together at different data rates.

- The most compelling technical advantages of DWDM are flexibility, transparency, scalability, and dynamic provisioning.

- Metro DWDM maximizes the service density per wavelength by supporting both subwavelength TDM and wavelength services.

- Metro DWDM is driven by demand for fast service provisioning, not fiber exhaust.

Key Terms

angular separation   A condition when the bulkhead is worn and allows some play in the alignment of two fibers, some light might be lost because the cores are not lined up completely.

attenuation   The decrease in the strength of a signal during transmission. Attenuation is a natural consequence of signal transmission over long distance.

dispersion   The condition in a TDM digital signal, when the variance of light speed, limits the spacing between bits of information and the rate at which bits can be sent.

DWDM (dense wavelength division multiplexing)   A technology that transmits multiple signals simultaneously at different wavelengths, allowing a single fiber to operate as if it were multiple fibers.

end-face separation   The condition when two fiber ends are separated, and loss occurs because of the spreading of light as it comes out of the first core.

IOR (index of refraction)   The ratio of the speed of light in a vacuum to the speed of light in a fiber.

macrobending   A bend that you can see. When you bend fiber, you can cause some of the light rays to exceed the critical angle, allowing light to leak out of the core and into the cladding.

microbending   The process that causes the light to exceed the critical angle and leak out of the core. It occurs on a microscopic scale and is not visible to the eye.

midspan meet   The capability to connect different vendors' equipment on a communication network and have them function properly with each other.

multimode fiber   A type of cable that is used to transmit many signals per fiber. Multimode allows many paths or modes for the light. The larger core of multimode fiber allows light to break up into many different modes.

(OA) optical amplifier   A device that amplifies an input optical signal terahertz (THz) of optical bandwidth near 1550 nm, nearly ideal noise performance, low signal distortion and crosstalk, and high-output saturation power.

optical filter   A filter that is used in fiber networks that is used to identify different wavelengths or lambdas.

optical-to-electrical converter   The process that occurs when the receiver is a semiconductor that changes light into a corresponding electrical signal.

reflection   A light ray that bounces off the interface of two materials at the same angle it hits. Reflection occurs when a flashlight beam bounces off a window or mirror.

refraction   The bending of the light ray as it changes speed going from one material to another.

SDH (Synchronous Digital Hierarchy)   This is the term used for the international equivalent of SONET.

single-mode fiber   The fiber optic standard that is used to transmit one signal per fiber. Single-mode fiber allows only one path for the signal to travel down the middle of the fiber. The entire signal travels the length of the fiber at the same rate, allowing for much higher data rates.

SONET (Synchronous Optical Network)   The standard for synchronous data transmission on optical media used in North America.

transmitter—A source of light, such as a light bulb.

WDM (wavelength division multiplexing)   Mixing two wavelengths of light on the same fiber without interference between them.

Check Your Understanding

1. Which of the following is not the key driver of optical networks?

    A. Efficiently meet capacity and scalability requirements in both metropolitan and long-haul network infrastructure

    B. Reduce costs and accelerate profitable new service revenue simultaneously

    C. Reach long distances

    D. Be adaptable through a closed-system architecture

2. Which of the following is true of IOR?

    A. It stands for index of reflection.

    B. It is a light ray bouncing off the interface of two materials.

    C. It is the ratio of the speed of light in a vacuum to the speed of light in a fiber.

    D. Two fibers with different IOR values cannot work together.

3. True or false: The light current is the electrical noise that occurs naturally in the circuit.

    A. True

    B. False

4. Which of the following is *not* a wavelength value that is used in fiber optics?

   A. 850 nm

   B. 1300 nm

   C. 1450 nm

   D. 1550 nm

5. Which of the following describe(s) fiber optics?

   A. High-speed transmission

   B. Long transmission distance

   C. More reliability than copper wires

   D. All of the above

6. Which of the following methods can amplify an input optical signal within the fiber?

   A. OADM

   B. SONET

   C. ROL

   D. EDFA

7. What is the typical multimode transmission rate?

   A. Hundreds of megabits per second

   B. Hundreds of kilobits per second

   C. Hundreds of gigabits per second

   D. None of the above

8. Which of the following is true of single-mode fiber?

   A. The signal travels through a single-mode fiber at a different rate.

   B. Single-mode fiber has a lower data rate than multimode fiber.

   C. Single-mode fiber allows multimode to travel down the fiber.

   D. Single-mode fiber allows one mode to travel down the fiber.

9. Which of the following is a possible problem of the fiber core?

   A. The core can be slightly off center from the cladding center.

   B. The cores might be slightly different sizes.

   C. The core might be noncircular.

   D. All of the above.

10. Which of the following is *not* a component of fiber-optic cable?

    A. A fiber core

    B. An inner cladding

    C. An outer cladding

    D. A protective outer coating

11. SONET was designed to standardize which of the following?

    A. Synchronous networking-enhanced operations, administration, maintenance, and provisioning

    B. Asynchronous networking-based operation, administration, maintenance, and provisioning

    C. Protections to the SONET facilities at the application layer

    D. Transmission standards for ATM

12. Which of the following is *not* one of the three levels of overhead channel for maintenance?

    A. SOH

    B. COH

    C. LOH

    D. POH

13. Which of the following could be a client-side device for a DWDM system?

    A. LAN switches

    B. Bridges

    C. Routers

    D. Hubs

14. Which device within the DWDM system is used to convert the SONET/SDH–compliant optical signal?

    A. Transceiver

    B. Transformer

    C. Converter

    D. Transponder

15. From technical and economic perspectives, what is the most obvious advantage of DWDM technology?

   A. The capability to transmit a limited amount data at the same time

   B. The capability to provide potentially unlimited transmission capacity

   C. Easy installation

   D. Low cost

Objectives

After reading this chapter, you will be able to

- Describe how to document a network
- Describe the major components of network security
- Describe how to deal with environmental factors that can affect a network
- Describe how to establish a baseline performance measurement
- Describe the administrative side of network management
- Describe how to monitor a network
- Describe how to troubleshoot a network

Chapter 18

Network Management

Now that you know how to design and build networks, you can perform tasks such as selecting, installing, and testing cable, along with determining where wiring closets will be located. However, network design and implementation are only part of what you need to know. You must also know how to maintain and manage the network and keep it functioning at an acceptable level. Network management involves many different areas, including network documentation, network security, network maintenance, server administration, and server maintenance. This is not an all-inclusive list, but it is more than enough to be covered at this time. Each one of the listed topics is just as important as the rest, and none of them should be overlooked.

Many administrators feel that when the network is up and running, the job is over. This statement could not be further from the truth. When a network setup is done, that is when the real job of a network administrator starts. This means that you must know how to troubleshoot problems when they arise. In addition, you must know when it is necessary to expand or change the network's configuration to meet the changing demands that are placed on it. In this chapter, you begin to learn about managing a network by using techniques such as documenting, monitoring, and troubleshooting.

Network Documentation

The first and most critical component for a good network is documentation. Documentation is the most talked about and least performed task in a network. Documentation represents the network administrator's memory. It consists of your Engineering Journal, but it does not stop there. Documentation also includes these components:

- Diagrams that indicate the path of the physical wiring layout
- The type of cable

- The length of each cable
- The type of termination for the cable
- The physical location of each wall plate or patch panel
- A labeling scheme for easy identification of each wire

Main Distribution Frame (MDF) and Intermediate Distribution Frame (IDF) Layouts

This document contains a physical and logical layout of the main distribution facility and all the intermediate distribution facilities in the network. The IDF is defined as a cable rack that interconnects and manages the telecommunications wiring between an MDF and workstation devices. Cables entering a building run through a centralized MDF, then each individual IDF, and then on to specific workstations. For example, an enterprise that encompasses a building with several floors might have one MDF on the first floor and one IDF on each of the floors that is connected to the MDF. It includes the physical layout of rack mounts, auxiliary equipment, and servers in the distribution facility. It also includes patch panel labels to identify cable terminations, as well as identification and configuration details of all equipment that is located in the distribution facility.

Server and Workstation Configuration Details

You must fill out server and workstation configuration details about each host that is attached to the network. Information on these sheets is standardized and contains such things as the make and model of the computer, its serial number, floppy drives, hard drives, DVD/CD-ROM drive, sound and network cards, the amount of RAM, and any other physical details of the computer, as shown in Figures 18-1 and 18-2. This information also includes configuration details about the computer, including the interrupt request (IRQ), direct memory access (DMA), and base memory address configuration details of the peripheral cards. Other items that are a good idea to include in a document such as this include the physical location, user, and network identification (IP address, Media Access Control [MAC] address, subnet, and topology) information about the computer. Also include purchase date and warranty information in this document.

Software Listings

A listing of standard and special software used on each machine in the network is also necessary to document the standard configuration installation details of each software package. This list includes the operating system and application software. (See Figure 18-3.)

Figure 18-1 Computer Hardware Configuration Worksheet

Computer Hardware Configuration Worksheet
One sheet per computer

File Server or Workstation:	
Physical Location:	
Make and Model:	
Serial #:	
Company Inv. #:	

Removable Media Drives:

Manufacturer	Drive Letter	Capacity	Internal/External	Internal drive bay #

Fixed Media Drives:

Manufacturer	Drive Letter	Capacity	Internal/External	Internal drive bay #

Memory current/maximum:	Current:		Maximum:	

Peripheral Cards:

Manufacturer:	Model:	Type:	IRQ	DMA	Base Memory Addr.

Network Interface Cards:

Manufacturer:	Node Addr.	Model:	Lan Driver:	IRQ	DMA	Base Memory Addr.

Comments:	

Maintenance Records

Keep a list of all repairs that have been done to equipment that is included in the network. (See Figure 18-4.) This helps you predict possible future problems with existing
hardware and software.

Figure 18-2 Printer Configuration Worksheet

Printer Configuration Worksheet One sheet per printer						
Physical Location:						
Make and Model:						
Serial #:						
Company Inv. #:						
Printer ID #:						
Memory current/maximum:	Current:			Maximum:		
Paper Bins	Bin #1 paper type		Bin #2 paper type		Bin #3 paper type	
Printer Configuration:						
Serial	Port	Baud Rate	Stop bits	Parity	Xon/Xoff	Interrupt
Parallel	Port	Polling				Interrupt
Network	IP addr.	Polling	MAC addr.			
Print Queues:						
Print Operators:						
Comments:						

Figure 18-3 Computer Software Configuration Worksheet

Computer Software Configuration Worksheet One sheet per computer					
Computer Inv. #:					
Operating System(s)					
Manufacturer	Version	Service updates	Network capable	Security	
Application software					
Manufacturer	Version	Service updates	Network capable	Install directory	Data directory

Figure 18-4 Computer Repair Worksheet

Computer Repair Worksheet				
One sheet per computer				
Computer Inv#:			Date:	
Type of problem:	Hardware:		Software:	
Problem Description:				
Warranty Coverage:	Yes:	No:	Location of Repair:	
Repair description:				
Department Charged:				
Authorized By:				
Repair Completed By:				
Comments:				

Security Measures

This document not only includes "soft" security, such as user rights, password definition, and firewall support, but it also addresses physical security. Physical or hard security includes things as simple as identifying how the MDF and IDFs are locked, who has access to these rooms and why, how the hosts are protected (security cables and alarms), and who has physical access to the system. (See Figures 18-5 and 18-6.)

Figure 18-5 Network Security Room Form

Network Security Room Form					
One per room					
Physical location:				Date:	
Physical security:	Door lock	Windows	False Ceiling	Fire suppression	Locking cabinets
Servers Tape Backup:					
Server Name:	Type	Media	Off-site Loc.	Tape set name	Start day-of-week
Server #1					
Server #2					
Server #3					
Authorized Access:	Name		Department		Function
Comments:					

Figure 18-6 Network Security User Form

Network Security User Form One per user				
Physical location:		**Date:**		
User name:		**User ID:**		
Department:		Dept. manager:		
Password length:		Home Dir:		
Date ID expires:		Local access:		
Access hours:		Print access:		
Remote access:		Admin. Access:		
Inclusive groups:	Group name	Group rights	Local/Global	Restrictions
Network Duties/Privileges:				
Comments:				

User Policies

User policies are documents that can be the most important and beneficial to the network administrator. They contain information on how the users can interact with the network. These policies include what is and what is not permissible on the network. This documentation should also include the consequences of violating user policies. Other aspects of user policies include what the minimum user ID and password length should be and rules for the content of passwords. User policies need to be created with the management of the company to make sure that they are acceptable and will be enforced. As a network administrator, you want to create the most secure and functional network possible for your company, while still ensuring that network policies do not conflict with company policies or limit the users' access to necessary resources.

The information that is recorded in the documents mentioned creates the network documentation set for your system. This documentation set helps ensure that maintenance and upgrades to the network work in a more orderly fashion. This documentation also gives the administrator a starting place to which to return if an upgrade goes wrong or if recovery from a network failure is necessary. One last point about network documentation is that it continuously needs to be updated with the latest upgrades and configuration changes to the network. If this does not happen, the documentation will not have much relevance to your current network implementation.

Network Security

Network security involves two major components. The first is keeping your network safe from unauthorized access, and the second is ensuring your ability to recover data from catastrophic events.

The first part of security refers back to the network documentation section of the chapter. It involves making the network as secure as possible against unauthorized access. You do this by establishing security policies, such as minimum password length, maximum password age, unique passwords (not allowing the same password to be repeated), and allowing the user to log on to the network only at particular times of the day or days of the week. You can directly control these parameters, and the network operating system will enforce them.

Security also involves making sure that users are aware of the company's network policies and that they follow those policies. Examples of such policies might be not letting users use family or pet names for passwords. Another example is making sure that users are logged out of the network or have a password-protected screen saver activated any time they leave their computer. These are the types of rules that can be followed only if the users understand and follow the established network policies.

Data Recovery

Data recovery, the second part of network security, involves protecting data from loss. Multiple methods exist for this, and usually more than one method is used at the same time to protect the data. As shown in Figure 18-7, three popular data protection methods are tape backup of data, fault-tolerant disk configurations, and the use of uninterruptible power supplies (UPSs) to prevent equipment shutdowns during electrical power outages. The following paragraphs will talk about the first two methods in detail. The third method is discussed in the "Environmental Factors" section.

Figure 18-7 UPS, Tape Backup Unit, and Disk Array

Data backup is the process of duplicating all stored data to magnetic tape or another storage medium such as removable hard disks, CD-ROM, or DVD-ROM. Tape is often used because of its cost and capacity. Tape cartridges are much less expensive and contain much greater storage capacity than comparable removable hard disks. The drawback of tape for general usage, however, is that it stores data sequentially, the same way that music is recorded on a tape cassette. This means that, just as trying to find a single song on a cassette is difficult to do efficiently, the same is true of trying to find a specific file on a data tape. But because the data for a backup is recorded sequentially and is recovered the same way, this isn't a problem for this usage. Tape might be the best backup for servers, but CD and DVD recorders are an easier and less expensive alternative for backing up workstations.

It is important to do a tape backup as completely and quickly as possible because it can be quite a drain on system resources (network bandwidth and server processor power). To allow the complete backup to occur most efficiently, different types of backups have been developed. Most of the backup types work with a flag or switch called the *archive bit*. The archive bit is stored with a file and is turned on whenever that file is created or modified. This flag tells the backup process whether the file needs to be backed up. If a file is stored to tape during the backup process, the flag normally is turned off, saying that the current file is backed up to tape. Most companies recommend that tapes and backups be stored in some type of fire safe or be taken off the premises in case of fire or water damage.

Backup Operations

The five types of backup operations are as follows:

- **Full backup**—All files on the disk are stored to tape, and the archive bit for all files is set to off.

- **Incremental backup**—This type backs up all the files that have been created or modified since the last backup. It is important to remember two things about an incremental backup. First, an incremental backup backs up only those files and directories with the archive bit turned on, after which it turns the archive bit off. Second, any file that is created or modified subsequent to a backup has its archive bit turned back on so that it will be saved to tape during the next incremental backup.

- **Differential backup**—This type backs up all the files that have been created or modified since the last full backup. This sounds the same as an incremental backup, but the difference is that even though the file is saved to tape, the archive bit is not reset. This means that each time a differential backup is done, all the files that have been modified or created since the last full backup are stored again.

- **Copy backup**—This backup type backs up user-selected files to tape. This backup does not reset the archive bit to off.

- **Daily backup**—This type backs up only the files that are modified on the day of the backup. This backup does not reset the archive bit to off.

The first three backup procedures are the most widely used. Here is a sample way of doing first an incremental backup and then a differential backup. To do an incremental backup, first do a full backup on Monday; this resets all the archive bits on the files. On Tuesday, perform an incremental backup to a separate tape. This stores all the files that were modified on Tuesday to tape and resets their archive bit. Repeat this process for all the other business days of the week, each with a separate tape. This gives a complete backup of all files that were modified during that week. On the following Monday, start the entire process over again. The advantage of this type of backup scheme is that it requires the least amount of time per day to do the backup, so it has the least impact on the network resources. The disadvantage is that if you need to restore the backup, it requires that you first restore the full backup tape and then all the incremental backup tapes in order, which takes a great deal of time. In addition, if one of the tapes is bad, you lose that information.

To do a differential backup, first do a full backup on Monday to reset all the archive bits on the files. On Tuesday, perform a differential backup to a separate tape. This stores all the files that were modified on Tuesday to tape, but it does not reset their archive bit. Repeat this process for all the other business days of the week, each with the same tape. This process also provides a complete backup of the network data. The advantage of a differential backup is that it requires only two tapes to make and restore the backup, if necessary. A disadvantage of this method is that each day, the files that you backed up on previous days are stored again, which takes more of the network resources per day. Also, if the deferential backup tape is damaged and you performed the restore on Friday, four days' worth of data is lost and must be re-entered.

NOTE

If you do a full backup each day, you need only one tape to restore the data; however, it is impractical to run a full backup each day because of the amount of dedicated time that it requires. Neither the copy backup nor the daily backup resets the archive bit, and both are used for backup of selected files.

Another important consideration when performing system backup is the data that is on the user workstations. Is the data stored on a workstation being backed up—and if so, how? The data that is stored on the workstations is just as important—if not more important—than the data that is stored on the network servers. The particular method of backup for workstations depends on the situation. The following paragraphs discuss different scenarios for workstation backup.

The first method is used for a workstation that creates and works on a large amount of data that is used only by that workstation. In this case, an individual tape drive might work best because it allows for large amounts of data to be backed up and does not impact the network throughput. The downside of this method is that it puts the responsibility for the backup in the hands of the user.

A second way to do workstation backup is to copy all data files to a removable storage device such as a floppy or ZIP disk drive. This saves the expense, time, and complication of doing a tape backup, but it still leaves the responsibility in the hands of the user.

The last method is to create directories on the servers for all users to store their data. This solution removes the user's responsibility of doing the backup. Instead, the backup is done when the servers are backed up, eliminating the need for special devices on the workstation to do the backup. The drawback of this solution is that the policies of where data is to be stored must be clearly defined. The users must understand where they are storing the data to make sure that it is done correctly. Also, if a network communication problem occurs, the data might not be available to the users until the problem is corrected.

As you have seen, all solutions have potential problems. Each situation has a best-case solution for that particular time and place. The only wrong solution is to ignore the need to back up data on the system.

Redundancy Techniques

The next method of protecting data is through fault-tolerant storage devices. This is categorized by Redundant Array of Inexpensive Disks (RAID) levels 0 to 10. The RAID types are as follows:

- **RAID 0**—Stripes data across multiple disks, with no parity, so there is no redundancy.
- **RAID 1**—Uses disk mirroring (disk duplexing) to write data to two identical partitions on separate hard disks, thereby creating an automatic backup. Disk duplexing uses two hard-disk controller cards as well as two hard disks to prevent the controller card from being the single point of failure for the system, as in disk mirroring.

- **RAID 2**—Writes data across multiple hard disks, with error checking. This system is not used anymore because it requires expensive disk modifications to work.

- **RAID 3**—Stripes data one byte at a time and has a dedicated parity drive. This is a good but expensive redundancy choice. Because of the expense, this solution is not used very often.

- **RAID 4**—Stripes data one sector at a time and has a dedicated parity drive. This is an expensive redundancy choice that is slow writing data to the disk. Because of the expense and the slowness of writing, this solution is not used very often.

- **RAID 5**—Stripes data and parity across multiple disks (at least three for RAID 5). By mixing the parity across all the disks, a separate parity disk is not required, but full data redundancy is achieved. Data writes to the disk are still slow, but the cost is not so high. Another important fact about RAID 5 is that on a Windows NT system, the boot and system partitions cannot be located on a RAID 5 disk array.

Other RAID levels exist, but they are beyond what is needed here. In fact, not all network operating systems support the RAID levels mentioned. The three RAID levels that most operating systems support are RAID 0, RAID 1, and RAID 5. The key points to remember are that RAID 0 is used for speed and provides *no* data redundancy (backup). RAID 1 provides full data redundancy but requires twice as much storage space because all data must be written to two separate disks; this method still involves a single point of failure in the controller card. This problem is taken care of by the other variation of RAID 1, which uses disk duplexing, in which the disk controller is duplicated as well.

RAID 5 requires a minimum of three disks (four in a Windows NT system because the system and boot partitions cannot be on the RAID set), and the partition size must be the same on each disk. RAID 5 is popular because it provides fast data reads from disk, which gives better throughput to the network. One last important point about RAID 5 and Windows NT is that, to have full redundancy, this disk type of disk arrangement must be done. You need at least five disks; the first two will be set up as RAID 1 (disk mirroring) for the system and boot partitions, and the last three data disks will be set up with RAID 5. This provides full redundancy with the speed advantage that RAID 5 supplies.

The last term that you will see when working with hard disk storage is volumes. A *volume* refers to a physical unit of storage. A good analogy would be to think of an encyclopedia set. Each book in the set normally is called a volume. Some books hold more that one volume (such as the XYZ volume). Finally, think of the whole set of encyclopedias as a single unit. This concept is true of the disk volume set also, with one volume name that includes space from multiple disks that are referenced as a single unit. This information is important because volume sets are used quite often in network systems. One last thing about volume sets is that they provide *no* data redundancy; they are just a way to refer to large storage areas as a single unit.

Environmental Factors

Another part of good network management is dealing with the environmental factors that can affect a network. Controlling these factors creates a more stable and reliable network.

When installing new equipment, always follow the owner's manual setup procedures. This resolves many problems that might come up by "doing it yourself." Make sure that all the equipment's power switches are *off* before hooking it up. This also holds true if you buy a new peripheral card (an accessory that goes with your computer): Make sure that the computer power is *off* before you install it and that you ground (discharge) yourself before touching the inside of the computer. The best way to ground yourself is to use a grounding strap. Without proper grounding, you might build up an electric charge as great as 20,000 volts. This charge can be created by just walking on a synthetic rug with leather shoes or by sliding around to get comfortable in a plastic chair.

Another cause of static is lack of humidity in the air; therefore, make sure that the rooms that hold equipment have proper temperature and humidity control. Static charges are sneaky; you might not even know that there is a charge built up until it is discharged, causing damage. A static voltage discharge can burn out many of the ICs (electrical components) in network and computer equipment. To eliminate this problem, consider purchasing antistatic or ground mats along with grounding straps.

Keep dust and dirt out of the keyboards, disk drives, and equipment air vents. You can do this by keeping the environment in which equipment is used clean and free of contaminants. Tar and nicotine are sticky contaminants that are a part of cigarette smoke. Smoking around computer equipment is a sure way to eventually damage the equipment. Never set coffee, soft drinks, or any contained liquid on or above a piece of network or computer equipment. If the liquid spills and gets inside the machine, then it almost certainly causes the machine to burn out (and sometimes actually burn up).

Do not let the equipment overheat; computers and other network equipment have built-in fans to cool them. Also, do not block any of the equipment's cooling vents. Your work area should leave the computers vents open. In addition, make sure that you place the computer on a solid support area. (Do not set it on a snack tray.) Vibration and sudden shocks can loosen components inside the computer.

Power Conditioning

Protect your equipment from irregularities in your building's electrical wiring. The easiest way to protect your network and computer equipment is to put it on separate circuits in your building. Doing so solves some but not all power-related problems. Other devices that you can use to control electrical irregularities are listed here:

- **Isolating transformer**—Controls voltage spikes and high-frequency noise.
- **Regulators**—Maintain a constant output voltage, despite changes in the power line's voltage over a long period of time. Regulators handle such problems as brownouts and voltage surges.
- **Line conditioner**—Serves as a regulator with an isolating transformer built in.
- **UPS**—Charges a battery that, in turn, powers the computer. This device allows the computer to run even if there is a power failure. Note that there are two types of UPS: Online and Standby. Most inexpensive devices sold as UPS are the Standby type, which only provides power when voltage drops to 80–90 V. The more expensive Online types are true UPSs, which power the computer and provide line conditioning at all times.

EMI and RFI

Another source of problems with network communications can actually be the equipment. Computer components, such as power supplies and monitors, as well as fluorescent lights, large electric motors, and electrical wiring, can cause electromagnetic interference (EMI) and radio frequency interference (RFI) that can be picked up by other equipment and improperly shielded cables. Components of a device might be failing, but those components make it look like another part is causing the problem. These types of problems can be difficult to diagnose and are usually discovered by the use of diagnostic software and hardware.

Software Viruses

All the previous topics that can affect the performance of a network have dealt with the physical aspect of the network. Another factor that can affect the performance of your network is software—specifically, a type of software whose sole purpose is to disrupt the operation of a network. The following paragraphs describe the different types of infectious software.

A *worm* is a program that propagates itself across computers, usually by creating copies of itself in each computer's memory. A worm might duplicate itself in one computer so often that it causes the computer to crash. Sometimes written in separate "segments," a worm is introduced unknowingly into a host or network system either for "fun" or with intent to damage or destroy information. The term *worm* comes from a science-fiction novel and has generally been superseded by the term *virus*.

A virus is a program that "infects" computer files (usually other executable programs) by inserting copies of itself into those files. This is usually done in such a manner that the copies are executed when the file is loaded into memory, allowing them to infect still other files, and so on. Viruses often have damaging side effects. The latest variation is to send these viruses over the Internet as e-mail attachments.

A *Trojan horse* is a destructive program that is disguised as a game, a utility, or an application. When run, a Trojan horse does something devious to the computer system while appearing to do something useful.

A backdoor is a hole in system security that is deliberately left in place by designers or maintainers. Some operating systems come out of the box with privileged accounts for use by field service technicians or vendor maintenance programmers. Consider getting rid of unused default accounts. A backdoor is not a virus (neither is a Trojan horse), but it is a common security problem.

The following tips can help you prevent an infection by a virus to your network or computers:

- Be careful about getting software from unknown origins. Many times, software that is distributed through illegal channels is a prime carrier of viruses. This is because no system has been established for checking the software.
- Be wary of other people using your computer with their disks. Any kind of file can carry a virus. It does not have to be a program file; it could just as well be a data file that has a virus infecting it.
- Use a current virus-checker on all computers. Many companies sell or provide virus checkers.

There are many other ways of detecting and preventing viruses that cannot be covered here. If you are worried about viruses, you can obtain other articles and reports through the Internet.

Network Performance

Along with network security and redundancy, another important consideration in network management is network performance. Network performance is a measurement of a network's quickness and reliability. An automobile serves as a good comparison to a network. You want your car to lock (security) and to have a spare tire (redundancy), but this is only part of the car. The other part is how fast your car can accelerate from 0 to 60 (quickness) and whether your brakes work (reliability).

You need to check these aspects of performance to see whether performance is being maintained. To continue our analogy, if your car is not performing well, you can take it in for a tuneup. The difference between networks and cars is that most car models have standard performance levels; most networks do not. Every combination of computer and network hardware, software, and cabling has a different network performance. To know when the network is performing poorly, you must have a measurement to compare the performance against. This measurement is called a *baseline*. A baseline is established after the network has been installed and configured properly.

To establish a baseline, you can use a network monitor package or tool, such as the Fluke LANMeter or Windows NT network monitor program. These tools record several types of network performance data, including network utilization percentage, collision counts, frame errors, and broadcast traffic. By establishing a baseline measurement when the network system is at optimum normal performance levels, you have a comparison value to use to determine the health of the network.

As the network grows and changes, you need to periodically update the baseline measurement, just like any other documentation. As you upgrade hardware, you should also update the software drivers that control that hardware. If you install an upgrade or new program, you need to reinstall the service or repair packs that the software company supplies. With new hardware installation, the old software driver might not take advantage of the new hardware features or might not be compatible at all. This could create a serious performance problem. You want to reinstall the service packs to prevent files that are part of the new program's installation process or that are older than the file that is in the service pack from causing problems.

When you are making changes to the network, such as moving a piece of equipment from one location to another (as shown in Figure 18-8), verify the proper operation of that piece of equipment in its new location before updating your baseline measurement. This is especially important when you are making changes to reduce network traffic on a particular network segment. Even though the device was working properly on the old segment, it might not be working for the new segment, and this has an effect on network performance. Always verify the operation of a device thoroughly after an equipment move; this includes network functionality and all critical applications.

Server Administration

As a network administrator, you need to be aware of two types of networks: peer-to-peer and client/server networks. Figure 18-9 shows a peer-to-peer network, which is also known as a workgroup network. A peer-to-peer network is designed for small numbers of workstations; Microsoft recommends no more that 10 users in a peer-to-peer network.

Figure 18-8 PC Moved from One Segment to Another

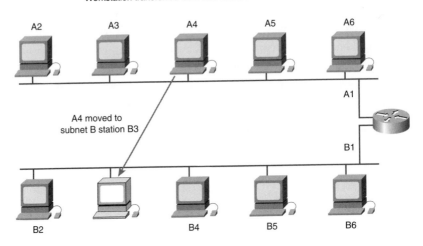

Workstation transferred from one subnet to another

A4 moved to
subnet B station B3

Figure 18-9 Peer-to-Peer Network

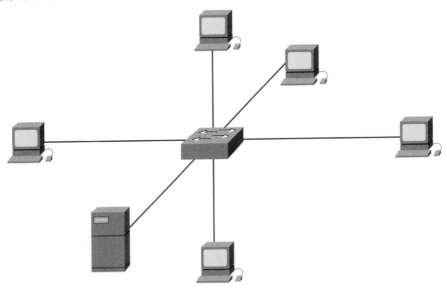

Some advantages of a peer-to-peer network are that it is cheaper to create and operate than a client/server network, it allows users to control their own resources, and it require no dedicated server or additional software besides a suitable operation system.

Among the disadvantages, no central point of management is provided, and each user must create IDs for each user who shares resources on a machine. Each time a user changes a password, you must change individually all passwords on shared resources. If a shared workstation is turned off or otherwise unavailable, then those resources are unavailable. The last disadvantage was mentioned before; if more than 10 users are currently on the network or if the network will grow to more than 10 users in the next year, a peer-to-peer network is not a good choice. Examples of peer-to-peer operating systems are Windows for Workgroups, Windows 95, Windows 98, and LANtastic.

Client/Server Network

The other type of network is a client/server network, as shown in Figure 18-10. Network operating systems are the heart of the client/server network. These systems control the resources and management of the LAN.

Figure 18-10 Client/Server Network

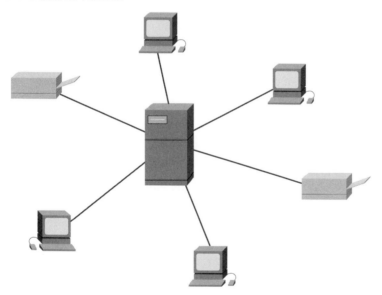

Among the advantages of client/server networks is a centralized point of user, security, and resource management. Dedicated servers also can be used to more effectively provide specific resources to clients. In addition, these networks provide access to all allowed resources with one network ID and password.

One disadvantage of a client/server network is that there is now a single point of failure in the network. If the server "goes down," no server resources are available to the clients. In fact, the clients cannot even operate without the server. Network operation and maintenance now require specially trained personnel to maintain the network. This, along with special network software and hardware, add greatly to the cost of operation. Even with the disadvantages, though, a client/server network is really the only choice for businesses that have more than 10 users. Examples of client/server operating systems are AppleTalk, UNIX, Novell NetWare, and Windows 2000/XP.

The UNIX operating system comes in many variations, as implemented by different companies. Companies that provide UNIX include Sun Microsystems, IBM, Hewlett-Packard, and Santa Cruz Operation (SCO). Free versions of UNIX also exist, including FreeBSD and Linux, the latter of which is popular at the present time.

UNIX is a multiuser operating system that supports multiprocessing, multitasking, and multithreaded applications. The operating system is kernel-based, which isolates the hardware layer of the computer from improperly operating applications and primarily uses the Network File System (NFS, which is Sun Microsystems's implementation). NFS provides for both file and directory security access on the server. UNIX also provides for centralized user and resource control through the operating system. Because of the multiple versions of UNIX in production, it is difficult to contrast all the variations and releases of this software. The previous description gives the common features that are available in all UNIX "flavors." Clients that work best with UNIX are usually specific to the developer of the operating system.

In discussing NetWare and Windows NT, it is important to talk about the different versions that have evolved over the years. The versions of NetWare that will be covered are version 3.X, version 4.X, and version 5.X. These versions primarily differ in their handling of directory services.

NetWare version 3.12 uses an object called the *bindery* to manage multiple users and resources. The drawback is that bindery services create a server-centric network, which is focused on the individual server as the point of control. This creates a problem with a multiple-server network. Each server still must have an individual ID for each user, even though the passwords could be synchronized so that changing one would change the password on all servers; this defeats the purpose of centralized management. To be fair, this is a time issue; version 3.12 was in existence before the great explosion of multiserver networks. This is one of the major improvements in NetWare version 4.11.

NetWare versions 4.11 and 5.0 use an object called *Novell Directory Services* to manage users and resources. The advantage over version 3.12 is that Novell Directory Services creates a network-centric network, which is focused on the entire network as the point of control. This focus consolidates management to a single point, and servers are treated just as objects within the context of the network. This allows a single ID and password to authorize users for all resources across the network, and it provides for easier network organization and management.

All versions of NetWare use a combination of two file services, the first of which is a file allocation table (FAT), which is the file system used for DOS. The second is the directory entry table (DET), which is a proprietary Novell file system that provides for both file and directory security on the server. Clients that work well with NetWare are numerous; they include all versions of Windows, DOS, Macintosh, and OS-2. NetWare's strong points are user and file resource management.

Windows NT is the last operating system to be discussed. There are two versions of Windows NT to cover: Windows NT 4.0 and Windows 2000 (also known as Windows NT 5.0). Windows NT version 4.0 server and workstation were developed with the Windows 95 user interface. This provides a consistent "look and feel" interface across all Windows products. Windows NT handles user and resource management through the use of domains (see Figure 18-11). A domain is a logical grouping of users and resources under the control of one server, called the primary domain controller (PDC). Domains also support the use of secondary servers called *backup domain controllers (BDCs)*, which balance the workload of the PDC and provide for redundancy of user and resource objects.

Figure 18-11 NT Version 4.0 Domain and Multiple-Domain Layout

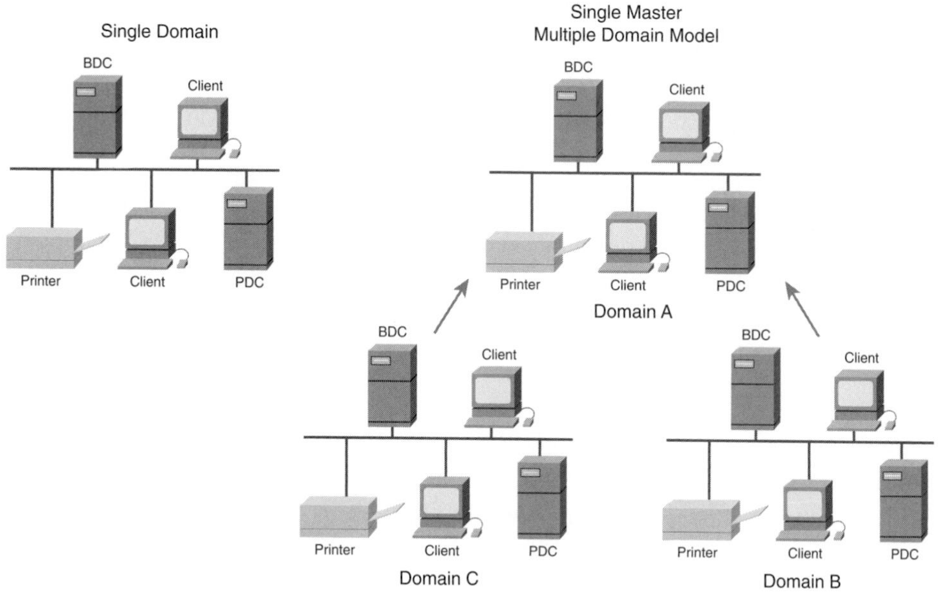

A third type of server, called a *standalone server*, is allowable in a domain. This server is primarily set up to support one particular application and to dedicate its resources to that application. Another variation of a domain is called a *multidomain model*. In

this model, separate domains are connected by trusting/trusted relationships, which allows users to cross domain boundaries to use resources.

The Windows 2000 Server is based on NT technology. However, the management structure has changed from domains to an Active Directory structure. Active Directory is based on a network-centric model, like NDS, rather that a domain-centered model.

Windows NT is just like UNIX: It is a multiuser operating system that supports multiprocessing, multitasking, and multithreaded applications. The Windows NT operating system, just like UNIX, is kernel-based, which isolates the hardware layer of the computer from improperly operating applications, and uses both the FAT16 file system and NT's own proprietary system, New Technology File System (NTFS). With FAT16, Windows NT provides only directory (also known as folder)–level security; no individual file security is provided. NTFS provides both file- and directory-level security and permissions.

The reason that Windows NT supports both of these file systems is that it has the capability to coexist with another operating system on the same machine. This does not mean that both systems can run at the same time, but the computer can run Windows NT or the other operating system. For the other operating system to have file access, the file system must be FAT16. Just as a point of interest, Windows 95 and 98 support FAT32; Windows NT does not. Therefore, FAT16 would be the choice for running Windows NT and Windows 95 on the same computer. Windows NT works best with its own client, Windows NT Workstation, but it also works well with Windows for Workgroups, Windows 95 and 98, and Macintosh clients.

No matter which network operating system is used, the main function of the NOS is to control the network. This is accomplished by establishing network user rights, login accounts (user IDs), passwords, and groups, along with system profiles and policies. These terms will be identified more completely in the following sections.

Network Control

A login account identifies the network user to the network system. This account, along with the user's password, identifies and gives access to the network system's resources. This account ID also holds the user responsible for actions on the network. This should be stated in the security documents identified earlier in the chapter. Just because the network user has an account does not mean that the network resources are completely available to this user. User rights determine the user's resource availability.

User rights are set by an administrator to permit or deny access to particular resources on a network. For example, even though a user is connected to the network and a network printer is also connected to the network, the user might not be able to print to that printer. If the user is not assigned the right or permission to use the printer, access to that resource is denied. If the user *is* assigned the right or permission, then the printer is available. This is true of printers, data and program files, and any other "resources" on the network. There is one administrative problem with assigning rights to users: If numerous users are on a network system, then assigning and modifying rights for each user can take most of the administrator's time. This problem is resolved by using groups.

Groups are a logical collection of users on the network. The rights and permissions are given to the group instead of to an individual user. If a user needs these rights, he or she is assigned to the groups and, by this action, is given the rights that are assigned to the group. This is also true if the rights to a resource need to be changed; a change to the group reflects that change to all the group's members. This does not mean that rights cannot be assigned to individual users, but the more efficient way in large networks is to work with groups.

The terms policy and *profiles* have nothing to do with system resources, but with how the user interacts with the workstation. Profiles allow a user to customize a user interface on a computer and then be able to use that profile at any computer that user connects to the network. This is called a roaming profile. Another type of profile brings up the same user interface for everyone without allowing changes to be made. This is called a *mandatory profile* and is used in situations in which many people must use the same physical computer. If users are on the same computers all the time and do not need to go to other computers, they might have a local profile. A local profile is stored not on the network like the first two profiles, but on the local computer.

Policies deal with the control of the resources on the local computer. A policy that prevents a user from storing data on the workstation's local hard or floppy drive can improve security by preventing data from being taken out of the building. Policies can also prevent users from accidentally making changes to their system configuration information. Things such as video card settings, hard disk configuration, and network card settings are aspects of the workstation that the majority of users have no need to change; if these aspects are changed, they can cause a lot of extra unnecessary work for help desk and network personnel.

All the aspects that we have just discussed can be summarized this way: Network rights, login accounts, passwords, and groups, along with profiles and policies, provide a way for the system administrator to control access and restrictions to network services and to control the local user workstation. Being a network administrator is also a set of rights and privileges granted on the network. Not all users have the right to change other users' rights and privileges; these rights are reserved for certain groups that have been given administrator rights. By being part of a group that has administrator rights, you are also an administrator.

The Administrative Side of Network Management

The view of a network is important. A network is a unified system of devices that interact with one another to provide communication. When a network administrator looks at a network, he should look at it as a whole entity, not as individual parts. In other words, each device in a network affects other devices and the network as a whole. As shown in Figure 18-12, nothing is isolated when it is connected to a network.

Figure 18-12 Basic Network Setup

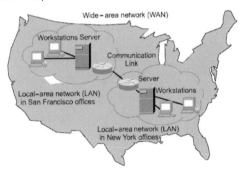

A good analogy for the network, in this instance, is an automobile. A car is a collection of parts that provide transportation. The engine provides power to move the car, but it does not work well if the fuel system goes bad or if the tires are flat. Brakes are also important components, but once again, without the hydraulic system, the brakes do not work and the car does not stop. Without all the components working together, the car does not perform its designated task: transportation.

The same is true with a network system. If the network server is set up to work with the IPX/SPX protocol and the hosts are not, then the two cannot communicate. Also, if the system is working fine and the administrator changes the protocols on only one end, then the system stops working. One device affects how other devices function. Another example is having a DNS server located at IP address 192.150.11.123. All your hosts are configured to find the DNS server at this IP address. If a network technician changes the IP address of the DNS server without changing the host identifiers, then the hosts no longer have DNS services.

The important thing to remember when dealing with a network is to view it as a single unit instead of a group of individual connected devices. This also applies to the wide-area connections that are used when connecting to the Internet. Changes that are made to the routers at your location directly affect the efficiency and reliability of communication throughout the entire system.

Understanding and Establishing the Boundaries of the Network

In an enterprise network, it is important that the network staff members know their responsibilities. Is it the responsibility of the network staff to diagnose problems on a user's desktop, or is it simply to determine that a user's problem is not related to communication? Does the network staff's responsibility extend only as far as the horizontal cabling wall plate, or does that responsibility extend all the way to the network interface card?

These definitions are important to a networking department because they affect the workload of each person and the cost of network services for the enterprise. The greater the responsibility of a network staff, the greater the resource cost. Imagine a restaurant that is owned and operated by a single individual. Only one person is responsible for all tasks, including cooking, serving, washing dishes, and paying the bills. The human-resource cost of the restaurant is relatively low, but possibilities for growth and expansion are limited until the owner hires cooks, waiters, bussers, and accountants. When responsibilities are divided, the restaurant can serve more people more efficiently. The trade-off, of course, is that resource costs have risen along with growth and expansion.

Just as the restaurant example showed, the job of network support can encompass all aspects of the network, or it can be limited to just certain components.

These responsibilities need to be defined and enforced on a department-by-department basis. The key to understanding this relationship is that making the responsibility area too large can overburden the resources of the department, but making the area too small can make it difficult to effectively resolve the problems on the network.

Costs of a Network

Network administration encompasses many responsibilities, including cost analysis. This means determining not only the cost of network design and implementation, but also the cost of maintaining, upgrading, and monitoring the network. Determining the cost of network installation is not a particularly difficult task for most network administrators. Equipment lists and costs can be readily established; labor costs can be calculated by using fixed rates. Unfortunately, the cost of building the network is just the beginning.

Some of the other cost factors that you must consider are the following:

- Network growth over time
- Technical and user training
- Repairs
- Software deployment

These cost factors are much more difficult to project than the cost of building the network. The network administrator must be able to look at historical and company growth trends to project the cost of growth in the network. A manager must look at new software and hardware to determine whether the company needs to implement them (and when), as well as to determine what staff training is needed to support these new technologies. The cost of redundant equipment for mission-critical operations should also be added to the cost of maintaining the network. Think of running an Internet-based business that uses a single router to connect to the Internet. If that router fails, your company is out of business until you replace the router, which could cost the company thousands of dollars in lost sales. A wise network administrator might keep a spare router on the premises to minimize the time that the company is offline.

Error Report Documentation

Effective network management requires thorough documentation. When problems arise, some form of error document should be generated, as shown in Figure 18-13. This error document is used to gather the basic information that is necessary to identify and assign a network problem. The document also provides a way of tracking the progress and eventual solution of the problem. Problem reports provide justification to senior management for hiring new staff, purchasing equipment, and providing additional training. In addition, this documentation provides solutions to recurring problems that have already been resolved. All the material presented so far in this chapter deals with the nontechnical issues of network management. The rest of this chapter deals with the tools that are available to monitor and diagnose problems on a wide-area network (WAN).

Figure 18-13 Error Report Documentation

Computer Repair Worksheet			
One sheet per computer			
Computer Inv#:		Date:	
Type of problem:	Hardware:	Software:	
Problem Description:			
Warranty Coverage:	Yes:	No: Location of Repair:	
Repair description:			
Technician Name:			
Department Charged:			
Authorized By:			
Comments:			

Monitoring the Network

Although there are many reasons to monitor a network, the two primary reasons are to predict changes for future growth and to detect unexpected changes in network status. Unexpected changes might include things such as a router or switch failing, a hacker trying to gain illegal access to the network, or a communication link failure. Without the ability to monitor the network, an administrator can only react to problems as they occur instead of preemptively preventing these problems.

In the previous sections, network management topics were covered with primary focus on LANs. Monitoring a WAN involves many of the same basic management techniques as managing a LAN. One of the major differences between WANs and LANs is the physical placement of equipment. The placement and use of monitoring tools becomes critical to the uninterrupted operation of the WAN.

Connection Monitoring

One of the most basic forms of connection monitoring takes place every day on a network. The process of users logging on to the network verifies that connections are working properly, or the networking department will soon be contacted. This is not the most efficient or preferable method of connection monitoring that is available, however. Simple programs can enable the administrator to enter a list of host IP addresses so that these addresses are periodically pinged. If a connection problem exists, the program alerts the administrator by the ping output. This is an inefficient and primitive way to monitor the network, but it is better than nothing. Another aspect of this type of monitoring is that it determines that there is a communication breakdown only somewhere between the monitoring station and the target device. The fault could be a bad router, switch, or network segment. The ping test indicates only that the connection is down; it does not indicate where the problem is. Checking all the hosts on a WAN using this type of monitoring involves many resources. If the network has 3000 hosts on it, then pinging all the network devices and hosts can use a great deal of system resources. A better way is to ping just a few of the important hosts, servers, routers, and switches to verify their connectivity. These ping tests do not give true data unless workstations are always left on. Again, this method of monitoring should be used only if no other method is available.

Traffic Monitoring

Traffic monitoring is a more sophisticated method of network monitoring. It looks at the actual packet traffic on the network and generates reports based on the network traffic. Programs, such as Microsoft Windows NT Network Monitor and Fluke's Network Analyzer, are examples of this type of software. These programs not only detect failing equipment, but they also determine whether a component is overloaded or poorly configured. The drawback to this type of program is that it normally works on a single segment at a time; if data needs to be gathered from other segments, the monitoring software must be moved to that segment. You can overcome this by using agents on the remote network segments (as shown in Figure 18-14). Equipment, such as switches and routers, can generate and transmit traffic statistics as part of their operating system. How is the data gathered and organized in one central location to be useful to the network administrator? The answer: the *Simple Network Management Protocol (SNMP)*.

Figure 18-14 SNMP Layout

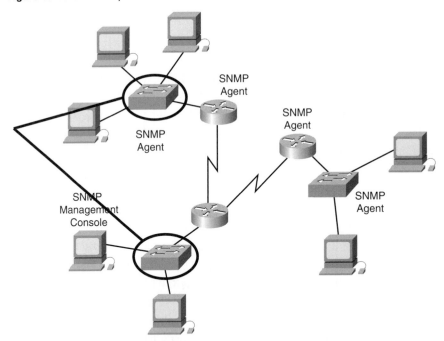

SNMP

SNMP is a protocol that allows management to transmit statistical data over the network to a central management console. SNMP is a component of the Network Management Architecture, which consists of four major components:

- **Management console (station)**—This is the network manager's interface into the network system. It has the programs to manipulate data and control the network. The management station also maintains a Management Information Base (MIB) extracted from the devices under its management.

- **Management agent**—This is the component that is contained in the devices that are to be managed. Bridges, routers, hubs, and switches might contain SNMP agents to allow the management station to control them. The management agent responds to the management station in two ways. First, through polling, the management station requests data from the agent, and the agent responds with the requested data. Second, trapping is a data-gathering method that is designed to reduce traffic on the network and reduce the processes running on the devices being monitored. Instead of the management station polling the agents at specific intervals continuously, thresholds (top or bottom limits) are set on the managed device. If this threshold on the device is exceeded, the managed device sends an alert message to the management station. This eliminates the need to continuously poll all the managed devices on the network. Trapping is beneficial on networks that have a large number of devices that need to be managed. It reduces the amount of SNMP traffic on the network to provide more bandwidth for data transfer.

- **MIB**—This has a database structure and resides on each device that is managed. The database contains a series of objects, which are resource data gathered on the managed device. Some of the categories in the MIB include port interface data, TCP data, and ICMP data.

- **Network management protocol**—This is used is SNMP. SNMP is an application layer protocol that is designed to communicate data between the management console and the management agent. It has three key capabilities: the capability to GET the management console retrieving data from the agent, to PUT the management console setting object values on the agent, and to TRAP the agent notifying the management console of significant events. The key word to remember in Simple Network Management Protocol is *simple*. When SNMP was developed, it was designed to be a short-term system that would later be replaced. But just like TCP/IP, SNMP has become one of the major standards in Internet/intranet management configurations. Over the past few years, enhancements have been added to SNMP to expand its monitoring and management capabilities. One of the greatest enhancements to SNMP is *Remote Monitoring (RMON)*. The RMON extensions to SNMP allow you to look at the network as a whole instead of looking at individual devices.

Remote Monitoring

Probes gather remote data in RMON. A probe has the same function as an SNMP agent. A probe has RMON capabilities; an agent does not. When you are working with RMON, as with SNMP, a central management console is the point of data collection. An RMON probe is located on each segment of the network that is monitored.

These probes can be dedicated hosts, resident on a server, or included in a standard networking device, such as a router or a switch. These probes gather the specified data from each segment and relay it to the management console. Redundant management consoles provide two major benefits to network management processes. First is the capability to have more than one network administrator in different physical locations monitor and manage the same network (such as one in New York and one in San Jose). Second is the all-important concept of redundancy. Having two or more management consoles means that if one console fails, the other console still can be used to monitor and control the network until the first console is repaired. (See Figure 18-15.)

Figure 18-15 Network with Dual-Management Consoles

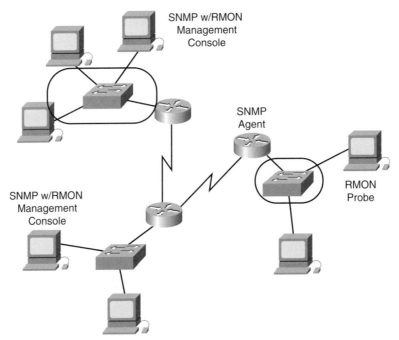

The RMON extension to the SNMP protocol creates new categories of data. These categories add more branches to the MIB database. Each of the major categories is explained in the following list:

- **The Statistics Group**—Contains statistics that are gathered for each monitored subnetwork. These statistics include counters (incremental that start from zero) for bytes, packets, errors, and frame size. The other type of data reference is an index table. The table identifies each monitored Ethernet device, which allows counters to be kept for each Ethernet device. The Statistics Group provides a view of the overall load and health of a subnetwork by measuring different types of errors, including cyclic redundancy check (CRC), collisions, and over- and undersized packets.

- **The History Group**—Contains a data table that records samples of the counters in the Ethernet Statistics Group over a specified period of time. The default time set up for sampling is every 30 minutes (1800 seconds), and the default table size is 50 entries, giving a total of 25 hours of continuous monitoring. As the history is created for the specified counter, a new entry is created in the table at each sample interval until the limit of 50 is reached. Then, as each new entry is created, the oldest entry in the table is deleted. These samples provide a baseline of the network and can be used to compare against the original baseline to resolve problems or to update the baseline as the network changes.

- **The Alarm Group**—Uses user-specified limits called thresholds. If the data counters that are being monitored cross the thresholds, a message or alarm is sent to the specified people. This process, known as an error trap, can automate many functions of network monitoring. Instead of having a person constantly and directly monitoring the network or waiting for a user to identify a problem with the network, the network process can send messages to the network personnel because of a failure or, more importantly, an impending failure. This is an important component of preemptive troubleshooting.

- **The Host Group**—Contains counters that are maintained about each host that is discovered on the subnetwork segment. Some of the counter categories maintained are packets, octets, errors, and broadcasts. Types of counters that are associated with each of the previously mentioned items could be, for example, total packets, packets received, and packets sent, along with many counters that are specific to the type of item.

- **The HostTopN Group**—Prepares reports about a group of hosts that top a statistical list based on a measured parameter. The best way to describe this group is by example. A report could be generated for the top 10 hosts that generate broadcasts for a day. Another report might be generated for the most packets that are transmitted during the day. This category provides an easy way to determine who and what type of data traffic most occupies the selected subnetwork.

- **The Matrix Group**—Records the data communication between two hosts on a subnetwork. This data is stored in the form of a matrix (a multidimensional table). One of the reports that can be generated from this category is which host utilizes a server. Reorganizing the matrix order can create other reports. For example, one report might show all users of a particular server, whereas another report might show all the servers that a particular host uses.

- **The Filter Group**—Provides a way that a management console can instruct an RMON probe to gather selected packets from a specific interface on a particular subnetwork. This selection is based on the use of two filters: the data filter and the status filter. The data filter is designed to match or not match particular data patterns, which allows for the selection of that particular data. The status filter is based on the type of packet looked at, such as a CRC packet or a valid packet. These filters can be combined using logical "and" and "or" to create complicated conditions. The filter group enables the network administrator to selectively look at different types of packets to provide better network analysis and troubleshooting.

- **The Packet Capture Group**—Allows the administrator to specify a method to use to capture packets that the Filter Group has selected. By capturing specified packets, the network administrator can look at the exact detail for packets that meet the basic filter. The packet group also specifies the quantity of the individual packet captured and the total number of packets captured.

- **The Event Group**—Contains events that other groups generate in the MIB database. An example is a counter exceeding the threshold for that counter that is specified in the Alarm Group. This action would generate an event in the Event Group. Based on this event, an action could be generated, such as issuing a warning message to all the people who are listed in the Alarm Group parameters or creating a logged entry in the event table. An event is generated for all comparison operations in the RMON MIB extensions.

- **The Token Ring Extensions**—Contains counters that are specific to Token Ring networks. Although most of the counters in the RMON extensions are not specific to any type of data-link protocol, the Statistics and History Groups are. They are particularly attuned to the Ethernet protocol. The Token Ring Group creates counters that are necessary to monitor and manage Token Ring networks by using RMON.

Remember that RMON is an extension to the SNMP protocol. Specifically, this means that although RMON enhances the operation and monitoring capabilities of SNMP, SNMP is still required for RMON to operate on a network. As a last point, it is important to mention that there are later revisions of both SNMP and RMON, labeled as SNMPv2 and RMON2. This curriculum does not cover all the new capabilities of these versions.

Network Troubleshooting

Problems happen. Even when the network is monitored, the equipment is reliable, and the users are careful, things will go wrong. The test of a good network administrator is the ability to analyze, troubleshoot, and correct problems under pressure of a network failure that causes company downtime. The suggestions in this section review troubleshooting techniques and offer other tools for troubleshooting a network. This is a review of previous techniques as well as some additional techniques for troubleshooting a network. As stated earlier, these techniques can be the best tools in curing network problems.

The first and most important thing in troubleshooting networks is to use your Engineering Journal and to take notes. Note-taking can define a clear path to diagnosing a problem. It can tell you what you have already tried and what effect that had on the problem. This can be extremely valuable to the troubleshooter so that previous attempts at resolving the problem will not be repeated needlessly. Taking notes is also valuable if the problem is handed off to another technician because it prevents that person from having to redo all that work. A copy of these notes should be included with the resolution of the problem when the trouble ticket on this job is completed. This provides a reference for similar problems that might occur.

Another essential element of preemptive troubleshooting is labeling. Label everything, including both ends of a horizontal cable run. This label should include not only the number of the cable but also where the other end is located and the usage of the cable, such as voice, data, or video. This type of label can be even more valuable than a wiring cut sheet when it comes to troubleshooting because it is located right where the unit is, not stuck in a drawer somewhere. Along with the wire labels, labeling each port on a hub, switch, or router as to location, purpose, and point of connection greatly improves the ease with which problems can be solved.

Finally, all other components that are attached to the network should be labeled as to their location and purpose. With this type of labeling, all components can be located, and their purpose on the network can be easily defined. Proper labeling, used with the network documentation that was created when the network was built and updated, gives a complete picture of the network and its relationships. Another important reminder is that the documentation is useful only if it is current. All changes made to the network must be documented both on the devices or wire that is changed and in the paper documentation that is used to define the complete network.

The Troubleshooting Process

The first step in network troubleshooting is to define the problem. This definition can be a consolidation of many different sources. One of the sources could be a trouble ticket or help desk report, which initially identifies a problem. Another source might be a phone conversation with the user where you discuss the problem to gather more information about it. Network monitoring tools can provide a more complete idea about the specific problem that needs to be resolved. Other users and your own observations will provide information. Evaluating all this information might give the troubleshooter a much clearer starting place to resolve the problem, rather than by working from any one source. Network troubleshooting is a systematic process that is applied to solve a problem on a network. A good technique for troubleshooting is the scientific method. The following list shows the scientific method specifically pointed at troubleshooting:

Step 1 Identify the network/user problem.

Step 2 Gather data about the network/user problem.

Step 3 Analyze data to come up with a possible solution to the problem.

Step 4 Implement a solution to the network to attempt correction to the system.

Step 5 If the problem is not resolved, undo previous changes and modify the data.

Step 6 Go back to Step 3.

Troubleshooting Techniques

The processes of elimination and divide and conquer are the most successful techniques for implementing a scientific method of troubleshooting.

The following scenarios explain these techniques.

The Process of Elimination Technique

Imagine that a user on your network calls the help desk to report that his computer can no longer connect to the Internet. The help desk fills out the error report form and forwards it to you, the network support department.

You call and talk to the user, who tells you that he has done nothing differently to get to the Internet. You check the hardware logs for the network and find out that the user's computer was upgraded last night. Your first hypothesis is that the computer's network drivers must be configured incorrectly. You go to the machine and check the network configuration information on the computer. It seems to be correct, so you **ping** the server on that subnet. It does not connect, as shown in Example 18-1.

Example 18-1 *Bad* **ping** *Output (Request Timed Out)*

```
C:/ping 110.0.1.1
Pinging 110.0.1.1 with 32 bytes of data:
Request timed out
Request timed out
```

Example 18-1 *Bad* **ping** *Output (Request Timed Out) (Continued)*

```
Request timed out
Request timed out
Ping statistics for 110.0.1.1:
Packets: Sent = 4, Received = 0, Lost = 4 (100% loss)
```

The next solution is to check to see if the workstation cable is plugged in. You check both ends of the cable and try **ping**ing the server again. Next, you **ping** 127.0.0.1, which is the loopback address for the computer (see Example 18-2). The **ping** is successful, so that eliminates a possible problem between the computer, the driver configuration, and the network interface card.

Example 18-2 *Loopback* **ping** *Output*

```
C:/ping 127.0.0.1
Pinging 127.0.0.1 with 32 bytes of data:
Reply from 127.0.0.1: bytes=32 time=1ms TTL=128
Reply from 127.0.0.1: bytes=32 time=1ms TTL=128
Reply from 127.0.0.1: bytes=32 time=1ms TTL=128
Reply from 127.0.0.1: bytes=32 time=1ms TTL=128
Ping statistics for 110.0.1.1:
Packets: Sent = 4, Received = 4, Lost = 0 (0% loss)
```

You decide that there might be a problem with the server for this network segment. Another networked computer is at the next desk, so you **ping** the server's address, and the result is successful (see Example 18-3). This eliminates the server, the backbone, and the server's connection to the backbone as the problem.

Example 18-3 *Successful* **ping** *Output*

```
C:/ping 110.0.1.1
Pinging 110.0.1.1 with 32 bytes of data:
Reply from 110.0.1.1 bytes=32 time=1ms TTL=128
Reply from 110.0.1.1: bytes=32 time=1ms TTL=128
Reply from 110.0.1.1: bytes=32 time=1ms TTL=128
Reply from 110.0.1.1: bytes=32 time=1ms TTL=128
Ping statistics for 110.0.1.1:
Packets: Sent = 4, Received = 4, Lost = 0 (0% loss)
```

You then go to the IDF and switch the port for the workstation, go back to the workstation, and try to ping the server again. The solution still does not work (see Example 18-4). This narrows your search down to the horizontal cabling or the workstation patch cable. You go back to the IDF, put the cable back in the original switch port, get a new workstation patch cable, and return to the workstation. You replace the workstation cable and try to ping the server again (see Example 18-5). This time, you are successful, so the problem is fixed. The last step is to document the problem solution. Do this on the error report form and return it to the help desk so that it can be logged as completed. Remember also to document the problem solution in your Engineering Journal for future reference.

Example 18-4 *Unsuccessful* ping *Output*

```
C:/ping 110.0.1.1
Pinging 110.0.1.1 with 32 bytes of data:
Request timed out
Request timed out
Request timed out
Request timed out
Ping statistics for 110.0.1.1:
Packets: Sent = 4, Received = 0, Lost = 4 (100% loss)
```

Example 18-5 *Successful* ping *Output*

```
C:/ping 110.0.1.1
Pinging 110.0.1.1 with 32 bytes of data:
Reply from 110.0.1.1 bytes=32 time=1ms TTL=128
Reply from 110.0.1.1: bytes=32 time=1ms TTL=128
Reply from 110.0.1.1: bytes=32 time=1ms TTL=128
Reply from 110.0.1.1: bytes=32 time=1ms TTL=128
Ping statistics for 110.0.1.1:
Packets: Sent = 4, Received = 4, Lost = 0 (0% loss)
```

As you can see, this example shows a step-by-step process of eliminating the possible causes of the network problem. Each possible problem was addressed in turn and individually eliminated. If you make multiple changes at once, the process can be confused, and the solution cannot be precisely identified. As the solutions were implemented and found not to resolve the problem, the data was re-evaluated and new problem solutions were formulated. This process continued until the actual problem was found and resolved. The problem was then documented for future use. No matter what type of problems will be encountered on a network system, the process for resolving them will be the same.

The Divide and Conquer Technique

Here, you combine two networks that work fine when they are not connected (see Figure 18-16), but when they are joined, the entire combined network fails (see Figure 18-17). The first step to correct this problem is to divide the network back into two separate networks and verify that the two still operate correctly when separated. If this is true, then you remove all the subnet connections for one of the connecting routers and reconnect it to the other working network. Verify that it is still working correctly.

Figure 18-16 Sample Network Example

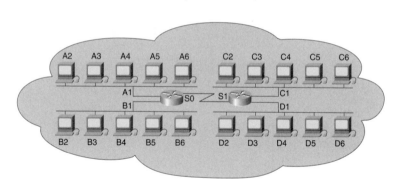

Figure 18-17 Network Without the A and B Subnetworks

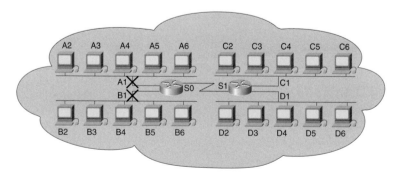

If the network is still functioning, add each of that router's subnetworks back into the router until the overall system fails. (See Figure 18-18) Remove the last subnet that was added, and see if the whole network returns to its normal operation.

If the network is again functioning normally, then remove the hosts from the network segment (see Figure 18-19) and replace them one at a time, again checking to see when the network fails (see Figure 18-20). When you find the offending device, remove it and verify that the network returns to normal.

Figure 18-18 Network Without the B Subnetwork

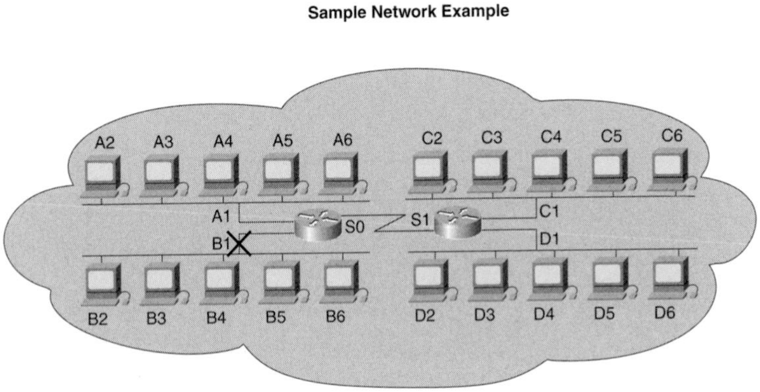

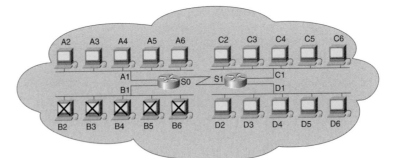

Figure 18-19 B Network Segment Without the Hosts

Figure 18-20 B Network Segment Without One Host

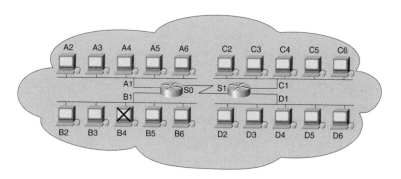

Sample Network Example

If the network still functions normally, you have isolated the faulty piece of equipment. You now can troubleshoot this individual piece of equipment to find out why it was causing the entire network to crash. If nothing proves to be wrong with this device upon analysis, it might be that this device, in conjunction with another device on the opposite network, is causing the problem. To find the other end of the problem, you have to repeat the process you used previously. First, reconnect the host that caused the network to fail. Then, disconnect all the subnetworks from the other router. (See Figure 18-21.) Check that the network has returned to operating status. If the network is functioning again, add each of that router's subnetworks back into the router until the overall system fails. Remove the last subnet that was added before the failure and see if the whole network returns to its normal operation.

Figure 18-21 Network Without the C and D Subnetworks

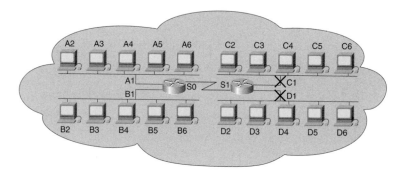

Sample Network Example

If the network again functions normally, remove the hosts from the network segment and replace them one at a time (see Figure 18-22), again checking to see when the network fails (see Figure 18-23). When you find the offending device, remove it and verify that the network returns to normal.

Figure 18-22 C Network Segment Without the Hosts

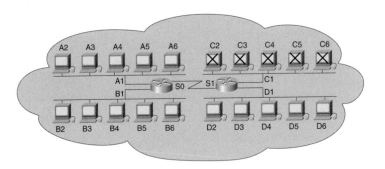

Figure 18-23 C Network Segment Without One Host

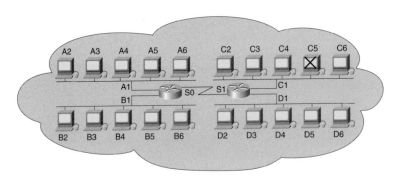

If the network still functions normally, you have isolated the other faulty piece of equipment. It is now possible to troubleshoot this individual piece of equipment to find out why it was causing the entire network to crash. If nothing proves to be wrong with this device upon analysis, compare the two hosts and find the reason for their conflict. By resolving this conflict, you will be able to reconnect both stations into the network, and it will still function normally. (See Figure 18-24.)

Figure 18-24 Complete Functioning Network

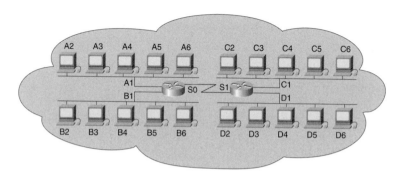

Sample Network Example

Software Tools

Along with the processes described previously, software tools are available for the network administrator to use to solve network connectivity problems. These tools can help in LAN troubleshooting, but they are especially helpful in a WAN troubleshooting situation. Certain commands are available to a network administrator in most client software packages. These commands include **ping**, **tracert** (traceroute), **telnet**, **netstat**, **ARP**, and **IPconfig** (WinIPcfg).

Command ping

Command **ping** sends ICMP echo packets to verify connections to a remote host. The output in Example 18-6 displays whether the **ping** is successful. The output shows the number of packets responded to and the return time of the echo.

Example 18-6 *Number of Packets That Responded to the* ping *Command*

```
C:/ping 127.0.0.1
Pinging 127.0.0.1 with 32 bytes of data:
Reply from 127.0.0.1: bytes=32 time=1ms TTL=128
Reply from 127.0.0.1: bytes=32 time=1ms TTL=128
Reply from 127.0.0.1: bytes=32 time=1ms TTL=128
Reply from 127.0.0.1: bytes=32 time=1ms TTL=128
Ping statistics for 110.0.1.1:
Packets: Sent = 4, Received = 4, Lost = 0 (0% loss)


C:/ping 110.0.1.1
```

Example 18-6 *Number of Packets That Responded to the* **ping** *Command (Continued)*

```
Pinging 110.0.1.1 with 32 bytes of data:
Request timed out
Reply from 140.189.8.65: Destination Unreachable
Request timed out
Request timed out
Ping statistics for 110.0.1.1:
Packets: Sent = 4, Received = 1, Lost = 3 (75% loss)
```

The syntax for the command is as follows, and it is explained in Table 18-1:

ping [**-t**] [**-a**] [**-n** *count*] [**-l** *length*] [**-f**] [**-i** *ttl*] [**-r** *count*] *destination*

Table 18-1 **ping** Command Options

Syntax	Description
-t	**ping** until interrupted
-a	Resolves host name and ping address
-n	Resolves host name and ping address
-l	Specifies length; send specified size echo packets
-f	Issues the "DO NOT FRAGMENT" command to gateways
-i	Here, *ttl* sets the TTL field
-r	Here, *count* records the route of the outgoing and returning packets
destination	Specifies the remote host to **ping**, by domain name or by IP address

tracert (Traceroute)

Command **tracert** (Traceroute) shows the route that a packet took to reach its destination. The output in Example 18-7 shows the **tracert** command.

Example 18-7 **tracert** *Command Output*

```
C:/tracert cisco.com

Tracing route to Cisco.com [192.31.7.130]
over a maximum of 30 hops:
```

continues

Example 18-7 tracert *Command Output (Continued)*

```
1    1 ms    <10ms    <10ms    198.150.221.254
2    2ms     1ms      2ms      198.150.15.252
3    4ms     2ms      2ms      198.150.12.1
4    23ms    4ms      4ms      ArizonaStateUniversity -s1 -0 -1.core.azst.net
     [140.189.64.9]
5    4ms     5ms      5ms      ArizonaStateUniversityISP -atml -0 -3.core.azst.net
     [140.189.8.65]
6    8ms     14ms     8ms      APhoenix1.core0.nap.net [207.227.0.201]
7    9ms     10ms     10ms     4.0.5.233
8    64ms    64ms     67ms     p2-1.paloalto-nbr2.bbnplanet.net [4.24.7.18]
9    67ms    65ms     69ms     p0-0-0.paloalto.cr18.bbnplanet.net [4.0.3.86]
10   66ms    75ms     75ms     h1-0. cisco bbnplanet.net [4.1.142.238]
11   66ms    68ms     70ms     Sty.cisco.com [192.31.7.39]
12   67ms    77ms     76ms     CISCO.COM [192.31.7.130]
```

The syntax for the command is as follows and is explained in Table 18-2:

```
tracert [-d] [-h maximum-hops] [-j host-list] [-w timeout] target_name
```

Table 18-2 **tracert** Command Options

Syntax	Description
-d	Specifies that IP addresses should not be resolved to host names
-h	*maximum_hops* gives the maximum number of hops searched
-j	*host-list* specifies the loose source route
-w	Specifies the timeout to wait the number of milliseconds that is specified for each reply
target_name	Specifies the remote host to trace, by domain name or by IP address

telnet

This is a terminal emulation program that enables you to run interactive commands on the Telnet server. Until a connection is established, no data will pass; if the connection breaks, Telnet informs you. This is good for testing login configuration parameters to a remote host.

netstat

Command **netstat** displays protocol statistics and current TCP/IP network connections (see Example 18-8).

Example 18-8 netstat *Command Output*

```
C:\netstat -a

Active Connections
   Proto  Local Address               Foreign Address            State
   TCP    matc-tag-phx:epmap          matc-tag-phx:0             LISTENING
   TCP    matc-tag-phx:microsoft-ds   matc-tag-phx:0             LISTENING
   TCP    matc-tag-phx:1028           matc-tag-phx:0             LISTENING
   TCP    matc-tag-phx:1041           matc-tag-phx:0             LISTENING
   TCP    matc-tag-phx:1073           matc-tag-phx:0             LISTENING
   TCP    matc-tag-phx:1074           matc-tag-phx:0             LISTENING
   TCP    matc-tag-phx:netbios-ssn    matc-tag-phx:0             LISTENING
   TCP    matc-tag-phx:1036           matc-tag-phx:0             LISTENING
   TCP    matc-tag-phx:1073           64.12.28.63:5190           ESTABLISHED
   TCP    matc-tag-phx:1074           64.12.27.164:5190          ESTABLISHED
   TCP    matc-tag-phx:1121           baym-cs39.msgr.hotmail.com:1863   ESTABLISHED
   TCP    matc-tag-phx:2025           currdev1.cisco.com:netbios-ssn    ESTABLISHED
   UDP    matc-tag-phx:epmap          *:*
   UDP    matc-tag-phx:microsoft-ds   *:*
   UDP    matc-tag-phx:isakmp         *:*
   UDP    matc-tag-phx:1030           *:*
   UDP    matc-tag-phx:1034           *:*
   UDP    matc-tag-phx:1046           *:*
   UDP    matc-tag-phx:1900           *:*
```

The syntax for the command is as follows and is explained in Table 18-3:

netstat [**-a**] [**-e**] [**-n**] [**-s**] [**-p** *proto*] [**-r**] [*interval*]

Table 18-3 netstat Command Options

Syntax	Description
-a	Displays all connections and listening ports. (Server-side connections are normally not shown.)
-e	Displays Ethernet statistics. This can be combined with the –s option.
-n	Displays addresses and port numbers in numerical form.
-p	*proto* shows connections for the protocol specified by proto; proto can be **tcp** or **udp**. If used with the -s option to display per-protocol statistics, *proto* can be **tcp**, **udp**, or **ip**.
-r	Displays the contents of the routing table.
-s	Displays per-protocol statistics. By default, statistics are shown for TCP, UDP, and IP; the -p option can be used to specify a subset of the default.
interval	Redisplays selected statistics, pausing *interval* seconds between each display. Press Ctrl+C to stop redisplaying statistics. If this is omitted, then **netstat** prints the current configuration information once.

arp

ARP gathers hardware addresses of local hosts and the default gateway. You can view the ARP cache and check for invalid or duplicate entries. (See Example 18-9.)

Example 18-9 arp *Command Output*

```
C:arp -a
Interface: 192.168.1.101 --- 0x2
  Internet Address      Physical Address      Type
  192.168.1.1           00-04-5a-2f-28-29     dynamic
C:\
```

The syntax for the **arp** command is as follows and is explained in Table 18-4:

```
arp -a [inet_addr] [-N [if_addr]]
arp -d inet_addr [if_addr]
arp -s inet_addr ether_addr [if_addr]
```

Table 18-4 arp Command Options

Syntax	Description
-a or -g	Displays the current contents of the ARP cache
-d	Deletes the entry that is specified by *inet_addr*
-s	Adds a static entry to the cache
-N	Displays the ARP entries for the specified physical address
inet_addr	Gives the IP address, in dotted decimal format
if_addr	Gives the IP address whose cache should be modified
ether_addr	Shows the MAC address in hex separated by hyphens

ipconfig (Windows NT)/WinIPcfg (Windows 95/98)

These Windows utilities display IP addressing information for the local network adapter(s) or a specified network interface card.

The syntax for the command is as follows and is explained in Table 18-5:

`ipconfig [/all | /renew [adapter] | /release [adapter]]`

Table 18-5 ipconfig Command Options

Syntax	Description
/all	Shows all information about adapter(s)
/renew	Renews DHCP lease information for all local adapters if none is named
/release	Releases DHCP lease information disabling TCP/IP on this adapter

These are the tools that enable a network administrator to remotely monitor and control the network. It is important to implement the proper security when using SNMP and RMON so that the network is not violated.

Summary

Now that you have completed this chapter, you should have a firm understanding of the following:

- The administrative side of network management
- Establishing the boundaries of the network
- Costs of a network
- Error report documentation
- Monitoring the network
- Monitoring the connection
- Monitoring traffic
- SNMP
- RMON
- Troubleshooting methods
- Software tools for troubleshooting

Key Terms

archive bit   Used to measure date since last backup by storing information with a file and is turned on whenever that file is created or modified. This flag tells the backup process whether the file needs to be backed up.

baseline   A measurement that is established after the network has been installed and configured properly. A Baseline can be used to compare the against future performance.

BDCs (backup domain controllers   Secondary servers that balance the workload of the PDC and provide for redundancy of user and resource objects.

bindery   An object that NetWare version 3.12 uses to manage multiple users and resources. The drawback is that bindery services create a server-centric network, which is focused on the individual server as the point of control.

data backup   The process of duplicating all stored data to magnetic tape or another storage medium such as removable hard disks, CD-ROM, or DVD-ROM.

mandatory profile   A type of profile that brings up the same user interface for everyone without allowing changes to be made. The mandatory profile is used in situations in which many people must use the same physical computer.

multidomain model   A model in which separate domains are connected by trusting/trusted relationships, which allows users to cross domain boundaries to use resources.

NDS (Novell Directory Services)   Novell Netware servers use this directory service to manage users and resources. The advantage over version 3.12 is that NDS creates a network-centric network, which is focused on the entire network as the point of control.

profiles   A system which allows a user to customize a user interface on a computer and then be able to use that profile at any computer that user connects to the network.

RMON (Remote Monitoring)   Extensions to SNMP that provide the ability to look at the network as a whole instead of looking at individual devices.

SNMP (Simple Network Management Protocol)   A protocol that allows management to transmit statistical data over the network to a central management console.

standalone server   A server that is set up primarily to support one particular application and to dedicate its resources to that application.

traffic monitoring   A sophisticated method of network monitoring that looks at the actual packet traffic on the network and generates reports based on that traffic.

Trojan horse   A destructive program that is disguised as a game, a utility, or an application. When run, a Trojan horse does something devious to the computer system while appearing to do something useful.

user policies   Documents that contain information on how the users can interact with the network. These policies include what is and what is not permissible on the network.

virus   A program that "infects" computer files (usually other executable programs) by inserting copies of itself in those files. This is usually done in such a manner that the copies are executed when the file is loaded into memory, allowing them to infect still other files, and so on.

volume   A physical unit of storage.

worm   A program that propagates itself across computers, usually by creating copies of itself in each computer's memory. A worm might duplicate itself in one computer so often that it causes the computer to crash.

Chapter 19

Network+ Certification Exam Review

This chapter provides a review of the topics that you need to know to successfully pass the Network+ certification exam that was developed in 1997. Each of the topics covered in this chapter corresponds to the topics on the Network+ certification exam.

The Network+ certification exam, covering the objectives, requires that the student has a proper understanding of the layers of the OSI model, can describe the features and functions of network components, and has the skills needed to install, configure, and troubleshoot basic networking hardware peripherals and protocols.

The objectives of the Network+ certification exam cover some of the latest technologies, such as wireless networking and gigabit Ethernet. The scope of networking systems that are emphasized on the exam includes Linux/UNIX, Windows 9x, Windows NT, Windows 2000, and AppleTalk as a network protocol. There is also an emphasis on hands-on experience knowledge needed in the areas of network implementation and network support including troubleshooting scenarios.

The exam tests four domain areas:

- Media and topologies (20 percent)
- Protocols and standards (25 percent)
- Network implementation (23 percent)
- Network support (32 percent)

For more information about the Network+ exam, visit the Comptia exam provider's website at www.comptia.org.

Basic Networking Topologies

In this section, you review the following topologies:

- Star
- Bus
- Mesh
- Ring
- Wireless

Star Topology

In a star topology, all devices are connected to a common central location, typically a hub or a switch. (See Figure 19-1.) When a node sends data to the central location, the central device retransmits the information and sends it to the destination. Because all cabling is connected to a central device, if one link fails, only that portion of the network fails. The rest of the network is not affected. However, if the central device fails, the entire network also fails. A star topology can have a maximum of 1024 nodes on a LAN and is commonly used for 10BASE-T (IEEE 802.3) and 100BASE-TX (IEEE 802.3u) Ethernet.

Figure 19-1 Star Topology

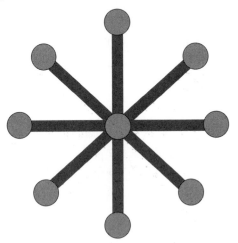

Advantages of star topologies include reliability and ease of maintenance and installation. You can maintain monitoring and troubleshooting at the central device, which provides easier maintenance. Star topologies allow for greater reliability because each node is connected to the central device by a segment. If one segment breaks, only that node loses access to the network, and the rest of the network is unaffected. Because each node is connected to the central device, star topologies also allow for an easy network layout, providing you with easier installation over the other topologies. A disadvantage of this topology is cost. With each device being connected to the central location, more cabling is required than with other topologies. In addition, there is the cost of the central device.

Bus Topology

A bus topology connects multiple devices onto one main cable and is sometimes referred to as a *backbone*, trunk, or *segment*. (See Figure 19-2.) You must connect terminators at each end of the topology to absorb reflected signals. If you use coaxial cable without terminators, reflected signals echo across the network, causing the entire network to be unusable.

Figure 19-2 Bus Topology

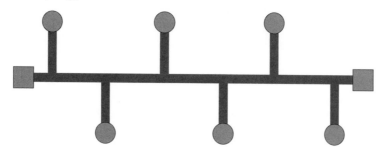

Advantages of a bus topology are cost and ease of installation. Because this topology uses a simple cable layout, it costs less and is easier to implement than the other topologies.

A disadvantage of a bus topology is that if a cable segment or the backbone breaks or fails, the network fails. Another disadvantage is that only one node can transmit data onto the network at a time. If two or more nodes attempt to send data at the same time, a collision occurs; this requires a recovery procedure, thereby slowing down the network. After the collision has occurred, you must resend all the data. A process called *carrier sense multiple access collision detect (CSMA/CD)* prevents the occurrence of another collision. CSMA/CD is a process by which each node waits its turn to retransmit data.

Mesh Topology

Normally used for WANs, a mesh topology connects every device on the network and provides a path to and from each device. (See Figure 19-3.) An advantage is that because all the devices are connected to each other, the network has a higher fault tolerance and reliability. If a cable segment breaks along the network, the devices find the quickest way to reroute the packet to its destination. Therefore, the data usually reaches its destination.

Figure 19-3 Complete Mesh Topology

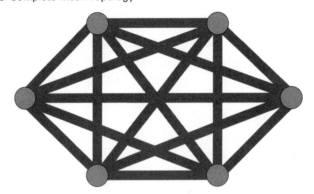

Disadvantages of this topology are cost and difficulty in management. Because there are numerous connections to and from each device, there are several cabling requirements, causing a mesh topology to be somewhat expensive. If a segment breaks on the network, with the complex design of the mesh topology, finding the exact problem location can be difficult. Therefore, maintaining the network can be complex.

Ring Topology

In ring topologies, each device on the network is connected with two other devices. (See Figure 19-4.) There is no beginning or end of the cable. This particular topology forms a complete ring. The devices on this network use a *transceiver* to communicate with their neighbors. Transceivers also act like repeaters to regenerate each signal as it is passed through the device.

Figure 19-4 Ring Topology

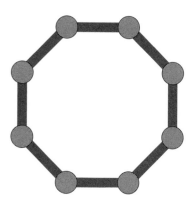

An advantage is better performance because each device receives a turn to transmit signals and has equal access to the network. An additional advantage is that each device that the data passes through, regenerates the signal, thereby preventing the signal from degrading.

A disadvantage of using this topology is that if one device on the cable fails, the entire network also fails. Locating the failure can sometimes be difficult. Another disadvantage is that if any changes are made to the network, including adding to or moving devices, the disruption causes the network to fail.

Wireless Topology

A wireless local-area network (LAN) topology is a flexible data communications system implemented as an extension to, or as an alternative for, a wired LAN. Using radio frequency (RF) technology, wireless LANs transmit and receive data over the air, minimizing the need for wired connections. Therefore, wireless LANs combine data connectivity with user mobility.

Wireless LANs have gained strong popularity in a number of markets, including health care, retail, manufacturing, warehousing, and education facilities. These industries have profited from the productivity gains of using hand-held terminals and notebook computers to transmit real-time information to centralized hosts for processing. Today, wireless LANs are becoming more widely recognized as a general-purpose connectivity alternative for a broad range of business customers.

The widespread reliance on networking in business and the rapid growth of the Internet and online services are big examples of the benefits of sharing data and resources with networking technology. With wireless LANs, users can access shared information without looking for a place to plug in, and network managers can set up or rapidly adapt networks without installing or moving wires. Wireless LANs offer the following productivity, convenience, and cost advantages over traditional wired networks:

- **Mobility**—Wireless LAN systems can provide LAN users with access to real-time information anywhere at work and in the home.

- **Installation speed and simplicity**—Installing a wireless LAN system can be fast and easy and can eliminate the need to pull cable through walls and ceilings.

- **Installation flexibility**—Wireless technology allows the network to go where wire cannot go.

- **Reduced cost-of-ownership**—Although the initial investment required for wireless LAN hardware can be higher than the cost of wired LAN hardware, overall installation expenses and life-cycle costs can be significantly lower. Long-term cost benefits are greatest in dynamic environments that require frequent moves and changes.

- **Scalability**—Wireless LAN systems can be configured in a variety of topologies to meet the needs of specific applications and installations. Configurations are easily changed and range from peer-to-peer networks that are suitable for a small number of users to full infrastructure networks of thousands of users that enable roaming over a broad area.

Segments and Backbones

This section reviews the terms segments and backbones.

Segments

In networking, the term segment has several meanings. First, in a narrow sense, segment can refer to a trunk (main line) of cabling that connects devices to a concentration device (hubs, media attachment units, or switches). Second, segment can refer to a logical grouping of devices that communicate within a given subnet separated ("segmented") by bridges, switches, or routers. The term segment is sometimes synonymous with a collision or Ethernet domain, as shown in Figure 19-5.

Figure 19-5 Segmenting Collision Domains

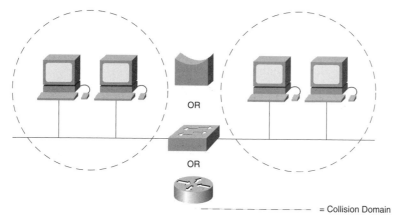

OR

OR

———————————— = Collision Domain

Backbones

The term backbone also has several meanings within networking. First, a backbone is most often the main cable (or trunk) to which all nodes and devices connect. Second, backbones are the foundations of both LANs and WANs where servers, routers, and concentrating devices (such as switches and hubs) are connected by a high-bandwidth connection. Because of its desirable electrical characteristics, such as immunity to noise and grounding problems, optical fiber is now more commonly chosen for backbone cabling than coaxial cable and unshielded twisted-pair (UTP).

The Major Network Operating Systems

In this section, you review Microsoft Windows NT/2000, Novell NetWare, and UNIX.

Microsoft Windows 2000 Server

Windows 2000 is Microsoft's latest operating system for the corporate desktop. Like the Windows 2000 server products, it is based on the NT kernel and includes many enhanced features. For example, Windows 2000 Professional provides a high level of security and stability for mission-critical tasks.

Windows 2000 Professional supports *Plug and Play technology*. Plug and Play can be installed on hard disks that are formatted with FAT32; it includes file encryption for securing data on the hard disk. Plug and Play technology is a useful tool that allows you to quickly and easily add components to the system. The operating system automatically recognizes and installs the drivers for the device. Essentially, after the component is "plugged" into the system, it "plays" automatically without additional configuration. Previously, when a new component was added, you had to install drivers and configure the device manually. Windows 2000 comes with a huge database of drivers for common Plug and Play devices.

Other advantages of Windows 2000 Professional as a desktop operating system and network client include the following:

- It offers better support for mobile users through Advanced Power Management (APM) and Advanced Configuration and Power Interface (ACPI). /.Windows NT does not support ACPI.

- It provides for more secure virtual private networking with Layer 2 Tunneling Protocol (L2TP) and IP Security (IPSec). Earlier versions of Windows supported only the Point-to-Point Tunneling Protocol (PPTP) for Virtual Private Networks (VPNs).

- The offline folders feature enables you to copy and synchronize documents from the network to your local system so that you can access them when your computer is not connected to the network.

- The Internet Printing Protocol (IPP) enables you to print to a URL and manage printers through a web browser interface.

- Built-in disk defragmenter and other tools and utilities help you maintain and manage the operating system. You have to purchase these separately from third parties for Windows NT.

- It supports Kerberos security (developing standard for authenticating network users) and the features of a Windows 2000 domain as an Active Directory client.

Windows 2000 Server

Windows 2000 Server includes all the features in the Windows 2000 Professional section as well as many new server-specific functions. Windows 2000 Server can also operate as a file, print, web server, as well as an application server. What separates Windows 2000 Server from Windows 2000 Professional is a complete set of infrastructure services based on Active Directory services. Active Directory, which is similar to Novell *NetWare Directory Services*, serves as a centralized point of management of users, groups, security services, and network resources.

Windows 2000 Server also supports four-way Symmetric Multiprocessing (SMP) systems and allows up to 4 gigabytes of physical memory. It includes the multipurpose capabilities that are required for workgroups and branch offices as well as for departmental deployments of file and print servers, application servers, web servers, and communication servers. Windows 2000 Server is intended for use in small-to-medium sized enterprise environments.

Some other enhancements that come with Windows 2000 Server are built-in support for the major network protocols that are in use throughout networks today, such as TCP/IP and IPX/SPX. Windows 2000 Server provides integrated connectivity with Novell NetWare, UNIX, and AppleTalk systems. A Windows 2000 Server that is configured as a communications server can provide dial-up networking services for mobile users. Windows 2000 Server can support up to 256 simultaneous inbound dial-up sessions as opposed to Windows 2000 Professional, which can provide support for only one dial-up session at a time.

Windows 2000 Advanced Server

Windows 2000 Server and Windows 2000 Advanced Server are the same except that Advanced Server provides hardware and software support that you need in an enterprise and extremely large network that might include several WAN links to offices all over the world. Advanced Server is a more powerful departmental and application server operating system that includes all the functions of Windows 2000 Server and adds the advanced high availability and improved scalability that is required for larger networks. Windows 2000 Advanced Server supports eight-way SMP, which would be ideal for database-intensive work. Advanced Server also provides support for higher-end hardware that supports an enterprise network. For example, Advanced Server provides support for more than 4 GB of physical memory.

Windows .NET Server

Microsoft has developed Windows .NET Server with the ability to provide a secure and reliable system to run enterprise-level web and FTP sites to compete with the Linux and UNIX Server operating systems. With the growing emergence of e-commerce, web-based companies, and companies that are expanding their services to the Internet, there is a need for a server that is capable of providing secure and reliable web and FTP services. Windows .NET Server, which is built on the Windows 2000 Server Kernel, is specifically tailored to provide these types of services. Windows .NET Server provides XML Web Services to companies that run medium- to high-volume web traffic. .NET Server provides support for companies that are just getting started in this new generation of business as well as businesses that have been providing Internet-based business solutions for some time.

Windows XP

There are two different versions of Windows XP: Windows XP Home Edition and Windows XP Professional. Windows XP's Home Edition is a less expensive version that is typically marketed to users and customers who use PCs in their homes and small businesses. Windows XP Home Edition is intended for inexperienced users who don't need to connect to corporate networks or the extra security options that Windows XP Professional contains. Windows XP Home Edition is compatible with any desktop or notebook PC that has a single CPU and a video display. The Windows XP Professional version includes everything in the Windows XP Home Edition, plus all the networking and security components that are required to join a Windows NT/2000/XP domain in a corporate network. Windows XP Professional also includes support for high-performance hardware, such as a dual-processor motherboard.

Windows XP Home Edition

Windows XP Home Edition includes many enhancements and features that are not included in Windows 2000 Professional or any of the previous Windows 9X releases. Some of these features include improved software and hardware compatibility, simplified security (Simple File Sharing versus Windows 2000 Sharing), a new login screen, fast user switching, enhanced multimedia support, and DirectX 8.1 multimedia libraries for gaming.

XP Professional Edition

The difference in the Professional Edition release of Windows XP is the additional security features. For example, in Windows XP Home Edition, each user is automatically assigned to the Owners local group, which is the Windows XP equivalent of the Windows 2000 Administrator account. This means that anyone who logs on to a Home Edition machine has full control of the operating system. The Backup Operators, Power Users, or Replicator groups do not exist in Windows XP Home Edition. However, Windows XP Home Edition does include a Restricted Users group, which grants limited access to the operating system for the selected users.

Windows XP Professional Edition includes the following features that are not included in Home Edition:

- **Power user**—The new Remote Desktop feature allows mobile users to remotely access their corporate desktop. As a system administrator, you can remotely administer clients on a network. Automated System Recovery (ASR) is included, which helps recover a system from a catastrophic error that might render the system unbootable. Windows XP Professional, like Windows 2000 Professional, supports dynamic disks. Windows XP Home Edition supports only the standard Simple Disk type. Windows XP Home Edition does not include the Internet Information Services (IIS) web server 5.1 software that you can find in Windows XP Professional Edition.

- **Management**—Windows XP Professional provides added operating system management features. Windows XP Professional Edition can be used to log in to an Active Directory domain. Group Policy support for domain users can be supported as well. Windows XP Professional Edition also includes a change and configuration management tool called *IntelliMirror*. This includes managing user data and central management of software installation, repair, updating, and removal, as well as user settings management.

- **Roaming profiles**—With Windows XP Professional, users have the ability to log in to any computer on the network and automatically receive their customized settings.

- **Corporate deployment**—Windows XP Professional is designed for use in corporate networks. It contains support for multiple languages. Windows XP professional also provides Sysprep support, which is used to install the operating system on multiple machines in a large or corporate network.

- **Networking features**—Windows XP Professional provides added networking features that are needed when deploying the operating system in a large corporate network. These include Simple Network Management Protocol (SNMP), the user interface for IPSec, SAP Agent, Client Service for NetWare, Network Monitor, and simple TCP/IP services.

Novell NetWare

Novell NetWare, also an extremely popular LAN operating system, is designed to support LANs such as Ethernet and Token Ring networks. To manage the resources that are available on the network, NetWare uses NetWare Directory Services, in which both a physical and a logical file system are used to arrange files and dates. NetWare's primary file system is a combination of the file allocation table (FAT) and the directory entry table (DET). Layer 3 protocols that are used in this operating system are the Internetwork Package Exchange (IPX) protocol and the Internet Protocol (IP).

Novell NetWare works well with many operating systems, including DOS, Windows 3.11, Windows 9*x*, and Windows NT Workstation.

Prior to its 5.0 release, Novell NetWare was mainly a text-based network operating system, with a few functions administered from the server console and most administrative functions executed on a client workstation (which was logged onto the server).

NetWare 3.*x* primarily used IPX/SPX as its protocol, whereas the newer versions Net-Ware 4.*x* and 5.*x* use TCP/IP or IPX/SPX as their protocols. Similar to the Windows platforms, NetWare uses GUI for its applications.

UNIX

Developed at the University of California, Berkeley, UNIX was designed for database management. UNIX is an important network operating system because its key features include multitasking, multiusers, and networking capabilities. UNIX has the capability to operate multiple processes while users are working with applications on the same machine. Multiple versions of UNIX exist, including Sun Microsystems' Solaris, IBM's AIX, Silicon Graphics' IRIX, Linux, and Hewlett-Packard's HP-UX. However, the operation of all versions is similar.

UNIX is a command-line–driven platform that is accessed by terminal sessions from other operating systems or on the same machine. Windows 95 clients can access UNIX by using terminal emulation programs. UNIX clients, such as Sparc (Solaris) workstations from Sun Microsystems, work best with their manufacturer's proprietary network operating system (NOS).

A recent relative of UNIX is Linux, which was developed as an open source operating system. Developers who want to modify the platform can purchase or download a copy of the source code and modify it based on their own needs.

Linux

In 1991, a Finnish student named Linus Torvalds began work on an operating system for an Intel 80386-based computer. Frustrated with the state of desktop operating systems such as DOS and the expense and licensing issues associated with commercial UNIX, Torvalds set out to develop an operating system that was "UNIX-like" in its operation but used software code that was open and completely free.

Although it was not his original intention, Torvalds' work led to a worldwide collaborative effort to develop Linux, an open-source operating system that looks and feels like UNIX. By the late 1990s, Linux had become a viable alternative to UNIX on servers and Windows on the desktop. The popularity of Linux on desktop PCs has also contributed to interest in using UNIX distributions, such as FreeBSD and Sun Solaris, on the desktop. Versions of Linux can now run on almost any 32-bit processor, including the Intel 80386, Motorola 68000, Alpha, and PowerPC chips.

As with UNIX, there are numerous versions of Linux. Some are free downloads from the World Wide Web, and others are commercially distributed. The following are a few of the most popular:

- RedHat Linux, distributed by RedHat Software
- OpenLinux, distributed by Caldera
- Corel Linux
- Slackware
- Debian GNU/Linux
- SuSE Linux

Linux is one of the most powerful and reliable operating systems in the world today. Because of this, Linux has already made inroads as a platform for power users and in the enterprise server arena. It is less often deployed as a corporate desktop operating system. Although GUI interfaces are available to make it user friendly, most beginning users find Linux more difficult to use than Mac OS or Windows. Currently, many companies (such as RedHat, SuSE, Corel, and Caldera) are striving to make Linux a viable operating system for the desktop.

Application support must be considered when Linux is implemented on a desktop system. The number of business productivity applications is limited as compared to Windows. However, some vendors provide Windows emulation software (such as WABI and WINE) that enables many Windows applications to run on Linux. Additionally, companies such as Corel are making Linux versions of their office suites and other popular software packages.

Recent distributions of Linux have networking components built in for connecting to a LAN, establishing a dial-up connection to the Internet, or other remote network. In fact, Transmission Control Protocol/Internet Protocol (TCP/IP) is integrated into the Linux kernel instead of being implemented as a separate subsystem.

Some advantages of Linux as a desktop operating system and network client include the following:

- It is a true 32-bit operating system.
- It supports preemptive multitasking and virtual memory.
- The code is open source and available for anyone to enhance and improve.

MAC OS X

Apple Macintosh computers were designed for easy networking in a peer-to-peer (workgroup) situation. In fact, network interfaces are included as part of the hardware and networking components built into the Macintosh operating system. Ethernet and Token Ring network adapters also are available for the Macintosh.

The Macintosh, or Mac, is popular in many educational institutions and corporate graphics departments. Macs can be connected to one another in workgroups and can access Appleshare file servers. They also can be connected to PC LANs that include Microsoft, NetWare, or UNIX servers.

Macintosh's new operating system, Mac OS X, is sometimes referred to as Apple system 10. Some of the new features of MAC OS X are in a new GUI called Aqua. The Aqua GUI resembles a cross between Microsoft's Windows XP and Linux's X-windows GUI. MAC OS X is designed to provide features for the home computer like Internet browsing, video and photo editing, and games, while still providing features that provide powerful and customizable tools that IT professionals need in an operating system.

MAC OS X is fully compatible with older versions of the MAC operating systems. MAC OS X provides a new feature that allows for AppleTalk and Windows connectivity. The MAC OS X core operating system called Darwin is a UNIX-based, powerful system that provides stability and performance. These enhancements provide MAC OS X with support for protected memory, preemptive multitasking, advanced memory management, and symmetric multiprocessing, which makes Macintosh a formidable player in the operating system competition.

Windows Directory Services

With the release of Windows 2000 Server, Microsoft made fundamental changes to its networking components that are even more drastic than those made by Novell in the transition from NetWare 3 to 4. The Active Directory is central to these changes. Whereas Novell Netware Directory Services functions as a service that works with the NOS, Microsoft Active Directory functions as an application that is deeply integrated with the operating system.

The following sections discuss the structure of the Active Directory database, Active Directory integration, and Active Directory information.

Active Directory Database Structure

Active Directory information is stored in three files:

- Active Directory database
- Active Directory log files
- Shared System Volume

The database is the directory. The log files record changes made to the database. The Shared System Volume (called Sysvol) contains scripts and group policy objects on Windows 2000 domain controllers. Group Policy is the means by which Windows 2000 administrators control user desktops, automatically deploy applications, and set user rights.

Windows 2000 Domains

The logical structure of Active Directory is based on units called domains. Although the same terminology is used, domains in Windows 2000 function differently from those in Windows NT. In both Windows NT and Windows 2000, a domain represents a security and administrative boundary, as well as a replication unit. However, Windows NT uses a flat domain structure, and Windows 2000 arranges domains in hierarchical domain trees.

The hierarchical tree concept works differently in Active Directory than in NetWare Directory Services. NetWare Directory Services does not divide the network into domains. Windows 2000 networks can have multiple domains that are organized into domain trees. In addition, these trees can be joined to other trees to form forests. A forest is the term that Microsoft uses for a collection of the different domain trees that are included in the Active Directory hierarchical structure.

Windows 2000 Organizational Units

Active Directory, like NetWare Directory Services, uses organizational units (OUs) to organize resources within domains. Administrative authority can be delegated to individual OUs. In contrast, NT networking enables administrative privileges to be assigned only at the domain level.

Active Directory and Domain Name System

Active Directory uses Domain Name System (DNS) naming conventions and depends on DNS to operate. There must be a DNS server on every Windows 2000 network. In addition, DNS zone information updates can be integrated with Active Directory replication, which is more efficient than traditional DNS update methods.

Windows 2000 supports Dynamic DNS (DDNS), which enables the automatic updating of the DNS database.

Active Directory Servers

To use Active Directory, at least one server must be configured as a domain controller (DC). It is recommended that there be at least two DCs in each domain for fault tolerance. Configuring the first domain controller on the network creates the directory for that domain.

Unlike Windows NT servers, Windows 2000 Servers that are running Active Directory have no primary domain controller (PDC) or backup domain controller (BDC). In Windows NT domains, only the PDC would contain a full read/write copy of the directory of user accounts and security information. The PDC would authenticate usernames and passwords when members log in to the network. The BDC would maintain a read-only backup of the PDC's master directory; therefore, any changes would need to be made on the PDC. Windows 2000 servers that are running Active Directory approach the DC concept a little differently. Unlike Windows NT Server, where a PDC must be accessible to make changes to the directory, Windows 2000 Server relies on the Active Directory multimaster replication model to update all the DCs within the forest when a change is made to any other DC. There is no PDC or BDC. All DCs are equal, and they all contain a read/write copy of the Active Directory partition. This information is kept up to date and synchronized through the process of replication. This process is discussed in the next section.

Active Directory Replication

Replication is the process of copying data from one computer to one or more other computers and synchronizing that data so that it is identical on all systems.

Active Directory uses multimaster replication to copy directory information between the domain controllers in a domain. Changes can be made on any domain controller, and those changes are then replicated to the others, except during the performance of a single-master operation.

Windows 2000 administrators can establish replication policies that determine when and how often directory replication takes place. This enables optimum use of network bandwidth. Controlling the replication schedule is especially important when domain controllers are located on opposite sides of a slow link, such as a 56K WAN link.

Active Directory Security

Each object in Active Directory has an access control list (ACL) that contains all access permissions that are associated with that object. Permissions can be either explicitly allowed or denied on a granular basis.

There are two different types of permissions:

- **Assigned permissions**—Permissions that an authorized user grants explicitly
- **Inherited permissions**—Permissions that apply to child objects because they were inherited from a parent object

You can assign permissions to an individual user or to a group of users. Windows 2000 enables you to control this process.

Active Directory Compatibility

Active Directory depends on the operating system and runs only on Windows 2000 servers. Because Active Directory is LDAP-compatible, services and information can be accessed or exchanged with other LDAP directory services. Microsoft also provides tools for migrating information from other directories, such as NetWare Directory Services, into Active Directory.

Novell NetWare Directory Services

Novell NetWare 3.*x* relies on a security database, called the Bindery, which uses only IPX/SPX. NetWare 4.*x*, 5.x, and later versions rely on NetWare Directory Services, which is a built-in directory service that uses TCP/IP or IPX/SPX. NetWare Directory Services is based on the Internet Directory Standard X.500, which uses a resource called the NetWare Directory Services tree to organize all user and resource information. The NetWare Directory Services tree allows users to log in to the network and access any of the resources that are available.

UNIX Directory Services

The UNIX directory services use a file system called the *Network File System (NFS)*. The NFS grants users permission to certain parts of the file system and controls the security of the UNIX systems. Because the shared files are transparent, NFS users can view and edit files on other UNIX hosts.

UNIX systems that are running *SAMBA* communicate by using Server Message Block (SMB). The SMB protocol runs on UNIX and Linux systems and allows Microsoft clients and servers to view UNIX and Linux systems as if they were Windows devices. UNIX also uses DNS to resolve transport layer names into logical network addresses.

IP, IPX, and NetBEUI: Associating Them with Their Functions

In this section, you review IP, IPX, and NetBEUI, along with their associated functions.

IP

IP is a routable protocol that works at the network layer of the OSI model and the Internet layer of the TCP/IP model. IP provides packet delivery and addressing for source and destination. Connectionless IP and the connection-oriented TCP are the de facto protocol standards of the Internet.

Because IP is a connectionless service, it is unreliable and does not guarantee the delivery of data or the order in which it was sent. Working with IP at Layer 4, the connection-oriented protocol TCP provides reliable and orderly delivery of packets.

IPX

IPX is a connectionless routable protocol that also works at the network layer of the OSI model. IPX is the network layer protocol that Novell NetWare uses.

IPX is efficient and scalable, has no performance issues, contains no addressing problems, and is capable of being used with Ethernet (1500-byte packet size) and Token Ring (4000-byte packet size) networks by using the proper network interface card drivers. However, IPX is largely being replaced by the IP protocol.

NetBIOS Extended User Interface

NetBIOS Extended User Interface (NetBEUI), which is commonly used for smaller LANs, is a nonroutable protocol that operates at the network and transport layers of the OSI model. Because NetBEUI is a nonroutable protocol, it is quick and easy to configure. Configuration is minimal after NetBEUI is installed and bound to a network adapter. However, because NetBEUI is nonroutable, it cannot participate in Internet communications. Therefore, NetBEUI is limited in its usefulness and scalability.

Redundant Array of Inexpensive Disks Overview

Redundant Array of Inexpensive Disks (RAID) is designed to allow some fault tolerance to prevent loss of data in the event of a disk drive failure on a network server. A disk drive is a mechanical device. Therefore, it is not a matter of *if* the disk drive will fail, but rather a matter of *when* the disk drive will fail. RAID accomplishes this fault tolerance or redundancy through disk drives storing parity or the same information to two different disk drives.

RAID level 1 uses duplication of the data to provide fault tolerance. RAID levels 3, 4, and 5 use "parity" information that is calculated from the bit patterns of the data being written to the RAID array to provide fault tolerance. When a disk drive fails in RAID 3, 4, or 5, the parity information can be used along with the data on the remaining disk drives in the array to calculate the data that was on the disk drive that failed. This allows the disk subsystem and the network server to keep functioning, although it will be a bit slower due to the calculations that are required to re-create the missing data. RAID level 2 is structurally different in that it does not use duplication or parity to provide fault tolerance. RAID 2 uses a special "hamming code" instead.

RAID is a term that is surrounded by a tremendous amount of misinformation. There is disagreement about how many levels of RAID are defined, whether the *I* in RAID stands for inexpensive or independent, and whether the *A* in RAID stands for array or arrays. RAID 6, 7, 10, 50, 53, and others can be found in many vendors' literature. This chapter focuses on the types of RAID that are used most often in a network environment.

RAID was defined in 1987 in the paper "A Case for Redundant Arrays of Inexpensive Disks (RAID)" written by David A. Patterson, Garth A. Gibson, and Randy H. Katz at the University of California, Berkeley. The original paper defined five levels of RAID (1, 2, 3, 4, and 5) and offered the RAID solution as an alternative to single large expensive disk (SLED).

In the past few years, many people have started using the phrase *redundant array of independent disks*, substituting the word *independent* for *inexpensive*.

RAID 0

RAID 0 was not defined in the 1987 Berkeley paper. In fact, it is not RAID at all; it does not provide redundancy. RAID 0 is just an array (or group) of disk drives used as a single disk. The data is written in chunks or stripes to all the disk drives in the array. This improves disk input/output performance in that several chunks of data can be written or read simultaneously. If a disk drive in the RAID 0 array fails, all data in the RAID 0 array is lost. RAID level 0 is often called disk striping without parity. Figure 19-6 shows an illustration of RAID 0.

Figure 19-6 RAID 0

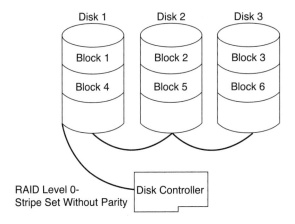

RAID Level 0-
Stripe Set Without Parity

RAID 1

RAID 1 requires a minimum of two disk drives (all other RAID levels, except level 0, require at least three disk drives) to implement. RAID 1 writes all data to two separate locations. To store 20 gigabytes (GB) of data using RAID 1, two 20-GB disk drives are required. This is a 50 percent loss of storage capacity.

There are two ways to implement RAID 1:

- Disk mirroring
- Disk duplexing

In disk mirroring, the two disk drives are connected to the same disk controller. The only problem with disk mirroring is that if the disk controller fails, there is no access to the mirrored data. Figure 19-7 shows a diagram of disk mirroring. To eliminate this single point of failure, use disk duplexing rather than disk mirroring.

In disk duplexing, each disk drive in the mirrored set is connected to a different disk controller. This eliminates the single point of failure in pure disk mirroring. The only additional cost is the additional disk controller. Figure 19-8 shows a diagram of disk duplexing.

Figure 19-7 Disk Mirroring

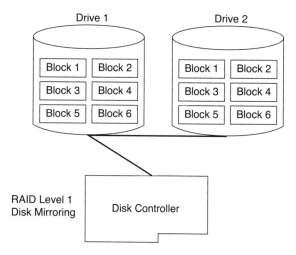

Figure 19-8 Disk Duplexing

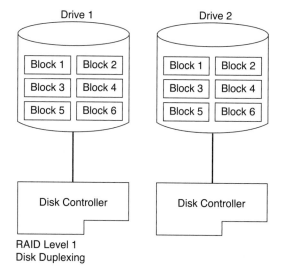

RAID 2

RAID 2 uses a hamming code to create an error-correcting code for all data to be stored on the RAID 2 array. The error-correcting code can detect and correct single-bit errors and detect double-bit errors. The error-correcting code has to be read and decoded each time data is read from the disk. RAID 2 is difficult and expensive to implement and has a high overhead (3 parity bits for each 4 data bits).

NOTE

A hamming code is an error-correction method that mixes three check bits at the end of each four data bits. When these check bits are received, they are used to detect and correct one-bit errors automatically.

RAID 2 has no commercial implementations due to the expense and difficulty of implementation. It requires a minimum of three disk drives to implement.

RAID 3

RAID 3 uses bit-level parity with a single parity disk to provide fault tolerance of data stored on the RAID 3 array in the event of failure of a single disk drive in the array. RAID 3 requires that all the disk drives in the array be synchronized with each other. The bits of the data and the parity information calculated from the data are written to all the disk drives in the array simultaneously. RAID 3 requires a minimum of three disk drives to create the array.

RAID 4

RAID 4 uses block-level parity with a single parity disk to provide fault tolerance to the RAID 4 array in the event of failure of a single disk drive in the array. On a RAID 4 array, data and the parity information that is calculated from the data is written to the disk drives in blocks. There is no need for the disk drives to be synchronized, and the disk drives can be accessed independently. A minimum of three disk drives is required to create the array. The problem with RAID 4 is that the parity drive is accessed on every write operation to the RAID array. This causes heavy utilization of the parity drive, which will probably fail before of the other drives in the array.

RAID 5

RAID 5 uses block-level parity, but it spreads the parity information among all the disk drives in the disk array. This eliminates the parity drive failure that is common in RAID 4 systems. The loss of storage capacity in RAID 5 systems is equivalent to the storage capacity of one of the disk drives. If three 10 GB disk drives are in a RAID 5 array, the storage capacity of the array will be 20 GB (a loss of 1/3, or 33 percent). In another example, if seven 10 GB disk drives are in a RAID 5 array, the total storage capacity of the array will be 60 GB (a loss of 1/6, or 16.67 percent). Figure 19-9 shows a diagram of RAID 5.

RAID 0/1

RAID 0/1 is also known as RAID 0+1 and it is sometimes called RAID 10. This combination of RAIDs provides the best of both worlds. It has the performance of RAID 0 and the redundancy of RAID 1. RAID 0/1 requires at least four disk drives to implement. In RAID 0/1, there are two RAID 0 stripe sets (used to provide high input/output performance) that are mirrored (which provides the fault tolerance). Figure 19-10 shows a diagram of RAID 0/1.

Figure 19-9 RAID Level 5

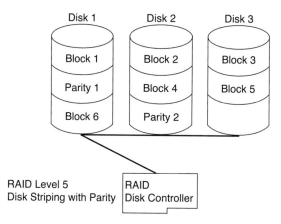

RAID Level 5
Disk Striping with Parity

Figure 19-10 RAID 0/1

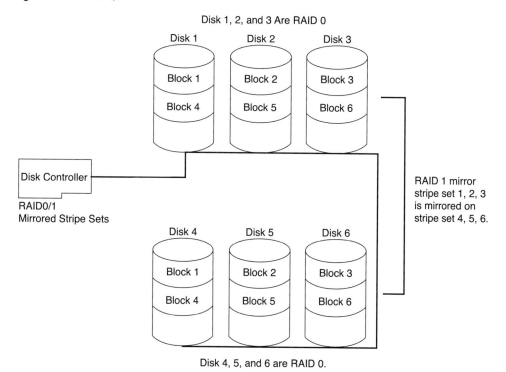

Mirroring

RAID 1, disk mirroring, is a common way to back up data. All information that is written to the first drive is also written to the mirror drive, making the two disk drives identical. A disk controller card connects to both drives and writes the data in parallel to each of them. This single controller card creates a single point of failure for disk mirroring. An advantage is redundancy. Disadvantages include cost and the amount of disk space that is required.

Duplexing

RAID 1, duplexing, provides fault tolerance for both data and the disk controller. Duplexing is disk mirroring with a separate controller for each drive. With its second controller, duplexing has improved fault tolerance over mirroring, and it is much faster than mirroring because the data can be written to both drives at the same time. The main disadvantage is the cost of the second controller card.

Striping

RAID 2, striping data, is a process in which the data is spread out onto a number of disks. A minimum of three hard disks is needed, with three or more different drives sharing the data. With more than one disk sharing the data, the process makes the input/output (I/O) faster. Parity is also an option with data striping. Striping with parity works on RAID 5, which provides redundancy by interweaving data onto several drives and has a distributed checksum for parity.

Volumes

Volumes is a method in which at least two volumes are on the server, on either the same physical disk or multiple disks. Normally, two volumes are used: a system volume and a data volume. The system volume holds all the operating system files, which allow the network to run. The data volume holds all the varieties of user data. Because of volumes, more physical disks can be added without administrative work being done to reorganize the logical structure of the storage.

OSI Model

In this section, you review the OSI model and the protocols, services, and functions that pertain to each layer.

Application Layer

The application layer (the seventh layer) of the OSI model provides network services, which are closest to the user. Programs such as Internet Explorer, Netscape Communicator, Eudora Pro, and other end user application software are examples of programs that utilize services provided by the application layer to the user. This layer establishes communication with intended partners and synchronizes agreement on procedures for error recovery and control of data integrity.

The protocols that function at this layer are SMB and Network Control Program (NCP).

Services that provide network access include these:

- Telnet and File Transfer Protocol (FTP)
- Trivial File Transfer Protocol (TFTP)
- NFS
- SNMP
- Simple Mail Transfer Protocol (SMTP)
- Hypertext Transfer Protocol (HTTP)

Devices that function up to this layer include *hosts* and *gateways*.

Presentation Layer

The presentation layer ensures that the information that the application layer of one system sends is readable by the application layer of another system. If necessary, the presentation layer translates among multiple data formats by using a common format.

The presentation layer also provides data encryption to ensure protection as data journeys through the network. When the encrypted data is received, it decrypts and formats the message before passing it along to the application layer.

Protocols include NCP. Data formats include ASCII, extended binary coded decimal interchange code (EBCDIC), Joint Photographics Expert Group (JPEG), Graphics Interchange Format (GIF), Motion Picture Experts Group (MPEG), QuickTime, Flash, WAV, AVI, and MP3. Devices that function up to this layer include hosts and gateways.

Session Layer

The session layer establishes, manages, and terminates sessions between two communicating hosts and provides its services to the presentation layer. It also synchronizes dialogue between the two hosts and manages their data exchange. In addition, the session layer offers provisions for efficient data transfer, class of service, security authorization, and exception reporting of session layer, presentation layer, and application layer problems.

The three types of dialogs used in the session layer are simplex, half-duplex, and full-duplex. A simplex dialog allows information to flow from one device to another without requiring a reply transmission.

A half-duplex dialog, which is also known as a two-way alternate (TWA) transmission, allows data to flow in two directions from one device to another; however, neither device can send a transmission until the previous signal has been completely received. When one device sends a transmission and requires the destination device to respond, the destination device must wait until the initial transmission is complete before it can send its response.

A full-duplex dialog, which is also known as a two-way simultaneous (TWS) transmission, allows devices to send data to another device without having to wait until the wire is clear. When a device transmits a signal, the destination device does not have to wait until the signal is complete to send a reply to the source device. Full-duplex enables two-way traffic to occur simultaneously during one communication session. A telephone is an example of a full-duplex dialog.

Protocols include NFS, Structured Query Language (SQL), remote-procedure call (RPC), X-Window System, AppleTalk Session Protocol, and Digital Network Architecture Session Control Protocol. Devices that function up to this layer include hosts and gateways.

Transport Layer

The transport layer segments data from the sending host's system and reassembles the data into a data stream on the receiving host's system. The boundary between the session layer and the transport layer can be thought of as the boundary between media-layer protocols and host-layer protocols. Whereas the application, presentation, and session layers are concerned with application issues, the lower three layers are concerned with data transport issues.

The transport layer attempts to provide a data transport service that shields the upper layers from transport implementation details. Specifically, the main concern of the transport layer includes issues such as how reliable transport between two hosts is accomplished. In providing communication service, the transport layer establishes, maintains, and properly terminates virtual circuits. In providing reliable service, transport error detection and recovery and information flow controls are used.

When the transport layer receives data from the upper layers, it breaks up the information into segments (smaller pieces) to be sent through the lower levels of the OSI model and then to the destination device.

Protocols that are used in this layer are listed here:

- Sequenced Package Exchange (SPX)
- Transmission Control Protocol (TCP)
- User Datagram Protocol (UDP)
- NetBEUI

Services that are used at this layer use TCP to provide connection-oriented communication with error-free delivery and UDP to provide connectionless communications without guaranteed packet delivery (unreliable delivery). Devices that function up to this layer include hosts and gateways.

Network Layer

The network layer is a complex layer that provides connectivity and path selection between two host systems that can be geographically separated. Layer 3 can be remembered as addressing, path selection, routing, and switching.

Protocols that function on this layer include these routed protocols:

- IPX
- IP

The following Layer 3 protocols also are involved:

- Internet Control Message Protocol (ICMP)
- Address Resolution Protocol (ARP)
- Reverse Address Resolution Protocol (RARP) Routing Protocols
- Routing Information Protocol (RIP)
- Interior Gateway Routing Protocol (IGRP)
- Enhanced Interior Gateway Routing Protocol (EIGRP)
- Open Shortest Path First (OSPF)
- Exterior Gateway Protocol (EGP)
- Internet Group Management Protocol (IGMP)

The following are grouped with routed protocols but are labeled as nonroutable protocols:

- NetBEUI
- DECnet

Services include software and hardware addressing, packet routing between hosts and networks, resolution of hardware and software addresses, and reports of packet delivery. Devices that function up to this layer include routers and *bridging routers (brouters)*.

Data Link Layer

The data link layer provides reliable transit of data across a physical link. In so doing, the data link layer is concerned with physical (as opposed to logical) addressing, network topology, network access, error notification, ordered delivery of frames, and flow control. Layer 2 can be remembered by frames and Media Access Control (MAC).

Ethernet CSMA/CD also operates at this layer to determine which devices should transmit at a given time to avoid collisions. The network interface card is responsible for CSMA/CD on Ethernet. If two or more devices attempt to transmit signals at the same time, a collision occurs. CSMA/CD instructs the device to wait a given amount of time before transmitting another signal to avoid another collision.

The data link layer is broken down into two sublayers by the IEEE 802 standards: the Logical Link Control (LLC) sublayer and the MAC sublayer. The LLC sublayer (IEEE 802.2) establishes and maintains communication with other devices and provides connectivity with servers when data is being transferred. LLC manages link control and defines service access points (SAPs).

The MAC sublayer maintains a table of physical addresses of devices. Each device is assigned and must have a unique *MAC address* if the device is to participate on the network. For example, the MAC address is similar to the individual's physical residence address, which the post office uses to deliver snail mail.

High-Level Data Link Control (HDLC) for WAN connections, including synchronous and asynchronous transmissions, are used at this layer. The LLC protocol (IEEE 802.2) provides flow control at this layer.

Technologies that operate at this layer include more than 18 varieties of Ethernet (specified in the IEEE 802.3 and other standards), Token Ring (IEEE 802.5), and other LAN technologies that rely on frames. Communications with the network interface card are also provided.

Devices that function up to this layer include network interface cards, bridges, and switches. Although routers and brouters are classified as Layer 3 devices, to perform their functions, they must operate at Layer 1 and Layer 2 as well.

Physical Layer

The physical layer (Layer 1) defines the electrical, mechanical, procedural, and functional specifications for activating, maintaining, and deactivating the physical link between end systems. Such characteristics as voltage levels, timing of voltage changes, physical data rates, maximum transmission distances, physical connectors, and other similar attributes are defined by physical layer specifications.

The physical layer is responsible for moving bits of data through physical media. Data, in the form of ones and zeros, is turned into electrical signals, pulses of light, or wireless signals. These signals are placed on the copper cables or optical fibers, or they are emitted as wireless signals by using a network interface card. When the network interface card receives data from the network, it turns the electrical signals, pulses of light, or wireless signals back into ones and zeros to be sent up the hierarchy of the OSI model.

Protocols are the cabling, signaling, and connection standards. Services include Ethernet, Token Ring, Fiber Distributed Data Interface (FDDI), and other LAN technologies. Devices that function at this layer are repeaters, multiport repeaters (also called hubs), media access units, and transceivers (transmitter/receivers for converting one signal type into another).

Networking Media

In this section, you review Category 3, Category 5, fiber optic, UTP, and Spanning Tree Protocol cable.

Coaxial Cable

Coaxial cable is braided, grounded strands of wire that can provide some shielding and noise immunity. (See Figure 19-11.) However, the installation and the termination of the cable can be costly. Coaxial cabling, which uses connectors called BNC (British Naval Connector or Bayonet Nut Connector), is used in forms of Ethernet, thicknet and thinnet, and in the older LAN technology, ARCnet, and cable TV.

Figure 19-11 Coaxial Cable

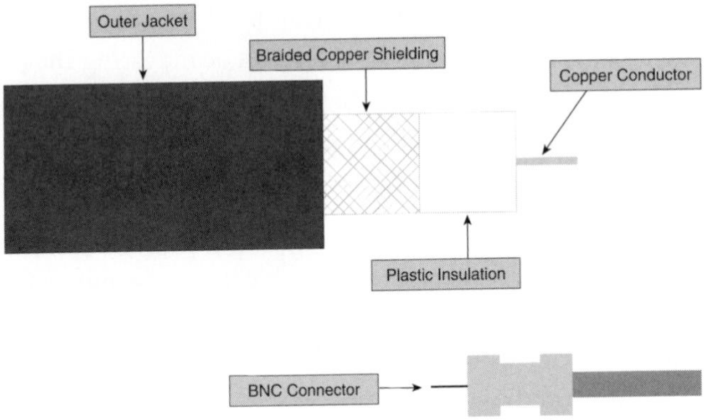

Cat 3 UTP and Shielded Twisted-Pair Cable

Category 3 (Cat 3) UTP and Spanning Tree Protocol includes applications as voice (telephony) or data (up to 10 Mbps). More commonly, Cat 3 is used on a network for cable segments to workstations or printers. Cat 3 is not recommended for data installations because its maximum bandwidth of 10 Mbps is rapidly being exceeded by many LAN technologies.

Category 5 UTP and Shielded Twisted-Pair Cable

Applications for Category 5 (Cat 5) UTP and Spanning Tree Protocol include voice (telephony) or data (up to 100 Mbps or, with certain technologies, 1000 Mbps). Cat 5 is sometimes used as a backbone, but it is restricted to 100 meters in length. It is currently the most popular cabling to connect workstations and horizontal cable runs because of its low cost, high bandwidth, relative ease of installation, and ease of termination with RJ-45 connectors.

Fiber-Optic Cable

Fiber-optic cabling carries signals that have been converted from electrical to optical (pulses of light) form (see Figure 19-12). It consists of the core, which is either an extremely thin cylinder of glass or optical-quality plastic that is surrounded by a second glass or plastic layer called the cladding. The interface between the core and the cladding can trap light signals by a process called *total internal reflection (TIR)*, in which the optical fiber acts as a light pipe. Protective buffer and jacket materials are used to cover the cladding layer. This type of cabling is less frequently used because it is somewhat more expensive; however, it is rapidly decreasing in both raw cost and installed cost.

Figure 19-12 Fiber-Optic Cable

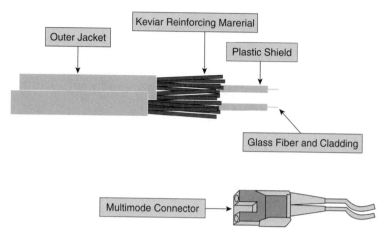

Fiber-optic cables are not susceptible to interference, such as radio waves, fluorescent lighting, or any other source of electrical noise. Fiber-optic cable is the common cable that is used for network backbones; it can support up to 1000 stations, carrying signals beyond 25 km. Fiber terminations include SC, ST, and a variety of proprietary connectors. Maximum data transfer rate is virtually limitless: tens and hundreds of gigabits per second, limited only by the electronics on each end of the fiber.

Unshielded Twisted-Pair Cable

Unshielded twisted-pair (UTP) cable is a set of three or four pairs of wires, with each wire in each pair twisted around the other to prevent electromagnetic interference. (See Figure 19-13.) UTP cabling uses RJ-45, RJ-11, RS-232, and RS-449 connectors. Because UTP is less expensive and easier to install than shielded twisted-pair or coaxial cabling, it is more popular. An example of UTP application is telephone networks, which use RJ-11 connectors, and 10BASE-T networks, which use RJ-45 connectors. UTP comes in the form of Cat 2, 3, 4, and 5 grades; however, only Cat 5 is recommended for data applications. The maximum length is 100 meters without using any kind of signal-regeneration device, and it has a maximum data transfer rate of 1000 Mbps for Gigabit Ethernet.

Figure 19-13 UTP Cable

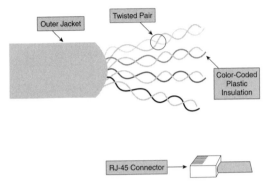

Shielded Twisted-Pair Cable

Shielded twisted-pair cable, like UTP, also has four pairs of wires, with each wire in each pair twisted together (see Figure 19-14). However, the difference is that shielded twisted-pair is surrounded with a foil shield and copper braided around the wires that allows more protection from external electromagnetic interference. Because of the shielding, the cable is physically larger, more difficult to install and terminate, and more expensive than UTP. For applications in electrically noisy environments, shielded twisted-pair uses RJ-45, RJ-11, RS-232, and RS-449 connectors. Like UTP, shielded twisted-pair also comes in Cat 2, 3, 4, or 5 grades; however, only Cat 5 is recommended for data applications. The maximum cable length without using a signal-regenerating device is 100 meters, with a maximum data transfer rate of 500 Mbps.

Figure 19-14 Shielded Twisted-Pair Cable

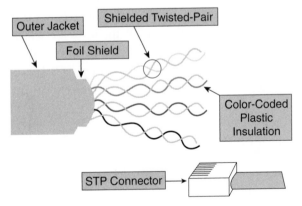

Baseband Signal

In this section, you review 10BASE-2, 10BASE-5, 10BASE-T, 100BASE-T, 100BASE-TX, and 100BASE-VG-AnyLAN.

10BASE-2

10BASE-2 cabling systems, which are also referred to as thinnet, thin wire, or coaxial, use coaxial cables. They connect no more than 30 nodes per segment, spaced at least half a meter apart. 10BASE-2 cabling is commonly used for small networks because it is inexpensive and easy to install.

The 10 in 10BASE-2 represents the rate of data transfer—in this case, 10 Mbps. Base is the type of signaling, either baseband or broadband; this type of cabling system uses a baseband signal. The 2 stands for the maximum distance of the cable; here, the 2 should stand for 200, but the maximum unrepeated distance is actually 185 meters. Therefore, this type of cabling system can transmit 10 Mbps, using baseband signaling, with a maximum distance of 185 meters.

10BASE-5

10BASE-5 cabling systems also use coaxial cables and are often referred to as thicknet, "Yellow Cable" (because of the outer yellow coating), or "Frozen Yellow Garden Hose." 10BASE-5 cabling can connect up to 100 nodes, spaced at 2.5 meters apart.

10BASE-5 cabling systems can transmit at 10 Mbps by using a baseband signal and can have a maximum unrepeated distance of 500 meters per cable. This type of cabling is expensive and is usually used in circumstances that require longer distances and use as a backbone. 10BASE-2 and 10BASE-5 cabling systems are normally used in bus topologies. However, this type of cabling is beginning to be used less often in structured cabling installations.

10BASE-T

10BASE-T cabling systems, which have become an extremely popular LAN technology, are normally found on Ethernet star or extended star topologies connected by UTP cables. They are usually connected to a central hub or a switch. This type of cabling system can carry 10 Mbps by using a baseband signal, with a maximum unrepeated distance of 100 meters.

100BASE-T

100BASE-T is the generic name for Fast Ethernet. It can carry 100 Mbps, using baseband signaling, with a maximum unrepeated distance of 100 meters.

100BASE-TX and 100BASE-T4

100BASE-TX and 100BASE-T4 are two variations of 100BASE-T, which is specified by the Institute of Electrical and Electronics Engineers (IEEE). Both cabling types carry 100 Mbps and use baseband signaling, with a maximum unrepeated distance of 100 meters per cable. 100BASE-TX uses Cat 5 UTP—specifically, two pairs of twisted wires—with the capability to transmit 100 Mbps. 100BASE-T4 uses Cat 3 and all four pairs of twisted wires to transmit 100 Mbps. 100BASE-TX is by far the most popular copper version of Fast Ethernet.

100BaseVG-AnyLAN

100BASE-VG-AnyLAN was developed by Hewlett-Packard and is similar to 100BASE-VG, which can transmit 100 Mbps using baseband signaling, using a Cat 3, Cat 4, or Cat 5 UTP cable for either Ethernet or Token Ring LANs. The maximum unrepeated length is 250 meters. The primary benefit of this technology is its versatility, including the cabling it uses and the type of LAN technology with which it can be used.

100BASE-FX and Gigabit Ethernet

Fast Ethernet 100BASE-T is 10BASE-T with the original Ethernet MAC at 10 times the speed. It allows three physical-layer implementations, all part of IEEE 802.3u: 100BASE-TX, which has two pairs of Category 5 UTP or Type 1 shielded twisted-pair cabling and is most popular for horizontal connections; 100BASE-FX, which has two strands of multimode fiber and is most popular for vertical or backbone connections; and 100BASE-T4, which has four pairs of Category 3 or better cabling and is uncommon.

Gigabit or 1000-Mb Ethernet is the 1998 IEEE 802.3z standard that includes the Gigabit Ethernet MAC and three physical layers. Gigabit uses 8B/10B encoding and encompasses three physical standards: 1000BASE-SX Fiber (horizontal fiber), 1000BASE-LX Fiber (vertical or campus backbone), 1000BASE-CX Copper (Copper-Twinax cabling), and 1000BASE-T.

Full- and Half-Duplex Operation

Three different terms are used to describe how transmitters and receivers interact during communications: simplex, half-duplex, and full-duplex. In simplex communications, the data travels only one way, and no response is needed or possible. An example of simplex communications is a school's public address system.

In half-duplex communications, data travels from a transmitter to a receiver and then from the receiver to the transmitter repeatedly, but never simultaneously. Simultaneous transmission and reception of data is not possible. Examples of half-duplex communications are walkie-talkies and 10BASE-T Ethernet.

In full-duplex communications, both the transmitter and the receiver can send and receive simultaneously. Clearly, this is the fastest way to communicate, but it requires more sophisticated electronics. Examples of full-duplex communications are the telephone and 100BASE-TX (Fast Ethernet).

WANs and LANs

A WAN is geographically unlimited, whereas a LAN is limited to a smaller region. WANs can span over cities, countries, and multiple locations, whereas LANs are limited to a single building or school campuses.

LANs operate within a limited geographic area, connecting workstations, peripherals, and other devices on a single network. LANs provide a business with complete computer technology to share devices on a network.

WANs are geographically unlimited and vary in size. They provide an efficient way to move information from one network (a LAN) to another network.

Servers, Workstations, and Hosts

Servers are typically powerful computers that provide resources and services to other computers on a network. Workstations (clients) are devices that are capable of locally processing data; they use resources and services that the server provides. Host is the special name given to any addressable computer system on a network that is running TCP/IP. Examples of hosts include workstations, servers, minicomputers, mainframes, and routers.

Server-Based Networking and Peer-to-Peer Networking

Two types of networks exist: server-based and peer-to-peer. A server-based network, also known as a client/server network, connects numerous hosts to a centralized computer. This computer acts as a server, providing security functions and access to the network and resources, allowing for a central security system. As the network grows and the number of nodes increases, this type of network can add specific servers to address specific needs and resources. Examples include file and print servers, application servers, domain controllers, and directory servers.

Client/server networks typically require a powerful server computer running a network operating system, and administration by highly trained personnel. Advantages are the variety of services that can be provided and the central administration of those services; however, the disadvantages include cost and complexity.

In a peer-to-peer network, there is no centralized server or security system. Each node on the network works as its own server, granting permission to the other nodes on the network to access its resources. This type of network is limited to approximately 10 nodes connected to each other. Advantages include simplicity, low cost, and ease of administration; disadvantages include slow speed and a severely limited range of services that can be provided.

Cables, Network Interface Cards, and Routers

To create a properly functioning network, the main necessities include cables, network interface cards, and routers. A cable is the physical medium that is used to wire networks. The cables that can be used to wire a network include UTP and shielded twisted-pair, coaxial, fiber optic, or wireless (if no cables are required). These physical media are used in combination with the network interface card, which allows the computer to communicate with the network. Another way to look at the network interface card is that it allows the workstation operating system to communicate with the local-area NOS. A router is a Layer 3 device that performs best-path selection and packet switching and that is used to connect one or more LANs to create a WAN.

Broadband and Baseband

Two types of signaling are broadband and baseband. Broadband is an analog signaling technique normally used in cable television. This type of signaling can carry video, voice, and data across a wire. It shares the medium's bandwidth over different channels, often using different carrier frequencies. One sharing technique is called *frequency-division multiplexing (FDM)*. FDM is a multiplexing technique that uses different frequencies to combine multiple streams of data for transmission over a communications medium. FDM assigns a discrete carrier frequency to each data stream and then combines many modulated carrier frequencies for transmission. For example, television transmitters use FDM to broadcast several channels at once.

Baseband is a digital signaling technique that uses the entire medium's bandwidth for a single channel at a time; it allows high throughputs (the actual measured bandwidths are possible due to this single-channel-at-a-time technique). Signals are in the form of voltage pulses on copper, light pulses on optical fiber, or electromagnetic waves in the atmosphere. A form of multiplexor (MUX) device is usually required so that multiple devices can take their turns using the medium.

Gateways

A gateway, which works as a translator, provides communication between different operating systems and frequently services the Internet. A gateway must exist if two different types of operating systems, such as Windows and UNIX, are to communicate. To communicate with a node on a different network over the Internet, the device must be connected to a LAN or a dial-up connection.

Gateway also refers to default gateway, where an IP address is used to forward packets from one subnet to another subnet, if no other routing information is available.

Understanding the Physical Layer

After installing or replacing a network interface card and experiencing problems accessing the network, it is important to troubleshoot the network interface card and follow a logical troubleshooting methodology:

1. Determine which areas are affected. Identify what caused the problem: a protocol or a device.

2. Identify the differences of the affected areas and the unaffected areas.

3. Restart the affected hardware. Often, the problem can be resolved if the hardware of the affected area is restarted.

4. Divide the network in half and segment the area.

5. Last, if you cannot identify the problem by using any of these methods, physical tools—from technical databases to diagnostics—might be necessary.

One form of technical diagnostics is called loopback testing. Either an external loopback adapter or an internal device is attached to the network interface card. Data is sent from the network interface card and is looped back in to verify whether the data received is the same as the data that was sent. Vendor-supplied diagnostics programs are usually available through a vendor's web page or technical support service.

The following questions provide information that a network installer must understand to properly diagnose network interface card problems.

Question 1: What does the EPROM on a network interface card do?

In the Erasable Programmable Read-Only Memory (EPROM) is a set of instructions built into a network adapter that allows the network interface card to perform its basic functions. In a diskless workstation, commonly in larger networks, a PROM often replaces the EPROM. The code in the PROM is unalterable and boots a workstation that has no hard disk or diskette; this feature can be added to the network interface card so that the system can be enabled to boot using files that are stored on the network.

Question 2: What do jumpers on a network interface card do?

Jumpers are pieces of plastic and metal that connect two metal posts on a NIC. They are most commonly used to change a network interface card's configuration, mainly the Interrupt Request (IRQ) and the I/O addresses. Because network interface cards have multiple connection options, jumpers determine which transceiver needs to be used on the network interface card, which transceiver to hook the cable to, and what the data rate transfer setting should be.

Question 3: What does plug-and-play software (usually packaged with network interface cards) do?

Plug-and-play software works with the plug-and-play BIOS to configure expansion components on a system, such as a network interface card and other devices. This involves minimal, if any, configuration issues when installing a device.

Question 4: What are network card diagnostics, such as the loopback test and vendor-supplied diagnostics?

When troubleshooting a network, you can use two diagnostics. First is the loopback test, which tests the inbound and outbound communications of a network interface card. In an external loopback test, a signal is sent from the network interface card, out through an adapter, and then back into the network interface card. The information is then verified to determine whether the information received is the same as what was sent. Internal loopback tests use the same idea, but they do not use an external adapter.

The second method in troubleshooting a network interface card is using vendor-supplied diagnostic programs. Normally, the manufacturers of a network interface card provide specific tests that can troubleshoot a network interface card. Generic diagnostics are available, but the vendor-supplied diagnostics tests are usually more reliable. These programs can be retrieved from either the vendor's technical support lines or from web pages.

Question 5: What does it mean to resolve hardware resource conflicts, including IRQ, direct memory access (DMA), and I/O base address?

Because there are many devices within a personal computer, hardware conflicts might arise when one device tries to communicate with another. To avoid such conflicts, there are three main ways for devices to communicate to another within a computer.

IRQ is a method by which a device can interrupt the processor and request a service. In a PC, 15 IRQ lines are available that are dedicated to devices such as disk controllers and serial and parallel ports. Some of the more common IRQs are IRQ 3 (for serial port COM port 2) and IRQ 5 or 10 (dedicated to network interface cards). In general, IRQs cannot be assigned to more than one device at a time, or a conflict occurs.

DMA is a method by which devices can access the computer's memory without involving the central processing unit (CPU). The DMA is managed by the DMA controller chip, which is generally faster than the CPU and works as if the CPU had managed the transfer of memory itself.

Input/output (I/O) base addresses allow the CPU to access each device in the computer. Each device is assigned a unique I/O address that cannot be shared. If more than one device contains the same I/O address, neither device can function properly. The CPU attempts to send information to the specified I/O address but, because two devices are assigned the same address, both respond and the data is corrupted.

Hubs

Hubs, which operate at the physical layer of the OSI model, are the central location to which cabling from most topologies connect. Three types of hubs include passive, active, and intelligent hubs.

A passive hub receives information through one of its ports and then transmits the data through another port to a destination location. It has no electrical power and does not possess signaling processing capability. Passive hubs allow communication only from one location to another to flow across the network, and they absorb some signal energy, causing a signal to weaken.

An active hub receives data through one of its ports and then works like a repeater, regenerating and retiming the signal before sending it through another port to a destination. Active hubs are also known as multiport repeaters. Most hubs "share" bandwidth among users; more users means less bandwidth per user.

Intelligent hubs have even more electronics than active hubs, and they allow network management (a "managed" hub) or even switching (a "switching hub," or, more commonly, a "switch").

Multistation Access Units

A multistation access unit allows multiple workstations, which are connected on a Token Ring network, to communicate with each other. Although multistation access units are not UTP hubs, they are commonly referred to as Token Ring hubs. They often have eight ports and use universal data connectors (UDCs) or RJ-45 connections. Multistation access units are not powered devices; however, occasional lights flash when they are connected to the network. Multistation access units add fault tolerance to ring networks.

Switching Hubs

A switching hub, also called a multiport bridge, is a device that automatically verifies the MAC addresses of each device that is connected to its ports. When a packet is sent to its network, the switching hub checks the MAC address before sending the data to the specified location. Unlike a standard passive or active hub, switching hubs do not broadcast signals to each segment on the network; instead, they transmit data only to a specific destination. Switching hubs (and switches) result in dedicated bandwidth per port, whereas other hubs share the total bandwidth with the number of users.

Repeaters

When a repeater receives data from an Ethernet segment, it decodes/codes the binary information and then retransmits the signal to the destination. Advantages of a repeater include the capability to extend the network a greater distance, the capability to increase the number of devices connected to the network, added fault tolerance by isolating breaks on a network to only that cable segment, and the capability to link different cable types. A disadvantage is that repeaters enlarge collision domains: If two computers send packets at the same time, a collision occurs and CSMA/CD is applied to the entire network, thereby slowing down the network.

A repeater does not manage the flow of traffic; it only repeats signals. A maximum of four repeaters can be installed on a single-segment Ethernet network.

Transceivers

A transceiver (transmitter/receiver) is a device that transmits and receives data to and from the network. This device attaches to the network interface card in two different ways: as an onboard or external transceiver.

An onboard transceiver is usually "on board," or attached to the adapter card, such as RJ-45 receptacles and BNC connectors.

An external transceiver makes a physical connection to the network interface card by using a small device, called an *attachment unit interface (AUI)* or a Digital-Intel-Xerox (DIX) connector, which is attached by an extension cable. A common external transceiver can also connect one side to an AUI interface and the other to an RJ-45 interface.

The Data Link Layer

Bridges are devices that connect two different networks or network segments and that filter traffic from each network. The bridge builds a table of physical (hardware) addresses, learning the hosts that exist on each of its ports. The bridge examines the destination MAC address of each frame; if the destination address is local (on the same bridge port, based on the bridging table), the frame is not sent. However, if the destination MAC address is of a different bridge port than the source address, then the frame is forwarded to the nonlocal destinations. Bridges provide connectivity with Layer 2 filtering. Some bridges connect networks of differing LAN technologies (such as Ethernet to Token Ring). Because the bridge operates at Layer 2, it forwards all upper-level protocols.

802.2 Logical Link Control

802.2 is the IEEE standard that defines the LAN technology-independent LLC. LLC manages link control and provides SAPs, all in software. LLC adds headers to encapsulated upper-layer data to identify which protocols a given frame can carry. It also provides communication between the hardware MAC sublayer and the software implementations of Layer 3.

802.3 Ethernet

802.3 defines Ethernet based on a modification of the original DIX Ethernet standard. Specifically, this standard defines the frame format to be used by a variety of specific media and topological implementations of Ethernet. The 802.3 standard also defines CSMA/CD, an algorithm for dealing with a situation in which two signals collide on a network. CSMA/CD sets the amount of time that each device must wait to send a new frame.

802.5 Token Ring

802.5 defines the "passing" of the token around a network to allow each device to transmit data across physical star or logical ring networks. A token is created by the first node and then passed along the network until another device wants to transmit data and grabs the token. The data flows along the network, past each node, until the destination node sees it and grabs the information. After the data has been received, the destination device transmits a reply to the source device to indicate that the information was received.

802.11b Wireless

802.11 refers to a family of specifications that the IEEE developed for wireless LAN technology. 802.11 specifies an over-the-air interface between a wireless client and a base station or between two wireless clients. The IEEE accepted the specification in 1997.

802.11b (also referred to as 802.11 High Rate or Wi-Fi) is an extension to 802.11 that applies to wireless LANs and provides 11 Mbps transmission (with a fallback to 5.5, 2, and 1 Mbps) in the 2.4 GHz band. IEEE 802.11b data is encoded by using direct-sequence spread-spectrum (DSSS) technology. DSSS works by taking a data stream of zeros and ones and modulating it with a second pattern, the chipping sequence. In 802.11, that sequence is known as the Barker code, which is an 11-bit sequence (10110111000) that has certain mathematical properties, making it ideal for modulating radio waves. 802.11b was a 1999 ratification to the original 802.11 standard, allowing wireless functionality comparable to Ethernet.

The Function and Characteristics of MAC Addresses

A MAC address is a unique address that is burned onto the memory of a network interface card. Ethernet requires each computer to have a MAC address, and any computer with a MAC address is called a node. MAC addresses use a 48-bit address, which is a unique identifier for each device that is used for delivering data to a specific location. MAC addresses (Layer 2 addresses, hardware addresses, and physical addresses) are crucial to the functioning of LANs, allowing local delivery of frames and packets. A MAC address is similar to a Social Security number or a personal identification number.

The Network Layer

If the MAC address matches the address that is burned into the network interface card, the data link layer passes the data to the network layer. If the MAC address is all 1s, then the data is also passed to the network layer. When the network layer receives the packet, it uses the packet's network address to route beyond the local network. Routing allows the network layer to transfer data packets across the internetwork from a source to a destination and to choose the most efficient path to deliver the packet.

Router

A router is a Layer 3 device that provides best-path selection and switching of data packets. To connect two different networks, a router must be used. Routers can be used to segment LANs, creating smaller collision and broadcast domains. However, the most important use of routers is as the backbone devices of WANs. Networks consisting of routers, all of which can communicate using routing protocols, can be built to allow reliable and flexible delivery of data. They make the Internet possible.

Routers are either static or dynamic devices and are normally connected in a mesh topology with other routers. Statically configured routers cannot communicate with other routers; they have a determined fixed route, which you enters manually. Dynamically configured routers can communicate with other routers to determine the best path to route a packet by a variety of protocols, including RIP, IGRP, EIGRP, and OSPF.

Brouter

A brouter is a combination of both a router and a bridge. It acts as a router for routable protocols and a bridge for nonroutable protocols. A brouter allows the network to resolve almost all of its connection problems by using one device; therefore, it is cost effective. However, brouters are decreasing in prevalence because their functions are being incorporated into separate categories of devices: Layer 3 routers and Layer 2 switches.

The Difference Between Routable and Nonroutable Protocols

A routable (routed) protocol can be delivered beyond a single LAN or WAN segment; its packets can be routed. For routed protocols, a best path can be selected, and the packet can be switched to the appropriate interface for that best path. Nonroutable protocols cannot leave the LAN on which they originate. Routable (routed) protocols include IP, IPX, and AppleTalk. NetBEUI is an example of a nonroutable protocol.

The Concept of Default Gateways and Subnetworks

The connection of a LAN to a WAN is achieved through a router; therefore, routers can segment LANs. The interface of a router, which resides on a LAN, is called the default gateway. (See Figure 19-15.) The default gateway is the location where all nonlocal network traffic that has no specific route to a destination is sent. The default gateway acts as an entry and exit point of a subnetwork.

When sending data to a remote subnetwork, the host sends the packet to the initial router that is specified as its default gateway. The router receives the packet and then must determine whether the destination location is on one of its local networks or whether to send the data to another router for delivery.

Figure 19-15 Default Gateway

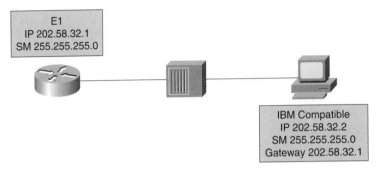

The Reason for Employing Unique Network IDs

Each device that participates on a network must have a unique ID: a MAC address (also known as a Layer 2 address, a hardware address, or a physical address). MAC addresses can be easily identified and maintained for LANs up to a certain size; however, the addresses become unmanageable for large unsegmented LANs or WANs. The Layer 3 or network addressing scheme, which is hierarchical, was created because a new addressing scheme was needed. By requiring that all networks that are connected to the router have their own network ID number, the router can refer to a group of hosts with one network layer (often IP) address. The router builds tables of device hardware and network addresses (typically MAC and IP addresses) and determines by which interface these networks can be reached. Thus, the routers use the network ID address to efficiently make best-path selection and switching decisions.

The Difference Between Static and Dynamic Routing

Two major types of routing processes exist: static and dynamic routing. You program static routing to determine which path a packet must take to reach its destination. You must maintain (including any kind of changes, additions, or deletions) the routes of each network routing device. Static paths are not flexible with changing network environments. When the static routes are programmed, the determined paths for packets do not change, regardless of changing network conditions. Static routes are most often used for security reasons.

Dynamic routing allows the router to select which path a packet must take to reach its destination. In doing so, a router uses routing protocols such as RIP, IGRP, EIGRP, or OSPF to communicate with other routers to determine which path is the fastest way to transport data across an internetwork (a network of networks). Using the routing protocols, routers "talk" to each other to update what paths are best to send data through, especially while network conditions are constantly changing. Without routing or its protocols, large networks such as the Internet would be impossible to maintain.

The Transport Layer

Connectionless communication is a fast way to send information to a destination; however, it is not reliable because there is no notification of receipt to the source location. Connectionless protocols include IP and IPX (Layer 3) and UDP (Layer 4).

Connection-oriented protocols include TCP (Layer 4) and SPX. Connection-oriented protocols, such as TCP, typically use an acknowledgment (ACK) process between source and destination. If a source does not receive an ACK from the destination, TCP retransmits the segment until an ACK is received. The processes of segmentation, handshaking/acknowledgment, flow control, and error checking are used to provide reliable transport.

The Purpose of Name Resolution

Name resolution is important for both local and remote delivery of data packets. Typically, layer hardware and Layer 3 network addresses must be resolved. IP uses ARP and IPX uses SAP to resolve host names ("abbreviations" of network addresses) to MAC addresses.

TCP/IP Fundamentals

TCP/IP is the most used protocol suite to date because every operating system and millions of hosts worldwide utilize it. TCP/IP is popular because it is flexible, compatible, and capable of performing well in both small and large network implementations. Because of historical reasons and the quality and versatility of its protocols, TCP/IP is the de facto standard set of protocols for the Internet.

Default Gateways

IP datagrams (packets) use default gateways as entry and exit points between subnets. The subnet mask for the default gateway and the network on which it resides must be the same. A default gateway is usually the computer or router that is connected to the local subnet or other networks, which can determine the best path for delivery to the destination network ID. Packets that are too large for the gateway are fragmented with three additional pieces of information: a flag to indicate that fragmentation has occurred, a fragment ID number, and a fragment offset number for reassembling the fragments into the original packet.

DHCP, DNS, WINS, and Host Files

Dynamic Host Configuration Protocol (DHCP) automatically distributes IP addresses to devices that are connected to the network. When a client tries to connect to the network, a request is sent to the DHCP server for configuration settings. When the server receives the message, the DHCP server sends a reply to the client that includes the configuration information; then it keeps a record of the addresses that have been assigned. DHCP uses the BOOTP protocol to communicate with clients. Clients must renew their IP addresses after 50 percent of the address lease life and again at 87.5 percent of the lease life by sending a DHCPREQUEST message. Client hosts keep their IP address until their lease expires or until they send a DHCPRELEASE command. IPCONFIG and WINIPCFG are utilities run from the command line that allow verification of the IP address information that has been assigned to the client host.

DNS

DNS is a name-resolution service that resolves (associates) host names to IP addresses. DNS keeps a record of IP addresses and host names in a process called a domain. DNS provides services along a hierarchical chain, with a database design that is similar to a file tree structure (root level/top level/second level/host name). DNS also services requests for host names that cannot be resolved locally. Large internetworks have several levels of DNS servers to provide efficient name resolution.

Windows Internet Naming Service (WINS)

Windows Internet Naming Service (WINS) works as DNS does to resolve IP addresses with host names. However, a difference exists between DNS and WINS: WINS uses a flat namespace by using NetBIOS instead of using a hierarchical one such as DNS. To resolve an IP address, a WINS client host registers its NetBIOS and IP addresses with the WINS server. Then the WINS client host sends a name query request to the WINS server, indicating that it desires to transmit to another host. If the desired IP address and host name are found in the server's WINS registry, they are sent to the original WINS client host. Requests that WINS makes are routable. The WINS proxy agent is used for non-WINS clients such as UNIX hosts; however, WINS does not provide support for Macintosh operating systems.

HOSTS Files

The *HOSTS file* is a statically configured host name to IP address translation file. This file is usable in all hosts' IP protocol stacks. If present, it will be referenced for name resolution before an external DNS search. LMHOSTS provides the same services in a WINS environment and is statically configured on Windows networking clients.

TCP

TCP is a connection-oriented protocol that operates at the transport layer of the TCP/IP and OSI models. TCP is the de facto standard of the Internet and provides full-duplex data transmission. When TCP receives data from the upper layers of the OSI model, it guarantees reliable delivery to remote networks. TCP is useful for transmitting large amounts of data reliably, but with the penalty of large ACK overhead consuming bandwidth.

UDP

UDP is a connectionless protocol that operates at the transport layer of the TCP/IP and OSI models. Because UDP is an unreliable delivery service, it does not require receiving protocols to acknowledge the receipt of a packet. An advantage that UDP has over TCP is that, because it does not concentrate on establishing a connection, it can transmit more information in a smaller amount of time than TCP. Useful for transmitting small amounts of data when reliability is less crucial, UDP lacks the overhead caused by ACKs.

Post Office Protocol Version 3

Post Office Protocol version 3 (POP3), which uses TCP port 110, is a mail protocol that is responsible for holding e-mail until delivery. When an SMTP server sends an e-mail message to a POP3 server, POP3 holds on to the message until a user makes a request to have the data delivered. Thus, POP3 transfers mail files from a mail server to a mail client.

Internet Message Access Protocol Version 4

Internet Message Access Protocol version 4 (IMAP4) allows a client to access and manipulate electronic mail messages on a server. IMAP4 permits manipulation of remote message folders, called mailboxes, in a way that is functionally equivalent to local mailboxes. IMAP4rev1 also provides the capability for an offline client to resynchronize with the server.

IMAP4rev1 includes operations for creating, deleting, and renaming mailboxes; checking for new messages; permanently removing messages; setting and clearing flags; searching; and selective fetching of message attributes and texts. Messages in IMAP4 are accessed by using numbers. These numbers are either message sequence numbers or unique identifiers.

IMAP4 is designed to be upward compatible from the IMAP2 protocols. In the course of the evolution of IMAP4, some aspects in the earlier protocol have become obsolete.

SMTP

SMTP, which uses TCP port 25, allows users to send and receive e-mail over the Internet. It is the SMTP's responsibility to make sure that the e-mail is sent to the POP3 server.

SNMP

SNMP, which uses TCP port 161, allows simple maintenance and remote monitoring of any device on a network. With SNMP, you can address issues such as problems with a network card in a server, a program, or service on the server, or a device such as a hub or a router.

When you are managing a network device by using SNMP, you can use the central management system and the Management Information Base (MIB). The management system allows you to view performance and operation statistics of the network devices, enabling you to diagnose a network remotely.

FTP

FTP is a fast, connection-oriented, error-free protocol that uses TCP ports 20 and 21. FTP allows data to be transferred between servers and clients. For FTP to connect to a remote server, the IP address or host name must be provided. FTP must be capable of resolving IP addresses to host names to establish a connection.

HTTP

HTTP, which uses TCP port 80, allows clients to transfer documents that are written in Hypertext Markup Language (HTML) over the World Wide Web for display by a browser. HTTP is the universal display language of the Internet.

Another protocol for transmitting data securely over the World Wide Web is Secure HTTP (HTTPS), which is designed to transmit individual messages securely.

IP

IP is a routable (routed), connectionless protocol that operates at the network layer of the OSI and TCP/IP models. IP is the de facto standard for the Internet and provides packet delivery and addressing for source and destination.

Because IP is a connectionless delivery service, it is unreliable and does not guarantee that the packets received will be in the order sent, if they are received at all.

Internet Domain Name System

The Internet Domain Name System consists of a root and a subdomain. The root represents the upper-indexed pointers to other DNS servers. For example, when a user—such as user@cisco.com—tries to send an e-mail to an international location—such as a student at the University of Cambridge in England, student@cam.au.uk—the DNS server first contacts the subdomain server, which is cisco.com. The DNS server sends the e-mail to the subdomain. After the subdomain, cisco.com, has been contacted, the e-mail is sent to the root, .com. The root passes it along the other roots to .uk, which stands for United Kingdom. The .uk root passes the e-mail message down its hierarchy to its subdomain, .au, and then to .cam. After .cam receives the data, the e-mail message sits on the POP3 server until the mail is requested.

Class A, B, and C Addresses and Their Default Subnet Mask Numbers

IP addresses are divided into classes to accommodate different sizes of networks. (See Figure 19-16.) Depending on the type of IP address, the first octets (through the first, second, or third octets) are issued by American Registry for Internet Numbers (ARIN) or other national agencies. The IP address has three parts: the network field (assigned externally), the subnetwork field (that you create locally), and the host field (assigned locally). To create more hierarchical networks with subnets, the extended network prefix—also known as the subnet mask, which allows the decoding of the IP address into its three parts (network, subnetwork, host)—is required.

The classes of IP addresses are as follows: Class A addresses begin with binary 0xxx xxxx in the first octet—that is, decimals 1 to 126. (0 and 127 are reserved for special test purposes.) Class B addresses begin with binary 10xx xxxx in the first octet—that is, decimals 128 to 191. Class C addresses begin with binary 110x xxxx in the first octet—that is, decimals 192 to 223.

Figure 19-16 IP Address Classes

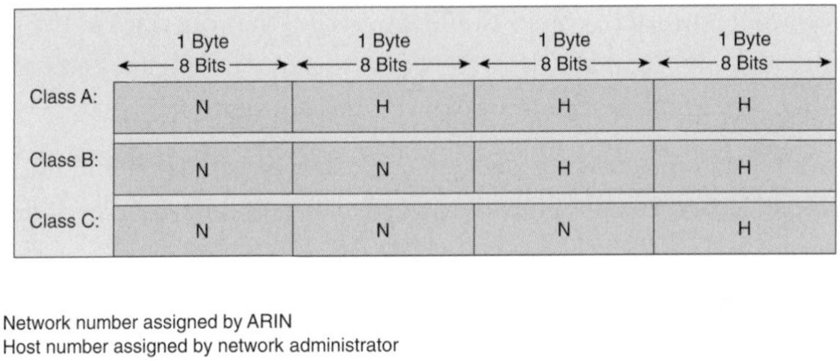

N = Network number assigned by ARIN
H = Host number assigned by network administrator

Class A IP addresses are reserved for the larger networks. This range allows Class A IP addresses to have a possibility of 126 networks. Each network has a capacity of more than 16 million unique hosts using a default subnet mask. The default subnet mask for this class network is 255.0.0.0.

Class B IP addresses are reserved for medium-sized networks. The range that is dedicated for Class B networks includes IP addresses from 128.0.0.0 to 191.255.0.0. The possibility of networks available for this subnet is a little more than 16,000 networks, with each having the capacity of a few more than 65,000 unique hosts using the default subnet mask. The default subnet mask for a Class B address is 255.255.0.0.

Class C IP addresses are dedicated for small local networks. Class C networks range from 192.0.0.0 to 223.255.255.0, with a capacity of more than 2 million networks, each with a capacity of 254 unique hosts using the default subnet mask. The default subnet mask for a Class C address is 255.255.255.0.

Other classes, which are not as popular, are Class D and Class E. Class D addresses range from 224.0.0.0 to 239.255.255.255 and are used mainly for multicasting to various amounts of hosts. Class D has the potential of having more than 268 million unique multicast groups. Class E addresses, which are experimental addresses blocked for future use, have a range of 240.0.0.0 to 247.255.255.255.

Various solutions to the problem of IP address depletion are being implemented, including network address translation (NAT) and private addressing, variable-length subnet masking (VLSM), classless interdomain routing (CIDR), and IP version 6 (IPv6, which is a version of IP with longer IP addresses—and far more addresses to assign).

Port Numbers

Each TCP/IP protocol has at least one specifically designated port number for the flow of network traffic between client and server. Note that the use of the word port here refers to a structure in software, not a hardware interface. Port numbers correspond to services to be provided for the upper layers. TCP/IP normally assigns well-known port numbers on the server prior to connections; however, these numbers can be changed. Because clients have the capability to dynamically log in to the server from any location, they do not have assigned port numbers. For instance, if an individual (client) were to call a friend (server) from anywhere in the country, the friend would be able to pick up his telephone. Common port numbers include HTTP (port 80), FTP (port 21), Telnet (port 23), and SMTP (port 25).

Proxies and Why They Are Used

A proxy server is a type of a go-between between the Internet and the users of a network. If a client needs information from the Internet, the proxy server searches for the destination and retrieves the information. This provides for higher security and faster service because the client does not directly connect to the destination.

A proxy server is used for a number of different reasons. Proxy servers enhance security by hiding the individual host addresses. When a server receives the request, the server sees only one address: the address of the proxy server, not the individual host. Because all requests are being made on one server, network traffic is less busy if more than one user requests the same location, enhancing performance. The proxy server copies each of the requested addresses. When another host requests the same destination, the server sends the cached version of that location.

Workstation Configuration

Normal configuration parameters for a workstation include the IP address and subnet mask, the DNS setting, the default gateway and subnet mask, the IP proxy, WINS, DHCP, the host name, and the Internet domain name.

IP Addresses and Subnet Masks

When you are assigning IP addresses, you must consider two important factors: The IP address needs to be unique, and it must be assigned a subnet mask. When a DHCP server assigns an IP address, it specifically assigns unique addresses to each device, not duplicating any address. If you are manually assigning IP addresses, it is important that no two devices have the same IP address.

Each address must also have a subnet mask to properly communicate with the network. The subnet mask determines the network and host IDs of an IP address; therefore, it is important that each IP address has a subnet mask.

Default Gateways and Subnet Masks

The interface of a router, which resides on a LAN, is called the default gateway. The default gateway is the location where all nonlocal network traffic that has no specific route to a destination is sent. The default gateway also acts as an entry and exit point of a subnetwork.

Host Name

You assign a host name to identify each device on the network. By default, on Windows-based machines, host names are the names of the computers.

Internet Domain Name

Internet domain names are registered for the public by accredited registrars who are governed by the Internet Corporation for Assigned Names and Numbers (InterNIC). The InterNIC is operated by Internet Corporation for Assigned Names and Numbers (ICANN).

The domain name consists of two parts: the host name and the domain. In the address www.cisco.com, www is the host name and cisco.com is the domain. Together, www.cisco.com becomes a fully qualified domain name (FQDN).

TCP/IP Suite: Utilities

In TCP/IP, ARP is used to bind (associate) the physical (MAC) addresses with a specific logical (IP) address. When a data packet is sent to a particular destination, ARP matches the addressing information against the ARP cache for the appropriate MAC address. If no matches are made, ARP sends a broadcast message on the network looking for the particular destination. A host responds with the correct address and sends a reply to ARP. Table 19-1 shows some variations on the **arp** command.

If duplicate IP addresses appear in the ARP cache, a Windows NT 4.0 TCP/IP stack is written, and a new ARP broadcast is sent to each computer that is affected by the ARP cache error.

Table 19-1 arp Commands

Commands	Action
arp -a	Displays a list of all IP and MAC addresses
arp -a -n *interface* Example: **arp -a -n 146.188.144.223**	Filters the display to show only the interface specified
arp -s *interface MAC_address*	Manually adds entries
arp -d *IP_address*	Manually deletes a dynamically entered ARP cache

Using Telnet to Test, Validate, and Troubleshoot IP Connectivity

Telnet, which uses port 23, allows users to log into and execute text-based commands when working on a remote server. To use Telnet, the user needs to run Telnet.exe at the command prompt or from the Start menu. (Choose Start, Programs, Accessories, Telnet; then select Connect, Remote System until a dialog box appears.)

To connect to a host, the client must be capable of resolving the name to an IP address. The user must also specify the port to connect to (Telnet port 23) on the remote server. VT100 is the default terminal emulation that is used.

If a user is having problems logging onto a server, Telnet might still be functional. In this case, the user can log on using Telnet and administer the problems that are associated with the server. For example, if a Windows NT server crashes and displays a blue screen and the server allows for a remote administration card to be plugged in, the user can Telnet to this card, determine the problem of the server, and reboot it.

Using nbstat to Test, Validate, and Troubleshoot IP Connectivity

nbstat displays information regarding NetBIOS names and corresponding IP addresses that have been resolved by a host. **nbstat** is used to troubleshoot two computers trying to connect via NetBIOS over TCP/IP (NetBT) by displaying the protocol statistics and current connection with each remote host.

Using tracert to Test, Validate, and Troubleshoot IP Connectivity

The **tracert** command-line utility traces the exact route that the data packet used to reach its destination. Using ICMP, **tracert** sends echo packets to the destination, which was the packet's original destination, to determine the exact route. Variations of the **tracert** command are shown in Table 19-2.

Table 19-2 tracert Commands

Command	Action
tracert *hostname* or **tracert** *ipad dress*	Displays the exact route taken by the packet to its destination
tracert -d	Specifies that an IP address should not be resolved to a host name
tracert -d -h *number_of_hops host_name* Example: **tracert -d -h 15 www.cisco.com**	Lists the maximum number of hops in a search
tracert -j *router_name local_computer*	Specifies the loose source routing to make the outbound datagram pass through the router and back
tracert -w *number*	Instructs the amount of time to wait in milliseconds before timing out

An example of displaying hops from one location to another is to use the **tracert -d -h 15 www.asu.edu** command.

Using netstat to Test, Validate, and Troubleshoot IP Connectivity

Use **netstat** to display the methods used by virtual circuits and network interfaces. **netstat** is available for troubleshooting specific TCP/IP issues by displaying protocol statistics and current TCP/IP connections. This utility is used to show the three-step handshake method when establishing and disconnecting network sessions.

Command **netstat** displays a list of protocol types, local addresses and port information, remote access and port information, and current state. The information displayed also explains what connections are open and in progress. Variations of the **netstat** command are shown in Table 19-3.

Using **netstat** enables you to troubleshoot TCP/IP-based connections by monitoring TCP protocol activity (by using **netstat -a**). Error counts and Ethernet interfaces can also be monitored using by **netstat**.

Table 19-3 netstat Commands

Command	Action
netstat -a *number*	Displays connections and listening ports.
netstat -e	Includes the number of bytes received and sent, discards and errors, and unknown protocols.
netstat -s -p *ipad dress*	Displays contents of the routing table. Allows users to view the current routes and active sessions and addresses.

Using ipconfig/winipconfig to Test, Validate, and Troubleshoot IP Connectivity

ipconfig and **winipcfg** display the current TCP/IP configurations on the local workstation and enable the user to modify the DHCP address that is assigned for each interface. **ipconfig** is used in Windows NT, and **winipcfg** is used for Windows 9x platforms. This utility enables the user to view the IP-related settings, such as DNS and WINS servers, and the network interface's physical address. Variations on the **ipconfig** command are shown in Table 19-4.

Table 19-4 ipconfig and **winipcfg** Commands

Command	Action
ipconfig /all or winipcfg /all (for Win 9*x*)	Displays all IP configuration information
ipconfig /renew or winipcfg /renew	Renews the DHCP lease information, if none is named
ipconfig /release or winipcfg /release	Releases the DHCP lease information and disables the TCP/IP on the adapter

Using FTP to Test, Validate, and Troubleshoot IP Connectivity

FTP, which uses ports 20 and 21, is designed to transfer data across a network. Variations of the **ftp** command are shown in Table 19-5.

To use FTP to connect to an address or target machine, such as Telnet, FTP must be capable of resolving the host name to the IP address of the destination machine. When the connection and login has been made, users can transfer files and manage directories.

Table 19-5 **ftp** Commands

Command	Action
ftp -v	Suppresses any display server response
ftp -n	Prevents automatic login
ftp -l	Turns off interactive prompting during file transfer
ftp -d	Displays all FTP commands between the client and server for debugging
ftp -g	Disables the gobbling capacity
ftp -s: *filename* Example: ftp -s:network.doc	Runs the text file containing specific FTP commands
ftp *hostname* Example: ftp www.cisco.com	Connects to the host

When you are connected with the remote computer, commands to navigate around the server include those in Table 19-6.

Table 19-6 Commands to Navigate Around the Server

Commands	Action
CD	Changes working directory
DELETE	Deletes files
LS	Lists current directory contents
BYE	Ends connection and logs out
GET	Downloads a file
PUT	Uploads a file
VERBOSE	Turns verbose mode on and off

A common use of troubleshooting with FTP is researching and downloading patches or fixes. For example, Microsoft provides an online FTP server, where patches, upgrades, and the like can be downloaded. Most vendors provide some type of FTP server for users to retrieve these utilities.

Using Packet InterNet Groper to Test, Validate, and Troubleshoot IP Connectivity

Packet InterNet Groper (ping) is a basic TCP/IP troubleshooting tool; ping is usually the first step to take when troubleshooting the network to verify whether a specific machine is active. Using ICMP, ping verifies connections between two servers by sending echo packets to remote servers and listening for replies.

PPP and SLIP

Serial Line Internet Protocol (SLIP) and Point-to-Point Protocol (PPP) allow users to log on remotely to a network by using a device such as a modem (a dial-up connection through an analog telephone line). Although SLIP is available for Windows 95 and NT desktops, it was originally designed to connect UNIX platforms to a remote network. SLIP was one of the first remote connectivity protocols. However, with new technology and better security, SLIP is being replaced by PPP.

PPP was designed to replace all the older technology of SLIP. It provides asynchronous and bit-oriented synchronous encapsulation, network protocol multiplexing, session negotiating, and data-compression negotiation while supporting protocols such as IPX/SPX, DECnet, and TCP/IP. PPP uses the HDLC protocol for data encapsulation during transmission and establishes and maintains connections by using the link control protocol (LCP). Using NCP with PPP, you can run different protocols simultaneously on the same line.

Advantages of PPP over SLIP include the fact that SLIP can be used only with TCP/IP, whereas PPP can use multinetwork protocols simultaneously during one session. PPP also uses DHCP to resolve IP addresses with the server and can handle a faster connection than SLIP. PPP supports data compression and IP address negotiation, neither of which SLIP does.

The Purpose and Function of PPTP

PPTP has functions that are similar to those of PPP. However, PPTP provides a secure transmission of data from the remote server. To use PPTP, the PPTP-enabled client must dial in to a PPP server and gain access to the remote server. When the connection is established between the PPP and PPTP servers, the PPTP server creates a connection with the client through tunneling. When a remote client sends a transmission, the transmission goes through the PPP server, is encrypted, and then is sent through the tunnel to the PPTP server. The PPTP server receives the transmission, decrypts it, and directs it to the appropriate host. These features of PPTP make secure connections possible across the Internet. PPTP facilitates the transfer of sensitive data: A user can log into an ISP, use the ISP as a gateway, and then log securely into an office network.

ISDN and PSTN (POTS)

The Public Switched Telephone Network (PSTN) was originally designed to carry analog voice signals across telephone lines. A technology called Integrated Services Digital Network (ISDN) was created to convert analog signals into digital signals to allow data transfer rates that were faster than PSTN.

One advantage of ISDN over PSTN is speed. The fastest connection that a modem can establish using a PSTN analog line is 56 kbps. Data is converted by the modem from the PC's digital signals to analog signals and then sent across the wires to a remote network, where the data is again converted from analog signals to digital signals. ISDN enables digital signals to travel over regular telephone lines in their digital form, transmitting data in half the time of analog modems. An ISDN Basic Rate Interface (BRI) line can carry data at 128 kbps, and ISDN BRI lines can be aggregated to create an ISDN Primary Rate Interface (PRI) line to carry 1.472 Mbps (T1) or 1.920 Mbps (E1). Another advantage of ISDN over PSTN is the capability to be connected to the network "all the time" without tying up the analog telephone line, which is especially useful for telecommuters.

Modem Configuration for Dial-Up Networking to Function

For dial-up modems to work properly with the dial-up network, the parameters, such as serial ports, IRQs, and I/O addresses, must be configured properly. Modems use a serial port for connection and attempt to use COM1 as the default. The EIA/TIA 232 serial standards determine how to connect a modem to a computer.

Serial ports, which are based on DB-9 (9 pins) or DB-25 (25 pins) connectors, are commonly known as COM1, COM2, COM3, and COM4 ports. Data terminal equipment (DTE) represents the computer side of the connection, whereas the data circuit-terminating equipment represents the modem connection. Modems should be set properly; depending on the serial port, modem setup can be done through the Start menu, Control Panel, Modems.

IRQs provide a device a way to send interrupt signals to a computer. In many cases, for more than one (if not all) attempts to transfer data into a CPU, each device is issued an IRQ. An I/O address, a four-digit hexadecimal number, enables the flow of data within the computer. Addresses are used to select the information to be accessed in memory or peripherals.

The maximum port speed is the speed that a modem can support in kilobits per second. An analog line, also known as a regular telephone line, can support speeds up to 56 kbps by using an analog modem.

The Requirements for a Remote Connection

The requirements for remote connection include the following:

- The user must have a valid ID and password to access the network remotely. This includes accounts with PPP, SLIP, or Remote Access Service (RAS).
- A remote server must be available to be accessed.
- The appropriate hardware device, such as a modem or an ISDN line, must be enabled to communicate with the server.
- Network protocols must be configured to access the remote server or network.

Security

Two types of network security exist for protecting the network: share-level security and user-level security. Said to be weak and difficult to manage, share-level security allows users to access certain information if you assign them a password. For an individual to access information on the network, that user must provide a password, which a you assign specifically.

User-level security specifies the rights and privileges of each user. You assign the user an account to access a specific computer or network. When an individual attempts to log into the network, the computer matches the user account ID and password(s) against the security database before providing the user access.

Many protocols are used to encrypt data and help secure incoming and outgoing traffic through the network. Some of the most popular security protocols that are used today include IPSec, L2TP, Secure Socket Layer (SSL), and Kerberos.

IPSec is a set of protocols that the IETF developed to support secure exchange of packets at the IP layer. IPSec has been deployed widely to implement VPNs. IPSec supports two encryption modes: Transport and Tunnel. Transport mode encrypts only the data portion of each packet but leaves the header untouched. The more secure Tunnel mode encrypts both the header and the payload. On the receiving side, an IPSec-compliant device decrypts each packet.

L2TP is an extension to the PPP protocol that enables ISPs to operate VPNs. L2TP merges the best features of two other tunneling protocols: PPTP from Microsoft and Layer 2 Forwarding (L2F) from Cisco Systems. Like PPTP, L2TP requires that the ISP's routers support the protocol.

SSL is a protocol that Netscape developed for transmitting private documents via the Internet. SSL works by using a public key to encrypt data that is transferred over the SSL connection. Both Netscape Navigator and Internet Explorer support SSL, and many websites use the protocol to obtain confidential user information, such as credit card numbers.

Kerberos is an authentication system developed at the Massachusetts Institute of Technology (MIT). Kerberos is designed to enable two parties to exchange private information across an otherwise open network. It works by assigning a unique key, called a ticket, to each user who logs into the network. The ticket is then embedded in messages to identify the sender of the message.

Standard Password Practices and Procedures

In both share-level and user-level security models, passwords are given to the user for access to the network or specific data. Passwords should always be kept secure and should never be written down where unauthorized users might stumble upon them.

Passwords should not be one of the following:

- The login, first, or last name of the user, or these names reversed
- A familiar name, such as the name of a spouse, child, pet, or relative
- Easily attainable information, such as personal information
- A word found in any language dictionary
- A combination of letters and numbers only
- A group of single digits or letters (such as AAAAA or 11111)

Passwords should have these characteristics:

- Be between six and eight characters in length
- Include nonalphanumeric characters
- Be set to expire periodically, ideally once every 30 days

Data Encryption

Data encryption provides the secure delivery of information being sent over the internetwork. It takes the information, which is written in plain text, and codes it into a text called ciphertext, which resembles nothing, making it unreadable. When the data is received, it is decrypted from ciphertext and converted back into its original text.

The Use of a Firewall

A firewall is used to protect the internal network from the public and insecure Internet. Firewalls can be implemented by using hardware or software. A software firewall is a set of programs on the gateway that monitors all traffic flowing in and out of a network; these are often implemented using specifically configured routers. All information must go through the firewall and be verified against a specific set of rules. If the information does not meet the specified rules, the data is bounced back and cannot continue until it meets the set standards. An example of hardware firewall is using specially configured routers to control inbound and outbound traffic.

Administrative Considerations

Before installing a network, you must consider the configurations of the network, physical location, topologies, physical structure of the network, administrative duties (including administrative and test accounts), passwords, IP addressing, IP configuration, connectivity requirements, and software.

Administrative accounts allow you unrestricted access to all the information and security on the network. These accounts should be created only for individuals whose job requires the need for unrestricted access, and they should be restricted to exercise these privileges only for administrative duties. Because your role as the administrator is to protect all the data on the network, this account should be sensitive and should have a strong password that must be difficult to break.

When you use your administrative account to make changes on the network, a test account should be used to test and verify the changes. Test accounts are similar to that of a normal user account, resembling other user accounts and privileges.

Both administrative and test accounts need to have passwords. Passwords are a form of computer security that enables privileged users to access network information. A strong password, which should be used for administrative accounts, is a password that is difficult for hackers to "crack." Some hackers use what is called the "brute force" attack, which uses dictionary files against a user's account. It is important to use a password that is an uncommon word not found in any dictionary, that consists of six to eight characters in length, and that is a combination of numbers, letters, and non-alphanumeric characters, as previously discussed.

You must also consider IP configurations and standard operating procedures (SOPs) when building your networks. IPCONFIG is a Windows utility that is used to determine TCP/IP settings. This utility verifies IP addresses, default gateways, subnet masks, DNS, and other IP-related settings. IP configurations are normally determined by the desktop used.

Although most networks have different names, they use similar SOPs, which is a baseline of the resources in day-to-day operation. SOPs might include backing up data on the network at the end of each day or each evening, having backup information in case a network goes down, or monitoring performance. To monitor performance, a tool called the "sniffer" can be used to monitor the amount of network traffic on the network. A sniffer is also used to analyze network traffic and provide solutions to problems that affect the infrastructure of the network.

The Impact of Environmental Factors on Computer Networks

Environmental factors should be considered when maintaining or creating a network. Computers and networking devices can easily be affected by extreme situations, such as temperature, moisture, vibrations, and electrical interference. If exposed to these situations, computers and networking devices might act irregularly and fail.

Room conditions should be at normal humidity and temperature to prevent electrostatic discharge (ESD) and overheating. Fluorescent lighting, space heaters, televisions, radios, and other electrical devices might contribute to electromagnetic interference (EMI), especially when copper cabling is the primary networking medium. Often, cooler and darker places, such as a basement, are ideal areas to store computer equipment.

Common Peripheral Ports

Common peripheral ports include serial and parallel ports. Serial ports are often used for a workstation's mouse or keyboard and are referred to as a slow port because data can flow only in one direction.

Parallel ports are used for devices that are quicker and that connect outside of the workstation. Data can be transmitted in both directions, making the connection faster. A printer, for example, connects to a parallel cable and port to speed up printing processes.

Data bus (DB) connectors are D-shaped connectors that are used to connect serial and parallel cables to the computer. DB connectors are usually referred to as DB-x, with x representing the number of wires; DB-9, DB-15, and DB-25 are most commonly used.

External Small Computer Standard Interface Connections

The Small Computer Standard Interface (SCSI) enables workstations to connect to and communicate with peripheral hardware, such as CD-ROMs, disk drives, and scanners. SCSI provides faster data transmission than the parallel port, is used for high-performance systems, and has the capability to chain together up to 7 or 15 devices.

Print Servers

Two types of print servers exist: dedicated and nondedicated. Both types receive requests from end users and direct the requests to a printer pool. A print server is secure because it has no client access into the network. The difference between dedicated and nondedicated print servers is that a dedicated print server is used only as a print server; a nondedicated print server also has some other network server functions.

Patch Panels

Patch panels, which are an integral part of structured cabling installations, consist of a row of female connectors (or ports), in which every cable from different work areas connects directly to the back of the patch panel. They provide support for UTP, shielded twisted-pair, fiber ports, and various Cat ratings of UTP cabling.

Uninterruptible Power Supply

An uninterruptible power supply (UPS) provides protection from spikes and sags that can come over the electrical wires. While the server is plugged in, the battery charger constantly charges the battery. If a power outage occurs, the fully charged battery can provide operations to continue or provide enough time for the server to shut down properly.

Network Interface Cards

Network interface cards allow the communication between a computer and the network, providing a physical connection. For the computer to interact with the network interface card, the computer must have the proper drivers installed. Each network interface card is assigned a unique address called the MAC address. This address is also the physical address and is burned onto the network interface card by its manufacturer. No two MAC addresses are or can be alike.

Token Ring Media Filters

A Token Ring media filter is a passive device that is used to convert output signals from a Token Ring network interface card so that it can be compatible with different media types, such as shielded twisted-pair cable or different terminations, such as a DB-9 connector. Media filters are also designed to eliminate unwanted high-frequency emissions and to adjust inputs when using UTP cable.

Analog Modem Installation into a Digital Jack

The technologies of an analog and a digital jack are different and are not compliant. Analog modems use a standard phone line to gain remote access; a digital jack is reserved to be used with an ISDN line or a PBX switch. A NIC or a transceiver can burn out if it is exposed to the voltages of an analog phone line. Likewise, an analog modem can be damaged if it is plugged into a digital jack.

Uses of RJ-45 Connectors Depending on Cabling

Registered jack (RJ) connectors were previously the standard for telephone connectors. More recently, RJs have been used to connect not only the telephones, but also 10BASE-T, 100BASE-TX, and Token Rings.

Telephone lines use the RJ-11 connector, which connects four-wire cables, with the two inner connectors for one phone line and the two outer connectors for another line. Modems are restricted to using RJ-11 because it is an analog connector. RJ-12, which is rarely used, is a six-wire version of the RJ-11 that is used for more complex telephone systems.

RJ-45 connectors have eight wires and are used for network technologies that require four pairs of wires, such as Ethernet and Token Ring networks. RJ-45 connectors are specifically designed for digital signals. If an analog modem uses an RJ-45 connector, either the connection will not function or the analog modem will stop functioning and burn out. RJ-45 connectors are used mainly to connect 10BASE-T cabling (or the like) to a hub or a bridge to connect to another media type, such as using a BNC connector for 10BASE-2.

Patch Cables: Contributors to the Overall Length of the Cabling Segment

Patch cables are typically 3 meters in length and often are used for either connecting two multistation access units (in a Token Ring topology) or connecting two Ethernet hubs. Patch cables also are used to "patch" a system with a network interface card to the digital jack on either a cube wall or a floor mount. The EIA/TIA-568-A standards govern horizontal cable installations. For Cat 5 UTP, the distance limitation is 100 meters, of which 3 meters are designated for workstation patch cables, 90 meters are designed for horizontal cable runs (from the outlet to the horizontal cross connect [HCC]), and 6 meters are reserved for patch cables/jumper cables within the HCC.

Maintaining and Supporting the Network

Test documentation normally is included with the software during packaging. Vendor patches, fixes, and upgrades usually occur after the product has been purchased. Vendors provide patches and updates of their products when bugs are found in the software or to make their software run more efficiently. If a bug is found in an earlier release, patches are provided to fix the bugs. The most current patch or fix is likely to be found on a vendor's web page. Normally, a search feature or online support guide on the vendor's web page is available to easily navigate the site to locate the specific patch that is needed.

Software upgrades are designed to improve current software and to make it more powerful. Normally, upgrades are free (or can be purchased for a fee) and can be downloaded from a vendor's web page in the same way that a patch would be downloaded. However, a backup should be made before installation to prevent loss of data.

Without antivirus software installed on the servers and workstations, no modern network will continue working efficiently. Depending on the user's needs, a wide variety of antiviral packages are available. An ongoing network maintenance strategy should be to update virus signatures frequently. Because new viruses are spawned frequently, within a few months, what was previously protective antivirus software can become useless.

Standard Backup Procedures and Backup Media Storage Practices

Each administrator who is maintaining a network should have a standard backup procedure that is implemented nightly. Backup procedures should include tape drives, tape automation, and full, incremental, and differential backups.

DAT and DLT are the two standard types of tape drives. DAT provides a complete digital recording method, which was originally used to record audio and video. DAT has a capacity of 24 GB, uses a SCSI connection, and is mostly used for medium-sized networks.

DLT has a capacity of up to 80 GB, and this is becoming the more popular method of the three backup standards. Although DLT is expensive, it is fast and reliable. Like DAT, DLT uses a SCSI connection.

Tape automation is a scheduled routine backup in which a tape backup is scheduled with an average of 20 to 25 tape rotations. The most common tape backup procedure is the 21-day tape rotation, where rotation is consistent for four days out of the week, Monday through Thursday.

Some rotations are scheduled for five days a week (Monday through Friday). Storing backup tape off-site is a good idea in case of a major catastrophe that could ruin the backed up information.

Three different types of backups exist: full, incremental, and differential. Full backup is the process in which all the information is backed up. Most companies perform full backups every day. However, this process requires the most tape out of the three backup processes.

Incremental backups back up files that have been changed since the last incremental or full backup was performed. This process is less time consuming and uses the least amount of tape. If the database needs to be restored, the last full backup and every incremental tape afterward are needed.

Differential backup is a process in which files that were changed since that last full backup was performed are backed up. This type of backup process takes less tape than a full backup. When you are restoring the information, only two tapes are required: the last full and differential backup tapes.

The Need for Periodic Application of Software Patches and Other Fixes to the Network

It is important to patch the software that is running on the client workstation and the server. There is always existing software on the client that will not be on the server, and vice versa; if software is upgraded or patched on a server and not on a workstation, problems might occur when users try to access the software with a different version.

The Need to Install Antivirus Software on the Server and Workstation

Because traffic flows from network to network via the Internet, there is a chance of a virus coming over the Internet and onto the network. To prevent a virus from destroying a system or a network, it is important to install antivirus software on the servers and workstations. Antivirus software scans all the files that come into the network off the Internet and scans all the files that are opened on the server that are considered to be outgoing. Without antivirus software installed on the servers and workstations, no modern network will continue working efficiently—all can be vulnerable to virus attacks and damages.

The Need to Frequently Update Virus Signatures

It is important to frequently update virus signatures that are used by the virus-scanning software when eliminating viruses. The vendor updates these signature files and either mails them to the user or makes them available on the web page.

Troubleshooting the Network

An example of a troubleshooting approach involves the following four steps:

1. Determine whether the problem exists across the network. Is the problem across the network or in a portion of the network? Identifying the scale of the problem will determine how many users are affected and might provide clues as to what caused (or is causing) the problem.

2. Attempt to isolate the problem. Is one workstation not functioning? Is that client capable of connecting to the network? Or is the entire workgroup not functioning? Are any of the devices capable of printing? Or is the problem affecting the entire LAN? Is it the entire Ethernet segment that is not functioning? Or is it a WAN problem, or a problem with the LAN-WAN connection? (For example, do the clients have Internet access?)

3. Determine whether the problem is consistent. Is the problem continuous and not intermittent? In other words, is the problem constantly present instead of occurring periodically or randomly? Can the problem be replicated? (Given the same conditions on the same machine or another, are the same errors present?) This information will help determine what might be causing the problems on the network.

4. Finally, determine whether the problems can be resolved by using tools. A set of standard tools for maintaining networks should be available. These tools include hardware tools (such as cable testers), software tools (such as protocol analyzers), workstation and server commands, software and utilities, web-based and text-based hardware and software manuals, and diagnostics that come with various network components, such as servers, network interface cards, hubs, switches, and routers.

Determine Whether a Problem Is Attributable to the Operator or the System

To troubleshoot the network for operator or system problems, first identify the issue. Is the problem protocol based, or is it a network issue? Second, identify what parts of the network are affected, and determine whether the problem exists on the cabling or the workstations.

When you are identifying the exact issue, begin with a broad view—say, the entire network. As you conduct the research, the problem should become more isolated. When you are dealing with network problems, re-creating the problem can provide assistance in learning the events that have occurred during the error. If the problem is complex and possibly will occur in the future, re-creating the problem might be beneficial for future reference. However, if the problem is simply to replace a network interface card or a piece of hardware, re-creating the problem might not be necessary.

Isolating the cause of the problem has two benefits. First, if the problem is isolated to a specific area or number of users, the rest of the network can continue to be functional. Second, by isolating the issue, it is easier to diagnose the problem among 3 to 5 workstations than it is on 500 workstations.

After you identify the problem, correcting the problem might be even more complicated. There might be more than one way to fix the problem. First, determine the various methods to correct the problem; sometimes a problem can be patched temporarily, or a software patch can provide a temporary fix. There is also a possibility that when you fix one problem, another problem will occur because of the fix.

Proper documentation (journals and equipment logs) and feedback, such as methods used to contain the problem and additional comments, can be helpful in case the problem arises in the future.

After you correct or temporarily patch the problem, consider having another operator re-create the problem and test it on another workstation. This allows verification that the problem can be re-created on other machines.

Next, have the operator re-create and test the problem against the original machine to verify that the problem can be created and fixed and to see if any other issues arise with the affected workstation. Having the operator follow the documentation that was originally created for the problem verifies whether other operators are following the SOPs.

Check Physical and Logical Indicators of Trouble

When you are isolating a problem, physical and logical indicators of trouble might exist. These indicators include the link light, power light, error display, error log and display, and performance monitors.

Link lights should be a steady green or amber, indicating that a device is connected to a network. The power light also should be a steady light. If this light is out on a machine, it could mean one of two things: First, there is no power in the device, or, second, the power light is burned out. Scope all aspects of the problem before determining that the device has no power.

Error displays often indicate a malfunction or a failure in a device. Errors can be viewed either as a dialog box that pops up or in the LED error display of the device. Logs and error displays maintain a listing of errors that have occurred. Although error logs and displays do not provide a solution to the problem, some documentation is provided to help lead to a solution.

Performance monitoring is accomplished with a tool provided by Windows NT called the Network Monitor. This monitor provides information regarding data coming in and going out of a workstation. It tracks the resources that components and applications use. Performance monitoring is useful when you are trying to identify bottlenecks in the CPU, memory, disk I/O, network I/O, and error trends. This feature monitors real-time system performance and performance history. By using this monitor, you can determine the capacity of the system and system configurations.

Given a Network Problem Scenario, Determine the Problem

Use the following techniques to determine the problem: recognize abnormal physical conditions; isolate and correct problems where the fault is in the physical media (patch cable or cable run); check the status of servers; check for configuration problems with DNS, WINS, and HOST files; check for viruses; check the validity of the account name and password; recheck operator logon procedures; and select and run appropriate diagnostics.

Question: What are some common issues to look for if a network is having problems?

First, consider abnormal physical conditions, such as power interruptions, presence of high heat or humidity where a networking device is located, or large amounts of electrical noise.

An extremely common problem, often referred to as a Layer 1 problem, is somewhere in the conducting path from a PC's network interface card to the nearest networking device (typically a hub or a switch). The patch cable from the PC to the outlet could be faulty: bad terminations, bent or crushed cable, or improper wiring sequences. The horizontal cable run from the outlet to the patch panel could be bent, crushed, cut, improperly mounted, or otherwise damaged. Alternatively, the patch and jumper cables from the patch panel to the networking device could be the incorrect type of cable or could be damaged.

Check all servers and resources to verify that they are functioning properly. Check servers and resources, such as DNS, WINS, and HOST files, for proper configuration. You can perform a virus scan to be sure that a virus has not tapped into the network, causing problems. Workstations must have all the proper settings.

Next, verify the validity of the user's account and password. Is the user typing the correct user ID and password? Does the individual have access? Verify the login procedures. Finally, if you cannot resolve the problem, run vendor-provided diagnostics.

Summary

Now that you have completed this review chapter, you should have a firm understanding of the following topics:

- Basic networking
- Major NOSs
- Wireless LAN technology and standards
- Backup and RAID technologies
- Physical layer
- Data link layer
- Network layer
- Transport layer
- TCP/IP fundamentals
- TCP/IP suite utilities
- Remote connectivity
- Security
- Security protocols
- Installation of the network
- Maintenance and support of the network
- Network troubleshooting

Key Terms

AUI (attachment unit interface) The portion of the Ethernet standard that specifies how a cable is to be connected to an Ethernet card. AUI specifies a coaxial cable that is connected to a transceiver that plugs into a 15-pin socket on the network interface card.

backbone Another term for bus, or the main wire that connects nodes. Backbone is often used to describe the main network connections that compose the Internet.

brouter (bridging router) A combination of both a router and a bridge. A brouter acts as a router for routable protocols and a bridge for nonroutable protocols.

CSMA/CD (carrier sense multiple access collision detect) A set of rules that determines how network devices respond when two devices attempt to use a data channel simultaneously (a collision). Standard Ethernet networks use CSMA/CD. This standard enables devices to detect a collision. After detecting a collision, a device waits a random delay time and then attempts to retransmit the message. If the device detects a collision again, it waits twice as long to try to retransmit the message. This is known as exponential backoff.

FDM (frequency-division multiplexing) A multiplexing technique that uses different frequencies to combine multiple streams of data for transmission over a communications medium. FDM assigns a discrete carrier frequency to each data stream and then combines many modulated carrier frequencies for transmission. For example, television transmitters use FDM to broadcast several channels at once.

gateway A node on a network that serves as an entrance to another network. In enterprises, the gateway is the computer that routes the traffic from a workstation to the outside network that is serving the web pages. In homes, the gateway is the ISP that connects the user to the Internet.

host A computer that is connected to a TCP/IP network, including the Internet. Each host has a unique IP address.

HOSTS file A statically configured host name to IP address translation file. This file is usable in all hosts' IP protocol stacks. If present, the HOSTS file will be referenced for name resolution before an external DNS search.

MAC address A unique address that is burned onto the memory of a network interface card. MAC addresses use a 48-bit address, which is a unique identifier for each device that is used for delivering data to a specific location.

NFS (Network File System) NFS grants users permission to certain parts of the file system and controls the security of the UNIX systems.

NetWare Directory Services   Novell Netware's directory service that uses TCP/IP or IPX/SPX. The NetWare Directory Services tree allows users to log into the network and access any of the resources that are available.

RAID (Redundant Array of Inexpensive Disks)   A category of disk drives that employ two or more drives in combination for fault tolerance and performance. RAID disk drives are used frequently on servers but are not generally necessary for personal computers.

segment   In networks, a section of a network that is bounded by bridges, routers, or switches.

SMB (Samba)   A protocol that UNIX and Linux systems run that allows Microsoft clients and servers to view UNIX and Linux systems as if they were another Windows device.

TIR (total internal reflection)   The interface between the core and the cladding on fiber-optic cabling that can trap light signals by a process in which the optical fiber acts as a light pipe.

transceiver   A device that transmits and receives data to and from the network. This device attaches to the network interface card in two different ways: as an onboard or external transceiver.

Objectives

After reading this chapter, you will be able to

- Understand what topics are covered on the CCNA exam
- Know what topics to study and pay particular attention to in order to pass the CCNA exam

Chapter 20

CCNA Certification Exam Review

This chapter serves as a review as you prepare for the CCNA certification exam. The first step in preparing for the exam is to review the exam objectives in conjunction with the curriculum topics. This chapter presents a review of the topics covered on the CCNA certification exam, which will assist in your preparation for the exam.

OSI Model

The overall goal of communication protocols is to allow a computer application on one computer to communicate with a computer application on another computer, regardless of the hardware platform or operating system of the two computers. The exam covers the seven layers and you need to know them.

Application Layer

The application layer identifies the communication partner and provides functions for particular application services, such as file transfer and virtual terminals.

Typical TCP/IP applications include the following:

- Telnet
- File Transfer Protocol (FTP)
- *Trivial File Transfer Protocol (TFTP)*
- Simple Mail Transfer Protocol (SMTP)
- Simple Network Management Protocol (SNMP)
- Hypertext Transfer Protocol (HTTP)
- *Bootstrap Protocol (BOOTP)*
- Dynamic Host Configuration Protocol (DHCP)

Presentation Layer

The presentation layer provides communication services by transparently converting the different data, video, sound, and graphic formats to and from a format suitable for transmission. This layer is also responsible for data compression, decompression, encryption, and decryption.

Although these can be specific protocols, they are usually built in to existing application layer protocols.

Some of the presentation layer standards involved include the following:

- **Text**—ASCII, EBCDIC
- **Graphics**—TIFF, JPEG, GIF, PICT
- **Sound**—MIDI, MPEG, QuickTime

Session Layer

The session layer controls the dialogue between devices or hosts. It establishes, manages, and terminates sessions between the applications.

Examples of session layer protocols include the following:

- Network File System (NFS)
- Structured Query Language (SQL)
- Remote Procedure Call (RPC)
- X Window System
- AppleTalk Session Protocol (ASP)
- DNA Session Control Protocol (SCP)

Transport Layer

The transport layer is responsible for end-to-end delivery of information, including error recovery and flow control.

Transport layer protocols can be reliable or unreliable. Unreliable protocols may have little or no responsibility for establishing connections, acknowledgments, sequencing, and flow control. Unreliable transport layer protocols may leave this responsibility to another layer's protocol. The reliable transport layer protocols may include responsibility for the following:

- Establishing connections and closing connections, such as the three-way handshake
- Transferring data
- Acknowledging what has been received or not received

- Making sure that packets arriving out of sequence can be sequenced in their proper order
- Maintaining flow control, such as in window sizes

The TCP/IP reliable transport layer protocol is the Transmission Control Protocol (TCP). Protocols that use TCP can include FTP, Telnet, and HTTP.

The TCP/IP unreliable transport layer protocol is the User Datagram Protocol (UDP). Protocols that use UDP can include TFTP, SNMP, NFS, Domain Name System (DNS), and the routing protocol RIP.

Transport layer protocols include the following:

- **TCP/IP**—TCP and UDP
- **Novell**—Sequenced Packet Exchange (SPX)

Network Layer

The network layer provides connectivity and path selection between two end systems (original source and final destination) that may be located on geographically diverse networks. Network layer addressing provides addressing for the original source address and the final destination address—in TCP/IP, these are the IP addresses. These addresses do not change along the path.

Examples of network layer protocols include the following:

- Internet Protocol (IP)
- Novell's Internetwork Packet Exchange (IPX)
- Address Resolution Protocol (ARP)
- Reverse Address Resolution Protocol (RARP)
- Internet Control Message Protocol (ICMP)

Data Link Layer

The data link layer provides reliable transit of data across a physical link. In doing so, the data link layer is concerned with physical (as opposed to network, or logical) addressing, network topology, line discipline (how end systems use the network link), error notification, ordered delivery of frames, and flow control.

The data link layer delivers the frame from one node to the next, such as from host to host, host to router, router to router, or router to host. The data-link addresses usually change, representing the current data link address and the next-hop, data-link address. In terms of Ethernet, this would be the source MAC address and the destination MAC address.

Data link layer protocols include the following:

- Ethernet
- IEEE 802.3
- Token Ring
- IEEE 802.5
- High-Level Data Link Control (HDLC)
- Point-to-Point Protocol (PPP)

Physical Layer

The physical layer defines the electrical, mechanical, procedural, and functional specifications for activating, maintaining, and deactivating the physical link between end systems. Such characteristics as voltage levels, timing of voltage changes, physical data rates, maximum transmission distances, physical connections, and other similar attributes are defined by physical layer specifications.

Physical layer standards include the following:

- 10BASE-T
- 100BASE-TX
- V.35
- RS-232

Bridging/Switching

This review of LAN switching reminds you that one way to help reduce network congestion is to use switches rather than hubs whenever possible. In addition, to increase the efficiency of the switch, you might want to utilize some or all of these switching features:

- Fast Ethernet (100-Mbps) switch ports and host network interface cards
- Full-duplex communications
- Cut-through switching

Full-Duplex and Half-Duplex Ethernet Operations

Two types of Ethernet communications exist:

- Half-duplex
- Full-duplex

Half-duplex communication allows two or more devices to communicate with each other, but with only one device at a time communicating. (See Figure 20-1.) If multiple devices attempt to communicate at the same time, a collision occurs. Those devices then back off, and a random algorithm within each network interface card (NIC) determines which device sends first.

Figure 20-1 Half-Duplex Ethernet Design (Standard Ethernet)

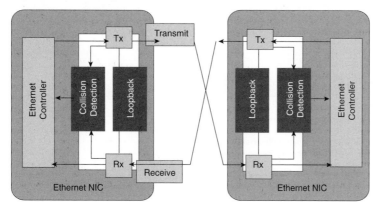

♦ Ethernet physical connection provides several circuits
♦ Most important are receive (RX), transmit (TX), and collision detection

Hosts that are connected to a hub must operate in half-duplex mode because they must be capable of detecting when a collision occurs (to stop transmitting).

Full-duplex communication allows two devices to communicate with each other simultaneously. (See Figure 20-2.) One of the limitations of full-duplex Ethernet is that there must be only one device connected to the switch port. That device can be a computer, a printer, a router, or another switch. If you have single devices attached to switch ports (no hubs), it is a good idea to have them operate in full-duplex mode.

Full-duplex operation doubles the amount of throughput on that link. On a standard Ethernet 10-Mbps link, for example, the throughput equals 20 Mbps—10 Mbps transmitted, plus 10 Mbps received. Virtually no collisions occur on a full-duplex connection because only two devices are in the collision domain.

Figure 20-2 Full-Duplex Ethernet Design

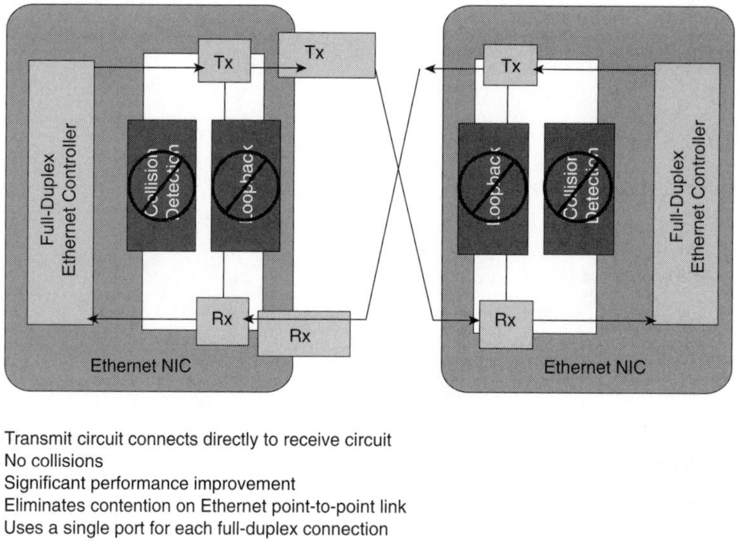
Tx
Tx
Tx
Rx
Rx
Rx
Full-Duplex Ethernet Controller
Full-Duplex Ethernet Controller
Ethernet NIC
Ethernet NIC
♦ Transmit circuit connects directly to receive circuit
♦ No collisions
♦ Significant performance improvement
♦ Eliminates contention on Ethernet point-to-point link
♦ Uses a single port for each full-duplex connection

Distinguishing Between Cut-Through and Store-and-Forward LAN Switching

The two main types of switching methods are store-and-forward and cut-through switching. Depending on the switch, this can be a configurable parameter on each individual port.

Store-and-Forward Switching

Store-and-forward switching is typically the default method on most switches. Before a switch forwards an Ethernet frame out another interface (by looking up the destination MAC address in the switch's source address table), it copies the entire frame into its buffers and checks the frame check sequence (FCS) against its own calculations. If the FCS and its own calculations match, the frame is forwarded out the proper port. If the FCS does not match its own calculations, the frame is dropped. Checking the FCS takes time—that is, causes additional latency in the switch—but all errors are filtered.

Cut-Through Switching

Most Cisco switches accommodate two types of cut-through switching:

- Fast-forward
- Fragment-free

Fast-forward switching begins to forward a frame out the proper switch port immediately after reading the Layer 2 destination address and looking up that address in the switch's source address table. The frame begins to be forwarded out that interface before the rest of the frame is copied into the switch. The FCS is not checked with fast-forward switching, so there is no error checking.

Fragment-free switching performs like cut-through switching, but it waits until the first 64 bytes of the frame are received before forwarding the first bytes of the frame out the outgoing switch port. According to Ethernet and 802.3 specifications, collisions should be detected during the first 64 bytes of a frame. Just as with fast-forward switching, the FCS is not checked in fragment-free switching, so there is no error checking. Fragment-free switching is faster (less latency) than store-and-forward switching, but slower (more latency) than fast-forward switching.

The Operation and Benefits of VLANs

Virtual LANs (VLANs) are used for several reasons, including the creation of separate broadcast domains within a switched network. Routers are necessary to pass information between different VLANs.

A VLAN can be thought of as a subnetwork. You can implement VLANs in several ways, but one of the most common methods is to separate subnetworks into separate VLANs.

Without VLANs, a Layer 2 broadcast, such as an ARP request, is seen by all hosts on the switched network. On a large switched network, these ARP requests can consume unnecessary network bandwidth and host processing cycles. Normally, only routers stop the propagation of Layer 2 broadcasts, such as these ARP requests.

Notice in Figure 20-3 that the hosts are on different subnetworks, but the ARP request is being received by all the computers. This can be an issue, especially in a network with Windows computers. Windows computers keep entries in their ARP tables for only 120 seconds. Therefore, if the ARP table hasn't communicated with a device for 120 seconds, the computer erases its IP address-to-MAC address mapping from the ARP table. The next time that the host needs to communicate with this same device, it must issue another ARP request. UNIX computers, on the other hand, normally keep entries in their ARP tables for approximately 20 minutes.

NOTE

VLANs are *not* necessary to have separate subnetworks on a switched network; as you will see, however, they provide more advantages when it comes to things such as data link layer (Layer 2) broadcasts.

Figure 20-3 All Switched Networks—Two Networks

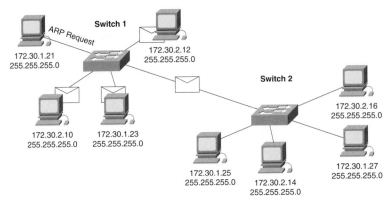

♦ Two Subnets
♦ Several Collision Domains
♦ One switch per port
♦ One Broadcast Domain

Routed Protocols

This review of routed protocols covers the following subjects, which may also appear on the CCNA exam:

- The different classes of IP addresses, including subnetting and private addresses
- Configuring IP addresses
- Troubleshooting IP address schemes
- Developing an IP addressing scheme to meet requirements
- Identifying the fundamental uses of various TCP/IP application layer protocols
- Converting among decimal, hexadecimal, and binary
- Defining flow control and describing the three basic methods used in networking
- Explaining the functions of the TCP/IP network and transport layer protocols

Different Classes of IP Addresses, Including Subnetting and Private Addresses

How does a user determine which portion of the address identifies the network and which portion identifies the host? The answer begins with the designers of the Internet, who thought that networks would be built in different sizes, depending on the number of computers (hosts) they contained, as shown in Table 20-1.

Table 20-1 IP Address Classes

Address Class	Number of Networks	Number of Hosts per Network
A	126	16,777,216
B	16,384	65,535
C	2,097,152	254
D (Multicast)	–	–

The assumption was that there would be a relatively small number of large networks, possibly with millions of computers. The designers envisioned a larger number of medium-sized networks, with perhaps thousands of computers each. Finally, they saw a great number of networks having several hundred or fewer machines. Therefore, the designers divided the available IP addresses into classes to define the large (Class A), medium (Class B), and small (Class C) networks, as shown in Table 20-2. Knowing the class of an IP address is the first step in determining which part of the address identifies the network and which part identifies the host.

Table 20-2 Identifying Address Classes

Address Class	High-Order Bits	First Octet Address Range	Number of Bits in the Network Address
A	0	0–127*	
B	10	128–191	
C	110	192–223	
D (Multicast)	1110	224–239	

*   Class A consists of networks whose left-most bit is 0 when written in binary format. Although the network 127 does start with a 0 bit, it has been reserved for special purposes. Therefore, Class A has 126, not 127, available networks.

IP has the job of forwarding packets from the network on which they originate to the destination network. This addressing scheme, therefore, must include an identifier for both the source and destination networks. By using the destination network identifier, IP can deliver a packet to the destination network. When the packet arrives at a router connected to the destination network, IP must then locate the particular computer connected to that network. This works in much the same way as the American postal system. When the mail is routed, it must first be delivered to the post office at the destination city using the ZIP code, and then that post office must locate the final destination in that city using the street address. This is a two-step process.

Accordingly, every IP address has two parts. One part identifies the network to which the system is connected, and a second part identifies that particular system on the network. This kind of address is called a hierarchical address, because it contains different levels. An IP address combines these two identifiers into one number. This number must be a unique number, because duplicate addresses are not allowed. The first part identifies the system's network address. The second part, called the host part, tells which particular machine it is on in that network.

The Internet's original two-level hierarchy assumed that each site would have only a single network. Therefore, each site would need only a single connection to the Internet. Initially, these were safe assumptions. Over time, however, network computing matured and expanded. By 1985, it was no longer safe to assume that an organization would have only a single network, nor that it would be satisfied with a single connection to the Internet.

As sites began to develop multiple networks, it became obvious to the IETF that some mechanism was needed to differentiate among the multiple logical networks that were emerging as subsets of the Internet's second tier. Otherwise, there could be no efficient way to route data to specific end systems in sites with multiple networks.

Subnetting

To create the subnetwork structure, host bits must be reassigned as network bits by dividing the host octet(s). This process is often referred to as borrowing bits, but a more accurate term is lending bits. The starting point for this process is always the left-most host bit, dependent on the IP class.

In addition its LAN-management features, subnetworking enables the network administrator to provide broadcast containment and low-level security on the LAN. Security, through subnetting on the LAN, results because access to other subnets is provided by the services of a router. A network administrator can configure access control lists to permit or deny access to a subnet based on various criteria, thereby providing security. Some owners of Class A and B networks have also discovered that subnetting creates a revenue source for the organization through the leasing or sale of previously unused IP addresses.

In such multiple-network environments, each subnetwork is connected to the Internet via a common point—a router, as shown in Figure 20-4. The actual details of the internal network environment are inconsequential to the Internet. They comprise a private network that is (or should be) capable of delivering its own datagrams. Therefore, the Internet must concern itself only with how to reach that network's gateway router to the Internet. Inside the private network, the host portion of the IP address can be subdivided to create subnetworks.

Figure 20-4 Subnetworks

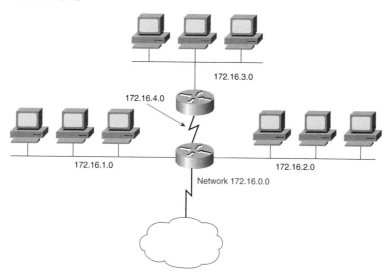

Because the subnet address is taken from the host number portion of Class A, Class B, and Class C addresses, it is assigned locally, usually by the network administrator. Like the other portions of IP addresses, each subnet address must be unique within its scope, as shown in Figure 20-5.

Subnetting provides another way to conserve IP addresses, like do classless interdomain routing (CIDR), IPv6, and private addresses. This method of dividing full network address classes into smaller pieces has helped prevented complete IP address exhaustion. Figure 20-6 shows a Class B network (131.108.0.0) divided into three subnetworks. It is impossible to cover TCP/IP without mentioning subnetting. As a system administrator, it is important to understand subnetting as a way to divide and identify separate networks throughout the LAN. It is not always necessary to subnet a small network; for large or extremely large networks, however, subnetting is required. Simply stated, subnetting a network means to use the subnet mask to divide the network and break up a large network into smaller, more efficient and manageable segments, or subnets, as shown in Figure 20-7. This is like the U.S. telephone system, first breaking the entire system up into area codes, then exchange codes, and finally local numbers. These elements of the phone system are comparable to network numbers, subnets, and individual host addresses, respectively, in an IP internetwork.

Figure 20-5 Subnet Address

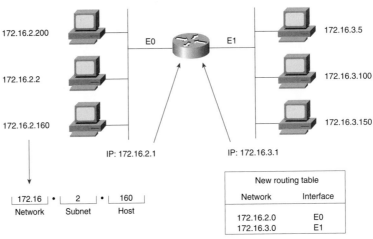

Figure 20-6 Addressing with Subnets

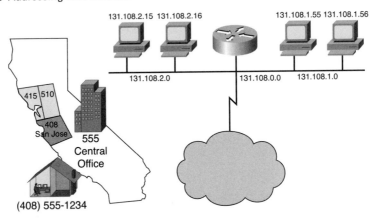

The system administrator must resolve these issues when adding and expanding the network. It is important to know how many subnet/networks are needed and how many hosts will be allowed to be on each network. With subnetting, the network is not limited to the standard Class A, B, or C network masks, and the administrator can exercise more flexibility in the network design.

Subnet addresses include the Class A, Class B, or Class C network portion, plus a subnet field and a host field. The subnet field and the host field are created from the original host portion for the entire network. The network administrator's addressing flexibility comes from being able to decide how to divide the original host portion into the new subnet and host fields.

Figure 20-7 Subnet Addresses

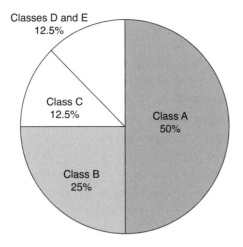

To create a subnet address, a network administrator borrows bits from the host field and designates them as the subnet field, as shown in Table 20-3. The minimum number of bits that can be borrowed is 2. If you were to borrow only 1 bit to create a subnet, you would only have a network number—the .0 network—and the broadcast number— the .255 network. The maximum number of bits that can be borrowed can be any number that leaves at least 2 bits remaining, for the host number. In this example of a Class C IP address, bits from the host field for the subnet field have been borrowed.

Table 20-3 Subnet Addresses

Decimal Notation for First Octet	Number of Subnets	Number of Class A Hosts per Subnet	Number of Class B Hosts per Subnet	Number of Class C Hosts per Subnet
.192	2	4,194,302	16,382	62
.224	6	2,097,150	8,190	30
.240	14	1,048,574	4,094	14
.248	30	524,286	2,046	6
.252	62	262,142	1,022	2
.254	126	131,070	510	–
.255	254	65,534	254	–

Converting Among Decimal, Hexadecimal, and Binary

There is usually more than one way to solve a math problem, and decimal-to-binary conversion is no exception. This section explores one method, but feel free to use another method if it is easier.

To convert a decimal number to binary, the idea is to first find the biggest power of 2 that will "fit" into the decimal number, as shown in Table 20-4. If you are using this process while working with computers, the most logical place to start is with the values that are the largest that fit into 1 byte or 2 bytes.

Table 20-4 2-Byte/16-Bit Number

2^{15}	2^{14}	2^{13}	2^{12}	2^{11}	2^{10}	2^9	2^8	2^7	2^6	2^5	2^4	2^3	2^2	2^1	2^0
32678	16384	8192	4096	2048	1024	512	256	128	64	32	16	8	4	2	1

As presented earlier, the most common grouping of bits is 8, which make up 1 byte. However, sometimes the largest value that can be held in 1 byte (255) is not large enough for the values needed. In such cases, you must combine bytes, so instead of having two 8-bit numbers you have one 16-bit number; or instead of three 8-bit numbers, you have one 24-bit number. The same rules apply as they did for 8-bit numbers: Multiply the previous position value by two to get the present column value. Table 20-5 documents those values (starting with a 2-byte/16-bit number that will be very important when learning the mechanics of subnetting.

Because those working with computers are familiar with references to bytes, it is easiest to start with byte boundaries and calculate from there, as shown in Table 20-5. Now calculate a couple of examples, the first being 6783. Because this number is greater than 255, the largest value possible in a single byte, we use 2 bytes. Start calculating from 2^{15}. Thus, $6783 = 00011010\ 01111111_2$.

Table 20-5 2-Byte/16-Bit Number

Position Power	Decimal Value	Position Value	Binary Count	Remainder
2^{15}	6783	32678	0	6783
2^{14}	6783	16384	0	6783
2^{13}	6783	8192	0	6783
2^{12}	6783	4096	1	2687

Table 20-5 2-Byte/16-Bit Number (Continued)

Position Power	Decimal Value	Position Value	Binary Count	Remainder
2^{11}	2687	2048	1	639
2^{10}	639	1024	0	639
2^9	639	512	1	127
2^8	127	256	0	127
2^7	127	128	0	127
2^6	127	64	1	63
2^5	63	32	1	31
2^4	31	16	1	15
2^3	15	8	1	7
2^2	7	4	1	3
2^1	3	2	1	1
2^0	1	1	1	0

The second example is 104. Because this number is less than 255, it can be done in 1 byte, as shown in Table 20-6.

Table 20-6 1-Byte/8-Bit Number

Position Power	Decimal Value	Position Value	Binary Count	Remainder
2^7	104	128	0	104
2^6	104	64	1	40
2^5	40	32	1	8
2^4	8	16	0	8
2^3	8	8	1	0

continues

Table 20-6 1-Byte/8-Bit Number (Continued)

Position Power	Decimal Value	Position Value	Binary Count	Remainder
2^2	0	4	0	0
2^1	0	2	0	0
2^0	0	1	0	0

Thus, $104 = 01101000_2$.

This method works for any decimal number. Consider the decimal number 1 million. Because 1 million is greater than the largest value that can be held in 2 bytes, 65,535, you need to have at least 3 bytes. By multiplying by 2 until 24 bits (3 bytes) is reached, the value is 8,388,608, meaning that the largest value that 24 bits can hold is 16,777,215. Therefore, starting at the 24 bit, follow the process until you get down to 0. Continuing with the procedure described, determine that the decimal number 1 million is equal to the binary number $00001111\ 01000010\ 01000000_2$.

Binary-to-decimal conversion is just the opposite. Just place the binary in the table and if there is a one in a column position add that value to the total. Table 20-7 demonstrates one example of this which shows converting 00000100 00011101 to decimal, resulting in 1053.

Table 20-7 2-Byte/16-Bit Number

Position Power	Decimal Value	Position Value	Binary Count	Remainder
2^{15}	0	32678	0	0
2^{14}	0	16384	0	0
2^{13}	0	8192	0	0
2^{12}	0	4096	0	0
2^{11}	0	2048	0	0
2^{10}	0	1024	1	1024
2^9	1024	512	0	1024
2^8	1024	256	0	1024
2^7	1024	128	0	1024

Table 20-7 2-Byte/16-Bit Number (Continued)

Position Power	Decimal Value	Position Value	Binary Count	Remainder
2^6	1024	64	0	1024
2^5	1024	32	0	1024
2^4	1024	16	1	1040
2^3	1040	8	1	1048
2^2	1048	4	1	1052
2^1	1052	2	0	1052
2^0	1052	1	1	1053

The material covered in this chapter, indeed in this whole book, focuses on the principle topics tested on the CCNA exam. Therefore, be aware that the topics covered in this section specifically relate to major objectives required to pass the exam and be prepared to demonstrate a full knowledge of this material.

Routing Protocols

A protocol is a standards-based set of rules that determines how computers communicate with each other across networks. A protocol also serves as the common denominator or medium by which different applications, hosts, or systems communicate. When computers communicate with one another, they exchange data messages. To accept and act on these messages, computers must have common understanding as to how a message is defined and what it means. Example messages types include establishing a connection to a remote machine, sending or receiving e-mail, and transferring files and data.

A protocol describes the following:

- The format that a message must take
- The way in which computers must exchange a message within the context of a particular activity, such as sending messages across networks

A routed protocol and a routing protocol are often confused because of the similarity in the terms. The following provides some clarification:

- **Routed protocol**—Any network protocol that provides enough information in its network layer address to allow a packet to be forwarded from one host to another host based on the addressing scheme. Routed protocols define the field formats within a packet. Packets are generally conveyed from end system to end system. A routed protocol uses the routing table to forward packets. Examples of routed or routable protocols are shown in the routing table in Figure 20-8 and include the following:

  — Internet Protocol (IP)

  — Internetwork Packet Exchange (IPX)

  — AppleTalk

  — Digital DECnet

Figure 20-8 Routing Protocols

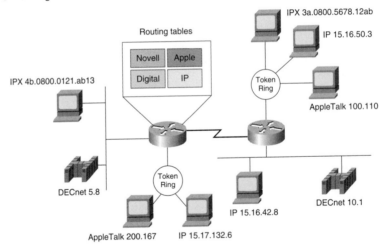

- **Routing protocol**—Supports a routed protocol by providing mechanisms for sharing routing information. Routing protocol messages move between the routers. A routing protocol allows the routers to communicate with other routers to update and maintain tables. TCP/IP examples of routing protocols include the following:

  — Routing Information Protocol (RIP)

  — Interior Gateway Routing Protocol (IGRP)

  — Enhanced Interior Gateway Routing Protocol (EIGRP)

  — Open Shortest Path First (OSPF)

For a protocol to be routable, it must enable an administrator to assign a network number and a host number to each individual device. Some protocols, such as IPX, only require that an administrator assign a network number, because they use a host's Media Access Control (MAC) address for the physical number. Other protocols, such as IP, require that a complete address be provided, and a network mask.

Both the IP address and network mask are required to have a routed network. A network mask is used to separate the network and host portions of a 32-bit IP address. IPX uses the MAC address concatenated with an administrator-assigned network address to create the complete address and does not use a network mask. With IP addresses, the network address is obtained by comparing the address with the network mask.

A network mask is used is to allow groups of sequential IP addresses to be treated as a single unit. If this grouping were not allowed, each host would have to be mapped individually for routing and that would not be possible with the millions of hosts that are currently on the Internet. All 254 addresses in the sequence of 192.168.10.1 to 192.168.10.254 can be represented by the network address 192.168.10.0. Therefore, data can be sent to any one of these hosts by just locating the network address, and routing tables need to contain only one entry of 192.168.10.0 rather than all 254 individual entries according to the Internet Software Consortium (www.isc.org). For routing to function, this process of grouping must be used.

Routing is an OSI Layer 3 function. It functions as a hierarchical organizational scheme that allows individual addresses to be grouped together and treated as a single unit until the individual address is needed for final delivery of the data. Routing is the process of finding the most efficient path from one device to another, as shown in Figure 20-9. The main device that performs this process is the router.

A router has two key functions:

- To maintain routing tables and make sure other routers know of changes in the network topology. This function is performed using a routing protocol to communicate network information to other routers.
- When packets arrive at an interface, the router must use the routing table to determine where to send the packet. It switches them to the appropriate interface, adds the necessary framing for the interface, and then actually transmits the frame.

A router is a network layer device that uses one or more routing metrics to determine the optimal path along which network traffic should be forwarded. The routing metric is a value used in determining the desirability of the route. Routing protocols use various combinations of criteria to determine the routing metric, as shown in Figure 20-10.

Figure 20-9 Network Layer Protocol Operation

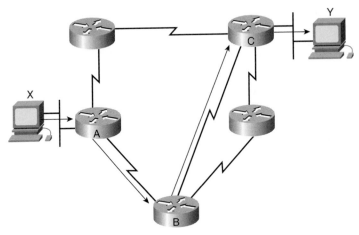

Figure 20-10 Routing Protocol Metrics

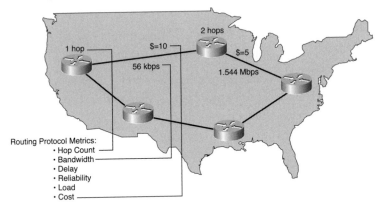

The metrics of hop count, bandwidth, delay, reliability, load, and cost are calculated together in various combinations to determine the best path through an internetwork. Routers interconnect network segments or entire networks. They pass data frames between networks based on Layer 3 information. Routers make logical decisions regarding the best path for the delivery of data on an internetwork, and then direct packets to the appropriate output port to be encapsulated for transmission. The encapsulation and de-encapsulation process occurs each time a packet passes through a router, as shown in Figure 20-11. Sending data from one device to another involves encapsulation and de-encapsulation. Encapsulation refers to breaking up the data stream into segments, adding the appropriate headers and trailers, and then transmitting the data.

De-encapsulation refers to the opposite process: removing the headers and trailers, and then recombining the data into a seamless stream. Routers take frames from LAN devices (for example, workstations) and, based on Layer 3 information, forward them through the network.

Figure 20-11 Data Encapsulation

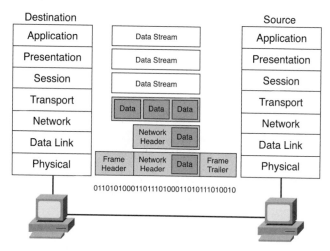

This section focuses on the most commonly used routable (or routed) protocol—IP. Even though the focus is on IP, you should know that there are other routable protocols (for instance, IPX/SPX and AppleTalk).

Protocols such as IP, IPX/SPX, and AppleTalk provide Layer 3 support and are, therefore, routable. However, some protocols do not support Layer 3; these are classed as nonroutable protocols. The most common of these nonroutable protocols is NetBEUI. NetBEUI is a small, fast, and efficient protocol that is limited to running on one segment.

Exterior and Interior Routing Protocols

Routers use routing protocols to exchange routing information. In other words, routing protocols determine how routed protocols are routed. Two families of routing protocols are the Interior Gateway Protocols (IGPs) and the Exterior Gateway Protocols (EGPs), as shown in Figure 20-12. These families are classified based on how they operate with regard to autonomous systems.

An autonomous system is a network or set of networks that are under the administrative control of a single entity, such as the cisco.com domain. An autonomous system consists of routers that present a consistent view of routing to the external world. The Internet Assigned Numbers Authority (IANA) allocates autonomous system numbers to the regional registries. These registries are ARIN (hostmaster@arin.net) for the Americas, Caribbean, and Africa; RIPE-NCC (ncc@ripe.net) for Europe; and the AP-NIC (admin@apnic.net) for the Asia Pacific region. This autonomous system number is a 16-bit number. Some routing protocols, such as Border Gateway Protocol (BGP), require that you specify this unique, assigned autonomous system number in your configuration.

Figure 20-12 IGPs and EGPs

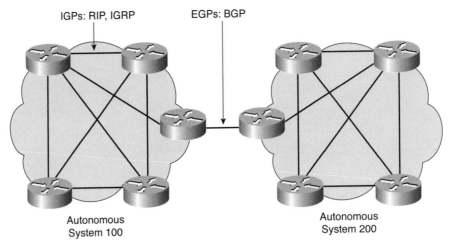

IGPs route data within an autonomous system. Examples of IGPs include the following:

- Routing Information Protocol Versions 1 and 2 (RIPv1) and (RIPv2)
- Interior Gateway Routing Protocol (IGRP)
- Enhanced Interior Gateway Routing Protocol (EIGRP)
- Open Shortest Path First (OSPF)
- Intermediate System-to-Intermediate System (IS-IS) Protocol

EGPs route data between autonomous systems. BGP is the most pervasive example of an EGP.

Enabling RIP and IGRP on a Router

The distance vector routing approach determines the direction (vector) and distance (hop count) to any link in the internetwork. Distance vector algorithms periodically (such as every 30 seconds) send all or some portion of their routing table to their adjacent neighbors. Routers running a distance vector routing protocol send periodic updates even if no changes occur in the network. By receiving a neighbor's routing table, a router can verify all the known routes and make changes to the local routing table based on updated information received from the neighboring router. This process is also known as "routing by rumor," because the understanding that a router has of the network is based on the neighbor's perspective of the network topology. Distance vector protocols use the Bellman-Ford algorithm to calculate best paths.

Examples of distance vector protocols include the following:

- **Routing Information Protocol (RIP)**—The most common IGP in the Internet, RIP uses hop count as its routing metric.

- **Interior Gateway Routing Protocol (IGRP)**—Cisco developed this IGP to address the issues associated with routing in large, heterogeneous networks.

Identifying Routing Metrics Used by IGRP and RIP

When a routing algorithm updates a routing table, its primary objective is to determine the best information to include in the table. Routing algorithms use different metrics to determine the best route. Each routing algorithm interprets what is best in its own way. The routing algorithm generates a number, called the metric value, for each path through the network. Sophisticated routing algorithms can base route selection on multiple metrics, combining them in a single composite metric, as shown in Figure 20-13. Typically, the smaller the metric number is, the better the path.

Figure 20-13 Routing Metrics

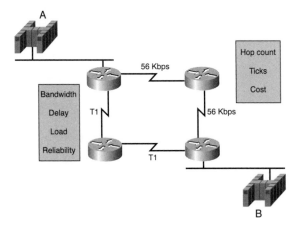

Metrics can be based on a single characteristic of a path or can be calculated based on several characteristics. Routing protocols use the following metrics most often:

- **Bandwidth**—The data capacity of a link. (Normally, a 10-Mbps Ethernet link is preferable to a 64-kbps leased line.)

- **Delay**—The length of time required to move a packet along each link from source to destination. Delay depends on the bandwidth of intermediate links, port queues at each router, network congestion, and physical distance.
- **Load**—The amount of activity on a network resource such as a router or a link.
- **Reliability**—Usually a reference to the error rate of each network link.
- **Hop count**—The number of routers that a packet must travel through before reaching its destination. Each router that data traverses is considered to be one hop. A path that has a hop count of four indicates that data traveling along that path would have to pass through four routers before reaching its final destination. If multiple paths lead to a destination, the router chooses the path with the least number of hops.
- **Cost**—An arbitrary value assigned by a network administrator—usually based on bandwidth, monetary expense, or other measurement.

Comparing and Contrasting the Key Operations That Distinguish Distance Vector, Link-State, and Hybrid Protocols

Link-state routing protocols were designed to overcome the limitations of distance vector routing protocols. Link-state routing protocols respond quickly to network changes, send trigger updates only when a network change has occurred, and send periodic updates (known as link-state refreshes), at long time intervals, such as every 30 minutes.

When a link changes state, the device that detected the change creates a link-state advertisement (LSA) concerning that link (route), and that LSA is propagated to all neighboring devices. Each routing device takes a copy of the LSA, updates its link-state (topological) database, and forwards the LSA to all neighboring devices. This flooding of the LSA is required to ensure that all routing devices update their databases before creating an updated routing table that reflects the new topology, as shown in Figure 20-14.

The link-state database is used to calculate the best paths through the network. Link-state routers find the best paths to destinations by applying the Dijkstra Shortest Path First (SPF) algorithm against the link-state database to build the SPF tree. The best (shortest) paths are then selected from the shortest-path-first tree and placed in the routing table.

Examples of a link-state protocol are Open Shortest Path First (OSPF) and Intermediate System-to-Intermediate System (IS-IS), as shown in Figure 20-15.

Figure 20-14 Link-State Routing Protocols

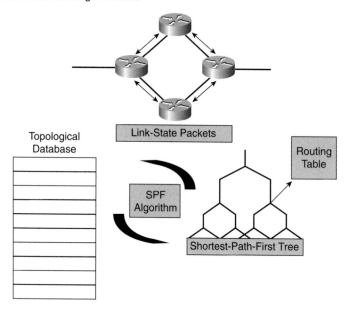

Topological
Database

Figure 20-15 Link-State Routing Protocols

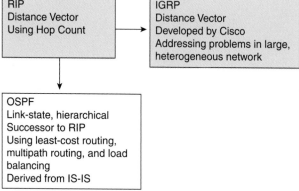

RIP uses hop count to determine the direction and distance to any link in the internetwork, as shown in Figure 20-16. If multiple paths lead to a destination, RIP selects the path with the least number of hops. Because hop count is the only routing metric used by RIP, however, it does not necessarily select the fastest path to a destination. RIP version 1 (RIPv1) uses only classful routing, which means that all devices in the network must use the same subnet mask because RIPv1 does not include the subnet information with the routing update.

Figure 20-16 RIP Uses Hop Count as Its Metric

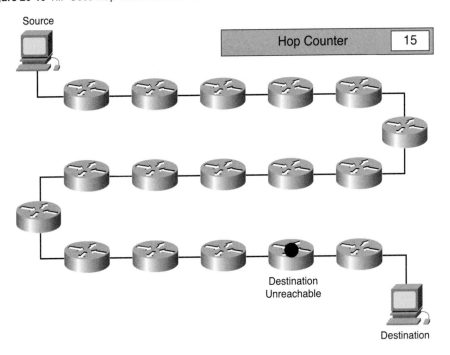

RIP

RIP version 2 (RIPv2) provides what is called prefix routing and sends subnet mask information with the route updates, in this way supporting the use of classless routing. With classless routing protocols, different subnets within the same network can have different subnet masks. The use of different subnet masks within the same network is referred to as variable-length subnet masking (VLSM).

IGRP

IGRP is a distance vector routing protocol that Cisco specifically to address problems associated with routing in large networks that were beyond the scope of protocols such as RIP. IGRP can select the fastest path based on the delay, bandwidth, load, and reliability. By default, IGRP uses bandwidth and delay metrics only and makes use of a 24-bit metric. IGRP also has a much higher maximum hop-count limit than RIP to allow the network to scale. IGRP uses only classful routing.

EIGRP

Like IGRP, EIGRP is a proprietary Cisco protocol. EIGRP is an advanced version of IGRP and uses a 32-bit metric. Specifically, EIGRP provides superior operating efficiency such as faster convergence and lower overhead bandwidth. It is referred to as an advanced distance vector protocol. EIGRP also uses some of the link-state protocol functions, hence the term hybrid is also used to describe EIGRP.

OSPF

OSPF, developed by the Internet Engineering Task Force (IETF) in 1988, is a link-state technology. RFC 2328 describes the most recent version: OSPF version 2. OSPF is an IGP, which means that it distributes routing information between routers belonging to the same autonomous system. OSPF was written to address the needs of large, scalable internetworks that RIP could not.

IS-IS

Intermediate System-to-Intermediate System (IS-IS) Protocol is the dynamic link-state routing protocol for the OSI protocol stack. As such it distributes routing information for routing Connectionless Network Protocol (CLNP) data for the ISO Connectionless Network Service (CLNS) environment. Integrated IS-IS is an implementation of the IS-IS protocol for routing multiple network protocols. Integrated IS-IS tags CLNP routes with information regarding IP networks and subnets. It provides an alternative to OSPF in the IP world, mixing ISO CLNS and IP routing in one protocol. It can be used purely for IP routing, purely for ISO routing, or for a combination of the two.

NOTE

CLNP refers to the OSI network layer protocol that does not require a circuit to be established before data is transmitted.

BGP

Border Gateway Protocol (BGP) is an example of an External Gateway Protocol (EGP). BGP exchanges routing information between autonomous systems while guaranteeing loop-free path selection. It is the principal route-advertising protocol used by major companies and Internet service providers on the Internet. BGP version 4 (BGPv4) is the first version of BGP that supports classless interdomain routing (CIDR) and route aggregation. Unlike common Internal Gateway Protocols (IGPs) such as RIP, OSPF, and EIGRP, BGP does not use metrics such as hop count or bandwidth or delay.

Instead, BGP makes routing decisions based on network policies, or rules, using various BGP path attributes.

The material covered in this chapter, indeed in this whole book, focuses on the principle topics tested on the CCNA exam. Therefore, be aware that the topics covered in this section specifically relate to major objectives required to pass the exam and be prepared to demonstrate a full knowledge of this material.

WAN Protocols

This review of WAN protocols covers the following subjects, which may also appear on the CCNA exam:

- Explaining key Frame Relay terms and features
- Configuring Frame Relay LMIs, maps, and subinterfaces
- Identifying ISDN protocols, function groups, reference points, and channels
- Differentiating among the following WAN services: LAPB, Frame Relay, ISDN/LAPD, HDLC, PPP, and DDR
- Identifying PPP operations to encapsulate WAN data on Cisco routers
- Using **show** commands to display network operational parameters so that anomalies are detected
- Configuring ISDN BRI and legacy dial-on-demand routing (DDR)
- Configuring a serial connection with PPP encapsulation

Key Frame Relay Terms and Features

With increasing demand for higher-bandwidth and lower-latency *packet switching*, communications providers introduced Frame Relay (FR). Although the network layout appears similar to that for X.25 (see Figure 20-17), available data rates are commonly up to 4 Mbps, with some providers even offering higher rates.

Frame Relay differs from X.25 in several respects. Most importantly, it operates a much simpler protocol operating at the data link rather than the network layer. The term *frame* is used for units at the data link layer.

Frame Relay implements no error or flow control. The simplified handling of frames leads to reduced latency. Measures taken to avoid frame buildup at intermediate switches help reduce jitter.

Figure 20-17 WANs with Frame Relay

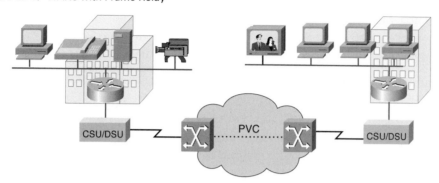

Most Frame Relay connections are based on *permanent virtual circuits (PVCs)* rather than *switched virtual circuits (SVCs)*. The connection to the network edge is often a leased line. Dialed connections, using ISDN lines, are available from some providers. The ISDN D channel is used to set up an SVC on one or more B channels. Frame Relay tariffs are based on the capacity of the connecting port at the network edge and the agreed capacity or committed information rate (CIR) of the various PVCs through the port.

Frame Relay provides permanent, shared, medium-bandwidth connectivity carrying both voice and data traffic and is ideal for connecting enterprise LANs together. The router on the LAN needs only a single interface, even when multiple virtual circuits (VCs) are used, and the (short-lease) leased line to the FR network edge allows cost-effective connections between widely scattered LANs.

Differentiating Among LAPB, Frame Relay, ISDN/LAPD, HDLC, PPP, and DDR

Data from the network layer is passed to the data link layer for delivery on a physical link, normally point to point. The data link layer builds a frame around the network layer data so that it can apply the necessary checks and controls. Each WAN connection type uses a Layer 2 protocol to encapsulate traffic while it is crossing the WAN link. To ensure that the correct encapsulation protocol is used, the Layer 2 encapsulation type to use for each serial interface on a router must be configured. The choice of encapsulation protocol depends on the WAN technology and the communicating equipment. Most framing is based on the HDLC standard.

HDLC framing is designed to give reliable delivery of data over unreliable lines, and so includes signaling mechanisms for flow and error control. The frame always starts and ends with an 8-bit flag field, the bit pattern 01111110, or $7E_{16}$ (7E in base 16, hexadecimal). Because there is the likelihood that this pattern will occur in the actual data, the sending HDLC system always inserts a 0 bit after every five 1s in the data field, so in practice the flag sequence can only occur at the frame ends. The receiving system strips out the inserted bits. Where one frame is transmitted immediately after another, the end flag of the first frame is used as the start flag of the next.

The address field is not needed for WAN links, which are almost always point-to-point, but is still present. It may be 1 or 2 bytes long. The control field indicates the frame type, which may be information, supervisory, or unnumbered. Unnumbered frames carry line setup messages, information frames carry network layer data, and supervisory frames control the flow of information frames, and if necessary request data retransmission in the event of an error. The control field is normally 1 byte, but for extended sliding windows systems is 2 bytes. Together the address and control fields are called the frame header.

Following the control field is the encapsulated data, and then a frame check sequence (FCS) using the cyclic redundancy check mechanism to give a 2- or 4-byte field.

Several data-link protocols, including subsets and proprietary versions of HDLC, are in use, and shown in Figure 20-18. PPP, included in the figure is discussed in detail in a later lesson. Both PPP and the Cisco version of HDLC have an extra field in the header, used to identify the network layer protocol of the encapsulated data.

Figure 20-18 WAN Frame Encapsulation Formats

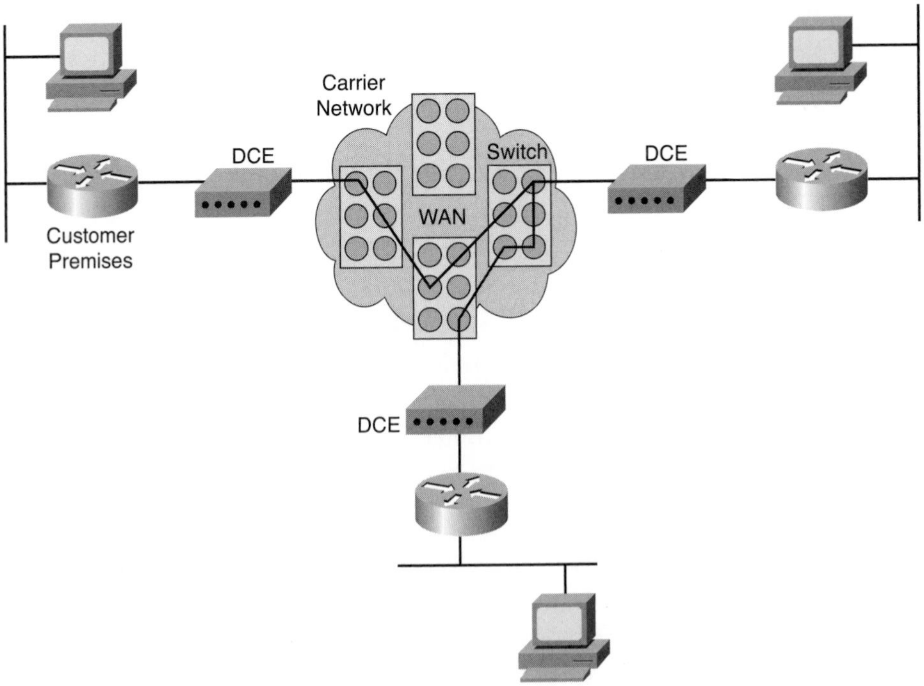

Configuring ISDN BRI and Legacy Dial-on-Demand Routing (DDR)

The internal connections or trunks of the Public Switched Telephone Network (PSTN) have changed from carrying analog frequency-division multiplexed signals, and now carry *time-division multiplexed (TDM)* digital signals. An obvious next step is to make the local loop carry digital signals resulting in higher-capacity switched dedicated connections.

Integrated Services Digital Network (ISDN) turns the local loop into a TDM digital connection. The connection has 64-kbps bearer channels (B) for carrying voice or data and a signaling (delta or D) channel for call setup and other purposes.

Basic Rate Interface (BRI) ISDN is intended for the home and small enterprise, provides 2 B channels with a 16-kbps D channel. For larger installations, Primary Rate Interface (PRI) ISDN is available. PRI delivers 23 B channels and 1 D channel in North America for a total bit rate of up to 1.544 Mbps. (This includes some additional overhead for synchronization.) In Europe, Australia, and other parts of the world, ISDN PRI provides 30 B channels and 1 D channel for a total bit rate of up to 2.048 Mbps (including synchronization overhead). The PRI D channel is 64 kbps, shown in Figure 20-19. Note that the rate of a North American PRI corresponds to a T1 connection. The rate of the international PRI corresponds to an E1 connection.

Figure 20-19 ISDN Channels

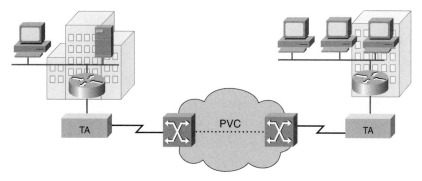

The BRI D channel is very underutilized with only two B channels to control. Some providers allow it to be used to carry data at low bit rates such as X.25 connections at 9.6 kbps.

For small WANs, the BRI ISDN can provide an ideal connection mechanism. BRI has a short call setup time (typically subsecond) and its 64-kbps B channel provides greater capacity than an analog modem link. Figure 20-20 shows WANs using ISDN. If greater capacity is required, a second B channel can be activated, giving 128 kbps. Although inadequate for video, this increase permits several simultaneous voice conversations in addition to data traffic.

Figure 20-20 WANs with ISDN

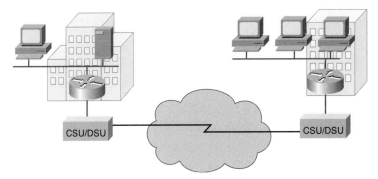

Another common application of ISDN is to provide additional capacity as needed on a leased line connection. The leased line is sized to carry average traffic loads while ISDN is added during the peaks. ISDN is also used when occasional failures of the leased line occur.

ISDN tariffs are similar to those of analog voice connections on a per–B channel basis. That is, two simultaneous 64-kbps connections cost twice as much as one.

With PRI ISDN, you can connect multiple B between two endpoints allowing for videoconferencing and high-bandwidth data connections with no latency or jitter. Multiple connections can become very expensive over long distances.

Configuration File Management Using TFTP

In a Cisco router or switch, the active configuration is in *random-access memory (RAM)*. The default location for the startup configuration in a Cisco router or switch is nonvolatile RAM (NVRAM). In the event the configuration is lost, this startup configuration should be backed up. One of these backup copies of the configuration can be stored on a TFTP server. The **copy running-config tftp** command enables you to back up the configuration. The following steps are used for this backup process and shown in Example 20-1:

- Enter **copy running-config tftp**.
- Enter the IP address of the TFTP server that is to store the configuration file at the prompt.

- Enter the name to assign to the configuration file or accept the default name.
- Confirm the choices by typing **yes** each time.

Example 20-1 copy running-config tftp *Command*

```
Cougar#copy running-config tftp
Address or name of remote host [] 192.168.119.20
Destination file name [Cougar-confg]?
!!!!!!!!!!!!!!!!!!!!!!!!!!
624 bytes copied in 7.05 secs
Cougar#
```

You can restore the router configuration by loading the backup configuration file from a TFTP server. The following steps outline this process to restore the configuration and are shown in Example 20-2:

- Enter **copy tftp running-config**.
- Select a host or network configuration file at the prompt.
- At the system prompt, enter the IP address of the TFTP server where the configuration file is located.
- At the system prompt, enter the name of the configuration file or accept the default name.
- Confirm the configuration filename and the server address that the system supplies.

Example 20-2 copy tftp running-config *Command*

```
Cougar#copy tftp running-config
Address or name of remote host [] 192.168.119.20
Source filename []?  Cougar-confg
Destination filename [running-config]?
Accessing tftp://192.168.119.20/GAD-confg...
Loading GAD-confg from 192.168.119.20 (via FastEthernet 0/0):
    !!!!!!!!!!!!!!!!!!!!!!!!!!!!!!!!
[OK-624 bytes]
624 bytes copied in 9.45 secs
Cougar#
```

How to Load a Software Image Backup

If you need to load the backup Cisco IOS version, again use the **copy** command **copy tftp flash**, which enables you to download the image that you previously uploaded to the TFTP server. After you enter the **copy tftp flash** command, as shown in Example 23-8, the system prompts you for the IP address (or name) of the TFTP server. This can be another router serving ROM or Flash memory software images. The system then prompts you for the filename of the software image. Example 20-3 shows sample output from copying a system image, named C4500-I, into Flash memory.

Example 20-3 copy tftp flash *Command*

```
Router#copy tftp flash
ILP address or name of remote host [255.255.255.255]? 117722..1166..1133..111111
Name of tftp filename to copy into flash []? c4500-I
copy C4500-I already exists; it will be invalidated!
Copy C4500-I from 172.16.13.111 into flash memory? [confirm] <Return>
xxxxxxxx bytes available for writing without erasure.
erase flash before writing? [confirm] <Return>
Clearing and initializing flash memory [please wait] ####...##
Loading from 172.16.13.111: !!!!!!!!!!!!!!!!!!!!!!!!!!!
!!!!!!! (text omitted) [OK - 324572/524212 bytes]
Verifying checksum...
VVVVVVVVVVVVVVVVVVVVVVVVVVVVVVVVVVVVVVVVVVVVVVVVVVVVV
VVVVVVVVV (text omitted)
Flash verification successful. Length = 1204637, checksum = 0x95D9
```

If you attempt to copy into Flash memory a file that is already there, a prompt tells you that a file with the same name already exists. This file is deleted when you copy the new file into Flash memory. If Flash memory has room for both copies, the first copy of the file still resides within Flash memory, but is rendered unusable in favor of the newest version; the [deleted] tag displays with the first copy when you use the **show flash** command.

If you abort the copy process, the newer file is marked (deleted) because the entire file was not copied and is therefore not valid. In this case, the original file still resides within Flash memory and is available to the system.

Configuration File Management

Capturing the output of the **show running-config** command is another way to create a backup copy of the configuration. You can create this backup from the terminal session by copying the output, pasting to a text file, and saving the text file. This file needs some editing before you can use it to restore configuration to the router. Figure 20-21 shows an example of cutting and pasting configurations.

Figure 20-21 Cutting and Pasting

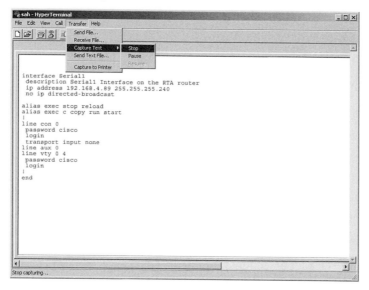

To capture the configuration in HyperTerminal text that displays on the screen to a text file, follow these steps:

Step 1   Choose **Transfer.**

Step 2   Choose **Capture Text.**

Step 3   Specify the name for the text file to the capture configuration.

Step 4   Choose **Start** to start capturing text.

Step 5   Display the configuration to the screen by entering **show running-config.**

Step 6   Press the **Spacebar** when each "—More—" prompt appears to continue with the configuration until you reach the end.

Step 7   When the complete configuration has displayed, stop the capture as follows:

- Choose **Transfer.**
- Choose **Capture Text.**
- Choose **Stop.**

After you complete the capture, you must edit the configuration file to remove extra text. To create this file in a form that is to be copied and pasted back into the router, remove any unnecessary information from the captured configuration. You may also add comments to the text to explain the various parts of the configuration. A comment is added by beginning a line with an exclamation mark (!).

You can edit the configuration from a text editor such as Notepad. To edit the file from Notepad, follow these steps:

1. Click **File => Open.**

2. Find the captured file and select it.

3. Click **Open.**

The lines that you need to delete contain the following:

- Show running-config
- Building configuration . . .
- Current configuration:
- —More—
- Any lines that appear after the word "End"

At the end of each of the interface sections, add the **no shutdown** command. Click **File => Save** to save the clean version of the configuration.

You can restore the backup configuration from a HyperTerminal session. Before the configuration is restored, remove any remaining configuration from the router by entering the command **erase startup-config** at the "enable router" prompt and then restart the router by entering **reload.**

You can use HyperTerminal to restore a configuration. To copy the clean backup of the configuration into the router, follow these steps:

1. Go into the router global configuration mode.

2. From the HyperTerminal, click **Transfer/Send/Text File.**

3. Select the name of the file for the saved backup configuration.

4. The lines of the file are entered into the router as if the lines were being typed.

5. Look for any errors.

6. After entering the configuration, press **Ctrl+Z** to exit the global configuration mode.

7. Restore the startup configuration with **copy running-config startup-config.**

Managing IOS Images with TFTP

Occasionally, the router needs to have the IOS upgraded or restored. The first time a router is used, the IOS should be backed up. You can store the IOS image in a central server with other IOS images to restore or upgrade the IOS into the routers and switches in the internetwork.

This server should have a TFTP service running. You can initiate the IOS upgrade from the privileged exec mode with the **copy tftp flash** command as shown in Example 20-4.

Example 20-4 copy tftp flash

```
Cougar#copy tftp flash
Address or name of remote host []?192.168.119.20
192.168.119.20 C2600-js-l_121-3.bin
Destination filename [C2600-js-l_121-3.bin]?
Accessing tftp://192.168.119.20/ C2600-js-l_121-3.bin
Erase flash: before copying? [confirm]
Erasing the flash file system will remove all files
Continue? [confirm]
Erasing device  eeeeee…eeeeeeeeeeeee...erased
Loading C2600-js-l_121-3.bin from 192.168.119.20 (via FastEthernet 0/0):
      !!!!!!!!!!!!!!!...!!!!!!!!!!!!!!!!!!!
Verifying Check sum........................OK
[OK-8906589 bytes]
8906589 bytes copied in 277.45 secs
Cougar#
```

The router prompts you to enter the IP address of the TFTP server. When prompted for the filename of the IOS image on the server, the router may then prompt to "erase flash." This prompt to erase Flash memory often happens if sufficient Flash is not available for the new image. As the image is erased from Flash memory, a series of the letter "e" displays to show the erase process.

As each datagram of the IOS image file is downloaded, an exclamation point (!) displays. This IOS image is several megabytes in size and may take some time to download.

The new Flash memory image is verified after it has been downloaded. The router is now ready to be reloaded to use the new IOS image.

Internet Control Message Protocol

IP is an unreliable method for delivery of network data. IP is known as a "best-effort" delivery mechanism. IP has no built-in processes to ensure that data is delivered in the event that problems exist with network communication. If an intermediary device such as another router fails or if a destination device is disconnected from the network, delivery does not happen.

Additionally, nothing in the basic design of IP allows for notification to the sender that a data transmission has failed. Internet Control Message Protocol (ICMP), a component of the TCP/IP protocol stack, addresses this basic limitation of IP. ICMP does not overcome the unreliability limitation that exists in IP. ICMP sends error messages to the sender of the data indicating that problems occurred with data delivery. Figure 20-22 shows where ICMP resides within the TCP/IP model.

Figure 20-22 ICMP

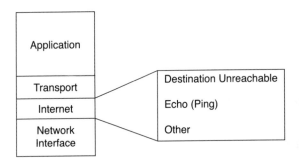

Router C does not notify the intermediary devices of the delivery failure. Therefore, Router C does not send ICMP messages to Router A and Router B or to the originating device. Neither does Router C know the path the datagram has taken to arrive there. Datagrams contain only source and destination IP addresses. Datagrams do not contain information about all the intermediary devices. The reporting device has only the sender's IP address with which to communicate. Although Routers A and B are not directly notified, they may become aware of the down interface on Router C. However, the dissemination of this information to neighbor routers is not the function of ICMP. ICMP reports on the status of the delivered packet to the sender. Its function is not to propagate information about network changes.

ICMP Message Delivery

ICMP messages are delivered using the IP protocol. ICMP messages are encapsulated as data in datagrams in the same way any other data is delivered using IP. Table 20-8 displays the encapsulation of an ICMP packet within an IP packet.

Table 20-8 CMP Encapsulation

Frame Header	Datagram Header	ICMP Header	ICMP Data
Frame header	Datagram header	Datagram data area	
Frame header	Frame data area		

Data is encapsulated within a datagram when it reaches the network layer. From there the datagram and its encapsulated data are further encapsulated into a frame at the data link layer. ICMP messages have their own header information. However, this information, along with the ICMP data, is encapsulated just as any other data would be within the datagram. ICMP messages are transmitted in the same way as any other data and are, therefore, subject to the same delivery failures. This creates a scenario where error reports could generate more error reports, causing increased congestion on an already ailing network. For this reason, errors created by ICMP messages do not generate their own ICMP messages. Therefore, it is possible to have a datagram delivery error that is never reported back to the sender of the data.

Error Reporting and Error Correction

ICMP is an error-reporting protocol for IP. When datagram delivery errors occur, ICMP is used to report these errors back to the sender of the datagram. For example, Workstation 1 in Figure 20-23 is sending a datagram to Workstation 6. When the corresponding interface on Router C goes down, Router C then utilizes ICMP to send a message back to Workstation 1 indicating that the datagram could not be delivered. ICMP does not correct the encountered network problem. In the example from Figure 20-23, ICMP does not attempt to correct the problem with the interface on Router C that is preventing datagram delivery. The only capability of ICMP is to report the errors back to Workstation 1.

Figure 20-23 Error Reporting

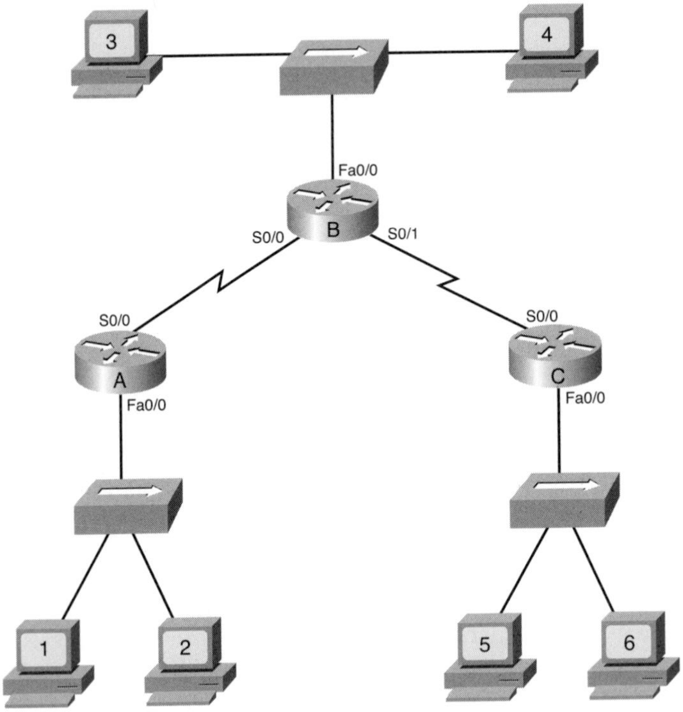

Unreachable Networks

Network communication depends on certain basic conditions being met. First, the TCP/IP protocol stack must be properly configured in the sending and receiving devices, including the installation of the TCP/IP protocol and proper configuration of IP address and subnet mask. A default gateway must also be configured if datagrams are to travel outside of the local network. Second, intermediary devices must be in place to route the datagram from the source device and its network to the destination network. Routers serve this function. Also a router must have the TCP/IP protocol properly configured on its interfaces and it must use an appropriate routing protocol.

If these conditions are not met, network communication cannot take place. For instance, the sending device may address the datagram to a nonexistent IP address or to a destination device that is disconnected from its network. Routers can also be points of failure if a connecting interface is down or if the router does not have the information necessary to find the destination network. If a destination network is not accessible, it is said to be an unreachable network.

Destination unreachable messages include the following:

- **Network unreachable**—This message usually implies routing or addressing failures.

- **Host unreachable**—This message usually implies delivery failures, such as a wrong subnet mask.

- **Protocol unreachable**—This message usually implies that the destination does not support the upper-layer protocol specified in the packet.

- **Port unreachable**—This message usually implies that the TCP port (socket) is not available.

Figure 20-24 and Figure 20-25 show a router receiving a packet that it is unable to deliver to its ultimate destination. The packet may be undeliverable because there is no known route to the destination. Because there is not a known route, the router sends an ICMP host unreachable message to the source.

Figure 20-24 ICMP

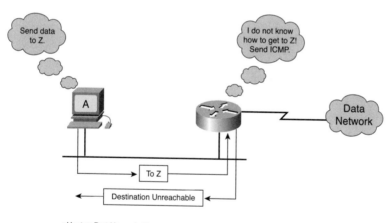

• Host or Port Unreachable
• Network Unreachable

Using ping to Test Destination Reachability

The ICMP protocol enables you to test the availability of a particular destination. Figure 20-26 shows ICMP being used to issue an echo request message to the destination device. When the destination device receives the ICMP echo request, it formulates an echo reply message to send back to the source of the echo request. If the sender receives the echo reply, this confirms that the destination device can be reached using the IP protocol.

Figure 20-25 ICMP

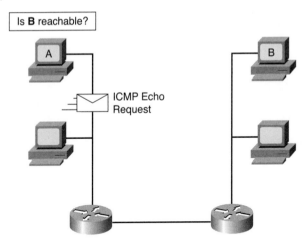

Figure 20-26 Echo Request

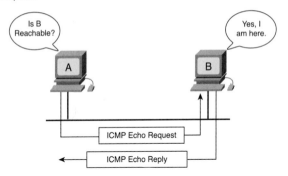

The echo request message is typically initiated using the **ping** command as shown in Example 20-5. In this example, the command is used with the IP address of the destination device.

Example 20-5 *ICMP* ping *Command Output*

```
C:\>ping 198.133.219.25


Pinging 198.133.219.25 with 32 bytes of data:


Reply from 198.133.219.25: bytes=32 time=30ms TTL=247
Reply from 198.133.219.25: bytes=32 time=20ms TTL=247
```

Example 20-5 *ICMP* ping *Command Output (Continued)*

```
Reply from 198.133.219.25: bytes=32 time=20ms TTL=247
Reply from 198.133.219.25: bytes=32 time=20ms TTL=247


Ping statistics for 198.133.219.25:
    Packets: Sent = 4, Received = 4, Lost = 0 (0% loss),
Approximate round trip times in milli-seconds:
    Minimum = 20ms, Maximum =  30ms, Average =  22ms


C:\>
```

You can also use the **ping** command as shown in Example 20-6, using the DNS name of the destination device (assuming DNS is available). In these examples, the **ping** command issues four echo requests and receives four echo replies confirming IP connectivity between the two devices. Table 20-9 shows Cisco **ping** return codes.

Example 20-6 ping *Command Output*

```
C:\>ping www.cisco.com


Pinging www.cisco.com [198.133.219.25] with 32 bytes of data:


Reply from 198.133.219.25: bytes=32 time=30ms TTL=247
Reply from 198.133.219.25: bytes=32 time=20ms TTL=247
Reply from 198.133.219.25: bytes=32 time=20ms TTL=247
Reply from 198.133.219.25: bytes=32 time=20ms TTL=247


Ping statistics for 198.133.219.25:
    Packets: Sent = 4, Received = 4, Lost = 0 (0% loss),
Approximate round trip times in milli-seconds:
    Minimum = 20ms, Maximum =  30ms, Average =  22ms


C:\>
```

Table 20-9 Cisco **ping** Return Codes

Code	Meaning	Possible Cause(s)
!	Each exclamation point indicates receipt of an ICMP echo reply.	The ping completed successfully.
.	Each period indicates that the network server timed out while waiting for a reply.	This message can indicate many problems: **ping** was blocked by an access control list or *firewall*. A router along the path did not have a route to the destination and did not send an ICMP destination unreachable message. A physical connectivity problem occurred somewhere along the path.
U	An ICMP unreachable message was received.	A router along the path did not have a route to the destination address.
C	An ICMP source quench message was received.	A device along the path—possibly the destination—may be receiving to much traffic; check input queues.
&	An ICMP time-exceeded message was received.	A routing loop may have occurred.

Access Lists

Network administrators must figure out how to deny unwanted access to the network while allowing appropriate access. Although security tools, such as passwords, callback equipment, and physical security devices are helpful, they often lack the flexibility of basic traffic filtering and the specific controls most administrators prefer. For example, a network administrator might want to allow users access to the Internet but might not want external users to use Telnet to access the LAN.

Routers provide basic traffic-filtering capabilities, such as blocking Internet traffic, with *access control lists (ACLs)*. An ACL is a sequential collection of permit or deny statements that apply to addresses or upper-layer protocols. In this chapter, you learn about using standard and *extended ACLs* as a means to control network traffic and how ACLs are used as part of a security solution.

In addition, this chapter includes tips, considerations, recommendations, and general guidelines on how to use ACLs, and includes the commands and configurations needed to create ACLs. Finally, this chapter provides examples of standard and extended ACLs and how to apply ACLs to router interfaces.

It is important to configure ACLs correctly and to know where to place ACLs on the network. ACLs serve multiple purposes in a network. Common ACL functions include filtering packets internally, protecting the internal network from illegal Internet access, and restricting access to virtual terminal ports.

ACL Overview

ACLs are lists of instructions you apply to a router's interface. These lists tell the router what kinds of packets to accept and what kinds of packets to deny. Acceptance and denial can be based on certain specifications, such as source address, destination address, and TCP/UDP port number.

ACLs enable you to manage traffic and scan specific packets by applying the ACL to a router interface. Any traffic going through the interface is tested against certain conditions that are part of the ACL.

ACLs can be created for all routed network protocols, such as IP and IPX, to filter packets as the packets pass through a router. ACLs can be configured at the router to control access to a network or subnet.

ACLs filter network traffic by controlling whether routed packets are forwarded or blocked at the router's interfaces. The router examines each packet to determine whether to forward or drop it, based on the conditions specified in the ACL. The ACL conditions might be the source address of the traffic, the destination address of the traffic, the upper-layer protocol, or other information.

ACLs must be defined on a per-protocol basis. In other words, you must define an ACL for every protocol enabled on an interface if you want to control traffic flow for *that* protocol, on *that* interface. (Note that some protocols refer to ACLs as filters.) If your router interface were configured for IP, AppleTalk, and IPX, for example, you would need to define at least three ACLs. As shown in Figure 20-27, you can use ACLs as a tool for network control by adding the flexibility to filter the packets that flow in or out of router interfaces.

Figure 20-27 ACL Example

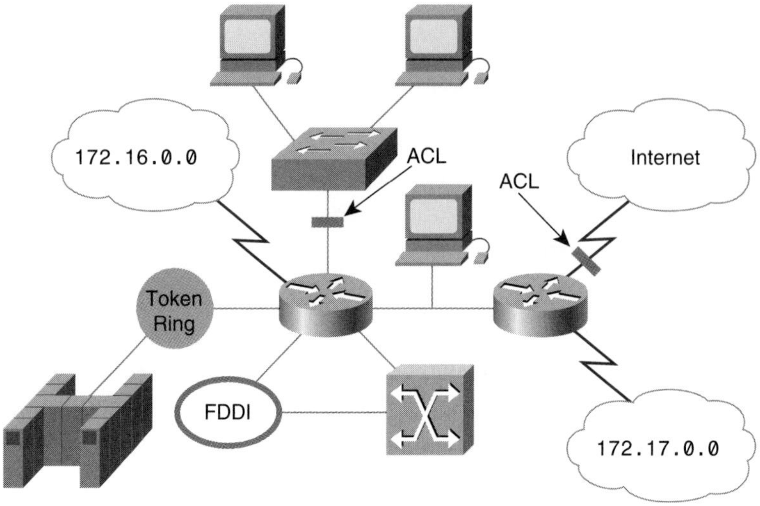

Reasons to Create ACLs

There are many reasons to create ACLs. For instance, you can use ACLs for the following:

- Limit network traffic and increase network performance. For instance, ACLs can designate certain packets to be processed by a router before other traffic, on the basis of a protocol. This is referred to as *queuing*. Queuing ensures that routers do not process packets that are not needed. As a result, queuing limits network traffic and reduces network congestion.

- Provide traffic flow control. For instance, ACLs can restrict or reduce the contents of routing updates. These restrictions are used to limit information about specific networks from propagating through the network.

- Provide a basic level of security for network access. ACLs can allow one host to access a part of your network and prevent another host from accessing the same area.

- Decide which type of traffic is forwarded or blocked at the router interface. For instance, you can permit e-mail traffic to be routed, but at the same time block all Telnet traffic.

The material covered in this chapter, indeed in this whole book, focuses on the principle topics tested on the CCNA exam. Therefore, be aware that the topics covered in this section specifically relate to major objectives required to pass the exam and be prepared to demonstrate a full knowledge of this material.

Cisco Equipment, IOS, and Network Basics

With regard to this review of Cisco equipment, IOS, and network basics, the following subjects are covered and included on the CCNA exam:

- Describing router elements (RAM, ROM, Flash, NVRAM, configuration register)
- Configuring router passwords, identification, and banner
- Using the context-sensitive help facility
- Using the command history and editing features
- Performing the initial router configuration (including using the setup mode)
- Using **show** commands to display basic network operational parameters
- Describing router startup sequence
- Establishing connectivity from a host to the appropriate network device to perform configuration tasks
- Interconnecting network devices in accordance with open standards

Initial Router Boot-Up Output

Each time a router is powered on, it goes through the following boot sequence:

1. The router goes through power-on self-test diagnostics to verify basic operation of the CPU, memory, and interfaces.

2. The system bootstrap software, the boot image executes and searches for a valid Cisco IOS image (router operating system software). The source of the Cisco IOS image, whether a Flash memory or a TFTP server, is determined by the configuration register setting. The factory-default setting for the configuration register is 0x2102. This indicates that the router should attempt to load a Cisco IOS image from Flash memory.

3. If after five attempts a valid Cisco IOS image is not found in Flash memory, the router reverts to boot ROM mode. This mode is used to install or upgrade a Cisco IOS image.

4. If a valid Cisco IOS image is found, the router searches for a valid configuration file.

5. If a valid configuration file is not found in NVRAM, the router opens the System Configuration dialog box so that you can manually configure manually the configuration file. For normal router operation, there must be a valid Cisco IOS image in Flash memory and a configuration file in NVRAM.

In Example 20-7 and Example 20-8, the messages displayed vary, depending on the interfaces in the router and the Cisco IOS release. The screen displays in this output are for reference only and may not exactly reflect the screen displays on the console.

Example 20-7 *NVRAM Invalid*

```
System Bootstrap, Version X.X(XXXX) [XXXXX XX], RELEASE SOFTWARE
Copyright (c) 1986-199X by Cisco Systems
2500 processor with 4096 Kbytes of main memory


Notice: NVRAM invalid, possibly due to write erase.


--- output omitted ---
```

Example 20-8 *Bootstrap and IOS Version*

```
--- output omitted ---
IOS (tm) X000 Software (XXX-X-X), Version XX.X(XXXX) [XXXXX XXX]
Copyright (c) 1986-199X by Cisco Systems, Inc.
```

Notice that in the first example the *nonvolatile RAM (NVRAM)* is invalid; this is possibly due to write erase. This tells the user that this router has not been configured for the first time, or that the NVRAM has been erased. A router cannot be used until it is configured.

In the second example, the user can determine the bootstrap version and the IOS version the router is using. The user can also determine the router model, processor, and the amount of memory the router contains. Other information listed in this output includes the following:

- How many interfaces the router has
- What types of interfaces the router has
- The amount of NVRAM
- The amount of Flash memory

Establishing a HyperTerminal Session

All Cisco routers include an EIA/TIA-232 asynchronous serial console port (RJ-45). Cables and adapters are needed to connect a console terminal (an ASCII terminal or PC running terminal-emulation software) to the console port. To connect an ASCII terminal to the console port, use an RJ-45-to-RJ-45 rollover cable with the female

RJ-45-to-DB-25 adapter. To connect a PC running terminal-emulation software to the console port, use the RJ-45-to-RJ-45 rollover cable with the female RJ-45-to-DB-9 adapter.

The default parameters for the console port are 9600 baud, 8 data bits, no parity, 1 stop bit, and no flow control. The console port does not support hardware flow control.

To connect a terminal to the console port on the router, follow these steps:

Step 1   Connect the terminal using the RJ-45-to-RJ-45 rollover cable and an RJ-45-to-DB-9 or RJ-45-to-DB-25 adapter.

Step 2   Configure the terminal or PC terminal-emulation software for 9600 baud, 8 data bits, no parity, 1 stop bit, and no flow control.

Table 20-10 shows a list of operating systems and the terminal-emulation software you can use.

Table 20-10 Terminal-Emulation Software

PC Operating System	Software
Windows 95, Windows 98, Windows 2000, Windows XP	HyperTerminal (included with Windows software), ProComm Plus
Windows 3.1	Terminal (included with Windows software)
Macintosh	ProComm, VersaTerm, ZTerm (supplied separately)

Logging In to the Router

To configure Cisco routers, the user interface must be accessed on the router with a terminal or by remote access. When accessing a router, a user must log in to the router before entering any other commands.

For security purposes, the router has two levels of access to commands, as shown in Example 20-9.

- **User exec mode**—Typical tasks include those that check the router status. In this mode, router configuration changes are not allowed.
- **Privileged exec mode**—Typical tasks include those that change the router configuration.

The user exec mode prompt displays upon login to a router. Commands available at this user level are a subset of the commands available at the privileged exec level. For the most part, these commands enable a user to display information without changing router configuration settings.

Example 20-9 *Router Modes*

```
Router
!User Mode
Router>enable
Password:
Router#
!Privileged-Mode
Router>disable
Router>
```

Keyboard Help

Typing a question mark (?) at the user exec mode prompt or the privileged exec mode prompt displays a list of commonly used commands. Notice the —More— prompt at the bottom of the sample display. The screen displays 22 lines at one time. The —More— prompt at the bottom of the display indicates that multiple screens are available as output, as shown in Example 20-10.

Example 20-10 *Keyboard Help*

```
Router#?
Exec commands:
access-enable    Create a temporary Access-List entry
access-profile   Apply user-profile to interface
access-template  Create a temporary Access-List entry
archive          manage archive files
bfe              For manual emergency modes setting
cd               Change current directory
clear            Reset functions
clock            Manage the system clock
configure        Enter configuration mode
connect          Open a terminal connection
copy             Copy from one file to another
debug            Debugging functions (see also 'undebug')
delete           Delete a file
dir              List files on a filesystem
disable          Turn off privileged commands
disconnect       Disconnect an existing network connection
elog             Event-logging control commands
```

Example 20-10 *Keyboard Help (Continued)*

```
enable              Turn on privileged commands
erase               Erase a filesystem
exit                Exit from the EXEC
help                Description of the interactive help system

--More--
isdn                Make/disconnect an isdn data call on a BRI interface
lock                Lock the terminal
login               Log in as a particular user
logout              Exit from the EXEC
more                Display the contents of a file
mrinfo            Request neighbor and version information from a multicast router
mrm                 IP Multicast Routing Monitor Test
mstat               Show statistics after multiple multicast traceroutes
mtrace              Trace reverse multicast path from destination to source
name-connection  Name an existing network connection
no                  Disable debugging functions
pad                 Open a X.29 PAD connection
ping                Send echo messages
ppp                 Start IETF Point-to-Point Protocol (PPP)
pwd                 Display current working directory
reload              Halt and perform a cold restart
resume              Resume an active network connection
rlogin              Open an rlogin connection
rsh                 Execute a remote command
send                Send a message to other tty lines
setup               Run the SETUP command facility
show                Show running system information

--More--
slip                Start Serial-line IP (SLIP)
start-chat          Start a chat-script on a line
systat              Display information about terminal lines
telnet              Open a telnet connection
terminal            Set terminal line parameters
```

continues

Example 20-10 *Keyboard Help (Continued)*

```
test              Test subsystems, memory, and interfaces
traceroute        Trace route to destination
tunnel            Open a tunnel connection
udptn             Open an udptn connection
undebug           Disable debugging functions (see also 'debug')
verify            Verify a file
where             List active connections
write             Write running configuration to memory, network, or terminal
x28               Become an X.28 PAD
x3                Set X.3 parameters on PAD
```

NOTE

At this point, the list of commands displayed is context sensitive. You see a different list when you are in user mode versus enable mode, and when in global configuration versus configure interface modes.

Whenever a —More— prompt appears, you can view the next available screen by pressing the **Spacebar**. To display just the next line, press the **Return** or **Enter** key. Press any other key to return to the prompt.

To access privileged exec mode, type **enable**. Typing **enable** causes the router to prompt the user for a password. Typing a question mark at the privileged exec mode prompt, (see Example 20-11) displays a longer list of commands than would display at the user exec mode prompt.

Example 20-11 *Exec Mode Commands*

```
Cisco#?
Exec commands:
  access-enable     Create a temporary Access-List entry
  access-profile    Apply user-profile to interface
  access-template   Create a temporary Access-List entry
  archive           manage archive files
  bfe               For manual emergency modes setting
  cd                Change current directory
  clear             Reset functions
  clock             Manage the system clock
  configure         Enter configuration mode
  connect           Open a terminal connection
  copy              Copy from one file to another
  debug             Debugging functions (see also 'undebug')
  delete            Delete a file
  dir               List files on a filesystem
```

Example 20-11 *Exec Mode Commands (Continued)*

```
    disable         Turn off privileged commands
    disconnect      Disconnect an existing network connection
    elog            Event-logging control commands
    enable          Turn on privileged commands
    erase           Erase a filesystem
    exit            Exit from the EXEC
    help            Description of the interactive help system
  --More--
```

Screen output varies, depending on Cisco IOS Software level and router configuration.

IOS Editing Commands

The user interface includes an enhanced editing mode that provides a set of editing key functions that enables the user to edit a command line as it is being typed. Use the key sequences indicated in Table 20-11 to move the cursor around on the command line for corrections or changes. Although enhanced editing mode is automatically enabled with the current software release, it can be disabled if written scripts do not interact well while enhanced editing is enabled. To disable enhanced editing mode, type **terminal no editing** at the privileged exec mode prompt.

Table 20-11 Editing Commands

Command	Description
Ctrl+A	Moves to the beginning of the command line
Ctrl+E	Moves to the end of the command line
Esc+B	Moves back one word
Ctrl+F	Moves forward one character
Ctrl+B	Moves back one character
Esc+F	Moves forward one word

The editing command set provides a horizontal scrolling feature for commands that extend beyond a single line on the screen. When the cursor reaches the right margin, the command line shifts 10 spaces to the left. The first 10 characters of the line cannot be seen, but a user can scroll back and check the syntax at the beginning of the command.

To scroll back, press **Ctrl+B,** or press the **Left Arrow** key repeatedly until you reach the beginning of the command entry. **Ctrl+A** returns you directly to the beginning of the line.

Router Command History

The user interface provides a history, or record, of commands that have been entered. This feature proves particularly useful for recalling long or complex commands or entries. The command history feature enables you to perform the following tasks:

- Set the command history buffer size.
- Recall commands.
- Disable the command history feature.

By default, the command history is enabled and the system records 10 command lines in its history buffer. To change the number of command lines the system records during a terminal session, use the **terminal history size** or the **history size** command. The maximum number of commands is 256. Table 20-12 shows command history commands.

Table 20-12 Router Command History

Command	Description
Ctrl+P (or just the **Up Arrow** key)	Recalls last (preceding) command
Ctrl+N (or just the **down arrow** key)	Recalls most recent command
show history	Shows command buffer
terminal history [**size** *number-of-lines*]	Sets command buffer size
terminal no editing	Disables advanced editing features
terminal editing	Re-enables advanced editing features
Tab	Completes the entry

To recall commands in the history buffer, beginning with the most recent command, press **Ctrl+P.** Continue to press **Ctrl+P** or the **Up Arrow** key repeatedly to recall successively older commands. To return to more recent commands in the history buffer, after using **Ctrl+P** or the **Up Arrow** key, press **Ctrl+N** or the **Down Arrow** key repeatedly to recall successively more recent commands.

When typing commands, as a shortcut, you may enter the unique characters for a command. When you press the **Tab** key, the interface finishes the entry. When the typed letters uniquely identify the command, the **Tab** key just acknowledges visually that the router has understood the specific command that was intended.

On most computers, additional select and copy functions may be available. A previous command string may be copied and then pasted or inserted as the current command entry.

Troubleshooting Command Errors

This lab introduces the Cisco Internetwork Operating System (IOS) command-line user interface. The task is to log in to the router and use different levels of access to enter commands in user mode and privileged mode. Become familiar with the commands available in each mode, whether user or privileged. Use the router help facility, history, and editing features. The IOS command interface is the most common method of configuring a Cisco router. Many commands are available, especially in privileged mode. Do not be overwhelmed with the large number of commands. Many of the commands are not used on a daily basis.

The Purpose of the Cisco IOS

Like any computer, a router or switch cannot function without an operating system. Cisco calls its operating system the Cisco Internetwork Operating System, or Cisco IOS. It is the embedded software architecture in all the Cisco routers and is also the operating system of the Catalyst switches. A router does not become functional until it loads the IOS. Without an operating system, the hardware has no capability. The Cisco IOS provides the following network services:

- Basic routing and switching functions
- Reliable and secure access to networked resources
- Network scalability

Operation of the Cisco IOS

The Cisco IOS devices have three distinct operating environments or modes:

- ROM monitor
- Boot ROM
- Cisco IOS

The router startup process normally loads into RAM and establishes one of these operating environments. System administrators can use the configuration register setting to control which of these modes is loaded into the router.

The ROM monitor performs the bootstrap process and provides low-level functionality and diagnostics. The ROM monitor is used to recover from system failures and to recover a lost password. You cannot access the ROM monitor through any of the network interfaces, but only through a console port session.

When the router is running in boot ROM mode, only a limited subset of the Cisco IOS feature set is available. Boot ROM allows write operations to Flash memory and is used primarily to modify the Cisco IOS image that is stored in Flash memory. You can modify the Cisco IOS image in boot ROM by using the **copy tftp flash** command, which copies an IOS image stored on a TFTP server into the router's Flash memory.

The normal operation of a router requires the full Cisco IOS image from Flash memory. In some devices, the IOS is established directly from Flash memory. However, most Cisco routers require a copy of the IOS to be loaded into RAM and also executed from RAM. Some IOS images are stored in Flash memory in a compressed format and must be expanded when copied to RAM.

To see the IOS image and version that is running, use the **show version** command, which also indicates the configuration register setting. The **show flash** command in Example 20-12 enables you to verify that the system has sufficient memory to load a new Cisco IOS image.

Example 20-12 *IOS Image*

```
Cisco>show flash

System flash directory:
File  Length    Name/status
  1   8022152   /c2500-i-l.121-16.bin
[8022216 bytes used, 366392 available, 8388608 total]
8192K bytes of processor board System flash (Read ONLY)
```

Cisco IOS Features

Cisco provides IOS images for devices spanning a wide range of network product platforms. To optimize the Cisco IOS Software required by various product platforms, Cisco is working to develop many different Cisco IOS Software images. Each image represents a different feature set that serves the various device platforms, available memory resources, and customers' needs.

There are numerous IOS images for different Cisco device models and feature sets. However, the basic configuration command structure is the same. The configuration and troubleshooting skills acquired on any one device apply across a wide range of products.

The naming convention for the different Cisco IOS releases contains three parts:

- The platform on which the image runs
- The special capabilities supported in the image
- Where the image runs and whether it has been zipped or compressed

The Cisco IOS naming conventions, name part field meaning, image content, and other details are subject to change.

After choosing the options that meet the network requirements, select a Cisco IOS Software release that is supported by the hardware. The software requirements of each device are listed in the Cisco Product Documentation section of the Documentation CD. The Cisco Software Advisor is an interactive tool that provides the most current information.

The show version Command

The **show version** command displays information about the Cisco IOS Software version currently running on the router, including the configuration register and the boot field setting.

- IOS version and descriptive information
- Bootstrap ROM version
- Boot ROM version
- Router uptime
- Last restart method
- System image file and location
- Router platform
- Configuration register setting

Router User Interface

Cisco IOS Software uses a command-line interface (CLI) as its traditional console environment. The IOS is a core technology that extends across most of the Cisco product line. Its operation details may vary on different internetworking devices.

You can access this environment in several ways. One access method to the CLI is through a console session. A console uses a low-speed serial connection directly from a computer or terminal to the console connection on the router. Another way to access a CLI session is through a dialup connection by using a modem or null modem connected to the router AUX port. Neither of these methods requires the configuration of network services on the router. Another way to access a CLI session is to Telnet to the router. To establish a Telnet session to the router, at least one interface must be configured for IP.

Virtual terminal sessions must also be configured for login and passwords.

Router User Interface and Modes

The Cisco CLI uses a hierarchical structure. This structure requires entry into different modes to accomplish particular tasks. For example, interface configuration mode must be entered to configure a router interface. From interface configuration mode, all configurations entered apply only to that particular interface. Each command mode is indicated with a distinctive prompt and only allows commands that are appropriate for that mode.

The IOS provides a command interpreter service known as the command executive (exec). After each command is entered, the exec validates and executes the command.

As a security feature, the Cisco IOS Software separates the exec sessions into two access levels: user exec mode; and privileged exec mode, which is also known as the enable mode.

The user exec mode allows only a limited number of basic monitoring commands, and is often referred to as a view-only mode. The user exec level does not allow any commands that could change the configuration of the router. The ">" prompt indicates that you are in user exec mode.

Cisco IOS Troubleshooting

Several things may prevent a router from booting properly, including the following:

- Configuration file has missing or incorrect boot system statement
- Incorrect configuration register value
- Corrupted Flash memory image
- Hardware failure

When the router boots, it looks in the configuration file for a boot system statement. This boot system statement can force the router to boot from another image rather than the IOS in Flash memory. To identify the boot image source, type the **show version** command and look for the line that identifies the image boot source, as shown in Example 20-13.

Example 20-13 *Image Boot Source*

```
Cisco>show version
--- output omitted ---


ROM: System Bootstrap, Version 11.0(10c), SOFTWARE
BOOTLDR: 3000 Bootstrap Software (IGS-BOOT-R), Version 11.0(10c), RELEASE SOFTWA
RE (fc1)
```

An incorrect configuration register setting prevents the IOS from loading from Flash memory. The value in the configuration register tells the router where to get the IOS. You can confirm this by using the **show version** command and looking at the last line for the configuration register, as shown in Example 20-14.

Example 20-14 *Configuration Register*

```
Cisco>show version
---- output omitted ----


Configuration register is 0x2102
```

Table 12-13 describes other helpful router status commands.

Table 20-13 Router Status Commands

Command	Description
show version	Displays the configuration of the system hardware, the software version, the names and sources of configuration files, the boot images, and displays the reason for the last system reboot.
show processes	Displays information about the active processes.
show protocols	Displays the configured protocols. This command shows the status of any configured Layer 3 (network layer) protocol.
show memory	Shows statistics about the router's memory, including memory-free pool statistics.
show stacks	Monitors the stack use of processes and interrupt routines.

continues

Table 20-13 Router Status Commands (Continued)

Command	Description
show buffers	Provides statistics for the buffer pools on the router.
show flash	Shows information about the Flash memory device.
show running-config (write term on Cisco IOS Release 10.3 or earlier)	Displays the active configuration file.
show startup-config (show config on Cisco IOS Release 10.3 or earlier)	Displays the backup configuration file.
show interface	Displays statistics for all interfaces configured.

The correct value varies in different hardware platforms. The Cisco IOS documentation should include a printed copy of the **show version** output. If that documentation is not available, you can check resources on the Cisco Documentation CD or at Cisco.com to identify the correct configuration register value. Correct this by changing the configuration register in the configuration and saving this as the startup configuration.

If a problem persists, the router may have a corrupted Flash memory image file. In such a case, an error message should display during boot. You can display the error message as follows:

```
open: read error...requested 0x4 bytes, got 0x0
trouble reading device magic number
boot: cannot open "flash:"
boot: cannot determine first file name on device "flash:"ú
```

If the Flash memory image is corrupt, you should upload a new IOS into the router. If the problem has not been identified in this section, the router could have a hardware failure. If this is the case, contact the Cisco Technical Assistance Center (TAC). Although hardware failures are rare, they do occur.

Summary

This chapter provides some insight into the main objectives and topics that are emphasized on the CCNA exam. Although this chapter is not an all-inclusive chapter that includes everything you will encounter on the exam, it does provide brief summaries of the main topics. Keep in mind that you need to study many commands, concepts, and scenarios to fully prepare for the CCNA exam.

Key Terms

ACL (access control list)   A means for controlling or limiting network traffic. An ACL compares different criteria to a defined rule set.

BOOTP (Bootstrap Protocol)   The protocol used by a network node to determine the IP address of its Ethernet interfaces to affect network booting.

extended ACL   Compares source IP address, destination IP address, TCP/UDP port number, and other criteria to the rules defining a standard ACL.

firewall   A router or an access server, or several routers or access servers, designated as a buffer between any connected public networks and a private network. A firewall router uses ACLs and other methods to ensure the security of the private network.

Flash memory   A special type of electrical erasable programmable read-only memory (EEPROM) that can be erased and reprogrammed in blocks instead of 1 byte at a time. Many modern PCs have their BIOS stored on a Flash memory chip so that it can be updated easily if necessary. Such a BIOS is sometimes called a Flash BIOS. Flash memory is also popular in modems because it enables the modem manufacturer to support new protocols as they become standardized.

NVRAM (nonvolatile RAM)   RAM that retains its contents when a unit is powered off.

packet switching   Networking method in which nodes share bandwidth with each other by sending packets.

PVC (permanent virtual circuit)   Virtual circuit that is permanently established. PVCs save bandwidth associated with circuit establishment and tear down in situations where certain virtual circuits must exist all the time. Called a permanent virtual connection in ATM terminology.

queuing   A process in which ACLs can designate certain packets to be processed by a router before other traffic, on the basis of some configurable parameter such as specifying a protocol.

RAM (random-access memory)   Volatile memory that can be read and written by a microprocessor.

SVC (switched virtual circuit)   Virtual circuit that is dynamically established on demand and is torn down when transmission is complete. SVCs are used in situations where data transmission is sporadic. Called a switched virtual connection in ATM terminology.

(TDM) *time-division multiplexing*   Technique in which information from multiple channels can be allocated bandwidth on a single wire based on pre-assigned time slots. Bandwidth is allocated to each channel regardless of whether the station has data to transmit.

(TFTP) *Trivial File Transfer Protocol*   Simplified version of FTP that allows files to be transferred from one computer to another over a network, usually without the use of client authentication (for example, username and password).

Objectives

After reading this chapter, you will be able to

- Describe how voice, video, and data networks have traditionally been implemented
- Compare and contrast voice-over-data technologies
- Describe voice, video, and data networks
- Describe the features and main building blocks of Cisco AVVID
- Identify emerging applications for converged networking and their functions
- Describe the effects of QoS in voice, video, and data-integration networks

Chapter 21

Introduction to Converged Networking

This chapter describes how traditional voice, video, and data networks are implemented and explains various types of voice-over-data technologies. In addition, this chapter describes the need for converged voice, video, and data networks and Cisco Architecture for Voice, Video, and Integrated Data (AVVID), along with new applications for converged networks. This chapter also discusses common issues with *quality of service (QoS)*.

Traditional Networks

Enterprises traditionally provisioned separate networks for data, voice, and video applications. These *traditional networks* have been deployed autonomously and have operated in isolation, often implemented and managed by separate teams.

These separate networks encompass the enterprise LANs and WANs and were built to interconnect private branch exchange (PBX) equipment, H.320 videoconferencing equipment, and routers. The networks have been provisioned over dedicated, leased lines for PBX and H.320 video, with a combination of leased lines, Frame Relay, and ATM for data. Figure 21-1 depicts a typical deployment of these disparate networks.

Figure 21-1 Typical Traditional Network

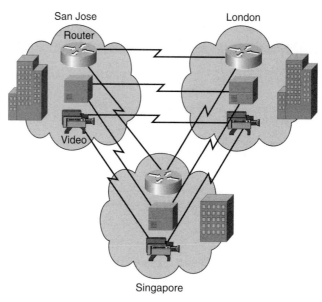

Introduction to Voice and Data Networks

Integrated voice and data networks support a variety of applications, all of which are designed to replace leased lines at lower costs. A voice-capable router can function as a local phone system for intra-office calls. In Figure 21-2, a user dials a phone extension that is located in the same office. The voice-capable router routes the call to the appropriate destination. A voice-capable router can also function as a phone system for interoffice calls, and can route calls within an enterprise network.

NOTE

CIR is the rate at which a Frame Relay network agrees to transfer information under normal conditions, averaged over a minimum increment of time. Measured in bits per second (bps), CIR is one of the key negotiated tariff metrics.

Voice over Frame Relay

Voice over Frame Relay (VoFR) technology consolidates voice and voice-band data (including fax and analog modems) with data services over a Frame Relay network. VoFR allows PBXs to be connected using Frame Relay permanent virtual circuits (PVCs). The goal is to replace leased lines at lower costs. With VoFR, customers can easily increase their link speeds to their Frame Relay service or their committed information rate (CIR) to support additional voice, fax, and data traffic.

A voice-capable router connects both a PBX and a data network to a public Frame Relay network (see Figure 21-3). A voice-capable router includes a voice Frame Relay adapter (VFRAD) or a voice/fax module that supports voice traffic on the data network.

Figure 21-2 Voice and Data Networks

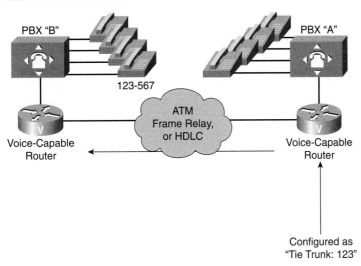

Figure 21-3 VoFR Network

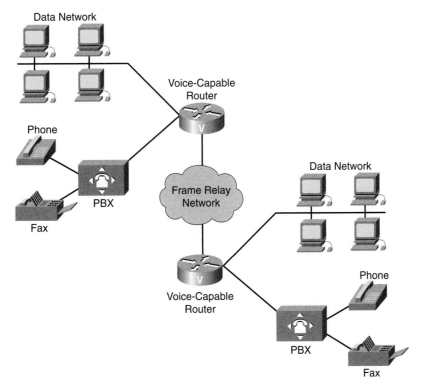

Sophisticated queuing techniques ensure QoS in voice over Frame Relay. Frame Relay provides the following benefits:

- Popular transport for multiservice networks because Frame Relay networks are common in many areas
- Cost-effective service that supports bursty traffic well
- Prioritization of voice frames over data frames to guarantee QoS

Voice over ATM

Voice over ATM (VoATM) is an ideal transport for multiservice networks, particularly for customers who already have an ATM network installed. ATM handles voice, video, and data equally well. A key benefit of ATM is its inherent design for handling the unique network transmission requirements of voice, video, and data traffic (see Figure 21-4).

Figure 21-4 VoATM Network

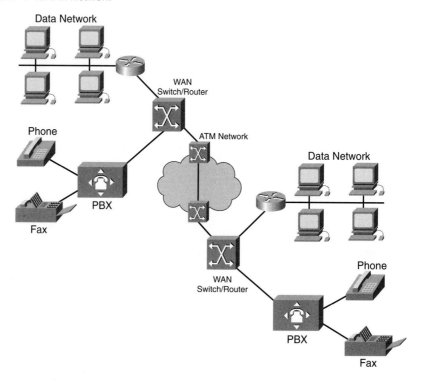

ATM supports several mechanisms for controlling delay and delay variation, including the following:

- **QoS**—Enables traffic to be provisioned with specific bandwidth and delay-variation guarantees.
- **Virtual-circuit queuing**—Treats each traffic stream differently. For example, voice traffic can be allocated priority over delay-insensitive traffic.
- **Small, fixed-length cells**—The 53-byte ATM cells reduce queuing delay and delay variations associated with variable-size packets, and also reduce delays through intermediate switches.

Voice over IP

The *Voice over IP (VoIP, often called Voice)* application runs over IP just like any other application. IP/User Datagram Protocol/Real-Time Transport Protocol (IP/UDP/RTP) headers encapsulate voice information as it passes through the IP stack; the information is de-encapsulated on the receiving side. RTP is utilized in addition to UDP to provide additional transport functions, such as time-stamping and sequencing of VoIP packets, that UDP does not provide. At the data link layer, VoIP packets can use any Layer 2 encapsulations, including Point-to-Point Protocol (PPP), High-Level Data Link Control (HDLC), Frame Relay, ATM, Ethernet, and so on. (See Figure 21-5.)

Figure 21-5 VoIP

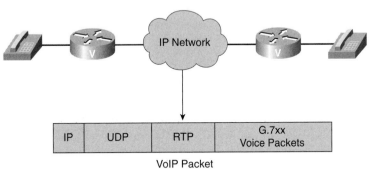

Users can choose VoIP as their voice-transport medium when they need a solution that is simple to implement, offers voice and fax capabilities, and handles phone-to-computer voice communications.

Comparing Voice-over-Data Technologies

Frame Relay, ATM, and IP are popular voice-over-data technologies that have been developed to meet the expanding needs of today's voice-over-data applications. As shown in Table 21-1, each technology has its advantages and its limitations.

Table 21-1 Advantages and Disadvantages of Voice-over-Data Technologies

Voice-over-Data Technology	Advantages	Disadvantages
Frame Relay	Deterministic Standards in place Services widely available	Tops out at T1/E1 speeds
ATM	Deterministic Granular class of service	Services not yet pervasive Equipment historically expensive
IP	Widely deployed for maximum savings potential Special class of service technologies	Connectionless Least deterministic

Voice, Video, and Data Networks

Using disparate facilities for each application transport is extremely inefficient. The volume of data traffic is growing faster than that of voice, driven by emerging and evolving technological innovations such as the World Wide Web, e-commerce, and applications such as videoconferencing or video streaming utilizing Internet Protocol (IP) multicast. Although growth rates vary by country and carrier, data transport will certainly dominate telephony networks. Data has already surpassed voice on some U.S. service provider networks and is the driving force behind global network growth. The challenge for the enterprise is to optimize networking to carry data, voice, and video traffic.

The rapid adoption and migration of vendors to the utilization of IP as a transport for data, voice, and video applications further endorses this transition to a converged networking architecture. Service providers (such as the telephone companies) that have historically used time-division multiplexing (TDM) infrastructures and relied on "Old World" practices are now relying on IP.

Converged networks are a continuing trend, and consolidating data, voice, and video is the natural evolution for multiservice networking. Utilizing IP as the ubiquitous transport offers the following benefits:

- Significant statistical gains in bandwidth efficiency in the enterprise
- Lower overall bandwidth requirements
- Ease of management
- The capability to deploy new applications rapidly
- On the LAN, a common infrastructure shared among data, voice, and video

A converged network allows the enterprise network to converge over a common IP transport. The number of WAN facilities is reduced, as is the number of devices required to terminate those facilities. Bandwidth can be added incrementally and can be shared statistically between applications, adding efficiency and reducing complexity. When voice is inactive, data can utilize the available bandwidth; when voice or video applications are active, they can be guaranteed the bandwidth required.

Cisco AVVID

Cisco Architecture for Voice, Video and Integrated Data (AVVID) is a standards-based, open-systems architecture for converged networking. Cisco AVVID is an enterprise initiative for integrated data, voice, and video over a common IP transport. Cisco AVVID comprises the following distinct building blocks (also illustrated in Figure 21-6):

- Clients, such as phones, PCs, PDAs, fixed and wireless IP telephones, H.323 videoconferencing equipment
- Network Platforms (LAN switches, routers, gateways, and other equipment)
- Intelligent Network Services (QoS, security, accounting, and management)
- Internet Middleware (distributed customer contact suites, messaging solutions, multimedia, and collaboration)
- Internet Business Integration (integrators, strategic partners, and customers)
- Internet Business Solutions (Oracle, Siebel, and Ariba enabled, accelerated, and delivered through Cisco AVVID)

Figure 21-6 Cisco AVVID Framework

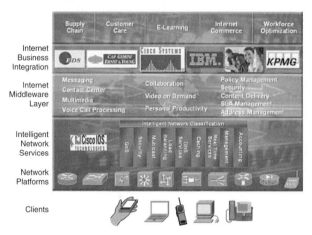

AVVID requires the appropriate infrastructure and design. Figure 21-7 depicts a converged network in which all data, voice, and video utilize IP as the transport; the IP WAN is the primary interconnect between sites, with the Public Switched Telephone Network (PSTN) being used as a secondary backup dialup connectivity method.

The use of open standards and the promotion of multivendor collaboration and interoperability are key benefits of Cisco AVVID. Because the network shown in Figure 21-7 is based on standards and open competition, interoperability with other applications is assured.

AVVID lowers costs and provides enhanced quality options for voice networking. It provides a highly scalable, reliable, adaptable network, and that permits the rapid deployment of new and innovative applications. AVVID allows the integration of products from multiple vendors to create a customized solution. No single vendor can provide a solution that fits all requirements for data, voice, and video. Specialized applications are often designed and implemented by only a single company and need to be integrated with the overall solution.

Converged Networking Applications

An important facet of converged networking is the enabling of new applications. Such emerging applications include desktop IP telephony, unified messaging, and the *Cisco IP Contact Centers*. A converged network offers the framework that permits rapid deployment of these new technologies.

Figure 21-7 Voice, Video, and Data Networks

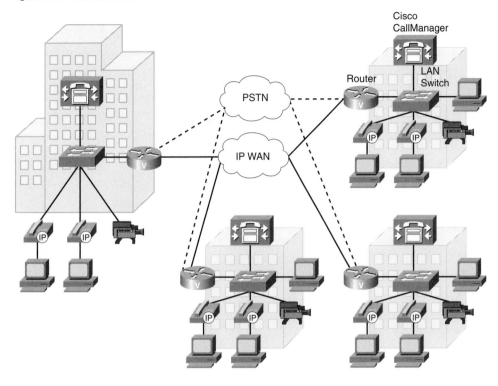

IP PBX

By using the Cisco CallManager, a PBX can be eliminated and replaced with IP telephony over a converged network. The Cisco CallManager provides call-control functionality and, when used in conjunction with the IP telephone, sets a soft telephone application that can provide the PBX functionality in a distributed and scalable fashion. A voice gateway connects the VoIP network to other network types, such as the PSTN, or to a PBX.

Unified Messaging

Today users have a wide range of communication and messaging media available to them: telephones, cell phones, pagers, fax, voice mail, and e-mail. Each of these requires distinct hardware and software components to function. *Unified messaging* combines voice mail, e-mail, and fax into a single application suite.

With unified messaging, a single application can store and retrieve an entire suite of message types. Voice-mail messages stored as WAV files can be downloaded as e-mail attachments while you are traveling, and a response can be recorded and returned to the sender, all recipients, or an expanded list. E-mail can be retrieved via a telephony user interface (TUI), converted from text to speech, and reviewed from an airport lobby phone or cell phone. Infrastructure is decreased because a single application can provide voice, e-mail, and fax. Productivity is increased because what were once disparate message types can be retrieved via the most convenient—or the user's preferred—interface.

Cisco offers unified messaging with its Cisco GateServer series of products. These products provide scalable solutions for service providers and the enterprise with open, standards-based interfaces. Figure 21-8 depicts a unified messaging model.

Figure 21-8 Unified Messaging

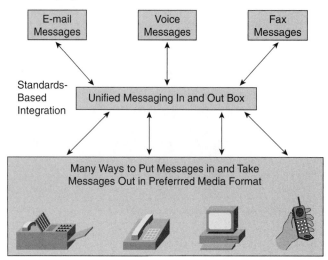

Cisco IP Contact Center

The *Cisco IP Contact Center (IPCC)* solution combines data and voice technologies to facilitate geographically independent multimedia customer interaction. This includes customer interactions originating from multiple, diverse contact channels, including IP voice, TDM voice, web, e-mail, and fax. Regardless of transport, whether the Internet or the traditional PSTN, the Cisco IPCC fully integrated contact-center architecture services all media types. (See Figure 21-9.) The Cisco IPCC architecture also provides a seamless migration path from the legacy call-center infrastructure to the IP-empowered, multimedia contact center.

Figure 21-9 Cisco IP Contact Center

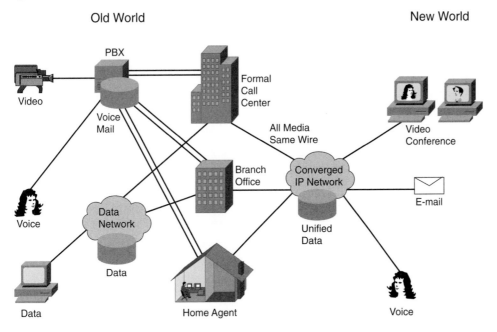

The Cisco IPCC solution also enables server and agent-level IP telephony to coexist with traditional TDM-based networks, existing automated call distribution/PBXs (ACD/PBXs), and installed desktop systems. The Cisco IPCC solution enables an organization to take advantage of new IP-based applications while preserving hetero-geneous legacy investments and taking advantage of existing IP data infrastructure. Cisco IPCC deployment can be incremental, adding IP telephony, new media channels, and new IP-based services at a rate that meets business demands.

Cisco IPCC business benefits include the following:

- Integrated multimedia queuing
- Enterprise-wide contact management based on a single set of business rules and supported by normalized, consolidated reporting
- Increased customer satisfaction through personalized customer interaction
- Geographic independence of both agent resources and IP-based application servers through the ubiquity of IP transport
- Carrier-quality fault tolerance and system reliability
- Scalability from single site to multisite to network service provider services
- Rapid solution deployment many times faster than traditional TDM solutions
- Single network, eliminating the overhead of multiple diverse data, voice, and video networks

Common Issues with QoS

Voice-over-packet networks can reduce cost and save bandwidth; however, these networks have unique QoS issues that you must consider. In a circuit-switched or time-division multiplexing (TDM) environment, bandwidth is dedicated, making QoS implicit. In a packet-switched environment, all kinds of traffic are mixed in a store-and-forward manner. So, in a packet-switched environment, a need exists to devise schemes to prioritize real-time traffic.

In an integrated voice and data network, QoS is essential to ensure the same high-quality voice transmissions as in a traditional circuit-switched environment. QoS issues for voice can be handled by VoIP, VoATM, or VoFR standards, or by an internetworking device.

Delay

Delay is the time required for packets to travel between two endpoints. In traditional data networking, delay can be tolerated with little or no impact on network users; however, in networks carrying voice traffic, delay is potentially quite significant because it can affect users' ability to carry on a telephone conversation. For example, delay can introduce pauses or gaps in the conversation, increasing the likelihood that one person will start talking before the other person is finished.

Because of the speed of network links and the limited processing power of many devices, some delay is expected. Telephone users normally accept up to approximately 150 milliseconds (ms) of one-way delay without noticing problems. You can measure delay using ping tests at various times of the day with different network traffic loads (see Figure 21-10). If network delay is excessive, you should reduce it before deploying a network that carries VoIP traffic.

Figure 21-10 QoS Issue: Delay

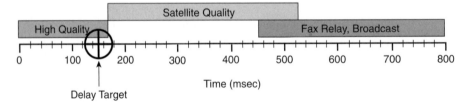

The types of delay most commonly found in today's telephony networks are as follows:

- **Propagation delay**—Propagation delay is caused by the characteristics of the speed of light traveling through fiber optic-based or copper-based media.
- **Handling delay**—Handling delay (sometimes called processing delay) defines many causes, such as compression delay, packet-switching delay, and packetization delay.
- **Serialization delay**—Serialization delay is the time it takes to actually place the bits onto an interface.

You can minimize delay using various Cisco IOS Software QoS tools, such as low-latency queuing and Point-to-Point Protocol (PPP) fragmentation.

Jitter

Jitter relates to variable interpacket timing caused by the network that a packet traverses. Simply stated, *jitter* is the variation of packet interarrival time. Removing jitter requires collecting packets and holding them long enough to allow the slowest packets to arrive in time to be played in the correct sequence, causing an additional delay.

Figure 21-11 shows that the amount of time required for packets A and B to send and receive is equal ($D_1 = D_2$). Packet C encounters more delay in the network ($D_3 ? D_2$) and is received after it is expected. This is why a jitter buffer, which conceals interarrival packet delay variation, is necessary.

Figure 21-11 QoS Issue: Jitter

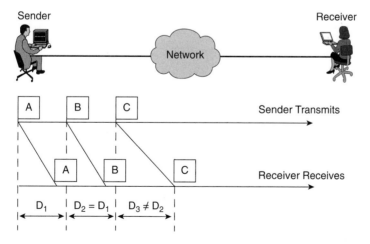

The jitter buffer in Cisco IOS Software is considered a dynamic queue. This queue can grow or shrink exponentially, depending on the voice packets' interarrival delay variations. Although many vendors choose to use static jitter buffers, Cisco has determined that a well-engineered dynamic jitter buffer is the best mechanism for packet-based voice networks. Static jitter buffers force the jitter buffer to be either too small or too large, causing the audio quality to suffer because of lost packets or excessive delays.

Lost Packets

Depending on the type of packet network, lost packets can be a significant problem. Because IP networks do not guarantee service, they usually exhibit a much higher incidence of lost voice packets than ATM networks.

Ideally, networks should be provisioned to have zero packet loss for applications such as voice and interactive video. For fax and modem traffic, very low loss is acceptable. Two sequential lost packets can cause a modem or fax call to drop. For VoIP calls from person to person, a much higher percent of packet loss is possible, but not desirable. To compensate, voice-over-packet software can send redundant information at the expense of bandwidth utilization.

Echo

Echo is present even in a conventional circuit-switched telephone network. This presence is typically acceptable because the round-trip delays through the network are smaller than 25 milliseconds (ms), and the echo is masked by the normal side tone that every telephone generates. Echo is caused by a conversion from two wires (local loop) to four wires and impedance mismatch.

Echo is a problem in voice-over-packet networks because the round-trip delay through the network is almost always greater than 25 ms. Hearing your own voice in the receiver after a delay of more than 25 ms can cause interruptions and break the cadence in a conversation. For this reason, echo-cancellation techniques must be used.

Echo-cancellation techniques compare voice data received from the packet network with voice data being transmitted to the packet network. For example, assume that user A is talking to user B. User A's speech to user B is called G. When G is echoed back to user A, user A can hear the delay several milliseconds after user A actually speaks.

To remove the echo from the line, the echo canceller keeps an inverse image of users A's speech for a certain amount of time; the echo canceller listens for the speech coming from user B and subtracts the G to remove any echo. In packet-based networks, echo cancellers can be built into the digital signal processor (DSP) or in software. Cisco includes all its echo cancellation on its DSP.

Cisco IOS Software QoS Technology

Cisco IOS Software provides QoS features and solutions for addressing the diverse needs of voice, video, and data applications. Cisco IOS QoS technology lets complex networks control and predictably service a variety of networked applications and traffic types.

The QoS features lead to efficient, predictable services for business-critical applications while ensuring high-quality VoIP services. As shown in Figure 21-12, with the QoS features enabled, the voice quality stays constant at a high level with varying network loads. In contrast, *not* implementing QoS makes the voice quality go down as the network load increases.

Figure 21-12 VoIP Traffic—QoS Enabled

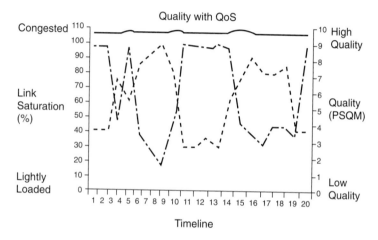

Summary

In this chapter, you learned the following key points:

- Traditionally, an enterprise has separate networks for data, voice, and video applications. Those networks usually operate in isolation and are often implemented and managed by separate teams.
- Integrated voice and data networks support a variety of applications, all of which are designed to replace leased lines at lower costs.
- VoFR is an inexpensive and easy-to-deploy service because of the wide availability of Frame Relay services.
- VoATM is an ideal transport for multiservice networks, particularly for customers who already have an ATM network installed.

- VoIP offers the capability to easily integrate advanced IP telephony features.
- A voice, video, and data-converged network lowers costs and provides enhanced quality options for voice networking.
- Cisco AVVID is an enterprise initiative for integrated data, voice, and video over a common IP transport.
- An important facet of converged networking is enabling new applications, such as desktop IP telephony, unified messaging, and the Cisco IP Contact Center.
- The Cisco IP Contact Center (IPCC) solution combines data and voice technologies to facilitate geographically independent multimedia customer interaction.
- Using QoS techniques throughout the network enables effective transmission of voice-over-packet switched networks. Through careful use of QoS techniques, network designers can overcome quality issues and produce circuit-quality voice at a fraction of the cost.

To supplement all that you've learned in this chapter, refer to the chapter-specific Videos, PhotoZooms, and e-Lab Activities on the CD-ROM accompanying this book.

Key Terms

AVVID (Cisco Architecture for Voice, Video and Integrated Data)   AVVID is a standards-based, open-systems architecture for converged networking. Cisco AVVID is an enterprise initiative for integrated data, voice, and video over a common IP transport.

Cisco IPCC (Cisco IP Contact Center)   The IPCC solution combines data and voice technologies to facilitate geographically independent multimedia customer interaction. This includes customer interactions originating from multiple, diverse contact channels, including IP voice, TDM voice, web, e-mail, and fax. Regardless of transport, whether the Internet or the traditional PSTN, the Cisco IPCC fully integrated, contact-center architecture services all media types. The Cisco IPCC architecture also provides a seamless migration path from the legacy call-center infrastructure to the IP-empowered, multimedia contact center.

converged network   When a single networks has been provisioned within an enterprise for data, voice, and video applications.

delay   The time it takes for packets to travel between two endpoints.

echo   Caused by a conversion from two wires (local loop) to four wires and impedance mismatch.

jitter   Relates to variable interpacket timing caused by the network that a packet traverses. Simply stated, jitter is the variation of packet interarrival time.

QoS) (quality of service)   Features that lead to efficient, predictable services for business-critical applications while ensuring high-quality Voice over IP services. With the QoS features enabled, the voice quality stays constant at a high level with varying network loads. In contrast, *not* implementing QoS means the voice quality goes down as the network load increases.

traditional network   When separate networks have been provisioned within an enterprise for data, voice, and video applications. These networks have been deployed autonomously and have operated in isolation, often implemented and managed by separate teams.

unified messaging   Combines voice mail, e-mail, and fax into a single application suite.

VoFR (Voice over Frame Relay)   Technology that consolidates voice and voice-band data (including fax and analog modems) with data services over a Frame Relay network.

VoIP (Voice over IP)   Voice is an application that runs over IP just like any other application. IP/User Datagram Protocol/Real-Time Transport Protocol (IP/UDP/ RTP) headers encapsulate voice information as it passes through the IP stack; the voice is de-encapsulated on the receiving side.

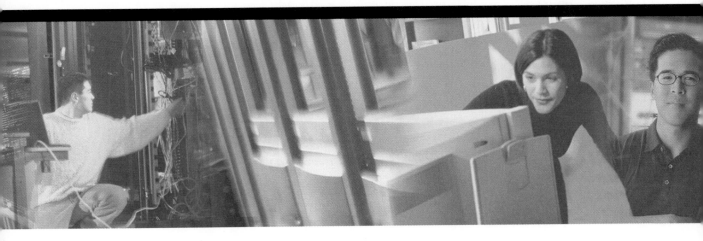

Objectives

After reading this chapter, you will be able to

- Describe network security design
- Describe security mechanisms
- Select security solutions

Chapter 22

Developing Network Security and Network Management Strategies

Security is one of the most important aspects of logical network design. Security is often overlooked during the design of a network because it is considered an operational issue rather than a design issue. However, if you consider security before you design your network, you can avoid scalability and performance problems that occur when security is added to the completed design. In addition, you can consider trade-offs while your network is still in the logical design phase, and you can plan a solution that can meet security goals.

You should complete security designs before starting the physical design phase because security designs might affect the physical design. This chapter helps you work with your network design customer to develop effective security strategies, and it helps you select the right tools and products to implement the strategies.

Network Security Design

To enterprise network designers, security is an especially hot topic these days because of increased Internet and extranet connections, increased e-commerce on the Internet, and more telecommuters and mobile users accessing enterprise networks from remote sites.

To help you address the issues that are associated with increasing security requirements, this chapter discusses the steps to develop a security strategy. This chapter also covers some common security techniques and solutions for typical security challenges, such as securing the Internet connection, dial-up network access, network services, and user services. You can find these techniques and solutions in RFC 1244.

The following steps help you design a network with security issues in mind:

Step 1   Identify network assets.

Step 2   Analyze security risks.

Step 3   Analyze security requirements and trade-offs.

Step 4   Develop a security plan.

Step 5   Define a security policy.

Step 6   Develop procedures for applying security policies.

Step 7   Develop a technical implementation strategy.

Step 8   Achieve buy-in from users, managers, and technical staff.

Step 9   Train users, managers, and technical staff.

Step 10   Implement the technical strategy and security procedures.

Step 11   Test the security and update it if any problems are found.

Step 12   Maintain security by scheduling periodic independent audits, reading audit logs, responding to incidents, reading current literature and agency alerts, continuing to test and train, and updating the security plan and policy.

Identifying Network Assets and Analyzing Risks

RFC 1244 states that *network assets* can include network hosts (including the hosts' operating systems, applications, and data), internetworking devices (such as routers and switches), and network data that traverses the network. Less obvious but still important, assets can include intellectual property, trade secrets, and a company's reputation.

Risks can range from hostile intruders to untrained users who download Internet applications that contain viruses. Hostile intruders can steal data, change data, and cause service to be denied to legitimate users. (These denial-of-service, or DoS, attacks have become increasingly common in the past few years.)

Analyzing Security Requirements and Trade-Offs

As is the case with most technical design requirements, achieving security goals means making trade-offs, as mentioned in RFC 1244. You must make trade-offs between security goals and goals for affordability, usability, performance, and availability. Also, security adds to the amount of management work because user login IDs, passwords, and audit logs must be maintained.

In addition, security affects network performance. Security features such as packet filters and data encryption consume CPU power and memory on hosts, routers, and servers.

Encryption can use upward of 15 percent of available CPU power on a router or server. Encryption can be implemented on dedicated devices instead of on shared routers or servers, but there is still an effect on network performance because of the delay that packets experience while they are being encrypted or decrypted.

Encryption can reduce network redundancy. If all traffic must go through an encryption device, the device becomes a single point of failure, which makes it difficult to meet availability goals. Encryption also makes it harder to offer load balancing. To maximize performance and minimize security complexity, a router that is running encryption should probably not offer load balancing. Load balancing can still be used, but only if it is done transparently to the routers that are providing encryption. Devices that are between routers offering encryption services can provide the load balancing.

Developing a Security Plan

RFC 1244 states that one of the first steps in security design is to develop a *security plan*. A security plan is a high-level document that proposes what an organization must do to meet security requirements. The plan specifies the time, people, and other resources that are required to develop a security policy and achieve technical implementation of the policy. As the network designer, you can help your customer develop a plan that is practical and pertinent. The plan should be based on the customer's goals and the analysis of network assets and risks.

A security plan should reference the network topology and include a list of network services that will be provided (such as FTP, web, e-mail, and so on). This list must specify who provides the services, who has access to the services, how access is provided, and who administers the services.

As the network designer, you help the customer evaluate which services are definitely needed based on the customer's business and technical goals. Sometimes new services are added unnecessarily simply because they are the latest trend. Adding services might require new packet filters on routers and firewalls to protect the services. Alternatively, it might necessitate additional user-authentication processes to limit access to the services, which would add complexity to the security strategy. Avoid overly complex security strategies because they can be self defeating. Complicated security strategies are difficult to implement correctly without introducing unexpected security holes.

One of the most important aspects of the security plan is a specification of the people who must be involved in implementing network security. Because of this, it is important to ask the following questions:

- Will specialized security administrators be hired?
- How will end users and their managers get involved?

■ How will end users, managers, and technical staff be trained on security policies and procedures?

For a security plan to be useful, it must have the support of all levels of employees within the organization. It is especially important for corporate management to fully support the security plan. Technical staff and end users at headquarters and at remote sites should buy into the plan.

Defining a Security Policy

NOTE

A security policy is a living document. Because organizations constantly change, security policies must be regularly updated to reflect new business directions and technological changes.

RFC 1244 states that a *security policy* is a formal statement of the rules by which people who are given access to an organization's technology and information assets must abide. A security policy informs users, managers, and technical staff of their obligations for protecting technology and information assets. The policy must specify the mechanisms by which these obligations can be met. Just like the security plan, employees, managers, executives, and technical personnel must buy into the security policy.

Developing a security policy is the job of security and network administrators. Administrators get input from managers, users, network designers and engineers, and possibly legal counsel. As a network designer, you must work closely with the security administrators to understand how policies might affect the network design.

After a security policy is developed with the engagement of users, staff, and management, top management should explain it to everyone. (Many enterprises require personnel to sign a statement indicating that they have read, understood, and agreed to abide by a policy.)

Components of a Security Policy

In general, a policy needs to include at least the following:

■ **An access policy**—Defines access rights and privileges. Should provide guidelines for connecting external networks, connecting devices to a network, and adding new software to systems.

■ **An accountability policy**—Defines the responsibilities of users, operations staff, and management. Should specify an audit capability and provide guidelines on reporting security problems.

■ **An authentication policy**—Establishes trust through an effective password policy and sets up guidelines for remote location authentication.

■ **Computer-technology purchasing guidelines**—Specify the requirements for acquiring, configuring, and auditing computer systems and networks for compliance with the policy.

Developing Security Procedures

Security procedures implement security policies. Procedures define configuration, login, audit, and maintenance processes. Security procedures should be written for end users, network administrators, and security administrators. These procedures should specify how to handle incidents (such as what to do and who to contact if an intrusion is detected). Security procedures can be communicated to users and administrators in instructor-led and self-paced training classes.

Security Mechanisms

This section describes some typical ingredients of secure network designs. You can select from these ingredients when you design solutions for common security challenges.

Authentication

Authentication identifies who requests network services. The term *authentication* usually refers to authenticating users, but it might also refer to verifying a software process. For example, some routing protocols support *route authentication*, when a router must pass some criteria before another router accepts its routing updates.

Most security policies state that to access a network and its services, a user must enter a login ID and a password that a security server authenticates. To maximize security, one-time (dynamic) passwords can be used. With one-time password systems, a user's password always changes. This is often accomplished with a security card. A *security card* is a physical device that is about the same size as a credit card. The user types a *personal identification number (PIN)* into the card. (The PIN is an initial level of security that gives the user permission to use the card.) The card provides a one-time password that accesses the corporate network for a limited time. The password is synchronized with a central security card server that resides on the network. Telecommuters and mobile users commonly use security cards. (Security cards are not usually used for LAN access.)

Authorization

Authentication controls who can access network resources, but *authorization* says what users or processes can do after they access the resources. Authorization lets a security administrator control parts of a network, such as directories and files on servers.

Authorization varies from user to user, partly depending on a user's department or job function. For example, a policy might state that only Human Resources employees should see salary records for people that they don't manage. Explicitly listing the authorized activities of each user with respect to every resource is difficult, so techniques are used to simplify the process. For example, a network manager can create user groups for users who have the same privileges.

Accounting (Auditing)

To effectively analyze the security of a network and to respond to security incidents, procedures should be established to collect network activity data. Collecting data is called *accounting* or *auditing*.

For networks that have strict security policies, audit data should include anyone's attempts to achieve authentication and authorization. It is especially important to log "anonymous" or "guest" access to public servers. The data should also log all attempts that users make to change their access rights.

The collected data should include usernames and host names for login and logout attempts, and previous and new access rights for a change of access rights. Each entry in the audit log should be timestamped.

A further extension of auditing is the concept of *security assessment*. With security assessment, professionals who are trained in the vulnerabilities that network invaders exploit internally examine the network. Part of any security policy and audit procedure should be periodic assessments of the vulnerabilities in a network. The result should be a specific plan for correcting deficiencies, which might be as simple as retraining staff.

Data Encryption

Encryption is a process that scrambles data to protect it from being read by anyone besides the intended receiver. An *encryption device* encrypts data before placing it on a network. A *decryption-device* decrypts the data before passing it to an application. A router, server, end system, or dedicated device can act as an encryption or decryption device.

Encryption is a useful security feature because it provides data confidentiality. It also can be used to identify the sender of data. Although authentication and authorization should protect the confidentiality of data and identify senders, encryption is a good security feature to implement, just in case the other types fail.

Encryption should be used when a customer has analyzed security risks and identified severe consequences if data is not confidential and if the identity of senders of data is not guaranteed. On internal networks and networks that use the Internet simply for web browsing, e-mail, and file transfer, encryption is usually not necessary. For organizations that connect private sites via the Internet by using virtual private networking (VPN), encryption is recommended to protect the confidentiality of the organization's data.

CAUTION

The audit process should not collect passwords. Collecting passwords creates a potential security breach if the audit records are improperly accessed. (Neither correct nor incorrect passwords should be collected. An incorrect password often differs from a valid password by only a single character or a transposition of characters.)

NOTE

Data that is encrypted is called *ciphered data* (or simply encrypted data). Data that is not encrypted is called *plain text* or *clear text*.

Encryption has two parts:

- **Encryption algorithm**—A set of instructions to scramble and unscramble data
- **Encryption key**—A code that an algorithm uses to scramble and unscramble data

Children sometimes play with encryption by using a simple algorithm, such as "find the letter on the top row and use the letter on the bottom row instead." A key might look something like this:

```
A B C D E F G H I J K L M N O P Q R S T U V W X Y Z
I N B Y G L S P T A R W Q H X M D K F U O C Z V E J
```

In this example, LISA is encrypted as WTFI. The key shows only uppercase letters, but many other possibilities are likely, including lowercase letters and digits.

The goal of encryption is that, even if the algorithm is known, an intruder cannot interpret the message without the appropriate key. This type of key is called a *secret key*. When both the sender and the receiver use the same secret key, it is called a *symmetric key*. The Data Encryption Standard (DES) is the best-known example of a symmetric key system. DES encryption is available for most routers and many server implementations.

Although secret keys are reasonably simple to implement between two devices, as the number of devices increases, the number of secret keys also increases, which can be difficult to manage. For example, a session between Station A and Station B uses a different key than a session between Station A and Station C, and so on. Asymmetric keys can solve this problem.

Public/Private Key Encryption

Public/private key encryption is the best-known example of an asymmetric key system. With public/private key systems, each secure station on a network has a public key that is openly published or easily determined. All devices can use a station's public key to encrypt data to send to the station.

The receiving station decrypts the data using its own private key. Because no other device has the station's private key, no other device can decrypt the data; therefore, data confidentiality is maintained. (Mathematicians and computer scientists have written computer programs that identify special numbers to use for the keys so that both the sender and the receiver can use the same algorithm, even though different keys are used.) Figure 22-1 shows a public/private key system for data confidentiality.

Figure 22-1 A Public/Private Key System Ensures Data Confidentiality

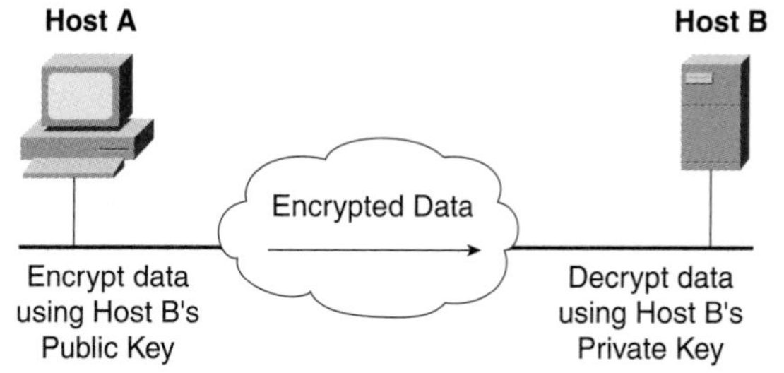

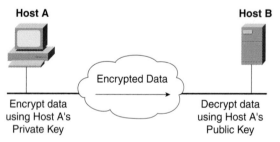

Public/private key systems provide both confidentiality and authentication features. Using asymmetric keys, a recipient can verify that a document actually came from the user or host that it appears to have come from. For example, you are sending your tax returns to the Internal Revenue Service (IRS). The IRS needs to know that the returns came from you and not from a hostile third party that wants to make it look like you owe more than you do.

You can encrypt your document or a part of your document with your private key, resulting in what is known as a *digital signature*. The IRS can decrypt the document by using your public key, as shown in Figure 22-2. If the decryption is successful, the document definitely came from you because no one else should have your private key.

Figure 22-2 A Public/Private Key System for Sending a Digital Signature

You can use the digital signature feature of asymmetric keys with the feature for data confidentiality. After you encrypt your document with your private key, you also can encrypt the document with the IRS's public key. The IRS decrypts the document twice. If the result is plain-text data, the IRS knows that the document came from you and that you meant for the document to go to no one but the IRS.

Some examples of asymmetric key systems include the Rivest, Shamir, and Adleman (RSA) standard; the Diffie-Hellman public key algorithm; and the Digital Signature Standard (DSS). Cisco Systems uses the DSS standard to authenticate peer routers during the setup of an encrypted session. The peer routers use the Diffie-Hellman algorithm to send information on a secret key, which encrypts data. The actual data is encrypted by using the DES algorithm and the secret key.

Packet Filters

Packet filters can be set up on routers and servers to permit or deny packets from particular addresses or services. Packet filters augment authentication and authorization mechanisms. They help protect network resources from unauthorized use, theft, destruction, and DoS attacks.

A security policy should state whether packet filters implement one of the following policies:

- Deny specific types of packets and accept all else.
- Accept specific types of packets and deny all else.

The first policy requires a thorough understanding of specific security threats and can be hard to implement. The second policy is easier to implement and more secure because the security administrator does not have to predict future attacks for which packets should be denied. The second policy is also easier to test because there is a finite set of accepted uses of the network. To do a good job of implementing the second policy, you must have a thorough understanding of network requirements. The network designer should work with the security administrator to determine what types of packets should be accepted.

Cisco implements the second policy in its packet filters, which Cisco calls *access control lists (ACLs)*. An ACL on a router or switch that is running the Cisco Internetwork Operating System (IOS) Software always has an implicit **deny-any** statement at the end. Specific **permit** and **deny** statements are processed before the implicit **deny-any** statement. (The statement is implicit because the administrator does not actually have to enter it; although, it is a good idea to enter it to make the behavior of the list more obvious.)

ACLs allows you to control whether network traffic is forwarded or blocked at interfaces on a router or switch. ACL definitions provide criteria to be applied to packets that enter or exit an interface. Typical criteria can include the packet source address, the packet destination address, or the upper-layer protocol in the packet.

Because Cisco IOS Software tests a packet against each criteria statement in the list until a match is found, ACLs should be designed with care to provide good performance. By studying traffic flow, you can design the list so that most packets match the earliest conditions. Fewer conditions to check per packet means better throughput. Good advice for ACLs: Order the list with the most general statements at the top and the most specific statements at the bottom, with the last statement being the general, implicit **deny-any** statement.

Firewalls

A *firewall* is a system or combination of systems that enforces security policies at the boundary that separates two or more networks. A firewall can be a router with ACLs, a dedicated hardware box, or software that is running on a PC or UNIX system. Firewalls are especially important at the boundary between the enterprise network and the Internet.

Intrusion Detection

Intrusion detection refers to the real-time monitoring of network activity and analysis of data for potential vulnerabilities and attacks in progress. Internal, authorized users who conduct unauthorized activity on the network—such as trying to transmit confidential documents over the Internet or illegally modifying network access privileges—can be detected in real time and stopped immediately. An external intruder who tries to break into the network can be handled in the same manner.

Real-time capability (as opposed to a periodic review of log files) can significantly reduce potential damage and recovery costs of an attack by eliminating the intruder from the network. A good intrusion system has the following characteristics:

- It must run continually without human supervision. The system must be reliable enough to allow it to run in the background of the system that is being observed.
- It must be fault tolerant; that is, it must survive a system crash and not require its knowledge base to be rebuilt at restart.
- It must resist subversion. The system can monitor itself to ensure that it has not been subverted.
- It must impose minimal overhead on the system. A system that slows a computer to a crawl will not be used.
- It must observe deviations from normal behavior and immediately alert someone if abnormal behavior occurs.
- It must cope with changing system behavior over time as new applications are added.

The capability to write customized detection rules for proprietary purposes should also be of interest to you. You might want to write customized detection rules to prevent a document that is labeled "confidential" from being e-mailed outside the network or to address vulnerabilities for custom or legacy systems. Such customization allows the system to be modified for use in almost any environment, even if those uses are not common enough to be included as standard features of a commercial product.

Physical Security

RFC 1244 states that *physical security* refers to limiting access to key network resources by keeping the resources behind a locked door. Physical security also refers to protecting resources from natural disasters such as floods, fires, storms, and earthquakes. Because physical security is such an obvious requirement, it is easy to forget to plan for it, but you should never overlook it or consider it less important than other goals.

Depending on your particular network design customer, physical security should be installed to protect core routers, demarcation points, cabling, modems, servers, hosts, backup storage, and so on. Work with your customer during the early stages of the network design project to make sure equipment will be placed in computer rooms that have card key access or security guards. Computer rooms should also be equipped with uninterruptible power supplies, fire alarms, fire abatement mechanisms, and water removal systems. To protect equipment from earthquakes and high winds during storms, equipment should be installed in racks that attach to the floor or wall.

Selecting Security Solutions

The previous section described some typical ingredients of network security designs. This section provides a few recipes for putting the ingredients together to meet the following security challenges:

- Securing the Internet connection
- Securing dial-up access
- Securing network services
- Securing user services

Securing the Internet Connection

The Internet connection should be secured with a set of overlapping security mechanisms, including firewalls, packet filters, physical security, audit logs, authentication, and authorization. Public servers, such as the World Wide Web and possibly File Transfer Protocol (FTP) servers, can allow unauthenticated access, but all other servers should require authentication and authorization. Public servers should be placed on a free-trade–zone network that is protected from other networks via firewalls.

If a customer can afford two separate servers, security experts recommend that FTP services should not run on the same server as web services. FTP users have more opportunities for reading and possibly changing files than web users. A hacker could use FTP to damage a company's website, thus damaging the company's image and possibly compromising web-based e-commerce and other applications. Security experts recommend that you never allow Internet access to Trivial File Transfer Protocol (TFTP) servers because TFTP offers no authentication features. Experts also recommend disabling ports and services that are not used or that are not essential.

Add Common Gateway Interface (CGI) scripts or other types of scripts to web servers with great care. Thoroughly test scripts for security leaks. Install e-commerce applications on web servers only if the applications are compatible with the Secure Socket Layer (SSL) standard.

E-mail servers have long been a source for intruder break-ins, probably because e-mail protocols and implementations have been around for a while and hackers can easily understand them. In addition, by its very nature, an e-mail server must allow outsider access. To secure e-mail servers, network administrators should keep up-to-date on well-known bugs and security leaks by subscribing to mailing lists that are dedicated to security information. It is important to keep up with installation of security patches. The SQL Slammer worm that disrupted the Internet might have been avoided if administrators of Microsoft SQL Servers had installed a security fix that had been available for more than six months.

Securing Internet Domain Name System Services

Domain Name System (DNS) servers should be carefully controlled and monitored. Name-to-address resolution is critical to the operation of any network. An attacker who can successfully control or impersonate a DNS server can wreak havoc on a network. DNS servers should be protected from security attacks by using packet filters on routers, as well as versions of DNS software that incorporate security features.

Traditionally, DNS had no security capabilities. In particular, there was no way to verify information that was returned in a DNS response to a query. A hacker could hijack the query and return a counterfeit name-to-address mapping. Digital signatures and other security features are being added to the protocol to address this issue and other security concerns.

Logical Network Design and the Internet Connection

A good rule for enterprise networks is that the network should have well-defined exit and entry points. An organization that has only one Internet connection can manage

Internet-security problems more easily than an organization that has many Internet connections. Some large organizations require more than one Internet connection for performance and redundancy reasons, however. This is fine as long as the connections are managed and monitored. Departments or users who add Internet connections without coordination from corporate network engineers should not be tolerated.

When selecting routing protocols for the Internet connection, to maximize security, you should select a protocol that offers route authentication (such as RIP version 2, OSPF, or BGP4). Static and default routing is also a good option because, with static and default routing, no routing updates could be compromised. Internet routers should be equipped with packet filters to prevent DoS attacks.

When securing the Internet connection, network address translation (NAT) can be used to protect internal network addressing schemes. NAT hides internal network numbers from outside networks and translates internal network numbers when outside access is required.

Organizations that use VPN services to connect private sites via the Internet should use NAT, firewalls, and data encryption. In VPN topologies, private data travels across the public Internet, so encryption is a must. The Layer 2 Tunneling Protocol (L2TP) is an Internet Engineering Task Force (IETF) standard for tunneling private data over public networks.

IP Security Protocol

The *IP Security Protocol (IPSec)* is a set of open standards that provides data confidentiality, data integrity, and authentication between participating peers at the IP layer. As IPSec gains industry acceptance, customers require support for it in internetworking products that they purchase. (IPSec is documented in RFCs 1825 through 1829.)

IPSec enables a system to select security protocols and algorithms and establish cryptographic keys. The Internet Key Exchange (IKE) protocol provides authentication of IPSec peers and negotiates IPSec keys and security associations. IKE uses the following technologies:

- **DES**—Encrypts packet data.
- **Diffie-Hellman**—Establishes a shared, secret session key.
- **Message Digest 5 (MD5)**—A one-way hashing algorithm that produces a 128-bit hash to authenticates packet data. Cisco uses hashes for authentication within the IPSec framework. Also used for message authentication in SNMP v.2. MD5 verifies the integrity of the communication, authenticates the origin, and checks for timeliness.

NOTE

Repudiation is a security feature that prevents a third party from proving that communication between two other parties took place. This is a desirable feature if you do not want your communication to be traceable. *Nonrepudiation* is just the opposite: A third party can prove that communication between two other parties took place. Nonrepudiation is desirable if you want to trace your communications and prove that they occurred.

- **Secure Hash Algorithm (SHA)**—Authenticates packet data by taking a message of less than 264 bits in length and producing a 160-bit message digest. The large message digest provides security against brute-force collision and inversion attacks.

- **RSA encrypted nonces**—Provides repudiation.

- **RSA signatures**—Provides nonrepudiation.

Securing Dial-Up Access

Security is critical for dial-up access. It should consist of firewall technologies, physical security, authentication and authorization mechanisms, auditing capabilities, and possibly encryption. Authentication and authorization are the most important features for dial-up access security. One-time passwords with security cards make sense in this arena.

Remote users and remote routers that use the Point-to-Point Protocol (PPP) should be authenticated with the Challenge Handshake Authentication Protocol (CHAP). The Password Authentication Protocol (PAP) offers less security than CHAP and is not recommended.

Another option for authentication, authorization, and accounting is the *Remote Authentication Dial-In User Server (RADIUS) protocol.* Livingston, Inc. developed RADIUS a few years ago; it has become an industry standard and is documented in RFC 2138 and RFC 2856. RADIUS gives an administrator the option of having a centralized database of user information. The database includes authentication and configuration information and specifies the type of service permitted by a user (for example, PPP, Telnet, rlogin, and so on). RADIUS is a client/server protocol. An access server acts as a client of a RADIUS server.

Dial-up services should be strictly controlled. Users should not be allowed to attach modems and analog lines to their own workstations or servers. (Some companies actually fire employees who do this.) It is helpful to have a single dial-in point (for example, a single large modem pool or access server) so that all users are authenticated in the same way. A different set of modems should be used for any dial-out services. Both dial-in and dial-out services should be authenticated.

If the modems and access servers support *callback* (which most do), it should be used. With callback, when a user dials in and is authenticated, the system disconnects the call and calls back on a specified number. Callback is useful because the system calls back the actual user, not a hacker who might be masquerading as the user. Callback can easily be compromised, however, and should not be the only security mechanism used.

Many operational security considerations with dial-up networks are outside the scope of a design book. Suffice it to say that modems and access servers should be carefully configured and protected from hackers who are reconfiguring them. Modems should be programmed to reset to the standard configuration at the start and end of each call, and modems and access servers should terminate calls cleanly. Servers should force a logout if the user hangs up unexpectedly.

Securing Network Services

Many of the recommendations for securing the Internet connection also apply to securing internal enterprise networks. Internal network services can make use of authentication and authorization, packet filters, audit logs, physical security, encryption, and so on.

To protect internal network services, it is important to protect internetworking devices, such as routers and switches. Login IDs and passwords should be required to access these devices whether the user accesses the device through a console port or through the network. Administrators who simply need to check the status of the devices can use a first-level password. Administrators who have permission to view or change configurations should use a second-level password.

If modem access to the console ports of internetworking devices is allowed, the modems must be secured just as standard dial-in user modems are, and the phone numbers should be unlisted and unrelated to the organization's main number. The phone numbers should also be changed when staff changes occur.

For customers who have numerous routers and switches, a protocol such as the *Terminal Access Controller Access Control System (TACACS)* can be used to manage large numbers of router and switch user IDs and passwords in a centralized database. Newer versions of TACACS include XTACACS and TACACS+. TACACS also offers auditing features.

Limiting the use of the Simple Network Management Protocol (SNMP) should be considered on enterprise networks where security goals outweigh manageability goals. One of the main issues with SNMP is the **set** operation that allows a remote station to change management and configuration data. SNMP version 3 (SNMPv3) supports authentication for use with the **set** operation and other SNMP operations.

As in the case with Internet connections, internal networks should run the most secure versions of DNS, FTP, and web software. Implementations of Network Information Service (NIS) and other types of naming and addressing servers also should be carefully selected based on the level of security offered.

Although it is obvious that services within a network (such as file servers) should require authentication and authorization, it might be less obvious that the network should also require these security mechanisms. Before a user can get to the point of logging into servers, the user should first be required to log into the network.

Securing User Services

User services include end systems, applications, hosts, file servers, database servers, and other services. File servers and other servers should offer authentication and authorization features. End systems can also offer these features if users are concerned about other people using their systems. Users should be encouraged to log out of sessions when leaving their desks for long periods of time and to turn off their machines when leaving work to protect against unauthorized people walking up to a system and accessing services and applications. Automatic logouts can also be deployed to automatically log out a session that has had no activity for a period of time. Another way to secure a workstation is to use a screensaver with password protection. Some screen savers allow workers to enter a password to cancel the screensaver and return to the desktop.

Security policies and procedures should specify accepted practices regarding passwords: when they should be used, how they should be formatted, and how they can be changed. In general, passwords should include both letters and numbers, should be at least six characters, should not be a "common" word, and should be changed often.

On servers, root password knowledge (or the non-UNIX equivalent) should be limited to a few people. If possible, guest accounts should be avoided. Protocols that support the concept of trust in other hosts should be used with caution. (Examples include rlogin and rsh on UNIX systems.) Hosts that permit guest accounts and support trusted hosts should be isolated from other hosts, if possible.

Kerberos is an authentication system that provides user-to-host security for application-level protocols such as FTP and Telnet. If the application requests it, Kerberos can also provide encryption. Kerberos relies on a symmetric key database that uses a key distribution center (KDC) on a Kerberos server. See the Kerberos Frequently Asked Questions (FAQ) document for the latest information on Kerberos (available at www.cmf.nrl.navy.mil/CCS/people/kenh/kerberos-faq.html).

A security policy should specify which applications are allowed to run on networked PCs and should give guidelines restricting the downloading of unknown applications from the Internet or other sites. Security procedures also should specify how users can install and update virus-protection software; virus protection is one of the most important aspects of user-services security.

Depending on the network topology, user-services security might incorporate encryption. Encryption is sometimes done at servers and end systems instead of within the network. Vendors such as Microsoft, Netscape, and Sun Microsystems offer encryption software for end systems, workstations, and servers.

To guarantee security at the user-services level, known security bugs in applications and network operating systems should be identified and fixed. Administrators should be required to stay current on the latest hacker tricks and viruses.

Summary

As a network designer, your goal is to help your customers develop strategies and processes for implementing security. You should also help your customers select tools and products to implement these strategies and processes. Security is a major concern for most customers because of the increase in Internet connectivity and Internet applications and because more users access the enterprise network from remote sites.

This chapter provided information to help you select the right processes and tools to meet a customer's goals for network security. The tasks involved with security design parallel the tasks involved with overall network design: analyzing requirements and goals, making trade-offs, characterizing network traffic flow, and developing an appropriate topology.

Security is often overlooked during the design of a network because it is considered an operational issue rather than a design issue. By considering security issues up front instead of waiting until the end of the design process or after the network is operational; however, your design will be more scalable and robust.

Key Terms

accounting (auditing)   The process of keeping track of a user's activity while accessing a network's resources, including the amount of time spent in the network, the services accessed while there, and the amount of data transferred during the session.

ACL (access control list)   A set of data that informs a computer's operating system which permissions, or access rights, that each user or group has to a specific system object, such as a directory or file.

authentication   The process of identifying an individual, usually based on a username and password.

authorization   The process of granting or denying access to a network resource.

callback   Callback is a method of verifying authentication where the system disconnects the call and calls back on a specified number, when a user dials in and is authenticated.

ciphered data   Data that is encrypted.

decryption-device   A device that makes data unreadable before passing it to an application. A router, server, end system, or dedicated device can act as an encryption or decryption device.

digital signature   A system in which software such as a document or e-mail has been encrypted with your private key.

encryption   A process that scrambles data to protect it from being read by anyone besides the intended receiver.

encryption device   A device that makes the data readable before placing it on a network.

firewall   A system or combination of systems that enforces security policies at the boundary between two or more networks.

intrusion detection   The real-time monitoring of network activity and analysis of data for potential vulnerabilities and attacks in progress.

IPSec (IP Security Protocol   A set of open standards that provides data confidentiality, data integrity, and authentication between participating peers at the IP layer.

Kerberos   An authentication system that provides user-to-host security for application-level protocols such as FTP and Telnet.

network assets   Can include network hosts (including the hosts' operating systems, applications, and data), internetworking devices (such as routers and switches), and network data that traverses the network. Less obvious but still important, assets can include intellectual property, trade secrets, and a company's reputation.

nonrepudiation   A system by which a third party can prove that a communication between two other parties took place. Nonrepudiation is desirable if you want to trace your communications and prove that they occurred.

packet filters   Filters that can be set up on routers and servers to permit or deny packets from particular addresses or services. Packet filters augment authentication and authorization mechanisms.

physical security   Limiting access to key network resources by keeping the resources behind a locked door. Physical security also refers to protecting resources from natural disasters such as floods, fires, storms, and earthquakes.

PIN (personal identification number   An initial level of security that gives the user permission to use the card. The card provides a one-time password that accesses the corporate network for a limited time.

plain text (clear text)   Data that is not encrypted.

RADIUS (Remote Authentication Dial-In User Server) protocol   A secure authentication protocol that gives an administrator the option of having a centralized database of user information. The database includes authentication and configuration information and specifies the type of service permitted by a user (such as PPP, Telnet, rlogin, and so on).

repudiation   A security feature that prevents a third party from proving that a communication between two other parties took place. This is a desirable feature if you do not want your communication to be traceable.

route authentication   An form of authentication that is used when a router must pass some criteria before another router accepts its routing updates.

secret key   A device that protects encryption by using an encryption algorithm so that an intruder cannot interpret the message without the appropriate key.

security assessment   A process in which the network is internally examined by professionals who are trained in the vulnerabilities exploited by network invaders.

security card   A physical device that is approximately the same size as a credit card and can be used to restrict access to rooms or computers.

security plan   A high-level document that proposes what an organization must do to meet security requirements.

security policy   A policy that states whether packet filters implement denying specific types of packets and accepting all else or accepting specific types of packets and denying all else.

symmetric key   A Public/Private key method in which both the sender and the receiver use the same secret key.

TACACS (Terminal Access Controller Access Control System)   A security protocol for customers who have numerous routers and switches, which can be used to manage large numbers of router and switch user IDs and passwords in a centralized database. TACACS also offers auditing features.

Objectives

After reading this chapter, you will be able to

- Describe Virtual Private Network (VPN) operation
- Describe VPN implementation
- Describe Cisco Systems VPNs
- Describe tunneling
- Describe Cisco Layer 2 Tunneling Protocol (L2TP) implementation
- Describe the end-to-end virtual dial-up process
- Describe highlights of the virtual dial-up service

Chapter 23

Virtual Private Networks

Networking is driven by the need to enable communications between applications and individuals in a faster, cheaper, and more robust way. In the majority of cases, networking is not driven by the need to handle these communications securely. Virtual private networking establishes a clear case for security as an enabler and a basic mechanism to do something new and different: to use public networks for private communications.

VPN Operation

A *virtual private network (VPN)* is a communications environment in which access is controlled to permit peer connections only within a defined community of interest. A VPN is constructed through some form of partitioning of a common underlying communications medium. This communications medium provides services to the network on a non-exclusive basis. A simpler, more approximate, and less formal definition of a VPN follows:

> A VPN is a private network that is constructed within a public network infrastructure, such as the global Internet.

VPNs can be constructed to address a number of specific business needs or technical requirements. A comprehensive VPN solution provides:

- Support for dial-in and other remote access
- Support for multiple remote sites connected by leased lines (or other dedicated means)
- Capability of the VPN service provider to host various services for the VPN customers (such as web hosting)
- Capability to support not just intra-VPN connectivity, but also inter-VPN connectivity, including connectivity, to the global Internet

VPN Advantages

Virtual private networking has significant advantages over previous forms of channel encryption and alternatives. Some of these advantages include the following:

- A single virtual private networking technology can provide privacy for multiple Transmission Control Protocol/Internet Protocol (TCP/IP) applications. Application-level encryption requires different methods for different services. Support for multiple protocols is also possible through tunneling IP using Point-to-Point Tunneling Protocol (PPTP), L2TP, or Layer 2 Forwarding (L2F) Protocol. Providing privacy for multiple TCP/IP applications is especially important in environments where you want to provide secure access for partners or telecommuters.

- Encryption services can be provided for all TCP/IP communications between the trusted client and the virtual private networking server. This has the advantage of being transparent to the end user. Because encryption is turned on, the server can enforce it.

Types of VPNs

A VPN is defined as customer connectivity deployed on a shared infrastructure with the same policies as a private network. (See Figure 23-1.) The shared infrastructure can leverage a service provider Internet Protocol (IP), Frame Relay, Asynchronous Transfer Mode (ATM) backbone, or the Internet. Three types of VPNs align how businesses and organizations use VPNs:

- *Access VPN*—Provides remote access to a corporate intranet or extranet over a shared infrastructure with the same policies as a private network. Access VPNs enable users to access corporate resources whenever, wherever, and however they require. Access VPNs encompass analog, dial, Integrated Services Digital Network (ISDN), digital subscriber line (DSL), mobile IP, and cable technologies to securely connect mobile users, telecommuters, or branch offices.

- *Intranet VPN*—Links corporate headquarters, remote offices, and branch offices over a shared infrastructure by using dedicated connections. Businesses enjoy the same policies as a private network, including security, quality of service (QoS), manageability, and reliability.

- *Extranet VPN*—Links customers, suppliers, partners, or communities of interest to a corporate intranet over a shared infrastructure by using dedicated connections. Businesses enjoy the same policies as a private network, including security, QoS, manageability, and reliability.

Figure 23-1 A Logical Topology View of a VPN

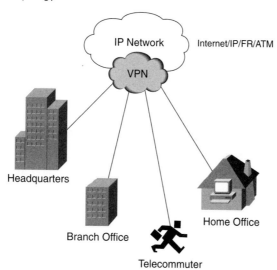

Service-Level Agreements

At this point, it is worthwhile to briefly examine the importance of *service-level agreements (SLAs)* regarding the deployment of VPNs. SLAs are negotiated contracts between VPN providers and their subscribers; they contain the service criteria to which the subscriber expects specific services to be delivered. The SLA is arguably the only binding tool at the subscriber's disposal to ensure that the VPN provider delivers the services to the level and quality agreed to; it is in the subscriber's best interest to monitor the criteria outlined in the SLA for compliance. However, SLAs present some challenging technical issues for both the provider and the subscriber.

For the subscriber, the challenge of SLAs is to devise and operate service-measurement tools that can provide a reasonable indication of the extent to which the provider honors the SLA. Note that a subscriber might use an SLA to bind one or more providers to a contractual service level, but if the subscriber's VPN spans multiple providers' domains, the SLA must also encompass the issue of provider interconnection and end-to-end service performance.

For the provider, the challenge of SLAs lies in honoring multiple SLAs from a number of service providers. In the case of an Internet public data network provider, the common mode of best-effort service levels is not conducive to meeting SLAs, given the unpredictable nature of the host's resource-allocation mechanisms. In such environments, either the provider must ensure that the network is generously engineered in terms of the ratio of subscriber access capacity to internal switching capacity, or the provider can deploy service differentiation structures to ensure that minimum resource levels are allocated to each SLA subscriber. Note that the first course of action tends to reduce the benefit of aggregation of traffic, which has an ultimate cost implication; the second course of action has implications in terms of operational management complexity and scalability of the network.

An Example VPN

In the example illustrated in Figure 23-2, Network A sites have established a VPN (depicted by the dashed lines) across the service provider's backbone network, whereas Network B is completely unaware of its existence. Networks A and B harmoniously coexist on the same backbone infrastructure.

Figure 23-2 A Virtual Private Network of A Sites

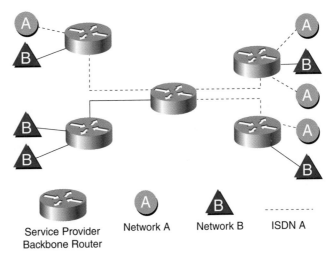

Service Provider Backbone Router   Network A   Network B   ISDN A

NOTE

The concept of virtualization in networking has also been considered in regard to deploying both research and production services on a common infrastructure. The challenge in the research and education community is how to satisfy both network research and production requirements.

VPNs of Network A Sites

The most common type of VPN has geographically diverse subnetworks that belong to a common administrative domain, interconnected by a shared infrastructure outside their administrative control (such as the global Internet or a single service provider backbone). The principal motivation in establishing a VPN of this type is that most of the communications between devices within the VPN community might be sensitive. (Again, a decision on the required level of privacy rests solely on a risk analysis that the administrators of the VPN perform.) Yet, the total value of the communications system does not justify the investment in a fully private communications system that uses discrete transmission elements.

On a related note, the level of privacy that a VPN might enjoy depends greatly on the technology that is used to construct the VPN. For example, if the communications between each VPN subnetwork (or between each VPN host) are securely encrypted as they transit the common communications infrastructure, then the privacy aspect of the VPN is relatively high.

In fact, the granularity of a VPN implementation can be broken down to a single end-to-end, one-to-one connectivity scenario. Examples of these types of one-to-one VPNs are single dial-up users who establish a VPN connection to a secure application (such as an online banking service), or a single user establishing a secure, encrypted session between a desktop and a server application (such as a purchasing transaction conducted on the Internet). This type of one-to-one VPN becomes more prevalent as secure electronic commerce applications become more mature and are further deployed in the Internet.

VPNs also have been considered as a method to segregate traffic in a network so that research and production traffic behave as ships in the night, oblivious to one another's existence. VPNs are so oblivious that major events, such as major failures or instability, within one community of interest are completely transparent to the other.

VPNs can be constructed to span more than one host communications network so that the state of the VPN can be supported on one or more VPN provider networks. This scenario is perhaps at its most robust when all the providers explicitly support the resultant distributed VPN environment. However, other solutions that do not necessarily involve knowledge of the overlay VPN are occasionally deployed with mixed results.

VPN Implementation

After you have made the decision to implement a VPN, you must take steps to ensure that the infrastructure is adequately secured and that the application and its goals are well defined before beginning implementation.

Security Audit

Running a security audit ensures that vulnerability in a firewall, remote-access application, or an authentication method is not exposed to a wider audience after the VPN implementation. These security issues justify a full audit of at least the network's perimeter, which might be attacked from inside and outside. This evaluation should audit all inbound connections to the intranet, including remote-access servers, router-based connections to subsidiaries, and extranet connections. In the case of an extranet VPN, this evaluation should also include the perimeter of an enterprise's partner organizations.

The Scope and Application Needs

After a security audit is performed, you must define the scope of the VPN by identifying the end user constituencies (such as partners, contractors, or telecommuters) that might access the VPN and the applications. This step includes evaluating the applications that the constituents will use and the sensitivity of the data they will transmit. Evaluating these applications allows for the selection of appropriate security services and adequate encryption.

Next, you must define and test the latency and QoS needs of all the applications that the VPN will support. Even applications that might be considered store-and-forward applications can have latency sensitivities in some configurations. These sensitivities affect whether the application is feasible for the VPN and help determine the nature of the underlying network.

Documentation

In the case of the extranet VPN, the enterprise should draft a statement of understanding for the extranet VPN users. In the remote-access case, the enterprise should update its remote-access policy to ensure that it incorporates this new form of access.

Security Policy

In the extranet case, for example, a virtual private networking policy regulates authentication and authorization.

Authorization should be based on generic roles that are defined by participating enterprises. (These roles should be mapped to individuals in the participating enterprises.) The generic role should have basic privileges—including network access and web server access—to the stock levels of the suppliers' products. These roles should then be mapped to a defined set of data and enforced through the VPN. Extranet policy should be incorporated in a statement of understanding among the involved users.

The virtual private networking remote-access policy should not differ radically from the already established remote-access policy. Key differences from traditional remote-access policy can include an "acceptable use" for access to the Internet, where applicable. Just as any Internet-based access should also have two-factor, token-based authentication in place, the policy should include a statement about how these tokens can be used most securely.

The Cisco Systems VPN Design

Cisco end-to-end hardware and Cisco IOS Software networking products provide sophisticated security for sensitive private transmissions over the public infrastructure, QoS through traffic differentiation, reliability for mission-critical applications, scalability for supporting large bandwidths of data, and comprehensive network management to enable a complete access VPN solution.

The following sections discuss how Cisco network access servers (NASs) and routers with Cisco IOS Software provide new functionality with virtual dial-up services. This functionality is based on the L2F protocol Internet Engineering Task Force (IETF) draft Request For Comments (RFC 2341). The L2F Protocol provided a standards-based tunneling mechanism for transporting link layer frames of higher-layer protocols, such as High-Level Data Link Control (HDLC), async Point-to-Point Protocol (PPP), Serial Line Internet Protocol (SLIP), or PPP ISDN. As of today, L2F has been combined with PPTP and essentially replaced by L2TP. *L2TP* is an extension to the PPP protocol that enables ISPs to operate VPNs. L2TP merges the best features of two other tunneling protocols: PPTP from Microsoft and L2F from Cisco Systems. Like PPTP, L2TP requires that the ISP's routers support the protocol. By using such tunnels, it is possible to divorce the location of the initial dial-up server from the location at which the dial-up protocol connection is terminated and the location at which access to the network is provided (usually a corporate gateway).

Tunneling Overview

A key component of the virtual dial-up service is *tunneling*, a vehicle that encapsulates packets inside a protocol that is understood at the entry and exit points of a given network. These entry and exit points are defined as *tunnel interfaces*. The tunnel interface is similar to a hardware interface but is configured in software.

The following sections supply additional detail about the interworkings and Cisco's implementation of L2TP. Using L2TP tunneling, an Internet service provider (ISP), or another access service can create a virtual tunnel to link customer's remote sites or remote users with corporate home networks. The L2TP access concentrator (LAC) that is located at the ISP's point of presence (POP) exchanges PPP messages with remote users and communicates by way of L2TP requests and responses with the customer's L2TP network server (LNS) to set up tunnels. L2TP passes protocol-level packets through the virtual tunnel between endpoints of a point-to-point connection. Frames from remote users are accepted by the ISP's POP, stripped of any linked framing or

NOTE

Currently, no standards exist that outline the software and hardware components of a VPN. Every vendor that provides a VPN service performs it in a method that is best supported by its own hardware platforms and software applications.

transparency bytes, encapsulated in L2TP, and forwarded over the appropriate tunnel. The customer's home gateway accepts these L2TP frames, strips the L2TP encapsulation, and processes the incoming frames for the appropriate interface. Figure 23-3 shows the L2TP tunnel detail and how user "lsmith" connects to the LNS to access the designated corporate intranet.

Figure 23-3 L2TP Tunneling Structure

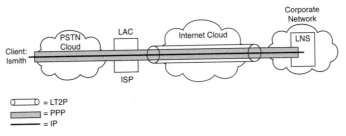

Tunneling involves the following three types of protocols, as shown in Figure 23-3:

- *Passenger protocol*—The protocol that is being encapsulated. In a dial-up scenario, this protocol might be PPP, SLIP, or text dialog.

- *Encapsulating protocol*—Creates, maintains, and tears down the tunnel. Cisco supports several encapsulating protocols, including the L2TP protocol, which is used for virtual dial-up services.

- *Carrier protocol*—Carries the encapsulated protocol. IP is the first carrier protocol used by the L2TP protocol because of its robust routing capabilities, ubiquitous support across different media, and deployment within the Internet.

Tunneling has evolved to become one of the key components in defining and using VPNs. Cisco IOS Software provides virtual dial-up service through a telecommuting form of a VPN.

Cisco Virtual Dial-Up Services

The following definitions fully describe the virtual dial-up service that Cisco Systems provides in its Cisco IOS Software:

- *Remote user*—The client who dials ISDN/Public Switched Telephone Network (PSTN) from either a home or another remote location.

- *NAS*—The telecommuting device that terminates the dial-up calls over either analog (basic telephone service) or digital (ISDN) circuits.

- *Internet service provider (ISP)*—The supplier that provides the dial-up services. It can provide for services itself through the NAS or it can deliver the dial-up remote user to a designated corporate gateway.

- *Corporate gateway*—The destination router that provides access to the services that the remote user requests. The services could be a corporation or even another ISP.

Remote users (using either asynchronous PPP or ISDN) access the corporate LAN as if they were dialed in directly to the corporate gateway (although their physical dial-up is through the ISP NAS). Figure 23-4 shows a topological view of how these conventions would be deployed within a virtual dial-up service.

Figure 23-4 Remote User Establishes PPP Connection with Corporate Network to Complete Virtual Dial-Up Topology

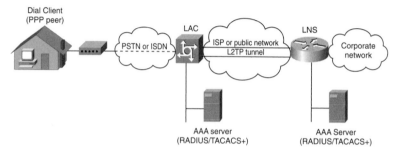

Cisco L2TP Implementation

Following are the key management requirements of service provided by Cisco L2TP implementation:

- Neither the remote end system nor its corporate hosts should require special software to use this service in a secure manner.

- Authentication is provided by dial-up PPP, the Challenge Handshake Authentication Protocol (CHAP), or the Password Authentication Protocol (PAP)—including Terminal Access Controller Access Control System Plus (TACACS+) and Remote Authentication Dial-In User Service (RADIUS) solutions, as well as support for smart cards and one-time passwords. The authentication will be manageable by the user independently of the ISP.

- Addressing will be as manageable as dedicated dial-up solutions; the remote user's respective corporation—not the ISP—will assign the address.

- The corporation's remote users will manage authorization because it will be in a direct dial-up solution.
- Accounting will be performed by both the ISP (for billing purposes) and by the user (for chargeback and auditing purposes).

These requirements are primarily achieved because of the functionality provided by tunneling the remote user directly to the corporate location using the L2TP protocol. In the case of PPP, all Link Control Protocol (LCP) and Network Control Protocol (NCP) negotiations take place at the remote user's corporate location. PPP is allowed to flow from the remote user and terminate at the corporate gateway.

L2TP is an emerging IETF standard that combines the best features of two existing tunneling protocols: Cisco L2F and Microsoft PPTP. L2TP is an extension to PPP, which is an important component for VPNs. VPNs allow users and telecommuters to connect to their corporate intranets or extranets. VPNs are cost effective because users can connect to the Internet locally and tunnel back to connect to corporate resources. This not only reduces overhead costs that are associated with traditional remote access methods, but it also improves flexibility and scalability.

Traditional dial-up networking services support only registered IP addresses, which limits the types of applications that are implemented over VPNs. L2TP supports multiple protocols and unregistered and privately administered IP addresses over the Internet. This allows the existing access infrastructure—such as the Internet, modems, access servers, and ISDN terminal adapters (TAs)—to be used. It also allows enterprise customers to outsource dial-out support, thereby reducing overhead for hardware maintenance costs and 800 number fees, and allows them to concentrate corporate gateway resources. Figure 23-4 shows the L2TP architecture in a typical dial-up environment.

End-to-End Virtual Dial-Up Process

To illustrate how the virtual dial-up service works, the following example describes what might happen when a remote user initiates access. Figure 23-5 gives you step-by-step details of this end-to-end process.

Figure 23-5 Steps Required for Remote VPN Client and Corporate LAN to Communicate

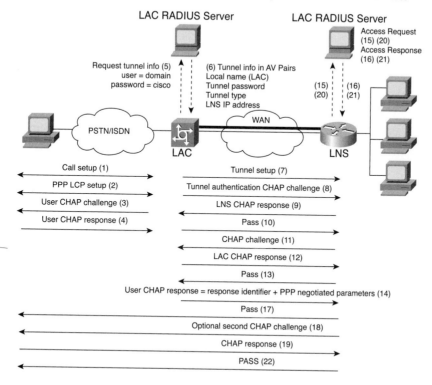

A virtual private dial-up network (VPDN) connection between a remote user, a LAC at the ISP point-of-presence (POP), and the LNS at the home LAN using an L2TP tunnel is accomplished as follows:

1. The remote user initiates a PPP connection to the ISP, using the analog telephone system or ISDN.

2. The ISP network LAC accepts the connection at the POP, and the PPP link is established.

3. After the end user and LNS negotiate LCP, the LAC partially authenticates the end user with CHAP or PAP. The username, domain name, or dialed number identification service (DNIS) determines whether the user is a VPDN client. If the user is not a VPDN client, authentication continues, and the client accesses the Internet or another contacted service. If the username is a VPDN client, the mapping names a specific endpoint (the LNS).

4. The tunnel endpoints—the LAC and the LNS—authenticate each other before sessions are attempted within a tunnel. Alternatively, the LNS can accept tunnel creation without the LAC's tunnel authentication.

5. After the tunnel exists, an L2TP session is created for the end user.

6. The LAC propagates the LCP-negotiated options and the partially authenticated CHAP/PAP information to the LNS. The LNS funnels the negotiated options and authentication information directly to the virtual access interface. If the options that are configured on the virtual template interface do not match the negotiated options with the LAC, then the connection fails and a disconnect is sent to the LAC.

The end result is that the exchange process appears to be between the dial-up client and the remote LNS exclusively, as if no intermediary device (the LAC) were involved. Figure 23-5 offers a pictorial account of the L2TP incoming call sequence with its own correspondingly more detailed sequence numbers that are unrelated to those in the preceding list.

Highlights of Virtual Dial-Up Service

NOTE

The functionality that Cisco NASs offer is intended to provide for both the virtual dial-up and traditional dial-up services.

The following sections discuss some of the significant differences between the standard Internet access service and the virtual dial-up service with respect to authentication, address allocation, authorization, and accounting.

Authentication and Security

In a traditional dial-up scenario, the ISP that is using a NAS in conjunction with a security server follows an authentication process by challenging the remote user for both the username and the password. If the remote user passes this phase, then the authorization phase begins.

For the virtual dial-up service, the ISP pursues authentication to discover the user's apparent identity (and, by implication, the user's desired corporate gateway). At this point, no password interaction is performed. As soon as the corporate gateway is determined, a connection initiates with the authentication information that the ISP gathered. The corporate gateway completes the authentication by either accepting or rejecting the connection. (For example, the connection is rejected in a PAP request when the username or password is incorrect.) When the connection is accepted, the corporate gateway can pursue another phase of authentication at the PPP layer. These additional authentication activities are outside the scope of the specification but might include proprietary PPP extensions or textual challenges that are carried within a TCP/IP Telnet session.

For each L2TP tunnel that is established, L2TP tunnel security generates a unique random key to resist spoofing attacks. Within the L2TP tunnel, each multiplexed session maintains a sequence number to prevent the duplication of packets. Cisco provides the flexibility of allowing users to implement compression at the client end. In addition, encryption on the tunnel can be done using IP security (IPSec).

Authorization

When providing a traditional dial-up service, the ISP maintains per-user profiles that define the authorization. Therefore, a security server can interact with NAS to provide policy-based usage to connect users based on their authentication. These policy statements range from simple source/destination filters for a handful of sites to complex algorithms that determine specific applications, time-of-day access, and a long list of permitted or denied destinations. This process can become burdensome to the ISP, especially if the ISP must provide access to remote users on behalf of corporations that require constant change to this policy.

In a virtual dial-up service, the burden of providing detailed authorization based on policy statements is given directly to the remote user's corporation. By allowing end-to-end connectivity between remote users and their corporate gateway, all authorization can be performed as if the remote users were directly dialed into the corporate location. This setup frees the ISP from maintaining a large database of individual user profiles based on many different corporations. More importantly, the virtual dial-up service becomes more secure to corporations that use it. The virtual dial-up service allows corporations to quickly react to changes in their remote user communities.

Address Allocation

For a traditional Internet service, the user accepts that the IP address might be allocated dynamically from a pool of service-provider addresses. This model often means that remote users have little or no access to their corporate network's resources because firewalls and security policies deny external IP addresses access to the corporate network.

For the virtual dial-up service, the corporate gateway can exist behind the corporate firewall and allocate addresses that are internal (and, in fact, can be RFC 1597 addresses that are reserved for private networks or non-IP addresses). Because L2TP tunnels operate exclusively at the frame layer, the actual policies of such address management are irrelevant to correct virtual dial-up service; for all purposes of PPP protocol handling, the dial-in user appears to have connected at the corporate gateway.

Accounting

The requirement for both NAS and the corporate gateway to provide accounting data can mean that they might count packets, octets, and connection start and stop times.

Because virtual dial-up is an access service, accounting for connection attempts (in particular, failed attempts) is of significant interest. The corporate gateway can reject new connections based on the authentication information gathered by the ISP, with corresponding logging. In cases where the corporate gateway accepts the connection and continues with further authentication, the corporate gateway might subsequently disconnect the client. In such scenarios, the disconnection indication back to the ISP can also include a reason.

Because the corporate gateway can decline a connection based on the authentication information that the ISP collects, accounting can easily draw a distinction between a series of failed connection attempts and a series of brief successful connections. Without this facility, the corporate gateway must always accept connection requests and must exchange numerous PPP packets with the remote system.

Summary

What is a VPN? As you have learned, a VPN can take several forms. It can exist between two end systems, or it can exist between two or more networks. A VPN can be built by using tunnels, encryption, or one of the virtual router methods. A VPN can consist of networks that are connected to a service provider's network by leased lines, Frame Relay, or ATM, or a VPN can consist of dial-up subscribers that connect to centralized services or other dial-up subscribers.

VPNs are a fairly quixotic subject; there is no single defining product, or even much of a consensus among VPN vendors as to what comprises a VPN. Consequently, everyone knows what a VPN is, but establishing a single definition can be remarkably difficult.

Every organization has problems that it must solve, and each of the tools mentioned in this chapter can be used to construct a certain type of VPN to address a particular set of functional objectives. More than one tool is available to address these problems, and network engineers should be cognizant that VPNs are an area in which many people use the term generically—there is a broad problem with many possible solutions. Each solution has numerous strengths, weaknesses, and vulnerabilities. No single mechanism exists for VPNs that will supplant all others in the months and years to come. Instead, a diversity of technological choices in this area of VPN support will continue to emerge.

Key Terms

access VPN   A VPN that provides remote access to a corporate intranet or extranet over a shared infrastructure with the same policies as a private network.

carrier protocol   A protocol that carries the encapsulated protocol. IP is the first carrier protocol used by the L2F protocol because of its robust routing capabilities, ubiquitous support across different media, and deployment within the Internet.

corporate gateway   The destination router that provides access to the services that the remote user requests. The services could be a corporation or even another ISP.

encapsulating protocol   A protocol that creates, maintains, and tears down the tunnel. Cisco supports several encapsulating protocols, including the L2F protocol, which is used for virtual dial-up services.

extranet VPN   A VPN that links customers, suppliers, partners, or communities of interest to a corporate intranet over a shared infrastructure by using dedicated connections.

intranet VPN   A VPN that links corporate headquarters, remote offices, and branch offices over a shared infrastructure by using dedicated connections.

ISP (internet service provider)   The supplier that provides the dial-up services. It can provide for services itself through NAS, or it can deliver the dial-up remote user to a designated corporate gateway.

L2TP (Layer 2 Tunneling Protocol)   An extension to the PPP protocol that enables ISPs to operate VPNs. L2TP merges the best features of two other tunneling protocols: PPTP from Microsoft and L2F from Cisco Systems. Like PPTP, L2TP requires that the ISP's routers support the protocol.

NAS (network access server)   The telecommuting device that terminates the dial-up calls over either analog (basic telephone service) or digital (ISDN) circuits.

passenger protocol   The protocol that is being encapsulated. In a dial-up scenario, this protocol might be PPP, SLIP, or text dialog.

remote user   The client who dials ISDN/PSTN from either a home or another remote location.

SLA (service-level agreement)   A negotiated contract between VPN providers and their subscribers. SLAs contain the service criteria to which the subscriber expects specific services to be delivered.

tunnel interfaces   Entry and exit points of the VPN tunnel. The tunnel interface is similar to a hardware interface but is configured in software.

tunneling   A vehicle that encapsulates packets inside a protocol that is understood at the entry and exit points of a given network.

VPN (virtual private network)   A private network that is constructed within a public network infrastructure, such as the global Internet.

Part V

Appendixes

Glossary of Key Terms

2B+D   In reference to the ISDN BRI service, two B channels and one D channel.

access layer   The layer that feeds traffic into the network and performs network entry control. End users access the network via the access layer.

access VPN   A VPN that provides remote access to a corporate intranet or extranet over a shared infrastructure with the same policies as a private network.

accounting (auditing)   The process of keeping track of a user's activity while accessing a network's resources, including the amount of time spent in the network, the services accessed while there, and the amount of data transferred during the session.

ACL (access control list)   A set of data that informs a computer's operating system which permissions, or access rights, that each user or group has to a specific system object, such as a directory or file. A means for controlling or limiting network traffic. An ACL compares different criteria to a defined rule set.

angular separation   A condition when the bulkhead is worn and allows some play in the alignment of two fibers, some light might be lost because the cores are not lined up completely.

application layer   Layer 7 of the OSI reference model. This layer provides network services to user applications. For example, a word-processing application is serviced by file-transfer services at this layer.

archive bit   Used to measure date since last backup by storing information with a file and is turned on whenever that file is created or modified. This flag tells the backup process whether the file needs to be backed up.

ARP (Address Resolution Protocol)   An Internet protocol used to map an IP address to a MAC address. Defined in RFC 826.

asymmetric switching   A switching method that provides switched connections between ports with different bandwidths, such as between 10-Mbps ports and 100-Mbps ports.

ATM (Asynchronous Transfer Mode)   International standard for cell relay in which multiple service types (such as voice, video, or data) are conveyed in fixed-length (53-byte) cells. Fixed-length cells allow cell processing to occur in hardware, thereby reducing transit delays. ATM is designed to take advantage of high-speed transmission media such as E3, SONET, and T3.

attenuation   The decrease in the strength of a signal during transmission. Attenuation is a natural consequence of signal transmission over long distance.

AUI (attachment unit interface)   An IEEE 802.3 interface between a media attachment unit and a network interface card. The term AUI can also refer to the rear panel port to which an AUI cable might attach, such as those found on a Cisco LightStream Ethernet access card. Also called a transceiver cable.

authentication   The process of identifying an individual, usually based on a username and password.

authorization   The process of granting or denying access to a network resource.

backbone   The structural core of the network, which connects all the components of the network so that communication can occur. The part of a network that acts as the primary path for traffic that is most often sourced from, and destined for, other networks. Another term for bus, or the main wire that connects nodes. Backbone is often used to describe the main network connections that compose the Internet.

balanced-hybrid protocol   A protocol that combines aspects of the link-state and distance-vector protocols.

baseline   A measurement that is established after the network has been installed and configured properly. A Baseline can be used to compare the against future performance.

Bc (committed burst)   Negotiated tariff metric in Frame Relay internetworks. The maximum amount of data (in bits) that a Frame Relay internetwork is committed to accept and transmit at the CIR.

BDR (backup designated router)   Backup to the designated router

Be (excess burst)   Negotiated tariff metric in Frame Relay internetworks. The number of bits that a Frame Relay internetwork attempts to transmit after Bc is accommodated. Be data, in general, is delivered with a lower probability than Bc data because the network can mark Be data as DE.

BECN (backward explicit congestion notification)   A bit set by a Frame Relay network in frames traveling in the opposite direction of frames encountering a congested path. DTE devices that receive frames with the BECN bit set can request that higher-level protocols take flow control action as appropriate.

best-effort delivery   This delivery occurs when a network system does not use a sophisticated acknowledgment system to guarantee reliable delivery of information.

BID (bridge ID)   This is the number with which the bridge or switches use to identify priority and root bridge or switch selection. The root bridge is the bridge that has the lowest BID.

bindery   An object that NetWare version 3.12 uses to manage multiple users and resources. The drawback is that bindery services create a server-centric network, which is focused on the individual server as the point of control.

BOOTP (Bootstrap Protocol)   The protocol used by a network node to determine the IP address of its Ethernet interfaces to affect network booting. Originally defined in RFC 951 in 1985. BOOTP is the predecessor of DHCP, and it shares some operational characteristics. Both protocols use UDP ports 67 and 68, which are well known as "BOOTP ports" because BOOTP came before DHCP.

BPDU (bridge protocol data unit)   A Spanning Tree Protocol hello packet that is sent out at configurable intervals to exchange information among bridges in the network.

BRI (Basic Rate Interface)   An ISDN interface that is composed of two B channels and one D channel for circuit-switched communication of voice, video, and data.

bridge   A device that connects and passes packets between two network segments that use the same communications protocol. Bridges operate at the data link layer (Layer 2) of the OSI reference model. In general, a bridge filters, forwards, or floods an incoming frame based on the MAC address of that frame.

bridging   A technology in which a bridge connects two or more LAN segments.

broadcast   A data packet that is sent to all nodes on a network. Broadcasts are identified by a broadcast address. *See also* broadcast address, broadcast domain, and broadcast storm.

broadcast address   A special address that is reserved for sending a message to all stations. Generally, a broadcast address is a MAC destination address of all 1s. *See also* broadcast.

broadcast domain   The set of all devices that will receive broadcast frames originating from any device within the set. Broadcast domains are typically bounded by routers because routers do not forward broadcast frames.

broadcast storm   An undesirable network event in which many broadcasts are sent simultaneously across all network segments. A broadcast storm uses substantial network bandwidth and, typically, causes network time-outs.

brouter (bridging router)   A combination of both a router and a bridge. A brouter acts as a router for routable protocols and a bridge for nonroutable protocols.

bus topology   A linear LAN architecture in which transmissions from network stations propagate the length of the medium and are received by all other stations. Compare with star topology.

callback   Callback is a method of verifying authentication where the system disconnects the call and calls back on a specified number, when a user dials in and is authenticated.

CAM (content-addressable memory)   Memory that is accessed based on its contents, not on its memory address.

carrier protocol   A protocol that carries the encapsulated protocol. IP is the first carrier protocol used by the L2F protocol because of its robust routing capabilities, ubiquitous support across different media, and deployment within the Internet.

CDP (Cisco Discovery Protocol)   Provides a single proprietary command that enables network administrators to access a summary of what the configurations look like on other directly connected routers.

CHAP (Challenge Handshake Authentication Protocol)   A security feature that is supported on lines using PPP encapsulation that prevents unauthorized access. CHAP does not prevent unauthorized access, but it identifies the remote end; the router or access server then determines whether that user is allowed access.

CIDR (classless interdomain routing)   Classless routing protocols based on route aggregation. CIDR allows routers to group routes together to reduce the quantity of routing information the core routers carry. With CIDR, several IP networks appear to networks outside the group as a single, larger entity. With CIDR, IP addresses and their subnet masks are written as four octets separated by periods, followed by a forward slash and a prefix that represents the subnet mask.

ciphered data   Data that is encrypted.

CIR (committed information rate)   The rate (in bits per second) at which the ingress access interface trunk interfaces, and egress access interface of a Frame Relay network transfer information to the destination Frame Relay end system under normal conditions. The rate is averaged over a minimum time interval Tc.

circuit   A communications path between two or more points.

circuit switching   Switching system in which a dedicated physical circuit path must exist between sender and receiver for the duration of the "call." Used heavily in the telephone company network.

Cisco Architecture for Voice, Video and Integrated Data (AVVID)   AVVID is a standards-based, open-systems architecture for converged networking. Cisco AVVID is an enterprise initiative for integrated data, voice, and video over a common IP transport.

Cisco Internetwork Operating System (IOS) Software   Cisco system software that provides common functionality, scalability, and security for all products under the CiscoFusion architecture. The Cisco IOS software allows centralized, integrated, and automated installation and management of internetworks, while ensuring support for a wide variety of protocols, media, services, and platforms.

Cisco IP Contact Center (IPCC)   The IPCC solution combines data and voice technologies to facilitate geographically independent multimedia customer interaction. This includes customer interactions originating from multiple, diverse contact channels, including IP voice, TDM voice, web, e-mail, and fax. Regardless of transport, whether the Internet or the traditional PSTN, the Cisco IPCC fully integrated, contact-center architecture services all media types. The Cisco IPCC architecture also provides a seamless migration path from the legacy call-center infrastructure to the IP-empowered, multimedia contact center.

CO (central office)   Local telephone company office to which all local loops in a given area connect and in which circuit switching of subscriber lines occurs.

collision   In Ethernet, the result of two nodes transmitting simultaneously. The frames from each device collide and are damaged when they meet on the physical medium.

collision domain   In Ethernet, the network area within which frames that have collided are propagated. Repeaters and hubs propagate collisions; LAN switches, bridges, and routers do not. Also called a bandwidth domain.

congestion   Traffic that is in excess of network capacity.

converged network   When a single networks has been provisioned within an enterprise for data, voice, and video applications.

convergence   The speed and capability of a group of internetworking devices running a specific routing protocol to agree on an internetwork's topology after a change in that topology.

core layer   The backbone of the campus-switched network. The switches in this layer can make use of many Layer 2 technologies.

corporate gateway   The destination router that provides access to the services that the remote user requests. The services could be a corporation or even another ISP.

CPE (customer premises equipment)   Terminating equipment, such as terminals, telephones, and modems, that is supplied by the telephone company, installed at customer sites, and connected to the telephone company network.

CSMA/CD (carrier sense multiple access collision detect)   A set of rules that determines how network devices respond when two devices attempt to use a data channel simultaneously (a collision). Standard Ethernet networks use CSMA/CD. This standard enables devices to detect a collision. After detecting a collision, a device waits a random delay time and then attempts to retransmit the message. If the device detects a collision again, it waits twice as long to try to retransmit the message. This is known as exponential backoff.

CSU (channel service unit)   Digital interface device that connects end-user equipment to the local digital telephone loop. Often referred to together with DSU, as CSU/DSU.

cut sheet   A rough diagram indicating where cable runs are located and the numbers of rooms they lead to.

cut-through switching   A packet-switching approach that streams data through a switch so that the leading edge of a packet exits the switch at the output port before the packet finishes entering the input port. A device that uses cut-through packet switching reads, processes, and forwards packets as soon as the destination address is looked up and the outgoing port is determined. Cut-through switching is also known as on-the-fly packet switching.

data backup   The process of duplicating all stored data to magnetic tape or another storage medium such as removable hard disks, CD-ROM, or DVD-ROM.

data link layer   Layer 2 of the OSI reference model. This layer provides reliable transit of data across a physical link. The data link layer is concerned with physical addressing, network topology, line discipline, error notification, ordered delivery of frames, and flow control. The IEEE divided this layer into two sublayers: the MAC sublayer and the LLC sublayer. Sometimes, this layer is called simply the link layer. This layer roughly corresponds to the SNA model's data link control layer.

datagram   A logical grouping of information sent as a network layer unit over a transmission medium without prior establishment of a virtual circuit. IP datagrams are the primary information units in the Internet. The terms cell, frame, message, packet, and segment are also used to describe logical information groupings at various layers of the OSI reference model and in various technology circles.

DCE (data circuit-terminating equipment) (EIA expansion) or *data circuit-terminating equipment* (ITU-T expansion)   The devices and connections of a communications network that comprise the network end of the user-to-network interface. The DCE provides a physical connection to the network, forwards traffic, and provides a clocking signal used to synchronize data transmission between DCE and DTE devices. Modems and interface cards are examples of DCE.

decryption-device   A device that makes data unreadable before passing it to an application. A router, server, end system, or dedicated device can act as an encryption or decryption device.

default gateway   A router interface that is normally referenced with an IP address.

default route   A route that a device will automatically select if you do not specify a substitute.

default router   A router that has at least one interface serving as a default gateway.

delay   The time between the initiation of a transaction by a sender and the first response that the sender receives. Also, the time required to move a packet from source to destination over a given path.

designated bridge   The bridge that incurs the lowest path cost when forwarding a frame from a segment to the root bridge.

DHCP (Dynamic Host Configuration Protocol)   Provides a mechanism for allocating IP addresses dynamically so that addresses can be reused automatically when hosts no longer need them.

digital signature   A system in which software such as a document or e-mail has been encrypted with your private key.

dispersion   The condition in a TDM digital signal, when the variance of light speed, limits the spacing between bits of information and the rate at which bits can be sent.

distance-vector routing protocol   A routing protocol that iterates on the number of hops in a route to find a shortest-path spanning tree. Distance-vector routing protocols call for each router to send its entire routing table in each update, but only to its neighbors. Distance-vector routing protocols can be prone to routing loops, but are computationally simpler than link-state routing protocols. Also called Bellman-Ford routing algorithm.

distribution layer   The layer that provides a boundary definition in which packet manipulation can take place.

DLCI (data-link connection identifier) A value that specifies a PVC or an SVC in a Frame Relay network. In the basic Frame Relay specification, DLCIs are locally significant. (That is, connected devices can use different values to specify the same connection.) In the LMI extended specification, DLCIs are globally significant. (That is, DLCIs specify individual end devices.)

DR (designated router) OSPF router that generates LSAs for a multiaccess network and has other special responsibilities in running OSPF. Each multiaccess OSPF network that has at least two attached routers has a designated router that is elected by the OSPF Hello protocol. The designated router enables a reduction in the number of adjacencies required on a multiaccess network, which reduces the amount of routing protocol traffic and the topological database's size.

DSU (digital service unit) Device used in digital transmission that adapts the physical interface on a DTE device to a transmission facility such as T1 or E1. The DSU is also responsible for such functions as signal timing. Often referred to together with CSU, as CSU/DSU.

DTE (data terminal equipment) Device at the user end of a user-network interface that serves as a data source, destination, or both. DTE connects to a data network through a DCE device (for example, a modem) and typically uses clocking signals generated by the DCE. DTE includes such devices as computers, protocol translators, and multiplexers.

DUAL (Diffusing Update Algorithm) Convergence algorithm used in Enhanced IGRP that provides loop-free operation at every instant throughout a route computation. Allows routers involved in a topology change to synchronize at the same time, while not involving routers that are unaffected by the change.

DWDM (dense wavelength division multiplexing) A technology that transmits multiple signals simultaneously at different wavelengths, allowing a single fiber to operate as if it were multiple fibers.

dynamic routing Routing that adjusts automatically to network topology or traffic changes. Also called adaptive routing.

echo Caused by a conversion from two wires (local loop) to four wires and impedance mismatch.

EIGRP (Enhanced Interior Gateway Routing Protocol) An advanced version of IGRP developed by Cisco. Provides superior convergence properties and operating efficiency, and combines the advantages of link-state protocols with those of distance-vector protocols.

encapsulating protocol   A protocol that creates, maintains, and tears down the tunnel. Cisco supports several encapsulating protocols, including the L2F protocol, which is used for virtual dial-up services.

encryption   A process that scrambles data to protect it from being read by anyone besides the intended receiver.

encryption device   A device that makes the data readable before placing it on a network.

end-face separation   The condition when two fiber ends are separated, and loss occurs because of the spreading of light as it comes out of the first core.

enterprise network   A corporation, agency, school, or other organization's network that ties together its data, communication, computing, and file servers.

enterprise server   A server that supports all the users on a network by offering services such as e-mail or DNS.

Ethernet   A baseband LAN specification that was invented by Xerox Corporation and developed jointly by Xerox, Intel, and Digital Equipment Corporation. Ethernet networks use CSMA/CD and run over a variety of cable types at 10 Mbps. Ethernet is similar to the IEEE 802.3 series of standards.

extended ACL   Compares source IP address, destination IP address, TCP/UDP port number, and other criteria to the rules defining a standard ACL.

extranet VPN   A VPN that links customers, suppliers, partners, or communities of interest to a corporate intranet over a shared infrastructure by using dedicated connections.

Fast Ethernet   Any of a number of 100-Mbps Ethernet specifications. Fast Ethernet offers a speed increase 10 times that of the 10BASE-T Ethernet specification, while preserving such qualities as frame format, MAC mechanisms, and maximum transmission unit (MTU). Such similarities allow the use of existing 10BASE-T applications and network management tools on Fast Ethernet networks. Based on an extension to the IEEE 802.3 specification. *See also* Ethernet.

fast-forward switching   Switching that offers the lowest level of latency by immediately forwarding a packet after receiving the destination address.

FCS (Frame Check Sequence)   Extra characters that are added to a frame for error control purposes. The standard 16-bit cyclic redundancy check (CRC) that is used for HDLC and Frame Relay frames. The FCS detects bit errors that occur in the bits of the frame between the opening flag, and the FCS and is effective only in detecting errors in frames that are no larger than 4096 octets.

FD (feasible distance)   The lowest calculated metric to each destination.

FDM (frequency-division multiplexing)   A multiplexing technique that uses different frequencies to combine multiple streams of data for transmission over a communications medium. FDM assigns a discrete carrier frequency to each data stream and then combines many modulated carrier frequencies for transmission. For example, television transmitters use FDM to broadcast several channels at once.

FECN (forward explicit congestion notification)   A bit set by a Frame Relay network to inform DTE devices that are receiving the frame that congestion was experienced in the path from source to destination. DTE devices that receive frames with the FECN bit set can request that higher-level protocols take flow-control action as appropriate.

firewall   A router or an access server, or several routers or access servers, designated as a buffer between any connected public networks and a private network. A firewall router uses ACLs and other methods to ensure the security of the private network. A system or combination of systems that enforces security policies at the boundary between two or more networks.

Flash memory   A special type of electrical erasable programmable read-only memory (EEPROM) that can be erased and reprogrammed in blocks instead of 1 byte at a time. Many modern PCs have their BIOS stored on a Flash memory chip so that it can be updated easily if necessary. Such a BIOS is sometimes called a Flash BIOS. Flash memory is also popular in modems because it enables the modem manufacturer to support new protocols as they become standardized.

flooding   Process that sends information out all ports, with the exception of the port on which the information was received.

flow control   A technique for ensuring that a transmitting entity does not overwhelm a receiving entity with data. When the buffers on the receiving device are full, a message is sent to the sending device to suspend transmission until the data in the buffers has been processed. In IBM networks, this technique is called pacing.

fragment-free switching   A switching method in which the switch filters out the collision fragments, which are the majority of packet errors, before forwarding begins.

Frame Relay   An industry-standard, switched data link layer protocol that handles multiple virtual circuits by using HDLC encapsulation between connected devices. Frame Relay is more efficient than X.25, the protocol for which it is generally considered a replacement.

FS (feasible successor)   A backup route. These routes are identified at the same time that the successors are identified but are kept only in the topology table.

full-duplex   Capability for simultaneous data transmission between a sending station and a receiving station.

gateway   A node on a network that serves as an entrance to another network. In enterprises, the gateway is the computer that routes the traffic from a workstation to the outside network that is serving the web pages. In homes, the gateway is the ISP that connects the user to the Internet.

Gigabit Ethernet   Any of a number of 1000-Mbps Ethernet specifications. Gigabit Ethernet offers a speed increase 10 times that of the Fast Ethernet specification.

half-duplex   Capability for data transmission in only one direction at a time between a sending station and a receiving station.

header   Control information placed before data when encapsulating that data for network transmission.

Hello protocol   Protocol used by OSPF systems to establish and maintain neighbors.

hop   The passage of a data packet between two network nodes (for example, between two routers).

host   A computer that is connected to a TCP/IP network, including the Internet. Each host has a unique IP address.

HOSTS file   A statically configured host name to IP address translation file. This file is usable in all hosts' IP protocol stacks. If present, the HOSTS file will be referenced for name resolution before an external DNS search.

hub   Generally, a device that serves as the center of a star-topology network.

ICMP (Internet Control Message Protocol)   A network layer Internet protocol that reports errors and provides other information relevant to IP packet processing. Documented in RFC 792.

IEEE (Institute of Electrical and Electronics Engineers)   A professional organization whose activities include the development of communications and network standards. IEEE LAN standards are the predominant LAN standards today.

IEEE 802.3   An IEEE LAN protocol that specifies an implementation of the physical layer and the MAC sublayer of the data link layer. IEEE 802.3 uses CSMA/CD access at a variety of speeds over a variety of physical media. Extensions to the IEEE 802.3 standard specify implementations for Fast Ethernet. Physical variations of the original IEEE 802.3 specification include 10BASE-2, 10BASE-5, 10BASE-F, 10BASE-T, and 10BROAD-36. Physical variations for Fast Ethernet include 100BASE-TX and 100BASE-FX. Gigabit Ethernet includes 1000BASE-T, 1000BASE-LX, and 1000BASE-SX.

IGRP (Interior Gateway Routing Protocol)   A protocol developed by Cisco to address the problems associated with routing in large, heterogeneous networks.

inside global address   In a NAT configuration, the IP address that the inside local address gets translated to.

inside local address   In a NAT configuration, the IP address that is translated.

interface   1. A connection between two systems or devices. 2. In routing terminology, a network connection.

intranet VPN   A VPN that links corporate headquarters, remote offices, and branch offices over a shared infrastructure by using dedicated connections.

intrusion detection   The real-time monitoring of network activity and analysis of data for potential vulnerabilities and attacks in progress.

IOR (index of refraction)   The ratio of the speed of light in a vacuum to the speed of light in a fiber.

IP address   A 32-bit address assigned to hosts using TCP/IP. An IP address belongs to one of five classes (A, B, C, D, or E) and is written as four octets separated by periods (that is, dotted-decimal format). Each address consists of a network number, an optional subnetwork number, and a host number. The network and subnetwork numbers together are used for routing, and the host number is used to address an individual host within the network or subnetwork. A subnet mask extracts network and subnetwork information from the IP address. Also called an Internet address.

IPSec (IP Security Protocol)   A set of open standards that provides data confidentiality, data integrity, and authentication between participating peers at the IP layer.

ISDN (Integrated Services Digital Network)   A communication protocol offered by telephone companies that permits telephone networks to carry data, voice, and other source traffic.

ISL (Inter-Switch Link)   A Cisco-specific, proprietary trunking protocol that interconnects multiple switches and maintains VLAN information as traffic travels between switches on trunk links.

ISP (Internet service provider)   The supplier that provides the dial-up services. It can provide for services itself through NAS, or it can deliver the dial-up remote user to a designated corporate gateway.

jitter   Relates to variable interpacket timing caused by the network that a packet traverses. Simply stated, jitter is the variation of packet interarrival time.

Kerberos   An authentication system that provides user-to-host security for application-level protocols such as FTP and Telnet.

L2TP (Layer 2 Tunneling Protocol)   An extension to the PPP protocol that enables ISPs to operate VPNs. L2TP merges the best features of two other tunneling protocols: PPTP from Microsoft and L2F from Cisco Systems. Like PPTP, L2TP requires that the ISP's routers support the protocol.

LAN (local-area network)   A high-speed, low-error data network that covers a relatively small geographic area (up to a few thousand meters). LANs connect workstations, peripherals, terminals, and other devices in a single building or other geographically limited area. LAN standards specify cabling and signaling at the physical and data link layers of the OSI model. Ethernet, FDDI, and Token Ring are widely used LAN technologies.

LAN switch   A high-speed switch that forwards packets between data-link segments. Most LAN switches forward traffic based on MAC addresses. LAN switches are often categorized according to the method they use to forward traffic: cut-through packet switching or store-and-forward packet switching. An example of a LAN switch is the Cisco Catalyst 5000.

LAPB (Link Access Procedure, Balanced)   A data link layer protocol in the X.25 protocol stack. LAPB is a bit-oriented protocol that is derived from HDLC.

LAPD (Link Access Procedure on the D channel)   An ISDN data link layer protocol for the D channel. LAPD was derived from LAPB and is designed primarily to satisfy the signaling requirements of ISDN basic access. Defined by ITU-T Recommendations Q.920 and Q.921.

latency   The delay between the time that a device requests access to a network and the time that it is granted permission to transmit.

layering   The separation of networking functions used by the OSI reference model, which simplifies the tasks required for two computers to communicate with each other.

LCP (Link Control Protocol)   A protocol that provides a method of establishing, configuring, maintaining, and terminating the point-to-point connection.

link   A network communications channel that consists of a circuit or transmission path and all related equipment between a sender and a receiver. Link is most often used to refer to a WAN connection. It is sometimes referred to as a line or a transmission link.

link-state routing protocol   A routing protocol in which each router broadcasts or multicasts information regarding the cost of reaching each of its neighbors to all nodes in the internetwork. Link-state protocols create a consistent view of the network and are not prone to routing loops, but they achieve this at the cost of relatively greater computational difficulty and more widespread traffic (compared with distance-vector routing protocols).

LLC (Logical Link Control)   The higher of the two data link layer sublayers that the IEEE defines. The LLC sublayer handles error control, flow control, framing, and MAC-sublayer addressing. The most prevalent LLC protocol is IEEE 802.2, which includes both connectionless and connection-oriented variants.

LMI (Local Management Interface)   A set of enhancements to the basic Frame Relay specification. LMI includes support for a keepalive mechanism, which verifies that data is flowing; a multicast mechanism, which provides the network server with its local DLCI and the multicast DLCI; global addressing, which gives DLCIs global rather than local significance in Frame Relay networks; and a status mechanism, which provides an ongoing status report on the DLCIs known to the switch.

local access rate   The clock speed (port speed) of the connection (local loop) to the Frame Relay cloud. It is the rate at which data travels into or out of the network.

loopback   A special IP number (127.0.0.1) designated for a machine's software loopback interface. The loopback interface has no hardware associated with it and is not physically connected to a network.

LSA (link-state advertisement)   Broadcast packet used by link-state protocols that contains information about neighbors and path costs. Receiving routers use LSAs to maintain their routing tables. Sometimes called a link-state packet (LSP).

MAC (Media Access Control)   The part of the data link layer that includes the 6-byte (48-bit) address of the source and destination, and the method of getting permission to transmit.

MAC address   A standardized data link layer address that is required for every port or device that connects to a LAN. Other devices in the network use these addresses to locate specific ports in the network and to create and update routing tables and data structures. MAC addresses are 6 bytes long, and the IEEE controls them. Also known as a hardware address, a MAC layer address, or a physical address.

macrobending   A bend that you can see. When you bend fiber, you can cause some of the light rays to exceed the critical angle, allowing light to leak out of the core and into the cladding.

mandatory profile   A type of profile that brings up the same user interface for everyone without allowing changes to be made. The mandatory profile is used in situations in which many people must use the same physical computer.

media attachment unit   A device used in Ethernet and IEEE 802.3 networks that provides the interface between a station's AUI port and the Ethernet's common medium. The media attachment unit, which can be built into a station or can be a separate device, performs physical-layer functions, including the conversion of digital data from the Ethernet interface, collision detection, and injection of bits onto the network. Sometimes referred to as a media access unit or a transceiver.

memory buffering   A buffering technique whereby packets are stored in memory before forwarding.

microbending   The process that causes the light to exceed the critical angle and leak out of the core. It occurs on a microscopic scale and is not visible to the eye.

microsegment   Division of a network into smaller segments, usually with the intention of increasing aggregate bandwidth to network devices.

microsegmentation   The process of splitting a single collision domain into two or more collision domains to reduce collisions and network congestion.

midspan meet   The capability to connect different vendors' equipment on a communication network and have them function properly with each other.

multiaccess network   Network that allows multiple devices to connect and communicate simultaneously.

multidomain model   A model in which separate domains are connected by trusting/trusted relationships, which allows users to cross domain boundaries to use resources.

multimode fiber   A type of cable that is used to transmit many signals per fiber. Multimode allows many paths or modes for the light. The larger core of multimode fiber allows light to break up into many different modes.

NAS (network access server)   The telecommuting device that terminates the dial-up calls over either analog (basic telephone service) or digital (ISDN) circuits.

NAT (network address translation)   Only globally unique in terms of the public internet. A mechanism for translating private addresses into publicly usable addresses to be used within the public Internet. An effective means for hiding actual device addressing within a private network.

NDS (Novell Directory Services)   Novell Netware servers use this directory service to manage users and resources. The advantage over version 3.12 is that NDS creates a network-centric network, which is focused on the entire network as the point of control.

neighbor table   The table that routers running EIGRP use to maintain lists of adjacent routers. There is a neighbor table for each protocol that EIGRP supports.

NetWare Directory Services   Novell Netware's directory service that uses TCP/IP or IPX/SPX. The NetWare Directory Services tree allows users to log into the network and access any of the resources that are available.

network   A collection of computers, printers, routers, switches, and other devices that are able to communicate with each other over some transmission medium.

network assets   Can include network hosts (including the hosts' operating systems, applications, and data), internetworking devices (such as routers and switches), and network data that traverses the network. Less obvious but still important, assets can include intellectual property, trade secrets, and a company's reputation.

Network Control Program   A program that routes and controls the flow of data between a communications controller and other network resources.

network layer   Layer 3 of the OSI reference model. This layer provides connectivity and path selection between two end systems. The network layer is the layer at which routing occurs. Corresponds roughly with the path control layer of the SNA model.

NFS (Network File System)   NFS grants users permission to certain parts of the file system and controls the security of the UNIX systems.

NIC (network interface card)   A board that provides network communication capabilities to and from a computer system. The NIC has a MAC address assigned by the manufacturer that is used as the computer's physical address in a LAN.

nonrepudiation   A system by which a third party can prove that a communication between two other parties took place. Nonrepudiation is desirable if you want to be able to trace your communications and prove that they occurred.

NT1 (Network Termination type 1)   A device that connects four-wire ISDN subscriber wiring to the conventional two-wire local loop facility.

NT2 (Network Termination type 2)   A device that directs traffic to and from different subscriber devices and the NT1. The NT2 is an intelligent device that performs switching and concentrating.

NVRAM (nonvolatile RAM)   RAM that retains its contents when a unit is powered off.

Open Shortest Path First (OSPF) protocol   A link-state, hierarchical routing protocol proposed as a successor to RIP in the Internet community. OSPF features include least-cost routing, multipath routing, and load balancing.

optical amplifiers   A device that amplifies an input optical signal terahertz (THz) of optical bandwidth near 1550 nm, nearly ideal noise performance, low signal distortion and crosstalk, and high-output saturation power.

optical filter   A filter that is used in fiber networks that is used to identify different wavelengths or lambdas.

optical-to-electrical converter   The process that occurs when the receiver is a semi-conductor that changes light into a corresponding electrical signal.

outside global address   The IP address of an outside host as it is known to the hosts in the inside network.

outside local address   The IP address that the host's owner assigns to a host on the outside network.

overloading (also known as PAT)   Uses TCP port numbers to allow a group of inside hosts to communicate to outside hosts and "share" the overloaded address in a NAT configuration.

packet   A logical grouping of information that includes a header containing control information and (usually) user data. Packets are most often used to refer to network layer units of data. The terms datagram, frame, message, and segment also describe logical information groupings at various layers of the OSI reference model and in various technology circles.

packet filters   Filters that can be set up on routers and servers to permit or deny packets from particular addresses or services. Packet filters augment authentication and authorization mechanisms.

packet switching   Networking method in which nodes share bandwidth with each other by sending packets.

PAP (Password Authentication Protocol)   An authentication protocol that allows PPP peers to authenticate one another. The remote router that attempts to connect to the local router is required to send an authentication request. Unlike CHAP, PAP passes the password and host name or username in cleartext (that is, unencrypted). PAP does not prevent unauthorized access, but it identifies the remote end; the router or access server then determines whether that user is allowed access. PAP is supported only on PPP lines.

passenger protocol   The protocol that is being encapsulated. In a dial-up scenario, this protocol might be PPP, SLIP, or text dialog.

path determination   The decision of which path traffic should take through the network cloud. Path determination occurs at the network layer of the OSI reference model.

PDU (protocol data unit)   The OSI term for a packet.

physical layer   Layer 1 of the OSI reference model. This layer defines the electrical, mechanical, procedural, and functional specifications for activating, maintaining, and deactivating the physical link between end systems. Corresponds with the physical control layer in the SNA model.

physical security   Limiting access to key network resources by keeping the resources behind a locked door. Physical security also refers to protecting resources from natural disasters such as floods, fires, storms, and earthquakes.

PIN (personal identification number)   An initial level of security that gives the user permission to use the card. The card provides a one-time password that accesses the corporate network for a limited time.

plain text (clear text)   Data that is not encrypted.

point-to-point   communication between one receiver and one location.

port   An interface on an internetworking device (such as a router). A female plug on a patch panel that accepts the same size plug as an RJ-45 jack. Patch cords are used in these ports to cross-connect computers that are wired to the patch panel. It is this cross-connection that allows the LAN to function.

portfast   A command that causes a port to enter the spanning tree forwarding state immediately, bypassing the listening and learning states.

PPP (Point-to-Point Protocol)   A successor to SLIP, a protocol that provides router-to-router and host-to-network connections over synchronous and asynchronous circuits.

presentation layer   Layer 6 of the OSI reference model. This layer provides data representation and code formatting, and negotiates data transfer syntax. It ensures that the application can use the data that arrives from the network, and that the information the application sends can be transmitted on the network.

PRI (Primary Rate Interface)   An ISDN interface to primary rate access. Primary rate access consists of a single 64-kbps D channel plus 23 (T1) or 30 (E1) B channels for voice or data.

process identifier (process ID)   A numerical number assigned during the OSPF configuration process that identifies each OSPF process running on a router.

profiles   A system which allows a user to customize a user interface on a computer and then be able to use that profile at any computer that user connects to the network.

public data network   A network that is operated either by a government (as in Europe) or by a private concern to provide computer communications to the public, usually for a fee. Public data networks enable small organizations to create a WAN without all the equipment costs of long-distance circuits.

PVCs (permanent virtual circuits)   Virtual circuit that is permanently established. PVCs save bandwidth associated with circuit establishment and tear down in situations where certain virtual circuits must exist all the time. Called a permanent virtual connection in ATM terminology.

Q.931   A protocol that recommends a network layer between the terminal endpoint and the local ISDN switch. Q.931 does not impose an end-to-end recommendation. The various ISDN providers and switch types can and do use various implementations of Q.931.

quality of service (QoS)   Features that lead to efficient, predictable services for business-critical applications while ensuring high-quality Voice over IP services. With the QoS features enabled, the voice quality stays constant at a high level with varying network loads. In contrast, *not* implementing QoS means the voice quality goes down as the network load increases.

queue   1. Generally, an ordered list of elements waiting to be processed. 2. In routing, a backlog of packets waiting to be forwarded over a router interface.

queuing   A process in which ACLs can designate certain packets to be processed by a router before other traffic, on the basis of some configurable parameter such as specifying a protocol.

RAID (Redundant Array of Inexpensive Disks)   A category of disk drives that employ two or more drives in combination for fault tolerance and performance. RAID disk drives are used frequently on servers but are not generally necessary for personal computers.

RAM (random-access memory)   Volatile memory that can be read and written by a microprocessor.

RARP (Reverse Address Resolution Protocol)   A protocol in the TCP/IP stack that provides a method for finding IP addresses based on MAC addresses.

RD (reported distance)   The distance that an adjacent neighbor reports to a specific destination.

reference point   Several reference points that are defined to characterize the different interfaces for ISDN that are defined in ITU recommendation I.411 (V, U, T, S, and R reference points) will be defined (physical and electrical characteristics).

reflection   A light ray that bounces off the interface of two materials at the same angle it hits. Reflection occurs when a flashlight beam bounces off a window or mirror.

refraction   The bending of the light ray as it changes speed going from one material to another.

Reliable Transport Protocol   A transport-layer protocol that can guarantee ordered delivery of EIGRP packets to all neighbors.

Remote Authentication Dial-In User Server (RADIUS) protocol   A secure authentication protocol that gives an administrator the option of having a centralized database of user information. The database includes authentication and configuration information and specifies the type of service permitted by a user (such as PPP, Telnet, rlogin, and so on).

remote user   The client who dials ISDN/PSTN from either a home or another remote location.

repeater   A device that regenerates and propagates electrical signals between two network segments.

repudiation   A security feature that prevents a third party from proving that a communication between two other parties took place. This is a desirable feature if you do not want your communication to be traceable.

RIP (Routing Information Protocol)   A protocol supplied with UNIX BSD systems. The most common Interior Gateway Protocol (IGP) in the Internet. RIP uses hop count as a routing metric.

RMON (Remote Monitoring)   Extensions to SNMP that provide the ability to look at the network as a whole instead of looking at individual devices.

route authentication   An form of authentication that is used when a router must pass some criteria before another router accepts its routing updates.

Route Processor   Contains most of the system memory components and the main system processor.

route summarization   Consolidation of advertised addresses in OSPF and IS-IS. In OSPF, this causes a single summary route to be advertised to other areas by an area border router.

routed protocol   A protocol that can be routed by a router. A router must be able to interpret the logical internetwork as specified by that routed protocol. Examples of routed protocols include AppleTalk, DECnet, and IP.

router identifier (router ID)   IP address that identifies a router participating in OSPF. The router ID is taken from the active interface with the highest IP address, or from a configured loopback interface.

router   A network layer device that uses one or more metrics to determine the optimal path along which network traffic should be forwarded. Routers forward packets from one network to another based on network layer information. Occasionally called a gateway (although this definition of gateway is becoming increasingly outdated).

routing protocol   A protocol that accomplishes routing through the implementation of a specific routing protocol. Examples of routing protocols include IGRP, OSPF, and RIP.

routing table   A table that is stored in a router or some other internetworking device that keeps track of routes to particular network destinations and, in some cases, metrics that are associated with those routes.

RSTP (Rapid Spanning Tree Protocol)   RSTP defines the additional port roles and defines port states as discarding, learning, or forwarding.

SDH (Synchronous Digital Hierarchy)   This is the term used for the international equivalent of SONET.

secret key   A device that protects encryption by using an encryption algorithm so that an intruder cannot interpret the message without the appropriate key.

security assessment   A process in which the network is internally examined by professionals who are trained in the vulnerabilities exploited by network invaders.

security card   A physical device that is approximately the same size as a credit card and can be used to restrict access to rooms or computers.

security plan   A high-level document that proposes what an organization must do to meet security requirements.

security policy   A policy that states whether packet filters implement denying specific types of packets and accepting all else or accepting specific types of packets and denying all else.

segment   In networks, a section of a network that is bounded by bridges, routers, or switches.

session layer   Layer 5 of the OSI reference model. This layer establishes, maintains, and manages sessions between applications.

shortest path first (SPF) algorithm   Routing algorithm that iterates on length of path to determine a shortest-path spanning tree. Commonly used in link-state routing algorithms. Sometimes called Dijkstra's algorithm.

single-mode fiber   The fiber optic standard that is used to transmit one signal per fiber. Single-mode fiber allows only one path for the signal to travel down the middle of the fiber. The entire signal travels the length of the fiber at the same rate, allowing for much higher data rates.

SLA (service-level agreement)   A negotiated contract between VPN providers and their subscribers. SLAs contain the service criteria to which the subscriber expects specific services to be delivered.

SMB (Samba)   A protocol that UNIX and Linux systems run that allows Microsoft clients and servers to view UNIX and Linux systems as if they were another Windows device.

sniffer   A program and device that monitors data traveling over a network.

SNMP (Simple Network Management Protocol)   A protocol that allows management to transmit statistical data over the network to a central management console.

SONET (Synchronous Optical Network)   The standard for synchronous data transmission on optical media used in North America.

Spanning Tree Protocol (STP)   Bridge protocol that uses the spanning-tree algorithm, enabling a learning bridge to dynamically work around loops in a network topology by creating a spanning tree. Bridges exchange bridge protocol data unit (BPDU) messages with other bridges to detect loops; then they remove the loops by shutting down selected bridge interfaces. Refers to both the IEEE 802.1 Spanning Tree Protocol standard and the earlier Digital Equipment Corporation Spanning Tree Protocol upon which it is based. The IEEE version supports bridge domains and allows the bridge to construct a loop-free topology across an extended LAN. The IEEE version generally is preferred over the Digital version.

SPID (service profile identifier)   A number that some service providers use to define the services to which an ISDN device subscribes. The ISDN device uses the SPID when accessing the switch that initializes the connection to a service provider.

standalone server   A server that is set up primarily to support one particular application and to dedicate its resources to that application.

star topology   A LAN topology in which endpoints on a network are connected to a common central switch by point-to-point links. A ring topology that is organized as a star implements a unidirectional closed-loop star instead of point-to-point links. Compare with bus topology.

static route   A route that is fixed and not capable of action or change.

static routing   Routing that is explicitly configured and entered into the routing table. Static routes take precedence over routes chosen by dynamic routing protocols.

store-and-forward switching   A packet-switching technique in which frames are completely processed before being forwarded out the appropriate port. This processing includes calculating the cyclic redundancy check (CRC) and checking the destination address. In addition, frames must be temporarily stored until network resources (such as an unused link) are available to forward the message.

stub network   A network that has only a single connection to a router.

stuck in active   This refers to the state of a router if one or more routers to which a query is sent do not respond with a reply within the active time of 180 seconds (3 minutes).

subinterface   One of a number of virtual interfaces on a single physical interface.

subnet mask   A mask used to extract network and subnetwork information from the IP address.

subnetwork   A network that is segmented into a series of smaller networks.

successor   A route that is selected as the primary route to use to reach a destination.

supernetting   Aggregating IP network addresses advertised as a single classless network address.

SVC (switched virtual circuit)   Virtual circuit that is dynamically established on demand and is torn down when transmission is complete. SVCs are used in situations where data transmission is sporadic. Called a switched virtual connection in ATM terminology.

switch   A network device that filters, forwards, and floods frames based on the destination address of each frame. The switch operates at the data link layer of the OSI reference model.

switching   The process of taking an incoming frame from one interface and delivering it out through another interface.

symmetric key   A Public/Private key method in which both the sender and the receiver use the same secret key.

symmetric switching   A switching method that provides switched connections between ports with the same bandwidth, such as all 10-Mbps ports or all 100-Mbps ports.

TA (terminal adapter)   A device that is used to connect ISDN BRI connections to existing interfaces, such as EIA/TIA-232. Essentially, a TA is an ISDN modem.

TACACS (Terminal Access Controller Access Control System)   A security protocol for customers who have numerous routers and switches, which can be used to manage large numbers of router and switch user IDs and passwords in a centralized database. TACACS also offers auditing features.

TDM (time-division multiplexing)   Technique in which information from multiple channels can be allocated bandwidth on a single wire based on pre-assigned time slots. Bandwidth is allocated to each channel regardless of whether the station has data to transmit.

TE1 (Terminal Equipment type 1)   A device that is compatible with the ISDN network. A TE1 connects to a network termination of type 1 or type 2.

TE2 (Terminal Equipment type 2)   A device that is not compatible with ISDN and that requires a terminal adapter.

TFTP (Trivial File Transfer Protocol)   Simplified version of FTP that allows files to be transferred from one computer to another over a network, usually without the use of client authentication (for example, username and password).

TIR (total internal reflection)   The interface between the core and the cladding on fiber-optic cabling that can trap light signals by a process in which the optical fiber acts as a light pipe.

topology table   The table that is made up of all the EIGRP routing tables in the autonomous system to provide the router with knowledge of all the destination routes with the Autonomous system. *802.1Q*   A trunking protocol that can carry the traffic of more than one subnet down a single cable. The IEEE 802.1Q committee defined this method of multiplexing VLANs in an effort to provide multivendor VLAN support.

traditional network   When separate networks have been provisioned within an enterprise for data, voice, and video applications. These networks have been deployed autonomously and have operated in isolation, often implemented and managed by separate teams.

traffic monitoring   A sophisticated method of network monitoring that looks at the actual packet traffic on the network and generates reports based on that traffic.

transceiver   A device that transmits and receives data to and from the network. This device attaches to the network interface card in two different ways: as an onboard or external transceiver.

transmitter   A source of light, such as a light bulb.

transport layer   Layer 4 of the OSI reference model. This layer segments and reassembles data into a data stream. The transport layer has the potential to guarantee a connection and offer reliable transport.

Trojan horse   A destructive program that is disguised as a game, a utility, or an application. When run, a Trojan horse does something devious to the computer system while appearing to do something useful.

trunk   A single transmission channel between two points that are usually switching centers.

trunking   A physical and logical connection between two switches across which network traffic travels. A backbone is composed of a number of trunks.

tunnel interfaces   Entry and exit points of the VPN tunnel. The tunnel interface is similar to a hardware interface but is configured in software.

tunneling   A vehicle that encapsulates packets inside a protocol that is understood at the entry and exit points of a given network.

TTL (time to live)   A field in the IP that specifies how many more hops a packet can travel before being discarded or returned.

unified messaging   Combines voice mail, e-mail, and fax into a single application suite.

user policies   Documents that contain information on how the users can interact with the network. These policies include what is and what is not permissible on the network.

VLSM (variable-length subnet mask)   The ability to specify a different subnet mask for the same network number on different subnets. VLSM helps optimize available address space.

virus   A program that "infects" computer files (usually other executable programs) by inserting copies of itself in those files. This is usually done in such a manner that the copies are executed when the file is loaded into memory, allowing them to infect still other files, and so on.

VLAN (virtual local-area network)   Group of devices on one or more LANs that are configured (using management software) so that they can communicate as if they were attached to the same wire, when in fact they are located on several different LAN segments.

VoFR (Voice over Frame Relay)   Technology that consolidates voice and voice-band data (including fax and analog modems) with data services over a Frame Relay network.

VoIP (Voice over IP)   Voice is an application that runs over IP just like any other application. IP/User Datagram Protocol/Real-Time Transport Protocol (IP/UDP/RTP) headers encapsulate voice information as it passes through the IP stack; the voice is de-encapsulated on the receiving side.

volume   A physical unit of storage.

VPN (virtual private network)   A private network that is constructed within a public network infrastructure, such as the global Internet.

VTP (VLAN Trunking Protocol)   VTP reduces administration in a switched network. When you configure a new VLAN on a VTP server, the VLAN is distributed through all switches in the domain. This reduces the need to configure the same VLAN every-where. VTP is a Cisco-proprietary protocol that is available on most of the Cisco Catalyst Family products.

WDM (wavelength division multiplexing)   Mixing two wavelengths of light on the same fiber without interference between them.

window   The number of bytes a receiver can accept.

worm   A program that propagates itself across computers, usually by creating copies of itself in each computer's memory. A worm might duplicate itself in one computer so often that it causes the computer to crash.

Check Your Understanding Answer Key

This appendix contains the answers to the Check Your Understanding review questions at the end of each chapter.

Chapter 1

1. Which OSI reference model layer best describes 10BaseT standards?

C. The physical layer

2. Which of the following best describes the function of the OSI reference model's transport layer?

A. It sends data by using flow control.

3. Which of the following functions does a router use to relay data packets between networks?

B. Path determination and switching

4. Which of the following are two basic types of dynamic routing?

C. Distance-vector and link-state

5. When all the routers in a network are operating with the same knowledge, the network is said to have done which of the following?

A. Converged

6. Describe the purpose of data encapsulation.

Each layer depends on the service function of the OSI reference model layer below it. To provide this service, the lower layer uses encapsulation to put the PDU from the upper layer into its data field; then, it can add whatever headers and trailers the layer will use to perform its function.

7. Describe the main function of the OSI reference model's transport layer.

   Transport-layer services allow reliable data transport between hosts and destinations. To obtain such reliable transport of data, a connection-oriented relationship is used between the communicating end systems.

8. Describe the purpose of ICMP.

   ICMP is implemented by all TCP/IP hosts. ICMP messages are carried in IP datagrams and are used to send error and control messages. Examples of ICMP messages are ping and destination unreachable.

9. Describe windowing in a TCP/IP implementation.

   Windowing is a method to control the amount of information transferred end-to-end. Windowing is an end-to-end agreement between sender and receiver on how much data will be sent between acknowledgments.

10. Describe the main function of the OSI reference model's network layer.

    The network layer provides best-effort, end-to-end packet delivery. The network layer sends packets from the source network to the destination network based on the IP routing table.

11. What commands are used to associate a network with a RIP routing process?

    B. router rip

    network *network-number*

12. Which of the following best describes the TCP/IP protocol stack?

    B. Supports all standard physical standards and data link-protocols

13. Which best describes the structure of an encapsulated data packet?

    C. Frame header, network header, data, frame trailer

14. What technique is used with windowing to guarantee that a stream of data sent from one machine will be delivered through a data link to another machine without duplication or data loss?

    A. Acknowledgment and retransmission

15. What is one advantage of dynamic routing?

    C. Adjusts automatically to topology or traffic changes

16. Which best describes a primary function of the transport layer?

    A. Uses the TCP protocol to segment and reassemble data into a data stream

17. In the IP RIP routing protocol, how often are routing updates sent?

    A. Every 30 seconds

18. Which of the following statements is true?

    C. The MAC address resides at the data link layer and is hard-coded into the network interface card.

19. What is the advantage of using a layered model of networking?

    D. All of the above

20. A router routing a packet of data performs which of the following functions?

    B. Consults its routing tables to determine which of its ports it will need to send the data out on for it to reach its destination network

Chapter 2

1. Which two addresses are valid subnet addresses when 172.17.15.0/24 is subnetted an additional 4 bits? (Choose two)

    A. 172.17.15.0

    D. 172.17.15.96

2. What is the most efficient subnet mask to use on point-to-point WAN links?

    C. 255.255.255.252

3. Which of the following are features of CIDR? (Choose all that apply.)

    B. Supernetting

    D. Route aggregation

4. What is a summarization address for the networks 172.21.136.0/24 and 172.21.143.0/24?

    B. 172.21.136.0/20

5. Which routing protocol does not contain subnet mask information in its routing updates?

    C. RIPv1

6. Which method represents a collection of IP addresses within a single IP address?

    D. Route summarization

Chapter 3

1. Which state are OSPF network routers in after the DR and BDR are elected?

   A. ExStart

2. Which OSPF packet type establishes and maintains neighbor adjacencies?

   C. Hello

3. What is the default cost metric for OSPF based on?

   B. Bandwidth

4. Which multicast address represents all OSPF routers?

   D. 224.0.0.5

5. Which command can change OSPF priority on an interface?

   B. ip ospf priority number

6. Which multicast address is used to send LSUs to all DR/BDR routers?

   A. 224.0.0.6

7. What is a common feature associated with NBMA networks?

   B. Support for more than two routers

8. Which command allows OSPF routers to exchange routing updates without multicasts?

   A. ip ospf neighbor

9. Which command displays the routes known to a router and how they were learned?

   B. show ip route

Chapter 4

1. How do you configure the automatic redistribution between IGRP and EIGRP?

   C. Configure the two protocols with the same autonomous system numbers.

2. Which protocol combines the advantages of both link-state and distance vector routing protocols?

   D. EIGRP

3. Which algorithm is used to achieve rapid convergence?

   B. Diffusing Update algorithm

4. Which protocol does EIGRP support through the use of PDMs?

   C. IPX

5. Which table includes route entries for all destinations that the router has learned and is maintained for each configured routing protocol?

   B. Routing table

6. Which of the following establishes adjacencies in EIGRP?

   B. Hello packets

7. Which of the following guarantees ordered delivery of EIGRP packets to all neighbors?

   D. Reliable Transport Protocol

8. What does DUAL do after it tracks all routes, compares them, and guarantees they are loop free?

   A. Inserts up to four lowest-cost paths into the routing table

9. How does EIGRP prevent routing loops from occurring with external routes?

   D. By storing all neighboring routes that have loops identified in the routing table

10. On higher-bandwidth connections, such as point-to-point serial links and multi-point circuits, how long is the hello interval that EIGRP uses?

    A. 5 seconds

Chapter 5

1. Which of the following broadcast methods does an Ethernet medium use to transmit and receive data to all nodes on the network?

   B. A data frame

2. Characteristics of microsegmentation include which of the following?

   D. A and B

3. LAN switches are considered to be which of the following?

   D. Multiport bridges operating at Layer 2

4. Asymmetric switching is optimized for which of the following?

   A. Client/server network traffic, where the "fast" switch port is connected to the server

5. Describe full- and half-duplex Ethernet operation.

   In half-duplex Ethernet, the transmit (TX) and the receive (RX) circuits contend for the right to use the same single shared medium. In full-duplex Ethernet, TX and RX are separate circuits; therefore, there is no contending for the right to transmit data across the media.

6. Describe the main function of the Spanning Tree Protocol.

   The main function of the Spanning Tree Protocol is to allow redundant switched/bridged paths without suffering the effects of loops in the network.

7. How would each segment be considered in a network that is segmented by switches?

   C. Collision domain

8. In a full duplex Ethernet switch, which of the following is true?

   D. All of the above

9. Congestion causes which of the following effects?

   E. All of the above

10. Host A transmits to another host, Host B. The communication is such that Host A stops sending information content packets and then Host B begins sending packets. Similarly, Host B stops when Host A starts transmitting again. The transmission type would be classified as which of the following?

    B. Half-duplex

11. Which of the following statements concerning packet forwarding in a LAN is not true?

    D. Buffering is required in cut-through packet switching if the network connection or link is slow.

12. Which of the following is true for a LAN switch?

    B. It is a high-speed multiport bridge.

13. How many collision domains would a 16-port LAN switch create?

    D. 16

14. By creating a virtual circuit with LAN switching, what will result on that segment?

    D. Increased available bandwidth

15. How do switches learn the addresses of devices that are attached to their ports?

    B. Switches read the source address of a packet that is entering through a port.

16. What is the purpose of symmetric switching?

    A. It provides switch connections on ports that have the same bandwidth.

17. What device provides logical segmentation of a LAN?

    A. Router

18. In what ways does a router segment a LAN?

    D. Both A and B.

19. Which of the following is *not* a benefit of implementing Layer 3 devices in your LAN?

    D. It increases the size of the LAN.

20. Which of the following is an example of an enterprise server?

    B. DNS server for a school district

Chapter 6

1. What does the access layer provide?

    A. The entry point for users and servers into the network

2. Which of the following is true of the core layer?

    B. It operates as a high-speed switching backbone to forward traffic from one area to another.

3. Which of the following is a benefit of implementing Layer 3 devices in your LAN?

    D. All of the above

4. Which of the following devices provides logical segmentation of a LAN?

    A. Router

5. What does microsegmentation with switches do?

    C. It creates additional collision domains.

Chapter 7

1. What do characteristics of microsegmentation include? Select all that apply.

   A. Dedicated paths between sender and receiver hosts

   B. Multiple traffic paths within the switch

2. How are LAN switches characterized?

   D. Multiport bridges operating at Layer 2

3. For what is symmetric switching optimized?

   A. Client-server network traffic where the "fast" switch port is connected

4. In _____ switching, the switch checks the destination address and immediately begins forwarding the frame, whereas in _____ switching, the switch receives the complete frame before forwarding it.

   B. Cut-through; store-and-forward

5. Fragment-free and fast-forward switching are two forms of _____ switching.

   C. Cut-through

6. When you connect a workstation to a switch, what is the proper cable?

   F. Straight-through

7. Which communication method is characterized by one host sending and one host receiving?

   B. Unicast

Chapter 8

1. The goal of redundant topologies is to eliminate network outages that are caused by how many points of failure?

   A. One

2. What is the purpose of Spanning Tree Protocol?

   B. To maintain a loop-free network

3. When the network topology changes, _____.

   D. Spanning Tree Protocol reconfigures switch or bridge ports automatically

4. On the root bridge, all ports are _____.

    C. designated ports

5. How does Spanning Tree Protocol select the root port on a nonroot bridge?

    B. The root port is the lowest-cost path from the nonroot bridge to the root bridge.

6. Which bridge does Spanning Tree Protocol select as the root bridge?

    B. The one that has the lowest bridge ID

7. What composes Spanning Tree Protocol BID?

    B. Bridge priority and bridge MAC address

8. In what state can a port populate its MAC address table but not forward user frames?

    A. Learning state

9. In the revised IEEE specification, what is the cost of a 100-Mbps link?

    C. 19

10. What is the definition of convergence for Spanning Tree Protocol?

    D. All the ports have transitioned to either the forwarding or the blocking state.

11. What is the default max age for Spanning Tree Protocol?

    C. 20 seconds

12. What is Rapid Spanning Tree Protocol equivalent state to the Spanning Tree Protocol blocking state?

    C. Discarding

13. Which port role specifies a forwarding port that is elected for every switched LAN segment when using Rapid Spanning Tree Protocol?

    D. Designated

14. How does STP provide a loop-free network?

    C. placing some ports in the blocking state

Chapter 9

1. What do VLANs address?

    D. All of the above

2. Which of the following can a VLAN be considered?

   B. Broadcast domain

3. What do routers in VLAN topologies provide for?

   D. All of the above

4. What does the phrase *microsegmentation with scalability* mean?

   A. The ability to increase network size without creating collisions domains

5. Switches, as the core element of VLANs, provide the intelligence to do which of the following?

   D. All of the above.

6. Each _____ segment that is connected to a _____ port can be assigned to only one VLAN.

   C. hub; switch

7. Which of the following is *not* an advantage of using static VLANS?

   D. They automatically configure ports when new stations are added.

8. Which of the following is *not* a criterion on which VLANs can be based?

   D. All of the above are criteria on which VLANs can be based.

9. Which of the following is a beneficial effect of adding a VLAN? Choose all that apply.

   B. Broadcasts can be controlled.

   C. Confidential data can be protected.

   D. Physical boundaries that prevent user groupings can be removed.

10. Which of the following statements that pertains to virtual LANs is false?

    C. Bridges form one of the core components of VLAN communications.

11. Which Layer 3 function on a switch allows you to easily manipulate devices that reside in different IP subnets?

    D. VLANs

12. Which of the following devices is needed for a packet to be passed from one VLAN to another?

    B. Router

13. In which layer of the OSI model does frame tagging occur?

   B. Layer 2

14. _____ allows switches to share address tables, and _____ assigns a user-defined VLAN ID to each frame.

   C. Frame filtering; frame tagging

15. Why is it important to create VLANs?

   D. Both A and B.

Chapter 10

1. What is the primary advantage of using a trunk link?

   B. Efficient use of router and switch ports

2. Which protocol carries multiple VLANs over a single trunk?

   C. 802.1Q

3. Which protocol is Cisco proprietary and designed to carry traffic from multiple VLANs?

   D. ISL

4. To create or configure a VLAN trunk on a Cisco IOS command-based switch, configure the port first as a trunk and then specify the trunk encapsulation.

   A. True

5. VTP messages are encapsulated in either Cisco proprietary Inter-Switch Link (ISL) or what type of frame?

   A. IEEE 802.1Q protocol frames

6. Using VTP, each Catalyst Family Switch advertises which of the following on its trunk ports?

   D. All of the above

7. VTP switches can operate in which modes?

   D. All of the above

8. Two different versions of VTP can run in your management domain: VTP Version 1 and VTP Version 2. The two versions are interoperable.

   B. False

9. To create a management domain, use which command?

   D. Switch(vtp)#vtp domain Cisco

10. The default behavior of a switch is to propagate broadcasts and unknown _____ across the network.

    A. frames

11. Enabling VTP pruning on a VTP server enables pruning for the entire _____ domain.

    C. management

12. In switched networks, _____ are used to provide communication between VLANs.

    A. Route Processors

Chapter 11

1. Private addresses are assigned by what?

   A. The network administrator from RFC 1918.

2. Which of the following are valid RFC 1918 private addresses?

   B. 10.0.0.0/8

   C. 192.168.0.0/16

   D. 172.16.0.0/12

3. The BOX Company maintains its own public web server, and it is about to implement NAT. Which type of NAT should be used for the web server?

   B. Static

4. Which of the following applications does Cisco IOS NAT support?

   A. ICMP

   D. FTP (including PORT and PASV commands

5. Which of the following traffic types does Cisco IOS NAT *not* support?

   B. DNS zone transfers

   C. BOOTP

6. BOOTP supports <u>Static mapping</u> whereas DHCP supports <u>Dynamic mapping</u>.

7. Place the following DHCP messages in the correct order as they appear in the process.

   D. DHCPDISCOVER

   C. DHCPOFFER

   B. DHCPREQUEST

   A. DHCPACK

8. What does DHCP stand for?

   A. Dynamic Host Configuration Protocol

9. NAT conserves the legally registered addressing scheme by allowing the privatization of intranets.

   A. True

10. DHCP is not intended for use in configuring routers, switches, and servers because these hosts need to have static IP addresses.

    A. True

Chapter 12

1. Analog dialed connections are not suitable for which of the following traffic types?

   D. Video

2. Which of the following statements pertaining to ISDN is true?

   A. The ISDN BRI offers two B channels and one D channel.

3. A leased line is a _____ link that provides a single previously established WAN communication path from the customer to a remote network.

   A. Point-to-point

4. Which of these statements about X.25 networks is not true?

   B. Data packets are not subject to delay.

5. How does Frame Relay handle multiple conversations on the same physical connection?

   A. Frame Relay multiplexes the circuits.

6. Which of the following is *not* true about ATM technology?

   D. ATM cells are always a fixed length of 35 bytes.

7. Equipment on a subscriber's premises that connects to a service provider's central office is called:

   C. CPE

8. Devices that put data on the local loop are called:

   B. DCE

9. The customer devices that pass the data to the DCE are called:

   A. DTE

10. For digital lines a _____ and a _____ are required.

    A. CSU and DSU

11. For analog WAN services a _____ is required?

    C. Modem

12. Circuit-switched connections include the following except _____?

    D. SONET

13. In a packet-switched network, routes established when the switches are started are called:

    A. Permanent virtual circuits (PVCs)

14. In a packet-switched network, routes that are established on demand are called:

    B. Switched virtual circuits (SVC)

15. Which type of service characterizes an ISDN connection?

    C. Synchronous dialup

16. Which of the following is a DCE device?

    B. Modem

17. At which OSI layer does PPP operate?

    B. Data link

18. Frame Relay operates at which layer of the OSI model?

B. Layer 2

19. ISDN BRI is composed of which of the following?

B. 2 B channels and 1 D channel

Chapter 13

1. What does the first step in establishing connections over PPP links involve?

D. The originating node sending LCP frames to configure the data link

2. In PPP, what happens if LCP terminates a link?

D. LCP informs the network layer protocols.

3. Which of the following is the network layer protocol that PPP supports?

D. All of the above

4. PPP uses NCPs to do which of the following?

B. Encapsulate multiple protocols

5. In a PPP frame, what field identifies whether you have encapsulated IPX or IP?

C. Protocol

6. When would PPP most likely be used at a local workstation for Internet connectivity?

C. When the workstation needs dial-up access to the Internet.

7. When you are running PPP, LCP is responsible for which of the following?

A. Establishment, maintenance, and termination of the point-to-point connection

8. How many phases are involved in PPP session establishment?

C. Four

9. What type of handshaking occurs when PAP is the selected PPP authentication protocol?

B. Two-way

10. What command on the router can you use to check the LCP and NCP states for PPP?

    C. router# show interfaces

11. What protocol would you use to establish a remote connection over ISDN?

    A. PPP

12. When PPP is load balancing across several links, what feature is being taken advantage of?

    D. Multilink

13. What does the PPP link establishment require the LCP to do after opening a connection?

    A. Negotiate configuration parameters and send and receive a configuration acknowledgment frame.

Chapter 14

1. In ISDN, what is the channel over which data is transferred?

    A. The bearer channel with 16 kbps capacity

2. Which channel is used for ISDN out-of-band signaling?

    D. Delta

3. What is the first dynamically assigned TEI value?

    A. 64

4. What mechanism is used to pass call control information between two ISDN switches?

    D. Q.921

5. What is the primary purpose of the D channel in processing an ISDN call?

    D. To carry call signaling

6. To use a router in North America as a dial-in server using ISDN BRI, which ISDN interface is needed?

    B. ISDN BRI U

7. If a router has a U interface, what does that indicate?

    C. It has a built-in NT1.

8. Which of the following switch types is used in European BRI connections?

   A. Net3

   B. Net5

   D. VN3

9. Which of the following provides SPIDs?

   C. The ISDN carrier

10. What is DDR used for?

    B. Low-volume, periodic network connections over ISDN

11. Which of the following statements about DDR is false? (Choose four.)

    B. DDR creates permanent connections between two sites.

    C. DDR allows a router to connect to only one endpoint.

    E. DDR is the correct technology to deploy if you have a permanent WWW server.

    F. DDR applies only to ISDN.

12. What is the main limitation with Legacy DDR?

    C. Configuration is applied directly to the physical interface.

Chapter 15

1. How does Frame Relay handle multiple conversations on the same physical connection?

   B. It multiplexes the circuits.

2. Which of the following protocols does Frame Relay use for error correction?

   B. Upper-layer protocols.

3. Which of the following does Frame Relay do to make its DLCIs global?

   C. It sends out multicasts.

4. Which of the following is the data rate at which the Frame Relay switch agrees to transfer data?

   A. Committed information rate

5. Which of the following assigns DLCI numbers?

   D. The service provider

6. DLCI information is included in which of the following fields of the Frame Relay header?

   B. The Address field

7. Which of the following does Frame Relay use to keep PVCs active?

   C. Keepalives

8. How does Frame Relay use Inverse ARP requests?

   D. It uses the IP address-to-DLCI mapping table.

9. Which of the following does Frame Relay use to determine the next hop?

   C. A Frame Relay map

10. For which of the following does Frame Relay use split horizon?

    B. To prevent routing loops.

11. Frame Relay operates at which of the following layers?

    B. Layer 2

12. Which of the following statements is correct?

    B. Proposals for the standardization of Frame Relay were initially presented to the Consultative Committee for International Telegraph and Telephone (CCITT).

13. Which command is used (at the config mode prompt) to enter the configuration mode for the serial interface for Frame Relay packet encapsulation?

    D. # interface serial0

14. If a **show interface serial 0** command is executed and the message that appears is "Serial line is up, line protocol is up," what is the correct interpretation of the message?

    C. The Frame Relay connection is active.

15. What does show interfaces serial do?

    A. It displays information about the multicast DLCI, the DLCIs that are used on the Frame Relay-configured serial interface, and the LMI DLCI that is used for the LMI.

16. What are FECN and BECN?

   B. Congestion-notification mechanisms

17. Which of the following is true of Frame Relay VCs?

   D. They provide a logical, bidirectional communication path between network devices.

18. Why does Frame Relay implement a CRC?

   B. To perform error-checking functions

19. Which of the following is *not* one of the Frame Relay LMI extensions?

   A. Algorithmically generated MAC addresses

Chapter 16

1. A network baseline is the comparison value to measure a network's what?

   D. Performance

2. A peer-to-peer network establishes what type of relationship between end stations?

   A. Client-to-client

3. Which type of file system does Windows NT use for security purposes?

   C. NTFS

4. In a client server network, a user's ability to access certain files while not being able to access other files is the user what?

   B. Rights

5. What is the IP address of the internal loopback?

   C. 127.0.0.1

6. What is one way to prevent static electricity damage?

   D. Use a grounding strap

7. Which protocol supports network management?

   C. SNMP

8. To list your IP setting on a Windows NT computer, you would run the _____ command.

B. ipconfig

9. What is one troubleshooting method used in network troubleshooting?

B. Divide and conquer

10. If the server is set up by using IP, the clients must use which protocol to communicate with it?

C. IP

11. RMON is an extension of what protocol?

A. SNMP

12. What does the *-n* protocol option stand for in the **ping** command?

A. The network number of the ping area

13. How is the remote data gathered with RMON?

D. Probes

14. The cost of _____ equipment for mission-critical operations needs to be added to the cost of maintaining the network.

A. Redundant

Chapter 17

1. Which of the following is not the key driver of optical networks?

D. Be adaptable through a closed-system architecture

2. Which of the following is true of IOR?

C. It is the ratio of the speed of light in a vacuum to the speed of light in a fiber.

3. True or false: The light current is the electrical noise that occurs naturally in the circuit.

B. False

4. Which of the following is *not* a wavelength value that is used in fiber optics?

C. 1450 nm

5. Which of the following describe(s) fiber optics?

   D. All of the above

6. Which of the following methods can amplify an input optical signal within the fiber?

   D. EDFA

7. What is the typical multimode transmission rate?

   A. Hundreds of megabits per second

8. Which of the following is true of single-mode fiber?

   D. Single-mode fiber allows one mode to travel down the fiber.

9. Which of the following is a possible problem of the fiber core?

   D. All of the above.

10. Which of the following is *not* a component of fiber-optic cable?

    C. An outer cladding

11. SONET was designed to standardize which of the following?

    A. Synchronous networking-enhanced operations, administration, maintenance, and provisioning

12. Which of the following is *not* one of the three levels of overhead channel for maintenance?

    B. COH

13. Which of the following could be a client-side device for a DWDM system?

    C. Routers

14. Which device within the DWDM system is used to convert the SONET/SDH–compliant optical signal?

    D. Transponder

15. From technical and economic perspectives, what is the most obvious advantage of DWDM technology?

    B. The capability to provide potentially unlimited transmission capacity

Index

S

T